Not Hitler's Child

Christa-Maria's (Extra)Ordinary Life
Early Childhood to 2000

MEMOIRS, PART I

Christa-Maria Beardsley

Pen & Publish, Inc.
Bloomington, IN

Copyright © 2018 Christa-Maria Beardsley

All rights reserved. No part of this book may be reproduced or transmitted in any form or by any means, electronic or mechanical, including photocopying, recording, or by any information storage and retrieval system, without permission in writing from the publisher.

Published by Pen & Publish, Inc., USA

www.PenandPublish.com
info@PenandPublish.com

Bloomington, Indiana
(314) 827-6567

ISBN: 978-1-941799-96-3
Library of Congress Control Number: 2017957311

Printed on acid-free paper.

In memory of Mutti, my heroic mother; Doc, my humanitarian husband; and Bill, my wise friend.

The author is proud to donate all proceeds from the sale of this book to the following charitable organizations.

Doctors Without Borders, in memory of my late, beloved husband, Major Wayne Roscoe Beardsley, MD, and his deceased son, Captain Peter Beardsley, MD.

Doctors Without Borders USA, Inc.
333 7th Ave., 2nd Floor
New York, NY 10001
Attn: Planned Giving
Phone: (888) 392-0392
Web: donate.doctorswithoutborders.org

The Carter Center, also in memory of my late husband.

The Carter Center
One Copenhill
435 Freedom Pkwy.
Atlanta, GA 30307
Phone: (404) 420-5119
Email: gayle.beckner@cartercenter.org

The Christa-Maria Endowed Scholarship Fund, created by the author, which will provide scholarships annually to college students enrolled in the Vienna music program offered by the Institute for the International Education of Students.

IES Abroad
Advancement Office
33 W. Monroe St., Ste. 2300
Chicago, IL 60603-5400
Phone: (312) 261-5069 (Jennifer Jerzyk)
Web: www.iesabroad.org
(IES Abroad is a 501(c)(3) organization.)

Contents

PROLOGUE	17
I. Early Childhood to 1954	19
Christmas in Hannover, Germany, before World War II	21
Starting School – *Kristallnacht* (Night of the Shattered Glass)	25
World War II – The First Bomb – At the Mercy of Relatives	28
Evacuation – Villa Glück Auf!	38
Occupation – Allies and Refugees	48
Sankt Ursula – Boarding School in Duderstadt – Sisters of Mercy – Bonn	57
Adjusting to Life in Hannover – First Job: Kommerzbank	74
The Jesuits – Switzerland – Hans	80
II. 1954–1961	89
Auf Wiedersehen, Germany – Hello, America – Land of Dreams	91
Wetherbee Lake Farm, Michigan – Broken Promises	92
The Croft – A Beam of Light	97
Job Hunting in Chicago – A Nightmare	98
New Hope – New Beginnings – Forging Ahead	102
Beginning of Travel in America – Niagara Falls – Michigan's Upper Peninsula – Washington, D.C.	105
Doc	108
Grand Tour of America, Canada, and Mexico	111
Time Out to Reflect – Doc's Pursuit Bears Fruit	114
"Ah! Sweet Mystery of Life – Such a Place to Have Found You"	114

Yes, Doc, I Do – Christmas at the Croft	124
Honeymoon in Yucatán, Mexico	128
Joys and Sorrows at the Croft	132
Adieu, Doc . . .	136
"Even the Weariest River Winds Somewhere Safe to Sea"	137
Adjusting to Widowhood – Mutti Pitches In – US Citizenship – Working for Attorneys James and Hoff	138
Getting Burned by Odd Suitors – Falling for John	144

III. 1961–1972   149

A University Student at Last – Good-bye, Croft – A Trip with Mutti to Bavaria and Austria	151
Broken Pledges – Broken Hearts	157
New Places, Friends, and Lovers	160
In Pursuit of a Law Degree – Love at First Sight – Erich	165
Junior Year Abroad – Aix-en-Provence, France – Monte Carlo – Italy	168
Mediterranean Cruise: Sicily – Cyprus – Israel – Turkey – Greece – Malta	177
Au Revoir, Villa Phocéenne – *Buenos Días*, Spain – Morocco (Africa) – Gibraltar	179
Mont Blanc, Doc's Mountain – Switzerland and Paris	186
New Family Problems and Heartaches	188
Attorney James Dies – Student Life in Bloomington, Indiana – Good, Excellent, and Eccentric Professors and Fellow Students	191
My Acquaintance from Ghana, Africa, Descends on Me Big Time – Papa Passes On – I Fall in Love with Teaching	201

The Veterans Administration Comes Through and Makes Life Easier	206
Bizarre and Ordinary Friends, Lovers, and Relations	209
The Croft Burns – Dissertation Woes	214

IV. 1972–1984 219

Adjusting to Life as a German Professor, to Academia, and to Colleagues on Campus and Abroad – Planting the Seeds for a Summer Program in Bonn, West Germany, with the Padre's Help	221
So Long, Erich – Laying the Foundation for International Summer Programs	233
German Christmas Extravaganza with My Students at the Scottsdale Mall	237
Trials and Tribulations of the 1975 Summer Program in Bonn, Federal Republic of Germany – Fishing in Himmerod, Eifel Region – First Trip to Berlin	241
Harmonizing with Our Quartet in Residence – My Friend André Bourde from Aix Excites Hearts and Minds in Indiana, None More than Mine	250
The 1976 Bonn Program Adds Bayer AG and Berlin (East and West)	257
E. T. A. Hoffmann's Two-Hundredth-Birthday Celebration in Bamberg – Sojourn in Marseille	263
Research and Travel in the German Democratic Republic	268
Another String Snaps – Adventures in South America: Machu Picchú, Peru, Rio de Janeiro, Brazil, and Buenos Aires, Argentina	287
Tenure – Miles Is Sold to Bayer AG – Snowed In with Amadeus	297
Bonn with Lynne Tatlock and Summer Seminar at Humboldt University in East Berlin	302
Intrigues and Politics in Academia, Intermingled with Snow and Music	307

Escape from the Berlin Heat with Ingeborg Guenther to Colder Spheres in Canada — 314

Foreign Language Days at IUSB – Last Summer Program in Bonn — 320

A Mélange of Crumbling Relationships – Headaches in Academia – Writing in Self-Imposed Isolation – Visitors from Bamberg – Launching the Earn and Learn Program in Cologne — 324

The Padre Spins Another Tale – Catching Up with Mutti and Old Friends in Germany — 331

Tying Up Loose Ends on Campus and Off – Starting New Projects at Home and Abroad — 335

V. 1984–1993 — 341
Antonio — 343

February 24 – German Day – Thirty Years in America – Falling in Love Again — 343

New Summer Program with Bayer AG, the CDG, and One Week in the GDR — 345

Finalizing the Manuscript in Bamberg – Operatic Intermezzo in Munich — 349

Climactic Romantic Happenings – Multiple New Beginnings – Promotion to Full Professor — 353

Meeting Antonio's Children – First Pre-honeymoon – Captiva Island, Florida — 361

Second Pre-honeymoon – Crete, Greece — 367

Back to Reality – Mutti Moves into a Nursing Home – The "Vultures" Come Out of Hiding — 371

Hosting the Dissident Musicians from the GDR and Romania – Christmas in Florida — 375

Antonio's Story — 378

Friends or Foes? – Sexual Harassment on Campus – Summer Abroad Despite Gaddafi and Chernobyl	382
Third Pre-honeymoon – Italy	386
Trials and Tribulations with the Ex, Stepchildren, and Other Adults – Engagement and Commitments	395
Fourth Pre-honeymoon – Provence – Summer and Christmas with the Kiddies	403
The Prima Donna Goes on the Offensive – The Berlin Wall and the GDR Start to Crumble – Child-Custody Troubles Continue	410
Wedding Plans in Venice, Italy – Problematic Students	418
The Prima Donna's Kiss of Death	427
The Wedding Date Draws Closer	431
Prelude to the Wedding in Venice	432
Fairy-Tale Wedding in Venice on the Fourth of July	435
Honeymoon in Tyrol – Home via Germany and England on the *QE2*	439
Married Life with Tonio and the Children – The Fall of the Berlin Wall and a New Summer Program	443
A Real Family Christmas	446
Affirmative-Action Hassles Start – Tonio and I Visit Reunited Germany	450
Impromptu Detour to Childhood Places	454
Traveling along the Mississippi to New Orleans and along the Gulf of Mexico to Florida with the Children	457
New Addition to Our House – First Sign of Tonio's Temper	464
Jet-Setting to London – Shattered Friendship	468
Tenth-Anniversary Celebration of the Bayer Program in Leverkusen	473

Downsizing at Bayer AG and Miles Gains Momentum – Visitors from
  Bayer and Berlin   478

Escalation of Discrimination – Sojourns in San Francisco and Germany 483

Overture to Tonio's Relocation in Pittsburgh   489

Tonio and I Cruise the Caribbean at Christmas: Antigua, Dominica,
  Saint Lucia, Saint Vincent, Bequia, Martinique, and Montserrat   494

VI. 1993–1995   503
The Corporate Undertaker Buries Tonio Half-Alive – Tonio's Fascination
  with Native Americans Awakens – Our Lives Spiral Downwards –
  Mutti Dies   505

Gustl Runs Away from His Mother – The Charleston Dilemma   508

The Three Donizettis in Germany and Ireland   512

Tonio, Frank, and Gustl Go Camping, Tracking American Indian
  Ancestors Down South to Key West – Tonio's Temper Escalates   518

Gustl Enrolls at Howe Military Academy – Tonio Works at NAES
  College and Moves to Chicago   523

Holiday in Cancún, Mexico – Tonio Breaks with the Indians in Chicago
  and Lashes Out at Me   528

Researching Native American Ancestry in Atlanta – Vacationing on
  Grand Cayman Islands in the Caribbean – Tonio Abandons the
  Native Americans in Chicago   534

Full of Hope for a New Beginning in Princeton, New Jersey   537

Liesl and I Frolic at Our First German Wedding in Giesen, Germany   542

Early Clouds on the Horizon in Princeton – Lightning Strikes, Then
  Hits – Tonio Returns to Outplacement – He Seeks Solace at the
  Sweat Lodge – Wrestling with the Pain of Loneliness   548

Trying to Mend the Cracks with the Help of Dr. Alice and Her
  Husband, the General   558

A Shimmer of Hope in Cancún – Heading toward the Final Breakdown	563

VII. 1995–2000   575

In Search of a New Haven in Bloomington, Indiana, a Music Lovers' Paradise	577
Adjusting to Old and New Friends – A Musical Wunderkind Strikes a Chord – Antonio Lowers the Boom – Marriage-Dissolution Woes	585
The Music Starts: Schubertiades	598
Changes in Lifestyle and Friendships – Visiting Family and Friends in Germany	606
Exploring Southern Indiana with Liesl prior to Her Visit to Panther, Her Metamorphosed Native American Father	618
Strange Company from Cologne – New Neighbors – So-Called Friends – Tonio's Apology	622
More Schubertiades – Music Lovers – Miracle of High Tech: Doc's Return	631
Liesl and I Go Theater Hopping in Ontario, Canada	635
Trying Hard to Entertain Cousin Frank from Giesen	639
Bettina's Visit – Christmas with Friends in the Windy City – Visiting Doc's Offspring in the Big Apple	642
Local Gossip Lines among Friends and So-Called Friends	648
Liesl and I Cruise the Love Boat – MS *Sea Princess* – to Alaska	655
Doc's Grandson and Wife Come to Visit – Plans for Lake Louise – More Music, Disappointing Friendships, and New Wunderkinder	662
Interlude	668
1999 Christmas Schubertiade	671
Winter Wonderland with Liesl at Lake Louise – Turn-of-the-Millennium Denouement at Home	674

EPILOGUE IN TRANSIT 679
Fireball Lily – Victoria Falls – Zimbabwe, Africa 679

ACKNOWLEDGMENTS

My sincere thanks to all my worldwide friends who encouraged me to tackle this "magnum opus."

I am especially grateful to my sensitive, meticulous, and timely copy editor, John Rogers.

PROLOGUE

The snow is falling gently on this special Christmas Eve, the last of the twentieth century and of the millennium, spreading a white blanket over the grass behind the house and enveloping bushes and trees along the embankment until they glisten silvery in the moonlight.

I feel cozy, warm, and content within. The house is filled with the spirit of Christmas, inside and out. It still reverberates from the last house concert, the Christmas Schubertiade, which took place at the beginning of December. While soaking up the glow from the wood-burning stove in the glass-framed winter garden, I am sipping a glass of *Glühwein*, a brew of hot red wine, sugar, cinnamon, and orange juice, and listening to Christmas music piped in from the library. – I reminisce about my life and marvel at the many ups and downs, twists and turns, joys and sorrows. It seems nearly incomprehensible to have survived them all.

A German choir sings "O Tannenbaum," followed by "Stille Nacht" ("Silent Night"). Always at the sound of these melodies, a certain melancholy comes over me. My thoughts turn at once to my childhood and Christmas in Germany. – On this Christmas Eve, it's like a sign, a wake-up call that challenges me to start what I have been waiting to do for some time. I suddenly know I am ready to start writing about my life. And look, at this very moment, a couple of faithful friends, white-tailed deer, illuminated by the yellow spotlight, are feeding at their crib on the corn and bird feed I placed there earlier. Now, they turn their heads and look straight at me, and we wish each other a merry Christmas! St. Francis in the woods comes to mind. Tomorrow, I will start my memoirs with reflections on Christmas in Germany.

I Early Childhood to 1954

Early Childhood to 1954

Christmas in Hannover, Germany, before World War II

In my childhood in Germany, the Christmas season started on the first day of December. Each year, our parents put up a big Advent wreath with four large red candles in the living room. The candles were lit one after the other on the four Sunday evenings before Christmas. Each time, the family gathered around the wreath and sang Advent songs. My father accompanied us on the piano. On December 1, we children received a beautiful Christmas calendar. Mutti – German for "Mom" – hung the calendar against a windowpane so daylight could illuminate the pictures behind the little windows, which we opened each morning with great anticipation to discover the surprise figure or tiny toy behind each one. The calendar had twenty-four windows, numbered from one to twenty-four. We opened the first window on December 1 and the last on Christmas Eve. My two brothers and I had to take turns. The windows were embedded in sparkling winter-wonderland scenery. The snow covering the evergreen trees glittered silver and golden, the dark-blue sky was dotted with bright stars, and an orange-colored moon looked down from a place in the sky. Children dressed in bright-colored sweaters and caps were sledding down hills, their woolen scarves flying in the winter wind. Their little noses and cheeks were rosy and red. Underneath a huge, snow-covered pine tree, which took up much space on the calendar, were the outlines of the twenty-fourth window, actually a gate, which was massive by comparison with the others.

I will never forget the excitement that came over me whenever I gazed at our calendar, even when it was not my turn to lift the window. When a soft light or a candle on the Advent wreath hanging under the candelabra in the family room was lit, the sparkles seemed almost blinding, but oh so magical. The calendar had hypnotic powers. It was as though each window concealed a small wonder, keeping us children in suspense from one day to the next. The biggest surprise was unveiled on December 24, when the big gate waited to be opened. After we all gathered in front of the calendar, one of us was chosen, according to age, to climb onto the footstool to reach the gate. "Oh!" we exclaimed in a chorus when little Jesus, lying in the crib, was revealed. Mary and Joseph were admiring the infant, who had a halo above his curly head. A star, ever so bright, shone down from above on the newborn child, and a gentle angel dressed in a white, flowing gown stood behind the crèche, spreading his wings to protect the infant.

Our anticipation of Christmas and the arrival of the Christkind – little Jesus, or Santa, as the Lutherans called him – was intensified on December 6, St. Nicholas' Day. I shared a narrow and sparsely furnished bedroom with my two brothers, one older and the other younger than I. At that time of year, it was always cold in the room. My parents heated the small, coal-burning stove only when it was so bitter cold outside that the snow would crunch under the hooves of the horses pulling wagons through the cobblestone streets of Hannover. I cannot remember a winter when we could look down on the street without first having to breathe an opening into the windowpane, covered with glistening ice flowers. The fire in the stove usually died down during the night.

I could see our shoes on the windowsill. We went to sleep praying for cookies and candies the next morning. However, there was always the threat of finding lumps of coal. I was once particularly worried that St. Nicholas might remember something I did during the summer.

In an attempt to impress my older brother and his friend with how high I could jump at the age of five or six, I positioned myself smack in the center of my father's smoking room, which also served as the family room. Though an Oriental rug covered the parquet floor, I folded it back at one corner so I could stand on a bare spot. The boys counted, "one, two" – and at "three" I gathered all my strength and jumped as high as I could. I came down with an explosive plump, which earned me applause and bravos from my male audience. I beamed with pride.

Mutti was in the kitchen when, minutes later, the shrill doorbell rang loudly. Next, we all heard Frau Lang's voice, screaming at my mother. "What in heaven's name is going on up here? My beautiful crystal chandelier from Murano, Italy, an anniversary gift from my dear dead August, came crashing down on my precious mahogany table and burst into a thousand pieces. The entire table is covered with glass splinters – ruined, all ruined!" Frau Lang rented the apartment beneath ours.

Since my male audience was lacking in chivalry, I had no choice but to admit to the crime and endure the punishment. But my father chose not to let me escape with a sentence as light as waiting for St. Nicholas to bring me coals. That would take too long. Instead, he acted promptly on the day of the little mishap. Truth be told, his anger got the better of him. After all, my father had to pay Frau Lang for the damage, because I was penniless. Papa went into one of his rages. Since he was not very tall, he appeared scarier to me, especially when I was smaller. His jet-black eyes got so big they seemed to double in size. His typically whitish, pale skin turned crimson in a second. Indeed, his face was covered with red blotches as he screamed, perhaps even louder than I did at the moment of my corporal punishment. First, he called me a worthless child, a stupid goose, a devil, and whatever came to him. (*Devil* was not quite unjustified, since we lived on Little Devil Street when all of this happened.) Next, he grabbed the carpet beater, which was made out of nice cane, put me over his bony knees, pulled up my skirts, beat me mercilessly, threw me on the wicker basket filled with dirty laundry in the small closet, locked the door, and deserted me.

I was screaming at the top of my lungs to keep up my reputation of being the kid on the block who could cry the longest and loudest, a trait most likely inherited from Papa. When my voice gave out, I gathered my strength, as I had when I jumped. This time, I kicked against one of the little dark-green windows in the closet door. The glass broke and the splinters spread across the dining-room floor. My father, who was presumably too exhausted from raving and spanking, grabbed me and tossed me on my bed, where I finally dozed off after having cried long enough. I really don't know whether my fanny was black, blue, or green. I did not think of looking in a mirror. Strangely enough, since I do not recall ever finding coals in my shoes on St. Nicholas' Day, he must have thought I had been sentenced sufficiently. Perhaps he did not want to inject any dissonance into my Christmas hopes and dreams. After all, St. Nicholas is one of the kind and gentle fairy characters.

As far back as I can remember, each year on the Sunday before Christmas, Papa and Mutti treated us children to a performance at Hannover's opera house. Each time, I sat spellbound by the music and magic of Engelbert Humperdinck's opera *Hänsel und Gretel*. The fairy-tale opera was always followed by an enchanting show of Seppel Bayer's ballet *Die Puppenfee* (The Fairy Doll). How I wished I could fly across the stage on a broom like the witch in *Hänsel und Gretel* and dance as gracefully as the Fairy Doll!

With the opening of the gate on the glittering calendar on Christmas Eve morning, the holiday's spell began to take hold of me. It continued more dramatically after our traditional Christmas Eve meal of sauerkraut and *Bregenwurst* (the particularity of which I will spin out elsewhere in my memoirs) in the evening. Normally in Germany, people take warm meals at noon, while in the evening they eat pumpernickel and cold cuts. I do not know many children in America who like sauerkraut. We German kids all loved sauerkraut, be it with spareribs, pig knuckles, bratwurst, or *Bregenwurst*. It must be the reason why the world calls us *Krauts*. – The placement of a shiny red apple, resting on an evergreen twig, next to the plate filled with sauerkraut, potatoes, and sausage highlighted the entire meal, not to mention the table. A small candle was secured in the core of the apple. While we ate on Christmas Eve, the electric lights were turned out, and only the candles in the apples and the four candles on the Advent wreath were lit. It set the mood for what was to follow. My fondness for candlelight has been a constant in my life and is increasing with age.

After the sauerkraut, boiled potatoes, *Bregenwurst* with mustard, and applesauce were completely consumed, that is, when all plates were slick, we children were sent to bed to take a nap before Christkind came. We always went willingly and quietly, because the suspense, mixed with a speck of fear, continued to hold us captive. We did not have to undress fully.

Suddenly, the soft ring of a bell awakened us. Mutti called us with her gentle, song-like voice and encouraged us to get up quickly, because she had seen Christkind flying from the attic window. We jumped out of bed, ran through the doorway into the corridor, and followed Mutti, who climbed the stairway toward the attic window. She pointed toward the sky, and I swear I saw a bright light shooting up high into the star-studded heavens.

A bell rang downstairs the moment Christkind disappeared. Mutti asked if we heard it, and we rushed down to the corridor of the apartment. The corridor provided access to the various rooms. The doors were always closed, if not locked, and the dining room in particular was off-limits a couple weeks before Christmas Eve. Two doors led to the secret room, one from the hallway and one, a big door consisting of two wide wings, from the family room, where the piano had pride of place.

As we approached the family room, we heard soft music – *O Tannenbaum, O Tannenbaum*. My father was playing the song on the piano. As I entered, I felt as though I were penetrating a fairy world. All electric lights had been turned off. Candles burned on the Advent wreath, and before us, in a bay window of the big dining room, stood a tall Christmas tree on which many candles were burning bright, while sparkling streamers sizzled magically, lighting up the big, round ornaments – red, green, blue, golden, and silver. A golden angel adorned the top of the tree. At the foot of the tree, the Nativity scene was arranged on a bed of moss.

Next to the Christmas tree stood the big dining-room table. On it was a little electric train, running. Not far from the table, in an alcove space, stood the dollhouse and the doll carriage with my favorite dolls decked out in new outfits. Before we could touch the presents underneath the tree, we all gathered around the piano to sing "O Tannenbaum" and "Stille Nacht."

After having inspected all the gifts, which were never wrapped in boxes, and after trying on new pieces of clothing, we played with our toys. Mutti always sat next to the big, white tile stove, peeling oranges and apples and cracking nuts for us. Oranges were rare around our house. We received only one each at Christmastime. When the big grandfather clock with the Westminster chimes struck 11:00 p.m., Mutti served coffee and cake. She always baked huge sheet cakes at the bakery across the street for big holidays. They were yeast cakes topped with apples, butter, sugar, and almonds. Nobody could bake a better-tasting cake. I was never able to match Mutti in that department.

After coffee and cake, we all got bundled up in our new winter outfits and walked through the snow to attend Midnight Mass in our parish church, Sankt Heinrich. It was only a ten-minute walk from Kleine Düwelstraße. Midnight Mass at Sankt Heinrich was a rather festive occasion. I loved to listen to the organ playing majestically and the congregation singing joyfully. My mother had a beautiful voice. She always let me look into her hymnbook, and we sang together. It was heavenly. I relished the clouds of incense at the end of the Mass, because the fragrance reminded me once more of fairylands.

The first Christmas Day was spent with the immediate family, trying out new toys as soon as we returned home from Mass, and stopping only long enough to gather around the table to feast on Mutti's roasted goose and have more cake and coffee in the afternoon. – After *Abendbrot* (pumpernickel and cold cuts), we all stood around

Papa at the piano and sang more Christmas songs, while the Christmas tree flickered. When it was time to go to bed, we knew that in the morning we would get ready to visit Mutti's oldest sister, Aunt Anna, and her husband Uncle Wilhelm, in the place where their daughter Annie, with her husband Karl and son Rolf, would be. Uncle Seppel, Mutti's third-oldest brother, always joined us along with his wife, Aunt Ella. They had no children and brought the neatest toys.

– Throughout my life, the memories of prewar Christmas seasons on Kleine Düwelstraße have served as a model and inspiration for the others that followed. But never again did I experience the magic as intensely as I did during my early childhood. As though destroyed by the bombs of the war, the Christmases of the war period seem to have been wiped out of my mind almost completely. –

Starting School – *Kristallnacht* (Night of the Shattered Glass)

In 1938, shortly after Easter, my parents prepared me for my first day of school at the Kanonenwall (Canon Wall). Mutti, a devout Catholic, insisted I go to a denominational school, despite the fact that it meant a sixty-minute round trip each day across the big city in a streetcar, all by myself. One of the surprises of the first day of school was a new set of clothing and a brand-new square leather satchel to be carried on the back. It contained a slate, a slate pencil, and a first reader. A sponge and piece of cloth were tied to the frame of the slate, and they bounced merrily up and down alongside the satchel when I ran. Mutti hung the little square leather sandwich bag over my shoulder, and when I was almost ready to go, she disappeared and returned with a huge cone, about two feet long, made of cardboard and covered with pretty lacquered pictures, sprinkled with gold and silver tinsel. It was filled to the brim with cookies, candies, and chocolates, which were kept from falling out by ruffled crepe paper tied with a ribbon. All German children receive such a candy-filled cone on their first day of school. Mutti put it in my arms and took me by the hand, and we walked to the streetcar. Mutti and I climbed into No. 17 and rode to school together. The next time, I was on my own.

My daily rides on No. 17 went smoothly. I was not afraid. It was the same route each day through downtown and the older part of the city. I liked going to school, even though the building itself was a rather gloomy red-brick structure and the classrooms were anything but cheerful. A big black crucifix with a bronze-colored Jesus hung on the otherwise barren wall opposite our school benches.

One gray November morning – November 9, to be exact – everything came to a screeching halt. The streetcar stopped abruptly in the middle of the block in the old part of the city. The conductor told us to get out and continue on foot because the tracks were blocked. He said I should just walk along the tracks and that it would not be too far to school. Afraid I would be late, I went on my way. I looked down to avoid stepping on broken glass or stumbling over other pieces of debris. Nobody explained what had happened. It did not seem to matter that I was late. Other kids were behind schedule as well.

When I entered the classroom, a man in a brown uniform, a "Brownshirt," with an SA (stormtroopers) pin on his shirt, just as I had seen Papa wear, ordered me to sit down. I had not seen men in uniform in my school before, just the teacher in civilian clothes. The teacher stood against the wall, and other soldiers were lined up in front of her podium. Then, one of the brown men stepped forward. He announced, "Listen, tell your parents that starting right now, this will no longer be a Catholic school. It will be a public school!" He then commanded, "Stand up!" We jumped up from our seats. He said, "Starting today, you will no longer say a prayer before classes. Instead we will say, 'Heil Hitler!'" At that, he turned his back toward us and looked up at a big red flag with a black swastika in a white circle. It covered almost the entire wall. The crucifix was gone. He shouted, "Attention! Raise your right arm, stretch out your hand, look up, salute the flag, all together repeat after me, and say loud and clear, 'Heil Hitler!'" He turned toward us and said, "Now go home!" I never returned to the school at the Kanonenwall.

I went right back to the tracks and walked toward home. It was a long walk. I was not in a big hurry. The sun had come out. I strolled along the sidewalk next to the tracks. The streets were deserted in the old part of town. Deadly quiet. There was no one cleaning up or guarding the destroyed stores. I was fascinated by the disorder on the sidewalk. Brand-new pieces of merchandise were scattered around, some pieces of broken china, furniture, and God knows what. Store windows were shattered, as were windows in entrance doors to the stores. On some I saw a yellow star with a jet-black outline and the word *Jude* (Jew), also in black. I did not know what it meant. The windows at an old church-like building, a synagogue, were knocked out. Smoke came out of the openings. Mixed in with the big pieces of broken glass were tiny, flickering prisms. It was as though crystals had been sprinkled around. The glass splinters glistened as rays of sunlight shone on them. My heart pounded, and in front of the smashed window of a candy store, I stooped down to pick up some bonbons and chocolates that were strewn around. Not a single person or child was visible. The thought that I was stealing never crossed my mind. I tucked a few pieces into my coat pockets. As I came to the newer part of the city, the streets were clean, and I walked more quickly.

Mutti was glad to see me when I rang the doorbell. She did not object when I asked to play with my little friend Wolfgang, whose mother, a widow, owned a candy shop on Kleine Düwelstraße. Frau Fliess asked us on occasion to guard the shop when she had to run a quick errand. The reward was always oh so sweet; I mean the candy. But I have never forgotten when Wolfgang kissed me for the first and only time. We were playing together in the corridor of his apartment, upstairs above the store, and I was lying flat on my tummy on one of the benches in a kind of dark corner. He was sitting next to me when all of a sudden he pulled up my skirt, pushed down my panties and planted a big, fat smack on my "popo"! It was the first kiss I ever got from a boy.

Wolfgang lived at the end of our block. When I came to the shop, the door stood open, blowing in the wind. I called, but no one answered; no one was to be seen. It was deadly quiet. They were gone. Also gone was the nice lady from across the street. She used to sit on a bench in the playground and give us cookies. No one explained why and whereto she had disappeared. – Mrs. Streu, another occupant in our apartment house, whom I helped to make puppets, supposedly ended up in a concentration camp because she refused to answer "Heil Hitler" when someone riding in the same streetcar greeted her.

Unable to find Wolfgang, I went home, asked Mutti for a nickel, and headed to the corner drugstore to buy a few pieces of licorice, which I liked more than candy. Wolfgang was soon forgotten, and I concentrated on my other playmates, mostly boys, who lived close to the playground. When I was six, I had one female friend, named Ilse. Ilse was an only child and tied to her Mom's apron strings. She liked to play with dolls and dollhouses most of all. Ilse was a real sissy, cheated at checkers, and was too scared to join the male crowd when we engaged in such pranks as throwing a pebble in the street and running to fetch it just before an oncoming car could hit us. We did not even let her take part when we teased people by tying an empty old purse to a thin thread, laying it on the sidewalk while we held on to the thread behind a closed entrance door. The second a pedestrian bent down to pick up the treasure, we would pull it away and scare the poor soul. The boys got really nasty. They wrapped "horse apples" in small packages and put them on the sidewalk, watching for people to pick them up and encounter the stinky surprise when they unwrapped them. I did play along a couple of times when we spit down on people's heads from our third-floor balcony on Kleine Düwelstraße, but I don't remember the saliva ever hitting a hat or a head of hair.

I don't recall that any of my playmates ever wondered what happened to Wolfgang or the cookie lady on November 9, 1938. We did not know that the night's occurrences would later be referred to as *Reichskristallnacht*, that is, Crystal Night, or Night of the Shattered Glass. I find it incredible that on that gray morning in November, at the age of six, I was practically in the middle of it. I did not learn about the term and what it meant until I read about it in 1954 in the public library in Kalamazoo, Michigan, shortly after my immigration to America. Only then did I find out how it started: Hitler took advantage of an incident in Paris involving a Jewish teenager who shot the secretary of the German embassy to launch an entirely new phase in the government's persecution of Jews. It was not until I came to America and saw a documentary film on TV at Wetherbee Lake Farm, my sponsor's estate, depicting the horrors of the Holocaust that I began to grasp the enormity and full extent of the crimes against humanity that Hitler's Germany – including our fathers, either actively or by being silent – had committed. That part of history was not taught in schools, nor was it discussed at home, with friends, or in public. – I do not remember exactly when it was that I was told by my mother that the cookie lady was Jewish, as was Wolfgang's father, who had disappeared before that fateful night.

I must have been a good reader early on, because when I turned seven, our priest at Sankt Heinrich put me on his lap to test my reading from a prayer book. He concluded that I read well enough to go to First Communion early. It was a festive event at Sankt Heinrich. Both of Mutti's older sisters came; they were also my godmothers. Aunt Anna and Aunt Sissy. Aunt Sissy gave Mutti white silk with which to sew my dress, and Aunt Anna presented me with a silver bracelet, a matching necklace, and a crucifix pendant. Mutti baked sheet cakes at the bakery across the street, and together with a few other relatives, we had a special celebration with delicious cakes, whipped cream, and other pastries. In the evening, wine was served in the cobalt-blue crystal wine goblets. Papa played the piano and Mutti sang. It was the last festive event on Kleine Düwelstraße before our lives changed.

World War II – The First Bomb – At the Mercy of Relatives

In September 1939, not quite a year after Crystal Night, and a few months after my First Communion, we were suddenly roused by loud knocks at the heavy oak door at the entrance to our apartment house. My father got out of bed in the middle of the night. Several soldiers in greenish-gray uniforms told him to get dressed and come with them. From then on, he wore a uniform and a long saber at his side, even though he continued to go about his duties at the police (or county) court of Hannover. I believe he felt rather important in his role as warrant officer. Once, he took me along on an evening walk. It was dark outside, because as soon as the sun had set, the black shades in front of the windows cast in darkness the big city of five hundred thousand people. A soldier of lesser rank stood next to an unlit lamppost embracing and kissing his sweetheart. When he failed to respond to my father's "Heil Hitler," he stepped right in front of the lovers and asked the soldier in a commanding voice, "Don't you know how to say 'Heil Hitler'?" I was embarrassed and felt sorry for the man, but kept quiet until years later.

By and by, we were taught how to get ready for air raids. There were practice sessions conducted by the warden, Dr. Brasch, a philosophy professor, to condition the tenants to getting as quickly as possible from their apartments to the shelters. We children thought it all quite exciting. Once I tempted my playmate, Gisela Brasch, who lived in an apartment on the ground floor and was a couple of years older, to come with me to the top floor of the apartment-house stairs. I took along my half-size violin, stood right at the balustrade, and slid my finger up and down the D string, imitating a siren. The doors flew open; the tenants rushed with suitcases and gas masks toward the basement. Gisela's father stopped them at the basement door and informed them that I had played a trick. I was beaming, but Dr. Brasch and the tenants were not amused. I never tried it again, because not long after the incident, the first bomb fell in Hannover, right around the corner from us. That dampened my desire for tricks.

I had talked Ilse into going window-shopping with me downtown. It was in the early afternoon. We strolled arm in arm and paused at windows to look at pretty dresses, toys, and other things that interested us at that age. Out of the blue, sirens went off in the distance, followed by others in a staggered crescendo, until the wailing on all sides became so loud that we covered our ears. Shoppers and clerks were running everywhere, seeking shelter in basements and corridors. Within seconds, the streets were deserted and the traffic had come to a halt. Cars and streetcars stood empty in the street. Ilse and I started running together along the facades of the houses toward Kleine Düwelstraße, normally a thirty-minute walk.

As we turned the corner onto Sallstrasse, an air warden stopped us. He scolded us for being so careless and shoved us down the basement steps of a building. The cave-like interior had a dirt floor and was dimly lit by a blue light. The walls were black with soot, and the small place stank nauseatingly of rotten potatoes. It was crammed with people – whining children, old people on benches, men talking in low voices. A boy clutched a tin soldier, and a hoarse voice warned that enemy bombers were approaching Hannover. It was broad daylight. I whispered into Ilse's ear to stick close and told her we had to get out of the hole. Even a little kid could see that the place was not safe. As soon as the warden took his eyes off us, we sneaked up the stairs and stole our way homeward, ducking periodically into doorways. Two blocks from home, we heard the heavy drone of a plane. A zinging sound bore down on us, louder and louder. A shattering explosion threw us to the sidewalk. We were really scared. Ilse was crying. We crawled to the nearest basement and waited, trembling. – Not more than thirty minutes later, the sirens rang out again, signaling the end of the raid. We went home and fell into Mutti's arms. I got spanked by Papa with his favorite carpet paddle and got locked into the dreaded laundry closet, where I fell asleep crying. Ilse's mother did not even scold her.

I witnessed *Kristallnacht* and heard the first bomb hit Hannover. Miraculously, no one died. They were talking about a man who had been asleep in his bed on the fourth floor. When the bomb hit, he fell straight down to the ground floor, still in his bed and totally unharmed. However, I assume the rapid descent awakened him.

A story circulated that the bomb on Seilerstraße was an accident, that is, a stray bomb, dropped by a British bomber. At least, people hoped that was the case. In fact, after that "accident" in 1940, our lives were never the same, because the war began to escalate. Mutti went with us kids to a little village called Beendorf, where Aunt Sissy and Uncle Adolf, who was the director of a salt mine, lived in a magnificent mansion. In Germany, these big houses are called "villas." I was enrolled in a Catholic school for a few months only, because it was also closed by the Nazis, aka national socialists.

In Beendorf, we were aware of a big garden and park surrounding the manor, but had to adhere to stringent ground rules. "Take your shoes off the minute you step into the house," "don't raise your voices in the house," "don't step on the lawn or the flower beds." "Don't slide down the balustrade," "don't pick any fruit off the trees," "stay out of the garden," "don't leave your toys behind," "don't step on the carpet in the hallway," "don't play with Lux" (the shepherd dog), and so on. I thought it was so weird that my aunt instructed me not to tell my uncle that she had given me a pretty red dress and black patent-leather shoes for my birthday. We were also strictly forbidden to touch her navy blue Opel, which never had a speck of dust on it. She was afraid of fingerprints, which might be spotted by Uncle Adolf. We were also forbidden to tell him about the time she drove us back to Hannover. Uncle Adolf had ordered her not to. He himself had a chauffeur and never learned to drive. He was so short that he probably could not reach the gas pedal or see over the steering wheel. My aunt was about twice his size. To be fair, I must say that he was obsessed with mushroom hunting and did take us kids along on occasion to help him gather some. There were many beautiful forests with conifer trees close to his mansion, Villa Glück Auf ("Good Luck" for the miners). I loved the dark and spooky forest and its soft, mossy carpet. The scent of pine trees in the air was so refreshing.

Mutti always looked so nice in her snow-white apron frock. She was no taller than 5'5", and she had a pleasing figure and very shapely legs. She preferred to wear her light-brown hair combed back and gathered in a bun when she did not have a permanent. Her blue eyes must be attributed to her father, because her mother's eyes were brown. I believe Aunt Sissy ordered her to wear the white apron, to make sure she would not mistakenly be addressed as "Frau Bergwerksdirektor," an epithet the servants had to use whenever they addressed Aunt Sissy. Though she and her older sister had the advantage of having gone to a business school – a privilege not afforded Mutti – she never earned a single degree. Sissy was nevertheless a very attractive woman. She was tall and slender and had dark skin, brown eyes, beautiful curly black hair, and shiny white teeth. Mutti told us that when she was a little girl, the Gypsies, who had been begging in the village, got her confused with their own children and loaded her on their wagon. Her brother Franz spotted her just as the cart was about to leave the village.

Queen Sissy had a flock of servants, who had their quarters on the third floor of the mansion. I remember a cook who later took off with a priest, a cleaning woman who got pregnant by a soldier stationed in the area, a laundry woman who was too old to have fun, and a nanny who was constantly knitting for my little cousin. The gardener was as unfriendly as Uncle Adolf's chauffeur. They never spoke to us kids. Those in charge of cleaning were afraid of my aunt. Wearing white gloves, she would wipe her hands across surfaces and in corners to test for missed dust. Mutti might as well have been included with the servants. Though she did not get paid, she was always working whenever we lived with those relatives, and even when visiting others. Although she had to help with the coal business during World War I, the only training she had were lessons in sewing; thus, the relatives always took advantage of her. On the other hand, she never refused. Occasionally I had to babysit for my girl cousin, which I did not really enjoy. What I remember most is the time I found her standing in the crib, totally covered by a dark-green mush that looked like digested spinach. She must have liked it, unlike other kids I knew, because she was scooping it from the railing of her crib with her little index finger, which she stuck in her mouth in order to swallow the spinach a second time. I definitely did not like watching her go potty. Whenever she took too long, I urged her on with a pinch to her fanny, which resulted in her beginning to cry, thus prolonging the agony.

Aunt Sissy and Uncle Adolf's Glück Auf, like all of their impressive residences, was furnished luxuriously throughout. I always felt drawn to the extensive library, with massive bookcases, leather chairs and couches, and rich Oriental carpets. I was as fascinated by the round structure of the winter garden, enclosed with windows all around, heated in the winter, and housing beautiful potted trees, as I was by the lady's salon, outfitted with mahogany furniture. The chairs were upholstered with lilac velvet and sat on light-blue Oriental carpets. The glass cabinet was filled with Meissen and Rosenthal china figurines, with gold-rimmed cups and beautiful antique vases. Oriental carpets also graced the big entrance hall, and in front of the fireplace lay a huge stuffed brown bear, his pink muzzle wide open, flashing his big white teeth at us. Of course, all these rooms were off-limits to us, and so was the bear. We could look at him from three feet away only.

We had our more humble quarters upstairs, where we had a good view down on the pigeon loft, and on the part of the garage that housed the impeccable Opel, which like all privately owned cars was eventually confiscated by the German military. One Sunday morning, my older brother, dressed for church in his navy-blue suit, went to open the loft. He pulled on a chain below. A pigeon stepped out on the little platform and – plump – planted a white poop on his freshly combed and pomaded hair. I thought it was mighty funny. It reminded me of the time we kids sent down saliva from the third-floor balcony on Kleine Düwelstraße. We did not stay long in Beendorf and returned to Hannover, where we lived until we had to pack up again in 1941 and move in with Sissy and Adolf at their next mansion, in the snazzy resort Bad Helmstedt, where Uncle Adolf was in charge of another salt mine. Opposite the house was a beautiful lake. Again, everything was off-limits to us. Mutti enrolled me once more in a Catholic school, which I attended until Hitler closed it. I switched over to another public school, studying there until we returned to Hannover. From then until the end of the war, I "visited" many public schools. I attended a total of twenty-four schools in my lifetime.

Back in Hannover, I was now within walking distance to school. As the war escalated, food-ration cards were started as early as 1939, and groceries were increasingly shorter in supply. Fruits, candies, chocolates, and everything kids liked kept disappearing from the cupboards. We often went to bed hungry. When the situation got worse, Mutti would take us kids occasionally to her parents' home in a small village near Hildesheim, where everybody was Catholic and lived within walking distance of the small, but strikingly ornate, baroque church, in which all weddings and funerals were celebrated. A strong smell of incense, which I liked, was forever present. To get to Mutti's homestead we took the red streetcar, No. 11. It stopped every fifteen minutes or so. The trip to this antiquated village lasted over an hour, and it was not the most pleasant place to visit. There were no kids to play with, no open yards to run around in. The Germans are obsessed with building walls and fences around their properties. Every door or gate is locked. You have to ring a bell to gain entrance or risk being bitten by a fierce dog. No wonder I am still afraid of the four-legged barkers.

Mutti was the youngest and shortest of seven children – four brothers and two sisters. My grandparents were serious and sinister at all times. I never saw either of them smile or laugh. Though the term was unheard of at the time, they were probably suffering from ongoing depression. I am not sure whether Aunt Sissy and her older sister, the tall, blond, and blue-eyed Anna, were right when they complained about the shabby way in which Aunt Stingy and her husband, their older brother Hannes, were treating my grandparents. I read later in a chronicle that my grandmother was a "very vivacious woman" and a most capable business partner to my grandfather. I remember her as thin, petite, quick, and always dressed in black with a little white trim. Her hair was silver gray, parted in the middle, and twisted into a bun on the top of her head. Once, she visited us on Kleine Düwelstraße, when she was over seventy years old. I teased her by having her chase me around the heavy, round oak table in the family room. She had surprised me as I was cutting out a pattern in a tablecloth Mutti had crocheted. As I ran around the table, I pointed the scissors at her, calling out, "Catch me, grandma, catch me!" I don't think she laughed even when she caught me. She died when she was seventy-seven years old.

Grandfather hardly ever spoke to us kids. He was a tall man, bony, and physically very strong despite his various illnesses, which he treated himself, using Pastor Dr. Sebastian Kneipp's nature cures rather successfully. When he was sick, he simply asked the doctor for a diagnosis and then cured his ailments with herbs and other natural remedies. Mutti told me he had healed many people in the village by similar means and made quite a name for himself. Since Mutti had to stay home during World War I, she had to gather herbs for him in the surrounding fields and forests and help dry them in the attic. It was a habit she practiced herself all her life. Grandfather walked erect, but his head was always a little bent, probably out of fear of hitting the ceiling. He was very correct, a pillar of the community, a hard worker, and respected businessman. Over the years, he built a successful coal and threshing-machine business. His great passions were horse races and playing skat with his male friends in the corner pub on Sundays after Mass. I don't know if he had seven children because he liked children or because he was a devout Catholic. Grandfather died at age eighty-four, after his horse kicked him in the temple.

In reading my grandfather's (on my mother's side) chronicle recorded on Christmas Day 1942, during World War II (coincidentally, exactly fifty-eight Christmas Days before I started writing my own memoirs), I am filled with pride and admiration regarding my great-great-grandmother's strength of character. At age forty-one, Heinrich Engelbert Niele, a widower with a son named Ferdinand, married Josefa Katherina Reeke (who was twenty-three years old) in 1853. Four sons, including my grandfather, were born out of that marriage. Somehow, during their marriage, his mother lost both legs. She walked on crutches, or my grandfather pulled her in a cart or carried her around in a back-basket. He was proud of the fact that he and his brothers were physically very strong. All of them worked very hard. Grandfather, like his brothers, started working in the field when he was only eleven years old, for 40 cents a day. After his father's early death, at which point he and his three brothers were still underage, a legal dispute regarding the parcels of land left behind ensued. His crippled mother, in need of a decision from the court, hitched a couple of big dogs in front of the cart, rode to the nearest town, about five miles away, secured a judgement in her favor, borrowed money, and paid off Ferdinand, who immigrated to America and was never heard of again. She died at age fifty-two.

My grandparents had lived through World War I, at which time one of the sons, Uncle Franz, was injured by grenades. Empress Marie Louise had a medal made for him from one of the splinters. Another splinter was said to be traveling within his body and caused him to be termed an "invalid." He used to collapse unexpectedly. I very much liked him, as well as his wife Lisa and daughter Elisabeth. They were kind and more cheerful than Mutti's oldest brother, Hannes, and his grouchy and sinister wife.

Mutti's parents, her older brother, his wife and three children, and his younger brother Franz, along with his wife and daughter, all lived in a gloomy, L-shaped half-timber house, which was several hundred years old. Right at the main entrance door stood the iron water pump, where Grandfather was once hit by lightning. We fought over who got to pump when Mutti was fetching water for the kitchen. They had special red- and orange-colored enamel water buckets on a bench next to the stove. They were carried right through the sinister but spacious vestibule. The floor was covered with dark-gray stone. It was the spot where they put up the bier with my dead relatives before the pallbearers came to carry them through the main village street to the cemetery. The few windows in the house were too small for an escape in the event of a fire. Between the main house and Uncle Franz's place was a dark, tunnel-like stone walk to the horse stall and the toilet box, which was made of wooden planks and had a hole in the top. To get to it, one had to pass the horse, which tended to stick its head through the opening, underneath which it had its fodder crib. Scared, I would duck and then make a run for the box, which, like a throne, sat on yet another box where the stinky mess was collected for the vegetables in the garden behind the house. Instead of toilet paper, a column of square-cut 4" x 4" newspaper or magazine sheets was threaded on a string and hung on a hook next to the throne.

Grandfather had three or four small bedrooms upstairs. When grandmother died, I had to go to the narrow and dark room where she lay in bed. They made me touch her stiff big toe, to teach me what a dead person feels like. I'll never forget it. Before the funeral, she was displayed in the vestibule. The small living room, where Grandfather had a lectern, and where he also kept his long pipe and a bottle of whiskey with a spout and a shot glass, was next to the kitchen, which had a coal-burning cooking stove. I could watch as Grandpa poured a shot into a small glass and down his throat in virtually one motion. He also carried a little box in his jacket from which he would pinch a bit of powder, which looked like pepper, between his thumb and index finger. He held it close to his open nostril, squeezed the other one shut with the other index finger, took a deep breath, and instantaneously sneezed explosively. – A dining room for special occasions like funerals and weddings was also downstairs, to the right of the main entrance. It was not very big. The dining-room table took up the entire length of the room. When it was filled with guests, two of the younger ones had to sit in one chair. I have never again lived in a home where such bizarre practices were necessary.

When you entered the house's cobblestone driveway, you could not miss the big shed adjacent to the main house. It was the shelter for coal, which, in addition to other salvage, my grandfather sold to the villagers in big hundredweight sacks. At the entrance stood the big scale on which the sacks were weighed; they were then lifted by Grandfather, or whoever was helping, onto the big horse-drawn wagon. It was parked toward the back, next to the horse stall and the other big shelter, which housed the threshing machine he rented out to the farmers at harvest time. Mutti prided herself on having lifted many sacks of coal when she had to pitch in after her brothers had been drafted for World War I. I loved it when Grandfather let me sit on the seat next to him while he delivered coal to the villagers. Once, we had even more fun when he piled the cart full of hay and took us for a ride on the village streets. Since only a handful of people (150 or so) lived in the village, there were only a couple of streets. The main street led directly to the little river, the Innerste. Mutti was so proud when she told us that Grandpa would get up early in the morning during the coldest winters, run barefoot, dressed in bathing trunks, through the fresh snow to the river, break the ice, jump into the freezing water up to his waist, and return home to get dressed (a thirty-minute Kneipp exercise). Maybe that's the reason I like snow so much.

Mutti never visited her home to just sit and talk. It was obvious that her sister-in-law, whose harsh and ominous features are forever engraved in my mind, expected Mutti to work. Mutti was either mending at the sewing machine, digging, raking, pulling weeds in their various gardens (some of which were as much as a kilometer away), harvesting vegetables and preparing them for canning, scrubbing floors, or helping with the coal business. She helped because she was just that way; but deep down, she was hoping for a loaf of bread, a piece of ham, a can of lard, meat, wurst, or bacon. When we stayed overnight, we secretly hoped for a hearty breakfast in the morning. It meant a piece of pumpernickel with homemade sausage, or lard with cheese instead of the watered-down marmalade we got in Hannover. It was actually a mixture of berries, thickened with flour or grit. I have not forgotten the time that sinister aunt got her boys out of bed early to feed them a substantial country breakfast but, as soon as she saw us kids from the big city, replaced the sausage with marmalade similar to what we ate at home. When the first two of her three sons died in quick succession at the age of seven or eight, the relatives in the city felt that the good Lord had punished the parents for their avarice, which got worse after my grandparents passed away.

Mutti was better rewarded when she took us to help at hog-slaughter time in the fall. It was the time when one or two hogs, which they raised in the sty between the residences of the two brothers, were to be butchered right there on the premises. They were pigs and not cows, as my older brother tried to tell me when I was about two years old. It was always a sensation to watch the big, fat hog being half pushed and half pulled out of the sty. It had to cross a platform made of boards, which lay over a dung hole. Once, a true Wilhelm Busch caricature unfolded right then and there. (Busch, born in Hannover a hundred years before me, is famous for his satirical drawings and short rhymes exposing human weaknesses.) On this occasion, the fat swine was too heavy. The boards gave way, and the hog plunged with a big splash into the dung hole. The liquid manure came splashing out of the opening. Aunt Stingy raised both arms toward heaven and screamed, "Oh Gott, das schöne Schwein!" (O God, the beautiful pig!), and then cried, "Help! Help! My clean skirt, my apron, how dreadful, all that stinky mess!" She probably would have fainted if it had not been so important to retrieve the pink monstrosity from the liquid manure. Every available man and woman came to pull on the ropes around the hog and shove the boards underneath the pig's belly to eventually bring him up. The beast was screaming so loudly the people in the next village could hear it, I am sure. Aunt Stingy had pushed us kids out of the way when they poured buckets of hot water over the pig. The next scene I was allowed to witness was when Mutti pushed the large, white enamel bowl underneath the pig's neck. The butcher stuck a sharp knife into it, and a thick stream of blood gushed out into the bowl. Mutti stirred the thick, red blood with her wrist and hand. They needed it, along with pieces of tongue and white bacon fat, to make blood sausage. It tastes good on pumpernickel with lard and mustard.

Since these slaughter feasts took place during the late fall, Mutti made sure she got her share of *Bregenwurst* to eat with sauerkraut or kale on Christmas Eve. It is a specialty of Northern Germany and made from chopped pig brains, a fact I discovered only recently. Mutti took anything Aunt Stingy felt inclined to part with, including what normally was thrown into the garbage, like pig skin or bacon rind. Some used it to make soap, but Mutti put it in split-pea or bean soups, just to have a little extra fat. Since there were always many helpers around, they did not dare deprive us children of some meaty morsels. We ate as though we had been starving for years, lots of fat and plenty of mustard. I loved mustard so much that when Mutti sent me to the corner grocery across the street on Kleine Düwelstraße with an empty glass and a nickel to fetch mustard from their barrel, I had eaten a great portion of the yellow stuff with my index finger by the time I returned. – Mutti scolded me, claiming I would become stupid from eating too much mustard.

Each time we visited, Mutti made the rounds, calling on other farmers in the village. She used to take me along because I had no one to play with. I did not like my cousins, because they were rough and looked yucky. Nobody seemed to bother cleaning their noses. The green stuff was always running out of the nostrils. Mutti's old friends always gave her eggs, vegetables, fruits, or other food items, depending on the season. Before we went home, Mutti took us to the cemetery to pray for the dead and admire the elaborately decorated graves. They are status symbols. – I loved to visit my aunt and older cousin. They both had the prettiest brown eyes and dark-brown hair. Aunt Lisa was always joking and laughing.

Once, on the way home from the cemetery, Mutti decided to look for a few green apples under the trees lined up along the country road. They were no bigger than golf balls. She used them for apple jelly or heaven-and-earth soup (made with apples and potatoes), which she served with bits of bacon rind. If it did not cook long enough, the rind tasted like leather. After the detour, we stopped at Grimsel's. He was a wealthy farmer, a fact indicated by the huge dung heap at the entrance to his property. Any German knows that the richer the farmer, the larger the dunghill. It is the throne from which the rooster picks his hens. Oma Grimsel asked us to wait at the tree stump in the large cobblestone courtyard. When she returned, she was carrying a live chicken by its feet in her left hand and a hatchet in her right. It was screaming at the top of its lungs. She asked me to grip the fluttering bird by its feet. Before I knew it, I was holding the flustered screamer with both hands, as far away from my body as possible. I was seven or eight years old. Oma Grimsel grabbed its neck, pressed it down on the upright tree stump, and lifted the hatchet, which she brought down on the chicken's neck with a bang. The head fell to the ground; the blood dripped from the neck on the stump, which was brown from former victims, and trickled down on the cobblestone. I had trouble holding on to the chicken, which was jerking furiously as though it wanted to fly away. I yelled at Mutti to please take the bird. But the two women just stood there, laughing at me. Oma Grimsel said, "The chicken is for you!" Mutti finally took it, thanked Oma Grimsel profoundly, wrapped newspaper around the bloody neck, and stuck it in a paper bag; and we left behind another Wilhelm Busch scene. (I find the hatchet method more humane than that in vogue in America, where they grab the bird by the neck and spin it around until the neck comes off.) – On the way home, Mutti pointed to a garden behind a high and long red-brick wall. She told me she picked cherries there for the owner when she was young. While picking the fruit, she whistled continuously to ensure she would not be tempted to put a cherry in her mouth. Can anyone blame me for wanting, once the war was over, to get as far away from those bizarre people as possible?

But there is more. In 1941, when the Americans entered the war, the air raids accelerated. We got to be pretty good at trying on those stinky gray gas masks. They made us look like snorkeled monsters. We became experts at jumping out of bed at the sound of a siren and running downstairs with gas masks around our necks and our little suitcases in hand. At night, we wore double sets of clothing instead of pajamas and had no trouble finding our belongings in the dark-blue light. Dark blue, because in addition to the black shades, blue-tinted bulbs were used to prevent the *Amis*, as we called the Americans, from seeing our houses. In our basement stood bunk beds with straw sacks, in case we felt like sleeping. I never saw or heard of anybody sleeping during an air raid, except for the man on Seilerstraße. The women prayed whenever we heard bombers approaching or the shooting of anti-aircraft flak in the background, which was done in an attempt to hit a plane before it could unload on us.

My parents hardly ever went out at night, and we never had a babysitter. Occasionally they went to see a movie. One time, they decided to see the movie *Die grosse Liebe* (Great Love), with Zarah Leander, Mutti's favorite actress. It was a matinee performance. I begged them to take me along, but they refused. As soon as they left the house, I followed them down the stairway and along the facades of the houses on the way to the streetcar. When the streetcar stopped to pick them up, I waited until they stepped into the first car and got into the second one myself. Since I did not have enough money for the ticket, I waited in line directly behind them. When Papa noticed me, he was furious, but he restrained his anger. He had no choice but to take me along. I loved the movie even more than I would have otherwise, because it was like eating forbidden fruit. Fortunately, Papa forgot to punish me; he and Mutti got too involved in discussing the movie.

As time went on, the enemy bombers became less considerate and much bolder. When they challenged the flak and appeared on the horizon in broad daylight, Mutti stopped baking cakes or making meals that required any length of time to prepare. The menu consisted of endless varieties of soups, stews, and milk rice. I missed school with increasing frequency. Many times, my father called us into the living room to listen to Hitler's ear-piercing speeches from the radio on his desk. Later in life I could identify his voice the minute he opened his mouth. Mutti, a serious Catholic, did not like him, even though she fulfilled her duty, as was expected of all German housewives. She helped by sewing surgical dressings and the like for wounded soldiers, and collected every hair from her brush. Hair was saved, we were told, for the production of ammunition. Once, my father got extremely upset with her when she showed him a large poster made of white cardboard. She wanted to send it to Hitler, hoping he would repent and return to the Catholic faith. She had mounted several black-and-white photographs of Hitler with Eva Braun, Göring, Goebbels, Hess, and others, all in civilian clothes, and framed each photograph with fresh green myrtle, which has strong symbolic connotations and is worn by virgin brides on their wedding day or at Holy Communion. Underneath each photo was an inscription of a religious nature. My father shouted, asking her if she wanted us all to be killed. (In retrospect, I am inclined to believe he knew something of what was going on regarding the persecution of Jews and opponents of Hitler, even though he denied it repeatedly, even when Hitler was no longer a threat.) My father took the poster and stuck it behind the big wardrobe in the bedroom. I never saw it again; I assume it was burned at the time our house was destroyed by enemy bombers.

For the beginning of the 1942 school year, when I was ten years old, and when we children at times ignored the war or had just gotten used to it, I had to pass my entrance exam for admission to a lyceum, a high school for girls in Hannover. It was a big event. The exam lasted a week, and as it turned out, I was lucky. I was exempt from the oral part of the entrance examination as a result of my advanced reading skills. I was mighty proud when the examiner asked me to take her place at the podium and read a story out loud to the students taking the test.

My favorite subjects in school were music, geography, writing, English, French, religion, and sports. When visitors came to our classes, the teachers sometimes introduced me as "the child who writes nice essays." I had played the violin since I was five, and I played in school and other youth orchestras whenever possible. While arithmetic created the biggest headaches, I made up for it in sports. I won a couple of prizes as the fastest runner in the class, and excelled with four meters in the long jump. Kids envied me because I could climb a rope or a pole faster than anybody in my class. I must have inherited the genes from my father, who was a sports instructor at a police academy in his twenties.

Evacuation – Villa Glück Auf!

I had attended the high school in Hannover for only a year when the bombings became so severe that all mothers with children were ordered to evacuate to the country. Guess where we ended up? In Aunt Sissy and Uncle Adolf's third mansion, Villa Glück Auf, which was located in V., a village in the scenic and hilly region of the Solling. Sissy had persuaded Mutti to come to her because she did not want to house strangers. Deep down, she knew Mutti was a hard worker and would not dream of refusing to toil for her. She needed her desperately, because her staff was reduced to two, a cook and a laundry woman. After all, Mutti came gratis. At that point, anyone who lived in the country and had extra rooms to share was required to take in evacuees from the big cities. Besides, we children had already been conditioned to their strict rules. The lavish mansion stood on an extremely high hill, next to an exhausted potash-and-salt mine, aka "the Muna" (a large ammunition factory), where Uncle Adolf, though he claimed not to be a Nazi, had to watch what was going on. The mine was partially run by the German military, which had rented the facilities from Uncle Adolf's employer, Burbach AG, to manufacture ammunition and store it underground. Uncle Adolf was close to retirement age. We arrived at our future abode during summer-school vacation in August and just in time for school in September. Neither of my brothers made it to high school. I was the only one.

Because there was no high school in V., I had to take a train every morning, which was pulled rather slowly by a coal-fired locomotive to Northeim, a ride of thirty minutes or more each way. We were usually home by 2:00 p.m. The Solling region was predominantly Protestant. I soon dreaded going to that school, because as even my friends noticed, the female teacher, a stoic Nazi who looked as haggard, gray, and sinister as Aunt Stingy, had it in for me, most likely because I was the only Catholic in her class. I never saw her smile. She was a spinster, wearing mostly black or dark-gray dresses. She had a dark voice that sounded like a man's, and she constantly ordered me to stand up at my desk, even when I had not moved or whispered a syllable to a classmate.

As a result of increasing attacks on our train by enemy planes, I often arrived late or missed classes altogether. One time, the train stopped abruptly. The conductor told us to get out and seek cover in the bushes of the embankment along the railroad tracks. American planes zeroed in on us. They flew very low, aimed at our locomotive and at us in the bushes, and attacked with machine guns. No one was hurt. On another occasion, the train stopped in a tunnel we passed through daily. It was pitch-dark in both the train and the tunnel, which was not quite a kilometer long. The walls were covered with soot from the locomotive. We were afraid of being trapped, but got out in the end.

Seven weeks after our move to V., on the night of October 8–9, 1943, over 60% of Hannover was flattened by American and English bombers. We did not find out immediately what had taken place, but could see from the hill of our house, more than one hundred kilometers away, that the sky over Hannover was red. It was red for several days. Later, we learned they had dropped predominantly phosphor bombs, which burned down the city together with thousands of its innocent citizens. It was during that night that our house on Kleine Düwelstraße went up in flames, that Papa's much-loved black ebony piano was reduced to ashes, and that my violin teacher, Frau Ritter, left her bombed house with only the Stradivarius under her arm and moved to Silesia. It was also the night my favorite cousin, Elisabeth, burned to death.

The reports about what happened in Hannover reached us little by little. We had no telephones, and the lines of communication were destroyed. My father was sound asleep in bed on the fourth floor and was awakened abruptly by the flames that surrounded him. He had not heard the sirens. Dr. Brasch, the warden, did not know my father was in the house. To protect important data from bombs, the court had been moved from Hannover to Hildesheim, where my father lived after we had moved to V. My father was in charge of the transport, and his crew loaded the dining-room furniture on the van, which went through Mutti's hometown. He had hoped to store the furniture in the big shed, where the threshing machine was housed. He had acted without first asking, as there were no phones. When the van showed up in their driveway and he asked Aunt Stingy, she flatly refused to let the furniture be stored, even though there was enough room and my father was willing to risk the furniture's possibly getting damaged by the weather. She remained stubborn, and my father was forced to move the furniture back to Hannover, where he left it unassembled in the corridor. It was late. He was too tired to return to Hildesheim that night and went to bed. When he noticed the fire, he jumped out of bed. Still in his underwear, he grabbed his saber and barely made it to the stairway, which had not yet collapsed because the frame was made of iron. As he reached the stairs, the rooms came crashing down around him.

The tenants in the basement were surprised to see him. He told them what he had just witnessed. Dr. Brasch ordered everybody out of the basement and into another shelter through an opening in the basement wall. He watched at the opening to make sure everybody was accounted for, but did not follow. Much later, we heard that after he knew his wife and two children were safe, he committed suicide. At that point, he feared, the Nazis would discover he was Jewish and he would most likely be imprisoned and his family endangered. He also believed his life's work, a number of books on philosophy that he had published, had been reduced to ashes. His will to live had been extinguished. – He would have been pleased to know that his wife and children survived and moved back to Hannover, where his son had a practice as a medical doctor and Gisela was enrolled at the University of Goettingen.

Mutti felt it was very fortunate that we were all alive. It did not matter that we had lost the dining-room furniture and other belongings. After all, we had moved the living-room and master-bedroom furniture to V., where Aunt Sissy had allocated three rooms to us: a kitchen, a small living room, and a bedroom. When the news reached us, a couple of weeks after the bombing, that Elisabeth had burned to death in the house of her employer, we were devastated. It had been so unnecessary. Elisabeth was employed as a governess for a family originally from Italy. They owned Eisstuben, an elegant café on the south side of Hannover, not far from their residence. The family had been evacuated with their children to a village in the vicinity of Hannover. Elisabeth's fiancé, the son of a paint-store owner, whose building shared a wall with the house of Elisabeth's employer, had asked her for a date on the night of October 8. She had the weekend off and visited her parents in Großförste. She wanted to take the red No. 11 to Hannover. Her parents pleaded with her not to go, but she insisted, changed into her good dress and Italian leather shoes, a gift from her boss, and took the electric streetcar to Hannover. Just as she arrived, the sirens sounded. She made it to her basement but never came out alive.

Uncle Franz and Aunt Lisa waited for almost a week to hear from their daughter. Finally, my uncle, insisting he wanted to go alone, took the No. 11. He was devastated when he realized the extent of Hannover's destruction. Smoke was still coming out of the rubble everywhere. Hitler Youths and others were collecting charcoaled corpses leaning against the facades of burned-down houses. The stop was not far from the house. He made his way over stone rubble and debris. Since it was a one-family home and three heavy bombs had fallen on it, it was nothing but a huge pile of stones. Uncle Franz searched for an opening and was relieved when he spotted a small hole among the rubble. Smoke came out of it. Still, he was optimistic that Elisabeth might have escaped, because she was slender and quite athletic. Just then a couple of Hitler Youths came along. They asked him what he was looking for. He uttered, "I am looking for my daughter, my only child." The young men offered to help him search by going down into the opening. One of them tied a rope around his waist, and the other let him down slowly. When the first youth returned, he said he had touched two corpses. They called for additional help and started to dig.

Meanwhile, at home, Aunt Lisa had become restless. She followed her husband to Hannover and arrived at the very moment they pulled out the first scorched corpse. It had shrunk so much that it fit into a laundry basket. Even Uncle Franz was unable to identify the body. Aunt Lisa stumbled toward the group. My uncle put his arm around her and said, "Oh, Mutter! You should not have come." She looked at the basket and said, "Unsere Lisabeth" (our Lissy). She had recognized her daughter by the Italian shoes. The second corpse was Elisabeth's employer. They recognized him by a golden tooth. Both had been smothered because the coal had started to burn. They were trapped. Elisabeth's fiancé reported later that although he had heard someone knocking at the wall, he could not get out to help, because his house was also destroyed.

That night, the homes of Mutti's two other siblings, Seppel and Anna, were bombed and totally destroyed. Aunt Anna and her husband had to seek shelter in a big underground bunker. Uncle Wilhelm was almost trampled to death on the stairway leading down to the bunker. People were scared; they rushed down to the shelter as the bombs were falling without consideration for others. Fortunately, his injuries were not serious. They moved to their little garden shed outside of Hannover, where they lived for years in the most humble circumstances until Uncle Wilhelm died. Aunt Anna, finally, years after the end of the war, found a small apartment.

The war wiped out everything Aunt Anna and her husband did own. They lost a big apartment house with a pub downstairs. Her daughter Annie lived in the same house, with her husband and son. While Annie's husband had been drafted, she and her four-year-old son, Rolf, had been evacuated to the country, where they lived with Annie's in-laws near Heidelberg. Ironically, they never returned to Hannover. Aunt Anna did not find out what happened to Annie and Rolf until several months later. Rolf had complained about pains in his side. My cousin went with him to Heidelberg on the train, but there was nothing wrong with him. On the way home, American planes attacked the passenger train with machine guns. Rolf was fatally injured in his mother's arms, and she died from the shock, according to an eye-witness report. Her husband never returned from the front in Russia. Aunt Anna and Uncle Wilhelm would not have minded losing all of their and their daughter's worldly possessions, if only their child and grandchild had lived.

Uncle Seppel, who worked in Hannover as a machinist at the big tire company Continental, and his wife Ella lost their possessions while they too were evacuated and lived with relatives in a village near Hannover. We children liked Uncle Seppel and Aunt Ella. They used to give us self-made items or useful objects from auctions. My uncle liked to comb the area where the famous Hannoverian Schützenfest, the annual fair for marksmen, took place to find coins that had been dropped at the merry-go-rounds. He was a chubby guy, bald, with blue eyes and a big smile. He bragged when he had filled his little sack with coins. Sometimes, before the war and in the beginning, he treated us children to a day at the big fair and bought us oxblood candy of red and white sugar, pink and sticky Turkish honey, burned sugar-coated almonds, a hard roll with herring or lox, or a bratwurst with mustard. He always drank a few beers with a shot of schnapps, a favorite drink at the fair in Hannover.

Uncle Seppel and Aunt Ella rarely came to visit us in the Solling. Like the rest of the relatives, they were not fond of Uncle Adolf. There was no need to be afraid of air raids in V. The Americans never bombed the village in a big way, because at first they did not appear to know the location of the Muna. A couple of bombs fell there, probably by mistake. One came close to hitting the villa and harming my little brother, Alfons.

Alfons had befriended some of the soldiers at the ammunition plant. One Saturday forenoon, his friend Ulrich asked him to come along to pick up milk in the village for the soldiers. Alfons, about seven years old, climbed up and sat next to him on the wagon loaded with big, empty aluminum milk cans. Two big horses were hitched in front of the wagon. The cobblestone road went downhill. Ulrich stopped at Antons, the village inn, to get a beer. He asked Alfons to wait for him on the coachbox and watch the horses. Suddenly, a humming sound was audible. It became louder and louder. The horses shook their manes and neighed. A bomb exploded in the field next to the road, about two hundred meters away. The animals became wild, raised their front hooves high, pulled at the harness, and stormed, along with the wagon and rattling milk cans, toward a steep and narrow path down a hill, a shortcut for pedestrians. Little Alfons sat up straight, pulled with all his might at the reins, and, just one yard before the descent, stopped the wagon. Ulrich came running, jumped on the wagon, patted Alfons on the shoulder, and praised him for being so quick and brave. On that day, the little hero definitely prevented a catastrophe. The bomb left a big crater in the field next to our street.

Surprisingly, no bombs were dropped on the Muna. Later I learned that an American plane was shot down not too far from V. and that the pilot was buried in the cemetery of a neighboring village. Toward the end of the war, the railroad tracks were destroyed, which blocked the transport of ammunition to the front, but more importantly brought my school travel to a screeching halt. I did not miss going to that dreaded school in Northeim. Mutti, determined to keep me occupied, engaged a Latin and violin teacher for me while my brothers continued at the local school. According to my report card, which bore the stamp depicting an eagle with a swastika, I missed class fifty-four times that year and had to repeat it.

In addition to an occasional sounding of sirens, a couple of minor bombings took place two or three kilometers from our house toward the end of March and the beginning of April. The first resulted in the death of a child. The other was most likely an attempt to destroy the Muna with phosphor bombs. Instead, it caused minor damage down the street from us to the grandiose house of Mr. Albrecht, also connected with Burbach AG. Our village decided at the last minute not to resist. With the exception of one farmer, who was killed when he ran toward a ditch for shelter as soon as he spotted the *Amis* on the tanks, no one was hurt. The farmer ignored the Americans' warnings to stand still. They thought he wanted to get a gun and shoot them. The teacher and hardline Nazi who advised Alfons to cleanse his chest in case a bullet hit him – something I never quite understood – was seen on the roof of the school waving a white bedsheet, capitulating.

I became friendly with the daughter of Frau Haupt, who came to wash Aunt Sissy's dirty linens in big tubs in the basement. Frau Haupt first boiled the laundry in a big copper kettle and then transferred it into large, oval wooden tubs, where she scrubbed the linens with soap on a washboard. After the laundry was rinsed several times, she would squeeze it through a wringer and hang it outside in the sun or in the basement to dry. I liked to go visit Marianne, who was much taller than I and very skinny, unlike her mother, who was stout, had a red face, and always wore a scarf on her head. They lived very humbly in a tiny house in a nearby village, called Schlarpe. It took about twenty minutes to walk there on a hilly road. When I visited, Marianne often had to take a couple of goats to the meadow. We sat in the grass chatting or reading while herding the goats. Every Easter, Frau Haupt gave us a butchered baby goat, which Mutti roasted for our main meal, which in Germany is at noon. It tasted so good, and we always could have eaten more. Along the road to Schlarpe were wheat and potato fields. The pupils were sent there to search for potato bugs, which English planes were said to dispense. I always took along a bag and a knife to gather grass for our rabbits, which we raised for food in little cages in back of the villa and next to the fence that ran along the embankment down to the railroad tracks. Snitching grass was risky, because the owner of the field, who used the grass to feed his own animals, sometimes stood guard and might catch you.

Marianne and I liked to go mushroom hunting in the little pine-tree forest close to the villa. Sometimes, we took a blanket and spread it out when we wanted to relax and dream. I loved the scent of the coniferous forests and enjoyed walking on the needle-carpeted or moss-covered ground. When spring came, we gathered bright-yellow primroses, white snowdrops and lilies of the valley, or blue forget-me-nots in the deciduous forests and were happy when a tiny ladybug crawled over an arm. In the summer, we picked blue cornflowers and bright-red poppies in the fields of the Solling and wound wreaths for our heads out of daisies. Mutti loved it when I brought her a bouquet and put it on the chest of drawers in our bedroom next to the white porcelain statue of St. Mary. We said our evening prayers at the little altar.

In the beginning, only a couple of Catholic families lived in V. On Sundays we had a long – almost forty-five-minute – walk to get to church in a neighboring village. It was hard during the winter. Mutti was quite strict. Because we could not miss church on Sundays, which was considered a cardinal sin, we were obedient. We did not want to go to hell. Aunt Sissy saw to it that a priest from Goettingen came to the villa on occasion. She transformed her big dining room into a church with an altar. My oldest brother had crafted an altar cabinet out of wood for the monstrance, which Mutti held in high esteem. Sissy later bought the land on which a Catholic church was built. The priest was rather tall and well nourished, a bald-headed man who was rather chummy with Aunt Sissy, who had a thing for priests, as did Mutti, who used to go to opera performances with the priest who baptized me. This priest came at first by bike, together with a tall, pale, black-haired nun. They traveled approximately forty kilometers to hold Mass. Fräulein Kipp, that is, Mater Herwiges, dressed in civilian clothes. She came from the cloister Sankt Ursula in Duderstadt, which had been closed by the Nazis. Mater Herwiges worked as a parish nun for the priest. Sometimes a few young women from Hitler's Labor Service, who lived in barracks in the fields, came secretly, which did lend an eerie sense to the service. Herwiges also held catechism in our small living room, which held the furniture we had saved. The tall and massive dark-oak grandfather clock, Mutti's pride and joy, was the only piece saved from the dining room. We were only a few children: my brothers, two cousins, Karl, Marie, and I.

On the occasions when Mater Herwiges did not show up, Mutti speculated about what might have happened – whether she got caught or sent away. We children did not give it that much thought. We spent much time outdoors. On hot summer days, we skipped down the many steps to the swimming pool, built by the Nazis soon after they came into power. It was just big enough for the people in the area and was surrounded by well-kept lawns. The hills nearby were covered with lush forests, and at springtime, the slopes were thick with flowering shrubs. I learned how to swim in this pool, but I gave up diving when I hit the bottom with my head. Alfons learned to swim there when one of the German officers, a mandatory boarder at Aunt Sissy's who was supervising prisoners of war at the Muna, picked him up at the age of eight or so and tossed him without warning into the deep end. Miraculously, he learned to swim in an effort not to drown. It was quite scary to watch him hit the water with a big splash and paddle his way to the top. Alfons, who was nothing but skin and bones, did not even scream. It was Major Haas who also took us skiing on those dreadfully makeshift boards that were difficult to control because they were rough and dull. He was a huge and husky man with slick black hair, dark skin, and a sharp voice with a strong Viennese accent, and he always wore an officer's uniform. He had good skis and was always ahead of us. He also liked to play chess with Mutti.

On the field across from the villa were six barracks built by the German military for prisoners of war who worked in the Muna. Women from the Ukraine occupied two barracks and Polish men the other four. Each barrack was fenced in with barbed wire. Though we children were forbidden to seek contact with the prisoners, it was just too tempting not to try. Sometimes during the summer, at dusk, Marianne and I would walk up to the fence and watch the women as they huddled together, talking. A strong and distasteful smell of disinfectant was always present in the air. I was told it was used to kill the lice. I loved to listen to the women when they all sang together in the evening. Their songs were filled with profound melancholy and sadness, and never sounded cheerful or uplifting. On one occasion, a woman came to the fence when I was watching all by myself. She handed me a walking stick carved out of wood with pretty, dark-colored designs, for which I thanked her with a smile and ran home. Rumors were buzzing around to the effect that the military supervisors had been observed terribly mistreating female and male prisoners by abusing them verbally and physically. They had been seen lashing out at them with a whip and kicking them with their boots. Stories surfaced as well about Uncle Adolf and his rough and tyrannical treatment of the miners underground before the Nazis were in charge.

I cannot attest to Uncle Adolf's treatment of the men under his rod underground, but I can attest to his tyrannical treatment of us children and Mutti. How many times did I wish Mutti had not let us be lured to V. by her older sister? Not a single relative had one good word to say about Adolf. We called him "the Gnome." He was about as unappetizing to look at as they come. It seemed like he had never been young. He was bowlegged and so short that even I could almost look down on his few slick gray hairs, which he parted in a straight line. He glued them with gel to his pink and shiny skull. Never did I see a single hair out of place, not even when he exercised Lux, his fierce sheepdog. Once a day, he took Lux for a walk on the road to Schlarpe. Before locking him back into his kennel, he put him through a thirty-minute ritual in which he tossed him a piece of wood, which the dog grabbed with his teeth and rushed back to his master, the saliva dripping to the ground. Other physical irregularities were Adolf's disproportionately long arms, the pudgy hands with fingers like little sausages, and his fat stomach, resembling a pouch of potatoes. It got in his way when bending down to pick up the stick for Lux. Word had gotten out that he ate extra-large amounts of potatoes to grow the stomach and look more authoritarian. We could hardly keep from giggling as we watched him from our hideout in the bushes or when we saw him lap soup, which ran down his chin like his dog's saliva. Even funnier were his repeated attempts to catch the dripping liquid with his spoon and the rhythmic clattering of his false teeth as he gobbled down potatoes. He was a queer fellow. He never smiled or laughed, and constantly yelled at us. "Pack!" "Scoundrel!" "Stupid goose!" and "Get lost!" were examples of his frequent outbursts.

Why did Mutti not take us to strangers to escape the bombs? Anything would have been better than life in the villa. The seven years with those relatives were tantamount to slavery. What we endured there never could and never will be forgotten. Once I gained the distance necessary to digest the situation, I realized that the exposure to the events in V. had a major and lasting effect on my life and my relationship with family.

We were used to the dos and don'ts from our stays at Adolf's previous villas, where we never stayed very long. The same rules were still in effect, and others were added or enforced, such as access to his library. However, I discovered where he hid the key to the book cabinet and managed to retrieve many books without being caught. We did not want to believe our own eyes when one morning, as we looked out our bedroom window, Uncle Adolf was engaged in counting the espalier apples and pears by pointing his index finger at each fruit. Trained to grow against the wall of the villa, they were more easily accessible to us than the rest of the fruit trees. Those were located in a garden a level below, about ten steps down, and could be reached only through a tightly locked gate. Adolf guarded the key in his pocket. Just as incredible was the fact that he had counted the cherries in a bucket he had locked in on a balcony on the same floor as our kitchen. At the age of seven, Alfons virtually risked his life by stepping from the windowsill in the kitchen onto the sill on the balcony to fetch a handful of cherries. When the Gnome suddenly screamed so loudly that the owners of the villa five hundred meters away could hear him, demanding the stolen cherries back at once, we knew he had actually counted the cherries in the bucket.

Actually, the counting of apples and cherries was relatively tolerable. What he did to our adorable puppy, Nelly, was inhumane. Though we had strict orders not to have a pet, we dared to disobey, never expecting the results that followed. We assumed he loved dogs, since he had Lux. We children saved enough bread stamps to exchange them for a puppy from the local butcher. It was hard, considering our constant hunger. In a box, we smuggled tiny Nelly into a corner of the kitchen, where we kept him during the day. At night we carried him to a room in the basement where only our belongings were stored. After a few days, we wanted to take Nelly outside for some fresh air. When the coast was clear, we carried him outside the entrance gate and let him waddle around on a leash. While we were having fun watching Nelly, we forgot about the tyrant, who again appeared unexpectedly on the scene of the crime. He took one look at Nelly and turned pinker but did not scream; he just stooped to the ground, scraped together a handful of sand and gravel, and tossed it into Nelly's little eyes. We begged, "Uncle Adolf, please!" The puppy squeaked, and we picked him up, put him into his box, and hurried upstairs, where we rinsed out his red eyes. He had blinded the puppy. A few days later, Nelly died.

Nothing, however, could compare to the cruelties Mutti had to endure. She had taken over all of the duties of their former gardener, only rarely being rewarded for all her spading, raking, weeding, harvesting, canning, etc. Adolf's ultimate vindictiveness occurred when Mutti once went against his instructions. – He had given orders not to hang up wash and linens next to the kennel and the fence along the railroad embankment, for aesthetic reasons. No clutter! All our wash was to be dried in the damp basement, where it took days to dry. Those who experienced war in Germany know of the shortage of soap and detergent. Every housewife took advantage of sunny days to hang the wash on the line to be dried and bleached by the sun. Our wash was doomed to hang in the basement. It began to look gray. – One bright and sunny washday, Mutti watched the tyrant disappear with binoculars, cane, and Lux into the little forest adjacent to the villa. She decided to risk the unthinkable by quickly stringing a rope across the forbidden space. She hung the wet linens on the line in the hope that the mild breeze would blow it dry before the tyrant reappeared. She was on the lookout at the kitchen window upstairs, enjoying the view of the linens blowing in the wind. Encouraged that all was quiet on the front, she began to peel potatoes. Out of the blue, she heard Lux's bark shattering the peaceful atmosphere. She dropped the knife, rushed to the open window, and stared into the courtyard. Her cheeks grew pale. She braced herself at the sill. Tears welled from her tired, pale-blue eyes, ran down her haggard cheekbones, and dripped on the bib of her blue-and-white polka-dot apron. In agony, she pulled herself together, picked up the laundry basket despondently, stole down the stairs covered with thick carpets, and went to the backyard. She gathered the soiled linens off the sandy ground with trembling hands, sobbing softly. The tyrant had returned from his walk unexpectedly. When he saw the fresh linen, he pulled out his pocketknife and cut the line. Only after Mutti had found refuge in a corner of the dark basement did she sink down on a stool and let her tears flow freely.

Later, my brothers told me that one evening, they jumped Uncle Adolf and beat him up.

Occupation – Allies and Refugees

Our more or less peaceful coexistence with the prisoners and the German military came to a full stop a day before my thirteenth birthday. Mutti called us children into our living room, sat us around the heavy, round oak table, and explained that the Americans were on their way to our village. She told my older brother, Hanno, who had just turned sixteen, that he had to get ready to defend the village together with my cousin, who was fifteen, and other boys their age, because everybody over sixteen had already been drafted. The German military had ordered them to dig holes a bit back in the woods alongside the Bollert Straße, where the tanks were expected to roll in. The boys were to hide in the ditches and throw two grenades, which each boy was handed, onto the tanks, in the hope of stopping the Allies from reaching the Muna, one of the largest ammunition factories in Germany.

Mutti also mentioned that the German military had dug four holes in the bridge that crossed the railroad tracks approximately forty-five yards from the villa. They put dynamite into the holes to blow it up, and they would block the tanks coming by way of Schlarpe, where Marianne lived. We all knelt down and said a prayer, and Mutti blessed Hanno. Next, she told us to gather some of our favorite things and seek shelter in the basement, where we could sit on the chairs and wait for the *Amis*. There were a couple of bunk beds with straw sacks for Aunt Sissy and Uncle Adolf. We were directed not to go outside under any circumstance. The basement windows had been covered with wire window grilles in case of glass breakage. Just as Hanno and Karl were about to leave, a message was delivered that the boys should stay home. Mutti sighed, "Gottseidank!" but we still had to hide in the basement, because we did not know what to expect from the *Amis*. Also, the bridge had not yet exploded, and it was still possible that the German military would decide to blow up the Muna, which was only a few hundred yards or so away from the house. The whole place was like a powder keg ready to blow sky-high.

We waited anxiously all night in the basement. In the distance, we heard heavy artillery. Aunt Sissy and Mutti clutched rosaries and mumbled Hail Marys while Uncle Adolf paced the floor like a dwarf in a slapstick routine. I found the situation somewhat amusing. The next morning, a sunny spring day, we heard a heavy, sonorous noise approaching outside. "Tanks, Mutti, tanks!" shouted Alfons. Everybody whispered, "Die Amis." Sissy ordered us to lie on the floor and cover ourselves with blankets. As we lay quietly, we heard the metal tread of the tanks gnash across the cobblestones. The noise grew louder and the ground began to shake. Next we heard a big crash. The fence. A window broke and the wire window grilles clattered to the floor. Finally, all we perceived were the tank motors idling in the front yard. The explosion never came.

I was itching to peek. Slowly, I snuck away and stole my way up the basement stairs. There was a narrow window that led toward the front yard, which in turn was enclosed by a wooden fence, painted dark green. From the window, I could see a massive brown tank with a white star on it. It had crushed the fence and planted itself fifty feet away, right on top of Sissy's prized rose beds, like a panting beast. I cracked the front door and peered out.

Suddenly, the hatch flipped open with a clank. First a helmet and then a black face emerged. I had once seen a Moor wearing a yellow-and-purple silk turban and a flowing white silk robe walking in a street in Hannover from a distance. Now, I stared at the first black man who had ever stood directly in front of me. He smiled, his white teeth gleaming, his dark skin, browner than his uniform, glistening in the sun. He motioned for me to come out. I edged toward him. The next thing I knew, he tossed me a big, bright, beautiful orange. What a birthday gift. Thank you, America!

I ran to the basement, held out my orange, a treasure not seen or tasted in years, and told them not to be scared, that the black man was very nice. We stood looking at the *Ami* and were shocked when a white American, an officer no doubt, walked toward us with a bayonet over his shoulder. He planted himself in front of Aunt Sissy and Uncle Adolf, who took cover behind her, and shouted in a harsh voice, "Out, you German pigs – one hour!" Within one hour, we had to collect clothing, bedding, and whatever food we had to take to an inn at the railroad station, where we were assigned one small attic room for Mutti, my brothers, and myself. Aunt Sissy got three rooms for the four of them, because she complained until they made concessions for "Madame Director."

Each bed in the villa had two feather beds, one to sleep on and a second to cover up. Mutti was clever. Quickly, she slipped the covers off the top beds and put them over the ones below. She tossed the stripped red beds, which were the warmer ones, out the second-floor window and into the garden below, where we kids caught and hid them behind the fence near the bridge. Mutti left the underbedding for the *Amis*. The last thing we grabbed was the aluminum kettle with the big dent. Mutti treasured it, because it was the only possession she retrieved from the ruins of our house on Kleine Düwelstraße.

No sooner did sixty American soldiers move into the villa than the prisoners in the barracks, who were freed by them, swarmed all over the place. I had never seen such a tumultuous scene as when I looked into our bedroom. It was broad daylight. In beds and on blankets spread out on the floor, soldiers were engaged in wild, acrobatic movements with the Ukrainian women. As I looked upon their naked buttocks in an utter stupor, an American officer appeared, pushed me aside, and yelled something to the soldiers I did not understand. They jumped up and motioned to the women to get out. The women pulled their panties up and their skirts down in a hurry and fled out the doors and down the stairs. I never again saw Americans together with Ukrainian women. Word had circulated that America and Russia were not buddies.

We thought the Americans were very sloppy and wasteful, though we were glad of it, for each day we walked from the inn to the villa to sift through their garbage, which they tossed across the backyard fence and down the embankment toward the railroad tracks. We jumped with joy when we found such goodies as chewing gum, Nescafé, canned meat, Life Savers, or on occasion a whole loaf of white bread. – As soon as the tanks appeared on the horizon, the German military vanished without a trace. Word had it that they had provided for themselves by stockpiling food in their hideaways deep in the woods, but they left us behind to starve. Later, it was rumored that when the *Amis* settled in, the Germans fled to bluer horizons, leaving their provisions, some of their weapons, and their trucks behind. Meanwhile the Muna was open to the public. Though we never benefited from any food items, they gave us material that had been used to sew sacks for ammunition. We called it *Munastoff* (Muna material). Mutti used it to sew bedding, dresses, coats, tablecloths, and the like. It looked like heavy white linen. When it got wet, it was stiff as a board and therefore difficult to wash. Mutti had made a skirt for me with green and pink pastel stripes. It spread out as round as a plate when I whirled around while participating in my folk-dance group, wearing those terrible unbendable shoes with wooden soles.

One forenoon when I myself was actively involved in the turmoil of trying to acquire a bale of the *Munastoff* and other objects from their offices, as I came out of a building with some material underneath my arm, I heard a German yelling at me, "Halt! Stop!" At that moment, a gun went off, and I threw myself flat on the railroad tracks. Aunt Sissy screamed, "It's my niece, Herr Albrecht!" The bullet hit the tracks a few meters from me. I got up, grabbed my material, and went home. He thought I was one of the prisoners. I had pigtails like the Ukrainians, but was not very tall. At any rate, my appearance was irrelevant; the prisoners at that time were free and should not have been targeted with a gun.

The scene around the Muna had changed noticeably. American soldiers in brownish uniforms replaced the German guards, who wore green uniforms. Each American carried a gun over the shoulder to guard the wide entrance gate to the Muna. Instead of standing stiff and straight like the Germans, the Americans sat on a stool and stretched out their booted legs, smoking cigarettes or chewing gum. Their caps sat far back on their heads, and their guns leaned against the gatepost. Instead of being silent, they were constantly chatting with other soldiers. They were surely taking a vacation from warfare.

Aunt Sissy tried to ingratiate herself with the Americans, but since she spoke no English, her efforts were fruitless. Also fruitless were Uncle Adolf's repeated proclamations that he was no Nazi. He did not speak English either. I emerged as the only person in the village who could speak English in a comprehensible fashion, and was able to retrieve some valuables from the villa, such as sterling silver, china dishes, paintings, and Oriental carpets for Aunt Sissy. The soldiers liked me. They gave me a harmonica, chocolate, a deck of cards, chewing gum, toothpaste, and other goodies. I was quite proud when they took pictures of me sitting on top of their tanks – they assured me the photos would be shown on the TV news in America. I sat and read American newspapers with them. Jimmy, a medical student, said he'd come back to marry me when the war was over and I was older. They told me later that his jeep turned over and killed him. An officer had asked if I could find him a pretty girl, so I complied by introducing him to a very attractive, tall, and young brunette, a secretary. They smiled at each other and walked toward the little forest opposite the villa. I often wondered if he gave her chocolate and nylon stockings, if he took her back to America as a war bride, and whether the Americans liked or looked down on her, because in their eyes such war brides were often nothing more than prostitutes.

Because of my friendship with the soldiers, the officer in charge told me ahead of time that they were pulling out that night and we could move back in. He warned me, however, that the prisoners in the barracks had asked for the house and threatened to blow it up with hand grenades if the Germans offered any resistance. Aunt Sissy had asked the village police to help her if necessary. We moved in quietly in the dead of night. The Americans had left all the locks broken, so we barricaded the four entrances with piles of furniture. No sooner had we secured the doors than we heard men's voices outside. A crowd of Ukrainians and Poles surrounded the villa holding hand grenades. Soon, they were shouting for us to come out. "Help. Help! For God's sake, help!" Aunt Sissy screamed in her high-pitched voice from an upstairs window. How she could delude herself into believing she would be heard from up there was beyond reason. No help arrived. I found the scene rather amusing. – Uncle Adolf just sat on a chair doing nothing. He was almost too short to shout out of the window. In the midst of the madness, we heard Alfons crying in the backyard, "Mutti, Mutti, let me in!" He had disobeyed orders to stay behind at the inn. Mutti was beside herself, and she urged him from the bedroom window to be quiet and go back to the inn at once. – After a while, the liberated prisoners gave up and retreated into their barracks. No one knew why.

Aunt Sissy was more distraught than Mutti over the disarray of the house. The place was in shambles. A couple of her mattresses, a sofa, and an upholstered chair were slit open. Our "Old German"-style carved oak bookcase and desk, as well as Mutti's large oaken wardrobe, were marred by bayonets, and two of the carved panels of Papa's desk were pushed out. The charcoal outline of an iron on a white lacquered cabinet top had ruined the piece. The window box in the kitchen signaling service needed in the many rooms in the house was defunct, as was the bell suspended from the lampshade over the dining-room table, which Sissy rang whenever a servant was summoned to wait on them. All books had been dumped on the floor in the attic. Fortunately, they refrained from leaving behind bloated carcasses of dogs and cats, as they had in a neighboring villa. However, one day someone found a dozen or more pieces of sterling-silver cutlery buried in the garden. It was presumably hidden by a soldier and left behind, for whatever reason.

The big brown bear sprawled out in front of the fireplace in the entrance hall, whose fur I liked to straddle secretly and whose teeth I was forever tempted to wiggle, had disappeared. The antelope's head on the wall above the fireplace, the varicolored stuffed pheasant on a marble pedestal, and the stuffed boar with ugly tusks in one corner were missing. Also missing was Uncle Adolf's collection of multicolored stones and crystals, souvenirs from his days underground. The stunning pair of black porcelain panthers with glinting emerald eyes was miraculously left behind. Their heads and necks struggled away from a single body in a mirror-image pattern. The soldiers had used it as an ashtray, and Aunt Sissy never forgave them for staining the mother-of-pearl. Since the furnace was ruined, we could not move in. It did not matter, because the Scots were not far behind.

With the departure of the *Amis*, the garbage days were gone. The food situation got worse. My only entertainment lay in calling "how-do-you-do?" out of the inn's window to passing soldiers. My bed stood right under the window. I slept on a carpet, which they put on a board in the bed instead of a mattress. It was very hard, like sleeping on the ground. I struck up conversations with the soldiers who brought their laundry to Mutti. In exchange, they gave us a little food. They did not have much either.

That's how I met a sergeant by the name of James Rorrison. Rorrison, a Scot, taught me how to type on his typewriter. I typed out the lyrics to "You Are My Sunshine" so I could see them when he taught me to sing it. A highlight of their stay was when Rorrison asked me to translate for them at an entertainment event to which the villagers were invited. I was so proud to stand on the podium and translate from English to German. Several step dancers performed that night, which I will never forget. Rorrison also saved my life. I had lost fifteen pounds in a very short time and became skin and bones. Mutti thought I had tuberculosis, so she hired a car and took me to a specialist in Goettingen. I was ordered to stay out of the sun and in bed for three weeks. I was allocated one hundred extra grams of butter every two weeks. Instead of staying in bed, I visited Rorrison and spoke to him about the visit to the doctor. He told me to sneak away each day around noon, go to his room, and look under the helmet on his bed. Most of the time, I found a stick of butter, three or four eggs, a cup of sugar, and some cocoa. I think he stole it from the Army kitchen. He did not want me to tell anybody, but to whip it into a mash and eat it by myself. It tasted wonderful, and it worked. After a few weeks, I had gained weight and felt great.

The drab English replaced the friendly Scots. The Brits had pale faces and scrawny bodies, and they wore absurd berets on their slicked-down hair. I thought they looked rather comical with their white belts, spats, and funny boots. While the Scots had guarded the gate to the Muna in a more orderly fashion than the *Amis*,

Early Childhood to 1954

the English stood almost as straight and correct as the Germans. They hardly spoke to us, and I never got to be chummy with them. After all, they were considered bigger enemies than the Americans. The Germans "bombed the hell" out of the British.

In the middle of the night on September 30, 1945, a giant explosion threw us out of our beds at the inn. Dishes fell off a shelf. The walls shook as a series of detonations boomed in the distance. We went to the window and looked out. A pillar of flames more than two hundred feet high soared into the black sky not far away, lighting up the Muna and the village. The English, we were told in the morning, ran helter-skelter in their sock feet and underwear out of the villa and into their jeeps and drove off jabbering. The mines burned for several days, and three or four big explosions followed the first. Buildings were destroyed, and five Poles lost their lives as they ran across a field for shelter in the barracks. There was much speculation as to how it all started. One theory was that Poles or Germans looking for food, goods, or hidden treasures were careless with cigarettes and caused the fire. Many entered the mines secretly and by unsafe means. Later, it was learned that university libraries had stored thousands of volumes of books from their archives in the mines – and that the Nazis had hidden documents and museums had safeguarded paintings and other objets d'art in the mines as well. Reports came that the amber chambers from the czar's castle in Zarskoje Selo, in Puschkin, a gift from Fredrick Wilhelm I, had been stored there. – We did not care what was down there. All we knew was that we were stuck in V. and had nothing to flee with, no train, no car, no bike, no horse or wagon, and we were praying that the whole village with its beautiful surroundings, underneath which between 20,000 and 25,000 tons of ammunition were stored and carelessly abandoned, would not explode and kill us in the process. (I would like to thank Detlev Herbst, a teacher in V., for his well-documented book that records 750 years of V.'s history. The book was sent to me by Herbert Rückert after I visited V. decades later, and it refreshed my memory regarding the events. Mr. Rückert also sent a photograph of Rorrison, the Scot.)

The English stayed away, and we all moved back into the villa and continued to struggle in our search for food. Our territory, however, remained under English occupation. All food was rationed during the war, yet the more serious period of starvation started with the end of the war and the beginning of the English occupation. The daily supply of food per person consisted of seven ounces of butter, seven ounces of margarine, and one ounce of milk, and the four-week supply consisted of two pounds of pearl barley, one pound of meat, two pounds of fish, one-fourth pound of chicory, one-eighth pound of cheese, one pound of sugar, one pound of marmalade, one-fourth pound of cottage cheese, and four loaves of bread.

How many times did Mutti come home with her little two-liter aluminum milk can empty? She used to go down the hill from the villa to the village and knock at the doors of the farmers, one after another, offering to work in the field all day in exchange for two cups of milk. I don't recall ever seeing her bring home milk. After the grains had been harvested and the farmers had picked the fields clean, Mutti took us to search the same fields. Each of us clasped a little bucket as we crawled across the stubble, looking for wheat heads. It sometimes took hours to gather a mere pound. Mutti put the heads in a sack and pounded it with a hammer. She then poured the loose kernels into a coffee grinder and ground them until they were reduced to meal, which she kept in a sealed container. She saved the peels from potatoes no matter how old they were, and washed and crushed them in a meat grinder. She mixed the mush with the meal, added water and salt, shaped patties, and fried them in very little fat or salt water in the skillet. They were a rough modification of potato pancakes. Eggs were rare. If a recipe called for four eggs, we used one or two and added more water. We ate everything that was put on the table, no matter how yucky it looked. I got used to eating cooked nettles in place of spinach and dandelions as salad. Instead of a sandwich, we often had two round slices of rutabaga with a sprinkle of salt in between. For a while, we received yellow bread loaves made out of corn, a far cry from our favorite pumpernickel, but better than rutabaga. Even though the food was rationed, many times Mutti was unable to buy what was allocated, because supplies were limited. We walked forever along the railroad tracks to distant forests to look for wild blueberry or raspberry patches that had not yet been picked over by others. These berries were several times smaller than those growing in gardens. At times, we felt lucky when we found even half a pound. It took us forever to pick beechnuts, which we exchanged for oil or margarine, off the ground. It was like looking for needles in haystacks; it took a big sack full of nuts to exchange for one pound of margarine. When Mutti made marmalade from the berries, she always stretched it with flour or cream of wheat. Since sugar was scarce, the women made syrup out of sugar beets.

The entire process was a ritual. After the farmers had screened the fields for bits and pieces of sugar beets right after the harvest, they allowed people to pick up what they missed. Mutti, together with a couple of other evacuees, but never Aunt Sissy, took a train to Moringen, a village outside of Northeim, where I had gone to school. They walked several kilometers to the field, where they got busy gathering chunks of beets that were stuck in the ground, cut off by the blade of the plow. At the end of the day, Mutti walked to a farmhouse and asked if they would kindly load the sacks, weighing one hundred pounds each, on a cart with horses and take them to the train station. They refused, but offered Mutti the use of their cart and two oxen. She went and hitched the oxen to the cart and took them to the field, where the women loaded the beets. Mutti, who had experience hauling coal with horses, escorted the load to the train station. They transferred the sacks on a freight train. After that, Mutti returned the oxen and cart to their owner. Back in V., my brothers waited with our hand wagon at the station to haul the beets uphill to the villa. Someone in the village owned a sugar-beet press, which was passed around. The beets were rinsed, scrubbed with hand brushes, poured into the big copper kettle normally used for boiling linens, and transferred to the press when soft. A couple of men or strong women cranked the iron bar, squeezed the juice into a bucket, and poured it into the kettle until all the beets were pressed. It took hours for the sweet liquid to thicken into molasses. On top of the syrup, a white, sticky foam collected, which we kids loved to scoop off with a spoon and eat like candy. But the dark-brown syrup was used to sweeten everything imaginable. It's the reason so many foods calling for sugar looked light brown.

Making syrup was not the only labor of love Mutti was engaged in. She had no choice, because my father was sent to the front in Poland at the last minute. Once, he mailed us a goose, which was like a gift from heaven, even though it was not completely plucked clean of feathers and looked rather unappetizing.

Generally, the Germans looked down on the Poles, but my father was talking about the possibility of moving east and finding a much better life for us once the war was finished. He must have believed in Hitler's dream of a Third German Reich. But when he realized the war was lost, he escaped the Russians with his troops. He disobeyed orders, forfeited a promotion to a higher rank, and headed west as fast as the horses could run while pulling the canvas-covered cart, on which he sat with his men. He was convinced a miraculous dust storm prevented the Russians from pursuing his troops. They drove right into an American prisoner-of-war camp instead of a Russian one.

Though my father was starving in war prison through no fault of his own, Mutti always seemed to be the one who looked out for us. She was only 5'4" but physically and mentally very strong. She was stronger than my father, who was more of an artist and at times a bit absentminded, like me. I will never forget the day he came home with just a rolled-up sheet of parchment paper under his left arm. Mutti had asked him to bring home a couple of smoked herrings for *Abendbrot* (supper). When she asked for them, he noticed that the fish had slid out of the parchment paper, which was open at both ends. He tried to find them in the stairway, but they were gone.

Papa, it always seemed to me, shied away from demanding physical labor. He certainly did not help us with the move from Hannover to V., which I did not like. In addition to providing food, Mutti, though again she had no choice, was ready and almost eager to tackle the chore of fetching wood for the cooking range. A forester had marked a bunch of felled trees for us in the woods on a rather steep hill about three or four kilometers away. Mutti took us three children along. It was a long and strenuous climb, because we had to tug a handcart up the bumpy path. Mutti and Hanno sawed the stumps into pieces. Alfons and I loaded them onto the cart. Back home, we unloaded the wood, and Mutti and Hanno took turns splitting the pieces on a tree stump. Alfons and I stacked it next to the rabbit cage. We had to repeat the entire ritual several times before we had enough to last the winter. Once, while Hanno was splitting the wood with the hatchet and Mutti was picking up the pieces, the hatchet slipped and fell directly on Mutti's head. Blood gushed out and streamed over her face. Hanno yelled at me to run upstairs and get the yellow cotton to stop the bleeding. I fainted, fell, and came to when all was well. Hanno never let me forget it.

We were really glad when one day, quite unexpectedly, my father appeared at our doorstep. From the American prison, east of Berlin, he had walked home for days along the railroad tracks. He had stopped at Aunt Anna und Uncle Wilhelm's humble shed. I was upset with him, because he did not leave them one of his blankets, for which they had asked him. They were freezing. Now, five of us were squeezed into one bedroom, and the worry about my father's reinstatement at his old job, at the court in Hannover, began. He had to be denazified and, more importantly, find an apartment in that destroyed city.

* * *

Meanwhile, under British occupation, the flow of people coming to V. increased steadily. They were largely escapees from the Russian Zone. There was much unrest, and a new kind of fear emerged, that of rape. Gruesome stories were told of the Russians' ruthless deeds against women and men. Someone reported that they tied a man who had tried to defend a villager to the back of a horse-drawn wagon. They whipped the horses, which then ran through the village, dragging the man across the cobblestones until he was dead. My father's niece had to watch as Russians stormed into her apartment in Berlin, grabbed her fiancé and his father, who were hiding, lined them up against the wall, and shot them dead right in front of her. She never forgot – and never married. Later, she was a private secretary to the CEO of Mercedes-Benz in Stuttgart. She spoke three foreign languages fluently and enjoyed the privilege of having her own chauffer.

In 1946, the population in V. increased by 100%, to about 1,700. Many refugees and several hundred Jews who had been freed from concentration camps were sent to V. because of the existing barracks. The shortage of food was almost unbearable. Locals as well as refugees were ill-disposed toward each other. Aunt Sissy had to take in a family of five from Silesia. Every nine months they had another baby. They stopped when there were nine of them in two rooms. In addition, three other roomers were moved in, two elderly women and a gray-haired man, who had something going with Aunt Sissy. I caught them on several occasions in a most bizarre and compromising situation in the kitchen, once on the long white table. He was much taller than Uncle Adolf. Someone once wondered how Adolf and Sissy managed to have kids in view of their great difference in size.

The influx of refugees had one positive consequence for us children. We finally had a bunch of friends to choose from, boys and girls. On the other hand, the food supply was stretched even further. But Aunt Sissy was not doing badly. She would ride her bike down to the village at night and make the rounds. She was obviously much more successful than Mutti, because we watched her pushing the bike uphill slowly, huffing and puffing. The steering wheel and the back seat were always loaded with bags filled to the brim with food. She unpacked secretly in the kitchen, hoping to lock it into the larder before anyone, including Mutti, her youngest sister, could see the loot. Of course, she had money and valuables galore with which to milk the black market. We called her the black hamster. She probably gave some of her booty to the obese priest and to her favorite roomer who, to be honest, looked a bit undernourished. While we all resembled walking skeletons, her kids and Uncle Adolf, who never shed his potato belly, were in pretty good shape. She knew where she could get the most in exchange for her goods. Once, she even bribed the principal of my cousin's high school with a suitcase full of food. My cousin had flunked a grade, but Sissy's booty caused the principal to change the verdict to "pass." It did not help, because Karl was always lagging behind.

It was at Villa Glück Auf that I began to learn the difference between the haves and the have-nots, the power of money and what it is like to be the underdog. Most of all, I learned survival skills and how to rise above a situation when the chips are down.

Sankt Ursula – Boarding School in Duderstadt – Sisters of Mercy – Bonn

At Eastertime in 1938, I started my first day of school at a Catholic elementary school in Hannover. Thanks to Mutti's persistence and Mater Herwiges's insistence, my father, pleased to have regained his former job and to have found a room to rent in Hannover, agreed to send me to Sankt Ursula, a Catholic high school for girls in Duderstadt, a town of about ten thousand inhabitants, dating back to the mid-thirteenth century and not far from the scenic Harz Mountains. I started high school around Eastertime in 1946. Five Ursuline Sisters from Erfurt, Germany, founded Sankt Ursula in about 1700. Here, at a place which some might liken to a prison, I enjoyed four uninterrupted, happy years of going to school. About one hundred nuns lived in the half-timbered structure which stood to the left of the twelve-foot-high wrought-iron fence and entrance gate. They were of all ages and vocations – educators, administrators, gardeners, cooks, house cleaners, farm-animal keepers, etc. To the right of the entrance stood the cloister church, where we went to Mass every morning before school and where we confessed our sins to the antiquated priest, who was hard of hearing. Once the nuns entered the order, they remained behind the cloister walls for life, and could not even go home for funerals. Instead, the funeral processions would go past the cloister, so the grieving nun could look out the window to get a quick look at the casket of her dead parent, sibling, or such, provided they lived in the same town. Only the Pope could release the nuns from their final vows and only after years of waiting, which was tantamount to living in hell. I often wondered whether they seriously thought ahead when they went through the sacred and no doubt ecstatic ceremonial moments of their acceptance to the order. It was awesome to observe these nuns, brides of God, standing next to each other on the steps to the altar, genuflecting all at the same time and then spreading out before finally lying on the steps, flat on their stomachs. Their bodies were completely covered with rich white veils. Each nun wore a myrtle wreath on her head, accentuating her virginity. Intermittently, the previously inducted nuns chanted in a chorus.

The Ursulines had the reputation of being the best educators in Germany. Graduating from the school was a stamp of excellence. It was also the school of the haves. The rich and famous, lawyers, doctors, professors, and nobility sent their precious and often very spoiled daughters to Sankt Ursula from as far away as Spain and Switzerland. Big farmers, contractors, and mill owners, that is, those who could contribute food and other edible commodities, were not exactly the order's first choice, but in those dire times, these haves could gain entrance for their daughters in exchange for food. The few have-nots at Sankt Ursula, including me and a couple of friends, got in due to connections. – My friend Nanni, whose father had a small block-ice-producing business, was the niece of Mother Superior, and I got in because Mater Herwiges intervened on my behalf. Mater Ursula, who was in charge of my group when we were not in class, made no bones about the fact that I was merely tolerated. After all, my father was only an inspector at the courts and not a judge. Another friend, whose father had a bakery, was marginal as well. When Mater U., who herself was no more than a sewing, knitting, and needlework instructor, told her one day that her father was only a bakery owner, the baker yanked his daughter out of the school so fast it made their heads spin. Along with the girl, the tuition money and the flour donations, both substantial, went out the window at midyear. Annie was a nice girl, too, and not nearly as conceited as the daughter of some duke from Spain, who was wooed left and right by Mater U. She was pretty, I must say, and had a beautifully ringing name with lots of vowels, *a*, *o*, *i*, and *e*, Angelika Serano Philippi. Mater U. praised her artistic talent endlessly. I could not vouch for her intelligence, since I was never in the same class with her. She was a couple of years older and probably expected to marry a prince.

Sankt Ursula was closed down for several years and converted into a hospital for wounded soldiers by the Nazis. But after the war, the Ursulines opened their iron gates and their three heavy oaken doors, one after another, as soon as they exchanged their civilian clothes for the long, heavy black robes made of gabardine. The only ornament on their sinister attire was a long black rosary, dangling down their sides like a sacred saber. Their hair and a good part of their faces were hidden by heavily starched white linen, over which thick black veils hung down to their lower backs, below their waists. They covered their breasts, if they had any. It was hard to see what exactly was hidden. We could single out Mater U. more easily than the other nuns by her height. In her costume, which included a towering headdress, she was over six and a half feet tall. She supposedly had only one breast. All the nuns wore the same ugly black shoes, black stockings, and a wedding ring on their right ring finger, a symbol of their marriage to Jesus. Upon entering the nunnery, they always disappeared behind two big doors. The first was covered with a thick layer of leather upholstery; the second was massive and made of dark oak. The doors groaned when they were pulled or pushed shut. What lay behind them was *clausur* (closed to the world). An outsider who dared to enter the forbidden territory would be kicked off the premises in a jiffy, be excommunicated, and henceforth be unworthy of partaking in the holy sacraments. Any nun emerging through those double doors had our instant respect, mixed with a dose of fear. It was as though God presided in their realm. They all seemed to wear halos.

Inasmuch as Nanni and I were of lower birth, we did not gain entrance to the Gothic-like sanctuary on the day of our arrival. We were put up temporarily in the house of the mayor. It was a block away from the cloister and right across the old city rampart, which was about three kilometers long and took from 1500 until early 1700 to be completed. We really did not mind, and to be honest, the family was nice. In contrast to the thirty other students, who had to share a single dormitory, we had a cheerful bedroom and bathroom to ourselves. Their cubicle-shaped cells were gloomy and narrow, consisting of three shaky wooden panels just over six feet high, inviting anybody to look into one's sanctuary whenever it pleased them. All one had to do was stand, like Mater U., on one's toes, or step on the prayer bench in one's cell. The bench had a lid for shoes and brushes. It stood at the end of the narrow single bed, a few feet away from the nightstand. Each cell was painted white and had a white bedsheet curtain for a door. The walk across the ancient, squeaky, dark wooden floors to the bathrooms and washrooms took a few minutes, and instead of sinks with running water, we had a mere enamel washbowl and a pitcher on the nightstand with cold water, ice-cold in freezing winters.

Nanni and I were sworn to the same strict rules as the girls "inside"; that is, all lights had to be turned off and all reading had to stop at 9:00 p.m.; in short, we had to be in bed, not uttering a word, and asleep by 9:00. We had to be at the cloister at 7:00 a.m. for prebreakfast Mass. In view of the fact that no one supervised us, these rules were ridiculous, but we did not want special privileges and complied. The thought of going for an evening walk on the beautiful path along the rampart never crossed our minds. My most vivid memory of our short time with the mayor was the wonderful meal with which Nanni surprised me one evening after we had returned from that nauseating supper "inside." We first had a soup made with warm water, chicory coffee grounds, and salt. Afterward, we ate a barley pap with a smattering of rhubarb. Nanni had brought a can of meat from home. She opened it, and we consumed the entire one-pound contents at once, without any bread. It was one of the most delicious meals I had eaten in years. After we were finished, Nanni asked, "Krimi, do you know what you just ate?" "No, what?" She laughed, uttering, "Hüh, hüh," which is the sound German coachmen make when they want horses to stop running. Her father had butchered an old horse, exhausted from pulling ice blocks to the pubs, and canned the meat for human consumption. I could have eaten more. I was always hungry.

When we moved into the cloister, we had to pass through five doors, including the iron gate. All doors were opened by the push of a button from the little room at the first regular entrance. A nun was the doorkeeper, who let people in. Anybody who was not properly identified was guided into the small waiting room opposite the nun's post. All rooms were stacked with crucifixes and statues and pictures of saints. One never spoke in an ordinary voice after the first two sets of doors, or five total, locked behind you. Everybody whispered and the air smelled of incense, which came through the church doors, which in turn opened to the dim hall where a larger-than-life statue of Sankt Ursula greeted the guests.

The darkness of the eighteenth-century hallways persisted as one walked up the wide and dark-brown oak stairway. Eerie noises accompanied every step. The same eeriness persisted when you reached the foyer outside the church, from which you could climb a few steps to enter the gallery, where I sang in the choir and at times joined the nuns to sing Gregorian chants. If you turned right at the top of the stairs, you saw another big door, over which a broad white sign with the word *Internat* (living quarters in boarding school) was mounted. Since I had a penchant for pranks, I was brave enough later to climb up on a chair and paste over the words a strip of white paper with the word *Theater*. It took a while for the nuns to notice it, but it caused quite a stir, along with the appropriate punishment, that is, a letter to my parents and the threat of being kicked out.

Behind the doors to the *Internat* was a long dining room with windows on one side. The floor was a highly polished light-oak parquet. Three rows of long tables with white linen tablecloths and wooden stools underneath were set up as straight as soldiers. Each table had enough drawers to hold each student's linen napkins, silverware, and breakfast china separately, so it could be examined for neatness. *Silentium* was the most frequently heard expression at Sankt Ursula. There were about one hundred girls at each meal. We had to approach the table quietly, stand behind the stool quietly, and pray in chorus before each serving of food; we then had to sit down quietly, ten students per table at a time. If the supervising nun heard but one scratch of a chair against the parquet or any other sound, the entire table had to repeat the sit-down ritual until it was perfect. When we were finished eating, we had to wash and dry the silverware directly at the table. At the end of each table stood a little enamel bucket filled with soapy water and a brush. A second bucket filled with plain water and a dishtowel was passed around after the first. Students on opposite sides of the table had to wash and dry the silverware in absolute silence. If a noise was heard, the students had to stop, regardless of whether the water would get cold. It's amazing how quietly and quickly we learned to execute our tasks.

One Sunday morning at breakfast, all hell broke loose. We ate breakfast after church, because at that time you had to receive Communion on an empty stomach if you did not want to be excommunicated. We smiled as we entered the room. The sun was shining and a boiled egg, rarely seen in 1946, stood in an eggcup next to our plates. Properly seated, we were given the go-ahead by none other than Mater U., who stood about ten feet away from where I sat. I reached for the precious egg, held it with my left hand sideways on my pretty china plate, took the knife in my right, positioned it over the head of the egg, and with great force and exactness brought it down on the egg, decapitated its head, and shattered the plate. With a big sound, the head dropped and the broken pieces of my plate landed on the slick parquet and skidded directly toward Mater U.'s polished black shoes, where they stopped. *Quel malheur!*

I jumped to my feet more noisily than ever, picked up the pieces, curtsied, and apologized profoundly. It was to no avail. In a dictatorial voice, Mater U. ordered me, louder than was necessary, to our study hall at once without finishing breakfast, and without prayer. My peers pitied me, which did not sate my hunger. Mater U. repeated once more the rule that you never cut the egg with a knife, but crack it with a spoon and then peel the shell off, etc. I knew it all. I knew that rule as well as all the others she hammered into our brains: Never cut anything with a knife that can be separated with a fork. Never cut your salad with a knife and never a potato or any other vegetable. Tip your soup plate toward the table instead of your lap when finishing. Always eat with knife and fork. Hold stemware on the stem instead of the goblet when you are drinking or toasting. Place your left hand to the left of your plate if you eat with your fork only. Don't say *gesundheit* when someone sneezes. Apologize if you sneeze. Always wait to shake hands until the older person initiates the handshake. It's up to the lady to initiate the handshake when it concerns a man. Don't accept a second helping unless you first refuse twice. Wait to begin eating until the hostess starts, etc. Heaven knows why I deviated on this sunny day from the all-important egg-peeling rule. That night, I ate all the barley mush I could get my hands on, at least two terrines full. I volunteered to take Maria's place to assist with washing dishes. We had to take turns and help the nun in charge of dishwashing. It took about an hour. Maria gave me two apples, which her parents, who were big farmers in Dinklar, had sent in a food package. I was so grateful.

At Sankt Ursula I learned to eat very fast, because there was not always enough for seconds. As I belonged to the have-nots, I did not benefit from food packages. Aunt Sissy never surprised me with one, and Mutti had barely enough herself. Nanni and I tried to befriend some of the haves, like the blond, blue-eyed, and brawny Maria, the only student in my class who aced every math test; like Rose, with the dynamite figure, beautiful brown eyes, and the longest, thickest black eyelashes I'd ever seen; like Tina, a baker's daughter, who was a bit pedantic and not too bright; and like chubby Molly, who had dark, curly hair, always behaved, and consistently returned with food when she had visited her parents. I also befriended some of the have-nots, like the exotic Liesl, from Hungary. We loved to spend our free time philosophizing and psychoanalyzing. The fragile Karin, niece of one of the teachers, who played the piano and violin, was one of my favorites, as was the tall and healthy-looking Thérèse Descloux, from Freibourg, Switzerland, with whom I tried to converse in French as often as possible and whom I took home with me to V. during a vacation.

Sibby was the queen of the clique. She was the striking daughter of a big and husky contractor who looked like an Italian, helped to rebuild Hannover, and profited handsomely from it, but who declared bankruptcy before I emigrated and before he died an untimely death of cancer of the liver, caused by heavy drinking. It was not long after he declared bankruptcy, so Sibby told me, that he presented his wife with a bouquet of one hundred snow-white long-stemmed roses and a diamond-studded crown for her black hair out of gratitude for her promise never to cheat on him again. A week later, he caught her once more in her lover's arms. He was the first to construct a high rise in the center of Hannover, and he rebuilt Sankt Heinrich with his own funds after it had been bombed. He was a good Catholic, had a fabulous tenor voice, teamed up later with my music teacher Marianne in Hannover after she left Sankt Ursula, and on occasion sang with her at the opera.

Sibby, who could not sing quite as well as her father, was the apple of his eye. He spoiled her incredibly, and to make sure the nuns took good care of her, he trucked in loads of foodstuff. Sibby looked exotic with her long, jet-black hair and the forever-flirting pale-blue eyes underneath painstakingly plucked eyebrows, almost a carbon copy of her sinful mother. She was tall and slender and wore more beautiful and fashionable clothes than any of the other haves. After all, her mother, who carried on with a secret lover virtually throughout her marriage, had a full-time seamstress for herself and Sibby. Sibby, unlike the rest of us, was allowed mail and visits with boyfriends outside the cloister walls even during Lent. Her few shortcomings included millions of freckles all over her face and body. Her skin was white as bedsheets, her legs were shaped like oven pipes, and her lower lip hung down a tad.

Sibby was desirable most of all because she lived in the so-called Sleeping Beauty tower, the ultimate accommodation, especially when compared to our cells. On occasion, after having satisfied Mater U. that we were all asleep, we would steal our way across the screeching corridors to the tower. Sibby, who had smuggled in some rum, contributed it to our egg-liquor brew, which we whipped together with eggs, sugar, and some milk in an enamel bowl and sipped from glasses on our nightstand. Once, we rolled a few cigarettes with a few dried tobacco leaves, which the nuns hid in the attic for their black-market dealings. None of us liked it. In exchange for Sibby's generosity, Nanni and I volunteered to rub her arms endlessly with Swan lotion to get rid of the freckles. They would not fade an iota. We assured her that a face without freckles is like a sky without stars, but she pleaded with us to continue. She loved being adored by the world. Too bad for her that when she made her *Abitur* (that is, graduated from high school), she failed to bedazzle the examiner, who was sent by the minister of culture. He flunked her mercilessly, the only student in her class. Mater U. had summoned all one hundred nuns to pray for Sibby in church for the entire duration of the exam, but even God let her down. It was a monumental blow to her father, who had already sent out invitations to half of Hannover for the graduation party of the century. I was surprised when he said to me he wished Sibby had only an iota of what I had.

I wonder whether I could have advanced in America as much as I did without the solid education at Sankt Ursula. Next to the nuns, one of whom was my excellent German teacher, Mater Herwiges, I had several civilian instructors. Fräulein Schirduan, my beloved music teacher, was a refugee from a big estate in Pomerania, which she never stopped missing. She was a friend of our gym teacher, Miss Smith, who challenged us to run along the meandering paths through the spacious cloister gardens at 6:00 a.m., before Mass. I admired my English teacher, Miss Greif, not only because she was young and very attractive, but also because she had studied in England. Due to my exposure to the Americans, Scots, and English, I caught on to English quickly, and French came easily as well. Once, I dreamed about Miss Greif. She wore a beautiful wedding dress. I had heard that dreams of brides foreshadow sadness. When Miss Greif came to class the next morning, she wore black clothes and announced sadly that she would be gone for a few days. Her mother had passed away the night of my dream. I never told her, because it was not appropriate to discuss matters of a private nature with our teachers outside of the classroom. Then there was poor Monsieur Krach, my French teacher, who had to endure us girls and our little pranks. We would stare at his bow tie even when it was straight until he blushed and got nervous, but he never reached for the tie to straighten it out. Nobody taught history; it was taboo, because anything to do with Hitler was off-limits, as is obvious in retrospect. I don't recall ever hearing his name mentioned after the war was lost. There were no history books, because they had been ordered confiscated and burned by the Allies, as I found out years later.

Mater Irmgard taught us math, biology, geography, and physics. She lamented constantly that after the war, all we had to experiment with in physics were a few Bunsen burners, which is probably why I never excelled in either physics or chemistry in later years. She even laughed when we played a prank on her by writing busily on a piece of paper the word *nothing*. When she finally asked us what we were writing, we answered, "Nothing." She shook her head and smiled when she saw our scribbling. Mater Irmgard used to take us to the top floor of the school building at night and explain the constellations. In the mornings, she guided us into the cloister gardens, her pride and joy, to explain the plants to us in great detail. She was in charge of the landscaping of the big gardens, where the nuns used to walk endlessly, reading their breviaries or fondling the beads on their rosaries. It was the place in which, by some miracle, I learned how to whistle on two fingers, just like that. It was one of the most valuable functional skills, and one of the most envied, I acquired at Sankt Ursula – an ability which served me well throughout my life, especially when I traveled with my students throughout Germany. It saved my voice from being destroyed by screaming. – Thank you, Santa Ursula!

Mater U. tried her best to teach us the skills involving needles. I did sew a black-and-white skirt and a bright-red blouse to go with it (definite swastika colors!).

The grade depended on an apron with a bib made out of white linen. Sound simple? Not at all – the apron had to include all sorts of pockets on each side to hold kitchen tools. There were a thousand seams that had to be straight and exact and pass her hawk-eyed examination. You can imagine how many times I had to undo my seams before they passed her inspection. I am certain that apron put a curse on my cooking skills for life, even though I wore it only once or twice. Either I burn the food or I burn my fingers. I finally donated it to the Vietnam War Veterans in Princeton, New Jersey, during what seems like another lifetime. Mater U. did not really teach me how to knit. Mutti had taught me so well that I could knit mittens, socks, and sweaters in my cell bed at nighttime, without a flashlight.

I enjoyed teasing the nuns, even those I liked. One summer day, when the window to the classroom was open, fat black flies flew in from the barnyard, where the nuns kept a couple of cows and other farm animals for their home economics program, which was separate from our language- and science-oriented curriculum. They buzzed around and crawled over my desk close to the open, dried-out inkpot. Whenever Mater Herwiges turned her back to write on the blackboard, I caught a buzzer and stuck it in the inkpot, covering the hole with my left hand. Toward the end of the session, she came to my desk and requested that I lift my hand. I complied, and a swarm of flies buzzed straight into her face, which turned red in anger, but miraculously she did not explode. I knew Mater Herwiges liked my class essays, because I earned decent grades from her. Many times, when a student had written an exceptional essay, Mater U. asked her to read it during study time for the benefit of the others. Not once did U. ask me to read my essay.

I will remember Fräulein Schirduan forever for slapping my face on the country road that led to the border between the German Democratic Republic and the Federal Republic. As the nuns were not allowed to venture outside the cloister walls, she had the unfortunate duty of chaperoning us on our obligatory daily walks, either around the city rampart or down the monotonous country road toward the barbed-wire fence along the no-man's-land between East and West. Occasionally, we could spot an East German with a gun in a tower, eyeing us with his binoculars. Now and then we disobeyed orders and waved at the soldier when Schirduan was not looking; but he never waved back.

We actually preferred to walk around the rampart. It had colossal linden trees. They were centuries old and more than ten feet in diameter. Their branches hung over the path like huge umbrellas, providing cooling shade on hot summer days. We liked to crawl up on the broad roots to pose for photos. More importantly, from the rampart we could peek into the courtyard of the boy's boarding school, the Gymnasial-Konvikt Georgianum, the counterpart to Sankt Ursula, run by priests. It was constructed in April 1908 and was thus more modern.

Marianne Schirduan, who never married, though she was quite attractive, probably wanted us to stay clear of temptation, and on one historic day, she led us down the road to the border for the umpteenth time. Together with Karin, my younger friend from Silesia with a full head of black curls, I walked about fifty yards ahead of the group of twenty. Karin sang with me in the choir, directed by Schirduan, who liked us mainly because we could hold the tune. Karin and I had also acted in a couple of plays. Once, when she was sick, I took over her role on the spur of the moment and slipped into a Japanese kimono to play the part. The distance between us and Schirduan and the group had grown greater. We did hear her and the others calling that it was time to go back, but Karin and I acted as though we did not hear them and kept on walking. The calls grew to a fortissimo. We knew we were in too deep, and I strained my brain to come up with something to lessen the blow. I observed a brownish object, like a piece of wood, in the ditch to our right. I rushed to pick it up, intending to present it to Fräulein Schirduan for use in her wood-burning stove. She had a room in the dwelling of the tall and handsome provost, who came from Mutti's neck of the woods and used to stand up and applaud whenever Mutti acted in a play in the town hall. Schirduan liked him a lot. We hurried back with the object in hand. Unfortunately, it was not wood but a piece of sugar beet. But we had had good intentions. Caught up with Schirduan and the girls, I explained that I just had to pick up the piece of wood for her stove but that, regrettably, it was a beet instead. Before I knew it, she slapped me on the cheek with great force in front of everybody. I was enormously humiliated and quite angry. We all walked home in utter silence, sat down at our desks in study hall, and started on homework, as always in deepest silence. I took out a postcard and told Mutti in dramatic terms about the slap in the face, and I placed it open-faced on Schirduan's desk for mailing, so she would read it. Years later, whenever I visited her in Hannover, she never failed to reiterate how sorry she was to have hit me. We always laughed heartily. She had felt that I was making fun of her all along, because whenever I saw her outside of the classroom, I stopped momentarily, curtsied with a grin from ear to ear, and greeted her with a loud "Grüß Gott, Fräulein Schirduan." I smiled at her out of sheer adoration. Looking back, I feel proud that I was the chosen one, because it created a lifelong bond between us and was almost like having been knighted.

The curtsy was expected of us whenever a nun or teacher crossed our path. You can imagine how many times each day that happened. Mater U. could not get enough of being revered. She definitely had it in for me, especially ever since she had caught me at the dormitory window waving at the boys, who were cheering me on from the window of their high school, exactly opposite ours. She pulled me back and threatened to put me in a glass box. If she thought I had knocked at a door too loudly prior to entering, she sent me back to repeat my knock until she was satisfied. In retrospect, she probably would have benefited from a hot love affair.

The affair at the window cost me dearly. When the time was ripe for us girls to enroll in ballroom-dancing lessons, the climax of the years behind cloister walls, she forbade me to participate. Even Mutti, who came all the way from V., pleaded with her unsuccessfully. Once a week, when all my friends, Sibby, Rose, Maria, and the rest of our clique, would get dolled up and wait at the gate for their dancing partners, that is, the guys I waved at, I was allowed only to look on as they waltzed out the six doors to a few hours of freedom. If I cried, I made sure Mater U. did not notice. As you will see, I made up for it later on in life. And I got more daring within the confines of the red-brick walls. They were about twelve feet high.

Nanni and I had our eyes set on two friends, Hubert and the blond Heribert. Nanni, the blond, fell for Hubert, who had black, wavy hair, dark skin, and a classic profile and looked like a clone of Stewart Granger. Nanni went to see the movie *Madonna and the Seven Moons*, in which Stewart Granger played the lead, seven times after we had graduated. The ever-so-handsome Hubert looked even more dashing on his riding horse, a black stallion. He was the son of the owner of a big grain mill in town and did not live at the boarding school. Like Nanni, he was not good in school, and he was not crazy about her at all, as he confided in me later. I have seldom met a girl who pursued a guy as intensely as Nanni. She was constantly writing love poems and letters and sought out ways to see or talk to Hubert, which was extremely difficult, considering that boys were strictly off-limits. The closest Nanni ever came to him was at a school fair, when she borrowed a pair of leather pants from him. We had formed a four-girl Tyrolean band for the occasion and could hardly believe it when the nuns permitted us to wear men's pants. We stood next to the big Hänsel and Gretel house, which the home-economics girls had constructed and decorated with gingerbread, just as I did when I was a German professor later, in another life.

I had a crush on Heribert, who was a tall, handsome, Nordic blond-and-blue-eyed guy. Fortunately for me, we shared a music stand in the youth orchestra conducted by Schirduan or August Gümpel, son of the organist, who was also my violin teacher. We played first chair in the second violin section. Yet I don't think Heribert was ever aware of how much I liked him. No matter – he gave me an in with the boys that no one in our clique had. He was also a friend of the handsome Hans, who turned out to be the dancing partner of Rose. Thus, Nanni and Rose were constantly begging me to let them accompany me downtown on Saturdays under the pretext of going to confession in the church of the provost. We told the nuns that the priest at Sankt Ursula was rather deaf and could not hear our sins. Thus, on Saturdays, before confession, two of us always went promenading up and down the main street in Duderstadt, hoping to connect with our idol for at least a handshake, a couple of words, a smile – but no more. If we accomplished that, we would be ecstatic for the remainder of the week. We had to be quite careful, because the nuns, who did not trust us, had their spies in civilian clothes around town. Once, however, we beat them – at least temporarily.

We were just dying to see a movie, at least once, while at Sankt Ursula. We had no radio, no record player, no newspapers, and no access to worldly entertainment at all. Classical music, church music, and folk songs were the extent of our entertainment. We did put on the comic opera *Bastien et Bastienne* by Mozart, which was a musical highlight at Sankt Ursula, under the baton of none other than Marianne Schirduan. The lovely blond, blue-eyed Sophie von Zweel, who wore the thickest braids around her head, sang Bastienne ever so movingly.

It had come to my attention that the movie *Gefährlicher Frühling* (Dangerous Springtime) played in the local movie theater at 2:00 p.m. on a Saturday. Seven of us were willing to risk going. We gained access without interference and were back at Sankt Ursula by 4:30 p.m. The movie was a disappointment, because there was nothing "dangerous" to be seen. That evening, on the way to the dining room, Mater Irmgard stopped me in the gloomy foyer and asked me outright if I had been to see a movie that afternoon. I was momentarily shocked, pulled myself together, and with my famous grin assured her that I had not seen a movie in a long time. My friends behind me sighed with relief and thanked me for not getting us into trouble, that is, for not getting us kicked out. We had considered, though, that they probably would think hard before throwing all seven out at once. I hated to lie, especially to one of my favorite nuns. It was the first big lie I had told up to that point, and it bothered me until the day of reckoning.

Several months after seeing the movie, I got in late upon returning from vacation. Nanni zeroed in on me the minute I arrived at the convent. "Krimi, they know." She informed me that they were waiting for my arrival and that all seven of us had to be in study hall at 8:00 p.m. I never discovered how they found out. We arrived in study hall punctually at 8:00. Mater Stephanie, our room mother at the time, together with Mater Eugenia, the head mistress of the school, entered and in a somber voice told us to stand in a line, all seven of us. I was at one end and don't know why she started with me, the shortest in the group. Mater Stephanie conducted the inquisition: "Christa, did you see the movie *Gefährlicher Frühling* on Saturday afternoon, May 1st, in the Gloria Palace movie theater?" I muttered, "Yes," adding that I was sorry. At that, she raised her voice and shouted something to the effect that she could not understand how I could possibly have disappointed her so deeply and that she would never have expected it from me, etc. I looked at the floor silently and waited until she had finished with the others in a similar manner. We were not kicked out, but were forbidden to go downtown for at least two months. We never tried to see a movie after that, but thought of other, perhaps even riskier, ways to entertain ourselves. We did it not to lose our sanity.

What could have been more tempting than eating the forbidden fruit, that is, getting a taste of what boys, a definite no at Sankt Ursula, were all about? I had broken little rules all along, like reading books on the index in our cell after bedtime – with a flashlight, under the sheets. Three of us read *Gone with the Wind* in that fashion without getting caught. My friend Renate and I dared them all by openly walking out the gate at night to meet my cousin Karl and his buddy Jo. Both were enrolled at the boy's boarding school, the Georgianum, and both were quite handsome. Several of my friends adored Jo, who had black, curly hair and looked a bit exotic. Renate fell for Karl and vice versa. But Jo seemed to have chosen me, which I could never understand, since I thought I was not pretty enough. I did have a nice figure, but my face, with the snub nose and skimpy pigtails, did not come close to such beauties as Sibby and Rose.

I was not really turned on by Jo, but the risk excited me. After all, I was born in the street of the little devils. The risk was more enticing because we all knew that a girl had been thrown out in the middle of the night after a nun caught her kissing a boy on a wrought-iron bench in the cloister gardens. He had climbed the high cloister wall. Both were sent packing. He through the door and she to a hotel, where her parents picked her up the next day. Renate and I took advantage of the same bench on our escapades. We placed it directly underneath our classroom window on the ground floor. The building that housed the classrooms shared a wall with the dormitory building. Opposite was a second building with classrooms, but since the school had not returned to full capacity, that section was still used as a hospital for wounded soldiers. It was a safeguard for our nightly escapades. As soon as we left a classroom, the nuns locked it with a key. In order to get the key, I pretended to have left my fountain pen on my desk. I unlocked the door, but conveniently forgot to lock it behind me.

At bedtime, instead of getting undressed, we slipped under the covers in our bathrobes and waited for Mater U.'s final check. She peeked over the curtain, ascertaining that we were in bed, and headed for the door, which she closed noisily. We communicated in code by coughing, and nobody was told of our plan. We did not want to risk being held back or reported by one of the timid or jealous ones. As soon as the coast seemed clear, we got up, our coats underneath our bathrobes, and headed to the classroom, where we shed the robes, climbed out of the window, pulled the hoods of the coats over our heads, and walked toward the hospital section. We acted as though we were nurses leaving the building to go home. The rampart was only five minutes away from Sankt Ursula. Karl and Jo had escaped from their walls and waited for us on a bench on the rampart. We split up. Karl and Renate went in one direction and Jo and I in the opposite. We walked until we met again and returned to our respective quarters. We repeated the ritual of leaving the cloister on a number of occasions, and no one ever suspected or caught us. We met with the guys perhaps six or seven times until Jo tried to kiss me. It was my first kiss. I felt quite awkward. Still believing you could get pregnant from a kiss and being totally naïve when it came to the birds and the bees, I squeezed my lips together tightly and discouraged Jo from trying harder. I lost interest anyhow, since I liked the much taller Herbert a great deal more. But Renate continued to meet with Karl. She explored more intricate avenues, because she must have reacted differently.

You cannot imagine my disappointment when, many months later, we decided to reveal our secret to our clique. No one believed us. On the one hand, they did not think we had the guts, and worse, those who had a crush on Jo did not think he would fall for me. Deep down, they were probably jealous and just did not want to admit it openly.

After all, they knew I had guts. They had all seen me in action when I waited for Schirduan in front of her desk in study hall, which was one step down from the entrance, and poured a bucketful of cold water down the aisle between our desks in front of her feet. They had joined me when our first room mother, Mater Stephanie, stepped down into the same room and we all screamed, "A mouse!" and jumped on our chairs for safety. Mater Stephanie, over seventy years old, pulled up her black skirts and climbed on her chair, scared to death. We never told her it was a hoax. She was a very kind and gentle soul, liked by all of us, yet if you watched her day after day, reading her breviary while making sure we did not utter a sound when we did our homework, the temptation was simply too great. Once, I climbed on her desk, made tiny balls of white tissue paper, and moistened and stuck them on the ceiling above Stephanie's desk. We watched quietly and smirked as the pieces snowed down gently on Stephanie's black veil as they were drying. They created a nice polka-dot effect without her noticing a thing. My peers also knew I had dared to enter the innermost sanctuary of Sister Roswita, whose cell was next to mine. She had not yet taken her final vows, but her cell was considered *clausur*, that is, off-limits to us ordinary mortals, who were subject to excommunication if caught.

Sister Roswita was rather young and had no sense of humor whatever. Aching to play a prank on her, I consulted the others in the dormitory to back me up, come hell or high water. They promised they would, but left me to commit the crime all by myself. While a couple of girls watched the door, I drew open the curtain to my virgin neighbor's cell, took the shoe brush out of her prayer bench, and put it brush-side-up underneath her bedsheet where I thought her derriere would rest. I sewed up all of the openings on her nightgown and put it back underneath her pillow. I moistened her washcloth and stuck it underneath the sheet where her feet would lie. At night, we all waited in silence and listened as she approached the sacred cubicle and hung the clinking rosary over a hook. We pictured her stripping off the layered underwear and then reaching for the nightgown. As soon as she had experienced the full effect of my pranks, she screamed, "Who has done this?" When no one uttered a peep, she started banging on the cell wall next to me. It rattled badly and a picture in a glass frame fell and shattered on the floor. I yelled, "What's the matter?" She pushed back the curtain to her cell, which was twice as big as ours, and flew out the door. Five minutes later, Mater U. stormed in with giant steps and ordered all of us to get out of bed, get dressed, and be in study hall in ten minutes, which we were. Mater U. was furious, gave a long lecture about the gravity of breaking into a nun's sanctuary, told us to write a letter to our parents confessing our sins, which she would censor, and swore she would get to the bottom of it. Fortunately for me, she never did. This time we all kept mum, and in the end no severe punishment followed. Sister Roswita was not high enough in rank to warrant twenty dismissals.

Mater U. had an opportunity to push me out after she discovered my father had encountered difficulties coming up with the money for the high tuition at Sankt Ursula. In June 1948, the German Reichsmark was devalued 1:10. Every German received 40 German marks to start fresh, and since we were bombed out, which meant we had to look for new housing, etc., he scraped together barely enough money to keep me at the boarding school until I could earn a less significant diploma in 1950 that required two fewer years than the *Abitur*, which was needed to study at a university. By then, our family still had two living quarters, my father in Hannover and Mutti with the children in V. There were hardly any apartments available due to Hannover's destruction. I was disappointed, to say the least, because all efforts on behalf of Mater Herwiges to arrange for a stipend were denied. Aunt Sissy listened to Mutti's pleas for some temporary financial assistance but turned them down, as usual. She was always envious that I did better in school than her children. Each time Mutti was not punctual with the rent (it took time for the money to arrive from Hannover), she urged her to remove me from that expensive school.

Mater U. dealt her final blow when she found Nanni and me in bed together one night after 9:00 p.m. It was during finals time. We had ignored the decree never to sleep in the same bed with another girl and were busily listening to each other practice English vocabulary for a final the next day. We used a flashlight. Mater U. must have sneaked in. With a grand gesture, she pulled open the curtain to my cell and then ripped the cover away from us. We were in shock. All she could muster was "Ach, what do we have here?" Followed by a "just wait!" She turned and sped away, the length of the dormitory, only to return shortly in the company of the head mistress, Mater Eugenia. By then, Nanni had taken cover in her own bed. We were informed in no uncertain terms that this indecent and highly indiscriminate act – one never knows what can happen in such a narrow bed – called for drastic action. Years later, I figured out what she intended to insinuate by the phrase. The next day Nanni's aunt, Mater Superior, called us into the drab waiting room and informed us that under normal circumstances we would have been expelled at once, but that since it was the end of the school year, we could finish. We were strictly forbidden to go downtown thenceforth. At that point, we did not really care anymore. I was sad to leave my friends behind, but never forgot Mater U.'s good-bye: "Christa-Maria, I wonder what will become of you."

I don't know what possessed me to return to Sankt Ursula one last time only a few months after I had departed. My friends had flooded me with letters, begging me to visit and telling me they missed me. I missed them and Sankt Ursula as well. I longed to talk to them and chat with Mater Irmgard, who always told me not to snap my fingers during geography classes and let the others have a chance to answer. I missed Herwiges and Schirduan. I missed the entire atmosphere at Sankt Ursula. I especially liked the Advent season, when we lit candles and sat around the wreath on Sundays, singing songs and eating a big gingerbread heart. Karin and I played the recorder many times, and whenever St. Martin rolled around, all of us went for a procession through the corridors of the cloister, singing and carrying candles. We always ended up in the dining room and found a baked Martin's goose on our plate. I even looked forward to surprising Mater U., because all the negatives had turned into positives in my mind. I knew deep down that the years spent there were the best of my life so far.

Since I was penniless, my friends had assured me I could sleep in the dormitory, just as other alumni had done. With great anticipation, I dragged Mutti's antiquated bicycle out of the basement, scraped off the rust, and painted it with black lacquer paint. I packed sandwiches and some clothes in a backpack and, early one morning, headed toward Duderstadt. It was a long stretch in hilly territory, but I was determined to get there in one day. After many hours of pedaling, I ended up at the gates of Sankt Ursula and rang the famous bell, butterflies in my stomach. They were justified, and they fluttered wildly when none other but Mater U. appeared. She took one look at me and must have noticed my curly hair and a tad of lipstick. I curtsied and told her with a grin on my face that I had come to visit and wondered whether I could spend a night. She stepped back, looked down on me as though I had asked for the moon, and replied firmly, "Absolutely not – what are you thinking?" She never opened the iron gate, turned around, and marched toward the regular entrance doors, which opened and closed behind her with a bang. I was numb. Holding back tears, I picked up my bike, which I had leaned against the fence, and pedaled to the residence of the provost, Mutti's hometown admirer, whose housekeeper was also the godmother at my confirmation. They opened the doors wide for me, welcomed me in, fed me a good supper, and let me spend a wonderful night in the bedroom where the bishop or other visitors of high rank were privileged to sleep. The provost could not believe how cruelly Mater U. had treated me and vowed to take it up with the school later. The next day, I returned home through the hills without having seen either my friends or my favorite teachers. I did not return to Sankt Ursula until I heard Mater U. was dead.

* * *

My years at Sankt Ursula had not prepared me for any kind of meaningful job. The nuns might have loved for me to repent and join the convent, but I never considered it. There were no jobs in V., so to make sure I did not get involved with some boy, my parents decided to send me to Bonn, a small town near the Rhine River and the new capital of West Germany, to learn cooking. It was yet another place run by nuns and turned out to be a home for the elderly, run by a few Sisters of Mercy. Mutti was delighted to have found it, because it was free. How wonderful – I could learn the art of cooking in exchange for work. The institution was small and housed approximately 250 elderly residents, ten nuns, and three or four girls my age. They too belonged to the chosen few who enjoyed the pleasure of learning how to cook at this establishment adjacent to the beautiful Rhine. I shared a small but pleasant room with another cook-to-be on the ground floor; we had a view of a big garden full of trees and shrubs, bearing tons of fruit. It did not take me long to find out why there were so few girls to take care of and cook for 250-plus people. Two months prior to my arrival, between fifteen and eighteen girls had defected, none staying longer than a couple of weeks. They could not take it.

I gave the Sisters of Mercy, who could be merciless, my best shot. After all, I had lasted four years in Sankt Ursula, was used to taking orders from the Ursulines, and had endured a rigorous prep school at three villas Glück Auf. Here on the Rhine River, I got up at 5:00 every morning. The first duty was to prepare the kitchen for cooking. A huge coal-burning cookstove stood in the center of the kitchen, with a floor of white tiles. Every morning, when I opened the door, the white floor was black as coal. It was virtually covered with a blanket of the fattest, blackest cockroaches I had ever seen. I could hardly avoid stepping on the plague on the way to the faucets, where I filled bucket after bucket with scalding hot water and poured it over the roaches until all of them were flushed down the big drain underneath the stove. Next, I made a number of trips to the basement to carry up buckets of coal, two at a time, for the stove. Lucky for me, I had inherited the coal-carrying genes from Mutti, who lifted tons of coals for her father. After I started the fire, I fetched my skimpy breakfast and ravenously consumed the two slices of bread with a smidgen of butter, a drop of marmalade, a cup of chicory coffee, and on Sundays, a hard-boiled egg and a Danish, baked by us girls. It was starvation all over again, this time in what seemed like a land of plenty. Much of the food – butter, cold cuts, fruit, and the like – was stored in a walk-in refrigerator, where our humble allotments were set out on a designated spot on a shelf. As the meals served at noon and suppertime were just as skimpy, I brazenly began to help myself whenever I picked up my breakfast or sandwich for supper. I scooped out an extra morsel of butter, marmalade, or whatever looked inviting and gobbled it down in a hurry. I tried to survive without ever getting a day or even a couple of hours off to take a walk along the Rhine River or a ride on the boat to Drachenfels (Rock of the Dragon), which was less than an hour away.

A couple of times, I tricked a nun who took me down into the wine cellar to get wine for the elderly. On special holidays, they served their patients a decanter of fruit wine, which they made themselves from the cherries, raspberries, or blackberries in their garden. It tasted sweet and delicious. She told me to suck hard on the thin hose, one end of which was in the barrel, and instructed me to stop and direct the hose to the wine pitcher as soon as the wine began to flow. I followed her instructions up to the time when the hose should be pointed toward the pitcher. I acted as though nothing came, and instead of letting the dark and intoxicating liquid run into the pitcher, I let it seep down my throat until I felt a bit tipsy, which occurred rather quickly.

It was obvious that the nuns were a bit naïve in treating us like slaves. Besides, how could I learn to cook when each and every meal was prepared in mammoth quantities? Each Saturday, we had to bake hundreds of crescent rolls. A pound of salt had to be poured into the kettle to season soup. I did know how to fry fresh herrings after having fried hundreds of them. Once, an entire truckload of spinach was dumped on the floor in the room next to the kitchen at about 8:00 p.m. They ordered us girls to clean the spinach. After slaving away for an hour, I could not take it any longer. I got up and proposed to entertain them while they were picking the green stuff. Not even the nun protested. I got my violin and started playing for them. At one point, I sang a hymn to which we had changed the words at Sankt Ursula. I was sure they had not heard it. It was a prayer to St. Mary. The lyrics went somewhat as follows: "To love Mary was Joseph's intent. In the evening at 7:00 he sneaked to her abode. He helped her with the dishes and urged her to rush, because he wanted to neck with her in the bush while the moon was shining so brightly." I hate to think of what Mater U. would have done to me. The Sister of Mercy relished it as much as the girls.

The constant grind of slave labor got to me. I was starved for music. The movie *Eroika*, which focused on Beethoven's life and eponymous symphony, was playing at a local theater. I was determined to see it. After all, we were at the place of his birth. We were not allowed to go. Remembering my nightly escapes from Sankt Ursula, I resorted to the same tactics. My roommate and I crawled out of the window after dark and went through the iron gate as though we were visitors. The movie was much more exciting than *Dangerous Spring*, which we saw during the day in Duderstadt. Unfortunately, when we returned, the gate was locked and we had to search for a hole or loose brick in the wall, which was as high as the one at Sankt Ursula. We were lucky to find a gap in the darkness. I went first, but when I climbed to the top of the wall and looked down, I was shocked to realize that the descent was considerably longer than on the street side of wall. Along the entire length of the wall below, the ground was overgrown with thorny blackberry hedges and nettles. It had also started to rain, and I was wearing a white skirt. We had no choice but to slide down the wall into the hedges. Our skirts and legs badly soiled and scratched, we climbed through the window into our room and finally were under the covers. We sighed with relief because we had not gotten caught.

The final straw came when after four weeks of uninterrupted hard labor, the head mistress turned down my request to give us a day off once a week. She agreed only to one day off each month. The following Sunday afternoon, a couple of us took a trip on the boat to the Rock of the Dragon. We decided up there, not far from the Rock of the Loreley, that the situation was simply intolerable, as well as unlawful. I wrote a letter to my parents, and a week later they let me return home to V. I never found out how much longer the other girls stuck it out.

Adjusting to Life in Hannover – First Job: Kommerzbank

The odyssey of my youth ended with my parents' return to Hannover on November 7, 1950, when my father, after looking and waiting for five years after the war, found an apartment in the southern and nicer section of the city, not far from Kleine Düwelstraße. We lived on the fourth floor, without a lift. The house had been bombed and was rebuilt by the owner. The floor in the living room was a bit slanted. Our apartment had two bedrooms, a living room, a kitchen, and a bathroom to be shared with our very kind neighbors, who had only an efficiency apartment. The place held all the furniture we had saved, which was just dandy. My brothers got to sleep in one bedroom, and I had to sleep in the master bedroom between the wall and the long wardrobe. There was just enough space for a narrow single bed and a foot-and-a-half-wide crack from which to get into it. It was a dark hole, since there was neither an extra light nor a window. It was ever so much worse than the cell at Sankt Ursula. For entertainment, instead of a radio, I had the privilege of listening to my parents saw logs, that is, snore all night long.

As soon as we moved into the new apartment, discussions started about what to do with me. I pleaded with my father to send me for two years to the Academy of Music in Hannover, where I could have earned certification as a music, gymnastics, and dance instructor. It was much too expensive, and I should have guessed that the answer would be a decisive no. I needed to start earning money as soon as possible to help foot the bill for rent each month, since my parents felt they had to start over and, hopefully, save for a down payment for a house, Mutti's dream. My father decided to spend a few more marks to send me to another all-girls school, a *Höhere Handelsschule* (commercial college). It was an accelerated program, which I could finish in six months. For pupils who had not attended high school, like my older brother, it took two years. Having learned how to discipline myself at Sankt Ursula, I had no problem learning rather quickly. I earned better grades than at Sankt Ursula and found the college rather easy. I took courses in typing and shorthand, in Spanish, German, and English business correspondence, and in accounting, world geography, and other related subjects, all of which were skills and subjects that, coupled with what I had learned at Sankt Ursula, equipped me well to tackle what lay ahead.

I made new friends at Rackow, but a couple of male friends, Dieter and Rudi, continued to pursue me all the way from V., where they had been semi-rivals. Dieter was the son of a newcomer industrialist, a refugee from Silesia who took over part of the Muna to start a glass factory, producing crystal. Rudi's father, also from Silesia, was one of their employees. Dieter was a Protestant, had dark, wavy hair and gray eyes, wore glasses, and was rather short. He was quite handsome and a playboy par excellence. Rudi, on the other hand, was a Catholic who had reddish-blond, wavy hair and light-brown eyes and was taller than Dietrich. He was not a knockout, but was very intelligent. Dieter impressed me with crystal from his father's factory and invited me to bowl in their private alley, whereas Rudi and I liked to sit, debate, or philosophize. Unfortunately, he had a girlfriend from Silesia whom he neglected when I was around, it seemed. The two guys got into a fight when one discovered I had allowed the opponent to kiss me after a dance at Antons, the local inn. Believe me, kissing was not as intense then as it was much later in my life. When Dieter visited me in Hannover, I pretended to be busy and sent him out with my brother. Rudi, on the other hand, got to take me to the great graduation ball at the end of the commercial school. It was my first big dance. I had learned to dance despite the fact that Mater U. tried to keep me from it at Sankt Ursula.

Mater U. should have seen me in my dress, the most beautiful one I had ever owned. Mutti had made it from white organdy. It had a full, long skirt and was princess style, fitted with puffed short sleeves, a round collar, and several dozen tiny buttons, covered with organdy in the front. They started at the collar and extended down below the fitted waistline. A bright-red rosebud underneath the collar lent a final touch to the gown. They called me the dollar princess. Rudi and I danced all night and had a wonderful time. Unfortunately, he must have confused me with his girlfriend back home – after the dance, we sat on a bench at the Maschsee, a man-made lake close to where I lived, to reminisce and kiss. He tried to come too close, but I resisted instinctively, pleading with him not to get my dress too wrinkly, and suggested we better go home.

At boarding school, we were trained to guard our virginity until we married. It was the greatest gift a woman could give her husband on their wedding night. Besides, at that time, I was still rather naïve, though I no longer believed I could get pregnant from a mere kiss. After the failed connection, I sensed that Rudi, whom I did like a lot, slowly retreated. He tried to tell me I would never be satisfied with him because I lived in a fancy mansion, had attended a very prestigious school, and other such nonsense. Years later, I heard he married his childhood sweetheart and became a principal at a high school, mayor of a sizeable town, and an influential politician. Unfortunately, his wife died rather young. Dieter, who drank heavily, died at a very young age of cancer of the liver. His family was known for their fast lifestyle, which ultimately bankrupted their business. Ironically, Rudi's brothers took over and revived the company.

My father, the bureaucrat-artist who took a number of tests to advance in his position at the court, had a job lined up for me. It started a couple of days before my graduation. In fact, my clerk-secretarial position at the main branch of Kommerzbank AG, in Hannover, started on September 20, and I graduated on September 30. At that time, Germany was beginning to ease into the *Wirtschaftswunder* (economic miracle). Hannover rose like a phoenix from the ashes. They were building furiously all over Germany, the western part at least. With a new job, my first, I began to have a rather normal life, forever regretting, though, that I was not permitted to finish the *Abitur*.

I never really liked the job at the bank. I was constantly under pressure. All the supervisors were condescending, and often insulting, males. I was a fast typist and stenographer (120 words a minute) but was constantly worried that I would not be able to read back what I had written, at times at a very high speed. I don't know why they chose me, but I had to take dictation from the first director of the bank, Mr. Eyertt. He was the boniest-looking banker I ever met. He was a couple of inches taller than I and always wore black suits, white shirts, and dark neckties. The way to his office was long and frightening. I had to walk up two flights of wide stairs, covered with heavier carpets than I was used to, even at Sissy's opulent houses. The railings and walls were made of dark-brown mahogany, and portraits of old bank presidents in oil, framed in ornate golden frames, frowned down on me as I approached Eyertt's sanctuary. By comparison to Sankt Ursula, the atmosphere was rich and heavy and not austere. His huge office was just as daunting as the way to it. He sat in a big leather chair behind a massive mahogany desk. To the left was a big window with heavy, dark-green drapes and white curtains. A couple of oil paintings hung on the dark-paneled walls, two ships at sea. A mammoth bronze tiger was sprawled out on one of the bookshelves, which housed his banking library. It was reminiscent of Uncle Adolf's bookcases. My hands always perspired when I took dictation up there, and I could not wait to get back to my desk downstairs and start typing. Each document was placed in a big, book-like folder, which separated each letter with thick sections of blotting paper. At the end of the day, I had to take all of the letters in the folder to Mr. Eyertt and watch him scribble his name on them in black ink. Each time, I held my breath out of fear he would find a mistake, which I don't think he ever did. I got to be pretty good at erasing and correcting typos prior to my ascent.

Director Eyertt did have clout and was not so bad once I got to know him. He was at least decent, which could not be said of another fat and disgusting director, who was in charge of stocks and bonds. This director worked on the ground floor and always kept his door open to eye the girls. I always felt him undressing me with his eyes when I had to walk past his office. Once, he stopped me in the corridor and suggested that my legs were so nice I should consider a job as a stewardess. He most likely would have asked for special favors had I asked him for help instead of Eyertt. When I approached Eyertt and asked if he might be able to help my younger brother, Alfons, find an apprenticeship, which he was unable to get himself because of poor grades due to the handicapped years in school at V., Eyertt came through at once. He located a place for Alfons with a formidable industrial plant in Hannover, where he was trained as a machinist. The apprenticeship laid a sound foundation for his advancement later in life and earned him much praise for his achievements.

Next to my secretarial duties, I was trained in matters of foreign exchange, which also gave me access to bank clients dealing in imports and exports or needing foreign currency when traveling to other countries. I showed off my foreign-language skills whenever possible. I received marginal training in handling equities and balancing the accounts at the end of each month. At times, we devoted many hours of overtime to tracking down a discrepancy of a few pennies. We liked to earn the extra money because pay at banks was notoriously low. They gave us an extra month's salary at Christmastime. I earned about 250 marks net each month, but had to hand 50 marks to my parents for the honor of sleeping behind the wardrobe and to help with groceries.

While in Hannover, I enjoyed the freedom of making new friends or visiting with my old ones from V. and Sankt Ursula. Marianne Schirduan had moved to Hannover first. Mater Herwiges, now Fräulein Kipp, followed when she got permission from the Holy Father to break her final vows in exchange for another promise, that is, never to marry. After I had left Sankt Ursula, rumors were heard that Herwiges was heading toward a nervous breakdown. She would throw pieces of chalk at students who gave wrong answers. Rumor also had it that she clashed with Mater U. She was much happier teaching at the prestigious Käthe Kollwitz Lyceum (High School for Girls) in Hannover, the same school where Marianne Schirduan taught. – I have never forgotten the time the mother of one of the nuns died. Though she was not allowed to visit her dying mother, who lived in the same town, she was permitted to look out the window as the funeral procession went past the cloister. – Mutti's refugee friends, the Mischke sisters, who like Schirduan lost their big estates to the Poles, lived close to us. At times, we all took a train to the moorlands north of Hannover, where we gathered baskets full of bell heather to decorate our apartment, even though superstition dictated that heather brings tears. Mutti once painted a lovely picture of a field of heather on which a herd of white sheep was grazing. We also went on outings to Lake Steinhude, the biggest stretch of inland water in the northwest of Germany, watched the sailing boats on the water, and occasionally brought home a smoked eel, prepared locally according to an old secret recipe, which was terribly expensive but tasted delicious.

Hubert came to visit in his new car and confessed that he was interested not in Nanni but in me, which surprised me. He brought expensive gifts, and always a bouquet of flowers for Mutti, whenever he came. I treasured the little black velvet designer cap he bought after he had seen me admire it in a boulevard showcase. It was embroidered with dainty, shining, gold straw flowers and had a long black veil in the back. Hubert flattered me, but I never seriously fell for him. We double dated with Sibby and her friend Guenther. Hubert had failed the *Abitur*, just like Sibby, whom I consoled a lot when she came home from Sankt Ursula two years after I did, badly bruised. A couple of times, Hubert drove with me into the beautiful Harz Mountains, where we picnicked in a meadow filled with delicate, light-blue, bell-shaped flowers alongside a trout stream, in which we cooled a bottle of champagne. It is unimaginable that we did not steal a kiss in such a gloriously romantic setting.

If Nanni could have seen us, she would have been insanely jealous. I never told her. She lived more than an hour away, in Hildesheim, close to Mutti's stomping grounds, Großförste. She threw at least one wild party after Sankt Ursula, which I'll never forget. She had gotten hold of some eight different bottles and flavors of liqueur and challenged me to taste a small glass of each of them. I accepted, had a jolly good time chatting with a handsome blond student interested in music, and ended up totally intoxicated and sick. When I finally left the bathroom, I went straight to bed and swore never to drink the sweet stuff again.

I broke the promise to myself at the next bank outing. It was always a big occasion. The directors went all out and drove us in buses to an exclusive restaurant outside of Hannover, where we feasted, drank, and danced into the wee hours. I loved to dance with Charlie, a tall, dark, and handsome colleague of mine who once invited me to his parents' beautiful house outside the Eilenriede, a big, forest-like park in Hannover, where he made a serious pass at me in his bedroom, unsuccessfully of course. He was a bit daring, I must say. Once he kissed me rather unexpectedly at 2:00 a.m. in the middle of Georgstraße, the showpiece boulevard in Hannover. I forgave him the pass, because he was perhaps the most handsome colleague and the best dancer of the banking bunch. Remember, I was trying to make up for being deprived of dancing lessons at Sankt Ursula. Everybody thought we were the perfect couple. He was not Catholic, a definite minus at that time.

With Sibby only a few blocks around the corner from Bodenstedtstraße, our address, there was always excitement. By then, she had exchanged her admirer from Duderstadt, the son of the owner of the well-known establishment that produced Artmann Boonekamp liqueur, for her true love, Franzi, the son of the owner of big mill near my grandparents' place, in Giesen. In stature he resembled her gigantic father, except that he was blond. Like her father as well as his own, he made a name for himself as one of the town's biggest drunkards. No matter how much he had hurt Sibby, the minute he showed up at her doorstep or called on the phone, she dropped everything and rushed to his side. One night, she called and begged me to go with her to H., where Franzi, totally drunk, had gotten into a fight, breaking chairs and tables in his rage. He had given the authorities her name and number instead of his father's.

That night, Sibby dropped me off at Aunt Stingy's place and drove off in her white VW Bug without determining whether I would be permitted to wait there for her. Their children were out or in bed. My uncle took one look at me, which reminded me of Mater U.'s look at the time of my last visit, and told me he was not happy to have me wait there because I looked like a prostitute. He obviously objected to my permed hair, the lipstick, and the slightly traced eyebrows, which I had gotten used to since my return to the big city and working in the bank. They finally consented to let me wait on a stool in the kitchen, but spoke hardly a word to me until Sibby returned to pick me up. Come to think of it, they never talked to me much before, either. How my uncle could have become the mayor of that village of three hundred people is beyond me. The truth is, I began to dislike them even more intensely and left without a handshake.

I wonder what Aunt Stingy and Uncle Hannes would have said had they known what happened to my friend Renate, Karl's promenade companion, after she left boarding school. She was working at her sister and brother-in-law's practice. They were both medical doctors. We got together at times to reminisce about our daring outings and the pranks we played at Sankt Ursula. On one occasion, we had bought tickets for an operetta, *Blue Danube*. Since the opera house in Hannover was being restored, many performances were moved to the gallery in the beautiful baroque garden and park ensemble of Herrenhausen, founded in 1666 by Duke Johann Friedrich of Calenberg. It was preserved and further developed by Sophie, princess-elect of Hannover and mother of the first Hannoverian on the English throne. My parents used to take us to the gardens on Sunday afternoons to look at the magnificent flowers or run through the labyrinth of hedges, our favorite playground. Renate and I felt somewhat guilty, because Fräulein Schirduan had told us over and over again not to stoop so low as to listen to operettas. She considered all operettas tacky, the music second-rate. We loved the music. The excitement most likely loosened Renate's tongue, or she simply had to tell someone her big secret. It came out bit by bit: she was seven months pregnant. No, not from a mere kiss, but the regular way, I assume. She did not go into specifics. I was reluctant to believe her, because she did not look at all pregnant. Neither her sister nor her brother-in-law had discovered it, despite the fact that, since she lived with them, she was around them day and night. No one knew; and as far as I know, she never told the father of the child. She pulled the strings on her corset tight and fooled everybody until the day the child was born. It turned out that the parents, who she feared would throw her out and disown her, learned to adore the little boy. She ended up marrying a butcher and moved to Lake Constance, where I hope she lived happily ever after. I never attempted to find out what precious Mater U. had to say. I personally was glad I had not given in to those who wanted more than a kiss.

Sankt Ursula had succeeded in instilling within me the need as well as a strong desire to go to Mass and Communion daily. I did not miss a Sunday, because in addition to my own needs, Mutti and my Lutheran father, who had promised to support a Catholic upbringing of us children, made sure we all went to church on Sundays. I believed I would go straight to hell if I failed to go to Mass or set foot in a Lutheran church. I could never understand why my father, who most of the time went to church with Mutti, often just to pacify her, did not convert to Catholicism before he was on his deathbed.

The Jesuits – Switzerland – Hans

After Sankt Ursula, I rarely went to Sankt Heinrich with my parents, but became a regular at the Herz Jesu Kapelle (Chapel of the Heart of Jesus), under the scepter of the Jesuits. It was the place of worship frequented by the intellectuals, academicians, professionals, students, artists, etc. The chapel was famous for the Jesuits' superb sermons, guaranteed not to put you to sleep but to make you think. The chapel was not very large, which often meant standing room only if you were not early. Each Mass or High Mass was an inspirational experience in itself. I felt like I was on another planet as soon as I entered the chapel, always filled with a light fragrance of incense. I can still smell it when I close my eyes today. Whenever the padre superior, Father A., celebrated Mass and gave a sermon, the place was even more solidly packed. I was so mesmerized by the Jesuits that I had to go every morning at 7:00 on the way to the bank. It took fifteen minutes to travel from home to the chapel and another fifteen to travel from the church to the bank. Going to the Jesuits for confession was much more serious than going to the priest at Sankt Heinrich. Of course, to be pure for Communion, it was essential that I went frequently. I did have trouble thinking of sins, though, or making the ones I had committed sound more serious than they actually might have been. I tried to go to the same Jesuit if at all possible. Though they never let on that they recognized me, I am positive the padre superior, whom I came to call "the Padre," knew who I was the minute I started whispering my mea culpa(s). Maybe not at first, but definitely after he had lured me into his territory.

One morning, as I was descending the stairs to the chapel, the padre superior waited for me at the foot of the stairs. He was a stately man, perhaps five inches taller than I, and wore the usual long black robe. He had black, wavy hair, short but thick, his head was big with a strong jawline, and his skin was tanned. His dark-brown eyes behind his gold-framed glasses were piercing, as though he looked right through me as he stretched out his hand and wished me a good morning. He smiled and exposed a row of perfect white teeth when he asked me if I could spare a minute. I don't think he knew my name, but he came right out and asked me if I might consider giving some of my time to help him with secretarial work, typing lectures and correspondence. I was stunned and extremely honored all at once, and without considering whether I could measure up to his standards, I assured him that I would be glad to work for him.

From that day forward, I stopped daily at the Jesuits' chapel on my way home from the bank and donated four or five hours of typing to the Padre, the most respected and admired Jesuit around. He had a major influence on my life thenceforth and became something of a master figure to me, like Sarastro in Mozart's *Magic Flute*. He took it upon himself to screen any male friend I went out with. When I confided in him that a certain medical student from Teheran, Iran, Mohammad Tabasian, had kissed me with so much gusto I would have keeled over had he not pulled me back, the Padre lectured me about how condescendingly the men in Iran treated their wives, explaining that living there would not at all be as exciting as I might imagine it to be, despite the fact that his parents, as owners of a big carpet factory, were wealthy. The parents wrote a couple of letters to me. Their script looked to me like the pattern in an Oriental rug. Mohammad was very handsome and an excellent dresser, and he spoke German fluently and flawlessly. He was a terrific dancer and took me to elegant places to dance – until I followed the Padre's advice and broke it off. It was not so difficult for me, since I had not yet fallen for him.

The work for the Padre was demanding. I typed documents which were highly intellectual in nature, and the correspondence involved men and women of high standing in society. It was of a strictly confidential nature, dealing at times with annulments of marriages and the like. In lieu of monetary compensation (it is commonly believed that the Jesuits are poor!) I had the advantage of eating a free, tasty dinner each night I worked. I got to sit at the long table in the big kitchen in the company of the head chef, Josephine, another refugee from Silesia, who loved horses as well as cooking. A second honor was the trust I eventually gained to cross the busy street outside the chapel and buy a six pack of beer for the Padre and his friend Father H., who was in charge of the Catholic students at the Institute of Technology of Hannover. I took the beer trip around 10:00 p.m., right after I had finished my fifteen minutes of rosary praying in the tiny chapel next to the big one, before going home to sleep.

The Padre's office was not big, but it was full of light. A beautifully carved statue of a Madonna, about five feet tall, stood next to a large window and the big desk at which we sat on opposite sides whenever I took dictation. Against the wall stood a couch. Close to it was a Grundig hi-fi entertainment center. It was a present from a wealthy, unmarried lady from Switzerland. She used to arrive in her big Mercedes to take the Padre for a ride whenever she came to visit. She was related to the famous eye specialist at the renowned clinic for tuberculosis in Davos, Switzerland. He had operated on the Padre's eyes when he arrived there from Brazil, virtually blind from tuberculosis of the eyes. A rich Brazilian widow paid and arranged everything for this young Jesuit, who had been sent to Brazil during Hitler's regime. He contracted the disease shortly after he had finished building a small church out of timber. He was virtually brought to a halt at that time. It was difficult for the young priest, used to getting around on horseback. At Davos, he slowly regained vision in one eye and became a lifelong friend of the surgeon who operated on his eyes. The doctor's sons used to pick him up in their private plane in Hannover for special family celebrations.

I sometimes wished I had more money when doing my good deeds for the Jesuits. A couple of times, I gave the Padre a long cigar, four times the size of a regular one. He always lit it right away and blew the smoke toward the ceiling, smiling mischievously. He used to tease me, wondering how anybody could have a nose as "small" as mine. He cautioned me again and again that someday I would get into trouble as a result of speaking too much and interrupting people. A big plus was his dislike of Mater U. after I reported to him in vivid detail how she had tried to put me down. Both Schirduan and Kipp, aka Mater Herwiges, revered him. Sibby, more loyal to Sankt Heinrich since her father had rebuilt it, stayed away from him even though her beautiful and sinful mother lived in one of their thirty or thirty-one big apartment houses, next door to the Heart of Jesus.

Periodically, the Padre invited me to sit down on the couch next to him and listen to Haydn's *Surprise* Symphony. It felt like heaven when he sang along with some of the melodies in his full, sonorous voice. I doubt he spent such cozy moments with all the nuns who stood in line to see him. I was not envious of them, yet at times I was a tad resentful when those other women, often attractive, visited him either to unburden themselves of their problems or receive instruction for converting to Catholicism. A well-known actress from Hannover's leading theater came more often than others. After all, it could take years to become worthy of joining the Church. However, I believe her problems were of a different kind, because she was married to an actor who never came until the Padre had coaxed me into typing a manuscript of a play for them, which I did reluctantly – pro bono, of course. Ms. B., the young and beautiful, but Protestant, daughter of the owner of one of Hannover's leading cafés, Holländische Kakaostuben, who was engaged to be married to the dark and handsome Catholic organist and conductor of the chapel's choir, came for a long time before the Padre considered her ready. In America, she could have switched religions from one day to the next, as long she made a hefty donation.

The Padre had great connections with the theaters as well as the opera. Once, he invited me to a musical. I was excited and nervous at the same time. He had made it clear that we would have to be extremely discreet; that is, we would have to arrive separately and then just happen to sit next to each other. I was worried the whole time that someone might see us and found the entire evening rather nerve-racking. What might my colleagues have surmised had they seen us, especially those from our discussion group, which I had organized and which the Padre had happily agreed to conduct in his office twice each month? I had approached several of my agnostic colleagues with the Jesuit to discuss and debate topics of belief, and though none converted, they were impressed by him and participated enthusiastically each time we met.

* * *

I was eligible for a vacation in the summer of 1952. It was my first. I had saved enough money at the bank to take a trip by train to visit my boarding-school friend Thérèse Descloux, who lived with her parents, a brother, and a sister in Fribourg, Switzerland. I was full of expectations.

Early Childhood to 1954

The Descloux family owned a beautiful, spacious apartment on the outskirts of town, decorated with antiques. I loved the French atmosphere, café au lait for breakfast, tea hour in the afternoon with petit fours, and the French cuisine of Madame Descloux. We did not have to help because they had a maid. I had a mild crush on Thérèse's gallant brother, Jean, with whom I corresponded in French after I returned to Hannover. In fact, the entire family conversed almost exclusively in French while I was visiting. Mr. Krach would have been proud of us. The family took me to their summer cottage at Lake New Chatel, where I went boating for the first time.

The big vacation event was a bicycle tour to Gruyère, where we spent all day climbing a mountain, watching cows roam the meadows with ringing bells around their necks, tasting Gruyère cheese at a chalet, and admiring the mountain roses as we reached the top. Monsieur Descloux had rented a brand-new bicycle for me, and I borrowed a pair of heavy mountain-climbing boots from Thérèse. The weather was perfect, not a cloud in the sky. On the way down, I noticed I had a first-class sunburn. My arms were blistered and the skin was breaking. I put on a shirt with long sleeves, but kept quiet. The bike was new to me – it had hand brakes, and I was accustomed to using a coaster brake. Thérèse, used to mountain biking, was always quite a distance ahead of me on the way to Gruyère. I promised myself that on the way down, I would keep up with her, and I gave it my best when we started and increased my speed when I saw her disappearing around the curves downhill. The paved road, a two-lane highway, went downhill in serpentine curves. Not long after we started, and when Thérèse was no longer visible, I zoomed ahead and suddenly saw a car approaching from below, just around the bend in the road. I tried to use the hand brakes, but lacked the strength because I was going too fast. I knew I would hit the car if I followed the curve. I closed my eyes, let go of the brakes, and drove straight ahead, barely missing the guard along the curve in the road. When I woke up, I saw Monsieur Descloux bending over me. He and another man had crawled down the embankment, where I had fallen and landed on a narrow terrace about 150 feet below. They had carried me up to the road, where a number of cars had stopped, and laid me in the grass next to the shoulder. When I opened my eyes, I asked if the bike was OK. Monsieur Descloux explained that it had gotten caught in the bushes and did not have a scratch. An overhang at the edge of the cliff had blocked me from falling to my death hundreds of feet below, as others had at the same spot. I was muddy from the ground, which was soft because it had rained the day before.

Thérèse was long gone. Monsieur Descloux, who fortunately had stayed behind me the entire time, took me to a chalet located further down the mountain, where I cleaned up before we proceeded homeward. We made one more stop at a roadside chapel to say thanks to St. Mary for saving my life. I felt strongly that God had saved me so I could offer a special service to mankind. It seemed like a sign that I should follow the inspiration I had felt a few months before my trip to Switzerland.

Not Hitler's Child

I had heard a most moving speech at Sankt Heinrich by the bishop of Hiroshima, Japan, where the Americans had dropped the first atomic bomb, on August 6, 1945. He spoke of the suffering and the need for human assistance, and I was seriously considering going to Japan. While in Fribourg, I signed up with an order of nuns who sent missionaries to Hiroshima.

Upon my return, the Padre dampened my enthusiasm when I told him about my plans. He impressed upon me that it would not be an adventurous undertaking, but could be extremely hard. As I put the idea on hold, a care package arrived for us from Mutti's former schoolmate, Franz Neverbee, who had immigrated to Jones, Michigan, by way of Brazil. He had married an American and lived with his wife and two little children on a 250-acre farm, raising Hereford cattle and sheep for a living. In a thank-you letter to them, which I wrote in English, I expressed the wish to go to a foreign country. They responded quickly and offered to sponsor me and lend me the money for the flight, if my parents would permit me to go. I put my intent to go to Japan on hold and reasoned that I should first give America a chance and find out whether I would get homesick. I further felt that since my English was rather good, it would be the ideal place to strengthen my language skills. Having perfect English would surely open up new job opportunities for me that were more challenging than the one at Kommerzbank. – But I had another reason to let go, for a while, of my wish to cross the ocean.

* * *

The Jesuits' establishment housed approximately twenty-five Jesuits and as many male Catholic students, all of whom had to walk past me when entering or leaving through the main door, located next to the little entrance room, where I sat typing. Many moved in after I returned from my vacation and before the fall semester. The students were enrolled either in the School of Veterinary Medicine or the Institute of Technology. Still, it came as a big surprise when one evening, Theo, a tall and quite handsome student from the IT, started talking to me and, without much ado, invited me to a carnival costume party organized by his Catholic fraternity, Rheno-Guestphalia. I didn't think twice and let him know I would like to go very much. He asked when he could come to my house to ask my parents for permission. I told him I would clear it with my parents and that the following Saturday at 3:30 p.m. would probably be all right.

Theo appeared punctually, dressed in the appropriate suit and tie. My parents and I were pleased. He had perfect manners and appeared to be a gentleman in every way. The day of the party, I put on the costume Mutti had sewn for me, a yellow kimono with fitting apparel. I looked quite Japanese. Theo was a good dancer, and I had a lot of fun. As the evening advanced, Theo's even taller and handsomer brother, Hans, introduced himself and asked for a dance. From then on, Theo did not have a chance, because Hans insisted on every dance and would not let me go until his older brother came to fetch me. In accordance with the code of manners dictated by the fraternity, of which I became a *couleurdame* thenceforth, he escorted me home, where my parents awaited me. How lucky I was to work in a place and at a spot where all those handsome, well-mannered students had to pass by, including Hans. In addition to being the handsomest guy I had ever met, putting everybody else in the shade by way of looks, intelligence, and charm, he played the piano very well and was a devout Catholic.

Hans and I sought each other out whenever possible. We met daily for 7:00 a.m. Mass, after which he walked with me to the bank. At night, he waited for me until I had finished my work for the Padre and walked me home. On weekends we made music. He played the piano while I sang or played the violin. My parents loved it and thought Hans was a gem. Mutti could not get enough of Schubert's "Ave Maria" or the various arias from Mozart's operas. We even gave a recital for the fraternity a couple of times. Occasionally, we met at a popular meeting place, that is, under the "tail" of the horse, a monument carrying King Ernst August, who was responsible for the personal union between England and Hannover. The monument stands in front of Hannover's railroad station and miraculously escaped the bombings. Other times, we awaited each other next to the big clock at Kroepke, the elegant café in the center of town. This is where Hannover's more affluent female population likes to show off their precious jewels and fashionable outfits while sitting and sipping coffee and eating pastries with mountains of whipped cream behind the big windows. It is the most frequented meeting place for Hannover's petite bourgeoisie. When we felt like spending a day in the country, we took an electric streetcar and rode out into the Deister, the "little hills" of Hannover, and walked for hours through the well-maintained forests. We always treated ourselves to a piece of cake with a cup of coffee or an ice cream at a garden restaurant. Sometimes we took along a sandwich, and we had loads of fun hiking and blowing up long balloons until they burst in the bushes.

The good Padre channeled many free tickets to us, and we took full advantage of operas, concerts, plays, symphonies, and the like. It was paradise. Though Hans's fraternity had a rule that each student could invite the same lady only once during the semester, he managed to escort me each time. (He had been elected president of his fraternity.) We danced perfectly together. Once, I got carried away and danced for the fraternity on top of a round table. I was wearing a skirt as round as a plate and a pair of tennis panties underneath.

Hans also took me to parties thrown by other fraternities, such as the one for the veterinarians, St. Christopherus. One of the guys approached me one evening just as I was about to leave and begged me to come with him to a nearby hospital, where an old lady was dying because there was not enough blood for a transfusion. I went along. It was my first time in a hospital. I sat next to the bed of the patient. They stuck a needle at the end of a transparent hose into my artery and poked the other end with a needle into the old lady, who was breathing heavily. I avoided looking at her. I saw my blood traveling through the hose and right into the patient's artery until, unexpectedly, the needle slipped out of my artery and my precious blood splashed all over the white coat and bedding. I fainted. When I awakened on a bed, they told me to rest for a while. A nurse gave me a half pound of coffee and 250 grams of butter, which was to pep me up again. When I got home, my parents were upset, because I was not very strong to begin with. It was the first and last time I ever donated blood. I never found out if the patient survived.

At about the same time, the situation at home was becoming more tenuous. Though I did not object and at times found it interesting, I felt even more squeezed in when my parents decided to take in guests who came from all over the world to visit the industrial fairs for which Hannover was becoming known. Mutti arranged places to sleep in the kitchen for my brothers in order to free the bedroom and let some guests sleep on the couch in the living room. It was a good source of extra income, I admit, and most families took advantage of making an extra buck. A Swedish industrialist came for many years and brought a camera from Sweden, which I bought from him for 50 marks. I was impressed by my father's expertise at picking up guests in front of the railroad station. Since I worked for the Padre, I did not see him all that much, and I tried to avoid him because we argued constantly. I criticized him for leaving Mutti alone each year to have a good time at the spa in Bad Ems at the expense of the government, which I never approved of. While he was listening to the bands playing marches and waltzes in pavilions on the Maschsee, Mutti stayed home and cooked. I questioned the seriousness of his asthma, because I never witnessed any attacks. I did not like his spending Sunday afternoons at the soccer stadium, which they had built close to the Maschsee from stones collected at the ruins, instead of taking Mutti for outings. I nagged him about the money wasted on the soccer lottery. We quarreled about my education, which he regretted having spent so much money for. One Sunday at the dinner table, he lost his temper and slapped me so hard my tongue bled. Fortunately, he missed the goblet filled with white wine.

When I told the Padre about it, he suggested it was time for me to get out of the house. He supported my plan to go to America. Just as I had made up my mind to immigrate and set the plan in motion, I realized I had fallen in love with Hans. All along, while we were having fun, my resolve to follow through with my immigration plans drifted back and forth over our heads like light clouds. I waited a year and a half to receive my visa. I had to pick it up in Hamburg, Hans's hometown. I felt strange going to the Consulate and was sad that Hans had not felt comfortable telling his parents about me. They had strictly forbidden their sons from getting involved with a girl while they were enrolled at the university and required them to wait until they could provide for a respectable way of life. On the way home, I spoke with a couple of businessmen in my compartment. When I told them about my imminent immigration, one of them commented, "All of Germany's elite is leaving."

The last two months before my departure, on February 23, were packed with good-byes to friends and relatives, with entertainment, parties, dance teas, a couple of carnival bashes at different fraternities, and a performance of Verdi's *Turandot*. A highlight was when I sang Beethoven's *Missa Solemnis* with the Niedersachsen Chor in the big City Hall before some three thousand guests. Hans was much intrigued by my new camera; he experimented from all angles and snapped photos at every event so I could fill many pages in my photo album and leave a few pictures behind. When I showed the Padre a photo he had taken of Mutti and me, he smiled and sighed, exclaiming, "Ach, to have such a daughter!"

On January 28, Aunt Lisa, Uncle Franz's wife, died at the age of fifty-four, eleven years after her daughter Elisabeth had burned to death in Hannover. I attended the funeral, the last in Großförste. – As we were all gathered in their trophy dining room, sitting around the long table, Uncle Hannes ordered my cousin Rosi and me to share a chair, which we did. I was engaged in a lively conversation with one of the priests, friends of Aunt Anna. They had brought me along in their VW. Out of the blue, Uncle Hannes, who still had it in for me since my last visit with Sibby, ordered me to "shut up" and give the rest of the guests a chance to chat with the priests. As though they had been stung by a bee, both priests rose to their feet, excused themselves, and asked if I would like to ride back to Hannover with them. I accepted enthusiastically, waved good-bye to the crowd at the table and Uncle Hannes, and rode away with the black-frocked men, not to return for decades, never to send them a single greeting from the New World. Neither did they write to me.

Sankt Heinrich was packed on January 30 at 8:00 a.m., when I was still around to attend the big requiem for Sibby's father, who had died before he turned fifty. It was two days after Aunt Lisa's funeral. I skipped the funeral in Hannover and went to console Sibby afterward at home instead. The gravesite was covered with mountains of flowers and wreaths. Her sinful mother was draped in black, and one wondered whether she felt at all guilty and about what would happen with her longtime lover.

Even the Jesuits' reputation was a bit tarnished just before I left. The Padre had seen to it that the handsome Father A., the great preacher, was, if not defrocked, banished to a parish in East Germany. I had not expected the breach of confidence when I entrusted the Padre with a report of what some might consider inappropriate behavior, that is, that Father A. had put the palm of his right hand too far below my waist when the Padre was out of town. A. had wanted to pray with me together on the prayer bench in the Padre's office. A couple times, I had knelt on it when I was confessing my sins, but never together, side by side, with a Jesuit. I confided that he had resorted to a similar gesture once as he walked me home along the Maschsee late at night and tried to tell me he liked me as though he were my brother. Since my brothers and I were never very close, I had nothing to which to compare his behavior. Nevertheless, the Padre's drastic measures taught me thenceforth not to be so forthcoming in the company of the clergy. I wondered at times whether Father A. eventually married, just as the Padre's drinking companion, who was also a great orator and in charge of the students, did, much to the Jesuits' dismay.

II *1954–1961*

1954–1961

Auf Wiedersehen, Germany – Hello, America – Land of Dreams

The good-byes were a bit tearful. Sibby gave me a beautiful, pale-green cosmetic kit, which I held on to all my life. The Padre put an *Edelweiß*, which he had picked in Davos, into the golden locket from my grandmother, where it still is; and for the trip he gave me a tiny bottle of Chianti, which I kept for more than half a century. Hans surprised me with a copy of G. Terborch's *Concert*, featuring the girl playing the cello, which proves he knew even then that my greatest love would always be music. He also gave me a round jewelry box of green leather with a zipper, together with a matching address book and calendar, out of which I just transferred into these memoirs the exact time of my departure: My parents, Hans, and I boarded the bus at the railroad station in Hannover at 3:00 p.m. We went to the gate where the two-engine plane, KLM #210 to Amsterdam, took off at 4:35 p.m. I gave my father and Mutti a good-bye hug, turned to Hans, who put his arms around me, wished me good luck, and kissed my lips for the first time. Perhaps it was only a myth that kissing a girl at that time was tantamount to a marriage proposal.

The plane left on time. I sat at the tail end, which was going up and down like a seesaw. Though I was sure it could not happen to me, I got airsick halfway to Amsterdam and messed up my brand-new coat, for which I had paid one month's salary. The stewardess came with a liter bottle of 4711 cologne, cleaned the coat, and advised me to be careful about what I ate in Amsterdam, where a scrumptious meal was awaiting me upon my arrival at 7:20 p.m. I ate nothing. What a shame! KLM #631, a plane with four propeller engines, departed at 9:30 p.m. for New York, with stopovers in Glasgow, Scotland, and Boston. The flight went smoothly. I was spellbound by the sun rising like a ball of fire on the horizon, the formation of white clouds like snow-topped mountains beneath, the lakes glistening like diamonds below, and the waves washing along the shorelines. I thought the American next to me was sloppy; he threw magazines and newspapers carelessly on the floor, and I was tempted to stoop down and arrange them. Then I changed my mind. After all, it was a certain kind of freedom. As we approached New York City, I spotted the Statue of Liberty from the sky. An exhilarating sensation came over me. At 10:15 a.m., the plane landed at Idlewild Airport. It was February 24, 1954. I had arrived in America, the land in which a life so much more turbulent than the one I left behind was about to unfold.

A friend of my sponsor, Mr. White, picked me up at the airport and took me on a whirlwind tour of the Big Apple. It was a sunny day, the snow in the city had melted, and Mr. White was impressed and relieved that I spoke English so fluently, especially since he spoke no German. Our first stop was Rockefeller Center, where we watched the ice skaters, who were so much better than I could ever hope to be, show off. On the way to the Long Champs Restaurant for lunch, we passed the impressive St. Patrick's Cathedral. As he pointed out Cardinal Spellman's residence, he mentioned that he had hoped to arrange for a meeting with the cardinal, which was canceled. I was aghast when I saw Times Square, and found the billboards extremely repulsive. Just as vulgar did I find the many women who openly smoked in the streets, and wondered what the nuns might think. Never in my life had I seen so many black people, and I noticed that they moved around just as freely as the white people. When Mr. White told me Broadway was almost twenty miles long, there was no street in Hannover to which I could compare it. The subway was exciting and scary, but I beamed when we arrived at the South Ferry Station and looked straight up to the Statue of Liberty in all her glory, stretching her torch high into the blue sky. Mr. White afforded me a view of Wall Street, which I am sure Mr. Eyertt, from Kommerzbank, would have loved to see. From the business center, we went to the Empire State Building and, from the 102nd floor, had a magnificent view down on this intoxicating city of the New World.

I was grateful for having seen New York City. My United Airlines flight departed at 8:15 p.m., stopped shortly in some city in Ohio where it snowed heavily, and landed in Chicago just before midnight. Mr. Neverbee met me at the gate, and his wife waited at the exit. My first impression was mixed, because I had not even seen a photo of either. They seemed older than I imagined, almost fifty, I guessed. His wife, who was a bit heavy, had thick, dark-gray hair and wore a faded scarf. He was haggard looking, had a long nose, and was almost bald, with a few strawberry-red hairs combed back over the skull. Both were taller than I. He seemed coarse, with his strong German accent, while the wife, an American, seemed friendlier than he. I was taken aback when I noticed that she was clutching a detective novel in her left hand and holding a burning cigarette in her right, definite no-nos at Sankt Ursula. The cab, which took us to the South Shore Line, an electric train between Chicago and South Bend, Indiana, drove past the slaughterhouses. It was frightening, because the streets were not well lit. I had a distinct feeling of gangsters lurking in the background.

Wetherbee Lake Farm, Michigan – Broken Promises

I began to get a sense of the vastness of America when after a two-hour ride on the South Shore from Chicago to South Bend, it took another hour by car, an old Pontiac, to drive home to Wetherbee Lake Farm, two miles from Jones, Michigan. We arrived, tired, at about 2:00 a.m. on February 25, but I was not too tired to open the mail from my friends and colleagues at Kommerzbank, who had sent it before I left. I was thrilled when I read the poem they had written for me, their "Peggy," a nickname they gave me once the story of my immigration became known. They had cut their heads out from snapshots and glued them above the poem, with a photo of Charlie, the dancer, and I, cheek to cheek in the center of a heart. – For the first time in my life, I fell asleep in a room just for me.

The following five months were filled to the brim with new impressions, new experiences, and new challenges. Each day was very different from what I had known and learned in the Old World and even more so from what I had expected from my sponsor. I experienced a real culture shock. I was not told that Mrs. N. had a job as a social worker in Kalamazoo, Michigan. I had no idea that as soon as I arrived, she would leave the house at 7:00 a.m. and return at 7:00 p.m. I was not informed that I would be in charge of the children and the chores around the house. Yet I was eager to take advantage of every new experience that came my way.

The 250-acre farm was far out in the country on a hilly gravel road. A couple of days after my arrival, we were snowed in. The drifts were over four feet high. I had never seen so much snow. We were cut off from society until a snowplow came and opened the road. Although I was excited to see so much snow, I did welcome the spring on the farm, because I could venture out into the wild forests, which were a part of it. I learned not to be afraid of snakes and was thrilled when I spotted a raccoon or saw a turtle walk across the road. In April, Mr. N. took me to pick watercress at the two Wetherbee Lakes. They were located about five hundred yards from the small bungalow, which had replaced their former home after it burned down. I loved the wilderness, the crystal-clear water, and the glistening shells on the bottom of a small pond we passed. I was in awe when we made our way along a path where the Indians had been only eighty years before. The lake was named after English settlers who had come to the area around 1830 and were awarded the land free of charge in exchange for developing it. After four years, the Wetherbees became the owners of the land; hence the name Wetherbee Lake Farm.

In the early spring, we went to catch frogs in the swamps surrounding the lakes with the help of flashlights. The lights blinded the frogs and stopped them from escaping the burlap sack with which they were caught. From the same lake, Mr. N. once brought home a turtle. He was disappointed when I told him I had no idea how to prepare it. – It was hard to get used to the heat in the early summer, especially when Mr. N. dropped me off in the field and left me for hours to turn hay bales all by myself. I had never perspired so much. Each time I turned a bale over, a swarm of insects surrounded me. I helped Mr. N. plant 750 evergreen trees and thought it took forever. The Neverbees raised over sixty Herefords and owned more than two hundred sheep. When the new sheep were born, the mother of one of the lambs died, so I began to raise the lamb with a bottle.

Working in the fields, scrubbing floors, cleaning house, washing windows, doing laundry, ironing, taking care of two children (five and six years old), and cooking – none of these were my forte. Nevertheless, since I received much praise for how well I spoke English, I was constantly wondering when I might start working at a regular job. I had only brought $50 and needed to earn money to reimburse the Neverbees for the price of the plane ticket, which they had advanced because neither my parents nor I had enough money. Before I came over, they had promised me a job at a bank in Mishawaka, Indiana, about thirty-five miles away, where her father, a retired doctor, was a vice president. They had also assured me they would find someone to teach me English shorthand and continue my violin lessons. Most of all, I was to learn how to drive a car, which was a necessity out in the country.

Meeting new people and gaining insight into a new way of life was thrilling. Though nobody ever mentioned a violin teacher, I took advantage of every opportunity to play the violin or listen to classical music. Mrs. N.'s father did not mention a job, but they loved having me visit on a weekend with the children. They lived in a house on Diamond Lake, Cassopolis, which at the time seemed like a small castle. Their other daughter had studied music. A Steinway greeted me when I entered. The daughter and I played together on several occasions, and Mrs. D. and I listened to classical music whenever possible. They had a wonderful collection of records. There, I learned that Americans do not always shake hands when they meet or say good-bye. At first I thought they were rather unfriendly or did not like me, but I changed my mind quickly. Dr. D. at times picked up letters addressed to my friends in Germany. He paid for the stamps and mailed them. Mrs. D. also took me to a meeting of the Daughters of the American Revolution, where women wore genuine and custom jewelry all at once and decorated their hats with shiny pins. At times, I found it embarrassing to have to stand up, be introduced, and be applauded by the various groups whose meetings I was invited to. Church socials and jewelry parties were utterly foreign to me. I was not wild about the sweet angel food cakes, but relished the ice cream.

I had a hard time getting used to the small churches, the tacky decor, the mediocre sermons, and the choirs that always sang out of tune. (One time, due to my criticism, they stopped singing altogether.) It came as a surprise when contrary to what I had heard in Germany, the "negroes," as everybody referred to the blacks at that time, though very few in number, were not sitting separately from the white people in church. It looked comical when people wore handkerchiefs or Kleenex on their heads in church because it was a sin to enter the house of God without a cover on your head. – I frowned upon the domineering presence of the TV, which appeared to do away with family discussions and disengage the brain. At the movie theater, I found it odd that one could come half an hour late and stay longer to see the missed portion. Nobody cared if one got up in the middle of the show to get a drink or popcorn and consume it right there. It would have been impossible in Germany to bring infants and toddlers into a movie theater. Most of all, I liked to go to the drive-in theater, which, however, never happened while I lived at Wetherbee Lake Farm.

After more than a month at the farm, my reserves were dwindling. My clothes were suitable for office jobs only, and I had to buy a working outfit and toilet articles like toothpaste, as well as stamps and film for my camera. I took a deep breath and asked Mrs. N. about the job at the bank. She offered to start paying me for the work on the farm instead. Starting April 1, I was to receive $15 twice a month, and they would deduct $20 each month from the $351.05 they had advanced for my plane ticket. It sounded pretty good at first, but it would have taken me eighteen months to pay off the ticket. An even better job seemed almost within reach when in the middle of April, a friend of the Neverbees took me to a big high school in Mattawan, Michigan. My visit was a hit. I spent the entire day going to various classes and talking to students. The principal was so impressed that he asked me to speak to the entire student body in the big gym. Completely unprepared, I stepped into the arena and spoke about my flight and about Germany and answered many questions. All applauded loudly; the principal claimed never to have seen the entire student body so attentive. He was convinced they had understood every word. Two teachers wanted me to return soon to work with the seniors. When I related the events of the day to the Neverbees, pointing out proudly that the teachers and principal had praised my English, Mr. N. laughed sarcastically and suggested that he complimented me just to be polite. I was disillusioned, excused myself, went to bed, and wept.

I cried myself to sleep more frequently as time went on. While I painted a rosy picture in the letters to my parents and my many friends in Germany, and even in my diary, I was not unaware of Mr. N.'s increasing hostility. At times, I was reminded of Uncle Adolf, the nuns in Bonn, or Aunt Stingy. It hurt especially at night, when the Neverbees waited until I was in my room to serve the children a dish of ice cream, which had been so rare in Germany. As I had to feed a lamb whose mother had died at birth each day with a bottle, I knelt next to the fence and fed it through the wires. On one occasion, I fell backward, dropped the bottle, grabbed the wire with both hands, and received a frightening electric shock. N. stood next to me, watching and laughing piercingly. He had not told me the wires were electric. I was certain he was the one who had opened the kennel in which Susie, a huge and untrained Saint Bernard, big as a horse, was housed. One evening, it was dark outside when the neighbors dropped me off in the driveway. As I walked toward the house, the colossal Saint Bernard jumped me from the back and knocked me down. Seldom have I been so scared.

By and by, I was also becoming more afraid of what Neverbee might do if he found my letters in the mailbox, which stood close to the fence at the entrance to the driveway. I waited until he took off after breakfast to look after his cattle in the field and drive off in his truck to visit the divorcée who lived on the Long Lost Farm, at the edge of Jones, with whom I suspected him of having an affair. As soon as he was out of sight, I ran to the mailbox, seventy yards away from the house, and put in my letters, hoping the carrier would pick them up before N. returned home. I was forever watching for the mailman, because without the many letters from my friends, I would have had difficulty coping with the situation, which got worse when N. told me repeatedly to stop writing my friends in Germany, start making new friends in Michigan, and forget about Hans.

Neverbee was determined to break me down. I was boiling inside when he virtually forced me to go out on a date with a total jerk, a simpleminded GI who had just returned from Korea and took an instant liking to me. He was the nephew of a German war bride who had lived in Michigan less than a year, and he spoke German so badly I was embarrassed. She came to the farm to inform us that Fred wanted to get to know me better. When I tried to get out of the situation, the ogre assured her he would see to it that I showed up at their farmhouse (a shack) for a little party the next day. I protested in vain, because I had no desire to get better acquainted with him or his German aunt. The visit turned out to be what I expected. There was no real party, and the guy was mentally retarded and badly lacking in manners. Instead of helping me into my coat, he just stood there with his hands in his pockets. He must have gotten the message, though, because I never saw him again. However, I did like the ice cream.

Neverbee probably thought I was pretty good at cleaning house. He took the liberty of sending me to their friends in Jones to clean their home, which was an addition to their little grocery store. I cleaned all day and must admit, the place looked a lot better than when I started. In the hope that I would finally earn a couple of dollars, I went to the store to announce that I was finished. The woman pulled a small bottle of sample perfume out of a drawer and handed it to me with a loud "thank you." I could not have been more disappointed. When I opened the bottle, the fragrance stank so badly I tossed it into the trash can the next day.

The children undoubtedly picked up bad vibes from their parents, because they too behaved toward me with increasing hostility. I was devastated when Madeline yanked an arm out of my precious big doll, which I had protected since my childhood (I never owned more than two dolls) and brought for her as a gift. Her little brother tore a leather bow off my only good pair of shoes and lost it. The word *sorry* was never uttered while I was there. Once, when I had just finished cleaning the big picture window in the living room, the children ran outside, dipped their hands in a mud puddle, and put them all over the window, leaving marks all over. When I asked them why they would do such a thing, they responded that I was there to clean and should just do it over. They saw that on the few occasions I had been invited by neighbors for a Sunday-evening ride, the mother messed up the kitchen so badly that every utensil and bowl they owned was left dirty on the counters for me to clean when I came home. Many times, after I had just finished ironing all the ruffled dresses and dress pants, the children decided to exchange roles. The girl put on the brother's outfits, and the brother his sister's dresses, so that all were wrinkled and dirty again. The girl was nastier than the boy. I had burned my arm on the mangle while ironing bedsheets. Madeline came up to me unexpectedly and scratched the open wound with her sharp, painted fingernails, causing a bad infection afterward. I would have spanked her fanny a number of times had it not been strictly forbidden. My father would not have thought twice.

1954–1961

My exploiters seemed surprised when two weeks after my visit at the high school, a businessman from Dowagiac, a town about thirty miles away, offered me an office job for $50 a week. I was elated, but not for long. Both hastened to warn me. I could not work for the man, because he had a reputation with women, whatever that meant. Since I was at their mercy, I had no recourse, but began to wonder why they had made so many false promises. One would have thought that under the circumstances, they would be happy if I found a job and paid off my debt to them. But who would have taken care of the children?

I sensed that the Neverbees were becoming envious of my good relationship with Mrs. Neverbee's parents, because all of a sudden they decided to take me to church in Marcellus, which was in the opposite direction of Cassopolis, where her parents lived. Neverbee complained on a number of occasions that it cost him money every time he took the car out of the garage, implying that it would be wasteful to go for a ride in the countryside. Never once did they offer to teach me how to drive. Another broken promise!

The Croft – A Beam of Light

There was one place in the neighborhood to which I could walk on foot: the Croft. It was a walk of about ten minutes. Dr. and Mrs. Beardsley (Doc and Auntie Hazel) were the kind neighbors who welcomed me anytime, once we had been introduced by the Neverbees. Whenever time allowed, after I finished my chores on the farm, I took the children by the hand and we walked over to the Croft. Auntie Hazel was of German descent, as she proudly told me right away. She was a registered nurse when she married Dr. Beardsley, now a retired Army doctor. They had lived in various parts of the United States, including Hawaii, where Doc had been a chief surgeon in an Army hospital right across from Diamond Head, until he was forced into early retirement for medical reasons. He was also the medical director at the Cass County Hospital, after having been a surgeon at the Three Rivers Hospital. They had had two children, Gretchen and Peter. Gretchen lived with her husband and daughter in Flint, Michigan, and Peter had died at a very early age of a brain tumor. He left a widow and two sons, Wayne and Lee. Doc and Auntie Hazel had never gotten over the death of their son, who was also a regular Army doctor. Indeed, Wayne Peter was brilliant and earned his MD at the early age of twenty-one at the same school as his father, Jefferson Medical School in Philadelphia, Pennsylvania.

The Croft was a forty-acre country estate. The four-acre yard was like a park. I loved to spend time chatting with Auntie Hazel, helping with little chores like cleaning berries, weeding flowerbeds, or picking the meat out of black walnuts. Auntie Hazel had gray hair, brown eyes, and a medium-length nose. She was about my size, petite. She always walked erect and wore fitted dresses she made herself in her sewing room, using the fitting bodice. She liked to wear pretty aprons, which she made, and gave me several. Auntie Hazel enunciated each word very clearly at all times, and helped with my English, explaining slang expressions, such as *crab*, which I had picked up from the Neverbees. Neither she nor her husband was in the habit of hugging visitors, nor did they shake hands. We had a relationship of mutual respect.

On hot summer days, we liked to sit at a picnic table under the big walnut tree to benefit from a gentle breeze and the shade. Someone was always working in the huge yard, and Auntie Hazel was forever commenting on the working habits of the young helpers. When Doc came home, he greeted us with a big smile, and always gave his wife a kiss. The children and I usually went home when Doc arrived, because it meant getting supper ready for the Neverbees. The Croft was like an oasis, a place where I could relax and be happy. The Beardsleys called me their "Sunshine" and made me feel quite special. The parakeet could even say my name. Much to Auntie Hazel's sorrow, he flew away one day. Auntie Hazel once cooked a special dinner just for me. It was a meal fit for a king. A few times, the Beardsleys invited me out for a ride on Sunday afternoons and got permission for me to join them for dinner at a restaurant, which was a big event, because I had never eaten dinner in a restaurant before. They also took me to the Cass County Hospital, where I saw two newborn babies, one Indian and one black. The husband of the Indian woman had deserted her and was nowhere to be found, while the black woman was happy to have brought her sixth baby into the world. She could have fed four babies at a time, because she had a total of four breasts. I'm not kidding.

I tried my best to show a happy face during the day, but could not understand why the Neverbees stopped paying the promised $30 in June. I did not ask about the discontinued payments, but kept bringing up the matter of a job so I could pay my debts. It finally brought results. The Neverbees took me to their friends' house in South Bend, Indiana, where I was to spend the weekend; and at 7:30 a.m. on Monday, June 28, I took the South Shore electric train to go

Job Hunting in Chicago – A Nightmare

On my way, I observed the thousands of chimneys in Hammond and Gary, Indiana, puffing smoke of a diversity of colors into the air and tinting the otherwise blue sky gray. The high-rise buildings looked gigantic from a distance, but a thick veil of smog hindered the view. I will never forget the six or seven hours I spent in the Windy City, which I found to be much dirtier than New York. The traffic was stupefying, the high-rises overwhelming, the people intimidating. Mr. Mums had given me the address of a travel agency, which he claimed he had notified. I was quite anxious when I tried to figure out which El (elevated train) to take, where and how to buy a ticket, and when to get off. I walked forever in the heat of the day, overlooking the litter on the sidewalks and asking repeatedly for directions until I arrived at my destination, soaking with perspiration. It was not a big travel agency.

As I entered, I had the distinct impression that no one expected me. I handed the man behind the desk, who was presumably in charge, the letter from Mr. Mums.

The guy was about fifty, fat, and bald and wore gold-rimmed glasses, which sat low on his hawkish nose. He leaned back in his armchair, put his big feet on the desk, which I found to be extremely insulting, and glanced at the note. He wore no jacket and had rolled up his shirtsleeves. As he put the note on the desk, he grabbed his dark-red suspenders with both hands and started talking about the poor job market, informing me there were no jobs to be had at that time – in any case, he would let me know. I did not stay very long, thanked him for his time, and left.

Out on the street, I felt strange and had no appetite to stop and eat, and, as I did not have much money left, wanted to return to South Bend as soon as possible. From the El, I looked down with horror on the city's back streets and alleys. The tall buildings were blackened from the smog. Electric wires were everywhere. Here and there, a black woman leaned from a window out of which all sorts of colorful wash hung to dry. A scary feeling came over me. When I arrived back in South Bend, I was secretly hoping that a job in Chicago would never materialize. I went to bed at the M.'s dead tired.

The next day, I was alone in the house with Mr. Mums. The Neverbees were to pick me up in the evening. Though I had thought the couple to be quite friendly, I was taken aback the next morning when, shortly after I had gotten dressed and was sitting on the couch, Mr. Mums came over, sat down next to me, and without asking, put his head in my lap, stretched out his legs on the couch, and asked me to message his temples. I became suspicious, made excuses, and got up. I waited anxiously for his wife to come home and for the Neverbees to take me back to Wetherbee Lake Farm.

A week after the Chicago trip, Auntie Hazel introduced me to a group of Camp Fire Girls from Mishawaka. Each year they spent six weeks at Birch Lake, about two miles away from the Croft. They also spent two nights camping at the Croft. They liked to sleep on the lawn next to the red barn in which the Beardsleys used to keep a couple of riding horses. The girls awaited me eagerly, because Auntie Hazel had told them about me. We took an instant liking to each other. I got introduced to eating hot chili soup and toasted marshmallows and to annoying mosquitoes. When they had to pack up because it started to rain, I promised to visit them at their camp. For the first time in five months, I met girls with whom I could identify. It felt like being back at boarding school.

Whenever I visited my new friends at the campsite, we sat around a fire, where we talked and sang. It was moving to watch the fire flicker in many colors when the girls threw metal shavings into it. The reflections of the moonlight, which intermingled in the lake with those of the fire, were magical. Inside, we played games, made music, and chatted about my experiences in Germany during the war and the pranks I used to play at Sankt Ursula, and I played my mouse trick on the younger girls. They could not stop laughing when I stood in a corner with my back toward them and acted out "lovers." I crossed my arms so that my hands could caress my hair, slide down the sides of my back, and tighten around the waist while I whispered "I love you" and similar expressions of tenderness. It was wonderful. Whenever I got permission from the Neverbees to visit them in the evening, I went. I felt almost like a movie actress when they greeted me with applause, sang "Isn't She Sweet?" "For She's a Jolly Good Fellow," or "Stand Up," flashed their cameras, and stood in line to get my autograph when it was time to say good-bye.

Mr. Neverbee put a damper on my newfound happiness when he forbade me to let several of the counselors, whom I had befriended and who had offered to help, turn hay bales. Since they were from Mishawaka, the town where Dr. D. was vice president at the bank, he did not want it to become known that the girls would work on the farm of Dr. D.'s daughter. He also told me to start looking for friends around Jones and that it was high time I started a new life and forgot about my times at that "monkey school," as he called Sankt Ursula. He repeatedly criticized me for having "high-flying ideas."

Since nothing resulted from my job search in Chicago, and since I had continued to press for a regular job (I had only $7 left), he told me quite unexpectedly on July 13 that, if I wanted a job so badly, I should go back to Chicago and stay there until I found one. He added that I would not be good for anything but taking care of kids or the like. He asked me to write a letter right then and there to the YWCA in Chicago and include $4 to pay for the first night. He personally drove me in his truck to the post office in Jones, where I mailed the letter the same afternoon. With $3 left, I was not sure I had enough for the bus, which he wanted me to take this time. I had no idea where to look for employment. I was supposed to leave on Monday, July 17, 1954. My diary entries on July 14 and 15 read, "Sehr deprimiert" (very depressed).

I was desperate. Neither the Beardsleys, my new friends in Michigan, nor my friends abroad had any idea about what was going on behind the scenes. Only Hans must have sensed it, because as Mutti told me much later, he suspected that if I had the money, I would have come home. I was very careful not to let anybody in Michigan know what was going on and possibly drive a wedge between neighbors or friends or anger Mrs. N.'s parents. – I was getting more scared by the minute. On the evening of Thursday, July 14, I pulled myself together and walked over to the Croft. I broke down and told Auntie Hazel and Doc that the Neverbees were going to send me to Chicago on the 17th and that they wanted me to stay there until I found a job. I talked about my impressions of the previous trip to Chicago, about my dire financial situation, etc. Finally, I begged them to let me sleep in their basement for a while. They could not believe what I told them. Auntie Hazel insisted that it was extremely dangerous to send a young girl all by herself to the big city, especially since there was so much crime and rape going on. They did not want me to spend one more day at the farm. Doc told me to go back and inform the Neverbees that there was no need to go to Chicago because I already had a job offer. He wanted me to ask them for a written statement of what I still owed for my ticket and to instruct them that the Beardsleys would pick me up on Friday morning, July 16.

When I told the Neverbees I had a job, they were dumbfounded. Mr. Neverbee's face turned red in anger when I asked him for a statement. He accused me of having been dishonest, because I had wanted to join the mission in Japan when I first wrote to them, but after I had arrived I talked about staying for two years to earn money, spending two years in France and Spain, and then going back to be with my boyfriend. He reprimanded me for not having tried very hard to make a new life for myself and asserted that I probably felt I was on a vacation. He also rambled on about something to the effect that he did not see why I should have a better life than he did when he came over by way of Brazil. I remembered from what he told me that in Brazil, he had been attacked once and robbed of everything he owned. He accused me of selling myself to the Beardsleys and promised he would write to his family in Großförste and tell them what a low-down person I turned out to be. He reiterated that my parents should have sent me to a decent school instead of "that monkey school." (In that letter, he added that they should have spanked my bottom and taught me how to do physical labor and housework. He called into question Auntie Hazel's mental state and accused Doc of being antireligious.) When I came back into the kitchen after packing my few belongings, I spotted his statement on the table. It was in his handwriting on stationery with the Wetherbee Lake Farm letterhead, dated July 16, 1954. It read, "May 22 transportation from Hannover, Germany to Chicago Ill. $351.05 minus $60.00, leaving a balance of $291.05." $60 was the amount credited for my work from February 25 to July 15. I had also received a total of $60 in cash. When Auntie Hazel called to ask if I was all set and if I knew how much I owed, I told her.

On the morning of July 16, the Beardsleys appeared in their green Ford, Auntie Hazel's birthday present from Doc. The sun was shining. My suitcase was in the driveway. Mrs. N. was in Kalamazoo. Mr. Neverbee and I came outside. There was a brief hello, and then Doc proceeded in a rather businesslike fashion. He informed Neverbee that they would pay off my debt, that is, $290, and Auntie Hazel handed him the cash. At that point, Neverbee corrected Doc and said it was $291.05, whereupon Doc pulled out his billfold and gave him a dollar bill. N. corrected him again and pointed at the ".05." Doc grinned from ear to ear and pulled a big, mustard-colored burlap sack out of his hip pocket. On the sack, the name of the First National Bank of Cassopolis, Michigan, was printed in big black letters. He opened the palm of his big left hand and noisily poured a bunch of coins into it. He picked out, not a nickel, but one by one, five shiny copper pennies and counted them one after another into Mr. Neverbee's hand.

Doc had brought his own stationery, thank-you-note size and with an illustration of the Croft. It read, "Jones, Mich. July 16, 1954. Received of Mrs. W.R. Beardsley Two Hundred Ninety Dollars (290.00) in full for all claims against a Christa

Schmidt." Before he handed it to N. he got his fountain pen out, changed the first zero of "$290.00" to a "1" and the "00" to "05." Then he asked Neverbee to sign it, which, of course, he did.

The entry in my diary reads, "My new home: Dr. Beardsley's home. I am very happy."

New Hope – New Beginnings – Forging Ahead

I did not stay with the Beardsleys that weekend, but was invited to the home of my new friend, Nancy, who lived in Mishawaka. It was close to Elkhart, where the Garls, friends of the Beardsleys, lived. Mr. Garl, whom I had met once before and who was the director of a pharmaceutical company which delivered prescription drugs to Miles Laboratories, Inc., in Elkhart, had arranged a job interview for me on Saturday morning, July 17. Mr. Garl picked me up on Saturday morning in Mishawaka and took me to meet the president of the Export Division. The building, offices, and layout of Miles, famous for the manufacture of Alka-Seltzer, were impressive. One of Doc's cousins, Albert Raper Beardsley, had helped establish the pharmaceutical company and built what is now the Ruthmere House Museum in 1910. Doc at one time had been asked by his cousins to join the firm, but he turned them down because he did not want to have anything to do with "quack medicine," as he told me later. He preferred to remain a physician. It may have been the reason why he let Mr. Garl act as a go-between.

Mr. Koerting, the president of the Export Division, who was tall, slightly bald, and in his late forties, came directly from the golf course to interview me. He wore white pants and shoes and a navy-blue polo shirt. I felt encouraged the minute I met him, because he addressed me in perfect German, telling me his father had been a wine merchant in Hamburg. He liked the fact that I knew how to take German shorthand, type, and speak German, French, and Spanish, and he offered me a job at $70 a week starting on Monday, July 19. I was to begin as a file clerk, which included registering each letter in a big ring binder and appending a short synopsis, a task which required a background in foreign languages. He appeared pleased when I assured him I would take private lessons in English shorthand right away. I thanked him several times, and Mr. Garl, who took me back to Mishawaka, remarked that the Neverbees, thinking they had imported a cheap babysitter, had imported the "wrong girl." I was ecstatic. I had a job!

On Sunday, I moved into the nicest room in the YWCA for $9 a week. Auntie Hazel had lent me $20 to get started. I left for work at 7:30 a.m. I walked, but unfortunately lost my way when I turned off Beardsley Boulevard. I was a bit late, but no one chopped my head off. I quickly got used to my new and friendly environment and was happy to report to the Neverbees in a letter how "very very happy" I was, that I was earning an excellent salary, and that I had made sure I would never need them again. I thanked them profoundly for having brought me to this country and making it possible for me to meet so many wonderful new friends. I did question why they paid the promised $30 only in April and May, adding that I would appreciate an explanation if in fact they had considered my stay to be a "vacation."

I was intent on getting ahead at Miles. I took shorthand lessons from an excellent teacher in the Elkhart School of Business, enrolled in a night course in Spanish, and started violin lessons with the conductor of the Elkhart Symphony, which I joined in October. At that time, I also taught a German course for adults at the Elkhart High School. I thought it curious to see Doc's cousins Edward H. and Walter R. Beardsley walking through our office at times, but never spoke to them about Doc and Auntie Hazel. When I was finished with my files, I either practiced shorthand or helped Karlis, an actor from Latvia, sort mail in the back room. Strangely enough, he and his family had also been imported to a secluded farm in Jones, Michigan, by people whose ultimate goal was to exploit them.

I did not spend a single weekend at the YWCA. The Beardsleys, the Garls in Elkhart, or the Sears, who owned a stately mansion in Cassopolis, took turns inviting me to their homes. I was picked up at Miles on Fridays after work, driven to my violin teacher, and then driven to wherever I spent the weekend. Monday mornings, I was dropped off again at Miles. These elderly couples treated me like a daughter. With each family, I had my own room and bathroom. They always cared for me as though I were special, at times putting a little article about my visits into the local newspaper. The Beardsleys took me along on short weekend trips to Detroit to visit their daughter, asked me to join them to go to Doc's hospital for Sunday dinner, and took me to concerts or to visit other friends, including the Gebhards, who were special because Doc had successfully treated Mr. Gebhard for tuberculosis. Doc and Auntie Hazel had also taken Mary Gebhard's sister into their home to stay by her side when she was going through a difficult pregnancy. She had lost two or three babies, but this time the boy lived. I went to a wedding shower and a baby shower, which were new to me, and could not believe my eyes when I saw the countless dishes arranged around the big, fat, golden-brown turkey at Thanksgiving. Only two months after I had started at Miles, I repaid the Beardsleys what they had given the Neverbees for my ticket and sent another check for $100 to my parents.

Doc and Auntie Hazel introduced me to the beautiful countryside in Southern Michigan. I had never seen miles and miles of peach, apple, pear, and cherry orchards in full bloom. I could not stop gasping at the sight of the white, towering Warren Dunes of Lake Michigan, which were magnificent. Doc taught me how to thread a worm on a hook, catch my first fish at Eagle Lake, and clean, filet, and fry it in bacon fat for dinner. Mrs. Garl took me shopping for a black skirt for the symphony in the best department stores in South Bend and Fort Wayne. We finally found a three-quarter-length skirt with a fitted waist. It was of black taffeta and velvet and would look pretty with the ivory-colored damask blouse, with half-length sleeves and Mary Stewart collar, which Mutti had made for me. Both Mrs.

Garl, who always looked chic, and her equally well-dressed husband invited me along on a short business trip and treated me to a night in a first-class hotel, where Mrs. Garl and I attended an elegant fashion show before we drove home.

On Easter Sunday, April 10, 1955, Doc and Auntie Hazel had made reservations for our big group to have brunch at the Four Flags Hotel in Niles, Michigan, in celebration of our birthdays. Doc's oldest grandson Wayne and I had a birthday on the same day, but Doc, his daughter-in-law Dorothy, and Mr. Garl were also born in April. It was a sunny day. Everybody had a great time. Afterward, we were all invited to the Croft, where a beautiful cake with yellow sugar roses, mountains of ice cream, and yet another dinner with three roasted ducks and a ham awaited us. I was constantly amazed at the overabundance of food that was served wherever I was invited, be it in restaurants or families' homes. Doc always went overboard with his generosity.

I was happy to visit the Garls and the Sears, but preferred to visit the Beardsleys, where I really felt secure and at home. We were all one happy family. I had to pinch myself at times to believe my dreams were finally turning into reality. On December 20, 1954, I passed my driver's test! I almost did not pass. When the instructor told me to drive over to the curb and park, I pulled into a long and steep driveway instead, and stopped in front of the homeowner's garage. He asked me what I was doing there. I had confused *curb* with *curve*. He was kind and overlooked the misunderstanding. Both Doc and Mr. Garl let me drive their cars occasionally. They seemed so huge, especially Mr. Garl's brand-new Oldsmobile 88.

At work I progressed very well. Every free minute, as well as during lunchtime, I practiced shorthand. I took Spanish dictation in longhand, since none of the other ten or more secretaries knew how. It earned me high praise from the Spanish vice presidents, but I began to detect traces of jealousy among my coworkers. I overheard them saying once that in order to get ahead at Miles, one only needed to be a foreigner. Mr. Koerting enjoyed dictating letters in German, and when the secretary of Mr. Perez, another vice president, was on vacation, I jumped in whenever French letters needed to be written. After six months, I wrote 120 words per minute in English shorthand, which resulted in my being moved from the low end of the office to the front, where the VIPs sat. Mr. Koerting promoted me from file clerk to secretary to his assistant, Tony Podesta, a New Yorker and graduate from Harvard. I assisted with sending Christmas cards to a number of famous people, such as Cornelia Otis Skinner.

My circle of young friends grew bigger, and playing in the symphony was wonderful. The Beardsleys would come when we gave concerts, and the Garls always threw a party afterward. They were almost like parents to me. Mrs. Garl did not want me to wash dishes, because she feared it would ruin my hands for playing the violin. She was a little strange at times. When I gave her a bouquet of roses for Mother's Day, she was upset that I had spent money on her and refused to put them in a vase.

I saved every penny possible, ate soup at the YWCA every day for 25 cents, walked to work instead of paying 5 cents for a bus fare, hardly ever went to the movies, and bought only the most necessary clothes. I had a particular liking for one of my new dresses. I bought it for an exclusive office party. It was sleeveless, had a square décolleté neckline, and was light blue with an embroidered pattern of the same light blue, which contrasted well with my dark tan. It was princess style, with a very full skirt, and ideal for dancing. The party was at Mr. Perez's supermodern mansion in the most affluent residential area in Elkhart, on the St. Joseph River.

The Perez party was fabulous, with water skiing, dancing, games, and plenty of exotic and mouthwatering dishes. It was a truly international atmosphere. I almost fell for an extremely handsome Argentinian. He was tall and of athletic build, had golden-brown, wavy hair and a gorgeous tan, and spoke perfect English. He was the plant manager for the Miles plant in Argentina. I say I *almost* fell for him – I found out quickly that he was married. I did allow him to invite me to the movies a couple of times. He was called back to Argentina rather quickly. Besides, I was still in love with Hans, who was writing less frequently. He stopped altogether after my good friend the Padre, without discussing it with me, called him into his office and pressured him to decide, right then and there, if he wanted to marry me. All of this surfaced when Mutti went to confession at the Heart of Jesus Chapel.

Beginning of Travel in America – Niagara Falls – Michigan's Upper Peninsula – Washington, D.C.

A trip to Niagara Falls on September 19, 1954, was my first American journey. It was also my first voyage on an American train, the New York Center Express. Friends of the Beardsleys, who worked for Doc at the Cass County Hospital, took me along. We had reserved sleepers. In my diary, I noted that I found it amusing to see black heads sinking into soft white pillows. We left Niles, Michigan, at 10:30 p.m. and arrived in Niagara Falls at 7:30 a.m. I was in awe of the majestic panorama of the falls – and was overwhelmed by the seven million liters of water, which drop down at a rate of approximately two hundred yards per second. I could hear the monotonous roar long afterward. We saw the 185 tons of rock that had broken off of the formation a month earlier on the American side. I thought it was utter nonsense when I heard on the *Maid of the Mist* that six persons in a rubber barrel had decided to let themselves descend with the falls and three had died immediately. A third man survived the first attempt and was killed on the second. A husband and wife escaped without a scratch. We took in each and every important sight. I could not get over the accumulation of junk in the souvenir shops. I was ready to return to Michigan, which I did at 10:00 p.m., dead tired.

On August 15, 1955, Doc, Auntie Hazel, and I left for the Upper Peninsula in Doc's old black Ford, which he bragged about a lot, because it had mileage equivalent to several trips around the world. It was on its second motor, I guess. I learned to cope with tropical heat in a car without air conditioning, helped for the first time to change a tire on the road, went across the straits of Lake Michigan in a ferry transporting three hundred cars, and saw the mile-long bridge being built across the straits. It was expected to be finished in 1956. I spent my first night in a motel directly on Lake Michigan, which looked big as an ocean. I exclaimed "Oh!" and "Ah!" and "Look!" constantly, and even got excited about a swarm of big black ravens, which looked down on us like lords of the forest from their thrones in the treetops. We were in Indian Territory, where Indian heads, carved out of wood and painted in bright colors, gave road directions.

The Upper Peninsula was sparsely inhabited. On our way to Gogebic County, where Doc owned a cabin on eighty acres of woods, we passed fewer and fewer villages, small houses, and cars and saw nothing but vast stretches of forest, including virgin timber, as Doc pointed out. We passed many bubbling streams and lakes glistening in the sun like dark-blue aquamarine rocks and admired the accomplishments of the busy beavers, who had felled big tree stumps with their tiny teeth. The treetops dipped deep into the lakes or formed bridges across streams. Doc stopped the car for us to enjoy three golden-brown deer with big antlers. They crossed the road only a few yards ahead of us and disappeared into a lush, green pine forest. Nature at Wetherbee Lake territory paled in comparison to the environs of Watersmeet.

Without making a big announcement, Doc suddenly turned off the paved road onto a path I never would have found. It was almost completely overgrown with bushes and trees. The grass was four feet high and rubbed against the car. The path, leading through deciduous and coniferous forests approximately one and a half miles long, was hilly – and so bumpy I was afraid we would get stuck at any moment. I then knew why Doc kept his prized car, which was built much higher than his new Ford. All of a sudden, we came upon a clearing, and before us, in a heavenly peaceful setting, lay the rustic cabin. It was about one thousand square feet in size and constructed of cement blocks and logs. Auntie Hazel pointed toward the toilet, an outhouse, in the woods, while Doc unlocked the door. The inside of the cabin was paneled in yellow knotty pine. Four full-size beds stood one next to the other at the end of the one-room cabin, which Doc eventually planned to change into three separate bedrooms and a shower with sink and toilet. We all helped to remove the shutters from the fourteen windows, twelve of which looked down onto the murmuring and meandering trout stream, a branch of the Ontonagon River. It was about twenty steps down from the cabin. After we put in the screens, we could hear the gentle splashes of the stream all night long.

Doc hooked up the stove to a butane gas tank and filled the lamps with kerosene. We had plenty of wood for the big, barrel-like wood-burning stove in the center of the cabin, next to which stood a couple of comfortable leather armchairs and a rocking chair. Doc was desperate for ice, and we took off right after lunch. Since his usual source was out of ice due to the extreme heat, we had to drive all the way to

Ironwood, a town eighteen miles from Lake Superior. We had to wait three hours to load up the ice and did not return until 6:00 p.m. Without ice, we could not go fishing, the main reason for the trip.

The breakfasts at the long, knotty-pine picnic table, eaten after I bathed in the trout stream, were always scrumptious: French toast, ham, bacon, honey and butter, cocoa or coffee, and fresh peaches from the bushel basket, which Doc had picked up on the way. Right after breakfast, the three of us loaded up the boat and went fishing almost every day. We were each allowed seventy-five fish per day and had no trouble filling our lot rather quickly. Doc would not permit anybody else to fry them for consumption. Since they were not very large, I easily ate a dozen of the tasty, crisp morsels. The biggest fish I caught without even trying was a two-and-a-half-pound bass. I screamed a lot, because it was hard to remove the hook after the "monster" had completely swallowed it.

In the evenings, we often relaxed in the quiet and solitude of this heavenly spot, listening to the music of the creek and the birds chirping and singing in concert and hearkening to an occasional whiny sound – animals communicating with each other through the bushes. We felt the soothing effect of the gentle breezes as they browsed through the silken leaves, and looked toward the sky, where the evergreens bent their proud tops gently for the wind before reverting to their erect stature.

Before we headed home by way of the Wisconsin Dells, Doc showed us the town of Land-O-Lakes near the Wisconsin border, and took us up to Porcupine Mountain, the ultimate lookout down on Lake Superior, with its deep-blue, ice-cold waters, its stony shoreline, and the iron and copper mines in the distance. I loved the cooler air up north, which persevered as we went for a motorboat ride on the Wisconsin River, which flows through the Dells into the Mississippi. We could not have witnessed a more harmonious farewell from this striking land of the Indians. I felt both happy and melancholic at the sight of the setting sun, whose rays were flickering in the gentle waves of the eternally flowing river.

The trip up north was Auntie Hazel's last. On Sunday, February 26, I was invited to the Croft to celebrate Auntie Hazel's birthday and the second anniversary of my immigration to America. She was quite disappointed that Gretchen could not come. There had been a terrible snowstorm. When I said good-bye to Auntie Hazel to go back to Elkhart, she gave me a kiss, for the first time I believe, and made a special point of thanking me for having come for her birthday. I urged her not to work too hard. On March 1, Mrs. Sears called and told me Auntie Hazel had passed away at Doc's hospital at 11:30 a.m. It was a sad day for all. – I knew I would miss her terribly. I also knew my life would change, because my weekend visits to the Croft would stop. I felt very sorry for Doc and wrote him a nice note which I signed, "Love, Christa."

When I was sick in bed with a severe case of tonsillitis a couple of weeks later, Doc surprised me with a visit to Elkhart. He brought medicine and flooded me with all kinds of fruits and fruit juices. I was touched in particular by a porcelain eggcup in the shape of a chicken, in which he had planted a couple of snowdrop plants. Fortunately, I was better by the time my trip to D.C. started.

My campfire girlfriend Nancy from Mishawaka and my friend Maria from Sankt Ursula, who had spent a year at a small liberal arts college in Cresson, Pennsylvania, joined me for a week in Washington, D.C. It was my first ride on a Greyhound bus (a Scenicruiser). Nancy and I met up with Maria in D.C., where we stayed at the Y. I saw the sights well-known to anybody who has ever visited D.C., including the interior of the White House, the Smithsonian, and the Franciscan monastery, where I stepped into their sacred *Klausur* by mistake and was carted out immediately. Sounds familiar, right? In addition to the tourist attractions, I spent a few wonderful hours with Mr. and Mrs. Guillermo Espinosa, from the Pan American Union. He was a friend of Dr. Thierfelder, the conductor at the opera in Hannover whom I had known while singing in the Niedersachsen Chor. I immensely enjoyed being in the company of professional musicians, including John Haskins, at that time the leading music critic at the *Washington Evening Star* and best man of J. F. Powers. I took my two girlfriends to an elaborate dinner in the Embassy Room of the Statler Hotel, where we ate our first lobster, drank white Bordeaux, and watched a dazzling ice revue. Nancy discovered something wrong with her camera and dragged us to all the famous sights for a second time. We finished up at Arlington National Cemetery, where after watching the changing of the guards, I placed flowers on the grave of Doc and Auntie Hazel's son, Peter. Auntie Hazel was to be buried in the same grave as her son, on the first of April. Doc had promised he would take her urn to the cemetery personally.

That year, I spent Easter with the Sears.

Doc

It was not long after Doc returned from D.C. that he began to pay extra attention to me. He often gave me roses from their many bushes for my room when he took me back to the Y on Monday mornings. I missed the weekend trips and Doc's cheerful company. His blue eyes were always smiling. He derived genuine pleasure from joking with anybody and constantly probed and challenged the minds of his friends. To me, he was a Rock of Gibraltar, a gentleman of the world, a man I admired wholeheartedly, a man who made me feel secure. Doc seemed to pay more attention to his appearance as well. He had lost some weight, and as he was over six feet tall, he looked quite distinguished with his silky, silver-gray hair. He had three suits made by his friend Benjamin Goldblatt, the tailor in South Bend. The materials were from England. One suit was of light-gray flannel, a second of navy-blue wool, and the third of thick, light-brown tweed. Doc had lost most of his hair, which at one time was heavy and light brown. He made sure I knew he was voted "third-best-looking man" by his football team at Jefferson Medical School, where he was quarterback. He enjoyed pointing out to me that he would have gone into boxing if there had been a big enough interest when he was young, because he had knocked out a professional boxer years before. He played golf, swam, dived, and prided himself on having graduated from the top medical school without ever having taken a single note.

It was obvious in listening to Doc, who also excelled in chess games, that he had a photographic memory. He knew the Bible by heart and put Dr. Swengel, his colleague, to shame in front of a big group of guests because he had misquoted a passage from the Bible and given the wrong chapter and verse. He once boasted that he could read a fat novel in a few hours and I could quiz him about each page afterward. I was in awe of him when he mentioned rather en passant that he had climbed Mount Rainier and Mont Blanc in the French Alps and had a certificate to prove it. Since he had completed a postgraduate course in surgery at the University of Montpellier, France, he spoke French fluently and impressed me one day by citing an entire poem by Heinrich Heine from memory, in perfect German. He claimed to have taught himself German when he was going to school in Vandalia, Michigan. One of his friends made a point of telling me that Doc was known to have been the best student who ever graduated from that school. Considering that he went to school only during the winter, because he had to help his widowed mother farm the homestead, it was quite an accomplishment. He considered himself an autodidact and was of the opinion that one did not need to go to school to learn, just to get the certificates.

Doc was proud that he was born in a log cabin on the homestead, which his father, Hubbel Beardsley, farmed. He told me his grandfather was a Baptist minister, whose religion he did not want to take on because the sermons, instead of focusing on cheerful matters, constantly focused on hellfire and brimstone. His great-grandfather, Darius Beardsley, was a notable pioneer figure and one of four brothers who settled on the central Indiana–Michigan line around 1830. He was equally proud of being a descendant of the English artist Aubrey Beardsley and Elijah Beardsley, who was his great-great-grandfather as well as a Revolutionary War soldier who took part as a teenager in the Boston Tea Party. Whenever we drove to Elkhart, he stopped on Beardsley Boulevard to pay a visit to the beautifully decorated monument of his great-great-uncle, Dr. Havilah Beardsley, who founded the city of Elkhart, Indiana, in 1831.

Doc, confident as he was, let me know rather nonchalantly that he loved me and was sure I returned the affection because I had signed my note of condolences "Love, Christa." At first, I tried to avoid any discussion of my feelings, because the whole concept was so new to me. In part I was still hurting from losing Hans, who had stopped writing a while before. I also felt it was rather soon after Auntie Hazel had passed away and was naturally concerned about what people might say.

Doc impressed upon me that he had learned long before that people talk no matter what; that is, they talk if you do and they talk if you don't. How right he was! When Doc offered me an engagement ring, I refused to accept it, but I took it as a gift for my name day because he threatened to throw it away.

Instead of growing apart, Doc and I grew closer and closer. He wrote many wonderful letters to me in Elkhart. I got excited when he suggested going to Cresson, Pennsylvania, for Maria's graduation from Mount Aloysius College. He wanted us to pick her up, take a detour to Niagara Falls, and bring her back to the Croft, where both of us could stay in the same room. There was also Effie, who lived in the caretaker's cottage on the premises. She was part Indian, part black, and part Irish and was in charge of the household and the grounds. Doc thought it would be quite appropriate for us two girls to live at the Croft and offered to let me use the new car to commute to work.

When we were in Cresson, we stayed with Maria's friends the Knielings, a German couple who treated us royally. Everybody loved Doc, who was an exciting conversationalist. He was more charming and entertaining than I had ever seen him before. Anna and the young graduates swarmed around him, and when I confided to them that he actually wanted to marry me, each and every one of the girls thought I was stupid to be so reluctant. On the one hand, I had hoped they would try to talk me out of it; on the other, I was seeking their approval. Doc, Maria, and I had a wonderful time at Niagara Falls, and I will never forget the lobster dinner at the Niagara Hotel. Doc told us he used to order fresh lobster and other seafood from Maine in barrels for parties at the Croft. It was my second lobster dinner. Doc ordered two big ones for each of us, and I have loved lobster ever since. I guarded the big bib with the red lobster for years.

The next months were filled with sheer happiness. Doc went to church with us girls on Sundays, and he took us to see a baseball game between Boston and Detroit, where I rooted wildly for Boston, making use of the whistling skill I learned at Sankt Ursula. It resulted in the spectators moving away from us until we sat there alone. Doc informed me never to cheer against the visiting team during a home game. Boston won 13 to 2. We also went to Chicago, which I liked a whole lot better the second time around. The Cinerama Holiday show was simply tremendous. Of course, we went to the dunes of Lake Michigan, where we soaked up the sun and cooled off in the tantalizing waves. Doc, the gentleman, took time to teach Maria how to drive his old Ford, and decided not to report the accident to the police when she nosedived the car into a swamp along Robbins Lake Road. He did not want her to get a ticket.

All of Doc's efforts were not in vain. Indeed, when Doc offered to take us on a more extensive trip through America, or anywhere I wanted to go, I could hardly believe it. Maria and I had intended to take a trip through America on the Greyhound bus. Doc asked me to work out a route with the help of the American Automobile Club and wanted to take us on the trip despite my insistence on returning to Germany before I could agree to marry him. He felt he deserved a vacation, since he had not taken one in years. When, almost to the day two years after I started, I gave notice to Miles that I would leave them, they said their farewells with speeches full of high praise and assured me in writing that they would have a job waiting for me should I wish to return. Doc made arrangements for his assistant, Dr. Copeland, to look after his practice and the hospital while we were gone. We took off at the break of dawn on August 4, 1956.

Grand Tour of America, Canada, and Mexico

Maria and I saw more on our trip of 12,600 miles in seven weeks than many people see in a lifetime. We went west through Illinois and Iowa, where we crossed the grand Mississippi, which had taken a while for me to learn to spell in Mater Irmgard's geography class at Sankt Ursula. The river was ever so much broader than I had imagined. It was obvious where the Badlands in South Dakota got their name, but I was struck by the long stretches of gray and barren yet fantastic stone formations, resembling columns, domes, and turrets. While the crocodiles displayed by a private owner behind a rather small fence in Billings, Montana, looked a bit scary, the presidents' faces carved into Mount Rushmore in the Black Hills of South Dakota looked down on us mortals unblinkingly.

In Yellowstone Park, in Wyoming, we pitched our tent close to the Yellowstone River but decided to move into a motel the next night, because a big brown grizzly bear banged the lid to the trash can, not far from the tent, all night long. Both the hot springs and Old Faithful performed their miracles for us, and the Grand Tetons gave us a preview of the majestic mountain ranges that were to unfold as we climbed across the Rockies toward Montana's Glacier National Park, which showed off fields of mountain roses. Naturally, Maria and I had to stage a snowball battle before crossing the Columbia River, in Washington, where we had our only flat tire. Heading toward Vancouver, Canada, we gazed at the dark-blue waters of the Pacific Ocean, blinded by the reflection of the setting sun. The vivid colors of the lush flowers along Marine Drive stayed with us as we left behind the silhouettes of Lions Gate Bridge and tall totem poles on the way to Mount Rainier, conquered by Doc years before and sprawling out before us in all its white-hooded glory. We had to get a feel for the snow at Chinook Pass before heading south along the rocky Oregon coast, where we missed a rockslide which, the day before, had thrown two honeymooners and their car into the ice-cold waters of the Pacific.

Doc put a special emphasis on our stay in San Francisco, where I bought a red silk kimono in Chinatown and found a bouquet of two dozen dark-red long-stemmed roses from Doc on the table in our suite. I lost my glasses, which I kept in a little brown bag, at no other place than the Golden Gate Bridge. Miraculously, they were found and mailed to the Croft and awaited my return weeks later. Perhaps it was the result of a prayer to St. Aloysius, who assists in finding lost objects. I lit a candle at the strikingly beautiful Mission Dolores, where the burgundy and pink bougainvillea climbed high against the snow-white stucco facades of the church; the roses in the cemetery were as vivid as those in Victoria Park, on Vancouver Island. As we navigated the California hills, we had no luck when looking for gold at an old mine, but we did not mind, because the wonders we encountered at Yosemite, including the mammoth Grizzly Giant sequoia and the equally huge redwood trees, with trunks big enough to drive a car through, simply left us speechless.

After seeing what LA had to offer by way of Hollywood, including the spectacular houses of such actors as Marilyn Monroe and the footsteps of the famous in the pavement in front of the Chinese Theater, we welcomed a day on Santa Monica Beach. Doc made sure we took in as much as possible, not forgetting a rodeo, our first, in the Rose Bowl Stadium. He absolutely refused to stop in Las Vegas, where we would have loved to cool off in one of those enticing pools along the strip. Doc reminded me that I had wanted to see the desert in the daytime and that today was the day to do just that. He had a thing against gambling. He told us about a friend who had broken the bank in Monte Carlo only to end up penniless at the Croft one day. Doc bought him a new suit and gave him a hundred-dollar bill to start fresh. I forgot to ask what happened to him later. We were lucky to make it through the Mojave Desert to Lake Mead, the Hoover Dam, and the Grand Canyon without a breakdown of our car, which did not have air conditioning at that time. The sunrises and sunsets at the Grand Canyon were beyond comparison, as those who have witnessed them will agree.

My first and only disappointment on our entire journey was the Floating Gardens of Xochimilco, as we continued south to Mexico City via Ciudad Victoria. The only flowers to be seen were those being sold by the women paddling around in their decorated boats on the rather stagnant waters of the floating gardens. Maria and I loved seeing our first banana trees and coconut palms. We looked in vain for monkeys, but had to stop now and then to pass a donkey, carrying heavy sacks along the roadside. On the way to Guadalajara, we drove through orange groves and spotted a few huge cacti. As I drove along the Paseo de la Reforma of Mexico City, I felt that if I could drive there, I could drive anywhere in the world. I had hoped Doc would take us to see a bullfight, even though he did not like them, and he did not disappoint us. He was surprised I was so bloodthirsty. I had wanted to see all of it and not leave the stadium before the final blow. And a bloody massacre it was. It would have been more dramatic had we sat much closer to the action instead of high up in the bleachers. Nevertheless, the excitement of the thousands of spectators did have an effect on me, and I joined in with the crowd. The next morning, a large, round bowl of gardenias sat in the center of a round cocktail table in our suite at the Hotel el Bosque.

Acapulco, here we come. The closer we came to this world-renowned, exotic beach-resort town on the Pacific, the more excited we got, and we were not disappointed in the least. The striking hotel, painted light blue and embedded in red and yellow hibiscus, burgundy bougainvillea, and pink oleander bushes, was like paradise. With an oceanside view and a big balcony, we listened to the music of the waves day and night. We swam in the deep waters of the ocean, lounged in chairs on the beach, shaded by the umbrellas made of thatched palm leaves, sipped piña coladas out of empty coconuts, and held our breath as we watched a deeply tanned youth risk his life by diving hundreds of feet from a rock into the sea.

Both Maria and I had acquired a tan almost as dark as that of the natives. Doc, of fair complexion, wore a panama hat most of the time. We girls already looked forward to the beach in Corpus Christi, Texas, as we drove north through rice fields. We were in grand spirits as we got ready to cross the border in Brownsville, Texas. Unfortunately, Doc got quite upset with me when I joked with the customs official. He asked if we had anything questionable in our car, and I stated that we had an atom bomb in the trunk. He ordered us to pull over and searched the car more thoroughly than I had ever seen a car searched. Doc told me firmly, without raising his voice, that one must never joke about things like that – a lesson I never forgot. We tried out the beach and the Gulf of Mexico in Corpus Christi after we had endeavored unsuccessfully to locate one of Doc's cousins in Raymondville, Texas. Doc pointed out that the town had been named after his cousin, though I do not recall why.

Since we had planned to swim in the Atlantic on our journey through the good old United States, we went by way of New Orleans, where Doc invited us to eat a scrumptious meal at one of America's top ten restaurants, Antoine's in the French Quarter, for which I still have the menu, all in French, signed on August 5, 1956, by one J. P. Le Blanc. I had my first oysters à la Rockefeller and have never since tasted oysters which surpassed those served at Antoine's. At that time, "filet de boeuf Robespierre en casserole" cost $5 and was the most expensive entrée listed. I can recommend the place highly. – Yes, we did stop at the cemetery where the graves are above ground because of the high moisture content of the soil. On the way to Miami, Florida, we saw the first gracious and radiantly pink flamingos in the tropical gardens, which far surpassed the floating ones of Xochimilco. The AAA map took us along the Gulf Coast to Miami and from there to Daytona Beach, where we cooled off by swimming in the Atlantic, although the wind was so strong that the fine sand found its way into the rooms through the tiniest openings and cracks and finally caused us to leave. On the beach itself, the sand is so fine and closely packed that they have car races on it.

We had to be back in Michigan in time to pack and get ready for the sailing of our ships from New York to Bremerhaven. Our maps took us home via the scenic Smoky Mountains of North Carolina, which gave us a chance to pick a few balls of cotton from the fields in Georgia. After all, even though we did not visit Atlanta to see the Tara Plantation from *Gone with the Wind*, we could tell those friends from Sankt Ursula with whom I had secretly read the long novel with a flashlight underneath our covers what the fields in which Scarlett O'Hara picked cotton with her slaves looked and felt like.

How happy we were to have returned home to the Croft safe and sound and without getting sick; and how pleased Doc was to sense, rightly, that the two of us had grown even closer as we journeyed through his beloved homeland, for which he had risked his life at war and whose people he strove to serve as long as he lived.

Time Out to Reflect – Doc's Pursuit Bears Fruit

I had decided to go to the United States before I had met Hans, no matter what, and had planned to return to Germany two years later, no matter what. – Maria and I got ready for our trip across the Atlantic with record speed. I packed the big trunk to capacity with all I had accumulated since I arrived, squeezing in the twenty volumes of Charles Dickens's collected works, which I had fallen for while at the Croft and which Doc insisted I take as a good-bye present.

Doc had reserved two rooms in a downtown hotel in New York City. Maria's ship left a day before mine, the SS *America*. After we waved good-bye to Maria, Doc took me to dinner and afterward treated me to the Rockettes in Radio City Hall. Yes, I still resisted Doc's ardent attempts to convince me to stop fighting nature, which was even harder because we had sipped tequilas at the Rainbow Room while looking down on the tantalizing city. They were much more potent than the ones in Acapulco. I had to water mine down with a 7 Up, which cost an astronomical and thus sobering 75 cents at the time. I insisted on separate beds. I did not trust myself. It was not easy, because Doc was an expert when it came to the anatomy of the human body. He had kissed me more passionately than any of my German boyfriends, which left no doubt in my mind that I would soar to seventh heaven.

"Ah! Sweet Mystery of Life – Such a Place to Have Found You"

Before I put the Atlantic between us two budding lovers, it would be seriously remiss of me not to share with you the contents of some of the many letters Doc wrote while courting me. They bear testimony not only to his deep love for me, but more importantly to his unconditional love of mankind, his philosophy of life, his understanding of the forces of nature, and the enjoyment he derived from the multitude of her beautiful gifts. He surprised me repeatedly by quoting just the right line of poetry to enhance his thoughts or feelings, be it in French, German, or English. It never failed to touch my heart. How many times did he look at me with his blue eyes under his bushy white-and-black eyebrows and quote Heinrich Heine's "Du bist wie eine Blume / So hold, so schoen, so rein. / Ich schau Dich an und Wehmut / Schleicht mir ins Herz hinein" (You are like a flower / so lovely, so beautiful, so pure. / I look at you and sorrow / creeps into my heart)? Thus, it did not come as a surprise when the same poem showed up in a letter which he started with "Ah! Sweet mystery of life – such a place to have found you" and continued with "we will have to believe that time is purely 'relative'. . . . Maybe it was already written that I should so greatly love you when I learned German. . . . I am afraid Heine was a little bitter at times: 'Du hast mich zugrunde gerichtet / Feinsliebchen was willst du mehr?'" (You have tortured me sweet love, / what more do you want?). But the letter changed over to a more optimistic tone by quoting the "Blume" poem, to which he added, "It looks like we will just have to leave love to nature and not try to explain it. 'Ich hab darueber nachgedacht schon manche tausend Jahre' [I have thought about it many thousand years]. 'Seek not to know the unknowable / nor sink the string of thought into the fathomless.' Good morning darling. Have been watching the sunrise. Am quite a sun worshiper. It wasn't quite in the East, but it will be in four or five days more. The clock struck seven very close after it had risen."

Doc's constant companion was Elbert Hubbard's *Scrap Book*, which was always handy in the library: "Have been reading the scrapbook considerably this week. It is the talking and communing with the great of the earth. There is much beauty there also."

Among my favorite letters are those he wrote in the spring, when the fields of daffodils, narcissuses, and violets were in full bloom at the Croft. Doc must have had them planted because he "saw fields of them on the shores of the Mediterranean Sea. The other flowers are coming fast. Regular mass of violets to the north of the house. A large white violet is also in bloom." In the same letter, he wrote that "the daffodils are blooming great" and quoted Wordsworth: "I wandered lonely as a cloud / That floats on high o'er vales and hills, / When all at once I saw a crowd, / A host of golden daffodils; / Beside the lake beneath the trees / Fluttering and dancing in the breeze. . . . For oft, when on my couch I lie / In vacant or in pensive mood, / They flash upon that 'inward eye' / Which is the bliss of solitude; / And then my heart with pleasure fills, / And dances with the daffodils."

Doc was aware that in nature, every movement, no matter how seemingly insignificant, plays its part:

Darling little one, spent a beautiful evening sitting on the bench in the back yard just looking at springtime. It is now thundering and lightening, also part of spring. Dreams of Love and mountains of kisses. . . . The rains have made the grass very green and there are many more flowers out. . . . The winds are sobbing faintly with a gentle unknown woe. . . . The soughing of the wind is making me drowsy so will give my darling many kisses and wish her good night. Oceans of love. "Doc."

Doc's love of nature kindled within me the flame as well. How many times have I quoted his favorite saying, "Observe nature and think about it"? Thus, when I came to that point in my memoirs where I had to go back in time to be with Doc, I felt compelled to search for a special place, away from wires and voices. I could not have found a more ideal spot. One day, in exploring the scenic marvels along the grand Ohio River in Southern Indiana, I discovered, quite accidentally, the perfect sanctuary: River Haven. I knew right then and there that this was the refuge from which to share with you Doc's own words and wisdom. It was as though an invisible force led me to this big and beautiful river, almost one thousand miles long. This stream flows into the even bigger Mississippi, just as the smaller Mosel runs into the Rhine River in Germany. The two rivers start out running their separate ways, but they unite before immersing themselves in the waters of the Gulf of Mexico, which wash the beaches of Texas and Florida, where we traveled with Maria, as well as those of the Yucatán Peninsula, where Doc and I spent three months of our heavenly honeymoon outside the little fishermen's town of Progresso, where we found our haven in a tucked-away tropical paradise.

I was tucked away in my cozy river cabin, a house easily one hundred years old. It sat on a narrow clearing on a ridge about 150 feet above the river. Behind the house, a rock formation rose another one hundred feet. It was covered with broad-leaved trees. The east side of the five-room house was decorated in Southern Indiana country style, mostly blue, white, and pink, with wooden floors, the most comfortable easy chairs, couches, and rocking chairs, and warmly shining table lamps throughout. There was a large, screened-in deck looking down toward the river. On the southeast side was a front porch with rocking chairs, a porch swing, and a picnic table, all painted white and all affording a view of the river. Underneath the white painted porch balustrade was a flowerbed of deep purple petunias, lavender phlox, and lemon-colored daylilies. Southern hospitality was evident all over the place. At both main entrances were handcrafted welcome signs. A bouquet of wild flowers stood next to the sign on the porch. You could look down on the river from six windows, all with light-blue curtains, in the cheerful master bedroom and the inviting living room. I preferred the ceiling fans to forced cool air even in the quaint blue country kitchen. I had longed for the atmosphere of yesteryear. The river was forever present, forever flowing quietly, forever changing gently. I had not felt so peaceful in many years.

The harmonious solace was intoxicating. I felt hypnotized by the surface of the stream, which mirrored the trees on the bank. I was mesmerized by the ocean of oleander-pink and white blossoms on three or four trees halfway down. Their leaves were like those of ferns, and the branches spread out like huge umbrellas. The blooms above the leaves were lacy and delicate. Black-and-white butterflies and hummingbirds were ceaselessly hovering above, inserting their long beaks into the pink and white lace to suck up the sweet nectar. I reminisced about the first hummingbirds I saw at the Gulf of Mexico, as they peeked out of their tiny nest in a coconut palm tree under which Doc was lounging. Birds were chirping in concert all around me as I soaked up the atmosphere. A lone cardinal ruffled its scarlet feathers in the distance. A young gray fox strolled across the freshly cut lawn on the slope in front of the house, paused, and looked at me while a chipmunk darted into a bed of orange daylilies underneath the deck. It crossed my mind that the rascal had stowed away in my trunk.

As the sun began to set behind the treetops, small birds, like swallows, sailed across the surface of Mr. River, resting for a few seconds in the barren treetops here and there before they shot again through the air swiftly, only to coast close to the river's face once more before disappearing into nowhere. Were it not for the occasional monstrous barges floating up and down the river or an occasional car going by below, I could have imagined myself at our cabin in the North Woods. The barges reminded me of an article I found after Doc had passed away. Humble as he always was, he never told me he had been cited for his "heroic labors" in a supplement to the *New York Times*. In 1927, he was the chief surgeon on the influenza-ridden *Château* Thierry as it crossed the Panama Canal on the way to San Francisco. They arrived with fifty-two sick passengers and four dead mates. "Too much praise cannot be given to Captain Beardsley and his men – not forgetting those two nurses. They worked in twenty-hour shifts caring for the sick. . . . Besides more than one thousand military passengers the transport carried fifteen members of a Congressional delegation and their families" on the way to a peace conference in Honolulu. Doc brushed the praise aside with a mere "it was all in a day's work." His only regret was that they "could not have saved the four boys."

Rereading the letters out here in nature's stimulating seclusion made me realize once more how hard it had been to reason my way out of Doc's way of thinking:

Little lover, it took me nearly a lifetime to learn that nature (others call it god) is the all powerful thing in the world and its rules and regulations are the vital things to follow. So when one refuses its natural gifts, nature has offered, especially, as my whole lifetime has shown how very fundamental the conduct between male and female is, you must not expect me to applaud. . . . The chaos will leave my little one's mind when she decides to follow nature's law and completes her love.

He did his utmost to console me, being fully aware of my inner turmoil:

I know it appears very selfish of me, but knowing how few women receive the greatest rewards life has to offer (and being as you said an expert) and as the French say: how we are "en rapport" with each other, I might honestly be thinking of your happiness also. You are sure of the great chaos going on in your feeling. I sure understand the war between the fundamental laws of nature and made rules and regulations of mankind. You can be sure of my great love and sympathy with young mental struggles.

Doc always practiced what he preached:

First, it has always been a cardinal principle with me that one's body is their private property and their ownership should be respected by others. If they give it to an other, that is different. Your real desires in the matter will be respected by me. "Within yourselves deliverance must be sought, each one his own prison makes."

At another time, he wrote,

Now little one, you will have to come to me completely and unreservedly of your own will if you are ever mine. So do not fear me in any way, I expect to pretty much drop the subject of union between us. But as long as your mind is in a chaotic state, I will still hope. Oceans of love and millions of kisses. "Doc."

He was unwavering in his belief that I returned his feelings:

Now little lover although I do love you with a great love and desire nothing more than to spend the rest of my days with you, I would not urge you the slightest unless I had seen our great love in your eyes and the joy and happiness and peace when you were with me. I think this is the last time I will present what I believe to be facts in this matter to you. Argument never changes any minds it generally sets them in their opinion. I wish my lover to think of these things very carefully as I feel the happiness of at least one if not two is at stake. Solemnly with everything he has, all yours. "Doc."

Another time, he observed,

The love light in my darling's eyes "The light that was never on land or sea" was wonderful and beautiful to see. It makes me so proud and humble to think my little one loves me so.

Doc cherished the times when he sat outside in the park by himself, watching the moonlight, reminiscing:

The evening we had together was so wonderful. Do not believe my little darling could love me more if I was a complete man instead of half a wreck of one. The more we see of each other the closer we become to each other. It seemed there never was a more beautiful moonlight night. No darling I have not lived my life as yet, maybe I have been learning how to live and feel that maybe the knowledge that I have accumulated would make up for some of the years that have gone.

I had gone to sleep a bit earlier out here in nature while communicating with Doc. All of a sudden, at 11:00 p.m., I opened my eyes because a light was shining into the room. I jumped out of bed, and appearing quite low, a huge gold-and-orange-colored fireball was over the river. The finest veil was in front of the ball, giving it the markings of a globe, with outlines of continents and oceans. To have a full and better view, I went onto the porch, sat on the swing, and gazed upon the phenomenon in the dark sky as though no human eye had ever witnessed anything like it. I was so moved by the experience that tears came to my eyes. As I swung back and forth gently, I heard the sweetest sounds softly, ever so softly, ringing at my ear. I hearkened into the night and became aware of the wind chimes six feet from where I sat. A faint breeze stirred the chimes. Their harmonious sounds resembled angels' voices or kind spirits whispering in the trees. Another, deeper, hornlike sound became audible from far away, slowly drowning out the chimes. Soon, a monstrous iron body forged through the night on the river, with the moon above. It faded away when another barge came crawling behind, sounding its foghorn. The front was lit up like a Christmas tree in blue and yellow lights. The dark silhouette crept down the river until it disappeared around the bend, leaving me behind, swinging and listening to the serenade of the crickets until I went back into the house.

I moved the cherrywood rocking chair close to a living-room window so I could observe the moon. As she moved higher, the orange hue changed to a much lighter glow. Still too excited by the phenomenon of the night, I rose and curled up in the big and ever-so-comfortable easy chair with an ottoman, big enough to please a husky guy. In thinking about Doc's letters, I recalled the lesson of compassion toward mankind he had taught me when one day, while sorting through the papers in his desk, I came upon a bunch of unpaid doctor bills, for the delivery of a baby to be exact. When I asked him why he did not bill the patient, he told me to get into the old Ford, in which he took me on his beloved back roads near Vandalia and passed a couple of shacks where black people lived. Cass County, Michigan, was one of the terminals of the Underground Railroad that took many Southern Americans to freedom before and during the Civil War. He stopped at a hut where several sparsely dressed black children played in mud puddles, the mother sitting on a stool near the house, feeding her newborn child. Doc pointed at her, turned to me, looked deep into my eyes, and asked me if I thought he should send her a bill. I was never so ashamed and thenceforth asked no more. How many times did he point out that as long as there is food on the table, there is no need for concern?

As my eyes continued to wander around the room, I found that the local knickknacks arranged in the white painted shelves against the wall were not without a special charm. The Raggedy Ann dolls, locally crafted baskets, pottery, green plants, bird figurines, and a bigger figurine of a young boy sitting at a girl's feet, entitled *First Love*, made me smile. A blue-and-white porcelain Madonna reminded me of the aesthetically more appealing Madonna I had received as a wedding gift, which was carved out of wood by a craftsman in Bavaria. When I was ready to go to bed, I wished my favorite Raggedy Ann doll, which was sitting in a toddler-sized rocking chair next to a window, "Happy dreams."

At 5:00 in the morning, I was roused by my inner clock and by the rising sun, blossoming over the river. It was a sight to behold! The entire riverbed was like an ocean of magical, deep orange-red. I recalled Doc's words when he was certain I would return:

My darling will enjoy the rising of the sun and the walks with nature. (God, "each in his own tongue.") Think our happiness will be full and overflowing. Love without end, kisses infinite.

Doc assured me again and again that he would take care of me:

The welfare of my darling is paramount with me. Don't worry about your old doc, he had that feeling when he was young to work for the welfare of his fellow men and felt it could be best done as a doctor in his case. The work has brought great rewards to him. Your welfare is all he wishes and in any way he can further it, he will try. – No darling, do not fear that I will ever be angry at my little one nor doubt my genuine interest in your welfare. You have already brought so much sunshine and happiness in my life that payment would be impossible.

As his letters attest, Doc also tried to appease my serious concerns about our differences in religion. I was raised Catholic, and Doc, extremely well versed in all religions, but favoring Buddhism, had never been baptized:

You tell me to be logical, so will try and not state anything but the truth. The only reason for there being both, man and woman in the world is the reproduction of their kind. Sex is as simple as that. As it is one of the fundamentals of living, several religions have mixed it in with their dogma in order to have a greater hold on the people. (Food and shelter are the other.) As to your religion it is the result of a Catholic mother. The chance of having one in the world, are 1 out of 25 figuring the total people and total Catholics. To a logical mind, I am afraid, that a 25 to 1 odds of a thing being right would be considered too great. As a lady poet said: "So many gods, so many creeds, so many paths that wind and wind. When just the art of being kind is all the sad world needs." But as the poet in the "Apotheoses of Man" said: "Thou wouldst offer on an altar that seems true to thee; Thy little moment of eternity."... Now as my little lover knows, I feel a great charity and kindness towards all religions. Have no quarrel with their aims to do good in the world. Man-made dogma, which is to be found in all of them, is a different thing.

Doc knew I was quite naïve and ignorant when it came to intimate relationships, and he enlightened me as follows:

Have been thinking that opening the subject of sex, which is one, if not the one, of most importance; might be and is often very vital to the individual; that maybe I can help my darling in life as she says and I believe her, knows very little. Through lack of the knowledge, statistics as near as can be obtained show that only one out of three married women have proper gratification and pleasure in the sexual act no matter how young a male they marry. Of course this is due to ignorance. Very often the sexual education of the male was from their contacts with the "nymphs de putain" as the French say (Heine Dirne (prostitute)), which is nothing but beastliness and not true sex at all; and they are using their wives like them. As Heine says: "Ein Tor ist immer willig, / Wenn eine Toerin will" [A fool is always willing if a female fool is too].... According to nature the only object of the union of the male and female is reproduction. When two truly love each other they greatly desire to have children together. Sex tends to become merely lust when people are too prosperous.... From a selfish point of view it would mean much extra care and work for me to marry, but I know that service for others brings the only real happiness. To marry in order to have somebody to use revolts me. Many young women nowadays have had themselves sterilized. Bah! "Blown buds of barren flowers." Now little one, I truly love you and if I can serve you in any way, I would appreciate your presenting any problems that you have to me. Maybe I can help you solve them. The more I can help the happier I will be.

Doc disputed my reasoning that

children of younger men will be stronger and more vigorous than those of an old one. . . . Just the opposite is borne out by statistics. The same applies to the statement that a young father has more time to play with and teach his children. In most cases he is so busy getting the means to feed and clothe them, that he has no time. Also the knowledge and understanding that comes with age makes the old ones more congenial with the young. As the saying goes, he reverts to youth. Might mention that when a woman starts bearing babies, the rougher sports and dancing generally cease. Also, the father who is taking care of them is generally too tired to indulge.

He pointed out that his daughter-in-law Dorothy

had only six years with Peter. She has as a result two beautiful boys, which is more than the average. Also statistics show that young widows have more chance to make a successful remarriage than single ones.

He had very much hoped I would bear his child, especially since his son was taken so early:

Darling you have enriched my life so much. Hope I can enrich yours. Will be so happy to see you with a babe in your arms. Do not think anything so enriches a woman's life as a babe of her own. What was most wonderful was how our love for each other grew the more we were together. It was a good omen that it would keep on growing. . . . Love to you, but "tongue and words" are a poor substitute for "acts and deeds."

Doc, in the letters he sent across the Atlantic, was untiring in his efforts to calm any possible fear and finally convinced me that his daughter would not object to our union:

Gretchen has some of the natural jealousy of her mother in her makeup. But she knows the terrible unhappiness it brought to her mother and I believe she will fight it and overcome it in time. . . . Gretchen came out this weekend and told me she had written you. She is a reserved individual but stated positively that she thought we were doing the right thing under the circumstances. . . . Now my beloved and beloved darling, again and again don't worry but depend on me to arrange things the way you want and when you want and where you want if it is at all possible. . . . She feels that it is a marriage of love so is content. You have just about taken entire possession of my thought. Love infinite. "Doc."

I had expressed concern that we should not rush into a marriage also out of respect for Auntie Hazel, who had passed away not long before and was taken aback when

Doc confided in me that the marriage had its rough spots, in particular after his wife had an abortion without his knowledge. At that time, he gave her the option of a divorce or staying together, but never "touched" her again. They stayed together, but this letter appears to shed light on the relationship:

By the way. Olive Schreiner, in one of her "dreams," mentioned a case where a couple had lost their love and wandered disconsolate for a long time. They finally found a greater one present and found it was <u>sympathy</u>. Olive wrote some lovely things and I found them very consoling over the years. Hazel had my sympathy and it was no empty word. She told me she would have done different if she had had another chance. I guess that applies to most of us. There is a great sense of loss present. As the French say, "A partir est à mourir, un peut."

He also was of the opinion that we should "let the dead be passed" and was fully aware of the passing of time and of life, even when talking of spring:

Spring is at its very best. But how fast it is going and how few there are till life is gone.

I cannot end this commemorative part of my memoirs, composed at the river, without quoting from another of Doc's favorite poems, Algernon Charles Swinburne's "The Garden of Proserpine," which I heard him recite from time to time at the Croft:

> *From too much love of living*
> *From hope and fear set free,*
> *We thank with brief thanksgiving*
> *Whatever gods may be*
> *That no man lives forever,*
> *That dead men rise up never;*
> *That even the weariest river*
> *Winds somewhere safe to sea.*

Now, having reread and rethought Doc's letters almost half a century later, I am again overwhelmed at the depth of his love, the nobility of his heart, and his great wisdom, which over the years have given me the drive, the desire, and the strength to forge ahead repeatedly when it seemed adversity would overcome me. Doc kindled within me a truly genuine and eternal love, which I am convinced is rare and hard to find. I made a promise to myself when Doc left this world that I would keep his memory alive, for without his compassion and generosity, without the confidence he instilled within me, I would not have mastered my life as I did. Doc laid a foundation on which I could build, a foundation for which I am perpetually grateful.

* * *

1954–1961

The SS *America* left New York Harbor on September 27 in the late afternoon, with the band playing the national anthem as soon as the almost 34,000-ton vessel was set into motion. Doc stood at the pier in his light-gray flannel suit, raised his hand, and threw me a kiss as the ship left shore. With both hands in white gloves, I touched the purple orchid in the corsage Doc had pinned on my navy-blue princess-cut coat, raised my fingers to my lips, and threw him a bunch of kisses back. We gazed at each other until the ruffled waves of the Atlantic sparkled like silver from the rays of the sinking sun.

That same evening, when the ocean cruiser was gliding east on the open sea, I wrote Doc a letter telling him that I would come back and marry him. – The only excitement I remember from the passage is winning first prize in a dance contest. I won a golden charm bracelet with the letters *SS AMERICA* dangling from it. My partner was a Japanese. That is as close as I ever came to the mission in Japan. On my arrival, Mutti took me into her arms as though she would never let me go, tears streaming down our cheeks. She pulled seven letters out of her purse – seven letters from Doc – and said, "I know you are going back."

During the two months at home, Mutti and I combed the fashionable boutiques in Hannover, looking for the perfect gown and accessories. I visited my friends, and announced happily that I would return to America to be married to Doc. All were happy for me, even the Padre, who gave his blessing, noting that ultimately love, not age, was the deciding factor. I did receive a letter from Dr. Swengel's wife in Cassopolis, who expressed concern because her husband was seventeen years older than she and she wished it were otherwise. Later, Doc told me she had made inappropriate advances toward him during an office visit. I knew there were other opportunities for him, such as the widow in Florida who kept urging him to join her in the Sunshine State. Receiving the letter of approval from Doc's daughter meant a lot; and his cousin Francis Moorhouse, from California, was all for it. She confessed to having had a "thing" for Doc when she was younger, but since they were related, it was not advisable. Hmm . . .

While at home, Doc, the perfect gentleman, also wrote a letter to my parents in which he asked for my hand in marriage, telling them how deeply he loved me and spelling out in detail the steps he had taken to provide for me in case something should happen to him. He signed the letter with his signature and rank, as in a legal document. In another letter, Doc asked me to go shopping for the best-sounding and most advanced hi-fi entertainment center I could find and to bring it back as my wedding present.

Doc, determined not to waste one more minute of separation, had arranged the entire wedding as I wished, including a civil ceremony in front of the JP, as is mandatory in Germany prior to the church wedding. Considering that Doc never had been baptized, to pull off a Catholic-church wedding was close to a miracle, no doubt about it, especially in view of what took place across the Atlantic while

I was bidding my maiden times good-bye: One day, while out on house call in the back roads of lower Michigan, Doc stopped the old Ford to help a man stranded on the roadside with a flat tire. The man turned out to be the priest of a church in Decatur, Michigan, approximately twenty-five miles away from the Croft. The two men befriended each other, and Father Berger became a frequent dinner guest at the Croft, where Effie, the cook, treated him to roast duck and other culinary delights. When Doc informed me Father Berger had assured him that a wedding in front of the altar was no problem, a big weight fell from my shoulders, as well as from my parents'.

On November 20, I was eager to return on the majestic and luxuriously decorated SS *United States*, known for making maritime history. At 53,300 tons, it was at that time the largest vessel ever built in America and the fastest passenger ship in the world. She made the transatlantic voyage in under five days and lay anchored at Bremerhaven ready for me to embark. – As soon as the shipmaster saw the huge, two-ton crate that held my prized wedding gift, the state-of-the-art SABA entertainment console, he objected strenuously to loading it. He insisted that there was a strike at the pier in New York and I would not be able to get if off the ship. I pleaded endlessly, telling him that the SABA had to play at my wedding and not to worry. I was convinced I would be able to get it off the ship in New York. My parents and I sighed with great relief when we watched the huge box hanging in the net that slowly lowered my treasure into the hull of the vessel. During the ocean voyage, I successfully persuaded those in charge of unloading in New York to assist in getting the SABA off the ship. When the vessel docked on November 26, Doc welcomed me with open arms, hugs, and kisses. Unloading my box was no trouble. The strike was over. A customs official, out of gratitude for my assistance in translating between him and another German bride, who was not so lucky, complied instantly when I asked him to paste a customs-clearance sticker on my crate.

Yes, Doc, I Do – Christmas at the Croft

Our wedding, on November 29, 1956, was a pure white wedding in every sense of the word. As though Mother Nature were aware of my fascination with snow, she had draped the Croft and its enchanting landscape in shrouds of white, fluffy lace. It harmonized with my own Christian Dior wedding dress, made out of snow-white lace. The gown was plain, with a long and richly gathered skirt, fitted waist, high neckline, and long, tapered sleeves ending in a slight point just above the back of my hands. I wore a small bonnet made out of white, pleated georgette with twigs of myrtle on each side, which I brought from Hannover. A veil of white tulle was attached to the back of the bonnet and hung down below the waist, covering the small, covered buttons. White gloves, a small white silk bag, and matching pumps with high heels completed the ensemble. My bridal bouquet was an arrangement of purple orchids, just like the one Doc had given me at the pier.

As Major Darmody and his wife drove us from the Croft to Decatur, we passed the snow-covered landscape along the road and saw the white steeple of the little church from a distance. We entered the chapel, which was large enough to accommodate our intimate group of friends and colleagues, and looked straight ahead to the altar, which was decorated, like the entrances to the pews, with all-white carnations offset by branches of blue spruce. A lady from the altar guild was playing on a small organ. Doc looked handsome and distinguished in his tailored black suit. He wore a white shirt with a silver-gray necktie and had a white rose in his lapel. As is customary in Germany, I walked to the altar on his arm. The guests turned and greeted us with smiles. The sun beamed through a blue-and-red-colored church window throughout the ceremony. Father Berger had found a soprano who sang the "Ave Maria" and other arias rather nicely. After the final blessing, the photographer took over and trailed us back to the Croft, where Effie and a couple of cooks had prepared a reception feast to please everyone's palate, not forgetting the big wedding cake. Champagne and wines were plentiful. Our guests admired the SABA, its beautiful sound, and the fine craftsmanship of the walnut cabinet. I felt loved beyond comparison, and so did Doc. –

The only disappointment came when the wedding photos came back black. The electricity had been out during the developing process.

Being married to Doc was more wonderful and exciting than I could have imagined. We laughed, joked, and played a lot and had an ongoing love affair, calling each other "honeybunch" or "lover bunch," and we never once quarreled. It seemed as though each day surpassed the last. We were inseparable, as Doc had predicted. He even came to help with the dishes on Effie's days off, just to be close.

Christmas was right around the corner. It was my first real Christmas after immigrating to America and is engraved in my mind as vividly as the prewar Christmases of my childhood. Indeed, the setting could not have been more conducive to a memorable Christmas. The Croft – in England, as Doc explained, the term refers to a small farm on a hill – was a forty-acre gentleman's estate located far out in the country on Robbins Lake Road, about four miles from the tiny village of Jones in Southern Michigan. The terrain was hilly, and the surrounding woods and fields had almost reverted to their natural state. Thus, the landscaping of the grounds was by nature English.

It was snowing gently outside as Doc and I got ready to set up and trim the Christmas tree. It was huge, much taller and statelier than the tree in Hannover. Jim, a black man, who helped with odd jobs and repairs around the Croft in exchange for free medical services, had cut it down in our small forest, where we had marked it. He then put it into the stand, carried it into the spacious library, and placed it next to the baby-grand piano, the first piece of furniture we bought after the wedding, and opposite the big red-brick fireplace, which was framed with a light-oak mantelpiece. The bookcases and paneling were built from the same material. Doc always pointed out with great pride that all of the wood in the house – including the paneling in the library, in the Oriental-style living room, and in the dining room, bedrooms, and bathrooms, as well as the staircase, the railing, and the frames of the sliding pocket doors – was solid wood, such as cherry, bird's-eye maple, and yellow and red pine. It also came from the woods belonging to the Croft, the Beardsley family estate. It was where Doc was born and raised and where he helped his mother work the fields after his father's untimely death.

Doc had lit a fire in the fireplace. The heat that penetrated the room made us feel toasty. Our tree stood on the plush Chinese carpet. It covered almost the entire white-oak parquet floor, approximately four hundred square feet in size. I have never again seen a carpet like it. It was woven out of rich mustard-golden wool and highlighted with bold yet graciously snorkeling navy-blue designs. It could have had its place in a palace.

The library was a well-lit room. Four big windows let in much sunshine. It was as though the inside of the rooms extended directly outward into the surrounding landscape. No curtains, drapes, or shades interfered with the view. Doc and I sat cuddled together on the black leather couch, admiring the upright stature and luscious blue-green color of the tree. The winged doors leading to the Oriental room were wide open. The SABA was piping soft Christmas music into the rooms and made us feel warm inside.

The gods seemed to be smiling down on us as the snow gently covered the grounds. It softly clung to the broad branches of tall blue spruces, whose spikes stretched toward the blue sky. It settled on the outstretched arms of the ancient, giant black walnut tree in back of the house that provided cooling shade on hot summer days. It landed carefully on the apple, persimmon, and maple trees, which had matured handsomely in the four-acre yard and begged to be admired by those who visited. The Croft enjoyed the reputation of being a showplace of Southwestern Michigan. On Sundays people often drove by slowly along the split-rail fence to admire the house and the landscape. Yet, on snowy days, the curious were reluctant to venture out on the slippery Robbins Lake Road unless they were lost. However, the winter-wonderland scene unfolding before them would most certainly have touched them. Whenever falling snow clung to the cedar shingles of the house and smoke puffed from the chimney, it looked like a magnified gingerbread house enveloped by a fluff of confectioners' sugar.

The spacious yard that embraced the home presented a continuous flow of colors. In the spring fields, bright-yellow daffodils, snow-white narcissuses, and snowdrops were followed by cobalt-blue violets and white lilies of the valley, which in turn welcomed armies of red, yellow, and white tulips. I will never forget the huge bush of white snowballs right at the corner of the red barn in which Doc used to house a couple of riding horses, or the sixty-foot-long and five-foot-wide bed of hybrid irises, each more gorgeous than the next. There were only perennials in the yard. The big bushes of lush red, pink, and white peonies were so vivid in color that one could not stop admiring them. Roses were all over the place. Pink hedge roses, as well as hybrids of all imaginable sorts, named after presidents and other celebrities, were spread around or arranged in beds. They reminded me of the Herrenhäuser Gardens, in Hannover, where my parents took us for Sunday-afternoon walks. With the exception of the section of the lawn kept immaculate for tennis, the lawn was rather wavy – especially the section behind the house, which extended from the terrace-like rock gardens and displayed an array of the most colorful mosses and vines in the spring. It was a welcome playground for blue racers and garter snakes and came in handy as an occasional resting place for turtles on their way to the goldfish ponds, on which pink and white lotus and water lilies floated from spring to fall. During the winter, fish and lilies were housed in a big tank in the room where the freezer stood, leaving behind the round-faced rocks framing the ponds and the dried-up reeds bending with the wind.

On this first Christmas with my husband, Christkind had brought winter fairyland magic into the landscape and with it my childhood memories. When the snow first began to flurry, the rock garden looked as though a white, lacy veil were being draped over it. As it continued falling, it resembled a bunch of down cushions piled together. The reed tops covered by soft snowflakes looked like cotton balls. A multitude of birds – red cardinals, black-white-and-orange orioles, woodpeckers with a red patch, and yellow finches – quickly roused the senses when we spotted them against the immaculate snow in the bushes or on the ground. Traces in the snow caused by playing squirrels or other wildlife often triggered a comment by Doc, who asked where the rascals might be hiding or expressed concern that the neighbor's cat may have snatched a bird. He loved all wildlife, and I started to appreciate and love living at the Croft. Doc was my teacher.

It was still snowing as I began to unpack the tree ornaments from the boxes, which Doc had carried down from the attic. I told him to take a nap while I trimmed the tree – just as we took a nap before seeing the tree when I was a child in Hannover. I wanted to surprise him when he woke up. He stayed on the couch in the library, drifting in and out of a light sleep.

Never in my life had I seen such beautiful and huge ornaments. Each one looked more precious than the next. They were up to five inches in diameter – gold, silver, blue, red, and green – with glittering, delicate hand-painted designs. For the treetop, I found a magnificent golden star, twelve inches in diameter, which had to be placed over a bulb so it would shine in the dark. Since I was only 5'2" and did not want to awaken Doc, I climbed a ladder to place the ornaments, the strings of blue, green, red, and yellow lights, and finally the star on the treetop. Every now and then, I stepped back from the tree to get a look at it and make sure the ornaments were aesthetically well-balanced. Before arousing Doc I took a final look at my creation, feeling rather pleased with the outcome. The Christmas atmosphere in the room was perfect. The fire was crackling and the music playing. Suddenly, my tree began to bow its top toward me and, with a crash, came tumbling down onto the plush carpet. I screamed, "Oh no!" and Doc, who missed the actual plunge, got up, looked at the scene, and chuckled. "What a shame, oh, don't worry, little one." I felt pretty bad. A great number of the beautiful ornaments were broken and scattered all over the carpet. We lifted the tree, tipped it back onto its designated spot, and rearranged the ornaments that were not broken. In the end, it did look quite lovely. If you had not seen the broken ornaments, you would not have known they were missing. I was amazed that Doc was not at all fazed by the incident. I wonder how my father would have reacted had I been involved in his tree crashing into the dining room in Hannover. Mama mia, watch out!

Doc loved to spoil me with material things. In looking back, I believe he felt he had to make up for the things I missed as a result of the war. He went overboard at Christmas, to say the least. Instead of one he bought two fur coats, an Alaska seal for Sundays and a muskrat for weekdays. He bought all of the classical records available at a music store in Three Rivers and, as usual, went overboard buying all kinds of food. He was over six feet tall and probably thought I could eat as much as he. Though he advised overweight patients that the best diet is to leave food on the table, he wanted to stuff me.

Honeymoon in Yucatán, Mexico

Doc had planned an incredible honeymoon on the Yucatán Peninsula and reserved a spacious suite at the Hotel Mérida, where an exquisite arrangement of flowers greeted us. We had driven to New Orleans and flew from there to Mérida, because no roads had been built through the jungle. We strolled happily through the streets in Mérida, stopping here and there in front of a villa to peek through high, black wrought-iron gates, which contrasted strikingly with the white, yellow, or orange stucco facades of the manors. We greeted the Mayan women as they passed us wearing snow-white dresses embroidered with the most vividly colored floral designs. I took home a couple. I looked on with amazement when the small women balanced urns of clay on their heads with one hand, holding a child with the other. We marveled at the lush tropical flora in the courtyards, where the bougainvillea climbed to the roof, and were convinced the gods had painted the skies above us with an even richer azure.

Eating breakfast at the courtyard of the Hotel Mérida was like feasting in a corner of paradise. Royal and coconut palms graced the corners and surrounded the big fountain in the center, splashing merrily day in and day out. Red, yellow, and blue birds fluttered past our table and even dared to sit briefly on the freshly starched white linen tablecloth to peck a crumb or two. Doc chortled and remarked, "Live and let live." At sunset, we relaxed in the deep-cushioned rattan lounges and sipped our favorite tequila, made with tropical fruit juices, and tried to guess what kind of bird was chirping in the oleander bushes. When the birds piped down, a couple of

Mayan singers serenaded us in the garden and accompanied their songs with the guitar.

When Doc and I tried to catch a glimpse of Mexican life behind the gates of the courtyards, we never dreamed we would actually have a chance to walk through them, but we did. On one of our shopping extravaganzas, we visited a jewelry store, because Doc had wanted to buy a diamond ring for me. We encountered the jeweler, Mr. Goldstein, who employed about three hundred men. Doc and Mr. Goldstein befriended each other rather quickly. Doc, as usual, went overboard, which pleased the proprietor immensely, I am sure. Not only did my husband end up buying a two-carat diamond in a baroque setting, a much bigger amethyst in a Tiffany setting, a square white amethyst, and a fourteen-carat oval alexandrite that changed colors and was designed by yours truly, but he added two coin bracelets, one in silver and the other in gold, to the bargain. We had admired the gold bracelets on some of the señoritas among the hotel guests, who made sure they were noticed as they clinked on their delicate or not-so-delicate wrists.

Doc's knack at making friends paid off royally, just as it did with Father Berger, you may recall. Mr. Goldstein offered Doc a fifty-peso commemorative gold coin, of which only one hundred were minted and which he had secured from his brother-in-law, who happened to be the president of the Banco di Mérida. He also invited us for dinner at his Mexican villa. Of course, I was totally enthralled by what I saw behind those gates, but concentrated more on talking to the mistress of the house and her young child while Doc and Mr. Goldstein got deeply involved in a discussion of Einstein's theory of relativity, which to me sounded more like Chinese than Spanish, or English. The connection between the two gentlemen doubtlessly went beyond Einstein; Mr. Goldstein's wife was also much younger than he – and to their credit, they had a young child. Thanks to Señor Goldstein, Doc and I also gained entrance to another estate, even more exclusive and exotic than that of the Cuban ambassador. We attended a party at the ambassador's house the night before the chauffeur Doc had hired whisked us happy honeymooners away to the white beaches on the Gulf of Mexico, not far from the fishermen's town of Progreso. Here, we exchanged two weeks in the lap of wealth and luxury for ten weeks of carefree, very leisurely living at Cocoteros, a small hotel recommended highly by an American.

Cocoteros, as the name implies, was situated in a grove of coconut palms, loaded heavily with clusters of golden fruits. Our own hut or cabin, equipped with modern facilities, yet covered by a thatched roof and no more than one hundred feet away from an immaculate beach, could not have been more ideal for honeymooners. There is nothing more soothing than watching the ever-changing ocean waves, nothing more exhilarating than swimming in their waters, nothing more thrilling than joining their rhythm, jumping up and down and screaming when they wash over your head without warning. There is nothing more calming than resting in the shadow of coconut palms after some time in the sun. At Cocoteros, palm trees were all around us. Two hundred feet in another direction was a kidney-shaped pool made of blue tiles, which Pablo, the maintenance man, scrubbed until it was perfectly clean. The pool water was always crystal clear, and Doc loved to show off his diving expertise or beat me in a chase from one end to the other after we had exhausted the pleasures of the ocean.

My Spanish was improving daily, to the point that some Mexicans thought I was a native. I was short, like the Mayan Indians, and had also acquired a deep-bronze tan that contrasted rather nicely with my favorite bathing suit, made out of mustard-yellow, olive-green, and brown diamond-shaped pieces of spandex crocheted together with chocolate-brown silk thread. At the time, I weighed about 105 pounds, and it should not come as a surprise that one of the male guests asked me if Doc, almost twice my size, was my grandfather. You should have seen his face when I replied, with my trademark grin, "No, my husband!"

The same "youth," in his early thirties, was suddenly in awe of Doc when he saw us climbing up and down the many steep steps to the top of the big Mayan ruin, the principal temple, the so-called Castillo. The temple covers one acre of ground and reaches one hundred feet above the plain at Chichén Itzá. Along the center of the pyramid, a rope was strung for climbers to hold on to. You should have seen us beam with pride when Diego, our chauffeur in the straw hat, took our picture sitting on the steps halfway up. It was strange that the youth should show up just then, because there were only a handful of tourists around. I found it even stranger that a healthy-looking individual like him would be so afraid to climb the steps of the pyramid.

I learned a lesson when falling in love with Doc. It is not the outer appearance, not the signs of age that matter, but the character, the heart and soul. You fall in love with the man and everything about him, be it the wrinkles or other physical imperfections. You don't even notice them when you are truly in love.

The Mayan ruins at Chichén Itzá and Uxmal were exciting and new to me, born as I was in the village of Gieboldehausen, Germany, and I could not get enough of crawling around, inspecting, exploring, and wondering. I can still see in my mind the deep, emerald-green well where they sacrificed the maidens. Just think!

It was wonderful to go sightseeing with a private chauffeur, but it was just as much fun when Doc and I went "native," which was most of the time at Cocoteros. We found the Mayan Indians ever so much friendlier and less boisterous than their relatives to the north and in the cities. Pablo, short as he was, always dressed in a white shirt and wore his straw hat. Each morning, he greeted us with the biggest smile, showing off a row of white teeth, when he came to our sanctuary, bringing us our daily coconut-milk drink with a straw in the hollow shell of the nut. It was our refreshment right after we returned from our leisurely walk along the wide beach, where we gathered a sizeable collection of the most beautiful shells, sea stars, and conches. I displayed each one on the wicker chest of drawers in our room. The floor was covered with beige tile.

Whenever we decided to venture downtown or to a nearby village, we waited with the natives along the roadside for the bus. It was adventurous to ride on the antiquated, half-broken-down green bus through the countryside. One never knew if or when the vehicle, which resembled a box on wheels, would break down or what kind of cargo would next be hauled into the bus, be it live or butchered chickens or just-killed game. It reminded me a bit of my own chicken experience with Mutti. The seats on the bus were wooden, which may have explained the constant rattling noise. Whenever the driver stopped, the brakes squeaked so dissonantly you had to put a finger in your ear. I don't recall ever seeing an American on those buses; even the couple we befriended, the one that said over and over how wonderful it was to see such a happy pair, would not join us.

There is no better way to understand a fishermen's village than to take the autobus. It goes slowly, so it is hard to avoid looking at the poverty-stricken countryside. Even the occasional orange trees or a rooster on a roof lose their uplifting effect. You cannot help but shake your head as you notice the warped huts made out of clay and straw with thatched roofs and a small hole for an entrance, which leads into the dark interior, where woven rugs on the bare clay ground or a hammock serve as places to rest. Half-naked niños and niñas play in puddles from which piglets and dogs lap the brown liquid, while an Indian mother sits on the ground nursing a babe with her breast and guarding other little ones at the same time. Always dressed in immaculate white dresses, the Mayan women spruce up the seemingly desolate countryside. They attract the eye when they pull a bucket of water out of a well or kneel over a stream to wash clothes before spreading them out on the stones along the stream or hanging them on lines for the sun to bleach. The skin of the Mayans is like dark, tanned leather, but their eyes look peaceful.

The way to the village or town puts you in the right mood for a look at the thousands of crafted items begging to find an owner – or almost forced upon you by those selling them. But now you know why. It puts you in the mood also for a casual visit to the outdoor marketplace. No doubt about it, it takes a special attitude or stomach to look at the assortment of plucked or not-plucked fowl, rabbits, goats, or beef and to inspect the freshly caught fish, staring at you with their glaring eyes as though they were still swimming in their waters, lying next to mussels, shrimp, octopus, and other slimy creatures from the sea. There are obvious traces of blood all over, and a mild smell cannot be disregarded, because buzzing flies show a special appetite for the catch. It's always advisable to finish the grand market tour at the fruit stands – which intoxicate the eye with the shades of orange of papayas and mangoes, the reds of pomegranates and melons, the greens of avocados and limes, or whatever your palate desires – before finding your favorite restaurant, where you want to rest, drink, and eat.

When we wanted a break from the restaurant, which served excellent food, we frequented a small taverna in Progreso, run by the family of a Mayan fisherman. None of them spoke English, which was ideal for me. They always greeted us smilingly when we came through the door, which was usually open to let in the ocean breeze. A man in a white shirt ushered us to a special table, spread a spotless, white linen tablecloth over it, and let us know what they were serving that day. The food was always excellent, though there were not too many choices. We tended to stick with fresh seafood or grilled chicken, and we drank a glass of wine or a Mexican beer to flush out the sting of the superspicy dishes, including the little green and yellow peppers, which Doc liked. Unlike me, he also relished hotly seasoned octopus, which was served in little pewter bowls. I am still amazed that neither Doc nor I got sick.

Before getting on the bus, Doc always looked for a little niño to have his shoes shined. He enjoyed watching the boy's eyes when he put an extra peso in his little hand and enjoyed seeing his smile when he mumbled, "Muchas gracias, señor." Doc loved children and liked bringing them into the world, as he told me many times. We talked about children when we saw them running over the sandy beach into the blue waters of the gulf and wondered whether we would be blessed as well. There was no place on earth more heavenly for conceiving a child than right there, where the waves rocked us to sleep every night. There was no place in the universe for a more blissful honeymoon. As I wrote to my parents from Progreso, "Doc and I are still on our honeymoon, which will last until eternity." One month after we returned to the Croft, we knew we were expecting.

Joys and Sorrows at the Croft

Doc and I were shocked back into reality when we turned into the driveway and saw Doc's precious old Ford smashed into one of the big maple trees beneath which we parked the cars when we were too lazy to drive them into the barn. It turned out that Effie, whom we had permitted to drive the car, had lost control. It was also sad that she had fed my pretty red-winged canary, which sang so beautifully, so much lettuce that it died. Effie had gotten entangled with a drinking companion and lover and lived a life of Riley in the little house which Doc had improved for her before leaving, even giving her a TV set.

These insignificant mishaps were forgotten soon after my cousin Karl arrived, whom Doc, generous as he was, had sponsored because he was unable to find a decent job in Germany and, more importantly, was hoping to fix things with his girlfriend, whom he had found through an ad in the paper and who had taken off for LA, leaving him in the lurch. The son of rich Aunt Sissy and Uncle Adolf did not stay long before we took him to the airport and put him on a plane, not without putting a $20 bill in his pocket. I have not heard from him in forty-four years, but found out inadvertently that he married the runaway girl, did well selling windows, acquired a couple of rental properties, and was last seen peddling watermelons at a roadside stand in Florida.

Our life at the Croft was great. We went on our morning nature walks and drove to church on Sundays, where Doc, always smiling, emptied a bunch of coins from his yellow sack into the second collection, that is, the one after the envelopes, and eagerly critiqued the sermons of Father Berger, who joined us in front of the church as soon as Mass was over. I was amazed when Doc, each Sunday afternoon or evening, would not stop until he cracked the chess games in the *Chicago Tribune*. He always kept up with the latest developments in medicine by reading the various journals, often while I watched TV. He had asked me if I would like for him to introduce me to the social scene of his cousins in Elkhart, but since I sensed that Doc was not particularly interested in their rather glamorous lifestyle and since he and Auntie Hazel had taken me along to Ed Beardsley's home only once, I felt indifferent.

As I was pregnant, Doc decided against buying a horse for me. We still had a good English saddle in the barn where they used to keep horses. He also advised me against playing tennis, even though we had a lawn tennis court at our disposal. He did take me each week to Mishawaka, to continue with violin lessons, and did give in to my pleas to let me watch him deliver a child. The black woman was screaming and cussing her lungs out, not really wanting this ninth child. As soon as I saw the infant's head hanging down from the grip of his big right hand, I fainted. When Doc turned around to ask for his wife, they told him they had placed me on the bed in the next room. I nearly passed out when a black mother brought her young son to the Croft – he had cut his heel open when stepping on a piece of glass. I had to sit on the couch and hold the boy while Doc sewed up the bleeding cut right then and there. I found it hard to believe when he told me that one day, another mother arrived with a son whose thumb had been cut off with a knife. He told her to hurry home, fetch the cut-off piece from the garbage can, and bring it back. He sewed it on, and the thumb grew back together.

All along, while serving as the director of the Cass County Hospital and making house calls at all times, night or day, no matter how far out in the country, he continued researching cancer. After his son died of a brain tumor, he began pursuing the cause of the deadly disease seriously. Since his daughter was enrolled in medical school in Ann Arbor, the two collaborated and published a case history, which revealed what Doc was convinced was a breakthrough in the treatment of carcinoma. At times, he expressed a deep disappointment over the medical profession's lack of interest in his findings, despite the fact that none of his patients diagnosed with carcinoma ever died of it. He chuckled when one of his female patients, whose life he had saved, put an article in the paper in which she thanked God for saving her life. Needless to say, he was equally disappointed that his daughter, whom he sent to the university for thirteen years, never completed her work toward an MD.

In May, my brother Alfons arrived. He had, with my help, persuaded Doc to sponsor him. He too was in search of a better life, having had bad luck with jobs in the old country. Doc, in sponsoring him, had an ulterior motive. He wanted me to have a member of my family nearby. I had always looked out for my little brother, who was over six feet tall. I was happy to see him, even though he did not speak a word of English. Doc switched back to teaching, which had been his profession before studying medicine; he brought Alfons a first reader and spent an hour or more each night teaching him English. Doc spruced up the old Ford with a new motor, taught him to drive it, and even paid for the insurance. Alfons had the biggest bedroom upstairs, the one with the open-faced stone fireplace. He was well compensated for any and all tasks he performed at the Croft, especially for building a forty-foot swimming pool, for which he was paid the same amount a contractor would have charged, even though it took him much longer to finish, and even though I went job hunting with him at the same time, acting as an interpreter. The hunt paid off with a job in Elkhart.

All along, Doc and I were elated that the stay at our hacienda had borne the desired fruits. On July 5, however, the unexpected happened. We were watching Alfons dig out the rest of the pool. He egged me on not to be so lazy, tossing me a shovel to help dig. I remembered Mutti's advice that my pregnancy should not stop me from performing physical tasks around the house. I picked up the shovel, stepped into the hole, disregarded Doc's warning not to do it, and threw a shovelful of dirt toward the top of the pile along the rim of the hole. At just that moment, I felt a tear in my lower abdomen, dropped the shovel, hurried into the house with Doc behind me, and lay down on the big, antique bed made of cherrywood. Doc tried to calm me down – in vain. One hour later I lost the child, which we buried on the grounds.

Doc, the eternal optimist, looked on the bright side and was glad to know I could get pregnant. We took another trip up north to our cabin, where we continued to honeymoon, went fishing, and observed the foliage, which was beginning to change color. One evening after dark, as we sat next to the crackling fire in the wood-burning stove, Doc suddenly went silent in the rocking chair. His face turned pale, sweat broke out on his forehead, and his head nodded forward. Frightened, I jumped up, not knowing what to do. I grabbed the arm of the chair and started rocking it furiously, calling his name until he started breathing again. I was more relieved than you can imagine. Doc put his arms around me and said, "I think my little one just saved my life." As on a couple of occasions before this incident, he wanted me to promise him that I would take him to a home for elderly veterans if the need arose, because he did not ever want to become a burden. He also impressed upon me that if at any time I desired to be free, he would let me go.

1954–1961

Doc went up to his beloved haven in the northern woods once more. Though he himself never desired to shoot a deer, he took along three of his hunter friends. He returned early because we missed each other so much. But we also had big plans for our first anniversary party, right after Thanksgiving.

The celebration was a splendid affair, unlike anything I had experienced in my twenty-five years. We engaged several women, two of whom were cooks, to prepare for the party. The mahogany dining-room table was pulled out to seat twelve people comfortably. The heavy tablecloth, which according to Doc was made by five women from Brussels and took them an entire year to complete, graced the table for the special occasion. The heavy silverware blended perfectly with the gold-rimmed Limoges china from Havilland, France. The crystal goblets stood ready to receive the golden wines. Sterling-silver candleholders were placed to each side of an exquisite arrangement of velvety dark-red and snow-white roses, which graced the center of the table. The twelve dining-room chairs, including two captain's chairs, were covered with navy-blue needlework. In the center of each chair was a bouquet of white lilies. Doc had embroidered the chairs when he was retired from the Army after only twelve years of service. He had contracted pleurisy when he was chief surgeon at the Army hospital in Hawaii, right across from Diamond Head. He embroidered the seat cushions to keep his fingers nimble for future surgery.

To accommodate all of the guests, we set up card tables in the Oriental-style living room and in the big library. Each table was set with china from the big collection of antiques. There were turquoise-colored plates, and a relief-type accent of snow-covered Mount Fuji, the extinct volcano in Japan, appeared in the center of the plates and cups. Another setting consisted of large, heavy, square glass plates from the yellowish-green-colored Vaseline glass collection as well as matching goblets and dolphin candlesticks. I found them rather unusual. Doc said they were rare, but the color nicely matched that of the Chinese carpet in the library. In the center of each table were stunning arrangements of red and white roses. While Vaseline glass candlesticks were placed on the tables set with glass plates, white candles in sterling-silver holders stood next to the flowers on the other tables, ready to be lit during dinner. The ladies who served wore black dresses and small white aprons with starched lace ruffles. On their heads they paraded stiff lace tiaras, just like the servants at Glück Auf, Aunt Sissy's villa.

The anniversary celebration will be etched in my mind forever, not only because it fell into the Christmas season, but mostly because an incident occurred which again proved to me how much Doc loved me and how utterly unselfish he was.

I had bought a navy-blue cocktail dress with a low-cut back for the occasion and had mentioned to our housekeeper and caretaker Effie that I thought a white orchid would look great with it. Shortly before the party, Doc handed me a white orchid – exactly what I had imagined. Effie told me later that Doc had originally bought a purple orchid, similar to the one he had given me when he took me to the pier in New York a year earlier. When Doc heard from Effie that I had spoken of a white orchid, he rushed to the car and drove all the way back to Three Rivers, a thirty-mile round trip, and exchanged the corsage for a white one just in the nick of time.

Adieu, Doc . . .

Only a few days after our first anniversary, after we had spent another playful and blissful evening together, Doc awakened me in the middle of the night, asking me to get his bag, take out a small bottle of morphine, fill a syringe, which I had never done before, and inject it into his thigh. At that point, the phone rang – a patient at the hospital had taken a turn for the worse. Doc said he would handle it, hung up, and called his assistant, Dr. Copeland, asking him to take over. I was at a loss for what to do. Doc had told me previously never to take him to a hospital. He had no confidence in doctors, because when he had a badly inflamed appendix and was wrongly assured that they had removed it, he almost died from the burst organ. He returned to the hospital, stayed awake during the entire operation with Auntie Hazel, who was a registered nurse, at his side, and told the doctors what to do and what medication he needed in this case. He was not afraid to die, but did not see any reason to be in a hurry about it. This time, I knew something was wrong, especially when he called Alfons to his bedside. He asked him to promise that he would stay with me and take care of me if something should happen, which he did. We decided to call Dr. Copeland and ask for his advice. He said he would send an ambulance immediately to take Doc to Lakeview Hospital at Paw Paw, Michigan, where he would meet us. On the way to the hospital, Doc said to me softly, "Honey bunch, last year was the happiest year of my life. I hope you are pregnant."

Doc assumed that something was wrong with his heart. Dr. Copeland, even though two EKGs gave negative results, insisted that Doc's assumption was correct. I called in a heart specialist, who found that there was no problem with the heart, but a problem with the lungs. Dr. Copeland still did not agree with the diagnosis, but he finally started Doc on antibiotics. It was obviously too late. He seemed to get worse. I called Father Berger and asked him to baptize Doc and administer the final rites. Doc had told me it would be all right to baptize him when he was on his deathbed. In the evening, around 7:30 p.m., while I sat at Doc's bedside, which I had not left since we arrived at the hospital two nights before, he gasped for air from the oxygen mask. There was no airflow. I rang frantically for help. No one came. There was no doctor in the hospital. Copeland had gone home. When a nurse finally appeared, it was too late. Doc had expired.

"Even the Weariest River Winds Somewhere Safe to Sea"

When I came home that night, I placed the white orchid on the piano.

1954–1961

The autopsy revealed, according to Copeland's written statement, that "his death was hastened by the chronic condition of his lungs dating back to the time of his army discharge in 1930."

Looking back, the discord triggered by the crashing tree on my first Christmas with Doc foreshadowed the following Christmas, because there was no tree. Even though my brother from Germany was with me, we decided against a Christmas tree and everything that went with it. I returned all presents and cancelled the order for a Cadillac, with which my bighearted husband had wanted to surprise me, despite the fact that I never expressed a desire for such a splashy car. My brother and I went to bed as soon as it got dark outside.

Mr. Garl, who had recommended the heart specialist, told me he had resigned from the case because Copeland was reluctant to follow his advice. I found it hard to believe that this young doctor, whom Doc had treated like a son, could be so negligent. Mr. Garl said I had grounds to proceed against Copeland legally, but I was in no condition emotionally to resort to taking such steps at that time. Ultimately, Doc was right in not trusting any doctor. Copeland later had his medical license revoked, because he was addicted to drugs. After things calmed down, Alfons confided in me that the doctor had also made inappropriate advances toward him on a couple of occasions when he let him drive his brand-new, bright-red Chevy Impala convertible. The last time it happened, Alfons stopped the car, jumped out, and hitchhiked home.

Doc's daughter came for the funeral services. I was a bit disappointed when I saw her smoking a cigarette and whistling as we selected a casket, and wondered what had happened to her when, a couple of days later, she was absent during the service. When we returned to the Croft, I learned that she, together with Doc's best friend, had hauled away several pieces of furniture and belongings while I was at the service. I was at a loss for what to do and began to rely on the advice of Major Darmody, who assured me that he would be glad to help Doc's widow, for Doc had treated him and his family members free of charge so many times. He was glad to repay him in this way for his services. He enlisted an attorney who saw to it that Doc's daughter returned everything she had removed, including the furniture she had promised Dr. Copeland. Later, she got it all back when she contested Doc's will. I always regretted that she did not ask me at the time, because I would have turned the items over to her without question.

In accordance with Doc's wishes, he was laid to rest in the grave of Auntie Hazel and next to Peter at Arlington National Cemetery, where I had placed flowers only nineteen months earlier, and where he wanted me to come when it was my time. It was a somber military ceremony. I still have the flag with forty-eight stars that was draped over the heavy casket, which was lifted from the horse-drawn cart by six soldiers. I can still envision the casket appearing on a horse-drawn caisson and hear the bugles playing "Taps," the military escorts firing their rifles, and the canon shooting. Doc had joined the military when the war between Germany and America broke out, because he felt that at least one Beardsley of his family should serve the country. Only three were at the grave, Alfons, Major D., and I. Neither spring flowers nor snow covered the ground, just an ocean of white grave markers.

Adjusting to Widowhood – Mutti Pitches In – US Citizenship – Working for Attorneys James and Hoff

Doc's departure came as a terrible shock. The thought that he might die so soon had never entered my mind. I had pushed it aside even after the scare at the cabin. I was a widow at the age of twenty-five and had not fulfilled his last wish. I was not pregnant. It seemed as though we had lived through an entire lifetime in a year and a half. The following months were painful beyond imagination, intensified by a hard winter. The void seemed infinite. I would hover for hours next to the register in a small bathroom upstairs, or seek shelter in the freezing car parked underneath the maple trees, forever crying and questioning why it had to happen to me, and why so soon. Afraid to sleep alone in the big, antique cherry bed, I asked Alfons to let me sleep in the other bed in his room. When he failed to keep his promise to Doc to stay with me until things were settled, I moved downstairs. A few months after Doc's death, my brother enlisted in the Army, where he hated every moment, to the point of refusing to fight in the Korean War. I never knew why he did this, especially since it was totally uncalled for. He had a job and did not have US citizenship. In retrospect, I now believe he knew that serving in the Army would facilitate his earning US citizenship, which in turn would empower him to sponsor his German girlfriend, daughter of a staunch Nazi, in order to join and later marry her.

Our caretaker, Effie, who became more of a burden, doing less and less, had to be let go, because my source of income was drastically curtailed with Doc's passing and the expenses of keeping up the grounds were increasing steadily. Everything started breaking down. The repairmen were like scavengers, charging exorbitant fees for services rendered. First the pump in the well house was in need of being replaced; then the sewer broke, and we poked around the yard for hours to locate the septic tanks. The icicles kept breaking the windowpanes that covered the winter garden, which was filled with terraces of exotic plants. The winter garden was an extension to the entertainment room in the basement. A rumor had spread that I was wealthy, simply because Doc's cousins at Miles, Inc., were all multimillionaires. Every repairman wanted a slice of the pie. Since Doc had taken care of paying all bills, I did not even know where to pay for them. To make it worse, after lengthy attempts by Major Darmody and General Byers, who had also married a very young wife from Korea, the compensation, which Doc had been convinced I would get, was refused, because I was married only one instead of three years. If a child had been born, the benefits would have continued. The miscarriage, though proof that the marriage had been consummated, did not count. I did not have much choice but to sell the

Croft, our paradise, together with many of the treasures inside, as well as the cabin up north.

My so-called friend Major Darmody had suggested I appoint him special executor of the estate. I compensated him dearly for each and every task he performed for me by filling his car with gasoline and inviting him and his wife to many dinners at the Croft. He ended up writing a check to himself in the amount of $1,000 before the estate was settled. Not a word was said about his former assurance to return favors for Doc. I learned right then and there that I could no longer trust anybody, and decided to take care of any and all repairs I could handle. I fixed the windowpanes above the winter garden downstairs when broken by icicles and sent a bill to the insurance company, which reimbursed me without question. I mowed the lawn, which took thirteen hours each time, and fixed the mower myself the many times it broke down. I mended electrical cords, pulled thousands of weeds in the flower beds, helped paint one hundred window frames and shingles, and worked many hours to keep the pool immaculate, all of it to have the grounds in perfect shape for prospective buyers. Unfortunately, my so-called friends showed up with a bunch of their wild kids whenever it pleased them, and they always jumped directly into the pool, getting it dirty all over again. One of the little ones almost drowned. The parents forgot to watch them, because they were busy raiding the icebox in my kitchen, without asking, of course. In the winter, I learned to cope with ice storms, broken tree limbs, electrical outages, and snowed-in roads. I learned to economize and cut my heating bill by more than 30%.

The closest highway was about three-quarters of a mile from the Croft. To reach it, I had to pass Wetherbee Lake Farm, and thus my archenemy, to whom I had not spoken since the Beardsleys bought me free. Indeed, I had seen them only once, in church. It did not bother me when I was with Doc or my brother, but when I was all alone, every time I passed the cursed place, I prayed my car would not break down or get stuck in a snowdrift, which happened twice, but fortunately one hundred yards from their farm. My friends the Gebhards feared for me more than I did. Our house had five different entrance doors. I registered a small revolver, which I found and kept next to my bed, and placed a rifle close to the porch entrance. Lost drivers occasionally stopped to ask for directions, so I wanted to be prepared. Mr. Sears had taught us to shoot a rifle when Maria had visited, but the police warned me not to shoot the revolver unless I wanted to kill myself in the process. Thus, I kept the arms solely as a scare device. I would not know how to load them, anyhow. Just to be on the safe side, I went to bed early to avoid turning on lights, which would invite people to stop and ask for directions if lost.

Mutti, also worried about my living alone, especially since Alfons had taken off, offered to visit and help me while the Croft was up for sale. I was overjoyed and sent her a round-trip ticket, and she arrived dressed in funeral attire and looking a bit overweight in her new black fur coat. I had told her it was not necessary for her to wear black, as it is not the custom in America. Used to living frugally, instead of buying an extra suitcase, she wore several layers of clothes. – Mutti pitched right in. She loved having a huge yard at her disposal and wasted no time planting vegetables and getting ready for the enormous strawberry harvest, which hardly fit into the double-door freezer in the basement. She tried to mow a couple of times, but I forbade her to do it, because I did not want her to collapse or harm herself. She could not imagine having such a big lawn and so many flowerbeds to care for. My friends loved her. She spoke almost no English, but always got her point across with her eyes and gestures. We were invited out a lot, and Mutti cooked up a storm to please our guests, who liked her roasts, stews, and chickens, especially Major and Mrs. Darmody, Father Berger, and Alfons, whenever he was home on furlough. I was glad I did not have to do it. Remember, cooking was not my forte then or later.

Mutti and I did not coexist without an occasional spat, but we got over it quickly. Her creative juices flowed freely at the Croft. She sang, wrote poems, painted, crocheted, sewed, wrote lots of letters, and almost got hooked on soap operas and *Perry Mason*. She did not shy away from pushing the car out of the ditch when it snowed, especially when it meant getting to church on time. We took a mother-and-daughter whirlwind trip to Niagara Falls in my brand-new white 1959 T-bird with red seats, which I bought when I had cancelled Doc's order for a Cadillac at Christmastime in 1957. We made the falls in record time, seven hours to be exact, and did not bat an eye when the speedometer hit 110 miles per hour. Not a single car passed us on the entire round trip. I advised Mutti not to speak to me while driving. It was too dangerous. She complied, and we had a barrel of fun. I got my first speeding ticket while going through Vandalia, where I had to visit the JP and pay my fine. I tried to get out of it, reminding him of the many free babies Doc had delivered, but ended up giving him a tip for a cigar before I left.

It was pretty awkward that Mutti ended up next door to her old school buddy Neverbee, the guy to whom she had sent a package with canned blueberries from the forest and other handcrafted gifts in appreciation of a care package we had received, which eventually led to my immigration. At that time, he rejoiced in the fact that my parents sent me to a school as great as Sankt Ursula. You may recall that by the time I left his farm, he called it a monkey school. After I was gone, he sponsored one of his nephews, Johann, who was fourteen years old, to replace me at the farm. The lad was strictly forbidden to speak to anybody at the Croft. An old field reverting back to nature lay between our farms. At times, we observed Johann on the lookout for us, with a rifle in his hand. We waved, encouraging him to come and see us, and a couple of times he did. We exchanged a few sentences and then let him return before all hell broke loose. We certainly did not want him to be deported.

On April 15, a day after Doc's birthday, I heard over the news that President Eisenhower's secretary of state, John Foster Dulles, resigned his office due to cancer. I sent him a copy of Doc's case history, which according to their letter of thanks was forwarded to Dr. Charles G. Zubrod, clinical director of the National Cancer Institute, who was one of the consulting physicians to General Leonard D. Heaton, the man directly in charge of the secretary's case. That was the last thing I heard from them. The secretary passed away shortly thereafter, on May 24, and like Doc was laid to rest in Arlington National Cemetery.

My father was really getting anxious for Mutti to come home. As I had bought a round-trip ticket, I booked a flight and in May took her to the airport with many more bags than she had brought. When we were ready to check in, we were informed in no uncertain terms that her ticket had expired one year after it was purchased. I was stunned, and I pleaded and used every ounce of persuasion I could muster. No deal. I did not want to pay for an extra ticket, and Mutti did not want me to. We loaded all the luggage into the car and returned to the Croft. I called my father, who went into a rage, questioning my intelligence, since I always seemed to know what I was doing. Mutti was convinced it was meant to be, because it would have been sinful to let all those strawberries, apples, and plums, as well as the vegetables she had planted, go to waste. We promised my father she would come home as soon as I straightened the matter out, which I finally did, but Mutti did not leave until August 1959.

In June 1959, the attorney for the estate called and suggested that I look for a job, since it seemed to be taking longer than anticipated to sell the Croft – and since it might be good for me to work anyway. He seemed to be impressed by the background information I had given him in the form of a thirty-five-page document, just in case there was a trial in connection with the contested will. Mr. Jones tipped me off to an opening in the office of two top attorneys in Dowagiac, Michigan, one who had recently been defeated running for prosecutor and another who was a Harvard graduate, which did not mean anything to me at the time. They were desperately in need of a secretary or two, since three had just quit. To please Mr. Jones, I called the office and set up an appointment, convinced they would not hire me – I was certain I could no longer take shorthand or type fast enough. In addition, I was unfamiliar with the legal terminology. I had not given any thought to returning to Miles, even though Mr. Reamer, a vice president whose son I helped get into medical school in Vienna, had contacted me when I was in Germany and offered me a top-notch position as his private secretary. Working for two attorneys did appeal to me. I wanted to learn how to better protect myself and to guard against being taken advantage of by the sleazy and greedy, like Major Darmody.

Attorneys James and Hoff chose me out of six applicants. I told them not to hesitate to send me home packing if I had not measured up by the end of the three-month trial period. I had lost my self-confidence when Doc passed away. I knew my shorthand and typing skills would be shaky and that mastering the legal jargon would be a tedious process. I had to be a notary public for the job, which required US citizenship. However, providence was on my side. On May 13, 1959, I became a US citizen in Van Buren County Circuit Court, only five years and two months after I had arrived. I did not want to wait a day longer, and had prepared myself by taking a correspondence course at the University of Michigan to pass the test, which, much to my surprise, I aced. Mutti was still in Michigan at the time, and I renounced my German citizenship without hesitation. I ceased to be proud of my heritage when I learned about all those barbarous crimes of the Hitler period. I started working for my two attorneys on June 19, 1959, a month later, and stayed on for seven years, during which I learned more than at any previous job.

I got a taste of what it would be like with the lawyers the first day on the job. My typewriter table was directly behind and a little lower than the counter where clients would stand when they came through the door to announce their arrival or ask questions. Around noon, a short black woman dressed in farmer's jeans and a blue shirt, her hair hanging in disarray over her forehead, like curtain fringes, almost covering her piercing eyes but not hiding the deep wrinkles on her face, rushed through the door and asked for Mr. James, who was out. She told me they had just fished her husband out of the Mississippi River, drowned dead. When my boss arrived, I discovered that this Bertha Wenston, who made excellent barbequed ribs in a little shack west of Dowagiac, was an old favorite because she always paid with ribs instead of money. It reminded me of some of Doc's country patients who paid with ducks and chickens instead of cash. Bertha's runaway "husband" was another of her common-law-marriage fellows, which unfortunately would not qualify her for a penny of inheritance, which was more likely than not, according to James's assumptions, nonexistent. He advised her to be quiet and to be grateful that she would not have to pay the drowned man's debt. She was quite a novelty, and her eatery made the news more often than not for shoot-outs between gamblers and jealous lovers. I liked her. She was a pistol, if you know what I mean. Whenever I had to pick up ribs for James, I was a bit scared that someone would jump me out of a corner. The place was so dark you had to wait for your eyes to get adjusted in order to see.

James had a philosophy similar to Doc's, that is, live and let live. He charged the poor little or nothing and added a few dollars to the bills of the rich. For many years now, I have held on to a letter he wrote on January 16, 1957, to the president of the James C. Fifield Company in answer to their offer to add his name to the latest publication of the *American Bar* for $50. The letter just about sums up what my boss was all about.

1954–1961

Dear Sir:

I have read with a great deal of interest your advertising letter of January 14 inst. And the printed folder enclosed all of which seems to invite me to join the list included in the American Bar.

I am sorry but I shall have to decline your invitation because of my lack of qualifications. I have no taste for fine cars or beautiful women, my car suits me and so does my wife. I have the good things of life and have had them for twenty-eight years, without a Rembrandt, Venus De Milo or a Royal Sarouk. I do not hang out in clubs and I spend my time with whom I choose, so it is obvious that I do not need your book.

It is enlightening to know that your list in the Continental Mark II of law includes those who are sleek, plain, low, high powered and that it costs two or three times as much as it is worth.

I am also glad to learn that I have been approved by my peers but would be more interested in learning the names of those whom you qualify as my peers. My clients think I am pretty good and conceitedly I share their opinion.

So you want me to become a Tiffany Lawyer? No, I am just a diamond in the rough and I think I had better stay that way. Let's see, a Tiffany Lawyer, that would be drawing a parallel between the perfect diamond and the members on your list, right? Flashy, brilliant, clean cut, perfect, very very expensive, definitely a luxury that only the rich can afford, and without any heart whatsoever, very hard, sharp cutting edges, and with the possibility of hidden defects that only an expert could detect. Personally I think this parallel is an insult to the legal profession and to the many fine Lawyers on your list. I suppose there are some to whom this literature will appeal but it has about as much appeal to me as Aunt Jemima pancakes have sex appeal. I have the $50 but thanks to your letter I will keep it. Yours truly.

Mr. James, a former Cass County prosecutor, was about fifty-eight when I started, had a deep, sonorous voice, and had a register of vocabulary at his disposal which I was forbidden to use when I parroted him. His dress was mostly casual. He loved to eat and never worried about his beer belly. He was about six inches taller than I. His eyes were blue, he wore metal-framed glasses, and he had lost most of his hair, which was gray. His hobby was acting, an art he shared with his first wife, the mother of his two children, who passed away unexpectedly when the children were in their teens. He had earned his law degree at the University of Michigan.

Jim Hoff, his partner from Harvard, was twenty-five years his junior, wore his full, dark-brown hair parted, and looked handsome in his suits, white shirts, and neckties. He was about six feet tall and slender, wore gold-rimmed glasses, and had warm brown eyes, like his wife and four children. Mr. Hoff enjoyed golfing. His Harvard degree, mounted on the wall, read "Doctor of Jurisprudence." He was more polished than his senior partner, very polite, and definitely more scientific in his billing practices. I had to keep track of every minute he talked to clients. Four years after they hired me, Jim left to open his own practice. Mr. James allowed Mr. Hoff to go, on the condition that I stayed with the former. Later, Jim Hoff became circuit judge of Cass County, Michigan.

In an ongoing effort to please both attorneys, I learned to adapt to two different personalities rather easily. I was always keen on learning various aspects of the law. They handled everything except criminal-law cases. Having had experience with probate as a result of settling Doc's estate, which had been closed in March 1959, I was eager to learn more about it and found out that appointing Darmody as a special executor had been totally unnecessary and a waste of money. It was easy to draw up simple wills, which Mr. James let me do on occasion. Since he refused to handle divorces in which children were involved, he allowed me to prepare bills of complaints. A couple of times, when they were waiting for Mr. James to sign the papers, I talked the parties out of divorcing before he arrived. James & Hoff represented a local savings-and-loan association, and I assisted with examining abstracts, preparing deeds, land contracts, and mortgages, and even closing real-estate transactions at times. After Jim Hoff was gone, Mr. James taught me how to prepare briefs and documents for forming corporations and let me go to probate court on occasion when he was tied up. Indeed, I worked so closely with so many major clients that they trusted my work as though it were James's. One major client, the widow of the owner of the Cadillac agency in Niles, Michigan, appointed me as executrix and trustee of her estate because she claimed not to trust anybody as much as me.

I often wondered if my knack for legal matters was due to my father's genes – he worked for the courts all his life – and due even more so to my mother's. My great-grandmother on Mutti's side, as I reported early on in these memoirs, exhibited enormous strength, physically and mentally, when it was a matter of right versus wrong. She had a great sense of justice.

Mr. James was like another Rock of Gibraltar to me. He was always ready to advise me not only in legal matters but also when it came to the male sex. At that time, many thought I looked like the well-known actress Jane Wyman. On the SS *United States*, after they posted the photos of the passengers boarding the ship, rumors arose that Jane Wyman was on board.

Getting Burned by Odd Suitors – Falling for John

Soon, the eager suitors began to trickle in at the Croft, because they thought I was the most eligible young widow around, and they were ready to marry me lock, stock, and barrel. It started with the guy who sold me the T-bird. He was a real macho, with dark, curly hair and of Hungarian background, handsome but not very bright. It was simply stupid of him to grab me right under the maple tree when he delivered the car, kiss me, and proclaim that I was so sexy. He stopped at once when

I pushed him away, threatening to tell his wife. I used to see the two with their five kids on Sundays at Mass. The next one was an optometrist, brother of another optometrist who worked next door to the James & Hoff office, who used to tell me I simply must meet his brother, a bachelor. The pale, medium-sized male, who had dark-brown hair and eyes, took me out once and tried to kiss me in the Oriental room while Mutti was upstairs. He rolled his eyes when I told him I was too old to kiss. He returned another time and asked whether I liked him better in contact lenses or glasses. I told him it did not matter. The third time, out of desperation to get rid of him, because he was about as boring as they come and looked more like a girl than a guy, I resorted to more devious means. He lived with his mother, who did not want him to smoke. I advised him that at twenty-eight, he was too old to pay attention to his mother, and that if I were in his shoes I would smoke all the time. He never came back.

It seemed as though all of Southwestern Michigan and Northern Indiana were trying to match me with Mr. Right. An owner of a big hardware store in South Bend sent his tall and skinny son, who looked like a skinhead but was the director of the United Way. He dressed in stark black, except for the shirt. He took me to another dull dinner, after which I informed him that dating would not be fair to him, because I was not ready. I also recalled what Doc had said about being careful with donations to charities, because a big chunk would end up in the pockets of the administration. At that time, I had been a widow for about a year and a half. After a rather nice blue-eyed Catholic dentist from South Bend took me out to an exclusive restaurant, he told the friend who had sent him that he was bothered that I still wore my wedding band. I decided to take it off. I thought it would be OK with Doc, who had said young widows have a better chance at remarriage. The dentist never returned.

My German friend Elfie, from Elkhart, brought out Clark Gable's clone – I am not kidding. The nickname saves me the work of explaining what he looked like. He impressed Mutti so much that she would go upstairs whenever he drove up in his shiny black Chevy Impala convertible. He always brought a brandy snifter with a white gardenia and showered me with seductive lingerie; you can guess why. – Around Christmas, we danced with the fire crackling in the fireplace. I loved the gown, which was a cloud of bright-red chiffon, one full skirt on top of the other, trimmed in delicate, black lace and with tiny buttons covered in black silk down to the waist. I liked it more than the soft, tapered silk pants with the matching off-white shirt with long sleeves and narrow cuffs. He really bedazzled me by taking me to the fanciest restaurant in South Bend, and introduced me to martinis. It was my first fling since Doc passed away. He was working for a big bank in Detroit. His job involved traveling to banks in Michigan. When he asked me to lend him a few hundred dollars, Mr. James told me to be sure to have him sign a promissory note, which he did.

I was crazy enough to drive to Detroit one night after Mutti had left, and semi-flirted my way out of two speeding tickets that night. It was raining cats and dogs. As I entered the house, I was shocked. By the looks of it, Gable's clone was married. Fortunately, the Mrs. was out. I turned around, jumped into my car, and raced back in the rain without being stopped. When he showed up a week later at my door to explain, I gathered the dozen brandy snifters, put them in a box with the rest of the gifts, including the red chiffon, and pushed it into his arms. I demanded the $300, pronto, and shoved him out the front door, which he never again dared to penetrate. My legal experience came in handy in collecting the debt, which I finally received after threatening to tell his wife and notify the president of the bank and, if that failed, to garnish his wages.

Though the thought of marrying Gable's clone had not entered my mind, I sobbed after I kicked him out, because he had betrayed me badly. While I was sobbing, the phone rang, and a male with a wonderful and charming voice introduced himself as John, a friend of an antique dealer who had known Doc. He wanted to invite me out for a cup of coffee, and I accepted just like that.

John, a biology teacher in Niles, Michigan, but born in Huntington, Indiana, was my age. He was not quite six feet tall, a bit on the chubby side, especially his rosy cheeks, and thus more cute than handsome. He dressed impeccably and wore his dark-brown hair short, and his dark-brown eyes were always shiny and smiling, like a cherub. He had a warm personality and was bright and witty, with a great sense of humor. It was love at first sight. Doc, consciously or unconsciously, had become my measuring stick, but I thought he would not object to John. He was, however, paying off student loans even though he had had a science-foundation scholarship at Purdue, where he still needed to take a couple of exams to earn his master's. I was not on the lookout for a guy with a pile of money, but would not have objected if it happened to be part of the bargain. John had something in common with Gable's clone. He too drove a black Chevy Impala convertible.

About two weeks after John and I met, on Valentine's Day (which I always thought a bit tacky, maybe because we did not celebrate it in Germany), he totally overwhelmed me. He brought a bouquet of dark-red long-stemmed roses and a giant, heart-shaped box of chocolates covered with red velvet and three fake and rather tacky red velvet roses, glued to the lid. He knelt down before me, took my hand, focused his loving eyes on mine, and told me in that warm and caring voice, which went right through my heart, that he could not live without me. Assuming his proclamation was tantamount to a wedding proposal, I made sure he knew I reciprocated his feelings. I did not expect a ring, because I knew he could not have afforded one. *No es importante.* He introduced me to his family in Indiana, who were landowners, known for making apple cider with an old-fashioned press for apple growers in the area. The press was a family heirloom. Everybody liked me, and vice versa. All of my friends, including Messrs. James and Hoff, thought Johnny was a super guy. My good friend Sally, Mr. James's beautiful daughter, who accompanied me on the piano whenever she visited, much to Mutti's joy, liked John, and so did her great love, Guillermo, her Colombian college sweetheart from the University of Michigan, whom she married with pomp and circumstance in the Catholic church of Dowagiac. They had a turbulent courtship, as is not unusual between lovers from different cultures. Her wedding was the only one for which I have ever agreed to be a bridesmaid. Right after the ceremony, the groom swept his bride away to South America, where he also shipped many an American bull by plane, to breed more bulls. I am not certain if they became victims at bullfights, which Guillermo frequented. There, in the city of Bogotá, Sally bore Guillermo five children, one after the other. Eventually, they had twelve grandchildren to gather around them – most likely with more on the way.

John came to the Croft often and occasionally spent the night. We went fishing together, and he searched the field for Indian arrowheads and even found a few. Several times, he shot a pheasant, which I roasted in wine sauce for supper. They turned out to be pretty good eating, because I followed his instructions. John helped out with the yard quite a bit and even installed a 450-foot-long split-rail fence along the lawn bordering Robbins Lake Road, which we hoped would help sell the Croft.

One of the flaws I detected in John was his insane jealousy of anything connected with Doc. He said frequently that I spoke of Doc as though he were God, and he constantly insisted that he would never be able to provide for me as Doc had. He resented it when I bought a dress that cost a tad more than I should have paid, though it was my money, and criticized Doc for having neglected to send me to take courses at the university. Finally, to prove to him I was over Doc, I tore up a photo of Doc and myself right in front of his eyes, an act I have regretted ever since.

III *1961–1972*

1961–1972

A University Student at Last – Good-bye, Croft – A Trip with Mutti to Bavaria and Austria

As getting a better education was the primary reason I came to America, John deserves credit for encouraging me to apply to Indiana University, where, based on my records in German schools, I was accepted unconditionally, that is, despite the fact that I did not have the *Abitur*, which I would have needed to study at a university in Germany. I had hoped to go to IU–Bloomington, but had to alter my plans because I was unable to sell the Croft. To stay focused, I opted to start out at the regional campus, which offered classes in Elkhart and South Bend. John drove me back and forth to my classes, which far exceeded my expectations. For the first time, professors, particularly in literature and philosophy classes, praised my work in front of the class. A philosophy professor once whispered to me while I was writing a final exam that I could stop working, because he felt certain I had written the best paper, even though it was unfinished. Thinking back to Sankt Ursula, I realized how stimulating and productive a pat on the back could be, but concluded that I would never go so far as to stop a student before he or she was finished. The professor's name was Polish and sounded something like "watch your house key."

In August 1961, I finally sold the Croft. My ownership of this house, with my job in Dowagiac and classes in South Bend and Elkhart, had turned into a situation in which I felt like a slave of my possessions. I hated to let my and Doc's paradise go, but under the circumstances, I saw no alternative.

The Croft went for not quite one-half of what the appraisal for the estate had figured. It was sold on a land contract.

On September 1, the big auction of other possessions took place, to which people came from all over the country. They parked their cars in the field for which I received subsidies – in exchange for not farming it. It was called "soil bank." My farmer friend Harold Gebhard cleared the field. Two auctioneers screamed at the top of their lungs in two different locations. Ladies from the altar guild served refreshments under the big maple trees. It was hard to watch people haul away what had taken Doc a lifetime to collect at places around the world and what had provided so much comfort and pleasure for so many years. I disliked parting with the big mustard-colored carpet in the library, the Mount Fuji set of dishes, the Chinese carpets in the Oriental room, the tall corner cabinets, the sizeable collection of antique glass pitchers, the big, antique cherrywood bed with the beautifully carved headboard, etc. I never understood why John, who had turned the fields over looking for arrowheads, did not stop me from letting go of the cigar box filled with Indian treasures, including a tomahawk. I had no choice but to part with my baby grand, but I kept the SABA and the objects I knew were dear to Doc. I was lucky to find a choice apartment in Dowagiac, within walking distance to the law firm.

I skipped the fall semester and, not having seen the rest of my family and friends in several years, went to Germany for a visit. Soon after my arrival, and still grateful to Mutti for having stayed with me so long after Doc's death, I decided to take Mutti on her dream vacation. I too was anxious to see more of my native country. Though I had been to Switzerland, I had seen more of America and Mexico than Germany. All her life, Mutti had longed to hear her favorite opera, Verdi's *Aida*, at the Vienna State Opera House. Mutti had only been to Berlin, where she spent a short honeymoon with one of my father's cousins. Each time she talked about it, she complained about having eaten smoked flounder each and every day while visiting. My aunt had been able to buy a box full of the fish at a bargain price.

Considering that my father and I had continued to drift apart, I was relieved when Mutti suggested we plan our trip south while Papa would be at the spa – one of those health-furthering vacations funded by the government for its employees. My father did not complain, and as I had rented an Opel, he was pleased when we dropped him off at Bad Pyrmont, southwest of Hannover, where he could go promenading in the park to his heart's content. It was planted full of lush red roses, and bright-red geraniums draped down in masses from white flower boxes alongside the pretentious white-stucco spa house. Red roses and geraniums were also planted alongside the casino and the hotel and all around the green-domed gazebo, where the band was playing German marches and Viennese waltzes when we arrived. The lawns behind the white painted benches, on which we sat down to listen for a while, were impeccably manicured. I was anxious to start on our journey, and Papa looked forward to drinking the mineral waters from Pyrmont's natural springs and soaking in the mud baths, all in the hope of being cured of whatever ailed him, being rejuvenated, and returning to work with a new lease on life.

Mutti and I traveled well together, and this time I drove slowly enough to allow us to take in the picturesque countryside on the way to what many call the most romantic city in Germany: Heidelberg, on the Neckar River. We stayed a full day in this medieval town, with its enchanting baroque and Renaissance architecture, and got a good look at Germany's oldest university, established in 1386. I insisted on visiting the sparse Studentenkarzer (Student Jail) in the old town, and had no trouble deciphering the aged scribbling that covered the walls. Students were jailed for up to several weeks when they drank too much and behaved roughly. – We could see from a distance the red-brown ruins of Heidelberg Castle, high above the Neckar Valley, and after having explored the castle grounds sufficiently, we crossed the Heidelberg Bridge to take a walk on the famous Philosopher's Road, a winding walking path along the hillside across the river, opposite the castle. I am sure Johann Wolfgang von Goethe and Mark Twain after him were inspired as much as we were by the panorama of the town from up there. Toward evening, we joined a bunch of jovial students chatting at a large, round table in the student hangout, the Zum Roten Ochsen (Red Ox Inn), a favorite since 1703. We ordered a Heidelberger Pils with fried potatoes and brats. –

We could not have wished for better weather, especially in Germany, where it rains more often than not. Mutti had a knack for spotting idyllic bed-and-breakfast lodgings, and we felt happy in the Bavarian-style house on the Herrenchiemsee, where we took a boat to visit the extremely extravagant and sumptuous replica of Versailles, built by "Mad" Ludwig II of Bavaria. The splendor of the twenty completed rooms, especially the Large Gallery of Mirrors, was overwhelming, and I was glad when we approached the Bavarian Alps, with their snowcapped mountain pinnacles stretching high into the blue sky and the green alpine meadows with colorful wildflowers at their feet. They had a soothing effect on us, as did the shiny, emerald-green, ice-cold water of the Königssee. The lake, almost six hundred feet deep, mirrored the magnificent Watzmann, at 8,899 feet the second-highest peak in Germany. Too many mountain climbers have fallen to their death in an attempt to conquer it. The captain of the boat to Sankt Bartholomäus (St. Bartholomew), the white pilgrimage church with red onion domes, which sits all alone and peacefully on a small island in the lake, stopped the boat opposite the rocky eastern slope of the Watzmann to let us hear the echo of a trumpet.

While in the area, we were curious to look at the well-known winter resort Berchtesgaden, where Hitler and other Nazi leaders had their chalets until the Americans came, bombed it, and then took advantage of the choice mountain terrain for their own vacations. Quite close to it was Hitler's private and very secret mountain retreat, the Eagle's Nest. Looking out the window down the steep and scary rugged slope, in a special bus that took us up the narrow one-hundred-meter road, the guide spoke of the hardships endured by the men building the access to the hideaway. Several had fallen down the cliffs while building it and were left severely handicapped or met their death. Yet their fate was not known until after the war, because everybody was sworn to absolute secrecy. The lift that Hitler had built to take him, and now us, to the summit, where the solidly built retreat Berghof stood, was impressive due to the solid brass frames and mirrored walls inside.

As we stood at the summit of the Obersalzberg, while eagles were perched not far from where we admired the panorama below and all around us, it would have been more uplifting if we could have avoided thinking about who used to vacation and hide up there. At our feet lay Germany and Austria, where we were headed to visit Mozart's place of birth, Salzburg, a much-sought-after town for musicians, who strive to pursue their dreams while studying with a master teacher at the Mozarteum. – But first, our little Opel climbed the road toward Austria's highest mountain, the Groß Glockner, 3,757 meters high and perpetually topped with snow. We climbed out of the car to get a good look at the mountain and the glacier that descends for six miles. It brought back memories of my trip with Doc to Glacier National Park. Here too, we had to wear sweaters because it was freezing cold; but Mutti and I refrained from making a snowball.

Not Hitler's Child

On the way to Salzburg, Mutti spotted before I did five or six brown-and-white alpine cows trotting toward us in the middle of the road. They carried blue or white crown-like ribbons on their foreheads, and heavy brass cowbells hung from a strap around their necks, making harsh and penetrating sounds, which I could have listened to forever. I stopped and jumped out of the car to snap a photo of the festive herd. A lad in leather pants wearing a green felt hat was leading the adorned cattle home from the pastureland on the mountainsides for the winter. He wished us a friendly "Grüß Gott!" I thought of Papa all dressed up in his gray flannel pants and black blazer, wearing a daisy in his lapel and promenading in the well-kept park. I wondered how he would have reacted if suddenly a pretty cow stopped in front of him, lifted its tail, and surprised him, as one of these cows surprised me, with a brown batch of cow dung.

Mutti and I laughed at the spectacle almost as heartily as we did the next day, when we visited Hellbrunn, the ostentatious and entertaining summer residence built for the Prince-Archbishop Markus Sittikus von Hohenems of Salzburg some four hundred years ago. It was a unique experience to wander around the aquatic gardens and be teased to the point of laughter by the ingeniously engineered water tricks and games devised for the sole purpose of impressing and entertaining the guests, mostly heads of the church. Just imagine a group of overweight bishops feasting happily at the big stone table in the park, not far from the pleasure castle that boasts Italian architecture. Suddenly, a spray of water gushes out of each opening in the benches, directly underneath the buttocks. – I leave the ensuing scene to your imagination. The playfulness of the instigator of the attractions was evident also when we watched the intricate movements of the little figures interacting in a big mechanical theater. Everything is driven by water from underground springs that come down from the mountains. I had never seen anything like it, and could imagine that youngsters would get a real charge out of a visit to Hellbrunn.

Mutti and I had located another charming bed and breakfast, which, in typical Austrian style, featured clusters of red geraniums on the balustrade of the wooden balconies. We opened the windows wide to breathe in the fresh and aromatic air drifting in from the meadows in the morning. I opened my eyes as soon as I heard the ringing of the cowbells in the pastures. Mutti and I both loved to chat with the friendly hostess, who served a hearty breakfast on the terrace so we could see the snowcapped mountains on the horizon as well as the red, steepled roofs of the many churches and the big dome of the cathedral more or less in the center of Salzburg. Our hostess gave us an array of sights to see, but we had decided to spend a day just walking along a meandering path through the meadows to a nearby forest, stop for lunch at an inn on one of the many lakes, and be back by suppertime for *Abendbrot* in their rustic Austrian dining room.

As we were running short of time, we had to limit our sightseeing somewhat, but we did make sure we gained entrance to Mozart's birthplace, which had been bombed in 1944, leaving the portal entrance and the Dancing Master's Hall intact. Having started playing violin when I was five years old, I was touched to see Mozart's childhood violin, but also his concert violin, viola, and clavichord. – A special, indescribable feeling overcame me at Mozart's residence at Markart Square, where he lived after he had been to Vienna. It was there that he composed several of his symphonies and many other unforgettable compositions. With Mozart on my mind almost constantly while walking around in the old part of Salzburg, I just had to see the baptismal font in which he was baptized, which stands in the big cathedral with the dome, modeled after the Renaissance dome of St. Peter's Basilica in Rome. – In the same cathedral, Mozart was court organist and concertmaster and composed many works of sacred music. – When it was time to drive on to Vienna, where Mozart lived from time to time and where he died, I promised myself that someday I would return to Salzburg and attend their legendary Mozart Festival.

Fortunately, driving and navigating in the imperial city Vienna on the "blue" Danube was not as challenging as I had anticipated. As soon as we accessed the Ringstraße, the broad boulevard encircling the old town in the center of the city, we noticed the four rows of tall trees flanking the Ring, which was commissioned by the emperor Franz Josef to replace the old city walls that protected the old town center. The monumental character of the buildings likewise excited us. They testify to the proud character and imperial power of the emperors, as does the royal palace, the Hofburg. It is a vast complex, built for the royal occupants, the Habsburgs, as a winter residence. Here, where they entertained their guests, the offices of the president, six museums, the National Library, the Spanish Riding School, and the like are located today. –

We had no trouble locating our hotel, not far from St. Stephen's, the soaring Gothic cathedral in the heart of the city, and could not wait to get settled in our pleasant room and head out to explore the maze of narrow streets and shops nearby. –

But first on our agenda was a trip to the State Opera House to secure tickets for a performance the next day, hopefully *Aida*, Mutti's favorite. We spotted the impressive Neo-Renaissance building easily. It was not far away from the equally imposing Burgtheater, built in the same architectural style and, like the opera house, rebuilt after being heavily bombed in 1945. – As we checked the repertoire, we could hardly believe *Aida* was in fact scheduled to play the next evening. I went immediately to the ticket widow and was devastated to learn that the performance was completely sold out. As there was no line, I began to plead with the lady behind the window, explaining that we had driven all the way from Germany, I myself coming from America, to see and hear an opera at the world famous Vienna Opera, and that it had been Mutti's lifelong dream. I don't recall how long I pleaded, but when I was almost at the point of giving up, the kind lady sifted through a drawer and, lo and behold, held up two tickets for us. I almost cried, and so did Mutti, who had now and then injected her own plea and looked at the lady with her big, blue, begging eyes.

We were so elated that we did not think twice about the price when we noticed, close to the opera, Hotel Sacher, the home of the famous Sachertorte. And as we had already planned to sip a cup of Viennese coffee with a piece of the best chocolate cake in the world, we entered and were seated in the Kaffeehaus, furnished in nineteenth-century style. We imagined what the royal family, who used to frequent the café and was portrayed on several oil paintings on the wall, might have thought to see us two commoners at a neighboring table. – We ate our piece of tart slowly and stretched out the coffee as long as possible, because a pianist played Johann Strauss waltzes and operetta arias. I had to beg Mutti, who began as always to hum along, to stop. But we vowed that the next day, we would have a Wiener schnitzel at another restaurant and treat ourselves to a goblet of Austrian wine.

Right after breakfast, we visited Schönbrunn, the imperial palace and summer residence of the Habsburgs, that is, Francis I of Lorraine, Maria Theresa, empress of Germany and queen of Hungary, who had commissioned it to rival Versailles, and Franz Josef and his wife, Empress Elisabeth, to mention a few of them. – We spent several hours looking at the splendor inside, and I tried to imagine the time when the child prodigy Mozart gave a candlelight concert in the lavishly decorated, rococo-style Hall of Mirrors at the age of six. Once you have seen the Bohemian crystal chandeliers suspended from the ceilings, you will see their fiery sparkle forever.

Mutti, who loved gardening and walking around in memorial parks and the Herrenhäuser Gardens in Hannover, tried to get some ideas for planting flowers at home as we strolled through the vast park on the way to the Palm House, in which flora from jungles of all continents were thriving. This satisfied my obsession with exotic and tropical plants. We discovered a restaurant at Schönbrunn, where a charming Viennese waitress, dressed in black with a white lace apron and a lace headdress on her black braided hair, served mouthwatering schnitzel which would be difficult for any cook to duplicate. The goblet of white wine set us in the right mood for the opera in the evening.

As soon as we were seated in the grandiose, horseshoe-shaped opera house, we found ourselves mesmerized by the splendor of the rich decor, the crystal chandeliers hanging down from the coffered ceiling, and the elegance of the opera lovers, who spoke in muted tones. The experience in Vienna surpassed all visits to the opera house in Hannover. It was special in every way, from the performance of the singers, who sang the Verdi opera in the original language, to the conductor, the choir, the orchestra, the staging, and the costumes. Mutti and I were moved to tears in the final act but joined in with the standing ovation, and we were among the last to leave the glorious house, with its unique iron curtain. The magnificence of the Vienna Opera stood out even more at night. It was illuminated like other architectural gems throughout the city. The baroque St. Charles's Church with its turquoise dome, which shines ever so brightly against the black sky, comes to mind.

We returned to the opera early the next day to take a tour of the house, which had been rebuilt after the war in a manner as true to its original grandeur as possible. We ascended once more the grand staircase we had climbed the day before during intermission, and looking up at the fresco-covered ceiling was a transcendent experience. The tour lasted perhaps an hour, just long enough to give us a better overview of and insight into what happens behind the scenes and how the stage is engineered. – There was so much more that could have lured us into spending more time in Vienna, but as always, we had to head homeward to pick up Papa in Bad Pyrmont. Though he was pleased to see us, he could not understand why we had simply driven past the Belvedere Palace, built in secular baroque style, and taken no time to visit the National History Museum or to attend a play at the Burghof.

Broken Pledges – Broken Hearts

Upon our return, I had agreed to meet with Hubert, James Stewart's clone, who, as soon as he had found out Doc had passed away, flooded me with letters, convinced we were meant to be together after all, that I was the right woman for him, etc. All of it had left me cold, because at that time I was still coping with the loss of Doc. A year later, Hubert announced he would break things off with his fiancée immediately if I could only give him some hope. He was eager to come and visit. To find out how I would feel when I saw him again, I agreed to meet with him on his own turf. After twenty-four hours with him, I was convinced Hubert was better off without me. Besides, by then, I was hoping things would work out with John.

A real flaw in John's makeup was his extreme fear of examinations. He wanted to earn a doctorate eventually, but was scared to death to take the exams for the MS, a degree we both felt he should finish before we got married. In the fall of 1962, I finally drove him to Purdue to take the exam, which he passed with flying colors. By then, I had helped him balance his checkbook and get rid of credit-card finance fees, and after the exam we stood outside a jewelry store looking at engagement rings. Nevertheless, my hopes were dampened, as they had been before when things looked promising. The ring never left the store, and it wound up on someone else's finger.

I shed many tears during this roller-coaster relationship and for the first time in my life even ended up in the hospital, the emergency room no less. (A midwife brought me into this world.) – John had been upset, because I frequently prepared steak for supper instead of more economical dishes like bean soup with ham shank. I fixed steaks because they were quick and easy to prepare and tasted delicious. One Sunday after church, to surprise John, I got out Auntie Hazel's pressure cooker, which I had never used, and put in white beans, some water, and a ham shank from the Loesers' Lou Ann Valley Market. I failed to read the instructions, and when the little lid started flipping up and down to let out steam, I approached the pot on the stove to take a peek and attempted to push off the lid, which was extremely tight. As soon as the lid moved, the beans, ham shank, and scalding-hot water shot to the ceiling and over my chest. I ripped open my white nylon blouse, the buttons rolling to the floor, grabbed the flour can, stepped into the empty bathtub, and poured the flour pot over the scalded parts of my bare arms and naked chest. I remembered Mutti saying one should dip a burned finger in a pot of flour. The pain was unbearable. I called Mr. James, who lived close by. He and his wife rushed me to the emergency room, where they put gauze soaked in Vaseline on the burning, red flesh and transported me to a hospital bed to wait it out. John appeared with a pot of flowers, making a long face. Since Doc's colleagues had continued to treat me free of charge, and since I had no insurance, that bean soup cost me around $300 in hospital bills, which would have bought many steaks. I asked John to peel the beans off the kitchen ceiling and feed the shank to a dog.

In the spring of 1963, three years after John had knelt at my feet, he mustered up the courage to bite the bullet without the traditional engagement ring. After all, by then I was over thirty years old. He agreed to a Catholic wedding, being himself Swiss Reformed. We even obtained a certificate of blessing from the Pope. The priest, who once had almost damned me to hell when I confessed to having eaten meat at the house of friends on a Friday, would not consent to marry us in front of the altar, even if John took the required lessons. He insisted on the sacristy. That ordeal put a lot of stress on both of us. John, I had no idea why, possibly due to extreme nervousness, broke out in a bad rash all over his arms and body. – John's reasoning seemed a bit questionable at times. I knew he was not keen on having children and was extremely anxious not to get me pregnant, which can put a real damper on intimate relationships. Though a student of biology, he was no match for Doc, the physician who wanted children so badly. John was afraid of another war, and having been on the front lines as an officer at the age of twenty-one, where he witnessed several of his buddies being shot, he did not want the same to happen to his children. On the way home from his parents' house, John suddenly announced that we should move to H. after the wedding, since we could use a portion of my savings to start raising grapes on his father's farm, which they had planned to sell off in lots because the land was in great demand. I reluctantly agreed, provided we could send our children to the Catholic school in H. – although I sensed this would not go over well with his folks, who were not too fond of Catholics.

We spoke little on the way home. The next day, I was to order the wedding invitations that would go out to a great circle of family and friends. When I came to my apartment door after work, a note from John (an actual Dear John letter) was taped to the door that stated he could not go through with it – the marriage, that is. The envelope contained a check for $505.50 to reimburse me for what he had figured was the cost of any and all presents I had given him over the previous three years.

My whole world caved in once more, only six years after Doc had left. I searched for the cowardly escapee in vain, until his brother, the psychologist, told me that because it was the end of the school year, he had taken off for a job on a fishing boat in Alaska. I also learned he had once left a bride virtually standing at the altar. That time, he escaped through an open window. I returned the pearl necklace and matching earrings together with his other gifts, but kept the grandmother clock. I promised myself never again to accept a string of pearls from a man, because superstition had it that pearls bring tears.

The story goes on. John broke his teaching contract with the school system, resulting in his being blacklisted. When I had become a professor after achieving a PhD, which he had desperately wanted but was unable to get, not for lack of intelligence but for too much fear, he knocked at the door of my old friend whose farm we had visited many times. Harold Gebhard reported that John, still a bachelor, had stopped by. He had lost most of his memory, causing the loss of his job, because a mosquito stung him when fishing on a lake, triggering a lethal disease. Perhaps it was a species related to the tsetse fly? Anyhow, he was a long way from Africa. Gebhard maintained that John did not remember me. I find that hard to believe, but will let it rest, because in retrospect I thank my lucky stars that I was saved from a disaster. I could have been pregnant.

Mr. James lent a sympathetic ear while I carried on about the runaway bridegroom, trying to figure out what exactly went wrong, since the note did not explain his decision and we never connected to talk. I resisted cashing the check, which I regarded as John's attempt to buy his freedom. When Mr. James threatened to fire me if I did not cash the check, I decided to team up with Mrs. Lowe to travel to Las Vegas to blow the money. We made reservations on one of the Santa Fe Railway's glass-domed Pullman cars. Mrs. Lowe, the widow of the owner of the Cadillac dealership, was a devout gambler. She played poker twice a month with a circle of widows in South Bend. She was one of a kind. She thought the world of Mr. James, who by then was running the firm without Jim Hoff. She was about 5'4" and in her sixties, and her white face, with black, sheepish eyes, was framed with short jet-black curls. Her voice sounded a bit hoarse. She looked like a Gypsy. The fingers on both hands were studded with diamond rings. Fat diamonds glittered on her earlobes, and diamond broaches were pinned on her bright-red coats and dresses. It actually looked tacky. She wore only red or black dresses, but never a black coat. She bought all her clothes at garage sales. Each year, she drove the latest and most exclusive Cadillac, bright red.

Mrs. Lowe had already started gambling on the Wagon Wheel gambling train, which we took from LA to Las Vegas after a visit to Disneyland. I was still excited about having met the real Tinker Bell on the bus from Disneyland to the hotel. She was a very petite, white-haired woman, over seventy years old, who brought joy to the crowds as she flew down from the castle on a cable each night after the fireworks. She autographed a postcard, which much later I gave to Liesl. I gambled $25 on each of the five nights in Vegas, playing the nickel machines, until I lost everything. When my friend, who played more serious games like blackjack, poker, and roulette, looked gloomy, I suggested we go across the street to our hotel and exchange her black dress for a red one, which would most certainly bring her more luck. She never revealed the amount of her losses, which were probably not small. I thought about Doc's view on gambling, but felt he would not mind my throwing away John's money.

During the day, I hung out at the pool, where Doc had refused to stop on our 12,600-mile trip, and thought about how refreshing it could have been to take a dip back then. We took in all the kitsch and glitter, the flamboyant and flashy exteriors and interiors of the casinos, and a couple of shows on the strip, like the *Folies Bergère*. I can still smell the fragrance of horse manure, which some mechanism dispersed out into the street from the Western Cowboy casino downtown. I have never again witnessed such a blinding barrage of electric and neon lights as in downtown Vegas. Never have I seen so many haggard faces and hollow, greedy looks staring on cards being dealt out on gambling tables, so many nervous faces chasing dice rolling across green felts, so many impatient arms cranking slot machines, waiting to cash in, so many expressions changing to disappointment or even despair when the loot failed to pour into their buckets. Drinks were guzzled down and cigarettes were puffed in abundance; the smoke hung like a suffocating cloud above the gambling crowd. My biggest loss occurred on the way home. I dropped both of my contact lenses in the bathroom sink on the luxurious Santa Fe train. Before she left for Germany, Mutti had persuaded me to have these lenses fit by the brother of the eager optometrist suitor.

New Places, Friends, and Lovers

Now that both the man and his money were gone and all the prayers in vain, I was still pining away – almost to the point of feeling suicidal. Mr. James was astoundingly patient with me, never complaining once about my wasting so many working hours while I sat opposite him at the big, half-circle desk discussing, ad infinitum, my messed-up love life. I spent more time lamenting my loss than grieving President Kennedy's assassination, which occurred on November 22, 1963. One day, about one and a half years later, catharsis set in and I knew which course to chart, that is, the serious pursuit of a law degree. Mr. James was excited and offered to cooperate in every way possible, which meant allowing me to attend daytime classes, provided I made up for lost office time by working longer hours or on weekends. He made the entire deal even more palatable by indicating that once the degree was in hand, he would love for me to take over his practice, since his son preferred to go into teaching.

At the same time, a very desirable property, the residence of the founder and owner of the then-shut-down Royal Oak Stove Company, was purchased by one of our clients, the contractor Mr. Phillips, and changed into four or five apartments. I was fortunate to be able to rent one of the choice flats upstairs. The mansion was built of big, round, and irregularly shaped fieldstones. It stood high on top of a beautifully landscaped lot of six acres. Behind it was the carriage house, also converted into apartments, and a six-car garage was available as well. When you drove up to the main entrance, there was an arcade for carriages or cars and another roof above the stairs going up to the big doors, where you rang a bell to gain entrance. When the door opened, you walked through a set of swinging doors into a huge vestibule paneled in light-colored curly-maple wood. A massive fireplace welcomed the visitor. Above its ornately carved mantel hung a huge mirror, framed by a rich, gold, hand-carved frame. Tall rubber trees stood next to the windows, which were more than twenty-five feet high and let in much sunshine. A wide, curved wooden stairway, flanked by a curly-maple railing and balustrade, let you imagine a grandiose descent. Because it was still graced by a rich crystal chandelier hanging from the center of the wood-paneled ceiling, you instantly felt swept back into the twenties, when life in this entrance hall was in its prime. – Just imagine a ballroom atmosphere with dancing and music resounding throughout and beautiful ladies carefully descending the sweeping stairway, lifting their heavily brocaded gowns in an attempt not to trip and fall, although it would have been right into the arms of their partners awaiting them at the foot of the stairway.

My apartment was part of that elegant atmosphere. Four bay windows, reaching almost as high as the ceiling, were the focal point when you entered. The SABA had her spot right in the center, with the bright-red *Gone with the Wind* lamp on it. I moved the red light away from the window after one of the vice presidents from the bank, whom Mr. James represented, and who was married, knocked at my door one night and made a pass at me because I had always been so nice to him at the office. When I threatened to report him, he headed for the door, mumbling something to the effect that the red light looked very inviting.

The estate showed numerous traces of materials imported from Italy, as was obvious from the marble fixtures with golden faucets in my bathroom. It provided the perfect ambiance for a young woman embarking on a new career, eager to prove to the Joes and Johns and the Neverbees of this world that not all women are preordained to be just caretakers and housewives, to prove to the nuns at Sankt Ursula that they should have risked finding a way for me to make the *Abitur*, and that just maybe they would not have been disappointed. I wanted to be a lawyer and enrolled in such prelaw courses as philosophy, logic, ethics, and government, and discovered in reading Plato's dialogues that my mind was much more challenged than when listening to the lulling sermons of the priest, who wanted to send me to hell for eating meat on a Friday. I quickly realized that the time used to go to church could be better spent studying for classes. I became greedy with my time and turned down many invitations, even from friends who were so supportive they promised to stay on as my clients should I take over the practice. But I always made time to get together with the Loesers, my good Jewish friends.

The Loesers had already immigrated to America in 1938, prior to *Kristallnacht*. The Ochs family from the *New York Times*, relatives of Anneliese, had sponsored them. Anneliese's father was one of the cofounders of the Salamander Leather and Shoe manufacturing company, still based in Stuttgart, Germany, which was Anneliese's home until she married Heinz. She, contrary to what her father had hoped for his daughter, chose to work on a farm. She loved animals and the land. Already as a teenage girl, she spent her free time at their friend's zoo in Stuttgart, feeding a baby elephant with a bottle. Heinz's father had died early, leaving behind a widow who ran a printing shop in Berlin. Heinz had studied horticulture, a skill that ultimately helped him secure a visa for the two to immigrate to America. The consul general picked him out of the long line of Jews waiting to apply for a visa. Heinz had stepped out of the line to speak to him. As soon as he found out that Heinz had studied horticulture, he took him to his office and issued a visa for him and his new wife promptly. He remarked that he had never met a Jew who had gone into farming.

Because of the increasingly alarming atmosphere, hardly any of their friends and relatives had shown up at their religious wedding in Baden Baden. They were anxious to leave Germany – still refusing to believe that what came to their attention at times was actually true. After all, Anneliese's father had fought and risked his life for Germany during World War I. Their courtship was unusual insofar as they met through correspondence. Heinz and Anneliese both belonged to a youth organization for young Jewish farmers. They had heard it might be easier to immigrate as farmers than as other kinds of tradesmen. Anneliese was still a teenager when she wrote to Heinz, who was three years older. They were miles apart and saw each other only a few times before they decided to get married, when she was twenty-one. Their decision was partially motivated by the fear of what could happen if they stayed. The couple was allowed to take along their wedding goods, such as furniture, but little money. Anneliese had to leave behind the beautiful baby-blue Mercedes cabriolet with the light-blue Moroccan-leather seats, a birthday gift from her parents when she turned sixteen. Despite the fact that she was raised in very privileged surroundings, material possessions had never meant much to her. Her father was imprisoned by the Nazis and released in exchange for handing over his Salamander shares to Hitler. He and his wife left behind their beautiful estate in Stuttgart and moved to Boston, by way of Switzerland, together with Anneliese's brother. The young couple finally ended up in a small farmhouse located on seventy acres of land outside of Decatur, Michigan.

Upon their arrival in New York City, the Ochs family placed them in an apartment, but they did not stay long. They purchased a secondhand car and drove to East Berlin, Pennsylvania, where they were put up in a farmhouse free of charge in exchange for working the land. At the farm, they also raised chickens and made noodles with a pasta machine, which they had brought along. Every night, they would dry the pasta by hanging it over chairs. They sold poultry, eggs, pasta, and produce door-to-door. A year later they had saved enough money to make a small down payment on a place of their own. They drove further west and fell in love with a humble but picturesque farmhouse nestled in a valley. There was a red barn, a stream not too far from the house, and a strip of forest on top of a hill where mushrooms grew in the spring. At first, they had only partial electricity and a hand pump in the kitchen. They tried to raise a few cattle in order to have kosher meat. Several times in a row, the rabbi found a blemish in the butchered calf, so the meat could not be used. Finally, they decided to disregard it. Heinz was especially reluctant because he had lived with an Orthodox rabbi for several years. The two began raising produce, which they sold in addition to poultry and eggs at a stand on the driveway to their valley farm. They added to their property and house year after year and acquired a small twenty-four-hour grocery store at a corner in Dowagiac, where two major roads met. It turned out to be a gold mine, because both worked day and night. Heinz's mother had joined them from Israel and took care of their two children, Rachel and Kermit, who were ten years apart.

I first met the Loesers at Mr. James's office, because they were clients. I noticed quickly that they were rather distant at first. I sensed it was because I was from Germany and had an accent like them. By and by, we got to know each other better, and I was surprised to learn that Anneliese's father was connected with Salamander. Mutti always bought Salamander shoes for us, because they were sturdy. Since their grocery business continued to grow, they came to the office frequently.

I became intrigued with their success, which was a direct result of their relentless effort to please their customers. They worked side by side, always calling out a cheerful "hello!" "how are you?" and "what can I do for you?" The husband-and-wife team blended right in with the farmers and other customers. The Loesers were the first to hire black help and promoted a black employee to a managerial position. I recall Anneliese telling me her father had been instrumental in constructing housing for the workers at the Salamander factory. They too had a genuine social conscience. I was proud to be involved in their progress, and could talk endlessly on the phone with Heinz about his newest ideas for the supermarkets, of which they owned three when I left. I had many conversations with Heinz about the Holocaust as well. He told me I should have believed my father when he claimed not to have known what went on, because they themselves refused to believe it for a long time. The Loesers were also my first Jewish friends who had had direct contact with fatalities of the Holocaust. Heinz related the experience of his best friend, who was put into a concentration camp together with his wife and two children and was forced to burn his family while the camp kept him alive, because he was trained as a welder. Later, he was an accountant in New York City and became an important witness at the Nuremberg trials.

It was not until John left me that the Loesers invited me to their house, which by then had been expanded and remodeled several times. Heinz's mother had died unexpectedly before I had a chance to meet her. The Loesers were like family. Heinz at one time had the rather far-fetched idea of building a small house for me on their land. They liked my SABA so much that they bought one, which was like mine, except Scandinavian in design. –

How many times did I jump into my black T-bird and drive to Decatur, my heart always beating faster at the sight of that idyllic spot in the valley? The big red barn shone in the distance. It had served as a model for their supermarkets in that they resembled big red barns. Kermit, with thick, black, curly hair and the biggest black eyes, always waited for me to play or to haul me around the field on a little tractor. It was at that time that I developed a mild ragweed allergy. Sometimes he played the piano for me and I brought my recorder, or the violin. I even joined in when his father taught him Hebrew to prepare him for his bar mitzvah. They took me along to the temple in Kalamazoo and introduced me to the rituals of Jewish holidays. I was not nearly as afraid of their big Saint Bernard, Heidi, as I was of the one at the Neverbees, and watched in amazement as he devoured huge quantities of hamburger and freshly butchered beef hearts. His house was not far from Lucky Lindy's fenced-in stall. Lindy was Anneliese's beloved horse, which she bought from the Amish and pampered to no end. You could see the horse from the grill close to the picnic table, next to the yellow bungalow, where we sat many times, eating the thickest and juiciest steaks, which Heinz had brought from his butcher and grilled. Whenever I visited, I had to take a peek at their greenhouse, adjacent to the residence. It was filled with the most exotic varieties of orchids. They were in bloom all year long, including at Christmas, which at times I spent alone by choice, but in Dowagiac, I always spent it with the Loesers. They came to my place for Christmas, which usually coincided with Hanukkah, which I spent with them.

At their farm, the celebration was in accordance with the Jewish faith, and at my place it was a vague reflection of my childhood experiences. They were extremely giving. I recall that they were in the habit of piling the gifts up to the ceiling, which admittedly was not high in the ranch-style home. Whatever I had mentioned throughout the year as something I needed or should buy, you can be sure it was in my pile at the farm. We always had a good time. Both Heinz and his son played German folk songs on the piano. Occasionally, I joined in with my violin or recorder. I loved listening to Kermit play, since I had no room for a piano in my new apartment. He was definitely more talented than his older sister Rachel.

Rachel and I did not see each other too much once she went to college and I started to study, but when she came to visit, we loved pulling out the couch bed in my living room to watch TV until late at night on Saturdays. I was blown away when her parents gave her a bright-red car as a graduation present. We were so proud of

Kermit when he was chosen valedictorian of his class and, because he had a knack for writing, wondered if he would become a journalist.

My friendship with Rachel began to deteriorate when I observed how determined she was to latch on to a guy she met during her college years. She was no beauty queen and constantly struggled to keep her weight down. It was hard to accomplish, because she liked to eat. Harry, the chosen one, was no Prince Charming either. He was tall, with reddish-brown hair and watery blue eyes, and walked with his toes pointed inward a bit, but he was rather colorless and had no charisma or passion. His father worked on an assembly line in Pontiac, Michigan. I have never met a young girl who chased after a male with such a vengeance. She knitted sweaters for him, and believed wholeheartedly in the theory that "love goes through the stomach." She virtually bombarded him with packages of home-baked cookies of all imaginable varieties, which he never acknowledged with the deserved enthusiasm. He had a bit of an ego and seemed to be ambitious, but broke no records in college. Much to his discredit was the fact that he was a gentile by birth. Yet, young as he was, we knew he had switched religions a couple times before to please a girl. Rachel did not care, but her parents, especially her father, did. They were able to stop worrying when, right after graduation, Harry, who at that time did not really know much of Rachel's background, had looked for greener pastures and broke her heart by grazing elsewhere. No cookie or even the red car could stop him. Her parents tried their best to find Rachel a Jewish replacement. No such luck.

In Pursuit of a Law Degree – Love at First Sight – Erich

Heinz Loeser was one of Mr. James's clients who had indicated that he would remain a client should I take over the firm. Thus, when I was in the midst of my sophomore year, I took the law-school-admission test at Notre Dame. I was the only woman who passed, because no other woman took the test. It was one of the most demanding tests I had taken up to that point. To add to the pressure, Notre Dame did not accept women at that time. I pleaded with the dean during a private interview, but to no avail. Since I wanted to stay in the area to be close to the firm, Mr. James suggested that I apply to the law school in Valparaiso, Indiana. I was elated when I was accepted as a special student, based on my scores and my practical experience at James & Hoff. The big disappointment came when we found out that in order to practice in Michigan, I first had to complete a BA and then earn a degree at a law school, which took three years. Since I could easily earn advanced credits for German by completing German literature courses at a higher level, I took that route, deciding to major in German, simply to get ahead faster. I also took placement tests for French and skipped a few courses in that language as well. Had I had the *Abitur*, I could have skipped four semesters. A bit of a disappointment came when I earned a D in economics, the first and only D of my entire college career. I always had to study extra hard for courses that required a foundation in math, in which, you may recall, I was very poor. It was partly related to my fragmented schooling in good old Germany. I bought all the books that dealt with the mathematics related to the courses and struggled through. I often wondered if it had something to do with the numbers being turned around in German as well as having been out of school for fourteen years at that point.

* * *

I tried to see my parents more frequently after I sold the Croft. When I visited between semesters in 1964, I fell in love for the third or, if you count Hans, the fourth time. Erich, a German in every sense of the word, was from Northern Germany and three years older than I. He was tall and athletically built, had beautiful blue eyes and an extremely captivating personality, and to top it off, was witty, intelligent, sensitive, and whatever else one could wish for. When he laughed two golden crowns stood out on a row of perfect, snow-white teeth, and his hair was prematurely gray. He had a degree in agriculture, had been very successful professionally, doubtless in part due to Germany's boom, and wanted to fulfill a lifelong dream of becoming a doctor of veterinary medicine. He had been drafted into the German Army at the age of fifteen or sixteen, tried his best to get out by exposing himself half-naked to extremely cold temperatures and sitting at an open window in the barracks, hoping to catch pneumonia. He came from a staunch Catholic background. His father, a teacher in a strict Catholic town in Northern Germany, had died by shooting himself accidentally, while hunting. He himself had to endure torture by American soldiers when they took him captive. They knocked some of his teeth out with a gun butt as he tried to resist. When he returned home, bombs had destroyed their one-family house. He finally found his mother living with neighbors. With the help of other villagers, who had survived an attempt on Hitler's life, he rebuilt the homestead. His mother took in boarders to earn a living and to send her son to study at the university. At that time, for some reason, he was unable to study veterinary medicine. He felt obligated to marry a local Catholic woman who claimed he had robbed her of her virginity. After three children had been born into the marriage, he discovered it to have been a lie. At that point, he fell in love with a distant cousin, separated from the wife, and moved into one of his several big apartment houses. The cousin, who was another committed Catholic, worked as a housekeeper for the parish priest.

Erich had accumulated sufficient wealth to provide for his family while embarking on his life as a student once more. He was renting a room from my parents. Soon after we met, he told me he had been in love with me ever since he saw my picture with the violin on the piano. To make a long story short, he swept me off my feet, and this relationship was, as they always are, a totally new experience. I fell head over heels for this man very quickly. What made it more tantalizing was the fact that we lived together in a comparatively small apartment. Remember the function of the sword in *Tristan and Isolde*? Since Erich occupied the bedroom, I slept on the couch in the living room – most of the time. My parents would have killed us both had they found out. We communicated by putting little notes underneath a doily in the bathroom, met for lunch in restaurants, took weekend trips in his Mercedes, and lived dangerously right under my parents' noses. We danced and enjoyed sparkling wines on the Drosselgasse, in Rüdesheim on the Rhine, or at places closer to home. We went to the opera, theater, concerts, and movies and were very, very happy. I had not yet experienced a relationship so passionate. He knew human anatomy very well, and you may remember what I said about the medical profession along these lines. I shed many tears when I said good-bye to cross the Atlantic. To keep the relationship hot, Erich sent many passionate letters and sizzling cassettes, which would cause me to blush if I listened to them today. I sent my letters to the address of another student, a friend of his, to keep my parents from finding out.

During my sophomore year, another major experience in my life occurred. My German professor, Jacob Sudermann, wanted badly for me to teach a German course for beginners. I was reluctant, because I did not want to become a teacher. Besides, I was only a sophomore, and to be an assistant instructor, one typically needed to have at least a BA, and preferably an MA. He persisted and sought special permission from the president of IU–Bloomington. Based on my German and IU course records, I got the green light to teach this university course. I accepted and was quite pleased with it.

When I visited Germany in the summer, the relationship with Erich intensified. He gave me a beautiful platinum ring with a pearl, which was surrounded by diamonds engraved with his initials and the date. Since he was getting close to finishing his degree, he wanted to get started on having his marriage annulled to make sure the Catholic Church would not chastise him. He tried hard to persuade me to stay with him in Germany during this process and break my teaching commitment with the university. I just could not bring myself to do it. Before I left, he gave me a check for $5,000 to open an account in his name. I promised to find out what would be necessary for him to earn a degree of veterinary medicine from Purdue, after completing work for the degree in Germany. At that time, I told my parents about the relationship, because I wanted to mail my letters to their address. They were stunned, raised many eyebrows, and were not happy. After all, he was still married, and they had met his wife once or twice. To make matters worse, all were Catholic.

I returned in time for the fall semester and prepared seriously for G101, the introductory German course. Despite my original misgivings, I discovered that I enjoyed teaching enormously. And much to my surprise, the student evaluations were excellent. One male student, perhaps in his early thirties, told me on the last day of class that he had been tempted to withdraw from the course when he saw me, a woman, enter on the first day. He admitted having been wrong and had enjoyed the class very much.

What would have happened had I given in to Erich and gotten out of the commitment to teach? It was perhaps halfway through the semester that the letters from

Erich stopped coming. It was impossible for me to find out what was going on. I was once more overwhelmed with grief; Mr. James reverted to his role of consoling me. Finally, Erich wrote, unloading all the misfortunes that had come to pass. Mutti had virtually bombarded him with reprimands to the effect that he would ruin my life, not to mention the lives of his wife and the poor children – that God would punish him and me. She asked him what the other tenants or the mailman might think if they received letters from the daughter in America. It got so bad he could bear it no longer and moved out. To make things worse, he had injured his back playing soccer with his boys. He fell backward, his vertebrae hitting the edge of a spade, and suffered excruciating pain. He felt he might be handicapped for life, or even confined to a wheelchair, and did not want to subject me to such a life with him. He explained that at times he collapsed without warning and knew he would have to switch gears once he earned his degree, in order to focus on something like poultry diseases instead of treating cows and horses. I tried to break it off after a few more letters, returned his money, and focused on my studies. It was extremely hard to do, because I was still deeply and passionately in love. I would have married him even if he was crippled for life.

Junior Year Abroad – Aix-en-Provence, France – Monte Carlo – Italy

In the 60s, students aiming for a BA were required to spend their senior year on the Bloomington campus. It got increasingly difficult to enroll in certain required classes at convenient times. I sat down with Mr. James and discussed my plan to terminate my position as his secretary and, instead of attending IU full-time, to spend my junior year abroad. As you may recall, I had always wanted to perfect my French-language skills and found the program offered by the Institute for American Universities in Aix-en-Provence, close to the Côte d'Azur, perfect. I could use the interest income from the sale of the Croft to defray the cost of tuition and other expenses. Mr. James was all for it.

Upon receipt of the letter of acceptance, we found a new secretary. I stored my furniture, loaned an air conditioner, my TV, and other household goods to my brother Alfons and his wife, who had returned from Germany to live in Detroit, and put the newly purchased 1965 T-bird Landau, which was the envy of everybody who saw it, in a private garage for a rental fee of $5 each month. Mr. James promised to drive the slender black beauty now and then to keep it in shape. It had retractable, black leather seats, moving windows, a dashboard comparable to the inside of a cockpit, and a mahogany interior. You could not tell my pet car had been in a head-on collision one night on my way home from school. The roads were so icy that about seven cars collided unavoidably. My beauty and I slid into three cars, two brand-new, that were already in the ditch. The damages we caused were astronomical, because one car was a brand-new Cadillac. If Mr. James had not warned the insurance agent that he would cancel all of his insurance policies with them if they canceled mine, they would have done so. Mr. James came all the way from Dowagiac to South Bend to pick me up, take care of the car, and drop me off at Mrs. Lowe's place in Niles, where I spent the night.

I made the rounds to say good-bye to my many friends, including the Gebhards on their homey farm deep in the woods outside Marcellus. They had both earned master's degrees in education when they were over sixty, and I loved to spend weekends with them, because they were always so kind and caring, like parents. I shed a few tears while bidding the Loesers farewell and tucked into my purse Mr. James's wonderful letter of recommendation, from which I quote: "In my forty years of practice I have had many secretaries and I record Mrs. Beardsley as the best." I held on to it all my life and was mighty grateful to him for taking me to the airport to send me off to spend a whole year on the other side of the Atlantic.

* * *

My parents awaited me at the airport in Hannover, where I stayed from the middle of May until it was time to head south, on about September 8, 1966. Thanks to Doc, I had the income from the Croft. However, obtaining it required constant prodding, because the buyers were repeatedly in arrears and only came through after I threatened foreclosure, in letters composed by me but signed by Mr. James. In addition to paying for my education, I was able to purchase a white VW Bug with red seats, a bit less splashy than my 1959 T-bird. My father and I picked it up at the Wolfsburg VW factory, and I was mighty proud of it, though I had not driven a car with a stick shift since I learned to drive. I also acquired an antiquated portable typewriter at a secondhand store to take to France, and was set to drive to the Côte d'Azur.

Before I left, Harry came for a short visit. He was not one bit sorry he had ditched Rachel, who was pining away, wondering if she should have baked a different sort of cookies. I showed him around Hannover. When we stopped in front of one of the big Salamander shoe stores, which was half a block long, and I pointed out that Rachel was the granddaughter of the cofounder of the Salamander Works, he was amazed. He had had no idea and could hardly believe it. I could just see the little wheels turning in his head. It didn't come as a big surprise when I received word from Rachel, even before I took off for France, that the defected boyfriend had parked his car at her doorstep the minute he returned. It was on again for Rachel, and the stove was back in business, getting at times overheated. Things had come full circle. Though I never told Rachel about what motivated Harry to make amends, it was obvious to those who knew him that his new motivation was "love and money," much to the even greater dismay of Rachel's parents. Personally, I seldom regretted anything more than having introduced Harry to Salamander AG.

* * *

My white Bug and I traveled happily, but with great speed, along the Autobahn (the one good thing Hitler had left behind) and made our way without incident all the way to Orange, Provence. I decided to look for a hotel, because I felt sick from a bad cold. It was difficult navigating the dark and narrow streets to get to my lodging. I started early the next morning, eager to arrive at my final destination. I resisted the urge to buy some of the delicious fudge, for which Orange is famous, offered at stands throughout the town.

The sun was shining – not a cloud on the horizon. The radiant blue sky so typical of the Mediterranean stretched out in front of me as far as I could see. I was rolling through the charming countryside of Provence, and soon I got a first taste of Aix-en-Provence, the town in which a multitude of water fountains are forever splashing, inviting passersby to linger and take in the refreshing sight. This city is a place in which art abounds and never ceases to captivate the eyes and mesmerize the mind. I had arrived in Aix, which was the capital of Provence in the Middle Ages as well as the place where Paul Cézanne was born, the place that stimulated the painter to create many of his masterpieces.

I had to drive around the Place de la Rotonde, for the first time seeing the big fountain with its twelve spouts and big, sculpted pairs of lions sprawling out at its base. I felt welcomed by the plane trees lining both sides of the wide boulevard, the Cours Mirabeau, like soldiers standing guard for a parade led by the famous Roi René of Anjou, who governed in the fifteenth century. On my search for the Institute in the Rue Du Bon-Pasteur, I could not miss St. Saviour's Cathedral, built between the eleventh and thirteenth centuries, where Cézanne was said to have sat many times underneath Nicolas Froment's triptych *The Burning Bush* and where his funeral took place in 1906.

I could not help but observe that many of the streets in Aix were so narrow my T-bird from the States could not have squeezed through. I passed several sidewalks that were no wider than a foot, and when I had to pass a parked car, it was impossible to do so without a mutual scrape. – No wonder that after I had lived in Aix for a few months and parked my Bug close to a friend's house one evening, someone lifted it and put it down so close to the wall of the house that I could not unlock the door on the driver's side until a few guys came to pick it up and move it over a couple of feet. – In approaching the Institute I was lucky, because next to some bikes parked in front there was a narrow space where I could park my VW. I had had no idea what to expect and found myself wondering what was to come as I approached the big door, above which the number 2, the correct address, was displayed.

The outside wall of the Institute resembled that of a Romanesque church or chapel. When I entered, a stairway, obviously added in recent years, led to the offices upstairs, where a tall, rather boyish looking Englishman greeted me and introduced himself as Mr. Booth, assistant to the director, Mr. Mazda, who emerged later and was a gentleman in his fifties, about 5'7" and with silver-gray hair. Everybody treated me kindly, and once I had collected the mail being held for me and had all of the information necessary to get settled, I found my way through another maze of streets to the stately home of Dr. Bourzeix, on Rue de la Violette, which was on the outskirts of town. The entrance to the house bordered directly on the street. In answer to the doorbell, an elderly gentleman opened the door, and he eyed me a bit suspiciously; perhaps he had expected someone younger. Also, because of my German accent, he noticed I was not a full-blooded American. We conversed in French only, which seemed to surprise him a bit. He asked me to enter and summoned a very young and pretty maid, named Michelle, to show me to my room.

I followed Michelle upstairs. My room was directly to the right. It was a rather small and narrow room, but big enough for a bed, a movable wardrobe, and a small table with a lamp and chair. I positioned my antiquated typewriter on the table and set down an unopened letter from Erich, which had awaited me at the Institute. I left it unopened for quite a while. My room had a sink in a niche, closed off by a curtain. The bathroom was in the corridor close by, and the big positive was a large terrace accessible through the glass door and shutters of my room, from which I could look down into the garden, read, soak up the sun, or relax with friends. – I decided right then and there that I would be content in my new place. After all, I had been exposed to a wide variety of private "milieus" since early childhood.

By the time classes started at 8:00 am on September 14, I had gotten acquainted with Aix-en-Provence, and I slowly fell in love with the narrow streets so close to the walls of the houses. I began to look fondly at the facades of the ancient quarters with the stucco or plaster peeling off and leaving blotches of orange-, brown-, and rust-colored brick surfaces bare. Once I looked inside St. Saviour's Cathedral, I knew that if I were to attend an occasional celebration of High Mass, I would remember the times when Mutti and I sang together at Sankt Heinrich while the organ pulled all of the registers. And I had quickly discovered an ideal spot in the peaceful Romanesque cloisters to read and reflect in peace.

I discovered a couple of places away from the grand Cours Mirabeau's elegant boutiques, luxurious jewelry stores, pretentious banks, and fancy restaurants with sidewalk seating areas underneath green awnings. It was exhilarating and calming at once to rest on a bench at the Place de l'Hotel de Ville or next to my favorite fountain, *The Four Dolphins*, and just bask in the local atmosphere. I was elated when I looked up toward the tall windows with brown shutters, which were pulled shut at noon to prevent the sun from heating up the spacious rooms, which were so refreshingly cool. I imagined what kind of precious antique might be housed in those rooms with high ceilings, whether it might be from Provence or the era of Louis XIV.

The spacious interior of the Bourzeix house was rather sparingly furnished. A grand piano occasionally played by the doctor and a few antique upholstered chairs with golden armrests stood in one of the rooms. White walls offset baroque light fixtures, carved out of wood, painted gold, and holding candles. A long mahogany banquet table with twelve ornate chairs took up the full length of the dining room. A crystal chandelier was hanging above the center of the table, and a big still life in a frame of natural wood hung on one of the walls. All of the floors, as in most of the residences in Provence, were covered with tile. The Bourzeixes had two small children, whom I did not often see. I never was invited to join the family in a private setting, and I never sought to intrude. The grandfather became more talkative when my French-language skills had advanced to the point that they could be considered near-fluent. We always talked at the foot of the stairs.

On my stroll through the town, I had also looked for places to eat, since the cafeteria of the Université d'Aix-Marseille, where we could take our meals, was quite a distance to walk. It was not difficult to locate several larger and more intimate restaurants or brasseries, which many students frequented at lunchtime. The customary lunch consisted of a spare piece of pizza, a pastry or a slender slice of grilled beef, and a piece of chicken, with French fries and salad. When we had no classes in the afternoon, we would order half a bottle of *vin ordinaire* (ordinary wine), a rosé from the vineyards of Provence, for less than a dollar. (I had fun visiting wineries and accumulating information, including sampling the wines, for a noncredit paper about the art of making wine in Provence.)

At night, my meals were simple. I had no access to a stove, but had brought a miniature heating coil with which I prepared many a mug filled with hot instant soups. I ate many baguettes with just butter or cheese, accompanied by a cup of tea or simply water from the faucet. On weekends I splurged by trying out the better restaurants in and outside of Aix. It was a way to develop a taste for gourmet food and to find out about the items on the menu. Once, when my Puerto Rican friend Carmen and I ordered a dish recommended by the waiter, we cringed at the sight of a tiny bird lying on the plate, roasted but with its eyes and beak wide open. I loved escargots, octopus, mussels, and the like, but the little bird looked too sad to swallow.

It did not take long for me to get to know a number of the coeds who came from different universities in the States or from one of many foreign countries to spend either a semester or, as was typically the case, a year abroad. I soon noticed that in general, I blended right in. Occasionally, one of them would ask me for a favor. Since I was the only student with a car, I was glad to help out hauling their suitcases when they moved to different quarters or to take them along when I drove to Cassis to go for a swim in the Mediterranean. Once, a twenty-year-old junior asked for my advice when she fell for a young Frenchman who owned several riding horses. She had promised her father she would return "intact" after her year in France. Since the owner of the horses was a couple of years older and obviously more experienced than she was, she was afraid he would not let her continue to ride the horses if she denied him the compensation he had hinted at. I sided with her father, after talking to her at length about the numerous consequences which may or may not have ensued. I also emphasized that the French males considered the American girls rather promiscuous. After that, she seemed to avoid me, and I wondered whether she had given in or had already sinned prior to talking to me.

It was a fifteen-minute walk to the Institute. The lecture hall, which I entered for the first time shortly before 8:00 a.m. on September 14, 1966, was unlike any I had seen before. It was indeed a remnant of the Middle Ages, a somewhat modified version of the interior of a Romanesque chapel. The thick walls had no windows, and the room relied exclusively on electric lighting. The study chairs were similar to those in the United States. They were arranged in rows, all on one level, looking toward the podium with the lectern. Actually, the room would have seemed rather gloomy had it not been filled with the forty or fifty young men and women chatting animatedly in an effort to become acquainted.

This very room quickly became one of the most intellectually stimulating and exciting forums I encountered during my career as a student. It was there that I first encountered some of the most extraordinary professorial minds. They challenged the intellect, seduced the soul, and opened new vistas. Three professors from the Université d'Aix-Marseille stood out. Professor Dr. Wençelius was a personal friend of one of my favorite French authors, Albert Camus. He lectured on twentieth-century philosophy. Professor Dr. Madame d'Anselme had earned her PhD in comparative literature at Harvard. Professor Dr. Dr. Bourde, with PhDs from Oxford and the Sorbonne, had had visiting professorships at many prestigious and Ivy League universities, not only in Europe, but also in Africa and the United States. He was a professor of history and fine arts as well as an accomplished and highly esteemed concert harpsichordist. He was doubtlessly the most illustrious, and flamboyant, of the three star professors. I must not forget the French professor, S. Preca, who in his letter of recommendation stated that the results of my studies had been "brilliant" and encouraged me to eventually teach French. He challenged me tremendously. I had not taken any French since Sankt Ursula, that is, in sixteen years. Much to my surprise, I was placed in fifth-semester courses – advanced grammar and stylistics – which greatly helped with my other courses when it was required that papers be written in French.

I soon discovered that classes in France were much more demanding than in the States. I had to work extra hard to stay at the top of my class, but thanks to Mr. Krach at Sankt Ursula and my professor from the Université d'Aix-Marseille, I succeeded to such a degree that when I started my MA in the States, I continued to excel in French literature classes. I might add that at the Institute, I gained the self-confidence to enroll in classes outside the Institute. I quietly signed up for two courses at the Institut d'Etudes Françaises pour Etudiants Etrangers, twentieth-century philosophy and "Compte Rendu," which at exam time required reproducing (in writing) a speech by Robespierre, which the professor speed-read. I was thrilled when I saw my relatively high score announced on the blackboard and beamed when several coeds and Mr. Booth had found out and congratulated me. Some of my friends thought it rather devious of me to sign up for special courses secretly; others were perhaps a bit jealous. They considered it strange that I spent weekends studying while they were traveling, mostly to France's neighboring countries.

My French professors always required more from me than the rest of the students. Whenever there were special reports to give, they challenged me, simply because I was older. Professor Wençelius, who introduced us to such modern philosophers as Sartre, Camus, Heidegger, and Kierkegaard, once shocked me when he requested I give a critique and summary of an article of a philosophical nature in *Playboy* magazine. Theretofore I had avoided looking at or even touching the "repudiated" magazine. To my utter surprise, I found the article sound, and it somewhat changed my attitude toward *Playboy*. The professor also invited me to his country house, from which I admired Paul Cézanne's magnificent and impressive mountain, Sainte-Victoire, for the first time as it sprawled out harmoniously and in all its beauty across the soothing landscape.

I don't recall ever writing as many papers as I did at the Institute. I composed so many for Madame d'Anselme, who lived in Avignon, city of the Popes, that she was unable to find one of them. Since I had aced all previous exams and papers, she gave me an A for the missing paper and explained that she felt justified, since I was the first American student of all those having studied comparative literature under her to receive straight As for the course. Professor d'Anselme exposed me to a long list of works in her comparative literature courses, which I thoroughly enjoyed reading in the original languages, whether Spanish, German, French, or English, but she was also effective in persuading me to give up the idea of studying law and to focus on a PhD in German literature instead. When I argued that I lacked the necessary intelligence, she shook her head and laughed out loud.

Professors Wençelius and d'Anselme were outstanding and thought-provoking professors, but Professor Bourde was capable of capturing my attention so intensely that I sat glued to the edge of my chair for two solid hours, starting the second he entered the room and headed like an arrow toward the podium. He would stand or move around, an imposing figure, tall and slender, with tanned skin, big, shiny, dark-brown eyes, and gold-rimmed glasses on a sculpted nose. His black hair was slightly gray. Though he was beardless, he resembled the sculpture of Poseidon at the National Archeological Museum in Athens, Greece. He would lecture, or entertain us, if you will, about art and everything pertaining thereto in the most detailed, fascinating, and colorful language and in a tone of voice more highly spirited than any I had heard before. Yes, André Bourde had a profound influence on my future perception of any form of art, be it painting, sculpture, architecture, music, or cooking. My philosophy professors had laid a solid foundation for future philosophy courses by commencing with the Greek philosophers. Professor Bourde provided the basis for understanding art by introducing us first to ancient Egyptian and Greek creations. He was so dynamic that everything that followed fell into place with ease. He breathed life into every form of art and taught me how to look at it with new eyes. Indeed, he trained me how to observe art and life less seriously and to acquire a renewed thirst for life.

I drove north to Hannover to spend Christmas with my family in Germany, which no longer reflected the fairy-tale ambiance of my childhood years. – In February, I took a short trip to Ventimiglia, Italy, not far beyond the border of the principality of Monaco. I wanted to experience how it feels to drive along the Côte d'Azur on the Corniche, which I remember as one of the most intoxicating and scenic drives in that part of Europe. I stopped in Nice to visit the Roman Catholic cathedral Ste. Réparate and light a candle. As though I were a guest, I walked past the porters who stood next to the huge and heavy glass entrance doors of a couple of luxury hotels opposite the famous Proménade des Anglais, and I was awed by the elegance of the spacious lobbies. Before I continued, I sat down on a bench on the Proménade, ogled the fashionably dressed men and women parading back and forth, and bathed my eyes in the azure waters of the Mediterranean. On the way, I could not resist stopping at Europe's perhaps most splashy resort, Monte Carlo, and parked my Bug near the Place du Casino with its picturesque gardens. I was able to gain entrance to the casino, which also houses the opera and the Foyer de la Danse, just to look around and was astounded by the sophisticated atmosphere throughout, a far cry from the tacky casinos in Vegas. I waited in vain in front of the palace to get a glimpse of Grace Kelley. The colorfully dressed guards at the entrance gate did not blink an eye; and I decided to head toward Ventimiglia, only four miles away from the French border, just to sample the flavor of an Italian town, before heading back to Aix to experience the same landscape, this time illuminated by the purple glow of the setting sun.

Professor Bourde took us on a number of exciting field trips, during which he pulled us even deeper into the realm of Provençal art treasures. Those trips were always spiced with an anecdotal event. When he took us to his place in the country, far out in the rough countryside near Lurs, he opened one of the shutters of the ancient, reclusive dwelling of gray stone and pointed toward the big branch of a tree that could be reached from the opening. He told us in dramatic detail that he would cover the branch with a yellow glue to trap little birds by their feet until he liberated them – ultimately to have them served at suppertime by his houseboy Swalili as morsels of great delicacy. Another time, after visiting the Museum of Fernand Léger, in Biot, we stopped for lunch in a small town. Professor Bourde felt compelled to introduce those of us who had never tasted it to a stew of couscous with lamb. He asked me to come along and took me straight into the kitchen of the family-style restaurant, asking the woman at the stove for permission to peek into the pots before he ordered. The cook nodded with a big smile. The stew was delicious.

On many of these wonderful field trips, André asked his mother, Madame Gilberte Bourde, to come along. We always sat next to each other and conversed in French only, since she spoke no English. We became such good friends that I was invited to visit her and her son at their beautiful villa in Marseille. I found out later I was the only student who had ever been invited. Villa Phocéenne, more than one hundred years old, was situated on a rather steeply sloped rock formation approximately two hundred feet below the Cathedral of Notre Dame de la Garde but still two hundred feet above sea level. To reach it, one had to enter an iron gate from a street below and climb about sixty steps that meandered through rock gardens below the villa. The view from the villa was one of the most magnificent views I had ever experienced. I looked down on Marseilles' Vieux Port (Old Harbor) with the sand-colored Château d'If reaching out of the dark-blue Mediterranean Sea. It reminded me of Alexandre Dumas' riveting novel *The Count of Monte Cristo*.

On my first visit, I felt like I was entering an old palace. The black houseboy, Swalili, whom Professor Bourde had brought from the Congo in Africa to take care of household chores, opened the door after I rang the bell and ushered me into the spacious, rather dark entrance hall with vaulted ceilings. He was short and about twenty-eight years old, had a big smile, spoke French fluently, and wore a white apron. I waited until Madame Bourde arrived and greeted me with her usual cordial embrace and kisses on both cheeks. She was slightly taller than I, slender, and dressed in dark silk. She called me *chère petite amie* (dear little friend). Professor Bourde arrived later, yet in time to savor the tasty meal Swalili had prepared following his and Madame Bourde's direction. It was served in the large dining room, graced with beautiful antique furniture, gold-framed mirrors, paintings, and a precious chandelier. It felt like being in a palace.

Each time I visited, Madame would go after dinner to the music room, where a big Steinway stood close to a flight of windows reaching almost to the ceiling. She invited me to find a comfortable seat and then played brilliantly. I always wished she would go on and on. She played compositions by Mozart, Beethoven, Schubert, and others. Each time, I felt overpowered with emotion. It was a special treat when André surprised us with an encore even more radiantly performed. Madame spoke of their musical friends who used to come and make music at the mansion, including Isaac Stern and other renowned artists. I was told that her husband, a prominent vascular surgeon, had been active in the underground movement, helping Jews escape from Germany, and had later become a victim himself. Once, Madame and her son invited me to an old private club on the Vieux Port for lunch. The rooms were paneled in mahogany and richly furnished with heavy, dark-brown furniture and burgundy leather upholstery. It was the first time I tasted bouillabaisse. I have never again had a bouillabaisse as delicious as the one I ate in Marseille.

I felt richly blessed to study in Aix, to experience French culture and the French people firsthand. I felt blessed even more so to have become a friend of both Madame Bourde and her son André. I relished the trips Madame and I took in my little VW along the Côte D'Azur, taking in the atmosphere and the sights at Toulon, Saint-Tropez, Fréjus, and Cannes. On other occasions, I would meet Madame at the Marseille Opera, where we attended several memorable performances, such as Wagner's *Tannhäuser* and Verdi's *Aida*. I also had my first, but not last, encounter with the great Russian ballet dancer Rudolf Nureyev in Marseille.

Mediterranean Cruise: Sicily – Cyprus – Israel – Turkey – Greece – Malta

My friendship with André and his mother Gilberte very much influenced my decision to sign up for a Mediterranean cruise at Eastertime. I considered it primarily an educational journey and wanted to see firsthand many of the treasures of antiquity Professor Bourde had lectured about and shown to us on slides and in art books. I wanted to gather material in Athens at the Archeological Museum for the extensive term paper for his course, which I had decided to write about Greek sculpture. Athens was one of the stops on the cruise, and I was fortunate to get a student special on the virtually brand-new *Renaissance* (it was only her second trip) for a mere $250.

The *Renaissance*, approximately eight thousand tons, was a comparatively small luxury liner with about two hundred passengers aboard. I had first-class accommodations, the food prepared by French chefs was superb, and the passengers were predominantly French, which meant we conversed almost exclusively in the French language. Perhaps the most interesting person I met was a medical doctor from Oran, in Northwest Algeria, who turned out to be a personal friend of Albert Camus, a native of that region. Since none of the other students had come along, I was free to investigate whatever I desired. The cruise was unlike my ocean voyages across the Atlantic, because we stopped at so many harbors where the senses were stimulated with new and exotic encounters each day, starting with visits to the ancient city of Palermo and the village of Monreale in the northwest of Sicily, close to the Conca d'Oro, where oranges and lemons are cultivated.

We were usually picked up at the ship by taxis or buses, which took us to the various sites, cathedrals, palaces, museums, churches, and remnants of antiquity – too many places to mention. In Cyprus, the ship docked in the harbor of Famagusta, the wealthy town of the Middle Ages immortalized in Shakespeare's *Othello*, which remains quite vivid in my memory, not only because of the great panorama visible from the citadel with the famous Othello Tower, but also because I saw my first flowering mimosa shrubs on Cyprus.

When the ship tried to dock in Haifa, Israel, it was so stormy that it was on the verge of capsizing. Two other, smaller ships had indeed capsized. It was Easter

Sunday, and it snowed in Haifa, an unheard-of phenomenon. I found the situation rather adventurous. The heavy chairs, cocktail tables, and music stands of the band all tumbled or slid across the parquet floor toward one side. Those of us not seasick went toward the opposite side to create a balance. It seemed to work, because we went safely ashore and were glad to get into the buses, which took us on a sightseeing tour of Jerusalem and other sites of historical significance. I was astounded by what the Israelis had accomplished through hard work and irrigation in this obviously arid "Promised Land" of the Bible. As we returned to the ship via Haifa, I wished we could spend a night in order to enjoy a concert by their famous symphony orchestra. When we traveled the next day through Galilee and walked through the village of Nazareth, St. Mary's home, which offered so many reminders of the Holy Family, I began to question the concept of immaculate conception. I had not been aware that Joseph lived only a few steps from Mary's humble abode. – On the way to the ship, we saw the blue waters of the big Lake Tiber and visited a kibbutz, which reminded me of what I had heard about cooperatives in the German Democratic Republic.

On our visit to İzmir, in Turkey, I was shocked by the extreme poverty, especially in the district close to the harbor. However, I was diverted from such thoughts as I sat on a camel, smiling down on two of my new young female friends from Grenoble, and on the Arabs who made sure the animals would not run away and throw me to the ground. A highlight of Turkey was a visit to Ephesus, known in antiquity for its Temple of Diana and as the place where St. Mary, St. John, and St. Lucas had lived. I was amazed at the grandeur as well as the extent to which the rich and ancient remnants had been and still were being exposed to view through excavations. I stood in awe before the Forum, the Odeon, the Library of Celsus, and the Great Theater, built in the Greek era, reconstructed in the Roman period, and maintaining its incredible acoustics. I imagined Antony and Cleopatra riding in procession along the Arcadian Way and was anxious to share my experiences with my friends back in Aix. Indeed, Ephesus was an ideal transition for what awaited us in Athens, Greece, where we docked at the ancient seaport of Piraeus.

In Athens, I spent half a day at the National Archeological Museum, conducting research for my paper. The rest of the day, I was engrossed in admiring once more what Professor Bourde had taught me about Greek architecture and sculpture. We lingered at the Acropolis, the magnificent white Parthenon, with its strong Doric columns through which the blue sky shines, the Nike Temple, the slender Ionic pillars of the Erechteum, the Porch of the Maidens, and the sculptured caryatids, carrying the heavy stones flat on their heads with such grace and ease. Everything appears more harmoniously composed when you stand in front of it than when you look at it in pictures or photos. The overall environment was even more magnificent than I had imagined. Since everything I had just learned was fresh in my mind, I was tempted at times to add to what the official guide told us. Little by little, I drifted away, and a group of passengers from the ship followed me, indicating they preferred my extemporaneous comments to those of the guide. I made sure I did not leave Athens without having purchased a bust of Socrates. –

Next, we stopped at Naples, to view the city and the excavations at Herculaneum and the island of Malta, where we walked through the streets of Valletta, the capital, and saw St. John's Co-Cathedral, a monument to the Grand Masters built in the sixteenth century. By comparison, the other sights were rather anticlimactic. The captain's farewell dinner was exciting, followed as on other nights by entertainment and dancing. This event was to be a costume ball. Many of the passengers referred to me as "the Merry Widow." Accordingly, I dressed the part for the big event. I put on my black, size-four cocktail dress. It had a fitted bodice, with a tight skirt and a slit on the left side. Narrow straps and a low-cut back gave it a rather sexy look. The black patent-leather sandals with spike heels and sheer black hose with a delicate rose pattern were perfect. I took a cone-shaped cardboard hat and draped my black lace mantilla from Mexico over it, letting it hang down in the back. I wore long, black gloves, put a cigarette into a long cigarette holder carved out of ivory, which I had saved from the Croft, and held it between thumb and index finger, blowing an occasional puff of smoke into the room. The long, dangling, gold-filigree earrings Doc had given me, together with a great assortment of other gold-filigree jewelry purchased after we had returned from our honeymoon, came in handy. Mr. Goldstein had sent a shipment to a jeweler in the States who canceled the order too late. Doc was happy to buy it all, and I loved it. My outfit was a hit, and a young, handsome, tall, blond, and blue-eyed man danced with me all night until it was time to go to bed. When the *Renaissance* docked in Marseille in the afternoon of April 3, 1967, I looked back on another exceptionally rewarding and exciting experience in my life. I was eager to get to work on my paper for Professor Bourde. My head was bursting with impressions and ideas waiting to be captured.

My efforts and my enthusiasm were handsomely rewarded when my fifty-page paper earned one of the two As in a class of over fifty and received the notation "intelligent and sensitive." The other A was given to Penelope Hunter, a fine-arts major, who later worked for the Metropolitan Museum of Art, in New York City. That paper, coupled with other accomplishments at the Institute, resulted in my being awarded the Certificate of European Studies and the Academic Achievement Medal, both presented to me during the graduation ceremonies in the courtyard of the L'Institut Pour les Etudiants Etrangères.

Au Revoir, Villa Phocéenne – *Buenos Días*, Spain – Morocco (Africa) – Gibraltar

One year under the spell of Provence could not have ended with a more precious gift from Madame and André than the one I have kept alive in my memories. Prior to my departure on a trip to Spain, Morocco, and Gibraltar, Professor Bourde invited me to the manor to play for me on the harpsichord a few compositions by

Scarlatti, Handel, Bach, and Telemann. He permitted me to record the performance on a cassette.

André's quarters were on the third and upper floor of the palatial estate. I felt as though I were ascending into another realm and wondered what treasures and secrets the various rooms we passed might hold. When André opened the door with an inviting "voilà," I stood still and in utter amazement. The room before me was filled with sunlight shining through the half-opened shutters outside the tall and slender windows, which were draped with heavy burgundy velvet and gathered on each side by thick golden cords with tassels. The walls were covered with burgundy damask. They were glistening from the sunlight. A delicately woven, light-blue Oriental carpet covered the center of the dark parquet floor. In one corner of the room stood a tall antique bed with gilded carvings at the head- and footboards. Above it was a lounge draped in the same burgundy damask as the walls. Pillows and covers were likewise of burgundy damask. Golden baroque candelabras with candles were attached to the walls of the room, illuminating oil paintings in gilded frames. Armchairs covered with purple velvet and contrasting with the golden, daintily carved back- and armrests stood on the carpet.

Next to the window sat a long and slender harpsichord of light wood with two keyboards. I noticed a second, smaller harpsichord sitting against the wall opposite the bed and a third one to my right. It caught my attention. The lid exposed a voluptuous and sensuous painting, which seemed to be of Ruben's period. André pointed out proudly that all of the instruments were antiques and each one had its special sound quality. But this afternoon, he sat down at the instrument next to the window. I believe it was made in Flanders. I had never listened to a harpsichordist up close and was fascinated and enchanted at the same time by the brilliancy yet fullness of the sound André brought forth so powerfully. The baroque atmosphere of the room harmonized with the music and took me back in time. The whole experience climaxed when the golden sun, orange, red, and purple, started to set behind the Château d'If in the immense Mediterranean Sea, tinting the room with a golden hue and endowing the musician at the harpsichord with an immortal shimmer.

I was still in a semi-trance as I packed my sexy black cocktail dress into the suitcase for my journey in celebration of the end of the year abroad. I had chosen Spain instead of Italy, because I felt I would need more time than I had at my disposal if I were to visit Italy. I did choose a tour that attracted French-speaking tourists, and was careful not to encourage any of my American friends to tag along. It was considered a deluxe bus trip, guaranteeing superior hotels, cuisine, etc.

I stepped onto the bus at a stop near the Rotonde, and off we went past Nîmes and Montpellier, where Doc had taken postgraduate courses in surgery, toward Carcassonne. As we approached the town, we saw the towers and double line of ramparts, with the twelfth-century castle in the distance. The evening air was pleasant, the charm of the town enticing, the group friendly and relaxed. Naïvely, I accepted an offer from the not-so-handsome guide, who took me to a few sites not included in the regular itinerary. At the hotel, I thanked him and went to my room. The guide, who had a face like an owl, suddenly stood right behind me at the door, obviously ready to cash in a reward for the detour. He wanted to come into my room. When I attempted to turn him away, perhaps too politely, he put his foot in the door to prevent me from closing it. I finally had to push him away. Luckily he was neither tall nor big. Regardless, from then on a dark cloud in the form of the obnoxious guide hung over my trip through Spain.

We did not spend much time in Carcassonne. We left right after we had walked through the medieval section of the city, whose narrow streets are still intact and have been fully restored. I personally prefer the medieval ambiance to the more ornate and colorful Spanish architecture, of which we got a first taste when we visited Spain's capital, Madrid, right in the center of the country. Of course, riding on the grand Paseo del Prado reminded me of my drive with Doc and Maria on the Paseo de la Reforma, in Mexico. In Madrid, I enjoyed the gardens and fountains and monuments. Just as impressive was the Prado, which connects two oval plazas. In the center of one is the *Fountain of Apollo* and in the other is an obelisk commemorating the uprising against Napoleon. We saw the Moorish influence on Spain's architecture when entering San Pedro, which is built on the site of a mosque, and spent a couple of hours in the Prado Museum to look at paintings by the numerous masters, before going to see the baroque Montserrat and many other imposing monuments, statues, etc.

It was easy to get used to the Spanish cuisine. The heavy wines helped to obscure the presence of the guide. He occasionally made a catty remark, which only hurt him, because a number of tourists in whom I had confided recommended that I report his actions to his superiors. Curiously enough, the plot thickened somewhat, because on the long drive to Toledo, the bus driver, Mario, took an obvious interest in me – maybe to protect me, I thought. He was very handsome; his background was French and Italian. He had dark-brown, wavy hair, tanned skin, black eyes, and a fabulous baritone voice. Most of all, he loved to sing arias from operas and operettas. Little by little, as I felt more confident, I joined him when he sang. Some of the tourists challenged us to sing duets, and before we knew it, we were entertaining the passengers by singing into the microphone. We earned much applause. The chemistry between us singers was intensifying, and our guide looked rather miserable.

Toledo, on the River Tagus, was only an hour southwest of Madrid. From a distance, it looked like a vast fortress. I did not know Cervantes described the main plaza in his *Novellas Ejemplares*. Of particular interest to me were the churches Santo Tomé and San Vicente. I saw several of El Greco's paintings for the first time inside a church. We visited a couple of the many chapels known for their impressive detail and their colorful windows of stained glass, and admired the restored gateway

Mudéjar Puerta del Sol before continuing on our long journey to Cordoba. There, we stayed at the well-known hotel Cordoba Palace, close to the Bullfight Museum, which housed the restaurant where we dined.

In this picturesque town, I fell in love with the narrow, winding streets typical of Moorish cities. The stucco of the houses was snow white. Many rust-colored clay pots filled with blossoming flowers – red, purple, yellow, and white – hung on the walls of the houses and sat on wrought-iron balconies or in front of black, stained window bars. Now and then an arch connected the opposite facades of the residences and accentuated the quaint look. The highlight of the stay in Cordoba was a visit to the *mezquita* (mosque), now a cathedral. It was founded by Abd al-Rahman, but at various intervals it was enlarged to its present size, a rectangle only a little smaller than St. Peter's in Rome. The labyrinth of hundreds of pillars perplexed me. They are about thirteen feet high and boldly combine marbles of many colors. The abundance of mosaic throughout the mosque felt overwhelming. When departing for Seville, we took the Moorish bridge with sixteen arches across the Guadalquivir River and left the Alcázar, or palace quarter, and the Tower of Calahorra behind us.

That morning, Mario handed me a small bouquet of wildflowers. It touched my heart. Some of my newfound friends teased me, the guide got nastier, and I retaliated verbally, in French, of course. At one point, he pulled me aside and offered me a free plane ticket back to Marseille, which my friends found preposterous. Mario told me to ignore the guy, which at times was not easy.

I had looked forward to Seville, and was not disappointed. You could sense the southern climate. I loved walking through the maze of narrow, twisting streets and the small, enclosed squares. Here too, the houses were built and adorned in the Moorish manner. I thought back to Mérida, when I had glimpses through doorways of beautiful little arcaded patios. Closer to the district near the cathedral and Alcázar, the layout of the city is more spacious. I recall the ceramic plaques bearing street names and others indicating houses and streets that figure in the works of Cervantes and other authors. I loved the picturesque quarter of Santa Cruz, which is associated with Dona Elvira, Don Juan, and Figaro, and was glad to hear the guide point out the rebuilt tobacco factory associated with the opera *Carmen*. We were taken to the splendid Alcázar Palace, dating back to the twelfth century, and stopped to see the impressive Torre del Oro, a decagonal brick tower. I will not list the numerous sites or the chapels with their sumptuous decor, be it Italian maiolica, brightly colored mosaics, or gold and silver decorative tiles. As the French used to exclaim, "C'est trop chargée" (It's overdone). We spent just enough time at the museum, and saw works by Goya and Murillo, among others.

A visit to Seville, famous for its bullfights, would not be complete without attending one of these Spanish national spectacles. I noticed right away that the arena in Seville was much smaller than the fifty-thousand-seat Plaza de Toros in Mexico City, where I had witnessed the show with Doc ten years before. Here in Seville, the event proceeded as in Mexico, starting with the grand entry procession. The costumes of the different participants were elaborate to the point of being luxurious, with gold and silver trim similar to that worn by their counterparts on the other side of the Atlantic. Six bulls were killed in as skillful a manner as possible. Each matador received an ear of the bull; one got both ears and the tail at the end from a dignitary, with the audience roaring. We sat much closer to the ring than in Mexico, where we sat high in the ranks. When the last bull began to bleed from the impact of the pike poles, I started to feel slightly sick and turned away. No more bullfights for me.

Later that night, after dinner, our group went to see a dance performance. Professional dancers presented an array of exotic dances. Their costumes were bright and beautiful, their movements and rhythm graceful and precise. We were invited to join them on the dance floor. The leader of the group, a very slender man of about thirty and a superb dancer, his hair combed back and glued to his skull, came toward me across the dance floor and invited me to dance with him. I was wearing my black dress – and felt flattered that he asked me. We danced extremely well together. I loved it, as I always do when I have a chance to dance. When it was time to return to the hotel, my Spanish partner did not want me to leave. Indeed, he was very insistent and offered to take me back to the hotel in a limousine. A couple of my friends came up to help, and finally I was able to break away. He kept saying, "J'ai tellement soif de dancer avec vous!" (I have such a desire to dance with you!). I think Mario was glad when I showed up at the bus. We were to leave early in the morning for the seaport of Cadiz, located at the inlet of the Atlantic, from which we would take a boat to Morocco, Africa, and spend a couple of days in Tangier.

It felt refreshing to cross over to Tangier on a boat and observe how the city rises almost like an amphitheater as it is approached. As we disembarked, it was exciting to be greeted by a crowd of men and women so differently dressed. Black men in long, blue-and-white-striped frocks wearing cylindrical, burgundy felt hats with a dangling tassel came to usher us into the waiting cabs, which took us through the streets of this exotic city to the exquisite El Minzah Hotel, in the center of the town. It was surrounded by beautiful gardens and offered a magnificent view down on the blue waters of the Straits of Gibraltar, which are only eight and a half miles wide. There, the waters of the Atlantic and the Mediterranean mingle. The El Minzah was by far the most luxurious hotel we had stayed in. My thirst for exotic atmospheres was abundantly satisfied. I loved the multicolored, round ottomans covered with Moroccan leather that rested on tastefully arranged Persian rugs spread out on highly polished parquet floors in the elegant foyer. From this point, an entire wall of glass doors led toward the gardens and a big swimming pool, framed with green lawns and palm trees. The ceiling was decorated with purple and golden mosaics. The dining-room decor projected a simple elegance. In the center of the courtyard was a splashing fountain, reminiscent of the courtyard at Hotel Mérida in Yucatán. Underneath the arcades were tables and chairs where one could sit at breakfast. Pots of hibiscus were arranged around the fountain, and palm trees stood next to the columns supporting the arcades, studded with mosaics.

We slept well in the exquisite suites reserved for us; and I felt almost guilty the next day, when I witnessed how devastating poverty contrasted with ultimate luxury in this city, which had a strong presence of Europeans and Muslims as well as other international cultures. When walking through the streets, I was intrigued by the women draped in white and carrying wares on their heads, who reminded me of the women in their white and embroidered dresses in Mérida, Mexico. Though I had seen poverty already in the countryside of Michigan, on the Yucatán Peninsula, and in the streets of İzmir, Turkey, it paled in comparison to what I observed along the sidewalks in Tangier. Perhaps it resulted from the fact that I stood right next to it. At one street corner, a tiny, very old, severely emaciated woman, draped in a light-gray cloth, barely revealing the hollow eyes in her haggard and tanned face, caught my attention. She sat on the sidewalk, bent over an old, crumpled newspaper spread out in front of her on which fewer than a dozen green apples, smaller than golf balls, lay spread out for sale. A feeling of great sorrow and helplessness overcame me. A small distance from her stood a thin little boy, barefoot. After I gave him a dollar bill while passing by, I suddenly noticed that the boy was following me. He clung to me for a long time. I was told I should not have given him a dollar, because to him it had an unusually high value. When we walked through the Sultan's Palace shortly afterward, I still had a hard time wiping the incidents from my mind.

I did like the Mediterranean ambiance and the proximity of the sea. I took a few hours to bask in the sun on the beach and go for a swim before venturing out toward the highest point of Tangier. I took in the grand panorama of the city with the bay below, the many boats, and the Rock of Gibraltar across the Straits. We were close to the desert up there, and I simply had to climb onto a camel once more. The Arab driver was particularly handsome. It was a fitting good-bye from Africa.

After we had set across the Straits, we settled quickly in the Rock Hotel in Gibraltar and took in a few sights, such as the Cathedral, the Governor's Palace, and the Promenade through the lush Alameda Gardens. But I remember Gibraltar most for the rock apes, who love to roam the Upper Rock, an open park. We bought bananas to feed the monkeys and had fun watching their acrobatics. At one point, my friend pulled me aside suddenly, telling me I had a huge blood stain on the back and lower part of my bright-yellow dress. I had no idea as to how that could be, and I borrowed a sweater and tied it around my waist. How embarrassing! We discovered later that a monkey had bitten the finger of a lady feeding it a banana as she stood behind me. The blood had squirted out and splashed on my dress. Watch out for monkeys!

The trip lasted sixteen days, and at this point there were six to go, which I will treat in a more summary fashion, since I do not want my memoirs to become a full-fledged travelogue. You can rest assured that wherever we stopped, the people who arranged the trip made certain we saw all the sights the city had to offer and then some, as my copious slides will attest. At times, they spiced the evenings with entertainment. In the ancient Moorish city of Granada, Andalusia, after visiting the Alhambra, we relaxed in the Grotto of the Sacred Mountain and watched a passionate dance by the fiery *Gitanos* (Gypsies) in their brightly colored dresses, accompanying their dancing with castanets. I thought once more of Bizet's opera *Carmen*. The same evening, we went dancing once more ourselves. A very handsome Spaniard asked to dance with me. A group of locals watched as we twirled across the polished dance floor. I was excited myself, but was in my mischievous mood. Actually, I had decided that in the future, I would try to be in greater control of my heart when it came to men. After all, I had experienced my share of disappointments and would make sure that no male interfered with my new career as a student. I flirted with the Spaniard, intentionally leading him on to the point that he began to press me tighter against his chest. The moment he thought he had me in his spell, I stopped, excused myself, and walked away to dance with Mario, who took over the lead gladly.

I would have been disappointed had they not taken us to the quarters of Santiago near Guadix to see the caves in which the Gypsies live. I was surprised how well these quarters in the hills were kept, at least those we were shown. We stopped briefly in Alicante and rested at the beach, and I wondered where Sibby's condo would be and whether she still saw the Count, with whom she went horseback riding on the beach almost daily and who sent her fresh flowers every day, even when she was back in Hannover. It was one of her many tales I never felt I could believe. In Valencia, considered the richest town in Spain, we saw more churches, the Plaza del Caudillo, and a good example of flamboyant architecture in the Lonja de la Seda (Silk Exchange), which I found to be quite showy, to say the least. We left the Hotel Astoria early and went to Barcelona by way of Tarragona.

After having seen an abundance of Barcelona's architectural jewels, I opted to take a tour to Montserrat, to see the mysterious and celebrated *Black Madonna*. It was well worth the fifty-mile trip. The Benedictine monastery was built into a massive conglomeration of gray stones of vast proportions, and it has an overwhelming appearance. The serrated stone masses, with their jagged pinnacles and spires, stretch high into the sky. While the mountain is over four thousand feet high, the monastery stands right on the edge, about three thousand feet from the base. One cannot but wonder what would happen to the structure in the event of a tremor or other unexpected natural phenomenon. Hopefully, the *Black Madonna*, originally brought here for safekeeping by the Moors, will protect it. She is now patron saint of Catalonia and is said to attract thousands of pilgrims each year. I had not yet seen a "black" Madonna. She was carved out of wood and very small, but dressed in luxurious robes studded with the most precious jewels. Once you have seen her, the image is impressed in your mind forever.

Our last night was spent in Montpellier after a scenic drive along the Costa Brava and a luncheon in the small town Figueras. Unfortunately, we arrived too late for me to visit the university or walk around the town, since a good-bye dinner was scheduled at the Hotel de la Metropole. As usual, wine was served with dinner. As we chatted, a group of Spaniards sang passionately, playing their guitars. Our guide walked around the tables, talking to each one of us in a last attempt to butter us up for a good-bye tip. I felt happy and was entertaining my table with stories from my days at Sankt Ursula – when I suddenly felt something liquid on the top of my head. Before I knew it, red, thick wine was dripping down my face and on my light-blue dress. I turned around and saw the guide, laughing while emptying a bota bag – made of sheepskin in the Basque region and filled with the rather sweet and syrupy local red wine which was served with the dessert – over my head. The people at my table were ready to tackle him, but I preferred to make light of his "sweet" good-bye gesture. He is still waiting for a tip. Instead of filing a complaint with his company in Nice, I got off the bus in Aix, waved good-bye, and gave Mario a hug. I was ready to pick up my trunk at Rue de la Violette and head back home to Germany in my Bug.

The drive north was great. I was more confident than before; my French had improved enormously. I felt free as a bird, because I was sure not even Erich could lure me back into his realm, even if I were to see him again. I took my time and chose a route homeward that would take me to places I had wanted to see for a long time, like Mont Blanc, in Chamonix, and Paris.

Mont Blanc, Doc's Mountain – Switzerland and Paris

I drove to Chamonix by way of Grenoble but did not drop in on my new friends from the Spain adventure, Francis and Elvira. Since I have a penchant for mountains, I took a detour whenever I saw a special scenic spot, stopping, spreading out a blanket, and consuming the snacks I had picked up along the way. The weather was perfect. I could see Mont Blanc, covered with snow and ice, in the distance. It was a monumental and majestic mountain massif, almost 16,000 feet high. Something inside me stirred. I stopped the car at a point where the mountain was in full view. I got out, stood in awe, and sent a silent greeting and a "thanks" to Doc. Before me stood the highest mountain in Europe. It was this mountain that Doc, together with two companions and two official guides, had successfully ascended forty-eight years earlier, on June 19. It was the end of June when I was there. According to the certificate, the summit was at 4,810 meters, and it took sixteen hours to reach. As I stood there, I remembered Doc telling me that at one point he had slipped into a crevice. Thanks to the rope around his waist and the guides' assistance, he was saved and continued. It was hard to believe I had been married to one of the few men who had conquered this mountain. I found it interesting that the first man to ascend the mountain, in 1786, was also a doctor, Michel Gabriel Paccard from Chamonix.

Chamonix was a most charming mountain resort, famous for attracting numerous famous poets, including Goethe and Victor Hugo, as well as members of royal families. It is also the place from which the majority of mountain climbers start their ascent. I located a lovely room in an inn right in the village, from which I could easily get around on foot. I marveled at the glaciers, which reminded me of the ones I had seen in Glacier National Park with Doc twelve years earlier and the one at the Groß Glockner, which I had seen with Mutti. A major attraction was a large, cave-like room carved out of a glacier. Its walls, like thick glass, shone in a radiant emerald green, and in the absence of other tourists, I felt removed into an ethereal realm.

En route to Paris, I found truly fairy-tale lodgings in Lucerne, Switzerland. Schloß Gütsch stood high on the edge of the city, with a view down over the red-tiled rooftops onto Lake Lucerne. My room was in the tower of the small, freshly renovated castle, and I wished Sibby could have seen it, because this round room, decorated in antique furniture from the region and offering the best view possible, was so much more beautiful than her room at Sankt Ursula; in fact, it surpassed any hotel room I had theretofore encountered. A major asset was a private terrace outside my room. I went sightseeing for a couple of days before driving to Paris, where I should have spent much more time than the few days I had left.

I cannot attempt to do Paris justice in these pages. Paris, on the River Seine, bursts with life and excitement day and night. As a newcomer, one does not have to think where to start. Paris spellbinds you from the minute you arrive and long after you have left. You do not need a fancy room at a hotel, because you fall into the short, narrow bed with a brass head- and footboard the minute you return from walking the bustling streets of this exhilarating place. I loved everything I experienced and saw, be it walking through the narrow streets, looking for a sidewalk café to sip a cup of coffee, watching an artist next to me sketching the wrought-iron gate in front of a house across the street, or pausing for a few minutes to listen to a couple of violinists play a Mozart duet. I allowed myself to be lured by a group of singers in front of the Notre Dame Cathedral. After having stood in wonder and stared at the huge rose window, I felt myself in agreement with everything Professor Bourde had taught us about Gothic architecture and cathedrals. Since the Sainte-Chapelle was nearby, I had to see this beautiful work of Gothic art, filled with the most invigorating pieces of stained glass. Like most tourists, I climbed the Eiffel Tower, almost one thousand feet high, and was lucky it was not raining, which would have spoiled the panoramic view of Paris by night. It was impossible to miss the Arc de Triomphe, located on the west end of the Champs-Élysées, and like most tourists, I went to the highest point of Paris to inspect the monumental Montmartre. I particularly enjoyed walking through the streets in Montmartre, with their old buildings and shops.

I took a tourist bus to the Palace of Versailles, the extraordinary lifetime achievement of Louis XIV, where I spent hours walking through its fabulous wings and formal gardens and met a high-school principal from Accra, Ghana, with whom I ended up exchanging addresses – something I came to regret a couple of years later. I spent less than a day at the Louvre, where I looked at the Old Masters and, right when I stepped into the spacious hall, marveled at the gigantic, yet exceedingly graceful, Nike, winged goddess of victory. I was particularly interested in Greek sculpture and drifted easily toward the Apollo, the Venus de Milo, and other Greek and Roman sculptures before ending my educational journey with a visit to the Impressionists and a farewell to Leonardo da Vinci's *Mona Lisa*.

New Family Problems and Heartaches

On my return, the atmosphere in Hannover was shockingly sobering and anticlimactic. I realized once more why I had left that city, and its rather monotonous environment, in 1954. I had a couple of weeks left to say good-bye to old friends once more. I drove to Münster to bring the Padre up to date. He was then head of a seminary for priests and seemed to like me even more than he did fifteen years earlier. As always, he put his arms around me, held me tight against his broad chest, told me to be silent for a minute and breathe deeply, and whispered a sonorous "God bless you" into my ear.

I had ignored Erich's various attempts to contact me in France. My studies were my priority. But since I was back in Hannover for a couple of weeks, I was suddenly tempted to contact him. For some inexplicable reason, passions flared up with him (as always), but I did not give in to his pleas to stay with him in Germany, because my trust in him had faded. We took a few day trips to the beautiful Harz region and the Steinhuder Meer. I felt good about myself. I had learned in Spain to control my emotions and shed no more tears when we kissed good-bye. Yet I did not tell him to stop writing.

Sibby, who received me in a bright-red silk kimono, which looked seductive against her arms and legs, snow white though still full of freckles, brought me up to date on some of our Sankt Ursula chums. Rose's first husband, a pilot, had died in a crash, but she found solace with a new husband, a former priest, no less. Maria, after several disappointments, had landed an attorney for a husband, and Nanni, the blond, married another blond after she had gotten over Hubert. The Padre's housekeeper, whom he left behind in Hannover to cook for the rest of the Jesuits, had suffered from severe depression, almost leading to suicide. They had sent her to recuperate on a ranch with riding horses. Her parents used to own a stable, where she rode horses until the Russians took possession of their land. She confided in me that my first and great love, Hans, after hearing about my marriage to Doc, married another Catholic girl, nicknamed "Little Red Riding Hood" because her hair was red. Mollie and several others had a bunch of children, and were presumably happy with what sounded to me like a very colorless, philistine existence.

But Sibby's own story turned out to be the most dramatic. The love of her life, Franzi, had married her mother's sister, wife of a well-known architect in Hannover. Sibby was shattered when he informed her that he wanted to break off the engagement. He had gotten her aunt, about fifteen years older, pregnant at a New Year's Eve party. Unsuccessful in conceiving from her husband for many years, she was able to have the marriage annulled. This was important, since all parties involved were Catholic. The affair caused quite a stir in Hannover. – Sibby then met and married a so-called stateless but very slick businessman of Hungarian background when she realized she was pregnant by him. The father-to-be was a few years older. Once the child was born, the father took up with the wife of the CEO of Royal Dutch Airlines and got her pregnant as well. Sibby divorced him only to discover that he had robbed her of a great portion of her wealth. She had entrusted him with her rather substantial financial affairs, and claims she never retrieved any of the money. He married the Royal Dutch Airlines divorcée and reportedly never once bothered to look after his daughter with Sibby. Sibby, after several unsuccessful attempts to commit suicide with the help of gas from her stove, met, fell in love with, and got engaged to a man more than twice her age, but not as old as Doc. The engagement was terminated when Sibby, who had taken up with one of the attorney's sons, considerably younger than she, had found herself pregnant once more. The father threw out the son, vowing to disinherit him. The son married Sibby shortly after their daughter was born. They had a son a year or two later.

Sibby's young husband was still completing his Army service when I met him. At that time, he was helping with chores and gardening around the house. He was a nice-looking chap and intelligent enough for Sibby to provide for him and his education at the university. The marriage seemed to be harmonious on the surface, until it became obvious to Sibby that her young husband was having an affair with another older woman right under her nose, that is, in her own house. When he asked Sibby to get involved in a ménage à trois, she filed for a divorce, which resulted in another case of nonsupport – this time for two children. I suppose they all figured Sibby was wealthy enough to take care of their offspring. In the midst of all these rather sordid goings-on, Franz appeared on the scene whenever it pleased him, often drunk, as the story goes. She was forever hoping he would divorce her aunt, but over the years they had had more children. Sibby looked as beautiful as always, yet a narrow strand of silver-gray hair revealed she was aging. My hair had started to turn gray not long after Doc passed away. I used a tint to hide it when I was twenty-seven years old.

I remained true to the promise I made to myself the day of Aunt Lisa's funeral service, when Uncle Hannes forbade me to talk to the priests. I avoided Großförste. I did go back once before leaving for the United States, but not to visit Aunt Stingy and her brute. When I came home from Aix, my Uncle Franz, the invalid with the traveling splinter from World War I, was living with my parents. They had taken him into their home because he had been squeezed out of his lifelong homestead, which, as you recall, was an addition to my grandparents' main house. When the economic miracle in Germany took off in the 50s, Aunt Stingy, thirteen years younger than her husband, my Uncle Hannes, took over the scepter with an iron hand, bought a used truck to replace the horse-drawn carts, added the sale of oil to that of coal, and sat next to the truck driver to supervise the delivery (in a chronicle, Aunt Stingy was referred to as "the motor" of the business). As the money rolled in and Uncle Hannes's health was failing, she prompted the downfall of the old homestead. It was replaced with a new, more modern, and bigger house. Bathrooms, kitchen, etc. were up to par. Then there was Uncle Franz, whose humble abode was sacrificed mercilessly. To compensate him, she put him up in a small room in the new house and tolerated his presence, at least for a while.

I sat next to Uncle Franz on the thickly upholstered couch in our living room and listened to his story. He really did not sob or express any anger, but spoke in a soft voice, filled with sadness. His spirit seemed broken and he was rather helpless. It was obvious that Aunt Stingy, as soon as her husband passed away, made his life in the house miserable until he finally found refuge in a neighbor's big, red-brick farmhouse. It was not easy to coexist in the village. It was a known fact that his sister-in-law did not treat him well. His older sisters, Aunt Sissy and Aunt Anna, used to complain about the cruel way in which they behaved toward their parents and, now, their second-oldest brother. Eventually, my parents invited him to stay with them in the apartment, because all of the children were gone and Erich had moved out.

During my discussions with Uncle Franz, it became clear to me that staying with my parents was not ideal for him either. As his attacks were totally unpredictable – he would fall to the ground without warning, depending on the location of the splinter – life in the city could be more dangerous than life in the country. I also learned that my father, dissatisfied with the monthly rent Uncle Franz paid for his room, tried to convince him to change his will to favor our family as opposed to dividing the inheritance among the rest of his siblings, that is, those who had children. I was disturbed when I found out about it and told him to do no such thing, because he was paying a monthly rent and was under no obligation to give more to us kids. Indeed, I told him he could do with his inheritance whatever he liked. He looked at me with his big brown eyes, smiled a bit, took my hand, and told me that of all the relatives, I was the most just. I asked him if he would like for me to help him find a place in St. Konrad, a home run by Sisters in his hometown. His eyes lit up, and he assured me he would really like that. I contacted the kind Sisters, who said they would love to take him, though their establishment was not very big. The home was almost next door to the cemetery, where he could visit the graves of his wife Lisa and daughter Elisabeth whenever he wanted. We agreed to a time when I could drop him off. I was lucky to have my little VW and was relieved to have done the right thing when we said good-bye at his new place. I was only a few hundred feet away from Aunt Stingy's house, but it never occurred to me to say hello. A year later, on May 12, 1968, Uncle Franz died and was buried next to his loved ones.

After all was settled, I had a heated discussion with my father. Mutti tried not to get involved. I was rather blunt about the matter of the will and told him in so many words that I disagreed with his code of ethics. The argument escalated when I crossed over into other territory, that is, the question that burned on my lips and had cropped up more and more frequently over the years: why did he join the Brownshirts? I don't know how many times he insisted not to have known what was going on with the Jews. I never could bring myself to believe him, even after Heinz Loeser told me I should have. I kept suggesting he could have packed up and left the country with us as others did, etc. His answer came like a refrain: "You don't know what you are talking about – where should we have gone?" He kept insisting that as an employee of the court, he had to join the party to protect his job and his family. Dad had a bad temper, and he almost threw me out each time I visited and drilled him with my questions. However, his anger always subsided rather quickly, and before I took off for America, he did everything possible to help me pack, carry suitcases, and run errands, and he assisted with the transport of my Bug to the port in Bremerhafen. He got over the Uncle Franz episode by the time my plane started in the direction of Newark, New Jersey, where I had to pick up the VW. I had shipped it to America on the SS *United States*.

Attorney James Dies – Student Life in Bloomington, Indiana – Good, Excellent, and Eccentric Professors and Fellow Students

My Bug was waiting for me at the pier, and I drove carefully through Newark. The streets were almost empty. I got a glimpse of the buildings and stores that were burned down and destroyed during the riots, which had taken place in Detroit and Newark during the months prior to my arrival and while I was still in France. The burned-out buildings and broken display windows reminded me vaguely of the streets in Hannover after Crystal Night. I was afraid, and made sure the car doors were locked. I was glad when I reached the highway, which took me homeward to Dowagiac, Michigan, where all my friends and Mr. James were anxiously awaiting me. I had agreed to substitute for Mr. James's secretary while she was on vacation, so I rented a room near the office until it was time to go to Bloomington, Indiana, for the beginning of the fall semester of 1967.

Mr. James had taken good care of my T-bird. When I backed it out of the garage where it had been stored, it seemed huge – as long as a cruise ship. It took a couple of days to get used to it. The difference between it and the VW, which I parked behind Mr. James's office, was enormous. – At the firm, the clients were happy to see me. Mr. James was relieved that I went to work immediately. He told me right away that during my absence, the income for the year had decreased by more than

$10,000. I discovered quickly that a number of important responsibilities, such as the Claspy rental accounts, had been neglected for months. My substitute had obviously been incapable of handling the many probate matters I had taken care of.

In an attempt to finalize my admission to the Bloomington campus, I ran into major difficulties. Although they had informed me over the phone prior to my leaving for France that there would be no problem transferring my credits, they suddenly reneged. I wasted no time, got into my T-bird, and sped to Bloomington in record time. After five hours of intensive discussions with various deans – waiting for more than an hour on the floor outside the office of one of them – I finally got results. After they had looked through my documents and transcripts from the Institute as well as the glowing letters of recommendation, they agreed to accept the credits, but not the grades, which eventually cost me the Phi Beta Kappa award.

I took advantage of my Bloomington trip to find an apartment and spent a night in a modest motel, from which I called more than thirty-five landlords. Apartments cost between $125 and $180 per month, much more than I could afford. At the point of sheer exhaustion, I found a humble place on Woodburn Street for $80, which I took, even though it was still more than I had expected to pay. It was a built-out attic with slanted walls throughout. There was a bed and a table behind a curtain between the living area and the place to sleep. A small gas stove stood on one side of the sink and a refrigerator on the other. A vinyl-covered couch sat in front of the curtain separating the living and sleeping areas, and a worn-down easy chair with an even more antiquated reading lamp stood opposite the couch. A table and four chairs were located in a space close to the refrigerator. The bathroom consisted of a narrow shower stall, a tiny lavatory, and a stool. I had to climb up a shaky wooden outside stairway that ended on a small wooden deck to gain entrance to my hideaway apartment. Believe it or not, there was room on one wall for my SABA, and the TV found a place in front of the window in the living area. The big advantages of the place were a sizable storage area underneath a portion of the roof and a detached garage located in an alley.

Mr. James was happy that my trip to the campus turned out comparatively well. Over and over, he told me how happy he was to see me and how pleased he was that my year abroad had been so successful. It appeared that the marriage to his second wife, Evelyn, was not as rosy as it should have been. I thought it was strange that he ate breakfast in restaurants and that at times his shirts were not ironed or lacked a button. Though he never complained, even before I left, he had told me Evelyn complained that he could get along without her but not without me. She was obviously jealous, yet I had no idea as to how strongly she resented me. It became clear to me over the years that since I had been married to a much older man, other older men tended to look at me as though they might have a chance, and some wives feared their husbands might like me too much.

1961–1972

Mr. James hated to see me get ready for Bloomington, yet assisted in any way he could. He helped find a buyer for my VW. On an installment plan guaranteed by a promissory note, Bertha, his unique black client, bought my car for a few hundred dollars more than I had paid for it. Mr. James was kind enough to take care of the paperwork and accompanied Bertha to transfer the title on August 25, 1967, a day after I had come back from Bloomington. He returned to the office at noon, locked the front glass door, leaned against the counter, and handed me the papers. He told me he was not feeling right and asked me to help him to the leather couch in his back office and library. His forehead was covered with perspiration as I helped him lie down on the couch. He asked me to hand him a wastepaper basket and get a damp towel. I wiped his forehead with the cloth and opened his belt. He turned pale, and I rushed to the telephone to call the hospital. Then I tried to call Evelyn, but she did not answer. The ambulance arrived minutes later and took him to the nearby hospital. That same afternoon, I was told he had passed away at 6:00 p.m. of a heart attack and severe emphysema.

Thus, almost ten years after Doc had passed away so suddenly and unexpectedly, Mr. James, who had been a true friend, counselor, and guardian for seven years, had left even more quickly. I was sad and devastated. To make it worse, Evelyn banned me from the office. She seemed to blame me for not notifying her sooner. I spent two nights with the Loesers and was glad I had talked Mr. James, whose will I had typed, out of leaving anything to me. The funeral had to be postponed, because his son Frank was visiting his sister Sally in Bogotá. Mr. Hoff, Mr. James's former partner and my former boss, called and told me to ignore Evelyn's resentment. He virtually begged me to come and help him with Mr. James's affairs, since nobody was better acquainted with his personal business and his practice than I. I relented and worked hard until late at night and on weekends, collecting data for Mr. Hoff to facilitate probating the estate. In fact, I worked until it was time to leave for Bloomington on September 9. The movers were scheduled to arrive on the 13th, and school started on the 16th. In the end, I was glad I could help. It was my thank-you to Mr. James for all he had done for me. I told Mr. Hoff I did not want to be compensated for my time.

I turned my personal files over to Mr. Hoff the day before I was ready to head south. As I cruised along the rather straight and uninteresting Highway 31 toward Indianapolis, where I picked up Highway 37 South to Bloomington, I reflected on the timing of Mr. James's demise. It was as though he had waited until I returned for a last farewell. I thanked him again, as I have many times since, for encouraging me to forge ahead with my academic ambitions and for teaching me about law and justice, fairness and compassion, and what strength of character is all about. I interpreted Mr. James's death as a final sign to follow Professor d'Anselme's advice. I was then certain that instead of law, I was destined to study German literature.

The rolling hills on Highway 37 were covered with forests and meadows, which reminded me of the countryside in the Sauerland in Germany. My big, heavy car cruised along the highway smoothly. I appreciated the wide roads, the open landscape, and the absence of heavy traffic. It felt good to drive into this college town, which was smaller than the adjoining campus. I was relieved to have a place to stay. My humble abode was cozy, quiet, and most of all, the perfect place to study.

While trying to locate the various buildings where my classes were held, I got acquainted with the beautiful campus, which covered almost two thousand acres and dates back to the 1820s. The aesthetically pleasing and homogeneous architecture of the light-gray limestone buildings impressed me. They contrasted invitingly with the well-kept lawns and a multitude of mature trees on the university grounds, transforming it into an enormous park. Carefully planted flowerbeds accentuated the beauty of the campus everywhere. Flowerbeds also highlighted the big *Showalter Fountain*, in front of the auditorium, and the Lilly Library, which houses rare-book collections. The large fountain, with Venus in the center and surrounded by dancing dolphins spouting water, reminded me of the Fontaine de la Rotonde, in Aix. Students sat chatting on benches and lawns near scenic spots. They relaxed beneath trees by a small, meandering brook flowing through the grounds close to Ballantine Hall and stole a quick kiss now and then. I felt lucky when I found a parking place next to the notable Memorial Union and close to Ballantine Hall, the high-rise, where I attended most of my classes. It felt good that I would finally be part of a real university.

I was then thirty-five years old and made a promise to myself to have my PhD in hand before I turned forty. I did not foresee any major problems, since I had made the honors list throughout my college years. I had to enroll in a host of required courses. Being a native speaker of German and having decided to major in German languages and literature, I was able to skip several 300-level courses and take the 400-level courses necessary to complete my major in German. I was also permitted to enroll in two instead of the usual four successive German honors courses required for graduation with honors. It meant writing an honors thesis of more than fifty pages by the time I graduated. Having written numerous papers in France, I did not anticipate that this would be a problem. I also found out that I could fulfill the language requirement for the PhD by taking French in depth instead of two additional languages. I continued with advanced courses in French, taking grammar and literature courses, which focused on works from the Middle Ages to the present. All of my French professors were excellent, though Professor Quentin Hope and Madame Gérard were my favorites. They seemed more at ease and thus more exciting and dynamic than their younger colleagues. All along, I continued corresponding in French with my good friends in Aix, Grénoble, and Marseille.

I was also permitted to take an overload of courses and completed six courses in the fall and five in the spring semester, earning a 3.38 GPA in the fall and a 4.0 in the spring. I had to take a psychology lab, which gave me headaches. It required more work than any of the other courses, because I had to deal with probability and had no idea what it was all about. Though I aced my homework with the help of review books for math and had a real knack for training the cute white rats to rotate the wheels in their glass cages, I earned poor grades on exams because I was too slow and very nervous and at times drew a blank. It was sheer luck that I earned a C. As it turned out, 1968 was the only year in which the IU football team went to the Rose Bowl. The psychology professor was so excited he did not give a final exam. Strangely enough, the football player who made the decisive goal that sent the team to the Rose Bowl later built the house in which I live today.

In the first semester, I had a young assistant professor who taught a survey course on German literature to 1750. In comparison to my professors in France, this professor, the offspring of the Wedgewood china manufacturer, was utterly disappointing. To make it worse, whenever he switched from English to German, it was so flawed that it was difficult to concentrate on the content of his lectures. I earned a B, which turned out to be the only B I earned in all the German and French literature courses I took in Bloomington or elsewhere, be it for the BA, MA, or PhD. The young man either left or was let go a year or two later. Rumor had it that he joined a commune.

Associate Professor Lawrence Frye introduced me, in his German honors courses, to works by German romanticists such as E. T. A. Hoffmann. He had written his dissertation on Novalis, another well-known German writer of the period. Much to my surprise, Dr. Frye taught the course in English, but he was engaging and knew how to get us three or four students involved in intense discussions by asking very thought-provoking questions. Yet, at times, I had no idea what he was leading up to, and neither did the other students in the class. Instead of probing to get the answer he wanted, he tended to follow up with a completely new question. I quickly became fascinated with Hoffmann's works. Besides, this genius had made his mark not only as a writer, but also as a composer, conductor, pianist, painter, music critic, and satirist. Further, he had been an outstanding and controversial judge and had changed his middle name from Wilhelm to Amadeus out of love for Mozart's compositions. I admired these qualities, talents, and skills greatly. I chose a topic for the honors thesis quickly: music and magic in E. T. A. Hoffmann's works. I could have written the thesis in English, but as a Germanist, I felt it was imperative to write in German. Professor d'Anselme had allowed me to write my papers for comparative literature in German whenever I was writing about books by German writers.

I enjoyed Dr. Frye's classes and ignored the rumors that were flying around. He was divorced and supposedly had been intimate with a host of graduate students. He was tall and slender, with brown hair and brown eyes, and not exactly unattractive. I personally had trouble watching him speak in front of the class, because white foam used to collect at the corner and lower lip of his mouth. It stayed there until he would swallow it. I found it distracting and nauseating. Whenever he called me to his office for a private audience, I tried to look past him and out the window. I never understood why some fellow students thought he had great sex appeal.

I was rather pleased when I earned my BA with honors at the end of the spring semester of 1968. It was during this semester that, shortly before finals time, on April 4, the world was shocked by the assassination of Martin Luther King Jr.

During the graduation ceremonies, I sat in the blistering sun in the huge stadium to receive my diploma, bound in soft, red leather, and vowed to myself that it would be the first and last time. I suffered through it mostly because the Gebhards had come to campus, as had my brother Alfons and his wife Gerda. I did not invite other friends, because I had not had time to form solid friendships and was not in the habit of hanging out on campus. I took pride in all the congratulatory telegrams and cards and wished Doc could have been there. He would have been so pleased. We snapped plenty of photos, even though I did not like myself in the gown and hat and felt the white honors cords with tassels looked rather skimpy.

As a result of graduating with honors in German, I was invited to join the German honorary society Delta Phi Alpha and was courted by three good institutions to pursue my graduate studies in their departments: the University of Illinois in Urbana, the University of Michigan in Ann Arbor, and Northwestern in Chicago. They offered excellent financial assistance as well. I had also considered applying to Harvard, but after lengthy consideration, I decided to stay in Bloomington. At that time, IU was known for having the number-one German department in the country. I knew my chances for a scholarship were slim and that I would have to cover my expenses without outside assistance. I had four strikes against me: (1) it was considered inbreeding, because I came from a regional campus, (2) I was older, (3) I was a woman, and (4) they thought I was better-off than others because I drove a T-bird and wore nice dresses instead of blue jeans.

I did apply for and was granted a modest National Defense Loan for four semesters. It was useful inasmuch as the payments from the sale of the Croft were not enough to cover tuition for graduate courses, the cost of books, rent, and my car, and other living expenses. I was reluctant to dip too deeply into my savings, and lived frugally. I had enough clothes from my secretarial days – and concerning food, unlike most of my friends, who lived to eat, I ate to live. I cooked big quantities of spaghetti, sprinkled some soy sauce and a couple of teaspoons of margarine on it, and never got tired of eating the same dish days in a row. It was a quick meal and satisfied my stomach. On Sundays, I treated myself to something different. I did not indulge in any form of entertainment, be it movies, theater, or going for a drive in Brown County.

1961–1972

Two months after Martin Luther King Jr.'s assassination and just before the commencement of the summer session, on June 6, 1968, Bobby Kennedy was assassinated while campaigning for the Democratic presidential nomination.

I enrolled in two graduate courses, audited Dr. Frye's course on German romanticism, earned a GPA of 4.0, and was content. One of the courses was "The Age of Goethe." It turned out to be one of the most memorable courses I took at IU. My professor was Hans Jaeger, professor emeritus of German. He had come to Bloomington from Germany by way of Princeton University, and he greatly influenced my love of literature, in particular of the Goethe period. I was well prepared for the class, because I had read most of the works twice by the time they came up for discussion. Some students had barely read the works at all. It got to the point that Professor Jaeger told me not to raise my hand each time and to give the others a chance. When nobody had anything to contribute, I think he was glad that at least one student had something to say. A couple of native German students made fun of me by greeting me with "good morning, Dr. Beardsley." I replied, "Professor Dr., please." I did ace the course, but found out later from Professor Jaeger that he was shocked when he first read my final exam. Every answer was wrong. He had looked at my blue book to get an idea as to how the rest of the class might do. When he noticed I had answered each question incorrectly, he was stunned – until he realized he had used old exams and by mistake given me a different test than the rest of the class. I found out later that several students had gained access to the old exams and prepared for the final accordingly. Of course, they did not do as well as they had expected. I never told Professor Jaeger.

Professor Jaeger's health was failing. He suffered from asthma so badly he had to use an inhaler frequently. He had sustained an injury to his leg and needed crutches to walk. Worst of all, his eyesight was weakening. He was a gem of a professor. His genuine love of literature and drama was evident. A most touching and memorable incident occurred one day. It had come to my attention that he excelled in reciting passages from plays. I asked him if he would read a passage from Goethe's *Torquato Tasso* for us. He answered sadly that he was afraid he would not be able to read the fine print. I apologized. Much to my surprise, toward the end of the next class, he told us that since a student had requested it, he would read Tasso's final words to Antonio. He pulled out several sheets of paper on which he had printed the text in big black letters. He read with his clear, sonorous voice the poet Tasso's gripping words, of which I will cite the final verses:

> Zerbrochen ist das Steuer, und es kracht
> Das Schiff an allen Seiten. Berstend reißt
> Der Boden unter meinen Füßen auf!
> Ich fasse dich mit beiden Armen an!
> So klammert sich der Schiffer endlich noch
> Am Felsen fest an dem er scheitern sollte.

(Broken is the rudder, the ship crashes on all sides. The deck beneath my feet rips open, bursting. I hold on to you with both arms. Just as the shipmate clings to the rock on which he was to run aground.)

We all sat quietly and were moved to the core of our hearts and souls. It was a moment I will never forget.

I spent the rest of the summer reading as much as possible to fill the gaps in my knowledge, and I started on the reading list for the fall courses. I bought the books as soon as they were available, or brought them home from the library to get a head start. I began to type on index cards a synopsis of each work I read, highlighting important points of interpretation in red, and I arranged them in a special file cabinet.

I was glad to have an excuse to turn down Rachel's request to be a bridesmaid at her and Harry's wedding. Almost a year after he had returned to Michigan, he weaseled his way back into her life after I introduced him to Salamander AG, diplomatically explored various religions, and to nobody's surprise, discovered that a conversion to Judaism would be the most profitable move. It would ensure against Rachel's possible disinheritance, to which her father had sworn if she were to marry a gentile. I was glad I did not go to the wedding. The scene her father made at the temple before and after the wedding was by all accounts horrific. It was not a joyful occasion, to say the least. They did manage a honeymoon to Bermuda, and Rachel, who always struck me as a little naïve, seemed happy, at least on the outside.

In the fall of 1968, I got special permission to take Professor Remak's course "Structure of the German Short Novel," which was open to PhD candidates only. Professor Remak, who held degrees in German and comparative literature, was highly recommended by my advisor. He had just returned from a visiting professorship at the University of Hamburg, Germany, and had also studied at the Universities of Bordeaux and Montpellier, France, where Doc had completed post-MD work. During the summers, he was in charge of the well-known summer program at Middlebury College. I thoroughly enjoyed the course. We read approximately thirty-four short novels and were required to have read twenty of them in advance. Professor Remak was a bit of a caricature. He was tall, skinny, and bald. To compensate for the baldness, he grew a small mustache. It highlighted the few locks sticking up on both sides of the hairy wreath framing the polished top of his head. He had a tanned complexion, and his black eyes twinkled mischievously on both sides of his long, thin nose. I cannot recall ever having an exchange of words with him that was not spiked with humor. He was lively, sharp, and ever so witty and spoke in a ringing, clear, and distinct voice. The classes were exciting because of the fascinating works we studied. At times, he invited us to his home, where the atmosphere was more casual, and the group once congregated in my humble but cozy abode. We all wrote papers over forty pages long and tried extra hard, because the professor had promised to devote a footnote to us when the book he was in the process of writing was published. I am still waiting.

I learned early on that one must guard against having one's ideas stolen by fellow graduate students. Since I had the reputation of being a thorough reader and was always eager to try out my ideas and interpretations prior to voicing them in class, I was shocked when one of the friends with whom I had discussed a literary work (which I knew she had not completed reading) repeated my ideas during class discussion. I also was shocked to discover that a student in a class requiring a compilation of biographical entries for a book the professor was writing on Gottsched, an author from the eighteenth century, intentionally steered us in the wrong direction in the library. The professor had announced that whoever produced the biggest number of entries would get an A. I finally went to the professor and made him aware that he should not have made such a statement, because it created a nasty, competitive atmosphere in the classroom. He agreed and retracted it.

During the spring semester of 1969, I was pleased to take Professor Jaeger's seminar on Goethe's *Faust I* and *II*. His health seemed to get worse. Since his wife was teaching, I offered to drive him back and forth between IU and his home for classes. On May 20 at 9:30 p.m., the phone rang, and Professor Jaeger asked if I would be so kind as to take over his seminar the next day. He was not feeling well. He also wanted me to locate an article he had published on the subject; he meant for me to retrieve it from the library. I felt quite honored, agreed, hurried to the library, and worked until after 1:30 a.m. on the preparation for this particular act in Goethe's *Faust II*. The class went better than I had expected. Several students came to congratulate me, and I felt great. I knew once more that I would love to teach literature courses in the future. Professor Jaeger was pleased.

A memorable event took place a couple of weeks after the second fire in three months had been set at the old library, which brought the total loss of books to over $1 million. A great percentage of the German collection had been destroyed. Ironically, the fires occurred shortly before the opening of the new library, in June 1969. They were attributed to a disgruntled employee. We were all shocked. The timing was terrible. I was concerned it would affect my research not only for the MA and PhD exams, but more so for my dissertation. I began to assemble my own library and ordered many books from bookstores in Germany. I also approached Professor Bareikis and, with his assistance, initiated a drive to raise funds with which to replenish the destroyed collection. I wrote to many of my friends in Germany as well as to big German bookstores and companies, such as Volkswagen, and asked Professor Bareikis to keep my efforts confidential.

During that time, the unrest at universities in the United States and abroad was spreading. Students rebelled loudly and boisterously. They insisted on more control over university affairs. Professor Dr. Schneider, chair of the German Department at the University of Hamburg, came to IU on a visiting professorship, and I enrolled in his twentieth-century drama course, which was another highlight of my graduate studies. I had been a bit anxious, because I had no idea what to expect from a professor from a big German university. It took a while for me to understand Expressionist plays, but once I was exposed to them repeatedly, and thanks to Professor Schneider's lectures and discussions, I soon found them fascinating. The professor was most generous when he gave Mike Lützler and me an A+. Later, I visited him in Hamburg, where he told me about the tumultuous events that took place there. I was shocked to hear that several students had stormed into his office and hit him over the head with a club. It did not matter that the Nazis had imprisoned him because he had published an article in the paper criticizing the regime. I recall apologizing on behalf of a German male student in our class who at times had been rather abrasive. He brushed it aside as "harmless" in comparison to what was going on in Hamburg.

I continued with graduate courses during the summer of 1969. I took a seminar on Friedrich Schiller with a younger associate professor, Dr. Piedmont. His specialties were teaching methodology and both late-eighteenth- and early-nineteenth-century literature, drama, and theater. He had taught at a German high school before coming to IU. He had earned his PhD in Bonn the year I immigrated, 1954. He was a lively professor, rather small when standing next to Professors Frye or Remak. He was slim, with thinning black hair and brown eyes; students described him as being quite picky, and at least one female student thought he was cute. His voice sounded as though he were on stage, which was an asset when he supervised the assistant instructors. Nobody could claim he was hard to understand. At times, he organized a group of students to put on a German play. I enjoyed his classes, of which I took two, because I myself was partial to drama, theater, and Schiller and I liked his approach to teaching literature. Some graduate students seemed to feel attracted to him because he was a bachelor. They could not understand why he imported a bride from Germany; in their view, he could have done as well or better over here.

As far as crushes were concerned, if I were not still trying my best to avoid men, and if Erich were not still pursuing me, I could have fallen for a tall, dark, handsome, and somewhat younger visiting professor from Germany, but he found an import from Denmark or Sweden, if I remember correctly. Besides, I did not want to go back to Germany. They married and lived in Cologne, to be divorced later.

I also found Bryon Mitchell, the very young assistant professor of comparative literature, fascinating. He had just arrived from England. He was a Rhodes Scholar with a PhD from Oxford, tall and handsome, with black, curly hair. He was very bright – and at least ten years younger than I. He had presented us with an extensive reading list, including James Joyce's *Ulysses*, before the session started. As the course called for literature of the twentieth century and included works written in stream-of-consciousness style, *Ulysses*, with Molly Bloom's endless interior monologue between waking and sleeping, was a must. We struggled through the fat novels in the short summer session and sighed with relief when the final was behind us. I believe our youthful professor was at times annoyed with me, because I tended to be too eager, a flaw that dates back to Sankt Ursula and has gotten me into trouble repeatedly.

I was glad when the summer session ended, but I dove right into my MA reading list, which seemed longer than it was because I was scheduled to take my written exams already in September and October. The big event that caught the world's attention and kept me glued to the TV occurred on July 20, when America sent the first man to walk on the moon.

My Acquaintance from Ghana, Africa, Descends on Me Big Time – Papa Passes On – I Fall in Love with Teaching

Only three weeks later, on August 9, I received a phone call from the acquaintance whom I had met in Paris and who had written to me occasionally from Ghana and other places in the world, always putting big, colorful stamps on the envelope. Nicholaus Ash-Mettle was from Accra, held a degree in economics from the University of London, and was well educated, as his letters reflected. He took great interest in my studies and achievements and always injected some philosophical comments about the great historical events that stirred the world during those years. He called from New York to apologize for not having written from Spitsbergen, where he received a certificate for crossing the Arctic Circle. He had lost my address when his briefcase was stolen. He was on another of his trips to see the world and wanted to take a detour to Bloomington on his way to San Francisco.

Never in my wildest dreams did I think the man from Accra was serious when he had talked about visiting me in his letters. I tried my best to discourage him, impressing upon him that I was swamped with work for my MA exam. He did not budge, calling me back the next day to announce he had reserved a room at the IU Memorial Union. – I got worried and asked my friend Udo, another graduate student from Germany (who later married a German he met through a newspaper ad), if he would come along with me to drive the man around a bit. Udo, though busy himself, consented. I drove with Udo, who was 6'3", played the guitar, and was prematurely gray, to the Memorial Union to pick up my African visitor. He stood there at the circle grinning from ear to ear, showing off two rows of snow-white teeth. He held up several unwrapped presents. In one hand, he clasped an Ibo mask carved out of teakwood as black as his hands, about twelve inches long. From his arm dangled a long necklace with two kinds of beads. Some were in the shape of penne pasta, approximately two and a half inches long and of a rusty, red, lacquered material; these were intermingled with tiny, black glass beads. In his other fist, he clenched two small llamas carved out of wood and covered with brown-and-white furry skins. He held the gifts toward me. I was embarrassed and accepted hesitatingly. He insisted on putting the necklace around my neck. Udo and I drove him around the campus, and to be polite, I had bought three steaks and a bottle of red wine and invited the two to my place for dinner. After a while, Udo excused himself and left me alone with the Ghanian, who was not at all good-looking. – The visitor from Ghana was about fifty years old, was short and plump, and talked all the time. He thought I deserved to live in a better apartment and suggested that he pay for any additional expenses himself. He also wanted me to visit him, and I suppose his five kids, his wife, and a mistress, who was a nurse at the school in Ghana where he was the principal. He promised to send me a round-trip ticket and had procured a secondhand Mercedes 190 sedan in which he wanted to chauffeur me around Ghana. I turned him down politely, appreciating his good intentions. – It was getting dark outside, and I informed him that I really had to get back to work. I got up, and so did he. Instead of going toward the door, he put his arm around me and started to push me through the closed curtain separating the couch from the bed. He kept telling me how sexy I was, and before I knew it, he had pushed me onto the bed, slouched above me, unzipped his pants, and unbuttoned the white shirt, which looked even whiter against his jet-black skin. He was breathing heavily and pulling on my skirt. His black face, with the big, white-rimmed black eyes and red eyeballs, was so terrifying when he attempted to kiss me. He was too heavy for me to push away. I turned my head. I was scared but tried not to scream out of fear for how he might react. I begged him to stop. He ignored my pleas. I began to cry, and when he saw tears flowing down my cheeks, he got up and asked me to take him back to the hotel. It took all of my strength to deliver him to the door and say good-bye. That was the last time I saw or heard from him. When I returned home, I threw myself on my bed and sobbed. It's as close as I ever came to being raped.

I passed both the written and oral exams for the MA with flying colors, being one of the three students among twelve who passed with an A. As a result, I was nominated for the Woodrow Wilson Dissertation Fellowship, which would have taken me to Princeton, New Jersey. It meant I had a few weeks to submit a dissertation proposal. I decided quickly to examine the function of the master figure in E. T. A. Hoffmann's works. The departmental committee approved the proposal and admitted me to the doctoral program. Unfortunately, I did not receive the fellowship. Instead, a male fellow student, who was married with two children and had earned a BA a year earlier, received the award. I also turned down an invitation from Harvard to continue my graduate work there, because at that time IU ranked as the number-one German department in the United States. But I received a job offer from the chairman of the Foreign Languages Department at IU–South Bend. Jacob Sudermann wanted me to join the faculty there as soon as I completed my PhD. When I was an assistant instructor in South Bend, he had already tried hard to talk me out of going into law. I needed to finish more linguistics courses before taking the PhD exams in the fall of 1970. In addition to an individual reading course in German romanticism, I enrolled in Professor Banta's "Middle High German" course and Professor Blaisdell's "Old Icelandic" course. Both professors were excellent teachers as well as very nice, soft-spoken, and serious scholars. Professor

Banta was tall and thin and had lost most of his hair. Professor Blaisdell was short and had short gray hair.

In early January 1970, just before Professor Banta's final exam, Mutti called and told me Papa had passed away. I was sad, but did not think I could return in time for the funeral, especially since my passport had expired. I will never forget when Professor Banta approached me and offered to let me take the final later. He offered to pay for my plane ticket so I could attend the funeral. I thanked him and assured him that I could afford it, but did not think I would make it in time. When I spoke to Mutti again, she sounded almost elated and announced that Papa, who had died of kidney failure, had agreed to let the priest come and guide him into the arms of Catholicism and, better yet, into the Kingdom of Heaven just before he died. She insisted it was the happiest day of her life. I was somewhat dumbfounded, yet remembered the many tears she shed on Sundays whenever Papa would not join her at Mass. Though it was not all that often. He never went to a Lutheran church and scolded us children when we wanted to stay home on Sundays. Indeed, I never understood why he did not join the Catholic Church earlier, knowing full well how much it would have pleased Mutti. Mutti wanted me to come later, when I could spend more time, and insisted there was nothing I could do anyhow. On the day of the funeral, I wrote the final exam for the course in Middle High German; I passed with an A-. As I reflected on my relationship with my father, I remembered a letter I had written to him not long before, in which I thanked him for having introduced me to music. I had assured him my love of music had a major influence on my love of literature.

Professor Blaisdell's "Old Icelandic" course turned out to be as tough as could be imagined. It involved translating sagas into English. We were practically on our own, with almost no explanation of grammar and a couple of books to help us struggle through. One text was a dictionary. In Old Norse, many words have as many as twenty-five meanings. It took me over five hours to translate the first five lines of the first assignment. What made it worse was that a fellow student, an attractive German woman who had marital troubles in addition to those with the course, called me one night in despair. She had slit her wrist with a razor blade and was on the verge of bleeding to death. Fortunately, I got help in time. – Old Norse got a bit easier as time went on, but when halfway through the semester I discovered inadvertently that the majority of the students in the class had worked with English translations from the library, I was really ticked off. No wonder their translations always sounded so much smoother than mine. It seemed to be my luck that whenever I had a sentence I was unable to crack, the professor would call on me. I always blushed and stuttered through whatever I had written down. It was a miracle that I passed with an A-. Linguistics courses were not my favorites, though I must admit, I was amazed that by the end of the term I was able to translate the sagas rather fluently.

Since I was quite certain I would write my dissertation on E. T. A. Hoffmann and had decided to write my PhD exams on literature from the period of Goethe, choosing German drama as a genre, I continued with an individual reading course in German romanticism. I also needed one last course in linguistics, and since no others were offered, I ended up in Professor Banta's "History of the German Language," which I thought would be a snap until I received a big red C on the midterm exam – a grade that was tantamount to an F in graduate school. Fortunately or unfortunately, I was not the only student in shock. I went home, cried, called Professor Banta, and set up an appointment, which resulted in my spending spring break in my apartment starting all over again. I spread out numerous sheets of lists with paradigms on the floor and started at the beginning, committing them to memory. I did much better on the final and ended up with a B+, the lowest grade on my graduate record. As someone said, "It proves you are human, after all." It was my last course before the PhD exam.

The shock was soon overcome by the joy I derived from teaching a senior graduate course in stylistics. Native faculty members usually taught the course. I considered it a privilege and ignored some of the snide remarks from fellow students, most of whom taught introductory courses. All PhD candidates were required to teach two courses, and the department counted the course I taught during my sophomore year as one of the two. I felt honored when one of the faculty members, an American, asked if she could audit my course. All of the students were bright or very bright, especially Lynne Tatlock, who easily ranks among the best students I taught during my career as a college professor. Lynne was not only brilliant and highly motivated, always going beyond what was required, but also very attractive and polite. She appeared to be quite fragile and overly sensitive, as she let her tears flow freely when others would have held back. When Dr. Vater, from Germany, had to give her a B+ on a midterm exam in modern linguistics, it seemed that all of the German professors on the sixth floor anxiously awaited Lynne's reaction. It was the first B+ she had received in her student career. As expected, she cried, but she did not suffer a breakdown. She pulled herself together and earned an A+ for the course. She once told me there is nothing wrong with showing your emotions.

I tried my best to make the class sessions interesting. Since there was always too little time for conversation, I decided to invite each student a couple of times during the semester to accompany me for dinner at Aley Hall, the German house on campus, where the students were required to converse in German at all times. After dinner, I would take my guest to a restaurant for a hot drink. They really appreciated the special attention. Their exams turned out superbly, as did the student evaluations. One student, Amber Challifour, who held a BA in French from the University of Wisconsin and pursued an MA in French with a minor in German at IU, put a thank-you note with a token of appreciation, a piece of choice facial soap, in my mail slot. I have never forgotten the kind gesture. We became friends shortly thereafter and remained friends for a long time.

1961–1972

The spring semester of 1970 did not proceed without turmoil. Students on our campus finally began to speak out against America's involvement in the war in Vietnam. There were sit-ins on the lawns and protests in Dunn Meadow, and I too began to feel strongly opposed to America's involvement, especially when they barricaded Ballantine Hall, forcing us to crawl out of the window in order to get out. My best friend, Jocelyn Haskell, and I stopped short of telling our male students to tear up their draft cards. It was during these years that I began to pay more attention to politics and political parties. I began to realize that not all human beings have the ability to pull themselves out of underprivileged environments. Many need help, help from the federal government, if necessary. By that time, I had seen much suffering resulting from extreme poverty. I had seen it in several countries in addition to America, the richest country in the world.

I had the greatest respect for Jocelyn, a brilliant young woman with four beautiful children between the ages of four and ten, three girls with rich, long, blond-and-brown hair like their mother's and faces like angels and a boy with light-brown hair and equally delicate features. All were musical and played the piano, which Jocelyn, an accomplished pianist herself, was teaching them. She also taught them to help in the kitchen and put a footstool in front of the stove so they could stir the pot. In the morning, they stood one behind the other combing each other's hair. Jocelyn was brilliant. She had started advanced courses for the doctoral program right away, and she took two courses and taught one or two each semester, because she had very little money. She never went to bed before 2:00 or 3:00 in the morning. Just before she came to IU, she awakened one morning to find her husband dead beside her. He left her penniless. I often think of her when I speak with women who use raising a child or children as an excuse for not having been able to pursue a degree. – Jocelyn's dissertation bridged two disciplines. She wrote about Hofmannsthal's libretto and Richard Strauss's music for the opera *Salome*. She was the daughter of an Army chaplain and had been to many parts of the world. She had a special insight into the human psyche, and we talked deep into the night about the problems of society and about our courses, professors, and fellow students. She laughed when I told her about Udo's reaction when I told him that in my opinion all Germanists are a bit nutty. He thought I was crazy and definitely did not want to be included. Jocelyn and I were both widows and about the same age. She agreed that I should politely decline the advances of the cute and handsome Mark Silverman, who was new on campus. He was about my height and had jet-black hair, big black eyes, and a short, pointed black beard. He was very intelligent and caused a big stink on the sixth floor of the German Department when he defied them and put a huge poster of Karl Marx on his door, for which I always admired him and still do. Yet, not being sure what he actually saw in me, I was careful and told him to find a nice, young coed when he asked me out to the opera at the newly opened Musical Arts Center. He looked like a small Mephistopheles when he went to the theater, wearing his flaring cape made of black wool with a bright-red silk lining and held together by a shiny, sterling-silver clasp. Mark was a good friend of husky Dave Scrace, who had a thick, light-brown beard and a full head of hair and smoked a pipe. He came from Ireland, and every female graduate student and others thought he was the sexiest male around. He had imported his chosen female from Germany, only to have the affair end up in smoke.

During that time, nobody wanted to believe my age, which may have sent the wrong signals to some of the males, but I always made a point of letting them know. Sometimes we would congregate at Jocelyn's place, where she played the piano, the most treasured piece of furniture in the tiny and very humble house, or we listened to antiestablishment songs by the latest folk singers, including Joan Baez, Bob Dylan, Peter, Paul, and Mary, and others. Eventually, Jocelyn befriended a red-haired graduate student from England. I was not too fond of him. He used to walk around wearing floppy sandals. I can still hear his bare heels clicking. He had the reputation of being gay, which worried me; but Jocelyn applied her magic touch and proved them wrong when he married her and took her and her four children back to England once they had their degrees in hand.

The Veterans Administration Comes Through and Makes Life Easier

Early in the spring semester, another event convinced me that someone up there kept an eye on me. It was sheer luck that in February 1969, I noticed an article in the *Daily Student*, the campus paper, which I decided to subscribe to for $5 because, to save money, I did not subscribe to any other newspapers. I felt it was important because I was teaching. I could hardly believe it when I read the headline "Veterans' Wives Get College Aid." Since I was close to the Veterans Administration's headquarters in Indianapolis, I acted immediately, hoping that maybe this time, thirteen years after Doc's death, I might be eligible. The law took effect on December 1, 1968. I had given up after numerous unsuccessful attempts to contact the VA even before I left for France. I was elated when I was informed that (1) almost ten years after Doc's death, on October 1, 1967, the five-year marriage requirement had been reduced to one year and (2) effective December 1, 1968, eligibility for educational assistance was extended to widows of veterans whose death was due to or the result of military service. – On March 4, I reopened my claim, and after a lengthy exchange of correspondence, they finally came through and authorized dependency and indemnity compensation (DIC) benefits, effective March 4, 1969. On July 27 and October 19, I was awarded the educational allowance. I had appealed their decision not to grant retroactive pay and appeared in person before a committee of high-ranking military officials in Indianapolis. I had been assigned a counselor who was very discouraging. As it turned out, he did not say one word on my behalf for the entire meeting. He listened quietly as I pleaded my case for almost an hour, and when I was done, much to his surprise, the board agreed to pay the educational allowance retroactively after all. I won and was flying high. I thanked Mr. James for having taught me how to argue a case (I had found a loophole in the wording of the law) and sent a kiss toward heaven for Doc: finally!

From that experience, I learned that one must constantly be on guard. I have never dealt with a government agency which made more mistakes and advanced erroneous information more frequently than the Veterans Administration. Naturally, had I been more alert when I first arrived on campus and read a newspaper, maybe I would not have had to push so hard to finish. I decided on the way home to Bloomington that after my PhD exams, I would visit my parents in Germany, go on a shopping spree, slow down a bit, and enjoy some of the cultural activities on our beautiful campus. How much luckier could I get? The fabulous Musical Arts Center, or MAC, whose combined opera house and concert hall is considered one of America's "major musical assets," was about to open its doors in 1971.

I enhanced the surroundings of my efficiency apartment with flower boxes, by attaching them to the balustrade around my deck and filling them with bright-red geraniums and white petunias. I invested in a lounge chair and sun umbrella and felt free as a bird in my humble paradise. At times, I interrupted my otherwise very intense reading schedule with a ride to a nearby park, and I made sure my circle of friends did not miss out on the cultural events that virtually inundated our campus. One sunny forenoon, I called Professor Jaeger and invited him and his sons out for lunch at the Nashville House, which was famous for barbequed ribs and deep-fried rolls. The boys, who had recently learned how to drive, were even more excited when I let them drive my T-bird.

The two written PhD exams were scheduled for October 10 and November 14. One covered the Goethe period, the other, German drama. I was happy to find out I was among those who passed. I then got ready for my oral exam, which was scheduled for December 5 and covered all the periods and genres I had not written about. Since I considered lyric poetry my weakness, Professor Jaeger kindly offered to drill me a couple of times before the 5th. I was much more confident after that and geared up the night before by going over the many notes arranged on my table. I planned to go over them once more in the morning, just prior to the exam.

My phone rang at about 5:00 a.m. Calling from Washington, D.C., Jocelyn's mother told me that Jocelyn's house had caught on fire – and that the children were safe but Jocelyn was in the hospital. I promised to check on her right away. Jocelyn lay in the hospital bed looking very pale. Her long, light-brown hair was badly singed. She had been studying late when she suddenly noticed smoke coming from her children's bedroom. She awakened them and rushed them out of the burning room. The cat had entangled its tail in the electric heater and, in a frantic attempt to free itself from the fire, had spread the sparks around the bedroom. I assured Jocelyn I would be back after my oral exam.

I arrived a couple of minutes before 9:00 a.m. at the sixth floor of Ballantine Hall, where five professors were waiting at the long table, ready to "torture" me. I briefed them first about Jocelyn's mishap, and Professor Poag, whose specialty was literature of the Middle Ages, opened by asking me smilingly to identify what I considered my weakness. I answered, "Lyrics," and he responded, "Well, then let's see what you do know." At the end of the two-hour session, which I actually enjoyed, they shook my hand and congratulated me. I rushed back to Jocelyn, who was soon to be released. While inspecting her badly damaged house, I was happy to find the book I had loaned her. It was Professor Schneider's *Zerbrochene Formen* (Broken Forms). The cover was blackened but the text unharmed. By Christmas, the Haskells moved back into the renovated house.

I departed to Germany via Detroit, where I wanted to spend the holidays with my brother, before flying to New York to attend the annual convention of the Modern Language Association, or MLA, in order to assess the job market. Before I left, Professor Jaeger called. He asked if I could check out a few philosophy periodicals that night. He was in the final stages of completing his book on Heidegger. It was snowing outside. I drove to the library and found the material. On the way back to the car, I slipped and fell down the stairs. I tied a scarf around the bleeding knee, dropped off the material at the Jaegers, and hobbled up my rickety stairway to finish packing. In Detroit, I rested. And in New York, I felt much better by the time I met with the interviewers from Dartmouth, and was encouraged when they impressed upon me that I should stay in touch, because their Hoffmann scholar was about to retire.

On New Year's Eve in 1970, I arrived dead tired in Hannover, but I loved it when Mutti sat at my bedside, stroking my back and telling me over and over how proud she was and how nice it would be if I eventually came back to Germany, where it was nice too. It was not long after my arrival in Hannover that David Scrace sent me the sad news that Professor Jaeger had passed away while sitting in his favorite chair.

My sojourn in Hannover was spent mostly with Mutti, who had become a widow, like me. As usual, she insisted I get together with my brother and his family and buy a big bouquet of flowers for them, which I resented somewhat because we were increasingly drifting apart. We did not have much in common. Aunt Ella and Uncle Seppel came over for coffee and cake with Aunt Anna and, as usual, gossiped about the rest of the family. I got together with several of my pals from Sankt Ursula, Sibby, Nanni, and Christa, all of whom were trying to raise their absolutely "gorgeous" kids properly. Some were not doing so well in school, which was really no surprise considering their respective genes. I was about as interested in listening to the stories of their everyday lives as they were in hearing about my life as a student. I found more satisfaction in talking to my former teachers, Mater Herwiges, the ex-nun, and Marianne Schirduan. Both expressed admiration for what I was doing with my life despite all the adversities that had come my way. I thanked them for getting together with Mutti off and on and told Marianne how much Mutti enjoyed the performances at the school, where her choir had an excellent reputation. I ignored Hubert, but when Erich popped up again, we did take in a couple of theater and opera performances, in addition to engaging in a few other activities of a more sensual nature. I did not like it when Mutti waited up for me until the wee hours in the morning, to the point of looking down the street from the window on the third floor. She preferred to see me spend time on my dissertation research at the Stadtbibliothek (City Library).

Bizarre and Ordinary Friends, Lovers, and Relations

In keeping with my resolve to partake in the pleasures of life again, as soon as I returned to Bloomington, I organized a group of four professors and four doctoral candidates who met at my place to read German plays every two weeks or so. We all drew names of characters and then proceeded to read the drama with much gusto. A bottle or two of wine served as an extra stimulus. One of the students tried her best to convince me to be less prudish and come to her place for a round of hashish while listening to music. She assured me the effects would be phenomenal. I did not want to risk it out of fear of possibly liking it too much, getting hooked, and then having a hard time getting unhooked.

Though I never dared to partake in any pot-smoking activities, I did have the weirdest recurring dream during my college years, usually before major exams: I dreamed I was losing my teeth. At first, they started to loosen. The harder I tried to push them back into my gums, the more they multiplied, to the extent that my mouth was filled with many loose teeth and I was unable to speak. As I discharged the mess into the palms of my hands, I woke up and realized with great relief that it was only a dream. A year or so later, I read in a German TV magazine an article entitled "Dreams of Stars," and I found to my surprise that the actor Ruth Maria Kubitschek, who portrayed women who were generally self-confident and strong, had the same dream, usually just before or during a first performance. Dr. Michael Boehm, the author of the article, asserted that "these kinds of dreams by women are known as 'Geburtsträume' (dreams of birth)" and that "Kubitschek's dream represents the inner conflict, which takes place in a professional, emancipated woman." He claimed that "she loves her profession and has invested a large part of her feelings and strength in it and that such dreams are most common during times of professional stress. It means that her subconscious is plagued by a very bad conscience. The 'soft' feminine side of the dreamer is quite prominent, but she does not have the courage to recognize it."

As I began to mingle more with my fellow students, I befriended several with husbands and some without. Amber's bearded husband, from England, was an associate professor of physics and mathematics who had come to IU by way of Princeton. He was a serious and promising young scholar. They introduced me to

Heinz Leutwieler, a mathematician from Switzerland with whom we got together to watch his wife, Anita, make a genuine and superb-tasting Swiss-cheese fondue at my place. Sometimes, I went to cocktail parties in a charming cottage-type house in the woods outside of town, hosted by my very German friend Rita and her American husband, who also had come from a university on the East Coast. I had met Rita during my senior year, in Wedgewood's class. She was shorter than I, and wore glasses and dresses, which made her look older. Her husband was a divorced man with a couple of children and considerably older. She had met him while crossing the Atlantic in a student ship. Several of us found him somewhat repellant. He was about Rita's height, at least as short as Uncle Adolf, which must have been the reason he always stood in front of guests while they sat on the couch, looking down on their heads while sipping cocktails, of which one never knew how many he had consumed, because his eyes seemed bloodshot and his face red most of the time. I avoided talking to him, because he always knew better and would go on and on pontificating. I never asked for the cause when I heard his motorcycle and old Mercedes were totaled. Many of us wondered if Rita just played naïve when the tongues of colleagues and their wives were wagging about the little professor, who had a tendency not to show up to teach or administer exams. He was in the habit of holding a soft-drink can in his hand as he walked the corridors. Rumor had it that the intent was to camouflage the actual contents.

Through Rita I met Karla, who had a PhD in German. Her ex, another scientist and a native of some underprivileged region of the world, had also come to IU from an East Coast university, but one day he just took off for some university out West without letting her tag along. She simply refused to accept it, called on him constantly, and continued to wear her wedding band in the hope that he would return. She never changed a single hair on her head. It was forever dyed peroxide blond, parted on the left, and cut short and straight. Karla was quite a bit taller than I. She was skinny as a beanpole and looked like someone from the 20s and much like an old maid. She was incapable of laughing happily and always looked toward the floor. Maybe she wanted to hide her exceptionally long teeth. She kept her house so sterile you could have eaten off the floor. I have never met anybody who scrubbed kitchen sinks, pots, and pans more thoroughly. I felt utterly restricted whenever I visited her house and never dared to sit down without asking on which chair I should sit. She was consumed by fear, constantly convinced that someone was trying to break into her house, even though I did not notice a thing anybody might want. I never quite knew why she clung to me; it was probably because I was unattached, treated her kindly, and let her sleep on that ugly and uncomfortable orange vinyl couch whenever she was afraid to sleep at her own place because she had heard a strange noise. Of course, there was the common denominator, which virtually obliged you to try to fit in: we were both born and raised in Germany. It is difficult to distance yourself once you have been drawn into that circle, especially in a small college town. In addition, Karla, a Protestant, was the daughter of a gentile mother and a Jewish father, which meant she had everybody's sympathy, at least as far as appearances went. He had disappeared at the onset of the Holocaust. After her mother passed away, she immigrated to a safer continent. We used to compare childhood experiences, and she always remarked how much happier her life had been as an only child, compared to mine. Of course, she was a lot older than I.

I really liked my pretty and petite friend Lotte Franklin, a brunette from Wiesbaden, Germany. She was married to an American who had served in the Air Force for twenty years. They had two children, and he was pursuing a PhD in psychology. We spent great times together. I helped her get a secretarial job in the department and encouraged her to take a few German classes. She had a hard time writing term papers. A couple of times, I ended up writing the bulk of her papers, for which she earned As. She was happy, and although I felt a bit guilty, I hoped she learned from it. She called almost daily and even more frequently when her husband flunked his first set of PhD exams. They were devastated, but I kept encouraging him not to give up. He passed the second time around. After he passed, Lotte stopped calling, and I heard no more from her.

Yes, I did have a couple of flings after my PhD exam. One was an affair, completely under my control, with a rather handsome and very masculine PhD candidate majoring in philosophy and fine arts. I never thought I could pull off a relationship in which I remained emotionally detached. The only thing that reminded me later of this somewhat younger man from Czechoslovakia was an abstract painting he gave to me when he said good-bye. I also befriended an even younger man, a good-looking Vietnamese who was majoring in French. It was mainly a friendship by phone, in which we conversed entirely in French. I forgot his name, but still have in my possession a beautiful good-bye gift, a piece of purple silk material for a kimono. It is embroidered heavily with white pearls and silver sequins, forming a mighty dragon. He had asked his sister to send it.

After the artist-philosopher was gone, I should have been content with telephone friendships, and just reminisced about the good time I had when Erich came from Germany to visit me for a few days. Those were also the days when many of us became more promiscuous. I myself was not getting any younger. The friend who wanted me to indulge in pot bragged openly about an affair she had carried on with a well-known, but married, visiting professor. Unforeseen circumstances threw me into the arms of a local businessman who was about my age. I was stunned when he told me his wife had died the same year Doc passed away. Somehow I felt a bond was created right then and there. Next thing I knew, he carried bunches of flowers up the unsteady stairs. After that, he brought a bottle of Scotch, though, unlike Gable's clone, no glasses filled with gardenias. Yet, come to think of it, the two did have something in common, even though this specimen was not nearly as good-looking as Gable's double. He too had a small mustache and tanned skin, but was taller and bald. More importantly, like Gable's clone, he turned out to be a great lover, to the point that I almost abandoned my "resolve." Almost, because in the midst of all that passion fueled by sufficient Scotch and water, about four weeks or so after it all started, it suddenly dawned on me that the guy never invited me out to a restaurant or such. I sobered up, and sat up too, and asked him why he had never showed me his place. After a bunch of excuses and detours, the answer was very simple: he had a wife and kids. Having had enough experiences with lying and cheating men, I jumped up and told him in no uncertain terms to get out and stay away. He appeared flabbergasted and stumbled down the stairway, only to return the next evening after dark. He knocked at my door, pleading, trying to convince me through the door that his marriage was on the rocks and to let him come in to talk, to explain. All those lines they feed you! When I threatened to write a letter to his wife, he was silent and trotted down the stairs. I thanked my lucky stars for endowing me with such wisdom. At 6:00 a.m., I was at my table pecking away on the typewriter and getting "turned on" by E. T. A. Hoffmann's tales.

It was the last time I fell for a businessman. Come to think of it, there were a couple of other married businessmen whom I had a hard time convincing I was not interested. Heinz too had tried to be more than a friend. I could hardly believe it. He was not only the husband of my best friend, but also had zero sex appeal. It was a delicate situation, to say the least, if you know what I mean. The Loesers came to visit me a couple of times in Bloomington and took me to my then-favorite French restaurant, Chez Jean, where I had taken Udo after I got my first check from the VA. I wanted to thank him for having chauffeured the African and me around.

Remember the VP from the bank in Dowagiac, Mr. James's client, who was attracted by the red lamp? Well, on his way to the Kentucky Derby he had tracked me down in Bloomington. I threw him out when what I thought was a friendly visit suddenly changed into a downright amorous ambush. He too kept knocking at my door, which rattled so loud I feared my landlady or her bedridden husband would wake up. Weinmann, who had a pacemaker installed and no sex appeal, did not give up, either. He continued his chase by calling me from his hotel every five minutes for hours. I covered the phone with all the covers and pillows I could get my hands on and finally fell asleep. That was it, at least for the time being. Can you imagine what it would be like to be in the midst of an acrobatic entanglement with a married man who had a heart attack?

During the same summer, Mutti wrote that my brother's wife, Gerda, had had a miscarriage as a result of defying doctor's orders not to fly to Germany. It happened right after the plane landed. My brother was heartsick about it – he had desperately hoped for at least one more child after Susan. And I was furious, because I knew right away it was no accident. I had observed my sister-in-law for a long time, and I frequently overlooked and tolerated her behavior toward my brother as well as me. I had tried hard to like her and to help both of them build a new life in America. She was never satisfied and had nothing but criticism for anything American, be it the brooms, the cleaning materials, the clothes, the furniture, the houses, the people, you name it. She once asked for a couple of ounces from my bottle of furniture polish because she did not want to buy a new bottle.

Gerda was not very bright and failed her driver's test at least three times. I finally went with her and asked the lady to allow her more time. After more than an hour had elapsed, she finally passed. She took an English-writing evening course at a high school, which she would have failed had I not helped her with an essay, which she aced. She was obsessed with the mighty American Dollar. On Sunday afternoons, they literally counted out their bills and coins on a little cocktail table. To test them, I asked for a possible loan in case I was in need. She agreed – on the condition that I gave her the golden coin bracelet Doc had made for me at a shop in Yucatán. What I resented most about her was her obvious racist attitude and her defense of Hitler, which coincided with her father's extremist views.

I had also observed my sister-in-law when I spent the week with them at Sleepy Hollow Resort, on Lake Michigan, the previous summer. It broke my heart to watch Alfons looking pale and thin and doting on his little, fragile daughter while his wife kept her distance. She was in my opinion a cold fish. She set the tone the minute we arrived at the cabin by announcing she would take the double bed for herself and Susan. She did not want to sleep with her husband, with whom she barely exchanged ten sentences while we were at the lake. I always thought her greedy and selfish, especially since I overheard her telling her daughter to be nice to me because she thought I "had money." I was proven right again. Once, there were five hot dogs on the table. Each of us ate one, which left one on the platter. When I was about to offer it to my brother, she yelled, "I take it!" and grabbed and devoured it. I asked my brother what was the matter. He hinted that she kept avoiding him. Later, she told me he wanted her to have another child but that she would do everything in her power to prevent it. I thought I heard wrong when she proclaimed that, in her opinion, sex between marriage partners is nothing but animalistic behavior. I remembered what I thought when my brother had said in jest that he virtually had to "rape" her to get her pregnant with their first child. I always considered her a cold and calculating manipulator who got what she wanted. There was nothing about her that was soft or gentle, traits I had always admired in my brother. Something was obviously wrong. This last incident diminished my respect for her and her parents, who did not discourage her from flying, though they were even more aware of the inherent risk. I distanced myself further. My mother slowly began to see the light as well, but as always when there was a conflict on the horizon, she remained silent.

I did not dwell on what was going on in Detroit and continued with research for my dissertation, which I wanted to finish by the end of the summer of 1972. I had made good progress and decided to accept a teaching position at DePauw University for the fall semester followed by a short winter session. It involved commuting two hours each day to Greencastle, Indiana. The pay for teaching one intermediate course was acceptable, and I thought it could not hurt my teaching record if I had experience at another institution. They called DePauw the Harvard of the Midwest, which was definitely overstating the case.

The Croft Burns – Dissertation Woes

Prior to embarking on my new job in late August, I had a sudden desire to visit the Gebhards up north and take a look at the Croft. I called, and my friends told me to get into my car and come. As soon as I entered the house, they asked if I knew the Croft had burned down the night before as the result of a fire, which had started in the kitchen. "No!" I responded, shocked. The Gebhards took me to see the Croft the next morning. The entire front and a large portion of the left side of the house were burned down. The rafters and beams were black with soot, there was no sign of the beautiful woodwork inside, no sign of the stairway, and the library gaped, blackened by the fire. It looked like a ghost house. The swimming pool had been reduced to a big hole covered with weeds. The lawns had not been kept up. I held back tears and stood in silence for a couple of minutes. I could not stay any longer and asked Harold and Mary to take me back to their farm.

On the way back to Bloomington, I could not wipe the sight of the burned house from my mind. The one good thing that would result from the fire was that the insurance company would pay off the balance due on the land contract. I had had my share of problems with the purchasers. It had come to my attention that one of the brothers who had bought the Croft, a contractor, was a big scoundrel, deep in debt and disliked by the entire business community. – I did not realize I was driving too fast until a state trooper stopped me outside of Rochester, Indiana. Not being in the right frame of mind to flirt my way out of it, as usual, I paid the fine. It was my second ticket since Doc had passed away.

I liked teaching at DePauw, but was surprised by how conservative the place was. We were not allowed to wear pants on campus, and students were strictly forbidden to let their hair grow. However, one of the senior professors, at whose house I spent the night on several occasions when the weather was bad, thought nothing of making a pass at me while his lovely blond wife, who attributed her immaculate complexion to Estée Lauder's lotions, was in a room downstairs. I decided I had to tactfully decline future invitations.

Among my students at DePauw were several who belonged to a sorority. I learned quickly that serious involvement in sorority activities could have a detrimental effect on the academic achievements of the young women. One student placed more importance on fulfilling the requirements to get a certain "pin" than on spending extra time studying to avoid a D in German. I found it extreme when one of my good students, whose very neatly kept hair came down to his cheekbones, asked me what to do. One of his professors had threatened to flunk him if he did not cut his hair. This particular student was bright and stood out because he kept an unusual journal. Not only were the entries written in excellent German, but each one was in a different script. He spent much time in my office discussing a conflict with his parents. He was an adopted child and had trouble convincing his parents that he did not want to study medicine. Years later, he tracked me down by phone and told me I had had quite an impact on his life and that he had gone into theology instead of medicine.

Commuting to Greencastle and preparing the classes did not leave much time for my dissertation, but it received my full attention as soon as the semester ended. The experience at DePauw benefited me insofar as I decided to steer clear of institutions that were too conservative.

The question as to who would be my doctoral advisor was settled quickly. Dr. Frye had not made a secret of wanting me as his candidate. He had very limited experience advising, but the senior professors felt it was time for the younger faculty to take on their share. As my topic was related to his specialty, I did not try hard to resist. I was concerned mainly because he was neither a native speaker of German nor a full professor. But since the dissertation committee was composed of Professors Remak and Weisstein, both native speakers, and Professor Chatin from the French Department, who also spoke German but represented my minor in French, the arrangement seemed satisfactory. I was afraid of Professor Weisstein, who had a reputation as a fierce doctoral advisor. Rumor had it that he found a dissertation by a fellow student totally unacceptable. I don't know if the poor guy ever finished. By the time I started, I had decided to write in German and had limited my topic to the master figure in E. T. A. Hoffmann's fantastic fairy tales.

Dr. Frye had impressed upon me from the very start that under no circumstances was I to discuss comments made by the committee with them. I found that rather bizarre, but far be it from me to anger my advisor, who did not enjoy an established reputation in the department anyhow. I knew he needed to be treated with kid gloves. I tried to disturb him as little as possible, and I completed my first draft of 350 double-spaced pages in the first six weeks, without contacting him. I then asked him to read it as soon as he could so I could start with the revisions. He knew I needed to have my PhD in hand by the end of the summer, because I had decided to accept the position in South Bend offered by Professor Sudermann. I felt a certain loyalty toward the campus where I had embarked on my college career and where I had already taught. I also felt drawn to the area because it was a bit like home. The Loesers still lived there, and I still had a number of other close friends in the area from my time at the Croft. When others had a hard time understanding why I would want to teach there, I explained that financially less privileged students deserved a good instructor as much as others.

Looking back, I still find it hard to believe that I finished my dissertation in six months. It turned out that L. Frye's behavior bordered at times on the insane or bizarre, to put it mildly. He had bought a farm far outside of Bloomington and tried to live like the pioneers with his attractive wife, herself a PhD in English, and a newborn baby girl. I never knew when I should try to reach him by phone. It happened more than once that when he heard my voice, he fell silent and hung up. I assumed he was upset because I might have awakened the baby, but was never certain. On a couple of occasions, he asked me to drive out to the farm to discuss my work. He took me out to the hill and told me to sit in the grass, which was several feet high, and talk to him while he planted cherry trees. It was hot and sultry, bugs buzzing around me, but when the big black German shepherd started messing around with the pages in the grass, I got up, gathered my things, and asked him to take me to the house to continue the discussion. He gave me a strange look, threw the spade on the ground, walked toward the house with me behind him, and sat down in the porch swing. I pulled over a stool. As soon as we were finished, I thanked him, went to my car, and drove away on the dusty gravel road that colored my black car gray by the time I reached the paved road. When I told my friends about it, they thought I was kidding.

It took all my strength to keep on writing, especially when I had to ask him when I might expect his comments on the next chapter. On one such occasion, a Friday, he said I had a choice: he could bring the chapter by that very night or I would have to wait until Monday. I told him I would very much appreciate his dropping the chapter off that night because I wanted to work on it over the weekend. It was late and dark outside when he came up the stairs. He came in and, as he sat down, asked, "Well, how about that massage you promised?" I was even more stunned when he asked, "Where is your nightgown?" I pulled myself together and, in a cocky voice, fibbed, "I do not wear a nightgown, but may I offer you something to drink?" He let it go at that, and I sighed with great relief when he stomped down the stairway and drove off.

I had finished the dissertation more than a month early and was ready to have it bound. Fortunately, none of the three professors on the committee raised questions that required major revisions. Professor Weisstein had been encouraging me to use more foreign words, while Professor Remak preferred pure German expressions. When he asked if I had any objections to commas, Karla volunteered to go over my dissertation with a fine-tooth comb, and I was grateful. She approached it as though she were scouring a copper pot, obsessed with removing each and every tiny black dot.

As L. Frye reviewed the finished manuscript while swinging back and forth in his porch swing, he suggested out of the blue that I still had enough time to rewrite the final chapter and use a completely different approach. I thought I had heard wrong. I found the idea absolutely absurd. Of course, I did not tell him what I thought, but explained simply that I disagreed with him and that I would not change a word. He grinned a bit and let it go. I have always thought this was his final attempt to prove his superiority.

1961–1972

When I felt safe, I did confide in Professor Weisstein about my bizarre experiences with his colleague. He shook his head in disbelief and said he would be careful never again to serve on a dissertation committee with Frye. In the middle of July, the committee met with me for the defense, which was kept short and was more like a stamp of approval. I shook hands with the committee members, thanking all of them profoundly, and left the room on the ground floor of Ballantine Hall with the PhD in my pocket, only three years after the BA. When they called me "Dr. Beardsley," I immediately thought of Doc and wished from the bottom of my heart that he could have been there.

A couple of weeks before my defense, I had gone to South Bend to find a place to live, which was not easy. When I was almost ready to throw in the sponge, Rachel drove around with me once more, and we came upon an L-shaped ranch-style home. It was close to the campus and in a fashionable neighborhood and had been newly decorated with state-of-the-art materials by the owner, who was an interior decorator at one of the upscale department stores. I thought it was perfect and offered $2,000 less than the $20,000 they asked. They accepted, and I made a down payment with the money I had just received from the insurance company for the Croft. I then went to order furniture at the elegant store where Sally James had been an interior decorator before marrying Guillermo in Colombia, and I urged her former boss, the owner, to have everything ready for delivery before I moved in. I felt let down by my brother, who once again broke his promise to Doc to stand by me. I had asked him to assist with the move. On the day I moved, they basked in the sun on the beaches of Hawaii instead.

Before I headed up north, Professor Jaeger's widow, Dele, threw a party for me, serving German strawberry punch. The day before my departure, several of my fellow students and I went for a beer at Regulator, the student restaurant. I almost did not get in, because the guy at the door asked to see my ID. I was happily puzzled and told him he should get a flashlight and take a good look at me. I was forty at the time. The IU–Bloomington campus was in a celebratory mood as well, because our own Mark Spitz had won seven gold medals at the Olympics just before the terrorists attacked the Israeli team in Munich.

As I bid farewell to Karla, who knew about the fiasco with the businessman, she asked if she could have him. I told her I did not care, never thinking that after what I had told her, and after witnessing her outrage, she would be at all interested. I should have known, though, that she was unpredictable and, to all appearances, desperate, because her behavior was at times noticeably peculiar. I did not know what to say when, on one occasion, she dug up a black-and-white photograph of what I first thought was a corpse in the nude stretched out on a bed. I was speechless when she said it was she. I often wondered whether I was the only person who had been privileged enough to see a photo of her in the nude. She probably thought I would compare her to Giorgione's painting of the *Sleeping Venus*, on display at

Dresden's Picture Gallery. She shocked us, or at least me, again at the New Year's Eve party at her house. At the stroke of midnight, she grabbed a very young male student, not known to any of those present, threw her arms around him, bent him backward, and kissed him so passionately we thought she would never stop. We stood like statuettes, afraid to move.

IV *1972–1984*

1972–1984

Adjusting to Life as a German Professor, to Academia, and to Colleagues on Campus and Abroad – Planting the Seeds for a Summer Program in Bonn, West Germany, with the Padre's Help

On my drive north, I thought about my new house, with its shingles freshly painted dark brown. I was content and ready to furnish it. I had not owned a home since I sold the Croft. This bungalow had at least the color of its shingles in common with Doc's homestead, and I knew the minute I entered it where my yet-to-be-bought baby-grand piano would reign supreme. Sally's boss had promised to deliver the bedroom furniture as soon as I arrived, since I owned no bed. When he did not show, I called the store and found out the workers were on strike. I believe it was due to my connection with Sally James that Mr. Ries himself finally appeared with a van and, with the help of a couple of guys, virtually smuggled the furniture into my house after dark. Everybody loved my little house on the hill, and my friends were happy to have me back. Rachel threw a surprise party for me. All of the Loesers stood around me as I struggled to slice the huge angel food cake, which was at least two feet in diameter and almost eight inches high. Big red roses and *congratulations*, written in green sugar letters, decorated the monstrosity. I tried hard to slice the cake, but the knife did not cut. All of a sudden, I realized the cake was a hoax. It was made of Styrofoam. We laughed, and Rachel brought out the real product.

IU–South Bend, popularly known as IUSB, was the largest regional commuter campus in the IU system, with about six thousand students when I arrived. It consisted of a few modern structures located on the bank of the beautiful St. Joe River, which contributed to its frequently being referred to as "Riverside High." I was troubled by that derogatory term as much as by the other nickname, "Rinky-Dink College," and was determined to fight the term by adhering to the same standards I had been exposed to when studying in France and at IU–Bloomington. I liked that it had a comparably strong division of music and communication arts and was a growing campus with ample room for innovation and improvement.

I adjusted to academia rapidly and approached my classes with an abundance of enthusiasm. I was bursting with ideas to enrich the learning experience of my students and quickly achieved the reputation of being a workaholic. Before I knew it, I chaired a couple of committees, including one in charge of promoting hot food on campus. Unfortunately, though we ended up with a hot-food program eventually, much time and money was wasted on architects. My suggestion was to serve the food at an indoor sidewalk café, which would cater to the three foreign languages on campus: French, German, and Spanish. By the beginning of the spring semester, I had been asked to revive and chair the International Studies Committee, which was right up my alley, and before long, three summer programs, one for England, another for France, and a third for Germany, were approved for students from our campus only.

Teaching a senior culture course for German majors required instant and major adjustments on my part. I quickly realized that several of these students, and one in particular, were not prepared to follow my lectures in German. The difference between these students' capabilities and the capabilities of those who took the advanced course I had taught in Bloomington was like night and day. I had to switch gears, lower my standards for lecturing as well as my expectations, and try to gradually bring them up to the desired level of achievement. One older student, a divorcée who turned out to be in charge of the language lab and prided herself on having a special relationship with the chairman, required additional hours in my office to earn a passing grade.

I virtually inundated my students with cultural activities and, in addition to starting a German-film series on campus, invited them on numerous occasions to my home for pizza and German conversation, holding review sessions, reading German drama, singing German songs, or looking at slides I took in Germany. I founded the German Uni-Klub IUSB and drove them to eat schnitzel and bratwurst at the Berghoff in Chicago, where we got lost on the way to Büchner's play *Woyzek*. After the play, we talked with the German actors. I invited Heinz to talk to the culture class about the Holocaust and drove with them to the Loesers' farm for a German dinner followed by a German-style hike, during which we sang as we marched down a country road. I even took the class to a German Lutheran church service in Michigan to listen to a sermon in German and invited anybody interested in speaking German to a weekly German lunch hour at a nearby restaurant. To top it off, I hung out with the students once a week for an hour in the student lounge to speak German only. It goes without saying that I taught an overload of courses.

Under the umbrella of the Uni-Klub, I began to host an annual Oktoberfest with bratwurst imported from a German butcher in Chicago, potato salad prepared by my German friends, sauerkraut cooked by yours truly, and Löwenbräu in a barrel from the liquor store. Everybody was invited, and at times more than one hundred people flooded the premises. Everybody had a barrel of fun. They sang German folk songs around an open fire and chatted at tables on loan from the university, which were set up in my backyard and covered with red-and-white-checkered tablecloths. Candles flickered, sausages sizzled on an open grill, and the multicolored lanterns, which I brought from Germany, dangled in the trees for atmosphere. Oktoberfest music drummed through the evening air from the loudspeakers in the backyard from beginning to end.

I felt I had to perform acrobatics in front of the freshman classes to keep them awake and stimulated. Now and then, I asked the students to stand up and sing a German song, or challenged them to a vocabulary game on the blackboard. The freshmen in particular wanted to be entertained, and they loved it when I acted out prepositions taking the accusative or dative case with the help of a little copper dog and a brass cigarette box with a lid, and even enjoyed memorizing Goethe's

Erlkönig (Earl King) and acting it or German fairy tales out in front of the class. I was forever preparing handouts focusing on vocabulary or grammatical rules and went so far as to write my own short stories based on real-life experiences, because the students preferred them to those in textbooks. They loved it when I recounted real-life experiences from Germany and wanted me to write a book about my life.

Judging by my chairman's evaluation of my first academic year, my performance met his expectations. After all, he had denied tenure to my predecessor, who by all accounts had failed to measure up. I was pleased when he commented, "[Ms. Beardsley] has completed her first year of teaching with flying colors, and with an absolutely astounding expense of energy. She is devoted to her profession and, as her annual report shows, full of ideas."

The chairman of Arts and Sciences once said to a colleague, "Christa is a dreamer." My colleague replied, "It's amazing how many of her dreams have come true."

* * *

I did have a dream right at the onset of my teaching career: I wanted to make it possible for the financially less privileged students and those unable to study for a year abroad to spend at least a few weeks during the summer in Germany.

I began to realize my dream when I became chairperson of the International Studies Committee. I learned what was involved in developing programs for overseas study. As my plans included a trip to Germany from May 11 to June 24, 1973, I made it a point to set the stage and was successful in meeting with the German Embassy and the director of the German Student Exchange, Dr. W. Holle, at the University of Bonn. After having neglected the Padre for several years, I surprised him with a visit to Bonn as well. He was stunned and beamed when I told him I had earned a PhD. Over a delicious meal complemented with an excellent wine from the Moselle, for which I paid, because the Jesuits professed to be so poor, we caught up and laughed a lot. He listened carefully when I told him about my plans for a summer program in Bonn, which had fallen on sympathetic ears in my preliminary discussions with the embassy and Dr. Holle. In the same breath, he assured me I could use a youth-activities room in their building as a classroom and introduced me to Maria Hoefer, an already-ancient widow who looked rather elegant with her wig of reddish-brown hair. I was to ask her if she would house the students in the apartment house a block down the street from the Jesuits' residence. She had restored this bombed-out house and rented out the six apartments to students from underdeveloped countries who were subsidized by the Carl Duisberg Foundation, and to visiting Jesuits and members from the Ministry of Culture who came to the capitol in connection with government sessions. Up to twenty students could easily be accommodated during the summer, when everybody was on vacation. I spent a couple of nights at Mrs. Hoefer's house and must say that we hit it off right away. I immediately detected that she was shrewd. Earning all that extra money during the summer, when few visitors came to Bonn and her foreign Duisberg students were on vacation, probably made her think twice about turning down my offer. Besides, she venerated the Jesuits and especially the Padre, whose sermons she hardly ever missed. On Sundays, she wore a special wig, covered it with a navy-blue velvet hat from which a soft veil hung over her white face, and was generous, I am sure, when the collection plate reached her. She did not think twice about agreeing to put up our group starting in 1975.

The fundamentals for my program were in place, and my spirits ran high. The Padre was eager to go for a ride with me in my rental car. He suggested we drive along the Rhine and the Moselle to Trier and referred to the two rivers as "father Rhine and his lovely daughter Moselle." We rolled along the ever-so-romantic and idyllic countryside, covered with endless hilly vineyards and bordering the two famous waterways. I had last savored the landscape on a weekend trip with Erich, when we drank too much of the golden wine at the quaint and intoxicating Drosselgasse, in Rüdesheim on the Rhine, where countless wine restaurants compete with each other. I knew my students eventually had to get a taste of this vibrant part of Germany. The Padre and I stopped at an inviting inn along the Moselle, where he, a native of the region and a great connoisseur of wines, chose a precious drink. He first swished it around in the goblet and then lowered his well-shaped nose to smell the bouquet before sipping a sample noisily. He swished it around in his mouth, making sure you saw his cheeks bulge, and finally let it roll down his throat. At the end of the ritual he exclaimed, "Oh, what a divine drop!"

The Padre had suggested we stop at Adolf Lorscheider's place in Trier, Germany's oldest town, founded by the Romans around 15 BC and also known as "Roma secunda." He was a wine inspector and, in addition to having his own wine press, produced a very dry apple cider, which, if you drink a glass each day, should decidedly prolong your life. The Padre wanted to buy several cases and take them back for his co-padres. I was totally smitten with the kind Lorscheider family and their wine cellar, and even more with the wines, which they let me taste from the big barrels in the dark and moist cellar. When I told them about my plans for the students, they said right away that I must bring them there for an evening of wine tasting when we came to Bonn. What an incentive! But there was more to our visit in Trier.

The Padre wanted me to meet his older brother, the bishop from Trier, and his two very old sisters, who with a number of servants kept house for the bishop. I followed the Padre up the thirty or more steps to the big oak portal, which was opened by one of the old maids after her brother had pulled a cord on which a brass bell was suspended and rang loudly. We awaited the bishop in a somber waiting room similar to that at Sankt Ursula, except the crucifix on the wall was bigger. The bishop, tall with silver-gray hair and very sophisticated, entered and greeted us. When he held out his hand, I was not sure I should kiss his ring, because I was not there for an audience. Since his behavior was casual, I skipped the ceremony. We did stay for a cup of coffee and a piece of cake, and before we left, I mustered up enough courage to ask him if in the future I might pay him a visit with my students when we came to admire Trier, with the big cathedral, the famous Roman ruins, and other sights. He thought it would be nice and said that if he turned out to be available, he would love to meet us in the gardens, show us remnants from the past, and grant us a look into his famous wine cellars.

Before leaving Trier, we drove past a few major ruins of antiquity, such as Hadrian's well-preserved amphitheater and the very impressive and massive Porta Nigra, the fortified north gate of the city, which may date back to the third or fourth century AD. We skipped the ruins of the fourth-century Roman baths and other noteworthy sights, because I knew I would be back. – Toward evening, we paused for a German evening meal of pumpernickel with cold cuts and a goblet of red wine from the Eiffel region, which is in the hinterland of the Moselle country. We sat at a table outside with a view of the lovely Moselle, which shimmered golden from the setting sun. The Padre reminisced about his childhood, and I cherished listening to the tales he liked to spin. He had a way of mesmerizing the listener with his dark and sonorous voice, the expressions on his face, and his piercing black eyes, which constantly searched for the slightest movement in my face.

He started a bit tongue in cheek:

As you know, there are children and then there are children. Some are _this_ way and others are _that_ way. Little Anton was like _this_. You could notice right away that Anton was like _this_. All you had to do is look at him. Unlike other boys he did not have a turned-up nose, but a nose that was a bit slanted and slightly pointed. If you overlooked the freckles, you might detect a slight tendency toward the development of a more sculptured nose, like that of Apollo, if you know what I mean. But that was as far as it went. Anton's sparkling black eyes stood in contrast to his mouth. Already at that young age he understood to close the narrow lips sternly. His head was neither oval nor round, but noticeably square, which again accentuated his being like _this_. Anton showed no trace of flowing locks of the Greek gods either, despite the fact that Mother Nature had endowed him with a full head of obstinate, dark curls. But each year they sheared his head just as bare as they sheared the little sheep on which Anton used to ride around the old giant linden tree in the center of the courtyard in front of the schoolhouse where his father taught.

Yes, no doubt about it, Anton just happened to be like _this_. Have you ever met a little chap who at the age of three or four has the idea to fry sparrow eggs, sunny-side up? I am not talking about chicken, duck, or goose eggs. It is quite possible that this or that chap will throw those in a skillet. But not Anton, the gourmet. Quite early he developed a penchant for finding pleasure in the extraordinary. Child of nature that he was, he stretched out his chubby hands boldly and helped himself to the bounty with which Mother Nature surrounded him.

The ancient linden tree whose broad branches spread cooling shade in front of the old homestead offered Anton its treasures liberally. The tree stretched out his arms and encouraged the chap to climb up the bony stem and secure for himself a lofty spot under the green roof where he would be surrounded by the aroma of its blossoms. Up there, the linden tree offered Anton the unique opportunity to observe from up close a sparrow's nest. He was fascinated by the discovery. He wanted to find out how many eggs such a female sparrow might produce in a certain amount of time. As soon as two spotted eggs appeared in the nest, he helped himself quickly by picking up the fragile morsels with thumb and index finger, and secured them in a bowl from mother's kitchen.

Mother sparrow laid her eggs for the little thief fast, as if she wanted to break a record. She seemed to know that the boy would need a bunch of the tiny eggs to execute his plan. As soon as he had enough, he carried the precious supply to the kitchen stove, climbed on a stool, broke the delicate shells with the tips of his fingers, and let them splash one by one into the spattering grease in the skillet where they clung closely together while being fried. The eggs were done in a jiffy. Anton slid them back into the bowl, which he clutched close to his little round tummy. The rascal climbed back into the tree, sat down next to Mrs. Sparrow, and did not think twice about pushing the delicacies into his little mouth and devouring them noisily under the eyes of his generous provider.

* * *

It was dark when the Padre and I bid our farewell in front of the residence of the Jesuits. The next day, I headed to Regensburg, a small city and the episcopal see of the Land of Bavaria, located on the Danube. I had an appointment there to meet Professor Dr. Wulf Segebrecht, who was, despite his youth, one of the foremost Hoffmann scholars at that time. One could not but greatly respect his sound and impeccable scholarship, with which I got well acquainted when conducting research for my dissertation. I was understandably nervous, because I knew he was a sharp critic, but wanted to ask him if he thought my dissertation should be published.

When the young professor opened the door to the bright and spacious apartment, my nervousness diminished. I had had no idea what he would be like and was pleasantly surprised when he held out his hand to greet me. His blue eyes looked very friendly as he invited me to come on in. He was very slender and tall and walked with noticeable elasticity, which gave him a youthful appearance, while the glasses with a thin metal frame lent him a distinct professorial look. He had a boyish haircut, and since he was from Luebeck, in Northern Germany, I was not surprised that his hair was light brown yet not very thick. His pleasant voice was soothing. While each word, sentence, or phrase was spoken with impeccable, print-ready correctness, he did inject an occasional humorous twist. Most of all, Professor Segebrecht was neither arrogant nor condescending, but polite and modest, and I was relieved and pleased when he promised to read my dissertation and let me know if he thought it should be published. He also liked the idea for an article I wanted to write, and he urged me to send it to him in time for the next publication of the E. T. A. Hoffmann periodical, of which he was the editor in chief.

Before I left to return to Hannover by way of Bamberg, Professor Segebrecht introduced his wife Ursel and his daughter Bettina. His wife was a strikingly attractive, very charming, and tall brunette. She was highly intelligent, held a PhD in German, and like her husband, lectured at the University of Regensburg. I enjoyed listening to her clear and ringing voice, colored by that appealing Bavarian accent. She was a native of the picturesque medieval town Rothenburg o.d. Tauber, Bavaria, and asked many questions about life in America. Bettina was a little three-year-old redhead, as cute as a button. She had freckles and a little snub nose, giggled a lot, and wanted everybody to play with her. It was obvious that her parents adored their Little Red Riding Hood. Before I left, Professor Segebrecht suggested I stop in Bamberg and meet Dr. Wirth, the president of the E. T. A. Hoffmann Society, and ask him to show me the E. T. A. Hoffmann house, which is opposite the civic theater where Hoffmann used to conduct and where his opera *Undine* was performed.

Dr. Wirth, while showing me the very humble residence of this great writer-composer, expressed interest in the publication of my dissertation as well as the planned article, and he invited me to a special meeting of the E. T. A. Hoffmann Society in 1976, which I assured him I would attend. I wanted to get to know Bamberg better as well, but I was a bit rushed to return to Hannover and then back home. We spent less than an hour looking at the three or four small rooms in the very narrow and humble abode where Hoffmann and his wife Mischa lived from 1808 to 1813 and where his beloved voice student Julia inspired him to write several of his best works. I was quite fascinated by the little room underneath the roof, his favorite writing place, and was amused by the human-sized puppet, dressed in black, wearing a top hat, standing in the window, and looking down on the street as though it were Hoffmann in person. I had been anxious to see the rectangular opening in the floor through which Hoffmann was known to suspend a bottle or puppet on a string to tease his wife in the room below. It was still there. I was thrilled to have met and made new friends à la Hoffmann and could hardly wait to return to this unique spot to meet other Hoffmann enthusiasts.

* * *

My parents, whom I visited shortly, were proud of my accomplishments. Erich did not quite know what to do with me, and though he could still turn me on, it was more obvious to me than before that there was no future for us and that I was to forge ahead alone.

A few weeks before the semester started, another family drama unfolded in the Loeser household. Their son, then in college, had fallen head over heels in love with a coed who was not received by his parents with open arms. He and Barb had decided to move in together. Heinz strongly objected. The young girl, about five feet tall, had long, straight brown hair, blue eyes, and a pale, grayish complexion and was rather bright. She was majoring in comparative literature at the time, aiming eventually for a PhD. Kermit was of dark complexion, had a head of long, wild, black curls, was perhaps 5'4", and majored in math. To all appearances, they were a good match. Since the parents had made it clear to them that they would no longer be welcome if they moved in together, they came to me in South Bend to talk about the situation. We talked until late at night. I found out little by little that Barb, one of seven or more siblings, had suffered abuse at home by her father, and on campus had gotten involved with a group of drug users. She was apparently in bad shape when Kermit pulled her out of the gutter, so to speak, and tried to help her get back on her feet. I found all of this quite commendable, but began to worry when she told me, after Kermit left the room, that she had really wanted Kermit's roommate and that they had experienced problems in other sensitive areas. Since there was no one else and Kermit was insisting on helping her in every way possible, she lacked the courage to open up to him. I finally sent them to bed and was a bit puzzled when they went to sleep in their jeans. They looked as though they had not showered in a long time, but I was not about to make a point of it. After all, I had met plenty of students who looked just as they did, that is, as though they had crawled out of bed the same way they crawled in. But I was not crazy about their big black Doberman, who ran through my house the minute I opened the door and went to the bathroom, planting a big, stinky mess on the new rug next to the tub.

When Kermit talked about getting married in order to avoid a break with his family, I tried my best to convince him otherwise, but was not sure I had succeeded by the time they went back to college. I called Heinz and urged him not to throw them out if they decided to move in together, because I sensed that these young people had a lot to iron out before (and if) they were ever to get married. I was convinced that, otherwise, their marriage would be doomed to fail and that Kermit, who was always supersensitive, would suffer immensely. The next I heard, they got married without the presence of the family on the shores of Lake Michigan. A while after that, there was a major break with his sister Rachel and her husband. During a visit, they had informed the two never to set foot in their house again dressed in such rags. Harry feared he might lose clients if they happened to come by and see them. The couple never returned to the sister's home, but they were occasionally invited to the parents' farm.

Rachel and her husband went to the other extreme and accumulated much wealth, not without the inheritances from Rachel's grandfather and Heinz. On several occasions, a couple of my Jewish friends remarked that they were aware of the reason why Harry became Jewish and joined the temple, that is, to recruit clients for his accounting firm. I lost respect for both when I witnessed Harry mercilessly evict a young family with children from one of his rental properties late in the evening. I have never forgotten the time the widow of a poor carpenter, who had worked for Heinz at the stores and taken care of maintenance jobs for me, came to me quite disturbed. She had asked Harry to help her with her income taxes. Even though she wanted to pay him, he refused, telling her he did not take clients in her tax bracket. Considering that his own father, a factory worker, was probably in a similar situation, I often wondered if he would have made an exception in his case. Little by little, I distanced myself from my old friend Rachel.

I also distanced myself from old Karla, whose visit I tolerated once, despite her obnoxious behavior. Though we never talked about it, I believed she did not go after the married businessman from Bloomington after all. She called me almost weekly, claiming she would rather spend the money on phone calls than on a psychiatrist. I regretted having offered to drive with her from South Bend to visit a friend in Chicago. She was extremely condescending, treated me like a child, and made me so nervous I took a wrong turn. At that point, she let me have it, asking me in a vicious tone of voice how I could be so "stupid" as to miss a turn at a place where I had lived for over a year. It was the last time I invited her for a visit by herself.

* * *

When the fall semester started, I was appointed by Vice President and Dean Merritt to serve on the IU System-Wide Overseas Studies Committee. I was secretly ecstatic. The position would give me the opportunity not only to gain greater insight into IU's international activities, but also to stay in touch with some of my professors. In addition, I would get to know colleagues with similar interests and visit my old friends. I realized it was important for our campus not only to develop international programs suited to a handful of students from our campus, as had been the case in the past, but also to develop overseas programs to which students from all IU campuses or any other accredited university could apply. I found out quickly that several of my colleagues and the administrators were reluctant to cater to students other than those from IUSB. It was a question of finances. There was no objection to including IU-Bloomington students if the Bloomington campus helped to fund such programs. However, I personally felt that since our campus would collect the tuition, and since Bloomington did not require our campus to contribute toward the costs of programs developed by them, we should operate under the same policy.

Nevertheless, to demonstrate to the administration that I would also make an attempt to seek financial assistance and support among influential members of the community and industry, I reconnected with my former but retired boss, Mr. Koerting, VP of the Export Division of Miles, Inc., as well as with Lehman Beardsley, head of the Miles Foundation and son of Doc's cousin, Ed, also from Miles, Inc. I joined the World Trade Club and met with the head of the Chamber of Commerce. Even if they did not contribute financially, I felt it was imperative to bring the academic and business worlds closer together. I even joined the German American National Congress, despite the fact that some of their members were still clinging to the German Reich as though it still existed. But they did come through with financial support for some of my programs, such as the film series, audiovisual material, and language courses for children, which I started under the umbrella of continuing education. Several of my native students majoring in German were hired as teachers for these classes. The same courses were offered for French and Spanish as well.

In an effort to become integrated into the academic community, I socialized more frequently with the young liberals than with the older conservatives. The males convinced me to join the American Federation of Teachers and be their treasurer. But I cancelled my membership as soon as I realized that they accomplished nothing. The feminists wanted me in their circle as well. Though I had been too busy to pay much attention to the feminist movement, and never liked being cast into a certain mold, I went to a number of their gatherings, mainly because I liked Professor G. A very bright former English professor of mine, she had asked me to quote the first ten lines of Chaucer's *Canterbury Tales* in her course. I was a frequent guest at her and her husband's beautiful home on the St. Joe River and was intrigued each time by their handsome collection of primitive art. I very much enjoyed their arty circle of friends and relished their gourmet cuisine. Unfortunately, I felt I had to distance myself after she approached me, gently, at a convention where we shared the same room. It was at about that time that I learned of her bisexuality. I was surprised that the more liberal male professors on campus zeroed in on her so mercilessly. Such behavior would have been unthinkable in Germany. On a professional basis, I participated in a course she and another female colleague had developed under the title "Interdisciplinary Analysis of Women's Role in Germany." Up to that point, I had been naïve enough to think I was immune to discrimination as long as I myself adhered to high standards.

I made a special effort to get to know the members of my department better, and threw a party for my Spanish colleague when his booklet of sonnets, *Gotas de Presente*, was published. His colleague from Peru told me that the thin paperback had been published, receiving no reviews whatever, by a fellow Cuban dissident who had set up a printing shop in his garage in Miami. I felt a bit sorry for the Cuban, who enjoyed the administration's sympathy because he was one of Castro's young lawyers who escaped. I was impressed by the law degree until another Spaniard explained that only four years of certain courses in college sufficed to earn one the title of "lawyer" in Cuba. My chairman had told me that the man had had a hard time obtaining his PhD at Indiana State University. He had trouble finishing his dissertation, which threatened his teaching position and led to a reduction of his teaching load and consequently a reduction in income. He finished the dissertation shortly after his wife had completed hers. Rumor had it that she played a major part in finishing his thesis. My chairman had a difficult time coping with the situation, because each Christmas the Cuban couple presented both him and the chancellor, as I was told, with extravagant gifts, like a silver coffeepot. In retrospect, I fail to understand why Mr. S. attached such importance to a PhD, since he himself, though he called himself a professor, did not hold one. But then again, I had learned that one of the full-time, non-PhD German instructors at Notre Dame enjoyed the same privilege.

I had invited most of my colleagues and their respective husbands and wives to the party. They seemed to enjoy themselves, including the wife of my chairman. Only a year later, Mr. S. divorced that attractive, elderly, white-haired lady and married the much younger divorcée and language-lab assistant who had been among a small group of students with whom he traveled throughout Germany in a VW bus. I turned down his offer to come along and noticed that he had treated me with increasing indifference ever since. I did not know what to tell the sobbing wife when she called me again and again on the phone to ask if I knew what was going on.

I very much resented that other married faculty members made passes at me. One, from the Department of Political Science, openly propositioned me when he came to my house just to talk, so I assumed, about university matters. Fortunately, once I set him straight, he did not try again. He was a bit weird, totally self-centered, not at all handsome, overweight, and rather sloppy in appearance as well as in his eating habits. He smacked his lips disgustingly loudly and continually wiped his sweaty hands on the ends of the arms of the upholstered chairs, into which he virtually flopped and squeezed his oversized body. His hips were too broad, and his stomach definitely carried an overload. I was always tempted to put a towel on the arms of the chair before he sat down, but tried to be polite out of fear he might accuse me of anti-Semitism. We hardly ever had a discussion in which he failed to remind me I was a native of Germany. I had not kept it a secret that I suffered from the collective guilt syndrome. Is it possible that he took unfair advantage of me? As long as I can remember, whenever he called, which for years was almost daily, he never once asked how I was, never introduced himself, and just talked endlessly, forever complaining about administrators and his colleagues, regardless of sex, religion, race, or color, on our campus and across the IU system. Nobody, and no university, escaped his wrath, especially the University of Wisconsin, where he had had trouble being tenured. Yet, when I observed him in the company of those he disliked, he was as sweet as honey. One of my colleagues enlightened me when I pointed out the hypocrisy. It was actually diplomatic, because stirring up trouble could result in one's salary being docked and being denied letters of support when applying for grants, etc. – I most certainly got an education in the politics of academia, especially of our campus, from him. He soaked up gossip like a sponge and was forever complaining about the difficulties of finding a willing student to have an affair with. He could not understand why one of his colleagues had no trouble finding willing learners. He had a reputation for not giving any grade below a B because he felt it was the best way to appease the administration, which had a thing about attrition and thus loss of income from tuition. He openly slept with one woman after another, despite the fact that he had just married a young and beautiful second wife, whom I knew well because she was a loyal auditor of my literature courses. She appreciated my approach to teaching literature, because, she claimed, I understood how to communicate with the students at their level, in contrast to a well-known professor whom she had had at Northwestern and who, according to her, lectured at a level way over the students' heads. We also submitted a proposal to Prentice Hall for a textbook entitled "Read What the Germans Read" in 1974. – By the way, the overweight professor very rarely greeted me in the corridors. Once, however, when we both got stuck in the elevator, he talked a mile a minute. He was horrified that we might have been stuck there forever. I gloated when at one point the elevator moved a bit, only to stop again, but leaving a gap of about one foot, which I used to squeeze out, wishing him good luck. There was no way he could have crawled to freedom with that belly. The opening was a bit tight for me too; while escaping, I did break the agate on my necklace. – This particular academician was devoid of any sex appeal; he still had a few disorderly gray hairs on his almost bald skull. He forever lugged around bundles of loosely gathered papers under his arm. If you had the misfortune to have to go to his office for some reason, there was no empty spot in which to sit. Chairs, desk, and floor were stacked with papers and books in a tumultuous mess several feet high. I had no idea how anybody could find anything. If there was one good thing about him, he did abide by university rules, at least to my knowledge, and unlike his friend from the English Department, who kept a bottle hidden in his desk drawer, did not indulge on campus.

It was his other friend, who had an ongoing affair with a female student, whom I should have reported to the administration as soon as the affair happened, but I was too new and thus afraid to say anything to anybody. Already, during my second semester, this tall, yet not exactly handsome, full professor with a sizeable lump in the vicinity of his long nose came to my office. There were no windows in my room, and the walls were of metal. As I opened the door, he immediately stepped into the room and asked me a question about something, which I have forgotten. What I never did forget was his behavior. No sooner had he entered my office than he locked the door behind him so nobody could come in. A big guy with dark eyes, a sickly, pale, white face, and some fringes of black hair on his square head, he said something to the effect that he found me very attractive. I was speechless and afraid. He continued by pushing my back against the wall behind my desk. While holding me in a clench and looking at my face, he bent his head toward me, telling me again that he really liked me, at which point I gathered all of my strength, forced a grin, pushed him away with both fists, and told him to wait until I had tenure. He smirked, released me, and left my office. – I was devastated, since by then I knew it could very well happen that this particular individual might in the future sit on a promotion, tenure, and reappointment committee to cast a vote for or against my professional advancement.

* * *

I continued to teach an overload of courses at various levels in addition to writing an article and serving on various minor and major committees, but I spent the bulk of my time in connection with overseas programs. Two of my male colleagues from the History and Fine Arts Departments had proposed a summer program focusing on history and art in England, which was rejected by the system-wide committee. My colleagues were furious, to say the least, but I succeeded in calming them down and encouraging them to rewrite and resubmit it. By then, I knew which areas needed to be strengthened. I had developed a relationship of mutual respect with the members of the committee as well as with Dean Nugent, also chair of the Overseas Studies Committee in Bloomington. I succeeded in rescheduling the meeting at which the England proposal was to be reconsidered. It would be held on our campus. I was thrilled when they agreed to come, even though it meant having to fly in a few members. To make it worth their while, I invited all committee members, those from the system-wide committee as well as the members of the IUSB committee, for a semi-business social gathering at my residence, which would provide an opportunity for all to get acquainted before the meeting. The party, complete with champagne and hors d'oeuvres, was a success, and it goes without saying that on the following Saturday morning, the revised England program was approved at the meeting on our campus. It was the first and last time the system-wide committee traveled to South Bend to attend a meeting.

So Long, Erich – Laying the Foundation for International Summer Programs

By the end of the spring semester of 1974, I was ready for a vacation. As was the case so many times before, Erich had pursued me vigorously by sending me passionate letters and cassette tapes. He succeeded in convincing me not to tell my parents when I would arrive in Hannover. He wanted to meet me at the airport and take me on a vacation. He was by then a successful doctor of veterinary medicine, specializing in poultry diseases, which necessitated his traveling extensively all over Europe, but predominantly to lesser-developed regions. At that time, chicken farms were mushrooming. His back did not seem to bother him too much. He had opted to focus on poultry diseases in order to avoid heavy lifting and was making money right and left. He picked me up in his big white Mercedes-Benz 480 SL, which had reclining front seats, and I was quite excited, looking forward to a fabulous vacation. But when he drove off the Autobahn onto a rural path leading to a beautiful forest, something did not seem right. I watched quietly as he parked the car in a clearing. It was May, and the sun was shining down on the open spot. He turned down the radio, which played something by Mozart, took my hand, looked deep into my eyes, and told me in a most compelling and lamenting tone of voice that he was so sorry to have to tell me he could not keep his promise to take me on a trip. My heart sank. Before I could ask him for the reason, he explained that he had had a fabulous opportunity to buy a mink farm with tanning facilities for a most opportune price. The owner had declared bankruptcy only a day earlier, and he had to be there to finalize the transaction. I could hardly believe my ears and felt very uncomfortable, because my parents had no idea I was already in Germany. I asked him what he intended to do with me, since I could not possibly appear unannounced at my parents' house without my parents, who had continued to oppose the liaison with him, throwing a fit. He suggested I come with him to his house, where he also had his practice, and spend the day reading or in the library. I was too numb, and too jet-lagged, to come up with a better idea. As he approached his large house, he asked me to duck to avoid being seen by the good citizens of Oldenburg, because they might tell his wife, who lived in a neighboring town with the children, that we had been together. I had never been so humiliated. As he opened the door to his house, I was amazed at the rich interior. The living room was furnished with beautiful mahogany furniture, and a rich sky-blue Oriental carpet was spread out on the light parquet floor. As the house was new, the big windows let in much sunlight, which shone on the big plants standing in various corners of the room. The walls were covered with books and artwork. Somehow, I felt intimidated and wanted to get out.

I spent the next day in the library, waiting. As soon as Erich arrived, I asked him to take me to Hannover. I called Mutti on the way and shocked her with my announcement of a surprise visit. The next day, when I tried to reach Erich on the phone, his answering machine picked up. I was so infuriated by the machine I left a firm message in English. It was crystal clear: "Go to *hell*." I do not recall ever saying those words before or after. Though I must confess, it's easier for me to say them in English than in German. I gave instructions to my parents to tell him I was not available if by chance he called. Mutti, who hoped it was all finished, looked at me with big, blue, questioning eyes.

I was anxious to get to Bonn, where I had planned to pick up and strengthen my contacts in an effort to ensure the success of my Bonn Program, which was to take place for the first time in 1975. I was fortunate to be able to combine my efforts with my attendance at the meeting of the American Association of Teachers of German. It took place in Bonn, and Mutti Hoefer was happy to rent a room to me. At this meeting, during a big party at the magnificent, baroque Rathaus (Town Hall), I had the opportunity to meet the Bundespräsident Walter Scheel and to enlist the support of the American ambassador Martin J. Hillenbrand as well as that of Hans Steger, the mayor of Bonn. I was pleased when the officials of the university's student association assured me that our students could eat for a nominal fee at the university dining halls. They were only a couple of blocks away from their residence. The Bonner Bureau of Information promised to forward brochures, maps, etc., to be given to future participants. I wanted to make sure my proposal would be accepted by all of the six or seven administrators and committees, whose go-ahead was needed for the program to proceed.

While in Bonn, I also met with Mr. Herbert Grundmann, chief editor and proprietor of the publishing house Bouvier, who had agreed to publish my dissertation, which had Professor Segebrecht's blessing. He was quite interested in all my activities, scholarly and otherwise. I was optimistic that knowing Mr. Grundmann personally would be fruitful in the future.

I must say that without the support of the Padre, it would have been difficult to start the program. We had been friends since 1951. He liked to venture out into nature whenever he had a chance. As he was partially blind, he was dependent on others to drive him. But he also knew the train schedule to the most desirable locations in the area by heart. He was an obsessed wanderer and fisherman. I had sent him a deluxe American collapsible fishing rod for his birthday as a thank-you gesture for helping me with the Bonn Program. He had been eager to take me fishing ever since I had told him about my fishing escapades with Doc up north, and he wanted to show off the rod. Thus, before I returned to Hannover, we took a trip to the Eifel region, where he introduced me to a secluded trout stream. It meandered through the meadows surrounding the castle, which belonged to one of his friends, a relative of the count von Stauffenberg, who attempted to assassinate Hitler in 1944. It was a magnificent day, and the scenery, with the proud castle on a hillock, looked strikingly romantic. The Padre handed me a small can with worms, and he waded upstream in his long rubber boots while I tried my luck from the shore and by climbing on fallen tree trunks. We caught enough trout for a meal and set up our cooking gear in the shade alongside the sparkling stream. The Padre, just like Doc, insisted on cooking. I had brought a bottle of Château Neuf du Pape, chosen for its saintly name, which, though a red wine, tasted even better here in the arms of Mother Nature.

On the way back to Bonn, the Padre, who always told me which roads to take, had a surprise up his sleeve. He was full of stories and laughter when he directed me to turn off the road onto a narrow, bumpy trail through a dark forest. It reminded me of the primitive path to our cabin up north. The view, which emerged before us after about five minutes, was a sight to behold. I have never again encountered a more idyllic spot. An old mill, with its wheel turning quietly in the murmuring stream next to the house, stood nestled in the forest at the bottom of the downhill path. Its white stucco shone extra white next to the dark-brown half-timbered beams. The roof was covered with brown tiles, and bright-red geraniums shone like illuminated lanterns in the black flower boxes beneath the small windows, which were guarded by black wrought-iron bars and framed by functional black shutters. We had to open the gate of a white picket fence and walk through a paradise of flowers and blooming bushes to get to the heavy oak door, which the Padre unlocked with a key. Inside, he turned on the lights in the wrought-iron lanterns and lamps so I could admire the rustic decor of the kitchen, the country-style, handcrafted oak furniture in the family room, and the stone hearth, which I imagined to be warm and cozy with a flickering fire in the winter. We had a couple of glasses of the red wine left, which the Padre emptied into a pair of tin cups. It was inside this secluded and idyllic place where I felt more in harmony with the Padre than ever before. It took all our strength to withstand the seductive forces of this old mill.

Before I turned the key to start the car, we took one last, nostalgic look at the picture-perfect spot. The Padre explained that it belonged to a woman of considerable wealth who had purchased the mill and invested a substantial amount of money to have it refurbished, to use it for a vacation home for her four or five adopted children. When he told me I could buy it for 500,000 marks, I knew it was time to leave the dream behind me.

It was getting dark on the Autobahn. I had to stop for gasoline. It was self-service, which I was not used to. In my confusion, I forgot to close the gasoline tank, and the Padre was very upset with me when I announced that I smelled gasoline long after we had left the station. The lid was gone, and so were the dreams.

Call it divine intervention or whatever, but when I arrived back in Hannover to visit my parents for a couple of weeks before flying home, they had a new renter. He was young, tall, and extremely handsome, had curly blond hair and light-blue eyes, and was studying engineering at the Institute of Technology, where Hans, my first love, had studied. His name was Norbert, but I nicknamed him "Apollo." He drove a French "duck" from Citroen. He was about twenty years my junior and simply refused to believe I was over forty. Of course, he was not the only one. I myself did not feel that ancient either. To make a long story short, I did not resist very hard when he fell for me. Because I would not be there too long, a passionate relationship developed very quickly. We exchanged notes and poems constantly, all without my parents suspecting anything. Not to worry – since this young Apollo was a devout Catholic and, I am sure, still pure, I knew when to engage the brakes. But, to be honest, we had a wonderful time exploring nature around Hannover. When I said good-bye, he gave me a copy of Ovid's love poems with the following inscription: "Quidquid agis, / prudenter agas, / et respice finem. [Whatever you do, / do it prudently / and look to the end] Dein Norbert – Apollo." A flood of hot and passionate letters crossed the Atlantic for quite a while. It was the antidote I needed to put to rest my feelings for Erich and to balance the platonic sentiments for the Padre, who wrote a letter apologizing for possibly having given me the wrong impression about his intentions.

As soon as I returned to the States, I got busy composing my proposal for the 1975 G210 Summer Program in Bonn, West Germany (intensive German). I spent countless hours on the telephone, wrote many letters, etc., to ensure that this new program would be successful. It was approved without a hitch by all channels. The brochures turned out well, and my recruiting and screening efforts on the various campuses paid off: by April 1975, I had a group of seventeen students anxious to go.

1972–1984

German Christmas Extravaganza with My Students at the Scottsdale Mall

I must have been a glutton for punishment during that time, not only because I taught an overload again, but also because, once my Bonn Program was in place, I started another project to promote student interest in studying German at IUSB. I planned a German Christmas market at the new Scottsdale Mall.

For any German professor teaching German language, literature, and culture at an American university, it was imperative to introduce students to what Christmas was like in Germany. I seized the opportunity to recapture my childhood magic and bring it into my classroom as soon as I started my career as a German professor. Foreign-language classes, it seemed, were always held in the least attractive rooms in the university. Mine was stuck in the basement. There were no windows. It would have been easy to imagine you were in a prison. The walls were made of some sort of metal. The only way to mount things was with magnets and Scotch Tape. I would have loved to hang a Christmas calendar on a windowpane. Since that was not possible, I decided to talk about the holiday, in German, of course. I brought an Advent wreath, burned candles, which was against university rules and considered unsafe by the administration, and sang German Christmas songs while they flickered. The students brought Christmas cookies, which they baked following recipes I gave them from my German cookbook. I usually scheduled these Christmas sessions for the last twenty minutes of class so as not to sacrifice too much class time. We knew how to make the basement come alive. A professor or maintenance person occasionally peeped in and smiled approvingly. At times, I even ventured so far as to organize a quartet and, after much prodding, consented to join my students and play second violin, or fiddle, if you wish. We performed in the rather colorless atmosphere of the cafeteria while students, professors, and an occasional administrator had lunch. The cafeteria did at least have windows.

One of the highlights of the Christmas season was an entire class session devoted to my students speaking in German about their most memorable childhood Christmas experiences. In exchange, I vowed to talk about mine on Kleine Düwelstraße. Several students dreaded the exercise, worrying about their pronunciation and correct grammar, but in the end were glad they suffered through it. I enjoyed talking about my Christmas memories even though I got a bit sentimental at times.

The big favorite each year was a Christmas party at my home, which no student dared to miss. I trimmed my tree in a way reminiscent of the one in Hannover. At first, I struggled to put up a real tree, in keeping with true German tradition. When it got to be a real nuisance, because I had trouble straightening it again and again when it tipped over, I capitulated and bought a fake tree, which at least looked very much like the trees in Germany. I bought it on sale in Phoenix, Arizona, when visiting the Loesers over Hanukkah. I knew full well my very German friends would nag me forever for putting up a fake tree, and indeed they still do. Yet my imported tree had, and still has, two big advantages. It never tips over, and I can put wax candles on it without fear of burning down the house. The silk needles merely get singed when touched by a burning candle. Of course, my students never failed to warn me that it was against the law. I argued silently that laws are made to be broken – selectively, that is.

Burning candles, a crackling fire in the fireplace, and piano playing lend the essential magic to any Christmas party, especially mine, as you must recall. Before my students and I sang "O Tannenbaum," accompanied by a student at the piano, all electric lights had to be turned off. Only then could we feel warm and sentimental inside and hide a secret tear. The lights also had to be turned off before I started the magic and the climax of the evening: brewing the famous *Feuerzangenbowle*, or *Krambambuli*, as the English call it. I started the *Krambambuli* tradition to give my German students a choice taste of German Christmas culture. Mutti had sent me a special and long-desired Christmas gift, a beautiful copper wine-rum bowl set with a holder for the sugar loaf and a burner on which to brew the concoction, to be served exclusively on cold winter nights, Christmas, and New Year's Eve. A mixture of a light-red wine and some orange and lemon juice is heated on the stove and then transferred to the burner. A sugar loaf, properly imported from Germany, is placed on the holder across the bowl. It is soaked in warm, 150-proof rum. At this point in the process, I would summon all the guests to surround the kettle and observe the magic, which I unfolded before their eyes. I lit a match, held it to the rum-soaked sugar loaf, and in a flash a big blue flame flared up and illuminated the startled faces surrounding the kettle. Next, the sensuous flame hovered around the cone and licked the melting sugar, which dripped into the brew as the guests waited in great anticipation of how it would taste. After the flames devoured the sugar cone, I served the hot and potent *Krambambuli* immediately. If nobody felt warm inside before, I assure you they began to glow once they sipped the bewitching mixture.

For Christmas of 1974 – three years after I started teaching – the students and I went all out. I had founded a German club, which attracted an enthusiastic bunch of students studying German at IUSB. We decided at the beginning of November to plan a Christmas celebration with German flair, partly to recruit more students to study German at IUSB, partly to raise funds to purchase audiovisual materials for use in the classroom, and mostly to bring joy to the community. We asked the big Scottsdale Mall to host the affair. Several local firms and individuals donated goods or cash to buy the materials with which to craft jewelry, straw tree ornaments, bookmarks, etc. We spent many evenings and weekends around my dining-room table making jewelry out of copper wire. A student designed pins which spelled out German words: *Treue, Hoffnung,* and *Liebe,* or *Weihnacht* (Faithfulness, Hope, and Love, or Christmas). We also made star-shaped tree ornaments out of straw, which Mutti sent to us from Germany together with other typical ornaments, such as angels made from burlap. I distributed recipes from my German cookbook and all pitched in, baking large gingerbread cookies in the shape of Christmas trees, hearts, Hänsels and Gretels, and Santa Clauses. They were suspended on a ribbon so that those buying them could wear them around their necks, as German youths do at Christmas fairs. Mutti had sent the glossy Santa Claus and Hänsel and Gretel stickers, which we pasted on the cookies. The male students built a gingerbread house big enough to walk inside and to hide a wicked witch, who was in charge of selling the cookies with which we trimmed the exterior of her house. Another group set up a stage in the mall on which to perform their skit, a German version of *The Newlywed Game*. Students in charge of our children's German classes got ready to present a sample of their activities next to the witch's palace. Others set up a Christmas tree and decorated it with the ornaments we had so diligently fabricated. I did restrain myself from burning real candles on the tree. We compromised and used white electric candles imported from Germany. They looked almost like wax candles.

As you might guess, music reigned supreme at our celebration. I had been fortunate to interest the manager of the mall's piano and organ shop in furnishing an organ and a piano for the day. They moved the piano to the center of the mall, where we set up the stage, the house, and the tree.

Several weeks prior to Sunday, December 8, I had placed an article in the paper asking interested persons in the community to join us at IUSB to rehearse singing German Christmas and folk songs. A student from the Division of Music volunteered to be the conductor, and another adjunct faculty member agreed happily to accompany our choir, which grew from twenty-six to over one hundred members within three weeks. I also found a superb native German soprano who claimed to have studied under both Wunderlich and a wonderful baritone. Our choir sounded quite impressive. All were eager to sing at the Scottsdale Mall on December 8, two days after St. Nicholas' Day. We scheduled three sing-along sessions between noon and 6:00 p.m. and set up overhead projectors and screens to display the German lyrics so that mall visitors could easily join us. Approximately three thousand visitors came to chime in or watch the activities throughout the afternoon. It could not have been more perfect. My soloists performed brilliantly. The transformed mall resounded with music. Excitement was everywhere. Masses of onlookers, many of German descent, stood, admired, and sang. I observed several women wiping away tears of joy. The Christmas spirit captured each and every person in attendance.

I recall several elderly women who approached me and explained that they had emigrated from Germany many years before but had not had such a wonderful Christmas experience since they arrived in America. It was the music which affected us all and lifted us to such heights.

We received much praise from the news media and from colleagues and administrators. They urged me to repeat the affair in subsequent years since we recruited a few students who took up a major in German. One of them climbed the ladder of success and became a German professor. Another, much older American friend who had brought that student to our choir practice was likewise so enamored of the Christmas splash that she too signed up for a German major, despite her age. She struggled ever so hard and occasionally invited me to go boating on their Chris-Craft at Lake Michigan or to celebrate Christmas Eve with her husband and their two dogs, Swedish style. I was reluctant to drive to their small farm when it was snowing, and I once lost my way in a snowstorm and was forced to take shelter in one of the worst shacks I had ever seen. I ended up at the front door by sliding down the driveway in my black 1964 T-bird Landau. I knocked reluctantly. A man in his late fifties, dressed in rags and smelling like whiskey, pushed the squeaky door open with much difficulty. Three giant black dogs stood behind him, barking so loudly I stepped back into the blowing snow at the doorstep. I was certain those monsters would pounce on me like the Neverbee's Bernard. The snow was blowing and drifting, and I was freezing even though I wore Doc's Alaska Seal. I asked if I could call my friends. He ordered the beasts to shut up, said, "Come on in!" and let me squeeze by a pile of garbage bags filled to the brim. A foul smell made its way to my nostrils. He said the phone was in the kitchen. I tried not to look around at the junk in the room we had to pass through to get there. Every spot in the kitchen, including the counter, table, and chairs, was cluttered with papers – old stuff, just trash. He finally located the phone book underneath a pile of cartons. I called my friends, who came at once in their truck and rescued my car and me. I do not recall ever relishing their white Swedish sausages more than on that eve. They tasted almost as good as Mutti's *Bregenwurst*.

One of the singing folks, a recruit from the mall splash and later a star student, was a tall and sexy peroxide-blond GI bride who was working as a secretary in some insurance office when we encountered each other. She was rather unique in several ways. She was the first German I met who had the same name as the heavyweight Saint Bernard who pounced on me that night at the Neverbees. Heidi was very bright because she was born with excellent genes. Her family came from none other than the great Johann Wolfgang von Goethe, which she vowed she could prove genealogically. As I look at my gigantic Goethe poster in the garage, I can see her resemblance to that literary genius right away. Were it not for her dyed hair, her piercing black eyes and long, pointed nose would have made her his look-alike. Regrettably, she inherited neither Goethe's utter disgust for tobacco nor an iota of his fortune. She was a chain smoker and, next to my ex-fiancé John, one of the poorest managers of finances I had ever encountered. Regardless of these shortcomings, I genuinely appreciated her tireless efforts to assist with whatever I asked her to do in building the German programs on our campus.

1972–1984

Trials and Tribulations of the 1975 Summer Program in Bonn, Federal Republic of Germany – Fishing in Himmerod, Eifel Region – First Trip to Berlin

Before I took off with my students for Bonn at the end of the spring semester, in addition to all of my committee work and meetings with local heads of internationally oriented businesses, clubs, and organizations, I attended a number of exciting lectures, focusing on a variety of countries, by professors of varying disciplines whom our International Studies Committee had sponsored. I was extremely fortunate that my publisher required no changes for the publication of my book, which I had decided to dedicate to the Padre, whom I looked on as my inspiration.

We were fortunate that the local press gave all of our projects good coverage and that the student paper did a good job of attracting attention as well. I personally enjoyed the good reporting regarding the philosophy and strength of my teaching, and I had no reason to complain along those lines, because the student evaluations were excellent across the board.

My former star student, Lynne Tatlock, was pursuing her PhD in Bloomington. We were both excited when my department asked her to teach the beginners' course while I was in Bonn. It was a good arrangement not only because she was an excellent teacher, but also because she could stay in my house. Lynne, her husband, and I had become good friends. We had gotten to know each other even better when traveling through Germany before they went to Spain in connection with her husband's stay in the Navy. I never forgot Lynne's eagerness to perfect her German. While on the trip, she wrote down on a pad each and every new word or expression she encountered and would commit them to memory at bedtime. I was content, knowing my students would be taught superbly.

Can you imagine that the journey, even after so much planning, started out with a shock? Dr. Yutzy, a member of my committee, had offered to drive the participants in his van from the South Bend area to the Chicago airport, where the Lufthansa flight was scheduled to depart at 11:00 p.m. We wanted to leave from my house at 7:00 p.m. At 5:00 p.m., the airline called to inform me the flight was delayed for twelve hours. I was unable to reach several students from Bloomington. They had already left, but they spent a good night at the Hilton and bragged about the great accommodations when we met them in the morning to share a substantial free breakfast before takeoff. I got reacquainted with the students I had already met during the screening and orientation sessions, and all were excited and ready for takeoff. On the plane, I made the rounds to speak a few sentences in German with each student. My constant reminder, "Deutsch bitte!" (German, please), must ring in their ears to this day. All felt good, except little Bonnie, who was quiet and complained of a sore throat. I tied a scarf around her neck and hoped an Anacin would lessen the pain by the time we landed in Frankfurt early in the morning.

In Frankfurt, I steered the group to the train station. We missed the first train because it took longer than anticipated to remove the suitcases from the carousel. We missed the next train because we discovered that all Eurail passes had to be validated and another student had forgotten to bring her train ticket, which I had mailed weeks before. She also did not bring much money, so I lent her 50 marks. A kind conductor urged us to jump onto the train that was arriving with great speed. He promised that with a change in Mainz, we would arrive in Bonn at 9:00 a.m. Those who have traveled in Europe know how difficult it is to lift several fifty-pound suitcases onto a train which stops for only a couple of minutes before the doors slam shut, which in our case happened when three or four students were still waiting to board the train. But the conductor made sure everyone was able to board. When we arrived in Mainz, all the students were more skilled in boarding trains. But, alas, Dewayne Goodrich's suitcase handle broke off as he swung his newly purchased case up the steps. We sympathized with him, the tallest and huskiest of all the male students. Yet his distraught face lit up when the magnificent, good old Father Rhine came into view. The river accompanied us all the way to our destination, calming us down and holding us spellbound until we got off in Bonn, where Steven Jones, who had arrived a few days earlier, greeted us and led us to the cabs that drove us to Mutti Hoefer's house. The ride afforded my group their first glimpse of the beautiful city, including the Beethoven Plaza, the big Bonner Münster cathedral, the fountains and parks, and the fine University of Bonn. The group was pleased with what they saw, and they liked their rooms and our eighty-five-year-old landlady, Mutti Hoefer, who fortunately did not speak a word of English.

Several students simply threw their luggage into their rooms and took off with Steven to inspect downtown and the university cafeteria, where they could eat a meal for 55 cents. I unpacked in my apartment on the second floor, and others slept. We decided to commence with classes on schedule, that is, five days a week from 9:00 to 11:30 a.m., with a 10-minute break.

Already on the second day, July 4 to be precise, one hour before class, someone knocked at my door. There stood Bonnie, her blue eyes filled with tears. She put her arms around me and sobbed heartbreakingly. It was not her throat but her wisdom tooth causing all the pain. It was getting worse by the minute. I took her across the street to a dentist and went to teach. Two hours later, she appeared in class, still weeping. The tooth had to be removed immediately, but the dentist, whose office was closing, was only willing to refer her to the nearby clinic. After unsuccessfully begging the dentist to perform the procedure, I succeeded at convincing the clinic, which normally closed on Friday afternoons for the weekend, to make an exception in our case. They scheduled an appointment for 2:00 p.m. When I looked for Bonnie, ready to go, I was unable to locate her. She had wandered off with others. I was disappointed. When she finally showed up, after the clinic was long closed, it took more telephone calls with Mutti Hoefer's granddaughter and her husband, who were both dentists in Cologne, to get some relief. By 7:00 p.m., I had picked up penicillin and antipain tablets in Cologne to suppress Bonnie's pain temporarily. Unfortunately the medicine was not effective enough for her to join the group on our first planned excursion, to the quaint wine village of Bacharach on the Rhine. Another mishap occurred when Doreen discovered at the railroad station that she had forgotten her Eurail pass and had to purchase another ticket. As soon as we had boarded the train, Doreen made another discovery. She had left all of her traveler's checks at the exchange office in Bonn. Fortunately, after we returned, she retrieved her bundle of money when their doors opened on Sunday.

The students were much enchanted by the charming village on the Rhine and the breathtaking view from Burg Stahleck, the old fortress, down to the meandering river, bordered by terraces of vineyards and accented by picturesque villages showing off their ornate church steeples. While some had lunch and a glass of wine or a soft drink in the village, a small group sat on the fortress wall singing German songs. At this point, Patrick Holbert confessed, in a voice filled with envy, "What a pity not to have been born a German!" We traveled back to Bonn on a riverboat blessed by much sunshine, which is rare in Germany. I took advantage of the opportunity to acquaint my students with a group of German high-school students on the boat. The minute we docked in Bonn at 8:00 p.m., some hurried to the marketplace, where a free outdoor concert was being given.

As a result of my ongoing effort to bring my students together with German students, they were invited to a garden party at the home of the friend of a contact of mine from South Bend. As usual, I played chauffeur, piling my VW full with students. At the party, where champagne strawberry punch flowed freely, friendships began to blossom. The timing had been perfect. The next day, we received an invitation from the Padre's successor, Father Poeppinghaus, SJ. He was the new director of the renowned boarding school for boys, the AKO, Aloysius College, run by the Jesuits. We had met several of the students at the party, and they picked us up in a VW bus at the train station in Godesberg. Canceling classes that day was justified. It would be an experience of a lifetime. The hospitality of the director, the tour of the fine school with visits to classrooms, the small church, the lunch in the modern cafeteria, and the coffee and tea served with a special kind of cookie, baked by one of the brothers, will not be forgotten. We were all in awe of the beautiful grounds, with their parks and ponds, and especially in awe of the unique castle on the hill, Stella Rheni, where the director allowed one of my students, a music major from Bloomington, to perform a brilliant musical interlude on the Steinway grand.

The next day, I drove with Bonnie to Cologne and held her hand while the young dentist extracted the wisdom tooth with great skill. Bonnie was happy. He did not charge a cent.

I was pleased by the budding friendships between my group and the young Germans, who continued to invite the Americans to their homes and gatherings and even engaged a couple in basketball games. But our calendar was full of cultural activities as well, including a lecture at Parliament, a visit to the American Embassy, a performance of Puccini's *La Bohème* at the elegant opera house on the Rhine, and plays by O'Neill and Cocteau at the Contra Circle, an intimate theater, which was a brand-new experience for most. The theater was so small we virtually sat on the stage.

No German program should exclude a *Wanderung*, an extended hike. I enlisted the help of two fine young German brothers, sons of von Loewenich, the *Ministerialdirigent* (minister of cabinet council), to organize a hike in the Ahr Valley, famous for its rugged and romantic terrain and, of course, its rich, red Ahr wine. We first had to take the train. Those students without a Eurail pass got a ride in my car. We met at the station in Rech, a quaint village in the valley. The brothers, knapsacks on their backs, led the way up Steinegger Mountain. The sun did not desert us – but did its best to exhaust us. Little Bonnie, halfway up, murmured that she probably was not ready for this. Stephany, somewhat younger than I – though feeling, as I did at times, that even a heart attack would be better than continuing the climb – was sighing. Goodrich, to whom I had entrusted my camera, was perspiring so intensely his white shirt began to turn brown beneath the leather strap. I kidded that I had been unaware his color would come off. He grinned from ear to ear and raised the big staff in his hand, either as a mock warning to me or to chase away the pestering flies. He was obviously furious at Bernie, who was skinny and always some fifty yards ahead of everyone.

The two brothers, who occasionally helped me correct my students' homework, took us straight up rather than in the more comfortable zigzag fashion. At the top, we took a deep breath and were in awe of the beautiful panorama. We took the inn by storm, and after a refreshing break, the brothers, despite our protests, led us on a descent as rough as the ascent. We went straight down, crossing tree trunks, sliding on bottoms, and grasping at branches, nettles, or thorns, whichever was handiest. The descent took a mere thirty minutes, compared to the three hours it had taken us to reach the summit. Before our departure, we sampled the well-deserved Ahr wine and sat chatting on the shore of the narrow but sparkling river. We returned home at 7:00 p.m., dead tired – and at 8:00, Dr. Dexheimer knocked on my door. I had contacted him at the American Embassy, following the recommendations of Dean Nugent and Mr. Haas. Dr. Dexheimer was a friend of Dean Nugent and in the process of finishing his second PhD, this one in political science, with Professor Diamond from IU. As the gentlemen had predicted, Dr. Dexheimer turned out to be a most valuable contact.

The students flooded me with questions all day long, so I hardly had a moment to myself. I finally resolved to get up at 5:30 a.m. to prepare my classes, including meeting with new contacts in an ongoing effort to improve the program. Dean Nugent arrived from Bloomington to visit and inspect the facilities. At a luncheon arranged by Dr. Dexheimer, we met with Mrs. Fischbach-Wilke, who offered to assist in locating German families who would take in students in 1976. I also met with Dr. Littmann, director of the Fulbright Commission, who was most supportive of the continuation of the program. –

Our weekend visit to Trier turned out to be better than I expected, though I did encounter difficulties in finding accommodations for the entire group. We left on Friday after class. The students went by train. I arrived late by car, due to heavy traffic and heavy showers. Our first stop was at the bishop's wine cellars, where Mr. Ludwig gave an informative lecture and offered some words of wisdom: "Wine brings out the happy nature in man" and "Wine keeps the family together." This was certainly the case with the Lorscheiders, where the wine tasted almost better than those Mr. Ludwig poured. Their wine cellar was much smaller than the bishop's and more rustic and moist. We siphoned the wine directly from the barrel, and Mrs. Lorscheider, who greeted me with a bouquet of flowers, had prepared delicious open-faced sandwiches for all of us. Their hospitality was overwhelming. They also helped find accommodations for all our students and drove them to their respective locations. Later on, the Lorscheiders and I got better acquainted at a restaurant over a glass of beer.

The bishop had been quite helpful and arranged for a special guide to show us the big cathedral, where we looked up to the golden shrine, which houses the most famous relic preserved, the Holy Coat of Trier. The most pious believe it to be the seamless robe of Jesus. It was supposedly presented to the city by the empress Helena. The guide was most accommodating. When there were puzzled looks, he switched from German to English. The students could hardly believe they would meet the bishop personally. He received us in his splendid gardens and greeted each student with a handshake, chatting and laughing. He took Goodrich's pulse and asked his old sister to fetch some medicine for the poor guy. Later, the sister pointed out various Roman ruins and sculptures in the garden and underneath the residence, which were off-limits to the general public. We had taken along two German friends, who did not mind showing the group many of the other Roman ruins.

A couple days after the Trier visit, I met with a gentleman from the Bundestag (House of Representatives) in Hessen and, more importantly, spoke with Mrs. Fischbach-Wilke, who was invited to a party given in honor of President Ford. She agreed to present the president with our greetings. Susan Briggs, an art major, made a giant sketch of the *Rathaus* (town hall) in Bonn, which all of us signed and which our new friend, after many security checks, succeeded in bringing to the attention of the president. The embassy sent a thank-you note, and in September, I received a special thank-you from Roland L. Elliott, director of correspondence at the White House, regretting that the president could not thank us personally, since the embassy had retained the card with the names. The letter ended as follows: "He [the president] believes that Americans and Germans alike are enriched by these exchanges and interminglings, and he asked that you extend to each of your students his best wishes for the future and especially for an enjoyable Oktoberfest." We had invited the president to join us.

Almost four weeks into the program, I took a Saturday off while the students were traveling around Europe on their Eurail passes. I went trout fishing with the Padre and his brother, the bishop, which was an experience worth sharing with you. – The sun was beaming in a blue sky as the Padre and I arrived at Himmerod Abbey, the Zisterciense monastery located in the backlands of the Eifel, about twenty or thirty miles from Trier. It was an impressive estate, surrounded by meadows and forests and accessible only by invitation.

The Padre had a standing invitation to go fishing in the lively stream. We secured our gear underneath a tree and stuck a bottle of champagne between a couple of rocks in a low spot in the creek, to keep it cool. The Padre waded upstream, and as usual, I crawled onto a fallen tree trunk, where I sat waiting for my float to bob. The air was calm, a lark was singing in the distance, and I sat in absolute silence. The Padre was nowhere to be seen. Suddenly, I heard someone approaching and calling out to me. A bearded forester in a green uniform, wearing a green hat with a chamois bush, yelled at me, asking what I was doing there and ordering me to come down promptly to show him my permit. He spoke to me as though I were a boy, which was understandable, because I wore jeans and had a Dorothy Hamill haircut at that time. I told him I had no permit but was with the Padre, who was upstream. At that point, the Padre appeared, laughed heartily, and explained that I had come as his guest.

No sooner had the forester left than a big, navy-blue, highly polished Mercedes-Benz made its way toward us and stopped. A chauffeur got out and opened the back door, and out came the bishop of Trier, tall, distinguished, and dressed in a greenish-beige fishing outfit. The chauffeur drove off, promising to return before it got dark. I could hardly believe I was there, fishing with two such highly esteemed men of the cloth. To top it off, each one of us caught a bunch of long and slender silver trout. The Jesuit did us the honor of frying a selection; I took care of the champagne and the serving. It was a feast for kings, or popes, if you wish. We had a great time, joking and laughing until the chauffeur returned to take the bishop back to Trier. Not wanting the evening to end, I got both men of the cloth to agree rather quickly to stop in at one of the cozy and quaint inns for a glass of red wine. The bishop expressed concern that someone might recognize him. I suggested that I would screen the people in the inn before we entered. We proceeded to drive along the winding road, the Mercedes trailing me, stopping whenever I thought I might have found a spot. I thought it was quite amusing. After having inspected about three or four places, I found one where the coast looked clear. The chauffeur had to sit in a separate room, which I thought a bit strange. While sipping from our goblets, we jested about the two ancient sisters who were doubtlessly looking out the window, waiting up for the bishop, worried what may have become of him. As it turned out, he did not know how to deal with the refrigerator in the bishop's kitchen, since he had never opened the door. He was not sure how and where to store the fish either. I was tempted to laugh or snicker, but kept quiet. When the bishop got seriously worried, we said good-bye. The Mercedes drove off into the night, and I took the Padre back to Bonn. The chauffeur never uttered a sound.

The aftermath was extremely bizarre, I thought, and the Padre agreed. The bishop was severely reprimanded by his older sisters for his inappropriate behavior. It so happened that a relative had stopped by and that the sisters were extremely embarrassed, because they did not know whereto their brother had disappeared. They made it quite clear that I, the abductress, would be banned from the bishop's quarters thenceforth.

While I was trout fishing, several students had traveled to Germany's former capital, Berlin, and fallen madly in love with it. In the evening, we sat on the stairway singing songs, including "Oh Berliner Luft, Luft, Luft!" (Oh Berlin Air, Air, Air!) At that time, I was already contemplating integrating a trip to Berlin into the program in the future. I had invited Dr. Dexheimer, who was working for the CDU in Bonn, to give a lecture about the German party system and the divided Germany, which was very fitting and much welcomed by all. Dr. Dexheimer had brought along his wife, Carroll, who had just returned from a seminar in Rostock on the literature of the German Democratic Republic. I was very impressed by Mrs. Dexheimer, who was in the process of finishing her PhD at Brown University; and because she indicated a strong interest in assisting me with the program in the future, I later recommended to the committee that the university engage her to be my associate director and team instructor in 1976.

That summer, my mother had to be content with a weekend visit to Hannover. Much of it was spent getting ready for exams and rehashing the family problems resulting from a long letter I had sent to my immediate family, and to relatives like Aunt Sissy, in 1973. In it, I set forth numerous disappointments stemming from our divergent points of view and tried to explain why I felt increasingly alienated. I reminded Mutti of how disappointed I was when she cancelled her visit to see me in Indiana so abruptly. I had fixed up a nice guest room for her shortly after I moved to South Bend, told her about the plans I had made, and sent her a plane ticket. One week before her departure, she called and informed me that she simply could not bring herself to come to America and leave her grandchild, whom she babysat now and then. I was deeply hurt, and it took a long time to put it behind me. I was afraid to invite her again out of fear of being rejected.

When I returned to Bonn in the evening, I had already put the family ordeal behind me and was concentrating on administering the final oral exams in order to determine how my students had progressed in conversational German despite living with other English-speaking students. I spent a total of twelve hours over the course of three days testing their conversational skills in my apartment. It was at this time that little Bonnie revealed to me that the dentist who had performed the extraction of the wisdom tooth free of charge had later, when she was alone, dropped by in his bright-red Porsche to "collect"; but she sent him home empty-handed. It was a precarious situation, since our landlady was his grandmother-in-law. I did not want to burden her with the shocking news, especially since she had been a bit distraught on a number of occasions. Much to her chagrin, two beds broke down, because the male students had been moving the bedsteads around a lot. She complained that too many students sat on a bed at one time. Howard was the main culprit. After his bed caved in, he received a new one, but the mattress, which came in three parts, bothered his back. The one time it rained, he was awakened by the raindrops which fell through the slanted window above his head. The boys complained most frequently about insufficient water – until the last day, when the water pipe on the fourth floor broke.

Mutti Hoefer, at one point, got upset because the students appeared to use too much toilet paper. One day she asked them if they were eating it. She was also somewhat disturbed that the students congregated in the evenings or early mornings on the entrance steps of the house. Goodrich sat there one morning looking like a peacock in his green-yellow-and-red-striped socks, purple shorts, and yellow T-shirt. It is not customary in Germany to sit on the steps in front of a house. Mutti Hoefer also asked me to caution the girls about wearing shorts while putting their legs up in the windows that faced the street. Pedestrians looked up at them, grinning. When I informed the girls that such behavior in Germany is customary only in certain districts, they quickly stopped.

My lowest point occurred when Steven, somewhat of an outsider, thought by some to be on drugs, and the poorest student in the class, told me at the end of his oral exam that he felt he did not have to come to Germany to learn what he did. He had hoped we would discuss Nietzsche's philosophy. I thought I did not hear right. I told him he did not have to come to Germany to study Nietzsche – and that I knew of no student in the third semester of German who could read German well enough to understand the philosopher's teachings in the original. I should have ignored his comment, but at that moment I was too exhausted to think straight. I cried my heart out. I felt almost suicidal.

In the end, all was harmonious and forgotten. Even Steven had changed his mind somewhat. Mutti Hoefer threw a good-bye party for the group on her terrace and told them over and over how nice they had been and how much she would miss them. They were surprised, because at that point they were convinced she was glad to get rid of them. She wrote down all their addresses, wept with the girls when they embraced her, and loved the bouquets of flowers with which they presented her. I myself cherished the navy-blue T-shirt they had made for me, with *Deutsch Bitte!* printed in big white letters. It was my most frequently uttered plea during the trip, although summoning them with my famous Sankt Ursula two-fingered whistle was a close second. I knew then that it had not fallen on deaf ears. I also knew I would treasure the sterling pocket corkscrew, which they had had inscribed with *Bonn 1975*.

I ended my report to the committee as follows: "As much as I enjoyed the experience, for it was highly rewarding academically as well as satisfying concerning the group experience, I must admit that towards the end (especially after the oral exams), I felt almost totally exhausted. In short, to be originator, organizer, director, instructor, tour guide, counselor, etc., of a new program abroad all at once, is simply too much." I kept to myself the many nights I could not sleep because the noise coming from the rooms above through the open windows was at times intolerable. Their radios were playing at full volume, as were their voices. I ended my report with a request that Mrs. Dexheimer join us in 1976.

Before meeting the group in Frankfurt for our return flight, I spent two days in Berlin. I had never before toured Germany's former capital and felt it imperative to get at least a quick impression before incorporating a week's visit to Berlin into the Bonn Program. I flew there with my student/friend, whose husband, an attorney from South Bend, was awaiting us and ready to give us a whirlwind tour of this exciting city. The tour began after we checked in at the prestigious Hotel Gehrhus, the former Palais Pannwitz, built between 1912 and 1914 to the tune of millions of gold marks and surrounded by beautiful parks. After living in cramped quarters in Bonn, I was overwhelmed at what I saw. The forty-room hotel was one of the few palaces that survived the war. The attorney made sure we understood that its builder, Dr. W. von Pannwitz, was also personal attorney to his Majesty Kaiser Wilhelm II. He built this palace in Gruenewald, the distinguished residential quarter, to house his personal and unique art collections, which were renowned throughout the world.

I would have loved to linger for a while and roam around the rooms furnished in valuable antiques, but the husband was rearing to go. Unfortunately, in front of the Reichstagsgebäude, the husband and I got into a long and serious dispute about the Third Reich, Hitler, and others whom this American lawyer clearly revered, which overshadowed my appreciation of Germany's great capital. Our opinions clashed so severely that upon our return to the States, he barred his wife from ever again enrolling in any of my courses. The wife did not share her husband's opinion, yet lacked the conviction and strength to oppose him. I was not at all surprised, because I had met many women who opted to buckle under rather than follow their conscience and risk a confrontation.

Prior to coming to Berlin, the same gentleman took part in a similar interaction with my friend Lynne in South Bend. I had asked him to look after her a bit while we were gone. Upon my return, Lynne was virtually in tears, because she too had had a bad confrontation with him about Hitler. She happened to be an expert on literature related to and connected with Hitler and was devastated by this person's highly aggressive, totally unfounded verbal attacks. I should have identified the obsession the first time I walked into their library and saw the shelves stacked full of works about Hitler and the era of the Third Reich. It was the end of our friendship.

Harmonizing with Our Quartet in Residence – My Friend André Bourde from Aix Excites Hearts and Minds in Indiana, None More than Mine

Over the years, I have learned that when a relationship, be it with friends or family, turns into nothing but heartache, it's better to let go, distance yourself, and concentrate on something more uplifting and joyful. And it was a joyful and uplifting occasion when, in 1975, a string quartet took up residence on our campus with a part-time position in the Division of Music, headed by Dr. P. C., aka "the Pompous Conductor," who weighed three times as much as was appropriate. From the neck down to the knees, his body was a wobbly, sack-like mass of fat, water, and the like. – The quartet arrived directly from the School of Music in Bloomington, where they had just graduated. Lutz Rath, a cellist from Germany, about 5'8", with brown hair, tanned skin, a goatee, and mischievous Mephistophelian eyes, was a former member of the Munich Philharmonic and had studied with several renowned cellists before coming to study with the world-renowned cellist János Starker. Chihiro Kudo and his wife Machie Kudo, two attractive violinists from Japan, both major prizewinners before arriving in the United States, studied with two other famous teachers, Josef Gingold and Franco Gulli. Violist James VanValkenberg, the youngest of the four, was American. He was tall, slender, blond, and blue eyed, wore frameless glasses, had earned a degree at the Interlochen Arts Academy, and had toured Europe as a soloist with the North Carolina School of the Arts Orchestra before studying with the celebrated Georges Janzer. All four were bright and intelligent. Lutz, the oldest, was more interesting than the others, because he spoke French fluently and seemed well versed in literature and the arts and sciences, having started his academic career as a medical student in Germany. The foursome was a welcome addition to our campus, and they truly sounded ready to climb the ladder of success in the World of Music.

I had been extremely excited when, shortly after my return from Bonn, I ran into Lutz in the corridor at IU. I had met him through Udo, a fellow IU graduate student. Udo had brought Lutz to my student abode once at Thanksgiving, when I invited a few "homeless" international students for turkey. I had no idea they were coming up north and immediately suggested we get together as soon as possible. Their arrival was like a breath of fresh air. I gladly cosigned a note for Lutz to upgrade his cello. – The Loesers had just told me they decided to sell their four big stores in the area as well as the beloved farm and move to Phoenix, Arizona. I was very disappointed, especially since I had accepted the position in South Bend mostly to be close to my longtime friends. It appeared that while I was away studying,

Heinz, known to have a penchant for attractive young women, had hired a young couple to manage his supermarket businesses. We all felt sorry for Anneliese, because her husband spent more time with the miniskirted blond than with his wife, who played naïve. He once indicated that hiring a husband-and-wife team would provide him with more opportunities, all under the pretext of discussing business affairs, to spend time alone with the blond. There had been others. He was constantly arranging outings or trips for the young couple, himself, and Anneliese. The husband-and-wife team benefited handsomely, monetarily and otherwise. Even their in-laws found a managerial spot in the Loesers' employ. When I was told that due to the severe allergic attacks suffered by the blond, they all decided to sell out and move to Phoenix, I was stunned. Everybody found it hard to believe that Anneliese, who could have blocked the move since she was the major investor, consented. Admittedly, she was very reluctant; she finally went on the condition that she could take along her horse Lindy, who had the pleasure of exchanging her stall in Decatur for an orange orchard in Mesa, Arizona.

I too looked for more exotic pastures, and my house turned very quickly into a hangout for the quartet. It did not take them long to figure out I had a fondness for music and musicians and that I enjoyed having them over. I sympathized with them when I saw how very humbly they were forced to live as a result of the university's substandard salaries. In the beginning, they had to get by with housing in less desirable quarters. The violist had a mattress on the floor, a couple of chairs, a card table, a lamp, and a secondhand sofa. Yet all four were enthusiastic about their music and eager to perform all over the world. Lutz, with all his connections, naturally played the role of manager.

I was immensely proud when, little by little, they asked for my input on the sound quality of an instrument they were considering purchasing, did not hesitate to co-sign a note at the bank for Lutz to purchase another cello, and was ready to go whenever they asked me to come to the concert hall to critique their rehearsal of a program. I believe I was more excited than they were about their success. They had chosen the perfect name for their quartet. Not long after they had taken residence, their engagements took them not only to American cities, but also to countries in Europe and South America. They called themselves the International String Quartet.

When my first book came out early in the fall, I threw a party and invited new and old friends, colleagues, and administrators. When everybody was gone, the quartet stayed and proceeded into my den, where the white walls were covered with books on glass shelves. It was my special place to work and relax. The rosewood desk stood directly in front of one of the windows covered with white mesh curtains from Germany. A bright-red, cone-shaped metal lamp with an extendable chrome rod matched the red upholstered desk chair, which had a chrome frame and rollers. Next to the desk sat a white couch with a chrome frame, from which I could watch

TV, listen to music piped in from the entertainment center in the living room through speakers mounted in two corners of the ceiling, or observe the cardinals feeding outside the other window. On the wall above the couch hung a hand-woven rug from the Ivory Coast. It was earth colored and had stylized animal figures and plants traced in thick black. A Scandinavian table with a triangular glass top, a gift from the Loesers, stood in front of the couch, flanked by two small, beige upholstered chairs with velvety brown, beige-patterned cushions. They harmonized with the coffee-brown wall-to-wall carpet. The quartet and I used to retreat here after parties to have a nightcap or two of brandy while chatting and gossiping away. We spent many happy times in the cozy room. During the quartet years, my liquor bill skyrocketed. I also learned to eat with chopsticks at the Kudos, and they introduced me to sushi and other Japanese delicacies. All four were lovers of gourmet food, and Lutz, who on occasion "composed" a meal in my kitchen, was an exceptional chef.

It goes without saying that we all got to know each other very well. All four of the musicians felt comfortable coming over to talk or relax when time permitted. Since I had known Lutz longer, he stopped by more frequently in the beginning. He was an exciting conversationalist, full of stories and full of dreams for the quartet.

When I told my musical friends about the previous year's Christmas bash at the Scottsdale Mall, asking if they would like to participate this time and replace the choir, knowing full well it would be a more muted affair, they readily agreed. Elsa and Heidi pitched in, since I had changed the location to a much smaller mall, the old brewery in Mishawaka, which had been remodeled. I left out several presentations, such as the play and the ornament sale; it would entail less work. The event was not as electric as it was in 1975. The administrators kept saying, "Chris, we appreciate what you are doing" – but words do not put bread on the table. I also felt that, as a professor, I could not justify getting my students fired up and asking them to sacrifice so much studying time for another large-scale celebration, just to please the administration. Instead, I accepted an invitation to the local TV station, took along several students, a small choir, and a display of German ornaments, and talked about my childhood Christmas experiences in Germany. I reached a larger audience than the one that filled the mall a year before. They called the show "Christmas with a German Accent."

As soon as I was satisfied that my 1976 summer program would proceed as planned, and that I could engage Carroll Dexheimer as a liaison in Bonn and integrate a week in Berlin into the program, I focused on bringing more speakers of international stature to our campus. As chair of the International Studies Committee, I was committed to enriching the academic offerings on the home campus as well. I had maintained correspondence with Professor Dr. Dr. André Bourde and with his mother and could not think of a more exciting speaker than my old friend and professor from Aix. I brought the idea to his attention before Christmas, and was elated when he wrote back with the news that he would love to come. The committee approved a modest amount for an honorarium, travel, and lodging, which I thought was insultingly low; but since the professor did not complain, I asked the dean to send a written invitation, to which he replied on February 20, 1976. I feel compelled to share this letter with you, if only to show you why I was in awe of this exceptional man:

Dear ——, The invitation of the University of Indiana arrived like dew on a thistle (I being the thistle) and it is symbolical of my life that it took me two months before I could fix a date and quite some time before I could answer you properly. Before all let me thank you deeply for having suggested my name and tell you how happy I am at the prospect of seeing you again (this great pleasure being more than shared by mother who will write you soon) and how proud I am that you have continued so brilliantly in your studies and forgotten but had become, through your paper, an inspiration for your successors.

Hard to believe that I should have been remembered in so handsome a fashion by your glorious – and charming – Ph.D. self. . . . Indeed I will be bringing with me your paper on Greek sculpture which got a straight A, would it only be to show you that in spite of time and space the memory of your stay in Aix and under my demanding scientific yoke is still alive.

Nine years ago . . . and the light of culture and of friendship still alive! That is the most rewarding thing for a teacher whose heart is warm with pleasure in spite of the snows that have fallen on his temples.

That was the year when the Maza students were in hot competition with my overseas travels and the maze of my personal and university problems and ambitions. Yet the mists of these remote times have not cancelled the memories of our classes, of our field trips in Provence, of your visits to my house. . . . But it seemed like a rule of the game that these American visits should end like those flowers that were once alive, then end – without losing their colors or their perfume – in a scented bag of dried petals. And see, one of these flowers had revived again like these seeds that were lying asleep in Pharaoh's tomb . . .

You will find me, I think, much as I was, only more weather beaten, but possibly mellowed, and possibly more sedate, like the old Aix houses (I dare not say "palaces"). More sedate but not more settled, for ever since 1967 I have gone on playing my part in the merry-go-round (not always merry) of existence.

The "revolution" of 1968 found me roaming through the Indian Ocean and I went back to France after having ministered exams in the most improbable places. I found my university in a crisis out of which it has not yet come. My time was divided between going abroad for lecturing or studies (twice to America, twice to India and Nepal, several times to Africa), trying to save my country house in Upper Provence from thieves (and not succeeding), and divorcing myself from the Department of History in order to organize the new Institute of Art, therefore exchanging lectures on the potato or the Spanish Succession against lectures on Venetian art or the baroque churches of Germany.

I still play the harpsichord and have been giving quite a number of concerts; I still look after the Maza boys and girls, but the style of present times has changed. The new university pretending to be less formal, I henceforth appear in pull-overs even for official occasions (yet have no fear, I will bring an old-fashioned suit with me). I no longer require spelling nor grammar from the students since they possess neither the one nor the other. But still sailing against the winds, I have become convinced of the value of what I teach, and that what is heartfelt in history and in the arts is finally as important as statistics. Some parts of my heart have become colder, others (most of it) have remained warm and, all in all, and in spite of everything, I keep hope and reasonable equilibrium. I am reasonably happy. Yesterday I went to Avignon for lectures and I came back through this ancient countryside bathed in blue sky and cool sun, with its old towns, where certain wisdom of life remains around their outwardly austere and inwardly magnificent buildings. And together with the prospect of coming to the New World soon, I felt very joyous, though no silver lining is without a cloud, as we know.

My mother is of course aging, but, thank God, in good shape and more intellectually active than ever. She hates my going away, but this time she is happy at the thought that it is not ONLY scholarship that has been calling me away. She is soothed by the thought that in Indiana I will be gossiping with you about Aix and our old garden and our old house.

Dear ———, in order to be able to answer this invitation, I had to disentangle myself from so many things, cut so many threads ranging from lectures and exams to relinquishing administrative duties, that I have had no time to plan my travel...

I am trying to arrange a lecture that would be both scholarly and interesting – I mean entertaining – and I will bring numerous documentary slides on things that are well worthy of consideration, especially on a region that is a "hot" one in the present news.... During my stay at South Bend I will be at your University's disposal for any session or seminar they would wish for. Since I do not intend to go back to France before the end of March: South Bend, Bloomington, etc.... I will be at your disposal. Besides my exotic lecture, should it interest them I will bring also a lecture (with handsome slides) on "Church of the Baroque: lights and shades in the Church of Provence in the XVIIth and XVIIIth centuries" (I have just published the XVth-XVIIths centuries chapters of the new History of the Diocese of Aix). Just in case... and of course no fee would be required. I would be only too glad to acknowledge thus my pleasure at visiting you.... A bientôt la joie de vous retrouver chère Christa Maria.... Votre viel ami et prof, André Bourde.

He looked the same as he did ten years before, and I was still mesmerized by his effervescent personality. Indeed, it was like old times when Professor Bourde arrived at the South Bend airport on March 15. I had made reservations for him at a nearby hotel. When he saw I had a spare guest room in my little house, he asked if he could stay there. I did not object, and he quickly took possession of the room. From then on, my house was alive with laughter and music. André rushed to my baby-grand piano, the Knabe, to give it a try the minute he spotted it in the corner of the living room. I was elated and energized and got ready for a week bursting with music, culture, intellectual discourse, and laughter. He played in the morning before breakfast, at noon instead of taking a siesta, and at night before bedtime.

The committee had asked for a lecture on "Culture and Art on the East African Coast," but he was so generous with his time and enthusiasm that we added several others. He spoke to my literature class about the importance of Greek art to Germany and her literature; he gave a lecture to an anthropology class about religion in Africa and another to a fine-arts class on baroque art in Southern France. He also talked to students in advanced French classes about students in France, before I drove him down to Bloomington, where he spoke about Greek art to students of German. I was glad my friend Lynne – who was then working on her PhD in German and, with the kind assistance of Professor Segebrecht, had spent the spring semester of 1975 at the University of Regensburg – got to meet my favorite, twice-knighted professor from France over lunch.

A couple of nights before his departure, I orchestrated an elegant party at my residence, assisted by caterers dressed in black dresses with white aprons and bartenders in white coats. Colleagues and university administrators were invited, as well as friends like the Koertings, my former boss from Miles and his wife, who had invited us for dinner at their spectacular mansion outside of Elkhart. And of course, my new friends, the International String Quartet, were among my favorite guests. I had wanted them to meet the professor from France who, as a well-known harpsichordist, might arrange a concert or two for them in and around Aix-en-Provence, which was frequented by renowned soloists all year around. And I was right; the minute they met, there was a special rapport between the five musicians, which resulted in a promise from the professor to arrange for several concerts. To top it off, he also offered them his country home in Lurs, free of charge, when they told him they were going to enter the International Chamber Music Competition, to be held in Évian, France, in the summer of 1976.

To sum up Professor Bourde's visit, I once more take the liberty of sharing his reactions with you and copy below his letter, written April 12, 1976, in Aix:

Dear ———, Enfin. (I notice that on an American typewriter there is no exclamation mark, which is very telling). Of course, as I told you on the phone, the Williamsburg days were so pointillist in texture as to leave no room for writing or even for thinking; so engrossed was I with the tiny little problems developed by my friends and colleagues there: a dog to feed and to amuse, a meaningless sentence to ponder over, a comparative analysis of gins, a dinner to prepare for where words and demeanor had to be carefully weighed and expressed. . . . All the propriety of a pseudo-British civilization, so different from the South-Bend spontaneity. After having minutely endured these virginal rituals, I was finally relieved by a last invitation into a Haitian family – anthropologists friends of mine – where I had my heart's content of French slang, hot sauces and big kisses on both cheeks (to the stupefied but condescending horror of the other guests, blonde and confirmed southerners, who may, yet, have picked an idea of behaviour here and there). New-York of course was dynamite and I spent my days combing Times Square for cheap watches and dirty post-cards, eating apple-pies at the Metropolitan Museum, riding escalators in Macy's and visiting diverse jewish families connected with the Met, Yehudi Menuhin, the late court of Russia or chocolate factories. I finally found my watch (digital and electronic) at an Algerian refugee's shop. He gave me a hearty French welcome, professed to be my friend and compatriot and swindled me of five dollars. I was invited by a black former acquaintance of mine, very Afro with gold earrings, streams of Caribbean necklaces, a red velvet maxi coat and a deep fruity voice. I drank gallons of sangria and never discovered if his constant trips to Washington had to be explained by his being a Senator, a stewart of National Airways or a proprietor of a massage parlor. A little of everything I suppose. Finding out about my charter flight took me two days, and when we were to take off we had to go back since they had received a message that the plane was carrying a time-bomb, so that we were thoroughly searched, our luggage disembarked and we left five hours late. Uneventful flight with French students, – girls mostly – exchanging impressions of Alaska or Guatemala and interspersing their discourse with innumerable "merde" – which has become a word proper for all occasions.

Paris seemed sweet and hectic, and I finally arrived in Marseille to find my mother enthralled by your letter "Cette petite ... quelle charmante, quelle personnalité si remarquable et si digne" so that there is little I can add to so many truths. Our garden was swept by the Mistral wind blowing over the bluest of waters; the house was resplendent with the smell of leek-soup (odour of sanctity of the French bourgeoisie); Swalihi was happy with the shirt I brought for him which was very much like my Negro friend's maxi; and my university was on strike for mysterious leftist reasons which I haven't had time yet to explore fully, inasmuch as I must prepare to fly again to Central Africa in ten days, teaching the Republic of Rwanda in three weeks what I taught my Indiana audience in one and a half hours. I have arranged for a concert of the International Quartet in Aix beginning July, but I am expecting their programs, leaflets and letter. More will be arranged no doubt in Marseille and region.

Please send me quickly names and addresses of people who have received me so charmingly; and, like Flora with rose petals, you must scatter around you my very best memories, thanks, appreciation and kindest thoughts.

Your reception, style, personality, wisdom, scholarship, house, rouladen, wines, conversation, dresses, way of driving, holiness at Mass, ice-creams, friends, musical taste, wit, gaiety, rational romanticism and healthy poetry made a cocktail of unequalable perfection. I would need another letter to repeat my thanks, my pleasure and my pride at having had you as a student. (Haven't seen Maza yet. Will do it to-morrow).

More compliments to come for when we shall be in my garden after your Bonn labours. Swalihi is preparing your room.

Impossible to lay down plans for future exchanges before I am back from Africa mid-May.

I am grateful. I miss your tinkling laughter. I never was tired a second. I had the most interesting, heart-warming, profitable time.

Take care of yourself. Clip your wings and soft-pedal your talents. "Virtutis comes invidia." Be happy. See you soon. André.

I am reluctant to disturb the mood which reigned throughout Professor Bourde's visit and will copy here a few paragraphs from my letter to him dated March 27, that is, a couple of weeks before I received his letter:

Dear ———,

When I returned to my little house on Tuesday afternoon it seemed almost vacant in one way (not only because of the empty closet), yet in another way as the atmosphere was still impregnated with your presence (your baroque spirit, to be precise). Indeed, the walls were resounding your exuberance, your wittiness, and your music. Any sensitive soul would have felt as I did then and still do this very instance: sadly joyous. Sad at the "vacancy," but joyous at the realization of having recaptured the abundant riches of an "old" acquaintance and a "young" friend.

The 1976 Bonn Program Adds Bayer AG and Berlin (East and West)

As soon as Professor Bourde left, I had to focus again on the Bonn-Berlin program, which was to last from May 14 to July 9, 1976. Thanks to the strong campus-wide enthusiasm and support for the 1975 program, I was optimistic that with Carroll Dexheimer's capable assistance, the program would be enriched and strengthened further. I had received many congratulatory letters from IU administrators as well as one from the executive director of the American Association of Teachers of German, who urged me to send an announcement for their newsletter. A couple of former professors applauded the program in writing as well. Professor Remak was pleased to see that Carroll, whom he knew personally, would join me, and he liked the *South Bend Tribune* article about the program, which had called it a "success story." Professor Piedmont, who had also recommended me for a position on the Selection and Screening Committee for the academic year abroad in Hamburg, Germany, labeled the report "brilliant" and thought the 1976 program proposal "excellent." Thus, I had the green light.

That year, I had decided to fly Iceland Air from Chicago to Luxembourg via Reykjavík, Iceland. Carroll, who had prepared for the group, knew just where to send the students, who piled into the cabs that awaited us at the bus station in Bonn. She had conducted an exhaustive search for host families by contacting friends and social clubs. She had distributed flyers to all the educational institutions and, finally, written an article about the program, which the newspapers agreed to publish. Finding hosts for our students was difficult, because ours was not an exchange program. Most Germans are reluctant to take in students if they don't get something besides money in return. Some may ask for tutorial services for their children or expect a counterinvitation to America for their child. German apartments tend to be small, not leaving much extra space for a guest. German housewives, moreover, are obsessed with neatness and often unwilling to tolerate a new source of disorder. Carroll had found that almost 50% of the host families who had signed up had been in the United States before. Several wanted to return the warm hospitality they had enjoyed when visiting the States.

Although in the end the students agreed that they benefited from their stay with a family, there were several problem cases, which tested our nerves to the utmost. One student in particular, Deloris, a minority student from the Bloomington campus who had made a very favorable impression during the interview, turned out to be the biggest headache. She felt the world owed her something. Though she had received plenty of financial aid, so much, in fact, that she was perceived as the best-dressed student in the group, she was constantly complaining – in English. Though she had been highly recommended by her advisor on the Bloomington campus, where she had earned straight As in courses entitled "Germlish," in Bonn her academic achievements were substandard. The Germlish courses were created particularly for minority students or others who had difficulty learning German in regular classes. I was horrified when I found out how utterly nonsensical this modified German language was. Deloris simply could not keep up with my method of teaching and was unhappy when she got a D in the course. Her advisor, who had tried unsuccessfully to convince me to offer such courses on the IUSB campus, was equally disappointed when I refused to change her grade to a better one after our return. Carroll finally had to find a new family for her. Her hostess contacted Carroll in the middle of the night to demand that the girl leave the house immediately. The hostess was already on edge, because her seriously ill husband had been in the hospital since the day of our arrival. I recall that Deloris complained endlessly about the gray toilet paper and, in the forest where the lady had taken her for an outing and a picnic, the bugs crawling around on the ground. The second family seemed to be an improvement. Another student complained about her host family's constantly conversing with her in English, which, after Carroll interceded, improved, as did the situation with Kevin, who at first had a conflict with his male host.

Carroll had gone out of her way to arrange extracurricular activities for the group, starting with an invitation from Mr. and Mrs. Robert Baker, from the American Embassy, on the first Thursday, May 20. The Bakers had invited the entire group, together with the host families, to their big, beautiful apartment overlooking the Rhine River. It would have been a perfect start had it not been overshadowed by four students failing to show up. Carroll and her husband had been awakened shortly after midnight on May 19. A student called and informed them that he and three others were in Rotterdam, but would be back the next day. Their hosts had not been informed until Carroll called them the next morning. They were quite concerned. Carroll and I were infuriated at the lack of consideration the students showed toward the families, especially after Carroll had tried her best to match students with hosts based on personality. We were angered not only by their juvenile conduct, but also because they missed a required field trip to Aloysius College that included class sessions, which took place before the party at the Bakers. To make matters worse, their adolescent behavior continued on our trip to Trier, despite the wonderful program, similar to the one in 1975, which we had worked out for them, with visits to the bishop, the Karl Marx house, and the Lorscheiders, among others. This time, the students were housed in a guesthouse for which there was only one house key. The "Rotterdam Four," as we called them, left a window open in order to be able to return later than the rest of the group. The German guardsman was very upset, threatening to make this the last time he let us stay there. We spoke with each student individually, warning them that the next show of juvenile conduct would be reported to the dean of students and their parents. After the incident, a definite split developed in the group. Several students allied themselves with the Rotterdam clique, forming an arrogant group of would-be jet-setters that excluded the others. It made our subsequent group activities rather unpleasant. I was only too glad to have Carroll along to vent my frustrations. Much later, it was rumored that the Rotterdam Four had gone to Rotterdam to buy drugs or pot, which might explain their blatant disinterest in learning what they had professed wanting to focus on during their interviews in the States. In short, they had come to Germany to have fun at a reasonable rate. Carroll and I vowed to be more thorough in the selection process in the future.

As Carroll was in charge of teaching the civilization section on two days of the week, I taught language and grammar on three days. I also read a play by Bertolt Brecht, *Herr Puntila und sein Knecht Matti*, with them. Carroll had secured tickets for us to see the play at the Berliner Ensemble, Brecht's own theater in East Berlin, on June 25.

Prior to our arrival in Berlin, Carroll had arranged a number of highly interesting field trips in connection with her lectures on the German educational system, German mass media, German political system, and social conditions of the West German worker. To accent the lecture on the West German worker, she had obtained an invitation to the Bayer AG site in Leverkusen, outside of Cologne, West Germany, where two representatives from Personnel and PR lectured on codetermination and the system of social security.

We were all impressed by the hospitality Bayer AG showed us throughout our visit. A company bus picked all of us up in front of Mutti Hoefer's house and let us out at the front door of one of the many imposing buildings in the vast Bayer AG complex, not far from the Rhine River and the huge, encircled Bayer cross, which can be spotted from miles away, especially at night, when it is lit like a Ferris wheel. The lectures and the following Q&A sessions went better than I had expected. I personally was a bit surprised when one of the gentlemen boasted that Bayer AG had come back even stronger than it was before its breakup after World War I, and referred to the company as "Bayer World." I was introduced to the director of the personnel department, Mr. Hans Knapp, and thanked him heartily for such a superb meeting. He was a most kind man, who right away told me how impressed he was by what I was doing to bring Americans and Germans together and offered to assist in any way possible, if I should ever need his help. I assured him that I welcomed his offer and would certainly take him up on it again next year.

After proper good-byes and thank-yous, we were taken to a private dining room in the magnificent Kasino, not to be confused with a gambling establishment, known for its deluxe hotel status and superb cuisine. Here, VIPs from all over the world were treated to the greatest comfort imaginable and feasted on unforgettable, succulent meals. We too were ushered into an awe-inspiring private dining room paneled with dark mahogany. We sat around a very large, oblong banquet table covered with a white damask tablecloth and matching napkins. It was set with fine bone china and heavy sterling-silver tableware. Several students felt as though they were in another world, one they had never experienced. Three waiters, hardly noticeable and dressed in white linen coats, poured wine into the crystal goblets and, after a mouthwatering dinner, offered cigars and cigarettes on silver trays. They poured old brandy into crystal brandy snifters for those who wanted it.

On the way home, the group seemed more harmonious than before, leaving no doubt that the afternoon at Bayer was a success. As the Bayer visit took place toward the end of the Bonn portion of the program, it was also a good ending to our time in the new capital. We looked forward to our stay in Germany's former capital, West Berlin, and to the visit to East Berlin, the capital of the German Democratic Republic.

Yet we wanted to say a special good-bye to Bonn and all the people who had given so generously of their time and hospitality to make our stay an unforgettable learning experience. We could not have been luckier. The International String Quartet was on their way to Lurs and Évian, France, where they were to compete in the International Chamber Music Competition. I had enticed them to come to Bonn and play a concert at Schloß Rheni, the beautiful castle where, the year before, one of my students had played for us on the Steinway. Padre Poeppinghaus had graciously agreed to let us say farewell to our Bonner friends in this musical fashion. The quartet played brilliantly, and our audience responded with passionate applause.

Carroll, very capable, vivacious, and motivated, had taken great care in preparing the class for the Berlin experience by way of supplemental lectures and films focusing on postwar development in the GDR and the divided city. Through her dedication and engagement, she had made it possible for us to integrate a week in Berlin into the program. She also made the students aware of the importance of the German Democratic Republic for anybody who studies German language, literature, and culture.

Carroll had found lodgings in a youth hostel for a mere $5.20 per person per night, including breakfast. It was in a central location, within walking distance of the Kurfuerstendamm, the main boulevard in West Berlin, where the ruined Kaiser Wilhelm Memorial stands in marked contrast to the adjacent contemporary memorial church. The taxi driver explained that the Berliners refer to the ruin as "the hollow tooth" and the memorial church as "powder puff and lipstick." He made us laugh when he went on to explain that the supermodern and unique congress hall is known as "the pregnant oyster." As soon as the students put down their suitcases, they took off for the city to soak up the exciting atmosphere of the Ku-Damm, with all its fascinating display windows, restaurants, sidewalk cafés, and neon lights, which were so bright it seemed like day even at night. Since there were no age restrictions, they enjoyed the liberty of ordering a beer without having to present an ID.

Carroll had organized an optimal program, starting with a three-hour tour of the city on Sunday, June 20, the day after our arrival. The tour was followed by an invitation to a German student's apartment for sandwiches, beer, and dancing. The day ended at one of Berlin's spectacular discotheques, which became a favorite spot for the students' successors in years to come.

The next day, Carroll afforded the group a view of several of the beautiful lakes and suburban residential areas, followed by a talk at the Information Center on the political, economic, and cultural problems of Berlin. Though students found it difficult to understand everything, they did attend a performance of the popular political cabaret *Die Stachelschweine* (The Porcupines). Thanks to outstanding acting and to Carroll's recapitulating the scenes during intermission, the event turned out to be another positive experience.

With the exception of two students, all of us went to East Berlin on June 22. We proceeded in the customary fashion, walking down the main boulevard, Unter den Linden, from the Brandenburg Gate to the Alexanderplatz, the meeting point of two main avenues in East Berlin. At the Brandenburg Gate, we climbed the steps to the outlook and shook our heads at the chilling sight of the Berlin Wall, covered with anticommunist slogans and graffiti, and we understood full well why several youths were spitting at the revolting structure, topped with barbed wire. We could not but notice as we proceeded on the boulevard that East Berlin had profoundly impressive historical structures, such as Humboldt University, the Berlin State Opera, the Berlin Cathedral, and the Berlin State Library, as well as magnificent museums, the Pergamon and others. We found it to be in bad taste that they had constructed the obnoxiously pretentious Palace of the Republic so close to the Berlin State Opera. Several students took the elevator to the top of the television tower on the Alexanderplatz to enjoy a panoramic view from the rotating restaurant.

Others peeked into the big department stores and were disappointed at the sparse and primitive offering of goods. Carroll had included a trip to the monumental Soviet War Memorial in Treptow and even arranged a meeting with East German students in an apartment, which once more resulted in an interesting exchange of words between the young people.

Carroll took us to an exhibition on German history in the appealingly reconstructed Reichstag building in West Berlin, from which we continued to the city hall for the borough of Schöneberg, where the group had heated discussions with a member of the House of Deputies. Perhaps the students were too tired to join us for a memorable performance of an Expressionist play, *Die Wupper* by Else Lasker-Schueler, in one of the best theaters in West Berlin, the Schaubühne am Halleschen Ufer.

Charlottenburg Palace was a must-see for the students, as was the striking Bust of Nefertiti, located across the street in the Egyptian Museum. But Carroll also took us to the Berlin Museum, which contained exhibits from all eras of Berlin's history and featured a special exhibit on E. T. A. Hoffmann in honor of his two hundredth birthday. There, we had lunch in the museum's unique *Weißbierstube*. It featured a rich buffet that offered a mixture of gourmet foods. The place was packed with jovial Berliners. The background music was classical. Most of us tried a Berlin white beer before we headed back to the hostel.

The last day, Friday, June 25, after a written exam asking for the students' impressions of Berlin, several of us returned to East Berlin to visit the cemetery where famous personalities are buried, such as the great philosophers Fichte and Hegel, Bert Brecht, the actress Helene Weigel (his wife), John Heartfield, and Heinrich Mann. I took several students to the monumental Pergamon Museum, where we marveled at the Ishtar Gate, the magnificent Pergamon Altar, and other treasures from antiquity. The gate was built by king Nebuchadnezzar II in honor of the goddess Ishtar, aka "the Lady of Heaven," who is considered the most important deity of the Babylonian pantheon. This gate, along with the high walls of glazed cobalt-blue bricks flanking the Processional Way, was brought there from Babylon and partially restored. It is the first big attraction upon entering the Pergamon and leads directly to the equally monumental Pergamon Altar, with the Gigantomachy frieze, built in 164–156 BC. I consider these treasures to be among the most splendid and impressive works of art the world has to offer.

The day ended with a superb performance of Brecht's *Herr Puntila und sein Knecht Matti* (Puntila and His Servant Matti) at the Berliner Ensemble. We all agreed that struggling through the play in class turned out to be worthwhile. It was an unforgettable experience. A perfect ending to a summer abroad – and a perfect beginning for those intent on extending their stay with further travel as well as for those returning to the States, where their lives would never be the same.

I was very fortunate to have Carroll Dexheimer as my codirector, and was grateful that she offered to take care of the group in Berlin on the Saturday I went to Bamberg to attend the long-planned E. T. A. Hoffmann conference in celebration of the author's two hundredth birthday.

E. T. A. Hoffmann's Two-Hundredth-Birthday Celebration in Bamberg – Sojourn in Marseille

I arrived in Bamberg just in time for Professor Lehmann's opening address in the Kaisersaal (Emperor's Hall) of the new palace. I attempted to attend as many lectures as possible, given my time constraints. I had to be back in Berlin by Monday. The organizers of the conference had planned the events in such a way as to take full advantage of the places Hoffmann himself had frequented during his stay. I made sure to join the Hoffmann enthusiasts for the matinee membership meeting held in Hoffmann's "catacombs," a place where he used to escape alone or with friends to sip a glass of wine or two. This meeting was fittingly accompanied by a generous amount of the red or golden fluid. I found it quite appropriate that Professor Motekat held his lecture on Hoffmann's short story "Don Juan," based on Mozart's opera, in the very theater where the author had conceived it, and where he had been engaged as conductor, director, composer, stage director, and artist from 1808 until 1813. He directed his favorite Mozart opera at the theater five times between 1810 and 1811. It was right there that I heard for the first time several of Hoffmann's compositions, which put me and other Hoffmann enthusiasts in the right frame of mind for a get-together at another of Hoffmann's favorite places, the Theaterrose (Rose Theater), a wine restaurant adjacent to the theater and opposite Hoffmann's residence. I went with two enthusiasts, Professor Segebrecht and Hans Guenther, the former attorney general of Berlin. Hans Guenther had been the last person to hold the post of justice of the Supreme Court in Berlin. He had recently published a book about Hoffmann's time in the capital.

The three of us talked until late at night, or rather early in the morning. I became very much intrigued with Hans Guenther's story. I must say at the outset that he was a man in his sixties. He was one of the most distinguished-looking gentlemen I have ever met or had the pleasure to call a friend. He was tall and very well built, with a full head of lightly wavy, silver-gray hair combed backward. His facial features were prominent and strong, his voice clear and sonorous, and his eyes big and almost black. The thick, black-rimmed glasses gave him a look of seriousness and underscored his composed demeanor. I felt drawn to every sentence he spoke because of the strong conviction that accompanied whatever he said. I was much impressed with Hans Guenther's account of an experience he had while pursuing a law degree, which coincided with the time when Hitler came to power. One day in 1933, at the age of twenty-three, when he entered the courtroom as a junior barrister, he observed the flag with the swastika and voiced his objection to its display in a courtroom, pointing out that it was no place for a party flag. A man affiliated with the Nazi party informed him that it would be best for him to leave if he did not like it. Hans Guenther got up and left the courtroom. His law studies came to a halt because he was barred for reasons of political unreliability. In 1936, after having been without a job for several years, he moved to Berlin, where he worked as a *lektor* for the Carl Duncker publishing house and as a *feuilleton* (entertainment section) writer for the *Deutsche Allgemeine Zeitung*, or *DAZ*, and the *Frankfurter Allgemeine*, two major German newspapers. He married Ingeborg, a librarian. She was an attractive lady with blue eyes and very long, reddish-blond hair, which she parted in the middle and twisted into a bun on the neck. She came from a sizeable estate in Prussia, where her favorite sport was horseback riding. Despite being his wife, and though she had accompanied him to Bamberg, she had preferred to rest at the hotel while we were reminiscing. – Over the course of the evening, I learned that Hans Guenther had continued his law studies after the war ended. He was very successful; by the time the partition of Berlin and of Germany took place, he had held influential positions at Berlin's county court, and in 1961, at the age of fifty-one, after having been active as a criminal-law judge for nine years, he was elected attorney general of West Berlin. I was fascinated when he talked about a case which had been in the news a few years before and in which he played a decisive role. A young, I believe fourteen-year-old, girl in East Berlin had murdered her father in retaliation for serious abuse and escaped to West Berlin prior to the erection of the Wall. The East Germans demanded that the girl be returned and tried in the East. Hans Guenther intervened successfully. He knew the girl would be executed if he returned her. As it turned out, she was saved from execution and stayed in the West.

My trip to Bamberg was wonderful, because I made new friends. One young scholar who had come all the way from Japan taught me a few Japanese phrases on walks from one place to another. I liked each and every one of the participants, not only because all were Hoffmann enthusiasts, but also because we had fun naming each other after characters from Hoffmann's tales. One friend, Werner Maschmeier, who lived in the Goethe Staße in Berlin, called me "Dörtje" after a female character in one of Hoffmann's fantastic fairy tales. As we parted, he presented me with a curious old book entitled *Der verhexte Genius* (The Bewitched Genius), with an even more curious dedication, which he signed "Dörtje's admirer: Peregrinus Thyss a.o. Professor in Hoffmanno." Hans Guenther handed me a copy of his last book on Hoffmann, dedicating it to "the generous Frau Professor Okay [I said 'OK' rather frequently] as a small remembrance of not so melancholic Bamberger nights." Professor Segebrecht asked me to promise to visit him and his family soon and to keep him abreast of my research plans. I was considering writing an article investigating the function of animals in the works of E. T. A. Hoffmann and possibly in works of other German romanticists. I knew I would see Hans Guenther, whom I later compared to Tonio Kroeger, Thomas Mann's protagonist in his novelette with the same title, when I returned to West Berlin the next week. There was no question that we would correspond. We were kindred spirits, as we had spent many nights bonding over goblets of red wine in the name of Hoffmann.

1972–1984

When Hans Guenther called me in Berlin to invite me out for dinner at the well-known restaurant Kempinsky, I was happy to accept. After dinner, he surprised me with a special gift, a big silver coin embossed with the likeness of Maria Theresa, framed to be worn as a pendant. He then took me to an exclusive bar for invited members only. I felt quite honored and will never forget that night, because we waited until almost dawn at the Kurfuerstendamm for a cab. No cab appeared, because everybody was stuck in front of the TV. Cassius Clay had a boxing match that night.

June 4, 2016 – Forty years after the great boxer Cassius Clay, aka Muhammad Ali, held the world spellbound and I was out with Hans Guenther, attorney general of West Berlin, Ali left this world. May he rest in peace.

The Bamberger interlude had two effects: it provided both the desired stimulus to continue my research on Hoffmann and a good reason to enjoy the last week of the Berlin program even more. As a German professor at a regional campus, I struggled constantly to maintain a healthy balance between research, teaching, service, and conducting programs abroad. At this point in my career, I was satisfied that I had succeeded in doing so.

At the close of the program, as soon as the students were on their way home, I flew from Bonn to Marseille, where André Bourde awaited me for my visit to the phenomenal Villa Phocéenne. I spent six glorious days there. It was wonderful to see Madame Bourde again, with whom I had corresponded in French since my departure. I had relished each and every letter, because they were written with great warmth and with an eloquence I have not encountered since. Both André and Madame took great care of me and treated me to the most delicious meals. André took me to the Marseille fish market to select seafood from piles of fresh and colorful fish while the merchant chased the flies away with a palm branch. In the evening, we drove along the seashore and, to be intoxicated once more by the setting sun at the bay of Marseille, parked the car at a special outlook. The sea sparkled in red-orange hues.

One day, André took me to his recently acquired house in La Ciotat. It was a stone house, more than a hundred years old, and it shared walls with others in the narrow street. André was in the process of furnishing it for weekend getaways, I believe. We had a lot of fun rummaging through secondhand and antique stores for suitable but reasonably priced treasures, such as furniture, pottery, rugs, and the like. – Each night, the palatial villa resounded with music and exhilarating conversation. Before retiring we relaxed with a glass of wine in rattan chairs on the big terrace, which overflowed with tropical plants in clay and porcelain planters. The only blemish on this memorable visit occurred on my way down to the villa from a visit to the cathedral Notre Dame de la Garde. I stumbled on the stony path, fell, and severely strained my right middle finger. I tried to hide the pain, especially since it was Saturday and I was scheduled to fly home on Monday. But my finger hurt so badly

I had to say something. We soaked it in warm water, which relieved the pain somewhat. We talked about the incident for a long time.

I returned to the States via Hannover on July 9. Unfortunately, I did not get a chance to connect with the members of the International String Quartet, who were staying at André's country house in Lurs, Provence, while getting ready for the Évian competition. I had to wait until September, when they returned victoriously from France. They had won the Grand Prix d'Évian, the highest distinction awarded. One of the benefits of this award was an invitation from several of the judges, members of the Amadeus Quartet, to come to London for further study with them.

I myself was swept away by their success and had called together a welcoming committee to meet the quartet at the airport. I brought a big bouquet of flowers and cheered as happily as the others who had come to congratulate the four musicians as they came through the gate.

All our successes that summer were deserving of a smashing celebration at my house, which I scheduled for the early fall, before the foursome took off again for London and other concert performances in Europe. Administrators and colleagues always showed up when I hosted a party. As the cellist once told me, nobody in South Bend could match my parties. Unlike others, I did not serve hot dogs and popcorn.

The fall semester of 1976 was jammed full of academia-related activities. I was successful in gaining campus-wide approval for a new summer program to be conducted in Salzburg, Austria, by the International String Quartet and was chosen to sit on the very time-consuming Arts and Sciences Promotion, Tenure, and Reappointment Committee as a nontenured member. In addition to much other committee work on and off the home campus, I held the traditional Oktoberfest at my residence, continued the popular German film series, and organized another public Christmas celebration. I filed lengthy reports about the Bonn Program, made new recommendations for improvement, and composed a proposal for a new course entitled "A Contrastive Analysis of the Two Germanys (BRD and GDR)."

My duties connected with the different international studies committees necessitated travel to the Bloomington campus. Carroll withdrew from participation in the Bonn Program for personal reasons, which meant I had to look for a replacement, a task difficult to accomplish from the States. I decided to skip the program for 1977 and assess the situation during my next trip to Bonn. I took advantage of the extra time and applied for a grant to visit the GDR in the summer of 1977, to gather information for my course proposal and to do research at the Goethe and Schiller Archive in Weimar at the same time. In addition to teaching twenty-four credit hours that semester instead of the required nine, I implemented a new "language reinforcement program" for all languages, and was successful in hiring Heidi, my star student, to teach G101, even though she did not have a BA. Since Professor

1972–1984

Suderman had set the precedent when he hired me in 1966, I had no trouble. As a result of being urged by several of my colleagues, I prepared my dossier for promotion to associate professor. This promotion was unusual insofar as I did not yet have tenure. Several suggested I go up for early tenure as well, but I decided to wait a year. I felt very secure about the promotion. I had a book in print by a reputable publisher in Germany, had received excellent student evaluations for all my courses, and had done more than many others by way of service to the university, the students, and the public. All of the committees and administrators supported me, which meant smooth sailing ahead.

* * *

During the Christmas break of 1976, I virtually collapsed from exhaustion. With the exception of getting together with my musical friends, especially the violist, to whose ardent pursuits I had succumbed first slowly, then surely, and finally with great crescendo and fortissimo, I spent most of my time reading and researching the function of animals in Hoffmann's tales. Since the Loesers were in Arizona and the roads were clear, I spent Christmas Eve with my friends Elsa and Leonard. I had gotten used to their two little dachshunds sitting beneath the dinner table and salivating in anticipation of a morsel from above. I did go boating with them now and then, and I spent a night on their thirty-foot Chris-Craft. I enjoyed the breeze and the sunsets while cruising around Lake Michigan and rowing along the outlet to the place where we bought freshly smoked white fish, but I eventually tired of the boisterous beer-drinking parties along the pier. Leonard Carlson always addressed me emphatically as "Sergeant." When Elsa, during a conversation, said out of the blue, "We [Americans] should do to the blacks what Hitler did to the Jews," I was shocked and began to distance myself.

My colleague Professor Annemarie Poinsatte, a full-blooded Parisian with a PhD in French and Romance languages and literature from the University of Chicago, was serving her two-year term in the rotating chairman position. Her annual evaluations of my performance were consistently highly complimentary. When she was on a sabbatical during the spring semester of 1977, I was appointed acting chairman, a rather risky position for me to be in, considering I did not have tenure and was under consideration for a promotion. I always felt that as long as I myself adhered to high standards, I would be in a position to hold others to the same standards. While sipping a glass of wine in a rustic restaurant in Trier, I once asked one of my Bonn participants, a philosophy major, if he had an idea about what other professors thought of me, and he confided that while they respected me, they were also afraid of me. I had a feeling I had been observed rather carefully when sitting on the Promotion, Tenure, and Reappointment Committee, at which time they must have noticed how strongly I felt about standards. Not everybody who applied was awarded tenure. I never again sat on that particular committee. Incidentally, the student who passed on the information had been extremely reluctant to join the Bonn Program out of fear he would not make it. Later, he could not thank me enough for virtually dragging him there. As a result of his participation, he earned a Fulbright scholarship, which gained him entrance into the University of Trier.

Research and Travel in the German Democratic Republic

My acting chairmanship went rather smoothly, and my promotion to associate professor came off without a hitch. I felt especially honored because one of my female colleagues from the Biology Department, who was a member of the Promotion, Tenure, and Reappointment Committee, was sufficiently impressed to recommend me to the Committee on Distinguished Teaching Awards for a 1977 All-University Teaching Award. I also received a couple of grants to explore the GDR and conduct research in Weimar for an article entitled "The Language of Mephistopheles," which Professor Jaeger had encouraged me to publish in graduate school. I wanted to research Goethe's handwritten manuscript to see if he had made any significant changes while writing *Faust I* and *Faust II*.

In February of that semester, I was lucky to be on the Bloomington campus for committee work at the same time my favorite quartet, which at that point included my heartthrob, Amadeus, was playing in Recital Hall. They enjoyed a standing ovation. I returned to South Bend so elated that I felt compelled to send a letter full of praise to the chancellor, who I knew loved having the artists on our steadily growing campus. By and by, I adopted the habit of speaking out without being asked whenever I observed someone deserving of praise. Neither did I refrain from expressing criticism in writing when I disagreed with the actions of my superiors. I wrote a strong letter faulting the chancellor for demoting our head librarian – a move my colleagues felt was politically quite daring, because at the time I did not have tenure. Yet, maybe because of it, they did not hesitate to approach me when a rather sizeable group of young tenured professors decided to ask for the removal of the dean of Arts and Sciences. I signed my name despite the fact that he had treated me personally rather fairly. I agreed with my colleagues, who felt that he lacked strong leadership qualities as well as the flexibility required for a growing campus. Rumor had it that he did not attach much importance to foreign-language studies because he had had trouble with such studies himself. I was disappointed when he eliminated funding for Russian 101 after one year. I had fought hard to have the course offered, especially since the International Studies Committee had approved a summer course in Russia. I felt that one year was not enough to get a new program started. Of course, he would not even give Latin a chance, despite the fact that we had assembled a petition demonstrating great student interest. I always felt that to justify calling itself a university, an educational institution had to offer courses some might consider esoteric, no matter how low the enrollment. I later regretted having signed the letter, which did result in his resignation. The person who replaced him was even less desirable.

The summer of 1977 was filled with more events and experiences than the previous one. Considering my love of music, it should not come as a surprise that my friendship with the charming violist, who was twenty years my junior, had intensified. Ever since I invited them to a party I threw after one of his recitals on our campus, even his very nice grandparents from Kalamazoo had taken a distinct liking to me. I think they were flattered by the floral arrangement I had sent to their hotel as a welcoming gesture. I had also been a guest at their lovely home and had started to correspond and speak on the phone with the grandmother on occasion. However, despite the strong feelings involved, the thought that my relationship with the violist might take a serious twist never entered my mind. I hoped that eventually we would just part as friends. –

Knowing I would be absent from my house until almost the end of August, I told Amadeus he could stay there during my absence. Incidentally, he resembled my German admirer Apollo somewhat. They were both slender, tall, blue eyed, blond, and very young, but Apollo was more handsome. I was scheduled to return to South Bend late on July 24 and leave again for Brazil a week later. Amadeus was overjoyed to stay at my house and very grateful. On the day of my departure, in the middle of June, he gave me a beautiful necklace, a delicate golden chain with small white pearls, which I wore around the clock.

I flew via Iceland Air directly to Luxembourg, where my friends the Lorscheiders, who had hosted a wine tasting for my students, had found a conveniently located inn for me. I was contemplating changing the location of my future summer programs from Bonn to Trier, but after lengthy discussions with teachers from Clark University and Georgetown who already had programs in Trier, I decided to hold off until I reassessed Bonn. My main concern was finding host families, but I was concerned also that too many American students in that small town would increase the temptation to speak English rather than German.

In Bonn, with the generous help of the Padre and good contacts from previous years, and after spending hours on the phone searching for host families, I decided to return to Bonn in the summer of 1978. With Carroll's help, I found a new liaison in Bonn, Helmuth Rafalski, from the School of Education. I renewed contact with Inter Nationes, who offered to furnish any cultural material for the students I wanted. I gracefully declined Clark University's offer to merge their program with mine in Trier.

I arrived in Regensburg, at the Segebrechts, late on June 25. It was wonderful to see the whole family again, if only for a short time. We discussed my research on the function of animals in Hoffmann's fairy tales and agreed that there was enough material to warrant another book. My mind was made up. I would spend my sabbatical, which would follow my being granted tenure, on a new book instead of an article. But for the next few weeks, I would put Hoffmann's animals out of my mind and concentrate on the present, that is, on my long-awaited visit to the GDR.

Back in the States, a surprising number of people did not know which country I was referring to when I told them I would spend several weeks in the "GDR." When my elaboration "German Democratic Republic" also resulted in blank looks, I rendered my final explanation: "East Germany." Many so-called friends and acquaintances reacted promptly by giving me a heavy dose of unsolicited advice aimed at dampening the enthusiasm which had led me to undertake the long-overdue *Bildungsreise* (educational journey) in the first place.

My original desire to discover for myself how accurate all these warnings were grew more intense as I approached the day of my departure. It was important to finally find out how freely I could move around in the GDR and how careful I would have to be in expressing my thoughts. I became anxious to ascertain whether I would indeed be – as many prophesied – under "constant surveillance," whether my telephones would be "tapped," my rooms "bugged," my correspondence "screened," my suitcase "searched," and all unprocessed films "taken away," and most of all whether I would in fact encounter that particular "friend" who would trap me into saying something which would be used against me and possibly result in my being jailed. I also wondered whether I would be one of those victims whose patience would be tried by the constant and deliberate delaying tactics of officials and whether I would become so depressed that I would desperately long for the day of my return to the West.

I had not been completely immune to those words of caution. In fact, I asked myself what I was doing when, prior to my departure for Luxembourg, that is, three days before June 17, I still had not received a permit to enter the GDR. I needed it to secure a visa at the border. After numerous attempts by my travel agent, a vague response came on the 16th that "an answer may be expected soon." It occurred to me that this might indeed be a deliberate delaying tactic. Yet I reminded myself that, in all fairness, I had experienced consternation when our university committee, which granted part of the aid for my educational journey, took its own time in making a decision, no matter how much I stressed the time constraints. I wondered how speedily the Western bureaucrats would have processed a request by a citizen from a socialist or communist country. In the end, upon the advice of my travel agent, I left for Germany without the permit. It finally caught up with me when I arrived in Bonn, where the Jesuits received the permit on my behalf on the 18th.

The Segebrechts took me to the train station early in the morning on June 27. I waved to them out of the window until they were no longer visible, and my long awaited journey behind the Iron Curtain began.

I should stress that I did not go to the GDR to aggravate, agitate, or trigger a revolution. I went primarily as a Germanist and humanist, as a teacher of German language, literature, and culture, seeking firsthand acquaintance with the GDR and the cultural treasures in which she abounds and of which she can be proud. Most of all, I wanted to meet the people, observe their modes of life, and hear about their aspirations and their discontents. I considered it imperative for any German professor to acquaint him- or herself with the country personally before lecturing about its culture and people. I felt it imperative to include the GDR in the German curriculum. It had been suppressed all too long from lectures dealing with the cultures of German-speaking countries. I held that German professors could ill afford to deprive their students of the opportunity to learn about a country which at that time ranked tenth among the countries of the world in industrial output. The students had a right to learn how the differences and similarities vis-à-vis the Federal Republic (West Germany) were manifested or were in the process of being manifested in that comparatively young socialist country.

Another desire nourished my preoccupation with experiencing the GDR personally. Having been born, raised, and partly educated in the FRG, and being well-acquainted with her culture and people, I had wrestled for years with the persistent question of a possible reunification of the two Germanys. I needed to find out personally what the sentiments of the people in the GDR were and the degree to which a united Germany really was desirable and likely.

Last but not least, my father was born in the eastern part of Germany and had last lived in Leipzig. I had never personally met either of his two brothers or his mother and father, both of whom died before I was born. I was curious to see what it might have been like for them. I had heard that the only son of his younger brother Erich was a policeman, who escaped one night across the border, leaving behind his wife and a young child.

As I boarded the train in Regensburg, the corridors and the compartment in which I found a last seat were jammed full. Many were over sixty years old, returning home from a visit to their relatives in the West. Young people were barred from travel to the West out of fear that they would defect or criticize their own regime. I had at times thought that the restrictions imposed on the general public in the GDR were exaggerated in the West and was a bit surprised when a woman in the compartment, about an hour before the train was to arrive at the border town of Gutenfürst, pulled a *Stern* magazine out of her suitcase, unbuttoned her blouse, pushed the magazine inside, and buttoned it up. Nobody said a word. *Stern* is a magazine for which I would not spend a dime. It is popular for its pornographic content, to put it bluntly. Pornography in the GDR was off-limits, which I did not necessarily view as a negative, except that it deprives one of freedom of speech.

Even before the train pulled into the border town of Gutenfürst, two border controllers made their way through the corridor, checking people's passports and some pieces of luggage. Everybody seemed rather quiet. When they started checking in my compartment, they seemed to focus on me. I handed them my telegram, which authorized my entrance visa and my passport. They looked at each other, frowned, and informed me politely that I had to get off the train. Everybody's attention was on me, the American who spoke perfect German. I asked what was the matter, and he explained that the cable referred to a man, "Mr." Dr. Beardsley, instead of "Mrs." I produced all available pieces of documentation in my briefcase to prove my identity. No use – I had to get off the train and await clarification. They were kind enough to carry my suitcase, which was very heavy, and ushered me to a modestly furnished waiting room at this station in the middle of nowhere. I had of course noticed the barbed-wire fences when crossing the border and the strip of no-man's-land between East and West, but did my best to focus on the positive. Here was my chance to observe their treatment of me while they tried to determine whether the cable was for a Mrs. and not a Mr. It took a mere five minutes for them to discover I was legitimate, but it was too late. I missed my train and went to the station's little restaurant, where I was served a decent meal for one-fourth of what it would have cost me in the West.

The unscheduled delay ultimately bore curious educational fruits. On the train to Karl Marx City, I met a few elderly people who half-mockingly told me they call the train crossing the border "the Mummy Express." When I asked what the "VEB" signs on factory buildings meant, one passenger explained that they meant *Volkseigener Betrieb* (factory owned by the people), or more precisely, *Vaters ehemaliger Betrieb* (father's formerly owned factory). On the train, I learned that those factory owners who had to turn their firms over to the state were being paid a certain sum in annual installments of 10,000 marks. If the sum was not paid off during the owner's lifetime, it became payable to the heirs. I was surprised when my travel companions unanimously proclaimed that they liked to visit their relatives in the West but preferred to reside in the East. I was bothered by one of the women, who was showing off all the goods she had been given by her relatives. Next to her sat a younger mother with a little boy who looked so sad when he saw all the treasures. It was obvious that his mother had no access to such resources. It was another example of the contrast between the haves and the have-nots.

I took advantage of my bus ride to Annaberg-Buchholz, Saxony, in the Ore Mountains, by talking with an unhappy student. As a result of his final grades at the high school, he was forced to enroll in an engineering school instead of the university, as he had wished. He was disappointed because once finished, he would earn less. At that time, children of nonacademic parents were given priority for admission to the university, provided their grades were competitive, a policy which made sense to me. In the West, they had *numerous clausus* (limited admission) for students wanting to study medicine. Only students with straight As were accepted. I spoke to a bunch of other pupils on the bus. With the exception of three, all professed to remember almost nothing about the Russian language, which they were required to study for eight years. Reasons ranged from the difficulty of the language to poor instruction and a lack of interest in the language as such. Two of the exceptions had excelled and studied at the university in Moscow. Another enthusiast was continuing with evening courses so he could become a guide for tourists from the Soviet Union.

The bus arrived in Annaberg-Buchholz at 7:00 p.m. on the 27th. My bus companion turned out to be the first of many people in the GDR who treated me with unforgettable kindness. The taxi service was very sparse in the little town of Buchholz. I think it was nonexistent. My companion carried my suitcase the entire distance to the hotel. The sidewalks were too uneven to pull it on its wheels. When I offered him a tip, he refused to accept it.

I had not had a choice of hotels. All reservations had to be prepaid in dollars in the States. A particular hotel was assigned to me at each stop. Any change of location was out of the question. The hotel where I checked in, which was more like an inn, was dimly lit and somewhat intimidating. It was called Hotel zum wilden Mann (Wild Man Hotel). My room was at the end of a dark corridor. The atmosphere was spooky, and I was a bit scared when a bearded guy, who was wild looking indeed, appeared out of the dark and explained to me at length how complicated the bus connection to Seiffen, my next stop, was. I got the impression he wanted to talk me out of going there, and he almost succeeded, because I would have missed all of my appointments had I been forced to rely on the bus. I was disillusioned and hungry and went into the small, modestly furnished restaurant. I asked a couple if I might sit down at their table since no free table was available. It was not uncommon in either the GDR or BRD to sit with strangers. This couple worked for a farm cooperative owned by the state. He was a tractor driver. They were vacationing in the Ore Mountains and staying in a two-bedroom bungalow for two weeks – for only 100 marks ($50). It was subsidized by the state. They turned out to be my saviors, because they insisted on taking me to Seiffen in their little Trabant.

While I was still chatting with my new friends, the bearded character suddenly entered the restaurant, walked directly toward our table, and swiftly, without asking permission, sat down next to me. He interrupted our conversation rudely by stating that he simply could not miss the extraordinary opportunity to talk to an American. Without giving me a chance to respond, he zeroed in on President Carter. He denounced the president's proclamations on human rights as a "hypocritical political front." He pronounced him a "dead duck," "as dead as Gerald Ford." When he started in on President Kennedy, my friends across the table got up and left, saying "good night." I decided that neither the place nor the time was suitable for what had the potential of turning into a heated political discussion. I excused myself and halfway promised the eager assailant to accept his invitation to his apartment for the next evening, when he also wanted me to meet his wife. Curiously enough, he failed to show up at the hotel at the agreed-upon time. I felt somewhat relieved, for in discussing the incident with my Trabant friends, I decided it was best to avoid a possible confrontation on my first day in the GDR. I was itching, though, to inquire about what would happen to him if he were to attack Honnecker, their own head of state, as openly as he did the US presidents.

As promised, my friends picked me up at the Wild Man Hotel at 8:00 a.m. on the 28th. My luck was changing, and my spirits had been lifted. My ride in the tiny Trabant – which my friends had to wait ten years to buy and for which they paid 10,000 DDR marks, or $4,800 – was comfortable but somewhat slow. The traffic on these roads through the Ore Mountains was almost nonexistent. The hills were partially covered with forests and meadows, and the villages we passed through looked a bit run-down and lacked the masses of flowers so abundant in the West. I reminded myself that unlike the West, the East did not benefit from the Marshall Plan and that, to compound the problem, the Soviet Union, partly in an effort to get hold of hard currency, systematically drained the regions of the bulk of their resources. If the citizens did not have more, it was not their fault; far be it from me to run them down.

My friends chauffeured me around all day. We were in time for all of my prescheduled appointments in the charming town of Seiffen, where centuries ago silver mining was active. We stopped at the big Toy Museum, which contained the most fabulous collection of wood-crafted toys. In the center stood a magnificent Christmas pyramid whose intricately carved and brightly painted figures reached all the way to the tip of the vaulted ceiling. The display of nutcrackers, wooden figurines, and toys, which I had admired occasionally at store windows in the West at Christmastime, was fantastic. It was a child's dreamland. My hosts also took me to a home industry, which was operated by father and son and had been in the family since the time of industrialization. They demonstrated the wood lathe for me, filling a package with animal figures and turning flowers that I could show my students. At another place, I was presented with a beautiful bright-red nutcracker, a couple of pyramids, and several small figurines depicting forest workers and the father and mother of Hänsel and Gretel on their way home from the woods. They carried a bundle of kindling on their backs and an ax and a lantern in their hands. I decided right then and there to display the pieces on campus at an exhibit, which I planned to put together upon my return.

After a stop at a commune-type toy industry, I saw a demonstration on a lathe still driven by water and concluded that the working environment there, if not flawless, was much more humane than during the times of exploitation in these villages at the commencement of industrialization.

On the way back to Buchholz, we stopped at the big VEB VERO toy factory, in Olbernhau, where I had a lengthy discussion with the director and head designer, Mr. Flade, and his two assistants. He expressed several times how pleased he was that a professor from the United States was personally visiting their place. It was a first. He informed me that the majority of their exports were to the West. I was disappointed to hear that the general public in the GDR had very limited access to the goods they produced for export. Very few items were for sale.

In the evening, my friends treated me to supper, or *Abendbrot*, pumpernickel with cold cuts and a beer, at their little vacation bungalow, which consisted of a bedroom, small living room, kitchen, and bath as well as a terrace with a view of the rolling hills. I was concerned about missing the bus for Karl Marx City at 7:00 a.m. My friends took me by surprise when they picked me up in the morning and drove me all the way to Karl Marx City, carrying my heavy suitcase up the stairs to the tracks and into the train when it arrived. When I offered them money, they refused, but they did accept a wooden candleholder I had bought in Seiffen. They were most grateful when they received my package from the United States. I had sent a $100 bill to the family who gave me all those presents; however, it never reached them.

On my way to Weimar, I had to stop in Eisenach. It is a must for any professor of German. I had to have a first look at this town in Thuringia, which lies at the foot of the stately Wartburg, an eleventh-century castle where St. Elisabeth lived and Luther translated the Bible. Here Bach was born, Fritz Reuter was put to rest, and Wagner was inspired to compose his opera *Tannhäuser*. I climbed up to the Wartburg, which is situated up high on a rather steep hill and still contains a part of one of the few preserved Romanesque palaces. I was awestruck to walk around the halls of the castle, where the minstrels Walter von der Vogelweide and Wolfram von Eschenbach competed in the contest immortalized in Wagner's opera. I was awestruck also when I saw the murals depicting the miracle of roses with Elisabeth, who was betrothed to Louis the Saint at the early age of four. My third-semester students always loved the legend, and now I could elaborate. I was equally in awe at seeing with my own eyes the place where Luther found refuge in 1521 and the room where he spent ten months translating the New Testament.

My short stay at the hotel gave me a chance to observe that Western music was definitely favored. During a discussion with three traveling businessmen from Dresden, I found it strange that one of the gentlemen, apparently the head of a company, apologized for not being able to provide me with his name or address, as his colleagues did. They wanted to contact me at the hotel in Dresden and invite me to meet their families, but I never heard from them again. Yet, during my visit to the Wartburg, I met a young couple who invited me to their apartment when I was in East Berlin. Thus, I proved those wrong who back in the States had insisted it would be impossible to establish contacts on one's own.

Upon my arrival in Weimar, at Goethe's favorite hotel, Zum Elephanten, I was pleased to finally receive a response from Dr. Franz, the head of the Gesellschaft Neue Heimat (Society New Homeland), located in East Berlin. One of the agency's aims was to establish connections between German immigrants and the GDR. I had asked him to kindly assist me in setting up meetings with various organizations and institutions in connection with my research. Professor Reichmann, from Indiana University, head of the Department of Western European Studies, had recommended I get in touch with Dr. Franz. Though one of the purposes of my ten-day stay was to conduct scholarly research at the Goethe and Schiller Archive in addition to soaking up the atmosphere where Schiller, Goethe, and their friends and supporters lived and flourished, I was equally interested in learning about the pros and cons of socialism.

My first meeting was with a professor of English at the College of Construction and Architecture, where I gained insight into methods of teaching foreign languages and problems with students, facilities, professors' salaries, etc. I found my discussion the next day with Professor Dr. Paul Michel, president of the National Center for Music Pedagogy in the GDR and of the Franz Liszt School of Music in Weimar, more fascinating. He was internationally known for his work with child psychology and music and turned out to be a friend of Deans Hoffer and Webb on the IU–Bloomington campus. I assured him I would do my best to get him invited to our campus in 1978, when he planned to attend seminars in Canada and on the IU campus. He was later forced to cancel for health reasons. Professor Michel was most gracious; he invited me to dinner at the hotel, showed me the marvelous School of Music, Liszt's pretentious mansion, the Belvedere Castle and its Diana Pavilion, and the orangery where Goethe pursued his botanical studies. I was envious of the music students, who were specially chosen to study at the Belvedere Castle. Professor Michel also took me to the cemetery to see the vault with Goethe's and Schiller's sarcophagi and drove me out to Goethe's beloved garden house. I was intrigued by Paul Michel's story. He seemed to be a committed communist. His father had been a communist in Hitler's time. Paul Michel was one of the students who did not have a chance under Hitler but who, with Hitler's demise, was able to advance under socialism. I could not help but notice a tone of envy in his voice when I told him about life in America. We corresponded for a while, and then there was silence.

I considered my visit to the Kinder-Kombination, a day-care center outside of Weimar, a highlight. They sent a chauffeur to pick me up. As the car approached the center, about sixty children awaited me on the steps out front. They sang a cheerful welcoming song for me, which reminded me vaguely of the song the campfire girls back in Michigan sang for me a few months after my arrival. I was quite touched when a little boy handed me a big bouquet of pink carnations, and I was impressed by the highly informative tour of the center given by the people in charge. It was a pleasure to see the extremely sanitary, bright, and thoughtfully designed facilities, the types of books and toys available, and the nourishing meals served to the children. It was gratifying to meet the young women specially trained to care for the youngsters. The atmosphere was inviting, and it was clear that a mother could easily entrust her child to their care. It cost 15 cents per day, to defray some of the expenses for meals. I considered such day-care centers one of the major and most essential establishments for bringing about equality for women in the GDR and elsewhere, and could not understand why America, the richest country in the world, was so lax in providing the same care for the children of its working mothers. As I sat chatting with the women over coffee and cake, one of the nurses handed me a cobalt-blue creamer with white dots as a souvenir. It was a piece of pottery produced in the region. I still treasure it today.

I was disappointed when I was told that the National Theater in Weimar, where I had hoped to attend a few memorable performances, was closed to the public because the Freie Deutsche Jugend (Free German Youth Organization) had their big annual gathering in Weimar. All performances were reserved for them. I could not recall a single occasion in my life when I was unable to gain entrance to a theater performance or an opera I wanted to see. I took the initiative, called Professor Christa Lehmann, the well-known actress, who was also director of the theater at the time, introduced myself, and related my disappointment, and the next thing I knew she told me to come backstage before the beginning of the performance that night, where her assistant would take care of me. Her assistant, Helga Schuld, who later became a good friend, arranged for me to visit five "closed performances" where I had front row seats, gratis. The two top plays were Schiller's *Kabale und Liebe* (Intrigue and Love) and Brecht's *Mutter Courage*, in which Christa Lehmann played a superb Mother Courage. I was also present when the leader of the Youth Organization delivered an enthusiastic opening address in the theater, free of attacks against capitalism. It was followed by heavy applause. The theater experience, which provided the opportunity to meet another actress and people from the theater in a social setting, was as exciting as the meetings with Professor Dr. Hahn, director of the archives, and Dr. Henning. He was the director of the Central Library of German Classics, founded by Goethe. It was closed, but he opened it especially for me. The most exciting moment came when he unlocked the fabulous Rococo Room so I could see the collection of rare bibliophilic treasures, which were placed there in part by the great Goethe himself. It was pretty amazing when, in the same room, I found a copy of my book on Hoffmann right next to Aubrey Beardsley's. I wish I could have told Doc about it.

It was nice to learn that both Professor Hahn and Dr. Henning, the author of the voluminous Faust bibliography, knew many of my colleagues in West Germany and in the States. Both were very supportive of my scholarly endeavors.

Professor Hahn arranged for me to read the priceless and well-guarded manuscript of Goethe's *Faust I* and *Faust II*. I was assigned a special place at one of the long oaken tables in the archives, from which I could look down on the River Ilm. Two archivists delivered the manuscript pages, arranged in big folders with thickly matted dividers which protected the at times thin pieces of paper on which Goethe had scripted his *Faust* verses in meticulously crafted language, with no noticeable changes as far as Mephistopheles was concerned. Each time a new volume was placed before me, I felt as though I were about to open a sacred treasure. It was absolutely quiet and somewhat dark in the somber room despite its high windows and ceilings. When I was finished with a volume, it was picked up and carried back to the vault.

I worked in the archives mostly on days when no meetings were scheduled, and enjoyed looking at all the art treasures in this middle-sized town dating back to the Middle Ages. Others may remember Weimar as the place where the national assembly adopted the constitution of the new German republic in July 1919. I considered myself fortunate not to have to rush through the place. There were few tourists present, which meant I could walk in a leisurely fashion through Goethe's big house, which resembled the houses built for noblemen at the beginning of the nineteenth century. The atmosphere was indeed awe-inspiring and stood in noticeable contrast to that of the much humbler Schiller house. From there, it was not too far to the former palace, also built under Goethe's supervision, at the same location where the old one burned down in 1774 and where I wanted to see the rooms dedicated to the great poets Goethe, Schiller, Herder, and Wieland. As I looked at the noble structure of the von Stein house, Goethe's long and intimate friendship with Charlotte, the wife of Karl August's master of the horse, crossed my mind. Now, whenever I read the poems inspired by Charlotte, I visualize Weimar and the proximity of their residences and Goethe's house in the garden. It is not difficult to understand how a genius like Goethe would easily be motivated by a kindred spirit in these idyllic surroundings.

It was on Sunday, July 8, that I mustered up enough courage to take a bus to Ettersberg, the location of the Buchenwald National Memorial. Here, as early as July 1937, the Nazis started one of Germany's major concentration camps. It is surprisingly only about seven miles from the town which, only a little over one hundred years before, was the center of the greatest German classicists and humanists.

The sun was approaching the zenith when the bus dropped me off at the entrance. It was my first personal encounter with a "KZ," as the Germans refer to concentration camps, probably because the abbreviation removes a bit of the harshness of the vowels in the words. As I approached the gate hesitatingly, I saw the big metal letters *JEDEM DAS SEINE* (to each his own) across the top of a wrought-iron gate and was shocked at the blatant sarcasm. Walking along the path, I was glad I had come alone and was relieved to see virtually no other visitors. It was dead silent around me as I looked down on the vast expanse where mankind had committed the most atrocious crimes. This evoked my childhood experience of *Kristallnacht*. Forty years later, a big, soft blanket of green grass covered the scene of the crimes.

The mostly reconstructed barracks, buildings, and museums explained in graphic detail the procedures of the many forms of torture and cruelty to which the prisoners were subjected. It felt like walking through hell without fire. I realized that seeing all this in person was more moving than reading about the misdeeds in books, seeing them on a TV screen, or even listening to a secondhand report. Though still removed from reality, here at the very place where the crimes were committed, the pain and guilt of knowing that my own compatriots were the criminals overcame me. The impact is harsher when, in this environment, you read about what you already knew: that big industries from the country of your birth, "Flick, Krupp, Thyssen, the IG-Farbenindustrie, the Siemens and the AEG trusts were among the main financial supporters of Hitler" and that "fascism served its masters with comprehensive armament orders, high dividends, the supply of slave labor from the concentration camps and the murderous oppression of the German working class." Even more heart-wrenching was the documentary film screened in the poorly lit, sinister room in one of the buildings – more heart-wrenching because the heinous crimes took place precisely where I watched the film.

When I lingered at the mass graves where victims from thirty-two countries lay buried, it suddenly occurred to me that the descriptions of the various sites and the commentary in the film focused more heavily on sufferers from the Soviet Union, and on communists like Ernst Thälmann and socialists who had fought against fascism, than on Jews. Though they did build a memorial to murdered Jewish prisoners. When I later inquired about it, I was told that no Jews were persecuted at Buchenwald, which I found hard to believe.

I was numbed by the experience in Buchenwald and could not endure more than a couple of hours at the place. As I sat on a bench waiting for my bus back to Weimar, I read through the pamphlet and very much agreed with its conclusion: "We must never again allow the world to be plunged into an abyss of blood and misery and the peoples to be pushed to the edge of a catastrophe. . . . The decision whether the peoples shall take the road of peace or steer towards the abyss of a third world war lies in the hands of peace-loving mankind." I made a promise to myself to share what I had experienced in Buchenwald with my students whenever I taught a German-culture course in the future.

On the train from Weimar to Leipzig, a city with a population of approximately six hundred thousand, or the size of Hannover, I got into a heated discussion with a couple of passionate young socialists. The minute they realized I was American, they began to criticize President Carter's stand on human rights, calling it highly paradoxical. It was around that time that the president's approval of the development of a neutron bomb made headlines. Any respect they may have felt for him initially for his views on human rights was immediately destroyed when he referred to the weapon as "a clean bomb" – clean insofar as it kills humans only, leaving the environment virtually intact. My personal views left me without defense, and I could not help but sympathize with the people in the GDR. I understood only too well why such an inhumane invention would constitute an extraordinarily precarious situation for them as next-door neighbors of the West. I could see the fear in their eyes. Almost as difficult for me to rationalize and to explain was the blackout and the resulting looting which occurred in New York while I was in the GDR. The people could not understand how a nation as financially powerful as the United

States, which strongly advocated supporting the needy of the world, could fail to fund technology which could have prevented a disaster of this magnitude. Radio broadcasts blamed capitalist-oriented industrial monopolies that preferred private monetary gain to providing measures which protect the people.

My three-day stay in Leipzig, the city taken by the US Army in April 1945 but later turned over to the Russians, was packed with meetings and activities. My first stop took me to Karl Marx University to meet with Professor Dr. Ursula Förster, director of the Herder Institute and author of several leading textbooks used to teach German to foreign students preparing for enrollment at GDR universities. She readily agreed to provide me with sufficient copies of books and material in connection with my course development. I was interested in understanding how the West was presented in their texts as opposed to those used in the socialist states as well as their textbooks' general approach to grammar and cultural topics. She added my name to her regular mailing list, and for several years IU was the beneficiary of the latest publications coming from the GDR. I was upset when, even before the unification, our new librarian took it upon himself, when having a book sale, to include many of the books I had channeled to our library as they arrived from the GDR. These books, which today are virtually unattainable, went for 25 or 50 cents apiece at the sale.

Professor Förster welcomed my criticism of a number of aspects of their magazine, *Neue Heimat* (New Homeland). I suggested they tone down their aggressive and at times inflammatory rhetoric directed toward the West. She agreed, and because she sat on the editorial board, she encouraged me to pass on my criticism when I visited Mr. Vierlich, the director of the leading publishing house in the GDR, Verlag Zeit im Bild. I had a meeting with him scheduled for my next stop in Dresden. They also invited me to write an article, which was published by them in 1983 under the title "The GDR – A Gratifying Encounter."

A woman psychiatrist who was actively engaged in the Liberal Democratic Party of the GDR and had been a former representative in the city government of Leipzig talked to me about the activities of professional women and government support of women. She confirmed what I had heard, that the most frequent psychological problems among the young stemmed from alcoholism. She also expressed great concern about a flaw in their abortion law, which failed to place a limit on the number of abortions a woman can have, thus opening the door to serious physical and psychological damage.

I was appreciative when she took me to visit an elderly couple in a high-rise apartment house. I had long wanted to get a look at one of these houses, which were obviously erected quickly and with little thought of making them aesthetically appealing. One looked much like the others on a given block. To be fair, after the cities had been reduced to ashes and because raw materials in the GDR were not plentiful, the people worked hard and untiringly to clean old bricks of brittle cement so they could be utilized when rebuilding fallen houses. They needed roofs over their heads fast. No wonder that many of those apartment houses shared a common facade. Though not fancy, they were functional, and rent was as low as 45 marks per month. As we took the elevator to the couple's apartment, I noticed that the walls were painted in pastels. The man was an invalid, and his wife, who worked for the city, greeted us at the door. I was pleased to find that even though their one-bedroom apartment was small, the place was as neat and inviting as comparable residences in the West. *Klein aber fein* (small but neat).

While on a quick detour in Erfurt, I caught a lucky break. After I collapsed from exhaustion on a sidewalk, a man who turned out to be a dean of the nearby Erfurt Cathedral on the Hill (built in 1200) took me inside to recuperate. I seized the opportunity to discuss with him the general welfare of the Church. I got the impression that though there was very little support for maintenance of the churches, the situation was not as grave as I had imagined. Attendance was low, but there was certainly no law against holding services; and one day I heard a rather moving sermon, not without hidden criticism, in one of the churches in the GDR.

As I lost a half a day in Leipzig due to my collapse, I decided to take a city tour by bus. I simply had to see the St. Thomas Church, where Bach played the organ for so many years, and was upset when I noticed it had several broken windows. I urged a man in a black frock to notify the proper authorities to have it repaired. We also stopped at the new Gewandhaus (Concert Hall), home of the famous Gewandhaus Orchestra, where, according to my father, my uncle Arthur played the violin. We went past the center of the book-trade quarter and saw the booksellers' exchange, and I stood in awe before the tomb of Bach and the Reformation Monument, with bronze statues of Luther and Melanchthon. In Leipzig, one cannot miss the monumental Völkerschlachtdenkmal. It is the monument commemorating the Battle of the Nations, which took place in the fall of 1813 and ended in the defeat of Napoleon and the Grande Armée. I personally was more eager to see Auerbach's Keller (Cellar), which Goethe immortalized in *Faust I*. I invited my new friend the psychiatrist and her friend for dinner at the Keller, which has an unusual old wine vault. It contains a series of mural paintings of the sixteenth century, representing the legend on which the play is based. The evening we spent in this vault was awe-inspiring, and the scenes from *Faust* in which Mephistopheles plays his tricks were so vivid in my mind it was as though they were unfolding at that very moment. The dark-red wine might have played a part in this.

It would have been more difficult to leave Leipzig if the next stop had not been Dresden, where the greatest German literary geniuses and philosophers used to congregate and hold university posts, where Bach's and Mendelssohn's music resonated, and which was named *Klein Paris* (Paris in miniature) by none other than Goethe. Unfortunately, due to the heavy bombings by the Americans in 1943–1944, the city still had not been completely restored to its former state.

Dresden, the capital of the Dresden Bezirk (district) of the GDR, where I was to spend three days, was formerly the capital of the land of Saxony and only seventy miles northwest of Leipzig. Before the war it was called "Florence on the Elbe." That wide river, the second largest in Germany, dramatically highlights the silhouette of Dresden's architectural gems, especially when you look across from the right bank toward the Dimitroff Bridge. As the world knows, over 60% of this magnificent city, filled with several of the most famous art collections in the world, was destroyed by artillery and phosphorus and high-explosive bombs by the Allies at the very end of the war, on February 13, 1945. Over 35,000 civilians lost their lives.

Though the GDR had made considerable progress in rebuilding the city and restoring several of its architectural gems, it was depressing to gaze upon the blackened, broken blocks of tumbled-down pieces of architecture scattered in the black ruins of the Frauenkirche, reaching into the sky as though eternally begging to be restored to their original beauty. Across a narrow path in back of the ruins grew a young tree, stretched out in horizontal position about ten inches from the ground. A skinny black cat crawled along the trunk toward the soft green leaves of the crown – a symbol of life, a shimmer of hope?

My meeting with Mr. Heinz C. Vierich, journalist and director of the publishing house, bore fruit because he not only listened to my publication recommendations, but asked Mr. Liebscher, who was in charge of the Readers' Letters department, to take me to their display room, where I was at liberty to pick out any books (and as many copies as I needed) for the students in my course. They assured me all of it would reach me in time for my course, and it did.

I was anxious to see the Grüne Gewölbe (Green Vault), in the Albertinum, but stopped first at the Zwinger, built in the very ornate Saxon baroque style. It was originally designed as a forecourt for a castle and holds, among other objects, a beautiful collection of porcelain. I went through a section of the Semper gallery, which contains paintings by the Old Masters, and stood amazed before Raphael's *Madonna di San Sisto*. Indelibly imprinted in my mind, however, is the delicate and most intricately crafted scene of the household of the Great Mogul, emperor of China, crafted by the famous goldsmith Dinglinger. The golden canapé above the throne, with the emperor and his household gathered around him, is studded with the most precious jewels – rubies, diamonds, emeralds, and sapphires. It is a glorious and priceless work of art.

The sun was shining brightly as I stepped onto the riverboat to take a trip on the Elbe to the resort town of Königstein. The trip passed through Saxon Switzerland, a rugged terrain of sandstone formation, which reminded me slightly of the formation at the Wisconsin Dells. On the way back, I talked with a young man who had studied in Moscow, where he married a Russian who had studied German; he had subsequently encountered difficulties finding a position at a university because he had been critical of socialism as it was developing in the GDR. He claimed to be a true advocate of communism as envisioned by Marx and Lenin.

Since I had not yet seen a movie in the GDR, I decided to go to a movie theater across from the hotel on my last night in Dresden. One of the movies was produced by a filmmaker from Russia and Finland, and the other was produced by a Hungarian filmmaker. I was pleasantly surprised when the previews attacked the Ku Klux Klan in America and praised Angela Davis, who was at that time an outspoken African-American sympathizer with the socialist cause in the GDR.

Luther was my main reason for stopping for a couple of days in the small town of Wittenberg upon Elbe, about sixty miles southwest of Berlin. Luther had been a professor of theology at the university, together with his friend and fellow reformist Melanchthon, a great humanist and theologian, whose residence was only four houses away from Luther's. The Augustinian monastery where Luther lived was converted into a museum. I was particularly interested in visiting the Schloßkirche (Church of the Castle) and seeing the door on which he posted his ninety-five theses, proclaiming his opposition to the papal sale of indulgences and thus starting the Reformation movement. I had not been aware that the old wooden doors had been destroyed by a fire in 1760 and were later replaced by the bronze doors on which the Latin text of the theses was engraved. When I was in the Stadtkirche (Church of the Town), where Luther had preached, and admired the works of the famous painter Lucas Cranach, Luther's friend, I had another discussion with a sexton regarding the state's financial support of the restoration of churches of historical importance. I was surprised he had not noticed the many small holes in the church windows, which most certainly would hinder the preservation of the valuable Cranach paintings. His assurance that he would take care of it immediately probably meant Monday, since it was Sunday. While making the rounds in Wittenberg from one historic place to another, I was impressed by the well-restored and well-preserved historical sites. I also noticed that, as I expected, care was taken in the labeling of displays and sites to emphasize positive traits of socialist movements and negative aspects of the exploitation of the poor during times of feudalism and capitalism.

My train from Wittenberg to Berlin left at 7:30 a.m., and there were no taxicabs in Wittenberg. Fortunately, the maintenance man of the little hotel offered to help me out. He picked me up at 7:00 a.m. with his ancient bicycle (ancient, because just as in the West, new bikes have a great attraction for thieves). He loaded my suitcase, which by then weighed at least sixty-five pounds and had lost the function of its wheels, on his bike and pushed it to the station, which was a twenty-five-minute walk. We talked about the drawbacks of the Russian occupation, which they seemed to like less than the Germans in the West liked the Western Allies. When we parted and he refused to accept a tip, I promised this good soul, whose hobby was collecting stamps, that I would send him a bunch as soon as I returned to the States. I kept my promise, but never heard from him again.

In East Berlin, I finally met Dr. Franz, who had asked his assistants Mrs. Zachrau and Mr. Bettke to schedule various meetings for me. We met in the office of Liga für Völkerfreundschaft (League for Friendship among Nations), where I learned they had taken such an interest in me because I had emigrated to the United States from Hannover, Germany. Both Mrs. Zachrau and Mr. Bettke, who throughout the following years were important liaisons, had degrees in history and literature from universities in the GDR.

Mrs. Zachrau and Mr. Bettke were pleased at the prospect of providing material for my course and for the exhibit, which I had begun to plan when meeting with Mr. Vierich in Dresden. They wisely suggested I seek approval from my university administration first, but promised to send ample material to make it a success. Mrs. Zachrau also arranged a meeting for me with two of the leading women of the Demokratischer Frauenbund Deutschland (League of Democratic Women). I was taken aback when I entered the room and was first greeted by a man who was obviously the head of the league. He asked me to sit down in a big, brown, upholstered leather couch chair and offered me a brandy, which I turned down in exchange for a cup of coffee. After a few introductory exchanges and before he called in the women, I expressed my surprise at the "capitalistic atmosphere" in this office, which boasted heavy leather chairs on thick Oriental rugs – and one could not miss the richly carved cabinets along the wall. I never forgot his answer: "It is the aim of communism to sweeten everybody's life."

He introduced the two women, Ms. Engelhardt and her assistant, Sylvia Zenschuer, who told me everything I wanted to know and then some. Coming from a country where women were being discriminated against, I was very much impressed by their achievements regarding the status of women. I detected no trace of discrimination in regard to salary, jobs, or other professional concerns. Women were strongly encouraged to study, and large amounts of money were devoted to furthering their education so they could fill positions often held by men only. Women in the GDR had many advantages in comparison to those in the West. Each woman, regardless of her marital status, had one day off each month to take care of household chores and the like. To encourage larger families, women were entitled to twenty-three weeks off with pay preceding and following the birth of a first child. Their jobs awaited them when they returned. When a second child was born, women were entitled to a whole year off of work, with 90% of their monthly salary continuing and their jobs held for them. There was no worry about medical care, since everything was taken care of by the state. Marriage was encouraged, in that couples found it easier to obtain an apartment. They could borrow up to 5,000 marks at 1%–2% interest to purchase initial household goods. I was convinced that all this information would provoke lively debates in the classroom. The women promised to send all this information and more in print, in both English and German.

I took a closer look at Humboldt Universität and went across the grand boulevard Unter den Linden to the magnificent Staatsbibliothek (Main Library), where I had informative discussions with a young female librarian before finding my way to the apartment complex to which my engineer friend from the Wartburg in Eisenach and his wife had invited me for what they considered their typical supper. It was not unlike what my mother served in Hannover. I could not find fault with their way of life, and found that these young people, like many others I talked to while traveling, appeared to be content to live in the GDR. The one criticism they voiced was the lack of freedom to visit countries in the West, which at that time were off-limits to them. They were allowed to visit all the Eastern Bloc countries provided they could afford it and could receive the needed currency, which was allotted in accordance with the availability of hotel space.

With the exception of the Pergamon Museum, I did not have much time to visit museums in Berlin; they were closed on Tuesdays. I did manage to spend an hour at my favorite museum, just to look once more in wonder at the monumental Gate of Ishtar and the magnificent Pergamon Altar.

Before crossing the border to West Berlin, I took a train to Potsdam, where I went on a sightseeing tour by bus, visiting the major points of interest, which I will refrain from covering in detail. I should not neglect to mention that the infrastructure in and around Potsdam had begun to crumble and was very much in need of repair. Nevertheless, I very much enjoyed walking through Sans Souci Palace, which Frederic the Great called his *Luftschloß* (summer residence), and could well imagine what it must have been like to wander through the beautiful park where the Neptune Grotto and the Chinese Teahouse still spoke of times past. At the big palace, built by Frederic I in the seventeenth century, I found the marvelously tiled stove with its built-in seat, where Voltaire meditated during his stay of several years, rather cozy and intriguing.

The tour bus had left, and I still had to see Cecilienhof Palace, a rather unpretentious English country estate built for the Emperor Wilhelm II in the New Gardens, outside of Potsdam. It was finished in 1916, just before his abdication. More importantly, the Potsdam Agreement was signed there. It was too far to walk from the Charlottenhof Palace, and I would have had to wait one and a half hours for the next bus. A university professor of whom I inquired directions was so kind as to drive me to the Cecilienhof in his Trabant. Thus, my visit to the GDR began and ended with an act of human kindness and helpfulness – and both times in a modest little car.

I felt strange in the surroundings at Cecilienhof, even though the sun was shining brightly through the high windows of the conference room. I stared at the heavy, large, round wooden table in the center of the big carpeted and wood-paneled room. It felt almost unreal to listen to the guide explain that Stalin, Harry S. Truman, Winston Churchill, and Clement Attlee (there was no French representative) had sat at this very table from July 17 to August 2, 1945, and decided the fate of Germany's future. I was thunderstruck when I heard that Harry Truman, Franklin D. Roosevelt's vice president, who had taken over the presidency upon the latter's death on April 12, 1945, had given orders to the US Air Force from this very room to drop the atomic bomb on Hiroshima on August 6, 1945. The bomb destroyed most of the city and killed more than 50% of the population, about two hundred thousand people. It was this act that ultimately led to my immigration to the United States.

Back in East Berlin, another friendly soul lugged my suitcase from the hotel across the very wide Alexanderplatz to the S-bahn (Underground), which sped me to Checkpoint Charlie, where I crossed the border without any problem whatever. The customs officer was most helpful as well. At that point in time, I was convinced that those who dreamed of a reunited Germany should keep on dreaming. It would never happen in my lifetime.

My first shock in West Berlin came when I learned that the price for a beer was 3.6 marks, a far cry from the 56 *Pfennig* (cents) in the East. I was equally shocked by the price of a ride on the streetcar, which was 2.5 marks, compared to 20 *Pfennig* in the East. However, I had complained in the GDR about their charging travelers from the West the hotel-room rates customary in the West, despite the fact that the accommodations were of much lower quality.

After having been turned down by three strong-looking men when I asked them if they would kindly assist me in lifting my suitcase into the train, I was almost afraid to ask someone else, but I did. A young man came to my rescue.

I squeezed in a short dinner with Hans and Ingeborg Guenther in Berlin and spent much time on the phone trying to find inexpensive accommodations for the 1978 summer program. I was happy to get a commitment from the Kolpinghaus, a place comparable to the YWCA.

I returned to Hannover on June 22 and spent a day and a half with my mother, who bemoaned the fact that I was taking off for the States via train to Luxembourg so soon. I arrived in good old South Bend, Indiana, at 11:00 p.m. on June 24, my name day, only to be confronted with a catastrophe of another kind.

1972–1984

Another String Snaps – Adventures in South America: Machu Picchu, Peru, Rio de Janeiro, Brazil, and Buenos Aires, Argentina

Amadeus seemed happy to see me, though I was dead tired from the flight. I went to bed without much delay and fell asleep immediately. I had six days to regroup and repack my suitcase for my big vacation to South America. I had dreamed about Brazil ever since befriending Theresa, a Brazilian beauty, who also worked at Miles. She had a head of the shiniest brown curls I had ever seen. Her big dark-brown eyes were always smiling. Her complexion was bronze-brown, and every male was dazzled by her well-shaped figure. She wore a fifteen-carat aquamarine set in gold on her ring finger, which I would have loved to call my own. I was sure that if I were ever fortunate enough to visit Brazil, I would try to find one just like it.

I was glad to see that my young man had kept the house in good shape. Yet, while unpacking my suitcase and picking up the clothes from the white bedroom carpet to transfer them to the washing machine, I noticed a couple of long blond hairs clinging to the carpet. Mine were not long. My heart seemed to stop – and I could feel the blood rushing to my head. I sat down next to my suitcase to calm down. My musician friend was out. I got up and started to examine the closet and the room a bit more closely. The next shock came when I observed a big black spot, about three inches in diameter, burned into the polished top of my still-new chest of drawers, close to the big mirror. It was obviously caused by a big candle that had burned down unattended and had not been placed on a holder. I had no trouble surmising what had transpired in my bedroom during my absence. The minute my unsuspecting houseguest stepped through the front door, I asked him not very kindly to gather his stuff and get out, because the honeymoon was over. He turned red as a tomato and accused me of being rather cruel, but had nothing to advance in his defense, except that it did not mean a thing, or something like that. Of course, I felt terribly betrayed, but had no time to stew about it or give into my pain, because I had a thousand things to take care of before leaving for South America. I was going with my friend Dele, the widow of Professor Hans Jaeger. Her oldest son had an assistantship at the university in Rio, and his younger brother was visiting as well.

I was to meet Dele in Miami to fly to our first stop, Lima, Peru, where I had arranged for a trip to Machu Picchu via Cuzco. Dele came from Indianapolis. I waited for her at the gate until the last minute. When she failed to show, I boarded the plane without her, hoping she would still come. I ended up flying to Lima without her. I was quite upset, not knowing exactly what had happened, and hoping we would eventually connect in Lima. The travel nightmare escalated. Due to political unrest in Lima, the travel route was changed in midair. Instead of flying directly to Lima, they decided to land in Quito, Ecuador. We arrived at the airport of Ecuador's capital, which is located only fifteen miles south of the equator, on August 1, and I had to get off the plane. The sun was shining brightly in the blue sky, and

Not Hitler's Child

I was amazed at the mountains all around us. Someone pointed out Pichincha Volcano, which is almost 16,000 feet high. The climate was very pleasant, not at all hot or humid, probably due to the high altitude. The minute I got off the plane, two policemen drove up in a jeep and asked me to get in. They spoke little English, but remembering some Spanish, I understood what they were up to. They took me to get a visa and a passport picture for entrance into Colombia instead of Peru. I followed all their instructions and felt like a puppet at the mercy of a puppeteer.

One hour later, I was back on the plane, and I arrived in Bogotá at about 11:00 p.m. I was tired and depressed and even more uncertain about Dele's whereabouts. I waited to pick up my suitcase, but it never came. I could not understand why this was happening to me. Stupidly, I had packed everything into the suitcase, including all toiletry articles, fluids, and the container for my contact lenses. Up to that time, I had never lost a suitcase. I filled out the claim forms half in tears and half on the verge of flying back home and forgetting about the trip. I was a nervous wreck. They were going to put us up in hotels and gave us vouchers. A Spanish-speaking couple let me share a cab with them. We got in. The driver started the car and could not get it to move. He jumped out, began to push, and jumped back in when it started. It was after midnight when we arrived at the hotel. I was halfway glad I did not have to lug my suitcase up the steps, because there were no porters. The man at the counter turned us away. The hotel was full. This time, the cab started without a push, and the next hotel took us in. By then it was about 1:00 a.m., and I had to be back at the airport by 7:00 a.m. to hopefully catch a flight to Lima. The room was dimly lit. I took a shower, put my contact lenses into two ashtrays, and decided to track down my friend Sally, who had moved to Bogotá, as you may recall. I knew Spaniards tend to stay up late. The phone rang, and I could hardly believe it when Sally answered. She was utterly surprised, and she urged me to forget about my trip and stay with her family until I felt more rested. I was tempted to accept her kind offer, but could not do it to Dele. Sally, who looked wonderful, picked me up early in the morning, drove me to the airport, and waited with me until I found a flight to Lima – without my suitcase.

One man on the plane was sure I would never see my suitcase again, because down there they rob you blind. Another passenger advised that if I wanted to enjoy my trip, I better stop fretting, adopt a different attitude, and accept that in South America everything is mañana. To make matters worse, I had realized in all of this chaos that Dele had never given me her son's address in Rio de Janeiro. Of course, I had not asked either. My plane landed at the Lima airport in the early forenoon. I clutched my purse and began to look for the baggage-claim counter. It struck me that the big hall outside the gate was rather empty. As I looked for the directions, I could not believe my eyes when there, in the middle of the hall, all by its lonesome, stood my dark-red suitcase waiting for me. I was overcome with joy.

On the way to the hotel, looking out of the cab window, I was shocked by the shacks and crumbling one-story barrack-like houses flanking the wide, busy street leading to the center of the city. People in rags were crouched on the ground; children sat on pieces of rubble near their shelters and stared sadly into space. It was poverty at its worst and was just a preview of what was to follow. In the lobby of the hotel, my next surprise awaited me in a heavily upholstered chair. As soon as I called out "Dele!" my friend jumped up and we embraced each other happily. She had missed our flight because her plane was late and she too was rerouted, but by way of a different route. Dele looked healthy; she was about 5'7" and stout, with short blond hair, blue eyes, and light-colored horn-rimmed glasses. Her voice was a bit sharp and somewhat intimidating, which is not uncommon for teachers. She taught German at a high school in Bloomington.

Our first concern was what to do about the missed excursion to Cuzco and Machu Picchu, the reason for coming to Peru in the first place. Dele was quick to suggest we forget about it and spend the day sightseeing in Lima. I strongly objected. After all, we had already paid for the trip. I insisted on finding a travel agency at once to see what could be done about it. The agent claimed it would be impossible for us to go the next day, since all seats in the special train had been booked way in advance. When I demanded an immediate refund, he suddenly found a couple of seats for us.

The plane landed in Cuzco, the capital of the thirteen provinces that form the Department of Cuzco, around noon. Landing in this city, the heart of the Incan world, felt like landing on another planet. My first impression of Cuzco, as the cab took us to the hotel, was that the architecture, though Incan-Hispanic, reminded me of what I had seen in Mexico and Spain. The man at the reception desk asked the concierge to take us to our room, which featured Peruvian decor. It had a balcony with a view of the cobblestone street below. We were served a light lunch in our room and urged to lie down on our beds and drink the tea the waiter poured for us. He explained that this tea would help us get acclimated to the high altitude, which ranged between 11,000 and 14,000 feet above sea level.

When we got up a couple of hours later to explore the town, I felt as though I were under a magic spell, which I attributed to the exotic atmosphere. The uplifting sensation persisted as Dele and I walked around Cuzco, which seemed like a vast museum housing the remains of a glorious era, that of the rise, splendor, and fall of the great civilization of the Incas and the subsequent Iberian culture. Every narrow street, every block of stone, every sunlit patio or Moorish balcony recalled those Indo-Spanish times and revealed the splendor of the history its people had lived.

The sky was blue and without a cloud. The temperature was a dry 72 degrees Fahrenheit as we strolled across the main plaza to go inside the cathedral and, afterward, into the Church of the Society of Jesus. Both were built on the foundations of ancient Incan palaces. I found the golden altars in the churches of Cuzco, especially that of the Church of Bethlehem, overwhelmingly ornate. However, I was struck by the beautiful image of *Our Lady of Bethlehem*. She stood in the niche on the upper part of the tabernacle and reminded me of the *Black Madonna* at Montserrat in Spain. Legend has it that the *Lady of Bethlehem*, which depicts the patroness of Cuzco, was found inside a box floating on the ocean, near Callao, and it is believed to be the remains of a Spanish shipwreck. Much of the gold leaf covering the carved altars came from the region. It seemed richer in color than what I had seen in European churches. The pulpit in the Church of San Blas is a masterpiece of carved wood. Most of the elaborate ornaments of the local Churriguera style are completely covered with gold. The skull on the upper part of the pulpit, believed to belong to the artist who created the masterpiece, struck me as somewhat bizarre.

I found the more primitive Incan gold pieces, such as the Walla Walla idol and the small gold container displayed next to it in the Archeological Museum, aesthetically more pleasing than the other ornaments, and was fascinated by the report that the idol was found in a canyon 4,600 meters deep and that it was probably a gift offered to the gods or crafted for the tomb of a noble Indian. We sought out several of the pre-Incan and Incan ruins. The stonework and architecture, so different from those typical of the Mayan ruins in Yucatán, Mexico, reflected an unusual skill in engineering. The mammoth, cube-like stones of the wall along the Incan Sun Street, or Loreto Lane, were hewn out of white granite and placed evenly in rows and columns. They came alive when a native passed along the wall dressed in heavy black, red, or earth-colored garments handwoven with llama hair or alpaca wool, which natives herd for their livelihood. The natives are rarely seen without some sort of head covering, be it a shepherd's hat, an umbrella-shaped black wool hat with a red rim, or a multicolored shawl or poncho. Red and black were the predominant colors also in the woolen scarves and stoles draped over their shoulders.

On the way back to the hotel, we checked out the bazaar to see what treasures we might want to take with us. We loved the beautiful knit sweaters, jackets, and blankets. Made from alpaca wool or fleece, they were soft and light and would keep us warm in the coldest winter. We bought several, since the prices were incredibly low. When I spotted a baby llama skin of the softest and silkiest snow-white fur I have ever felt or seen, I bought it on the spot out of fear that I would never find another one like it. It would be perfect on the white couch in my den and would contrast perfectly with the chocolate-brown carpet.

The train to Machu Picchu had only four cars and made its way slowly alongside the Sacred River of the Incas, the Vilcanota, called the Urumbamba River further on. As the mountain slopes got steeper, our little train virtually crawled like a caterpillar on its single track, making its way up in zigzag fashion, deeper into the Amazon Jungle. The higher it climbed, the more exotic, beautiful, and lush the vegetation grew, and the more enchanted I felt. A continuously changing panorama expanded before my wandering eyes. Bright-red tropical flowers entwined with big orchids in a multitude of colors and lush green bushes bursting with white, yellow, and pink blossoms adorned the embankment and the steep slopes alongside the track, surpassing any tropical flora I had seen before. In the distance, snowcapped mountains stretched into the azure sky. The atmosphere was so intoxicating no one uttered a word.

Occasionally, the train passed a few small stone houses built on a terrace in the slope, like miniature fortresses. They reminded me vaguely of the stone structures in Provence. The perpendicular green mountaintops of the Andes in the background accentuated the steep straw-thatched roofs. As the train inched up the last stretch to Machu Picchu (a Quechua term meaning "old mountain" or "ancient peak"), known also as the Lost City of the Incas and the sacred capital, a vast area of grass-covered terraces built on the high and steep Andean Mountains spread out before us. They were built to control erosion and to facilitate agricultural cultivation for the inhabitants of the citadel. The jungle hid Machu Picchu so well that the Spanish conquerors were unable to find this gem of Incan civilization.

Dele and I explored the site. We walked and crawled around the ruins for hours. The city is placed on irregular and abrupt terrain, and there are quite a few steps to navigate. It is a city of stairways. The steps, placed at short intervals, were made with blocks of white granite that came from the nearby mountains. They are rather easy to climb and not too tiring. However, at one point I dropped my camera, knowing instantly that my film was ruined. I had no other film with me and was quite disgusted with myself. –

Without going into detail about all of the remarkable structures, I must point out that all of the doorways and niches are trapezoidal and the lintels are monolithic and quite huge. In the more noteworthy sectors, the walls are made of hewn stones built without mortar and projecting like pads, as in the principal door leading to the city on the south side. Like the Mayan Indians, the Incas had their place of torture. It is a huge rock with a flat, table-like top and with steps hewn into it that presumably made it easier for the priest to climb when performing rituals or the final ceremony, in which the dead were placed in their tombs. There was a noticeable absence of murals and decorative work, both of which were hallmarks of Mayan culture. A narrow stream of crystal-clear water ran down a fountain built like a staircase. It was brought from far away by means of aqueducts and meandered like a silver thread through the narrow channels, a masterwork of engineering.

It was hard to leave this amazing archeological site, which claims to be the world's most beautiful. Looking down on one side, one could see the phenomenal zigzag highway leading to the citadel. It is named after Hiram Bingham, the professor from Yale who discovered this miracle on one of his field trips, in 1911. Looking down from another spot, I marveled at the sight of the Sacred River, which winds like an endless snake deep down along the foot of a big canyon bordered by great masses of granite. Wherever you turn, you are embraced by an awe-inspiring mystical presence, second to none I had ever experienced. I felt I had encountered the quintessence of all panoramas in the world.

Going down, the last car of the train became the first, and each of us exchanged seats to see the other side of the mountain. Here and there a small herd of llamas or alpaca sheep grazed while the herder rested nearby. As we got closer to Cuzco, I could not help but feel sad at the sight of the primitive shacks sheltering the herders, their women and children sitting on the bare ground in front, spooning their food out of dented tin bowls. The women and very young girls who stood at train stops looked more pleasant, dangling before them their distaffs, each of which held a bunch of alpaca wool and rotated while they spun with their fingers. Others, dressed in bright and colorful clothes representative of their region, spread out their produce, such as chili peppers, on handwoven blankets in the hope of selling it. A young Indian weaver smilingly displayed a red and beige rug, which she was weaving as she squatted on the cobblestones in front of a stone hut. Toddlers wrapped in blankets clung to their mothers, who carried them around on their backs. Little caps covered their heads, but their pudgy feet dangled barefoot against the mothers' waists – unforgettable scenes in unforgettable surroundings.

Back at the hotel, we went to sleep rather quickly. We had to return to Lima the next day and from there connect with the late flight to Rio de Janeiro. When I inquired at the desk about where I could buy some of that wondrous tea to take home, the man smiled and explained that it was unfortunately not for sale. When he elaborated that it was made from coca leaves (illegal in the United States), I realized why I had felt so wonderful as I wandered through the streets of Cuzco on the day of our arrival.

The pilot announced that the sky was clear for landing at the Santos Dumont Airport and that the temperature in Rio was 70 degrees Fahrenheit. I had a window seat. The sun was piercing. I put on my sunglasses and fixed my eyes on the landscape below. Our Avianca jet soared like a giant falcon. As the plane tilted slightly to the left, where I sat, a most spectacular and picture-perfect panorama unfolded below. It was a dream come true. What I had seen in pictures was so much more dazzling in reality. The famous conical rock, Sugarloaf Mountain, stood at the entrance of the bay; and the gigantic white statue of Christ the Redeemer stood almost as high as the Statue of Liberty, tall and slender and with outstretched arms, on the summit of Corcovado (Hunchback) Mountain. The waves of the Atlantic sparkled dark blue against the broad, snow-white beaches framing the semicircular bay, said to be the most beautiful in the world. The city, with its high-rises and clusters of white stone buildings covered by tile roofs, spread out for miles and contrasted strikingly with the mountain range, covered by a dark-green tropical forest and rising abruptly on the opposite side of the bay. When the plane landed, I was anxious to explore this marvelous city, where we planned to spend eleven days.

Going through customs was sobering. The security check and the passport inspection were much more intimidating and fear inspiring than at Checkpoint Charlie a couple of weeks earlier. The passport inspector sat in a cubicle with bulletproof windows, looking down on the passengers from a height of about three feet. It would be difficult to fire a shot at him from below. We were happy to see Stefan with Freddie, who took us to his efficiency apartment. It was a bit small for four people, but had a perfect location.

The apartment was less than a five-minute walk to the breathtakingly beautiful beach, the Copacabana, where I spent a few hours on sunny forenoons swimming, jumping the waves, basking in the sun, admiring the bronze-colored bodies of young men and women relaxing on the white beach, and watching nude children play near the water. They built sand castles only to have them disappear before their eyes under the rolling waves. Never before had I seen people with bodies as stunningly shaped and colored as those of the Brazilians on the Copacabana and Ipanema beaches. Dele's boys kept after me to buy a string bikini, but I stuck to my more modest one, which was navy blue with white polka dots and left sufficient bare surfaces for the sun to tan. After all, since I walked to the beach wearing just my bikini and sandals and a towel over my shoulder, I felt daring enough. One day, when I was almost alone at the beach, I became apprehensive when a young Brazilian male stared when walking past me. I presumed my blond hair was the focus of his attention. Most of my beach ventures included a treat on the way back to the apartment. I always stopped at a stand selling fresh, ready-to-eat fruit. I can still taste the sweet juice from the golden-yellow pineapple slices that dripped down my chin each time I took a bite. I have never since tasted fresh pineapple so delicious.

The Jaeger boys saw to it that we did not sit idle and that we saw close-up what we had seen from the plane, and much more. They took us up Sugarloaf Mountain by cable car to give us a 360-degree view of Rio and Guanabara Bay and followed through after supper with a ride on the funicular train for a closer look at the illuminated *Christ the Redeemer* statue. To look down on this magnificent city by night is tantamount to experiencing a miracle: an ocean of moving and flickering lights next to the vastness of a still and pitch-black sea! The ridges of the mountain ranges separate the glowing residential areas and spread like arteries from the shore, moving up the slopes that end in the mountains. At sunrise, these green trails make for an even more picturesque setting.

I quickly became intoxicated by the hustle and bustle of this sensuous and hectic city. I have never been more excited at a soccer game than I did at the one we witnessed at Maracanã Stadium, which holds two hundred thousand fans and is considered the largest soccer stadium in the world. At the end, the spectators went nuts, tossing thousands of seat cushions wildly into the arena. The enthusiasm exceeded by far that which broke out at the bullfight in Mexico City. I found it unusual that everybody sat on a cushion, but it was understandable, because sleeping on the narrow cot which had been set up for me in the apartment was like sleeping on a board. It was so hard I woke up every morning with a stiff back.

We walked around the Botanical Gardens and had to look for the tiny monkeys in the trees of the beautiful Tijuca Forest, which we were told is the world's largest urban forest. We visited the Museu Nacional de Belas Artes, which houses works by Brazilian artists and others, such as Picasso and Matisse, but we neglected to visit the Municipal Theater and the Candelária Church, as well as other sites. We did spend one night at a samba-club restaurant listening to and watching the Brazilians samba in their colorful attire to the exhilarating music. It was great! It brought back memories from my dancing adventure in Spain. –

I remembered that I must not forget my aquamarine ring, which I thought would be very reasonably priced, considering that Brazil has some of the largest gem mines in South America. Both H. Stern and Amsterdam Sauer have their headquarters in Rio. We strolled along Ipanema's Avenida, Visconde de Piraja, and many other streets and eventually found a jeweler by the name of Badofsky Jo Alheiros on the Avenida Copacabana. After a lengthy negotiation, he agreed to set a beautiful, light-blue, twelve-and-a-half-carat aquamarine in a platinum setting, which I designed, and to craft a matching bracelet with three one-carat aquamarines, both for a mere $500.

I liked Rio's culinary delights, which we sampled at various restaurants, including a Brazilian barbecue, or *churrascaria*, which operated under the *rodizio* (all you can eat) system. One night, I invited Dele and her boys for dinner at the fashionable Marina Yacht Club, which Freddie, the only person in our group who spoke Portuguese, had recommended. While the food was superb, I relished even more the view of the Atlantic with the setting sun.

Freddie also urged us not to pass up a shopping spree at the big flea market, where we could bargain to our heart's content for contemporary Brazilian art, leather goods, jewelry, and the like. He suggested taking the local bus, which stopped right on our eight-lane boulevard. The traffic was crazy. He told us to ignore all traffic lights, run across the street whenever there were no directly approaching cars on either side, and always be on guard against pocket thieves. We had to run fast to catch our bus, because they never stopped long. It was somewhat exciting to go full speed along the Avenida Rio Branco, lined with brazilwood trees, mosaic sidewalks, parks filled with flowers, and modern skyscrapers.

As we arrived at the huge bazaar, I was intrigued by the quantity and variety of items for sale. After spending hours sifting through leather goods, such as purses and billfolds, I bargained for a navy-blue purse for casual use. It was made of soft leather and had three zippers, one across the top. I emptied the contents of my smaller purse into the new one right on the spot, closed the zipper, and wore it over my left shoulder.

1972–1984

Our bus home was standing room only. I did not have to worry about falling or stumbling during this wildest of all the bus rides of my life, because I was squeezed like a herring between a bunch of young, brown, curly-haired, perspiring Brazilian males in white T-shirts. I had put my zipped-up purse in front of my chest. The bus was rocking, and the guys were leaning against me on all sides. I noticed my purse had somehow slid to the back; I pulled it back to the front. When it happened a second time, I looked down at the purse and noticed the zipper was open. I looked up, and one of the handsome youths was holding, high above my head, my billfold, which contained all of my money, my driver's license, etc., with his slender, brown, pick-pocketing hands. I looked into his big brown eyes and yelled, "Policia!" He instantly dropped my billfold. As I stooped down to pick it up, he pushed his way through the crowd to the front of the bus. It stopped and let the thief out.

I began to understand why people would resort to stealing after seeing one of Rio's sprawling hillsides, known as Rocinha, inhabited like a beehive by more than two hundred thousand people suffering the most crushing poverty. Seeing the poorest of poor people, emaciated, shrunk and crippled, clad in rags, and crowded together in their crumbling quarters, rivaled any of my previous encounters with poverty. What made it more compelling was the fact that this ghetto-like hill was not far removed from the quarters where tremendous wealth, luxury, and excesses were the norm. After having just visited a socialist country, I could not but think that communism might well benefit these unjustly deprived human souls.

After this depressing experience, the trip on the big yacht from Itacuruca to the small island of Jaguanum was a welcome antidote, despite the rain, which poured down in buckets. It was invigorating to stand on the sixty-foot yacht, dressed in a big raincoat, and let the warm sea wind splash rain into my face. The shower stopped as the ship dropped anchor close to the white-sand beach, which contrasted dramatically with the canopy of thick black clouds in the sky. Were it not for a quaint hotel with its units built randomly on the slope and almost hidden by the tropical trees, the island would have been uninhabited. Truly, a lovers' paradise! I wandered barefoot along the private beach, thinking about the blond rascal back home who had so blatantly betrayed me. I felt he would not be worthy of sinking his feet into the white sand on this heavenly piece of land. The sparkling emerald water was ever so soothing. The only sounds came from the gently lapping waves and the birds singing in the trees of the forest, which was bursting with flowers.

Later, I often dreamed about my paradise so far away, always wishing that someday I would return with a man of my dreams.

We landed in Buenos Aires in the early afternoon on August 19. During the descent, I looked down on the vessels anchored in one of the world's largest ports, built into the wide estuary of the Río de la Plata. The view was by no means comparable to that of Rio, but the sight of this magnificent capital on the west bank of the river was impressive. The cab ride from the airport to the hotel gave us a first view of the beautiful, wide boulevard Avenida de Mayo, lined with trees behind which striking modern structures, beautiful parks, and palatial homes emerged. There was the presence of a strong European, mainly French, influence in much of the more dated architecture, and we understood quickly why the city is called the Paris of South America. Later, when we toured the city by bus, we observed the distinct Spanish character of the buildings on the principal Plaza Mayo, such as the Roman Catholic Cathedral, the Government Palace Casa Rosada (Pink House), and the Banco de la Nación.

Dele and I enjoyed shopping at the Calle Florida's numerous boutiques and shops, where I bought several pairs of stylish leather shoes and an equally stylish purse of the finest leather, all quite reasonably priced. We were bedazzled as we strolled around the Recoleta, the most elegant district of Buenos Aires, where we sat down and treated ourselves to a cup of coffee and a piece of chocolate pastry. I had not suspected such elegance and the presence of a truly international flair in Buenos Aires. Germans, French, Portuguese, Poles, Russians, Italians, English, Turks, Spaniards – you name it – had been drawn to this capital. Any European who loves to participate in the life of a metropolis would feel right at home in Buenos Aires. Men and women were dressed more stylishly than in Rio, I thought. Since it was their wintertime, the women paraded along the fashionable streets in their luxurious furs and hats. I would have burned up in a fur, but might have worn it had we had opera tickets for a performance at the world famous Teatro Colón.

Having always had a penchant for dancing, I persuaded Dele to come along to a tango show in the Boca district, on the legendary Caminito Street. One must watch native Argentinians here, floating, striding, turning, twisting, and leaning forward and backward on the polished dance floor, in step with the great music of tango. Only in the place of its birth will you see a genuine tango. It is the same for an Argentinian barbecue, which cannot be matched anywhere else in the world. We did not regret taking a trip into the country for a fabulous barbecue, which was accompanied by an ensemble of happy gaucho guitar players, singers, and dancers.

The bus ride through the vast pampas region outside Buenos Aires had none of the excitement of the mountain vistas in Rio or Machu Picchu, but had a calming effect. I could well imagine what it must have been like for the gauchos when they roamed the unfenced pampas or grasslands to hunt down wild horses and cattle like cowboys. They were of Spanish descent, mingled with the Indians, lived off the meat and skin of slaughtered wild cattle, and are said to have been free-spirited vagabonds of a happy disposition.

After an hour's drive, the bus arrived at the immense ranch, where cattle and horses grazed in the distance. A cheerful group of gauchos, dressed in red, royal-blue, and black pants and white shirts, against which their dark skin appeared even darker, greeted us with a spirited, guitar-accompanied song. A girl wearing a purple dress with ruffles shifted her hips with the rhythm. They were standing in the shade of a group of big trees from which long moss was drooping, reminiscent of magnolia trees on Southern plantations. I could see the large, stately, white ranch house shining through the branches several hundred feet away. A handsome young Argentinian rode toward us on a well-groomed, reddish-brown stallion. He wore beige riding pants, dark-brown boots, and a white shirt with long sleeves. His brown, wavy hair, blue eyes, and tanned skin reminded me vaguely of the handsome Argentinian whom I had felt attracted to when first working at Miles, Inc. You may remember that he was called back to Argentina rather unexpectedly. The rider jumped off his horse, greeted us, and for some reason engaged me in a very pleasant conversation. When I told him I had ridden a horse on a few occasions, he offered to let me ride, but I was reluctant to comply. He was the son of the owner of the ranch, many thousand acres in size. While the gauchos entertained us, others started the barbecue. Half a calf had been lanced on a spit and was roasting over a long barbecue pit, smelling more delicious by the minute. We gathered around the pit in anticipation, and when the meat was being carved off the spit and placed on our plates, the juice dripped and sizzled in the coals. We sat at long picnic tables in the shadow of the trees and could not rave enough about how tender, tasty, and juicy the meat was. It melted in my mouth, and I can still taste it. There is no doubt about it – the last supper on the ranch was a perfect ending to my South American adventure.

On the flight home, the experiences of the previous two months raced through my mind. It was almost too much to digest, and as soon as I boarded the plane from Chicago to South Bend, the realities I had left behind started to overshadow what had excited me in South America. By the time I went to bed, the problems of my personal life and the numerous duties connected with my job came to the forefront, such as writing reports and proposals and making new plans, but they were temporarily silenced as I dozed off to sleep.

Tenure – Miles Is Sold to Bayer AG – Snowed In with Amadeus

I was glad my acting chairmanship had lasted only one semester. It was time to bring my dossier up to date and submit it for tenure. I was not in the least worried, because I had already been promoted to associate professor and much of the documentation could be resubmitted. I completed my part of the new course proposal rather swiftly and made sure it would be considered by the committee that had recommended me for the Distinguished Teaching Award. The new culture course was to be taught in tandem with my colleagues from the French and Spanish Departments. I found out later that while the department recommended me for tenure, the male colleagues withheld their support for the teaching award. Since nobody tells you the reason and you are not at liberty to confront anybody, you are left guessing. I guessed that both professional jealousy and the fact that I was a woman played a big part. Come to think of it, the chairperson who recommended me was a woman as well. Up to that time, it had been inconceivable to me that anybody would even think of discriminating against me, because my record in comparison to that of many others was so very strong that I felt untouchable. Perhaps the males were jealous when they saw the dedication one of my students had put into a book of poetry he had written and left in my mailbox one day. I had included numerous unsolicited complimentary letters in my file and added a copy of J. Daugherty's dedication. A senior who occasionally played the guitar at my house at student gatherings, he wrote, "Dear Frau Beardsley, not only were you the most vibrant professor I've ever had, but you are also one of the most beautiful people I've ever known. Never lose that love of life."

I was relieved when my recommendations for changes and new assistants in connection with the 1978 Bonn Program were approved and my proposal for foreign-language-workshop sessions was being implemented. All of the other extracurricular activities were continued, and I served on enough committees on and off our campus to satisfy the administrators. I was even more relieved when the top administrators gave their blessing to my planned exhibits that focused on theatrical, cultural, and sociopolitical aspects of the former GDR. I submitted my article "The GDR – A Gratifying Encounter" to our PR man for publication in the local newspaper, but no luck. It took me a while to realize that even in the United States, perhaps especially in a predominantly Republican state, there are limits to freedom of speech. As I mentioned previously, the article was eventually published in German in the GDR.

One morning during the first week of October, when I was waking up with the help of the radio, I was startled by a news broadcast announcing that Miles, Inc., was in the process of negotiating a deal with Bayer AG, whereby the German chemical company, the same that had hosted us in the summer of 1976 and used to be a part of IG Farbenindustrie, would take over Miles, Inc., in Elkhart, the same place where I had worked after the Beardsleys bought me free from the Neverbees. The thought that the Germans were bailing the Americans out, so to speak, was shocking. I immediately remembered that one of the lecturers during our visit had pointed out, almost gloatingly, that though America had broken up Bayer's monopoly at the end of World War I, the company was stronger than before. That very morning, I wrote a letter to Walter Beardsley, CEO at that time, who by then I had met socially at the Koertings. I told him about my encounter at Bayer and that the takeover disturbed me deeply. It never occurred to me that a country as strong as America would be in a situation whereby one of her big industries had to lean on the Germans to survive. Walter replied quickly, indicating that they had "no choice" and that Bayer was "the best company," since they had "the necessary financial muscle." I later learned that the Japanese were also in on the bidding. I had lengthy discussions about the matter with Bill Koerting, at whose stunning estate I was a frequent guest, and who liked to come to South Bend and take me out to lunch. He later gave me Borkin's book *The Crime and Punishment of I. G. Farben*, which revealed the fact that Bayer, among other companies, had played a major part in conducting highly deplorable experiments involving the Jews and other political prisoners at the Buchenwald concentration camp. The book also revealed that such big US companies as Standard Oil had been aware of what was going on.

Professor S., my former chairman, had retired, married the lab director, and left for greener pastures in Switzerland. We replaced him for one year only with a man fresh out of graduate school who held a PhD in German linguistics. He was a rather jovial and likeable person who loved the Oktoberfest parties in my yard and would have preferred to stay for a while. However, I needed a person who focused on the literature of a period distinct from mine, and there was no interest in German linguistics on our campus. When he tried to sell himself as a jack of all trades, I decided to find a colleague who would fill the vacancy more appropriately. Early in November, my chairperson, Annemarie Poinsatte, asked me to join her at the MLA convention in New York City right after Christmas in order to assist in interviewing the more than forty candidates we had selected from over two hundred applicants. She needed me because she did not speak German.

By that time, Amadeus and I had mended fences – and time permitting, when he was not circling the globe on some concert tour or rehearsing for hours in preparation for a performance, we went about our lives together as usual. We both loved the soft white llama hide on my white couch, and I earned high praise for my deep Copacabana tan for as long as it lasted. It looked even darker when the llama skin brushed against mine.

I always thought it would be exciting to spend Christmas in the Big Apple with a lover, and it did not take much coaxing to convince Amadeus to come along. I booked a room at the Hilton, close to the Sheraton, where the interviews were held. It was snowing softly in the city, and revisiting the old familiar sights, including a stop for a cocktail high up in the Rainbow Lounge, was exhilarating and exciting. You can imagine the rest. We had a wonderful time, and Annemarie and I managed to pick three candidates who, we agreed, looked promising.

Whereas Amadeus returned to the Midwest to visit his family, I flew directly to Phoenix to spend a week in Mesa, Arizona, with my friends the Loesers. There the sun shone in a clear blue sky, and the temperature was a perfect 70 degrees. My favorite palm trees, many varieties of cacti, and climbing bougainvillea were everywhere. I felt as though I were visiting a posh vacation resort. The Loesers' beige, stucco ranch-style house, with an overhanging roof covered with shake shingles, was situated on a one-acre citrus orchard. The trees were laden with oranges and grapefruits. I was surprised to see a vibrant green lawn and rose bushes with dark-red roses climbing up white trellises in the front yard, instead of rocks, sand, and cacti. The inside of the house was spacious, with a big fireplace in the family room. From the bright kitchen, a door opened to a large, beautiful, blue, kidney-shaped swimming pool. Extending outward from the kitchen was a big awning, underneath which lounge chairs with colorful cushions stood ready for sunbathers like myself. It was like the Garden of Eden. The oranges and grapefruits were ripe and waiting to be picked whenever you wanted them. They were bigger and juicier there than in any place I had ever picked them before. A few yards to the right of the swimming pool was Lindy's kingdom. Lindy had weathered the transport from Michigan well. Branches filled with oranges drooped down into her large, fenced-in stall, to let her take a bite whenever she wanted.

The week in Mesa was filled with more new experiences. Heinz had made dinner reservations for New Year's Eve at a splashy hotel in Scottsdale, where we danced and brought in the new year with champagne. Scottsdale was also a shopper's paradise. The mall housed the most exquisite shops, including Saks, where I found great bargains, thanks to my petite size at the time. Heinz drove me around the area so I could admire the palatial homes of the superrich and famous and smiled when I raved about the different species of cacti. The reddish Camelback Mountain seemed to be present wherever we drove in the big, baby-blue Buick. It was at its most beautiful in the morning, when the rising sun shone against it. At night, it faded away like a big shadow. I took advantage of every free moment to swim in the immaculate waters of the pool, which was kept sparkling clean by a maintenance service, despite the fact that hardly anybody ever swam in it. In only a few days, my Copacabana tan was back.

Before my vacation was over, the Loesers took me along to a ballroom-dancing competition at another high-class hotel in Scottsdale. I felt a bit awkward, since this was something rather foreign to me. I had no idea that Heinz had taken up dancing in such a serious way. I was introduced to his rather attractive and very young instructor, Candy. A brunette, she was about 5'7" and had big black eyes and an almost overly slim figure. She looked fragile, like the Meissen-china ballerina on the lamp Heinz once gave me. I thought she might break in half at any time. It was wonderful to watch them dance and win a couple of prizes. His wife appeared almost uninterested. Little by little, I learned that Heinz, who had a cancerous kidney removed while still in Michigan, felt better here. He had also stopped paying attention to the miniskirted blond who lured them to Arizona from Michigan, and instead became obsessed with dancing lessons and his instructor. He was so fixated on the china-doll dancer that he made sure she would not teach other males. It was no secret that he channeled ample sums her way to compensate her for the time she devoted to instructing him. I had the distinct impression that the doll, though married to a pilot, was taking advantage of Heinz, something he obviously did not mind and Anneliese tolerated.

I had perceived as soon as I got off the plane that Heinz looked different. Not only was his hair dyed black, but his suits, shoes, and neckties struck me as a bit tacky. I had never seen him wear jewelry. He wore a big turquoise ring, a silver tie clasp with an even bigger turquoise, a heavy silver necklace, and a bracelet. I attributed the change at first to the Arizona sun, but changed my mind when I took Candy into consideration. Since Anneliese made no issue of it, I kept quiet, but I could not help but sympathize with her.

* * *

Phoenix, a snowbirds' haven because of its glorious sunshine, had been a welcome interlude. Not long after I had settled back in at home, winter came down on us like a mighty lion, more angrily even than when I lived at the Croft. (They still talk about the snowstorm of January 25, 1978.) I loved it and will remember it until my dying days. It snowed and snowed and snowed ceaselessly. Snow piled on snow, and it did not let up until everything that was visible before, including Amadeus's long, bright-red Chevy, which stood parked in the street opposite my house, was invisible. White fluffy snow bent the branches and twigs on the trees – first gracefully, then heavily. All of the windows around my house were halfway snowed shut. I was unable to look out of the windows in my bedroom, which were positioned high up on the walls, because the snow had drifted and piled up in front of them. We could not open any doors that led outside because the snow was too high. In short, we were completely snowed in. I was in ecstasy. All classes had been canceled indefinitely. There was no plow, and after Amadeus managed to shovel a narrow path from the front door to the driveway, the snow walls of the path reached up to my chin. – The fire crackling in the fireplace had never felt more sensuous and romantic. We spread out the snow-white baby llama blanket in front of the fireplace and sipped a warm brew of red wine, sugar, and spices while watching the flames flicker and listening to Mozart. The hot drink had never made me feel so warm inside, and the white fur brushing against my skin never felt softer . . .

When we finally needed a few items, Amadeus tied a heavy cord to a cardboard box and pulled it downhill to the nearest grocery store and back. It was the ultimate snow paradise. I am still waiting for a repeat performance, even without a lover.

Boxes of materials, including books, posters, and documentary films, had begun to arrive at the university after I returned from the GDR in 1977. They came from East Berlin, Leipzig, and Dresden but also from their West German counterparts such as Inter Nationes in Bad Godesberg, from the Information Center in New York, and from almost forty travel agencies in the Federal Republic of Germany. I was overwhelmed by the wealth of material available for my exhibit and my new course. A couple of students helped to tape almost one hundred big posters on the long walls of the first-floor corridor. I was glad that in America I felt at liberty to exhibit these controversial pictures, which both dramatically attacked the social ills of capitalism and fascism and highlighted social progress as well as advancements in the arts, theater, and restoration of historic sites. My exhibit was a little slanted toward the GDR, because they sent more material; and I did want to make people aware that there was another Germany. At that time, most maps left the East German sector more or less blank.

Since the entrance to our library was also on the first floor, my library exhibit displaying the books close to the entrance made it very convenient for those interested. Next to the book display, valued at approximately $2,000, the librarian had put on view the figurines and pyramids I had brought back and received as gifts from Seiffen. The large quantity of booklets and leaflets furnished by East and West as handout material for visitors was a real bonus. My exhibits were up for almost two months, and I was a bit amused when a couple of my colleagues from the Political Science Department said I had "a lot of guts" to flood the corridors with the GDR posters. I found it strange that no administrators expressed their views either verbally or in writing. Although the event was rather newsworthy, no press release appeared, on campus or elsewhere. Looking back, I assume the administration may have feared a critical reaction from this or that taxpayer. It did create a dilemma for them. Had they opposed the exhibit, it would have been an affront to academic freedom, which, I am sure, my more liberal colleagues would have resented. And during those months, people had to cope with the endless snowstorms, which may have contributed to the silence.

Not long after we had dug out from under the snow, I received an invitation and a grant from the League for Friendship among Nations, of which I had become a member when in East Berlin. I was invited to attend a summer seminar at Humboldt University, in East Berlin, from June 28 to July 23, 1978. It was a seminar at which international Germanists from twenty-one nations would participate. I was one of four Americans (two of whom were from the University of Wisconsin and one of whom was from William and Mary). The theme was "theater in the GDR," a topic dear to my heart. We would meet leading actors, authors, government functionaries, and the like, and attend many performances. I felt honored to have been chosen and could not wait to go.

By the time I took off for the Bonn Program on May 18, 1978, I had tenure, and as usual, our group left prior to the commencement ceremonies.

Bonn with Lynne Tatlock and Summer Seminar at Humboldt University in East Berlin

Each year, the Bonn Program was improved in one way or another. I was very much relieved in 1978, because I had been successful in bringing my friend Lynne Tatlock along as my assistant. She had just been admitted to the PhD program at IU, and I could not have wished for a more excellent and highly motivated teacher. Helmut Rafalski, who replaced Carroll Dexheimer in Bonn, had done his utmost to find suitable host families and to ensure that all local activities came off without a hitch. Though we had arranged for visits to the same or similar institutions as previously, we always strove for improvement. This year, the students were treated to a first-class tour of Beethoven's place of birth. One of the host fathers was an official guide there.

In Trier, I made sure we visited Karl Marx's birthplace right after visiting the bishop. The wine-tasting stop at Lorscheider's cellar remained a favorite. A new field trip took us to the majestic and well-preserved castle Burg Eltz, which was built for Duke Eltz between the twelfth and sixteenth centuries. Sitting up high on the forest-covered hills, it shows off its numerous pointed towers, almost like the fairy castle in Disneyland. At its foot meanders the River Elz, a tributary of the Mosell*e* River.

In 1978, we also added a meeting with guest workers who were employed as housekeepers by the Jesuits. They served coffee and cake. It turned out to be a most remarkable afternoon, in that we learned about the often inhumane treatment of these foreigners. They were almost like the Jews during the Holocaust, shipped in with cattle wagons during Germany's economic miracle. Women and children were often housed miles apart from their men. They were squeezed together in small rooms overflowing with people. Their compensation was meager, and their medical treatment was so poor that it left lifelong scars on many. In short, they were imported under false pretenses. The deplorable treatment of the guest workers was in the news for a long time. The degree to which the foreign workers were resented became obvious to us when one of my African-American students became very upset one day after a German woman yelled at her, out of her apartment window in Bonn, "Guest-worker whore, go home!"

Lynne and I lived at Mutti Hoefer's. We made a good team. I introduced her to the Padre, and we hiked together through the picturesque Eifel region, where the golden *Genista* was in full bloom. On top of the mountain, the Padre paused frequently, asking us to look around in silence and then exclaiming in his deep, melodious voice, "How beautiful is God's world!"

We were all thrilled when the mayor of Bonn invited our group for an afternoon reception at the beautiful, pink Bonner Rathaus (Town Hall), built in 1737, and we relished the sparkling champagne and open-faced sandwiches. – We were still talking about it on the train to Berlin. To add some spice to our four-hour train ride, Lynne and I had reserved a table in the dining car for oral exams. Each student sat with us for about fifteen minutes and carried on a conversation in German. The students liked the idea, because it gave them a chance to show how well they spoke. – In Hannover, the train always stopped for twenty minutes. It was perfect, because Mutti never failed to show up to greet us. There she stood on the platform as our train rolled in, always dressed nicely with hat and gloves. The instant she spotted me waving and calling out to her, she started running alongside the train, continuing until it came to a full stop. My students waved and called out, "Hello, Mutti," as I jumped out and ran to her. We hugged, and there were always tears when she exclaimed, "Oh Christa, how nice to see you!" Mutti tried to talk to the students using whatever English words she remembered from her visit to the Croft. She never failed to hand out cookies and candies and sometimes brought sandwiches for all. A couple of times, she handed me a one-hundred-mark bill, urging me to treat the students to a glass of strawberry-champagne wine punch in Berlin. One year, in an effort to spend the money, a couple of students and I went from restaurant to restaurant on the Ku'damm to negotiate with managers for sufficient punch for the entire group, all for one hundred marks. We found a generous soul in an underground restaurant, where we ended up dancing until the wee hours.

Our program – which at this point, I felt, was the best it had been since its inception – ended on June 28, and the summer seminar in East Berlin started on the same day. All I had to do was cross the border. – Before crossing, I had met with Ingeborg and Hans Guenther at the elegant Kempinski Hotel. As usual, he gave me a commemorative silver coin, this time of the Rider of Bamberg. Meeting with my Berliner friends was always special, and they were disappointed when I told them that once I crossed the border, I was prohibited from visiting them while attending the seminar. I promised to call once I was settled in East Berlin.

We were put up in student housing, a twenty-minute train ride from Humboldt University in the center of Berlin. The buildings were about fifteen stories high. Built in the early 50s, they were already badly in need of repair, as were many of the postwar structures in the GDR. Paint was peeling, stucco was crumbling, and the plumbing made strange sounds. I shared a modestly furnished apartment with a rather robust female professor from the University of Warsaw, a Catholic private secretary to the minister of culture in Bucharest, Romania, who spoke Spanish fluently, talked about having met General Franco, and swore she was not a communist. She also had an obsession with shoes and cut quite a few classes to go shoe hunting. I liked the young French teacher of German from a lycée in Paris. She professed to be a true communist and openly criticized socialism as practiced in the GDR.

I had made up my mind before going to East Berlin that, while there, I would try to contact at least one author personally, even though we were told not to venture out on our own. I had managed to get Klaus Schlesinger's address from a colleague in West Berlin, and was excited when the renowned writer invited me to his apartment. Schlesinger had the reputation of being a pure communist. He led me from the corridor into a well-lit, spacious room. The walls were lined with wooden bookshelves. We sat down on a light-colored modern couch. Before we started talking, he introduced me briefly to his partner, Bettina Wegener, a well-known songwriter and singer, and mentioned that they had several children who were not at home. While Klaus Schlesinger was tall and slender, Bettina was petite, and she wore her brown hair parted in the middle and in a bun. We talked about life in the States and in the GDR, and I was surprised to hear him say that although the thought of dissenting would not have entered his mind only a few years before, he had begun to have second thoughts, because he had been pressured to make changes to one of his popular works to reflect stronger support of GDR ideology. The government threatened to stop publication of new editions if he refused to comply, which would result in a major reduction of his income and consequently threaten his and his family's well-being. I began to realize more and more how devastating it must be for a creative mind to be prohibited from expressing itself freely. – I was not surprised when I heard in 1980 that he did immigrate to the West, and I was happy to learn he had been among those writers who protested Biermann's expulsion and the conviction of their fellow writer Stefan Heym. The conviction resulted from irregularities in foreign-exchange matters. The regime was obviously displeased that Heym published the bulk of his works in the West. Heym was thrown out of the Writers' Association in the GDR before Schlesinger, who moved back to East Berlin in 1991.

It was that afternoon, after my visit with Klaus Schlesinger, that I called the Guenther residence in West Berlin. Ingeborg answered. I knew instantly something was wrong. When I asked about their well-being, she told me her husband Hans had died a few days earlier of acute leukemia. I was speechless and saddened by the sudden loss of my good friend, a dissenter against Hitler's regime. Unable to cross the border, I promised I would try to get in touch on the way home.

The next day, a colleague from Switzerland who had come by car invited a couple of us for a ride. She had smuggled in a few cassette recordings by Wolf Biermann, who in November 1976, while on a concert tour in the FRG, had been forbidden to return to the GDR because he had criticized socialism and the GDR in his songs. As she played them in the car, we daringly opened the windows, wondering if we would get caught and what would happen. Nobody paid attention. It might have been enlightening to discover what they would have done with us if they had noticed.

The best part of the seminar was the opportunity to go theater hopping. During the three weeks in East Berlin, I visited sixteen theater performances, including a Mozart opera. I heard *Die Zauberflöte* (*The Magic Flute*) at the National Opera. It was built like a Corinthian temple, and although it had been badly damaged during the war, it was rebuilt in 1955. The interior was in need of repair, and though the singers were excellent, their costumes, especially that of Papageno, had lost their luster. The feathers were rapidly fading and falling out. I felt instantly captivated when I entered the more charming and intimate, but highly ornate, Komische Oper, built at the end of the nineteenth century, and was very disappointed to have to settle for a mere tour of the theater. It would have been a real treat to experience another Mozart opera there.

A visit to the Freie Volksbühne (Free People's Stage), built from donations by workers in 1914, where the epoch-making Max Reinhardt was the first director, was most memorable. The theater was destroyed during the war and reopened in 1954. I saw an outstanding performance by the celebrated Ursula Schallemeidt in Brecht's *Der gute Mensch zu Sezuan* (The Good Person at Sezuan) and found the discussion with the actors after the show just as fascinating. I learned of the rivalries that took place between the Volksbühne and Brecht's Berliner Ensemble. The actors from the Volksbühne were not only highly critical of Brecht's capitalistic heirs, and their Swiss bank accounts, but deplored them for adhering too much to Brecht's original stage directions, thus leaving no room for improvisation. They felt the plays should reflect the changes of the times. Ekkehard Schall, Brecht's son-in-law and a well-known actor, who was a constant presence at the Berliner Ensemble, appeared to be another thorn in their side; he had too much authority in selecting the actors for the BE performances.

After three weeks in East Berlin, I began to feel rather comfortable roaming around the city. Olga the Romanian and I tried out several ethnic restaurants in the vicinity of the Alexanderplatz, named after the Russian Czar Alexander I. In the center of the huge plaza, ideal for roller-skating, stood the big, round World Time Clock, a popular meeting place, which always reminded me of the big clock in the center of Hannover, also a meeting place. I enjoyed sitting on the bench close to the fountain in the park opposite the old red-brick town hall, built between 1861 and 1869 by Hermann Waesemann, the architect responsible for the red-brick Church of Christ in my hometown, Hannover. A couple of times I went down into the townhouse cellar to spend some of the money they had given us on a cold beer or a cup of coffee. Once, I got into a heated discussion with a couple of students from West Berlin who, in contrast to their fellow students in the East, could take advantage of crossing the border to purchase books and other items in East Berlin at a drastically reduced price. I played devil's advocate by pretending to be an East Berliner and attacking them and several policies of their government. I criticized them for constantly bad-mouthing the GDR but thinking nothing of taking advantage of it when they could profit monetarily. Many Westerners came to East Berlin early in the day and bought books, records, and groceries in large quantities and at very reasonable prices – and when the East Berliners got out of work, the shelves were empty. At the end of the debate, I revealed my identity as an American. They refused to believe me. When I showed them my American passport, they were in shock. I got up and said good-bye.

It was hard to say good-bye to my new friends at the end of the seminar, which had at times been very demanding, especially when we were subjected to difficult exercises in advanced stylistics. At the end, we all agreed that a party was well deserved. My Polish colleagues offered to organize the event, which they generously subsidized with vodka and food. It was there in East Berlin and at that party that I learned to admire the Poles. I found them to be among the most intelligent, language gifted, humorous, fun-loving, and generous of all the nationalities present. I had not been aware how deeply saddened they were that the East Germans looked down on them. But it should not have come as a surprise, because when I was a child, the Germans already looked down on the Poles; and even today, regardless of how unjust and unfair it is, nothing has changed in Germany.

1972–1984

We had selected a Polish professor as the speaker for the farewell ceremony. It was an exceptional address, and the lecture hall resounded with applause – a standing ovation. From then on, I observed students with Polish backgrounds more closely and discovered that they generally learned German more easily than those of other nationalities. I kept in touch with several Polish professors, and when a few years later they encountered major food shortages, I sent care packages to Poland, which they deeply appreciated.

Intrigues and Politics in Academia, Intermingled with Snow and Music

After a two-day visit with Mutti, who always spoiled me, I returned home on July 29. Two days later, on the 31st, I started my two-year rotating term as chairperson of the Foreign Languages Department, leaving very little time to prepare for my advanced literature course – especially since I had come back determined to bring about some major changes in the department. Having carried once more an overload in the spring semester, I was scheduled to teach a regular load of nine credits. Still, I had to prepare for three different courses inasmuch as I tandem-taught the new culture course for the first four weeks of the semester. I was under additional pressure, because I had been granted a sabbatical for the spring semester, which meant I had to put in extra time to get a head start on achieving my goals for the department.

The morning I returned to the campus, I was shocked to hear that over the summer, "Pretty Boy," who had been assistant to "the Prima Donna," had been appointed temporarily to head my division. The Prima Donna's tenure had ended as the result of a rumored "exaggerated" heart attack. I was partially to blame for Pretty Boy's new appointment, since I had regrettably endorsed the departure of his predecessor in the hope that a strong leader would be brought in from the outside. It became clear to me and others that these new arrangements were politically motivated and that some in the top administration did not know what to do with them. I never understood why the heart-attack victim, who did look like a resurrected corpse, was not placed in the Division of Education, where he belonged. He was of pale complexion, parted his slick red hair in the middle, and groomed a square moustache above his upper lip, underneath a long, pointed nose somewhat like Hitler's. Unlike the rest of us, who held PhDs, he prided himself on a master's in French and an EdD. To put it simply, he not only lacked expertise in speaking French perfectly, but also had no experience teaching advanced literature courses in French, which would explain why his publication record in that respect was nonexistent. I was stunned when he called me – instead of his French colleague, who had been teaching French literature for years – into his office and asked for my advice about teaching literature courses. Be that as it may, he first maneuvered his way into our department by teaching one French course per semester and two in education, and I can only guess how he schemed to have Pretty Boy, his slender assistant with silky, prematurely silver curly hair, catlike green eyes, and a shapely figure clothed in well-tailored suits, transferred to Arts and Sciences. The Prima Donna had taken possession of the largest office on our floor by forcing out a powerless, nontenured psychology professor. While all faculty and chairmen on our floor sat squeezed into little square rooms, some without windows, the Prima Donna, or "Pompous A—," as one of his students referred to him, had an anteroom with a desk and a tilt-back upholstered leather chair, in contrast to our wooden ones, and a second, larger room with big windows and a scenic view. I suppose he needed to appear as important as the fat salary he was allowed to keep. Unfortunately, since the members of the department were never consulted to evaluate his academic credentials, some of us felt powerless to object after the fact, while at least one politically shrewd professor – you may be able to think of a more fitting term – wasted no time in teaming up with him.

Starting a chairmanship in this highly charged environment could have proven devastating, because I never believed in playing politics. – I decided to be congenial and signed up as one of the first professors for what Pretty Boy called "the dean's seminar." Once a month, faculty from Arts and Sciences read papers in a seminar room on the fourth floor. It was the "power floor," where Pretty Boy had his office and which housed the Departments of English, Philosophy, Political Science, and most importantly, History: the movers and shakers. The top brass showed up to hear my presentation, entitled "E. T. A. Hoffmann's Music and Fantasy." Pretty Boy as well as the new and much-respected dean of faculty wrote highly congratulatory notes, and so did our "Prime Minister," Dr. Fox, who was a professed music lover. He used to take various persons, myself included, out to lunch in an effort to sound us out regarding our dissatisfactions or other concerns. I always felt flattered and never hesitated to join him for lunch, with one or more cocktails or glasses of wine if I had no more classes to teach. He appeared to be proud to have among his faculty a former student and adjunct instructor, who had made it up the ladder of success. I always felt a bit puzzled when he said, "Chris, you are really a very sweet girl."

In an effort to build up the department and increase student enrollment in foreign languages, I approached Miles, Inc., which had contacted me to discuss the development of a program for their executives and employees to learn German. The Germans from Bayer AG were slowly but surely infiltrating their plant, and just as I had predicted, when the takeover was finalized, their promise not to replace the top management with their own was soon forgotten. They started slowly, and before the Americans knew what hit them, a whole regiment of German VPs invaded the plant, squeezing the US management right out of the door and ultimately into the street. The only American who seemed to evade the push was Lem Beardsley, who was harmless anyhow, because he never held any threatening position and did a reasonable job as MC at company parties. When he visited me at my house, I thought Doc's ghost was walking up the steps. However, the closer he came, the more the resemblance faded.

I and my new colleague, whom we had just hired, worked out a pilot project for teaching the executives, but when I insisted it would involve homework, tests, and examinations, they lost interest, later deciding to send several of their young chemists for periods of time to Bayer AG in Germany. – In connection with those initiatives, I succeeded in convincing Miles to subsidize a beginners' course in German for credit. It was to be offered in the evening at the Elkhart High School as early as the spring semester of 1979. Lem Beardsley, bless his soul, was effective in bringing it about. I was quite pleased, and so were my administrators. The benefits were threefold: (1) instead of Miles, who paid the instructors, IU pocketed the tuition money, (2) our department gained more visibility in the community, and (3) we increased student enrollment. – I took further advantage of my renewed connection in that I approached Mr. Buckley, one of the VPs, and asked him if he would put in a word on behalf of my Bonn Program students so they could work at Bayer during the summer. He helped place four or five students, thus paving the way toward an eventual change in my summer-abroad programs.

I was disappointed with the students in my culture course, and even mentioned in my self-evaluation that this group was "one of the most disinterested, dull, and amazingly 'low-standard groups' which I have ever encountered during my years of teaching." I wondered whether students were enrolling in the culture sequence to avoid foreign languages and whether they were lacking in intelligence or motivation, or both. By contrast, several of my students returning from Germany excelled to the extent that after taking a placement test, they skipped an entire semester of German. All the students who enrolled in my senior literature course measured up to my standards easily, and were excited when I brought new life into the course by playing recordings of Brecht directing his plays, given to me in East Berlin. A favorite was a recording of the McCarthy inquisition into Brecht's "un-American activities." As on other occasions, I frequently conducted my seminars in my house, where we all enjoyed watching plays we had read on my Grundig VCR. I had brought it back from Germany, because at that time there was no money in the foreign-language budget for such extravagances.

My trips to the Bloomington campus in connection with my international activities were a big bonus of my job. I felt pleased to have been invited by Dean Lombardi to represent our campus on the Selection and Screening Committee for the new Overseas Studies director. Thanks to my connections, I was able to bring to our campus Dr. Engels, from West Berlin, who had given me the address of Klaus Schlesinger and lectured on dissidents from the GDR. I eagerly accepted the invitation from Channel 34 in Elkhart when they wanted to interview me about my experience in the GDR on their program *Straight Talk*. But I was disappointed when I learned that, once again, I could not speak freely; whenever I was about to express criticism of the United States, the interviewer found a way to cut me off and change the topic.

In November 1978, perhaps because I sensed the chancellor would be supportive, I decided to request a salary-equity review, just as my female French colleague and the female chairperson from the Psychology Department had decided to do. After checking faculty salaries on an up-to-date list, which was on reserve in the library, I was confident I had a very strong case, and trusted in the fairness of those sitting in judgment, including my Spanish colleague, who had been the affirmative-action officer for several years and still sat on the committee. I was also optimistic that Pretty Boy would not rule against me. It was common knowledge among the faculty that my salary was very low when taking into consideration my achievements by way of promotions, teaching, scholarship, and service. Many of my colleagues from outside the department, especially my friend and colleague Darnella, had approached me repeatedly to point out how unfairly I was being treated and to urge me to do something about it. At the end of the semester, before my sabbatical, I submitted my request to the affirmative-action officer, who was, like the rest of the committee, appointed by the chancellor.

When in December I had all my ducks in a row, including the 1979 Bonn Program, which I had decided would be directed by my new colleague, I was ready to immerse myself in research on the animal world in the works of the German romantics. I kissed Amadeus good-bye, packed a stack of primary texts which I planned to read, and flew to the Loesers in Phoenix for Hanukkah. They had invited me to stay for a month, and I could not have wished for more heavenly and peaceful surroundings. I worked diligently on my new opus, reading and taking notes while sitting at a poolside table underneath an umbrella, surrounded by citrus trees loaded to the hilt with big, juicy oranges and grapefruits. I took a dip in the pool whenever I felt like it. I chatted with my friends in the evenings, and on weekends I went along for a ride or watched some ballroom-dance performances.

No sooner had I arrived up north than I came down with a severe case of bronchitis, but I refused to let it stop me from continuing with my research. Much of the preparation for the Bonn Program required my attention throughout my sabbatical, because my new colleague lacked the necessary experience.

Occasionally, I took a break to hang out with my musical friends. Toward the end of February, winter once more descended on South Bend with fury. It coincided with a solo recital by my friend Machie Kudo at the university. I had planned a glamorous party with champagne and culinary delights for approximately forty people. In the late afternoon on that Saturday, it began to snow. The inches accumulated in a very short time. It was so plentiful that snowplows stopped plowing. Machie called. She was extremely disappointed. They had canceled her concert. I was frustrated. What should I do with all the food? I asked Machie to help me call the guests who lived within walking distance of my house and ask them to come over if possible. Among those called was Mr. Fischoff, sponsor of the Fischoff competitions, who right away said he would come and bring his Guarneri violin. About fifteen guests made it. It was ever so cozy. A fire was crackling in the fireplace. I had pulled back the sheer curtains in front of the large picture window to watch the snowflakes, which sparkled in the beams of the big lantern in front of my house. When Mr. Fischoff asked Machie to give her recital right there, on his Guarneri, her eyes lit up. We sat down around the piano, where she stood and positioned the precious instrument to play. She made the violin sing as brilliantly as you have ever heard. It was an evening I will always remember vividly.

That semester, I had another, very different experience around the middle of March, when I returned after midnight from a concert performance of the International String Quartet at Goshen College. As the automatic garage door opened, I was surprised to see the kitchen door leading to the garage wide open. The kitchen lights were on, as were the lights in the living room, den, and master bedroom. The den looked like a battlefield. The contents of the desk drawers were dumped on the floor. The holster for a revolver lay on the bed in my bedroom. All of the drawers from the vanity set as well as my jewelry box had been emptied on the carpet. In the living room, a drawer from the bedroom sat on the piano bench, and a window in the entrance door had been smashed so the burglar could reach down to turn the knob inside and open the door.

The door leading from the garage to the backyard was ajar, indicating that the burglar escaped when I opened the garage door. Strangely enough, only one gold coin and a few silver coins were missing, though I was a bit shaken up. I called Amadeus, who came over and spent the night. The police never found the perpetrators, but conjectured that they were the same burglars who had broken into a doctor's house in my neighborhood a few days earlier, where they supposedly had stolen a pistol. I installed double locks, and nothing ever happened again.

If I was a bit shaken up by the burglary, I was more taken aback when toward the end of March, while deeply engrossed in the realm of the animal world, I received Pretty Boy's evaluation, in which he lowered the boom on me, severely questioning my administrative competency. He accused me of "exacerbating dissension, personalizing conflict among faculty, lacking fairness in decision-making and having seriously overspent the department's hourly funds." I had given him the perfect excuse to zero in on me when, in my own evaluation, after having become increasingly aware of the underlying emotional tensions among the foreign-language faculty, I pointed out very honestly, but quite naïvely, and after first indicating why I had been under extreme pressure during the fall semester, that I had come to realize it was most unlikely that I would ever acquire that particular trait desirable in a chairperson: equanimity.

It is commonly known that foreign-language departments at American universities excel in personality clashes. Our department had been termed a "zoo" by colleagues from other disciplines because of the temperamental outbursts at meetings. We could be heard at the ends of the corridors. Imagine two professors with Spanish, one with French, one with German, and two with American backgrounds, of whom one was overly emotional and had an ego as big as they come and another acted like a Prussian nobleman. To compound the problem, all the males in the department were obvious chauvinists and clearly predisposed against any determined female, but especially one with a German and thus a Nazi-related background. If prior chairs had been unable to control the bunch, how could I have dreamed that I or anybody after me could? Our meetings resembled what you can witness on talk shows like CNN's *Crossfire*.

Pretty Boy's evaluation opened my eyes, because I began to realize that things were going on behind the scenes. If I thought before that men were not crybabies, I must have been wrong. – I had discovered long before that gossip and backstabbing were the norm in academia. Neither the administrators on our campus, with the exception of the dean of faculty who replaced the Prima Donna, nor anybody else practiced restraint in my presence when talking about colleagues. Some were like sponges, soaking up any tidbit of news imaginable. All you had to do was walk down the corridors and look into open doors, and you could see them huddled together and griping about this or that colleague, administrator, or policy. Some were more subtle – or devious – than others. One colleague's motto was "you catch your flies with honey." Another male Iberian got to be a real nuisance. He called me night after night and tried to tell me what to do, what to check out, and whom to watch out for. It dawned on me then that I had become the scapegoat. Truths were twisted and revenge was in the works.

I surmised that the Prima Donna was intent on getting back at me because, when I was acting chairperson for one semester, I allocated a 50% lower salary increase to him than I had given to the rest of my department. Though the decision was backed at the time by Pretty Boy's predecessor, it triggered a flood of protesting memos by the guy who felt he'd been shorted. I was not alone in believing that not only did his administrative salary exceed his true value, but his inferior credentials in French did not justify an equal increase. I can assure you, he never forgot it. He must have been elated when his former assistant took over as chair of Arts and Sciences. It also came to my attention that Pretty Boy had been upset with me a couple of years before, because when I needed a quick answer in connection with my Bonn Program, I went over his and the Prima Donna's heads by talking directly to the top. They never confronted me directly, and I never understood why not. I also wondered why this negative evaluation had been written after all those years in which I chaired the International Studies Committee and earned nothing but praise and support from its members and deans in Bloomington. Our meetings proceeded in an orderly fashion and without crossfire. Why had not a single person complained to me personally when I was acting chairperson?

Pretty Boy dramatically inflated the matter of overspending. It was no more than $500, maybe even less. I had not had any input into the budget for the year when

I started my chairmanship, and I was fully aware that with the improvements implemented, it would be difficult to run the lab with the same funding. A colleague, the chair of the History Department, advised me that the only way I would ever get an increase in the budget was by overspending. It sounded like good advice. Besides, I had taught many courses without compensation over the years, saving the university thousands of dollars for adjunct salaries. I had spent well over $2,000 of my private funds in developing the Bonn Program, had continuously raised funds to subsidize various programs, classes, and events benefiting students and the university, and had channeled book donations to the library well worth $2,000. To top it off, my salary was lower than that of my male colleagues, despite the fact that I held a higher rank.

I decided to ignore the criticism for the time being, because I did not want to get sidetracked from my research by writing a defense, and remembered what Mutti always said: "If you think you need to explain something it is better to be silent." And Doc invariably remarked that arguing about a decision is fruitless. Once they have made up their minds, they get only more set in their convictions. I focused on the positive remarks in the evaluation, which praised my "active and hard-working university service, selection of an outstanding new faculty member, contributions to the Arts and Sciences curriculum review" and the solid "intellectual achievement" of my paper at the dean's seminar. Sounding as though he felt guilty, he added this comment: "The above evaluation of her administrative work should by no means reflect on her other important contributions to the university in teaching, research, and service. Her excellence, creativity, and high standards make her an excellent faculty member and a genuine asset to the university."

When a couple of months later the Affirmative Action Committee voted against recommending a salary-equity adjustment for all three women, I was not in the least surprised. Even without having Pretty Boy's negative response in front of me, which many years later found its way into my hands despite being marked as confidential, I knew he had played a major part in the decision.

After the chancellor, at one of the luncheons, suggested in the sweetest tone of voice that I might get more if I stopped asking, I stopped and got as much as before – nothing. I promised myself to never again teach an overload without compensation.

Thanks to having been granted a summer fellowship, as well as a travel grant from IU-Bloomington's Dean Lombardi, who always came through for me with overseas travel grants, I could forego teaching a summer course and take off for Germany on the same Iceland Air flight the students would take en route to Bonn. I spent a couple of weeks in Hannover, continued my research at the city library, and followed up with a visit to my beloved Bamberg, where I spent three weeks conducting research in the city library. I visited the Segebrechts briefly in Mainz and benefited tremendously from constructive discussions with my friend before traveling to Bonn for a short visit and a hike with the Padre in the Ahr Valley. He was glad I had a summer without the students. Before heading back home, I had another meeting with my publisher, who was anxious for me to get the monograph ready for publication.

Being practically next door to Bayer AG, in Cologne, I made an appointment to meet with Mr. Knapp in an effort to increase the number of summer jobs for my Bonn Program participants. Smilingly, he assured me that Bayer would secure ten spots for us in 1980. I was then ready to fly home and prepare for my vacation with my friend Ingeborg Guenther. It was her first transatlantic flight, and we had planned to fly back together. She awaited me at the airport in Luxembourg, where several students from the Bonn Program had also gathered to return to the States. We flew home via Reykjavík, where we liked to stock up on Icelandic sweaters, jackets, and the like.

Escape from the Berlin Heat with Ingeborg Guenther to Colder Spheres in Canada

I had invited Ingeborg, because unlike her husband, who relied on his chauffeur to get around and never stepped onto an airplane, she spoke near-perfect English and was also an excellent driver. She did not shy away from planes or ships. She wanted to see the world. It was steaming hot outside when we landed in the United States. No sooner had we entered my air-conditioned house than a severe tornado-like thunderstorm broke loose, bent some trees until their crowns kissed the ground, snapped power lines, and left us for a couple of days without electricity, and thus no air conditioning. Ingeborg had never experienced anything like it. Her face was red as a tomato from the heat. We wore as little as possible and, to cool off, drove around in my air-conditioned T-bird, visited friends, and sat on mall benches.

At night, we relaxed under a big tree in the backyard, and I listened to Ingeborg's fascinating tales. She spoke with great nostalgia about her childhood and teenage years as the only child in a much-privileged environment. Her father owned a large domain encompassing several thousand acres of rich, tillable land in Pomerania, a province in what was formerly known as North-Central Prussia, bordering the Baltic Sea and not far from Stralsund and Germany's largest island, Rügen. Seashore lovers and artists alike visit Rügen. The sheer, white chalk cliffs at its Jasmund Peninsula intrigue them. –

Ingeborg's voice took on an air of pride when she spoke of the property, which had eight buildings, eighty cows, forty-eight workhorses, two coach horses, and one riding horse, which she rode daily. She underscored her father's keen business sense. He kept two sheep herds totaling one hundred heads, which were guarded by a shepherd and his young helper. The sheep were shorn in May to provide income before the grain was harvested. People referred to Ingeborg as "Golden Mary," until misfortune robbed them of almost everything. Her father, an overly zealous patriot, had sold a smaller farm shortly before the end of World War I. He ignored the warnings of his father-in-law, a captain of a ship, who had just returned from sailing the South Seas and predicted in 1913, even before the war started, that Germany would lose a war. Her father, convinced Germany would win, loaned the government over half a million marks to help finance the war. He ended up losing everything but 25,000 marks, which ultimately was used in part to finance Ingeborg's education as a librarian. Out of both guilt and necessity, her father worked as a laborer at the docks to make ends meet.

During her student years, Ingeborg befriended a young Hungarian Jewish doctor. Shortly after Hitler came to power, in July 1933, her friend, compelled to bid her farewell, expressed his anger and his fear prophetically: "This pest will spread over all of Europe, if I marry, I must marry a Jewish girl." Only a short time after he had left for Hungary, coming home from a walk, as she took off her coat, Ingeborg found a slip of paper in a pocket, on which a warning was printed, of which she gave me a copy to show my students and which I will translate for you. The first line is printed in bold letters: **"You are dating a Jew!"** The text continues as follows:

It is unworthy of a German woman to even consider looking at a Jew – let alone to get involved. We are assuming that you are unaware of the seriousness of your actions and are warning you. Should our further observations reveal that this warning has failed to influence you, i.e. you continue to go with Jews, your name will be added to the register of those women who had no pride in their race and threw themselves away on a Jew. In the new Germany, so that every German man can recognize them, a visible mark will be branded into their faces. Do not for one minute believe this may be a joke or empty threats! You are herewith warned and will henceforth be watched.

Ingeborg made sure to point out the printing date in the lower left-hand corner of the slip. I was shocked to see the year "32" – the year I was born. Hitler did not come to power until January 30, 1933.

The heat torture lasted a few days, and by the time we took off on our deluxe tour to the Canadian Rockies, which I had booked before I left for Germany, everything was back to normal. I had planned the trip not only because I wanted to see the region, but also because I wanted us to get away to cooler pastures. – We flew to Calgary, where an exclusive bus awaited our group and drove west on the spectacular, scenic Trans-Canada Highway toward Banff National Park. I was awestruck at the magnificence of the mountains. It was not unusual to spot an elk, a moose, and other wildlife close to the road, standing still and staring at the motor coach or us tourists. We were ordered to be quiet. I was amazed at the vastness of the scenic wilderness and kept staring at the serrated peaks of the Alberta Rockies stretching into the skies, here and there still capped with snow. We passed the Grand Banff Springs Hotel, sitting like an English castle on the mountainside. About thirty minutes later, the bus stopped in front of the equally impressive Chateau Lake Louise, an Edwardian hotel, where we spent three glorious days at the diamond-shaped lake, which lies at the foot of the Victoria Glacier and its Ten

Peaks. We were overjoyed to have a room with a perfect view of the flower-rimmed lake, shimmering emerald green. Ingeborg could not get enough of hiking up the mountain trails originating at the lake. I was impressed by her stamina. She was more than twenty years older than I and never once complained.

However, her age may have accounted for her snoring so loudly that I had trouble sleeping. I had been unsuccessful in booking separate rooms and finally bought earwax to muffle the sound. Sharing the same room had another disadvantage: she had difficulty restraining her overprotective behavior. I felt like I was under constant surveillance. Though I am sure she meant well, she warned me not to sit in the rustic room with the big fireplace because the cigar smoke would harm my skin. She cautioned me against having a cocktail because it might be detrimental to my health. I had to stay out of the sun to avoid skin cancer, etc. However, Ingeborg did not scold me when I teased some of the tourists on the bus, most of whom, despite their obvious riches and advanced age, were surprisingly ignorant when it came to international affairs. I had a lot of fun teasing a couple of ultraconservative Texans after I discovered they had no idea where Berlin was located, that it was a divided city, and that Germany was a divided country. Ingeborg started referring to me as *la méchante*. I am sure nobody on that bus knew what it meant.

The trip included an excursion along Icefields Parkway, with its mountain vistas, ice fields, and glacial rivers, and Bow Falls, tumbling like a long white veil over sloping layers of limestone. A "snow coach" took us over a strip of the Columbia Icefield, which extends over 150 square miles and embraces more than one hundred glaciers. My penchant for ultraquaint lodgings was satisfied when we spent a couple of nights at the Park Lodge hotel resort with its multicolored gardens, not far from Jasper National Park. I later found out that Jasper, an old trading-post town, located in the broad valley where the Athabasca and Miette Rivers meet, owes its existence to the building of the railroad in 1907.

On the way to Edmonton, the capital of Alberta, we stopped for a barbeque, and met Ursula, an attractive singer with a guitar who had emigrated from Germany. She was dressed like a cowboy. Despite her German accent, she tried her best to perform country music, and she hoped to find a Canadian to settle down with. She wished us good luck as we departed to have a look at the big city, where the Klondike Days festival was in full swing and awaited us with music and fanfare.

We had a day and a half before the flight home from Edmonton and spent most of it enjoying the aesthetically striking architecture of the immaculately clean city, with a population of over three hundred thousand. We strolled up and down the main avenue, admiring the elegant displays in the windows, and spent most of our time at the festival frantically taking pictures of Edmonton's celebrating citizens. With their splashy, erotically daring, and elegant costumes, they had gone to great lengths to recapture the fashions of the Klondike times. One can only imagine what it was like when the mad gold rush started in 1896 in Klondike, a district in

1972–1984

Northwestern Canada, in Yukon Territory. By the end of the century, as many as thirty thousand prospectors had invaded the region. The output of gold reached a total of over $20 million before it dwindled almost as rapidly as it started, sending the prospectors in search of new treasures in Alaska.

The sun shone brightly on the cheerful crowd, portraying the golden times of only seventy years before, most likely remembered by some. Some may have had their costumes stored away in trunks belonging to their mothers or grandmothers. They looked very much original. The center of the activities was on a big plaza in the city, with apartment houses and high-rise buildings in the background. Many couples almost begged to be photographed, as though all the time and money spent on getting decked out had been worth it. They posed and smiled, the ladies in their ruffled pink, white, or crimson dresses with matching wide-brimmed hats, on which big wreaths of bright silk flowers sat or on which long ostrich feathers danced with the breeze. Some wore blue prize ribbons over their busts. One woman wore a very short, shiny, bright-red dress and carried an open and equally red umbrella too small to protect her husband, who wore a brocaded vest and a yellow bow tie. The black-lace garter over her knee and the tiny patent leather slippers did not leave much room for doubt that she was the clone of a call girl in a saloon. Another woman, more stunning than the others, could have just stepped out of a saloon as well. Her crimson, tight-fitting dress ended above her slim ankles in several layers of red ruffles. The upper portion of the dress was covered with black lace, matching the lace on her red ruffled bag. Her bare arms were covered with delicate black lace down to her hands, which held a matching ruffled silk bag. She wore a huge hat with a wide brim, spruced up with big, soft, red flowers. The gentleman next to her looked just as stunning in his crème-colored tuxedo, black patent-leather shoes, and light-gray top hat, with a gold-studded cane in his hand. As we made our way back to the hotel, we paused in front of a group of Native Americans, a family no doubt, dressed in multicolored Indian costumes, carrying shields of long, bright feathers, and dancing to the muffled sounds of a drum, which I could still hear on the flight home.

Once back on my home turf, I began to get restless and worried about having lost too much time for research. I was almost relieved when my guest, who tried in vain to unload a handful of dollar bills on me for having hosted her, departed. I knew the agenda of my chairmanship would represent an added set of demands, and I was anxious to continue where I had left off.

Our department had to be more visible, and in the absence of sufficient funds, I had to beg my outside sources, who came through for me. We ended up with a rather sophisticated brochure advertising the Foreign Languages Department, which even Pretty Boy praised as "excellent." The brochure was the result of an admirable team effort by our department, and so was the next item on the agenda: the planning of our first Foreign Language Days, coupled with poetry contests. March 25, 1980, would be devoted to French, followed by German on the 26th and Spanish on the 27th. A major undertaking, it necessitated extensive preparations in advance, since all area high-school students and their language teachers would be invited and transported by bus to our campus. It was an ongoing project, and its success depended on everybody pitching in actively. I gained the enthusiasm of the students enrolled in my first senior seminar on my favorite author: E. T. A. Hoffmann.

In addition to spending, as usual, over one hundred hours on the Bonn Program that year, I had a tenure case to present, involving a person whom I considered a highly complex personality. Pretty Boy, although he was never direct about this issue, spent much time trying to convince me to reassess my recommendation. The Senate Committee asked for detailed explanations, of which I furnished more than four long pages. In the end, I acted in accordance with my conscience, even though a complaint hinting at sexual harassment had come to my attention. After lengthy deliberations, the person in question failed to be promoted to the rank he asked for, but being granted tenure at that time was nothing to complain about.

In addition to the tenure trials and tribulations, I had to deal with a secretary who was obstinate and downright hostile. Our department, which should have had its own secretary, had to share her with the Sociology Department, which she favored. The chairman tolerated any and all of her transgressions, as she took care of his department first. To push me even more into her disfavor, Pretty Boy had asked me to watch her like a hawk and document all of her offenses. I was to keep track of her whereabouts, because she took the liberty of keeping highly irregular office hours and failed repeatedly to notify me of where she was. A few times, instead of sitting at her desk, I found her sleeping on a couch in the lounge. It goes without saying that though she smiled whenever I asked her to take care of something, she took her sweet old time to finish the task. She made told me bluntly that I "fabricated" too much work. Behind my back, she called me "Gestapo." Believe me, it is easier to block a faculty member from earning tenure than to get a secretary fired, especially one who is a couple of months pregnant. Having been a secretary myself, I knew full well what I could reasonably demand of her. Mother Nature and a graduating husband finally moved her elsewhere.

In listening to my eager Latin American colleague, I discovered there were enough native Spanish speakers in the area to warrant offering a degree in English–Spanish bilingual instruction. A regional campus in Gary, Indiana, had obtained a major grant from the government to implement the program. After meeting with the chair and several faculty members of the Spanish Department in Gary, I invited two representatives for a meeting with our top administrators and my two Spanish colleagues, who would be the major players on our campus. More importantly, they would have to write the grant proposal. There seemed to be enthusiasm during the meeting, but whenever I asked for a progress report, the Spaniards were silent. I finally gave up when I became aware of their substantial bickering behind the scenes. One of them constantly pointed out that the other's command of the English language was not good enough. I could think of other reasons, and I'm sure you can as well.

That semester, I also undertook to upgrade our adjunct Spanish instructors. As you will recall, I was intent from the day I started to fight the reputation of our campus as "Riverside High" or "Rinky-Dink College." I also remembered what the chairman, who had hired me, regretted not having done before retiring. He had admitted he lacked the strength to improve the Spanish offerings and replace the high-school teachers who, despite their lack of a command of grammatically correct English, had made their way into the department with the help of our full-time Latin American colleague. They had obviously received favorable treatment, in that they were personal friends and compatriots of their benefactor, who also felt it was unimportant for them to be versed in English grammar. I advertised the positions after getting clearance from Pretty Boy and found two top PhDs, wives of Notre Dame professors, who had been unsuccessful in finding teaching positions in Spanish in the area. One held a degree from the University of Michigan and the other from Harvard.

My Spanish source suggested that the wife of our Latin American colleague, who also had a PhD in Spanish, had received favorable treatment as well. She had been scheduled to teach beginners' courses for us in the morning, to avoid a conflict with her classes at the college, where she held a full-time position. A fringe benefit to her was the use of the same textbook at both institutions. When I wanted to schedule her to teach a literature class in the evening, her husband objected strenuously on the grounds that she needed to be home at suppertime and that her institution would not permit it. When I stood firm, he accused me of wanting to squeeze her out, which would mean "less money in his pocket," as he put it. I proceeded democratically by putting the matter to a vote in the department, and ended up with two excellent adjunct instructors, a new and better-qualified lab director, a superior lab technician, and three good language-reinforcement assistants. Pretty Boy felt I had handled the matter well, and in his evaluation, after praising the "immense amounts of time" I devoted to the department and the university, he commented that the "problems in the department to which [he] called attention a year earlier had relaxed somewhat, most notably the problem in budget control, although some personnel problems persisted."

Your guess is as good as mine, but since I had had an opportunity to set the record straight in the long and detailed letter relating to the tenure case, I assumed he realized I was not in fact the culprit. Going into the red the year before turned out to be a positive for the departmental budget, in that it was appropriately increased. I could not think of anything for him to criticize. In addition to receiving letters of gratitude from several of my students after they were accepted to elite graduate schools and having been invited to join a couple of scholarly societies myself, I had received a letter from my publisher expressing strong support for my book in progress.

I am sure the increase in the budget made "the Fly Trap," the next rotating chair, happy. What did not make him happy, I assure you, was my having relieved his compatriots and his partner in marriage of their ties to our department. From then on, I was definitely on his blacklist, which also meant that three of the four males in the department began to scrutinize my every move. The jury was still out on my new colleague. He did not have tenure. I was glad to get out of the maze halfway intact. I got a refreshing break at the MLA convention in my favorite city, San Francisco, from which I went straight to the Loesers in sunny Arizona before returning to the Snow Belt.

Foreign Language Days at IUSB – Last Summer Program in Bonn

After I earned tenure, I decided not to sell my house but to give it a major face-lift. I invested a sizeable amount decorating the interior and enhancing the exterior with shutters and flower boxes to give the home a more or less Bavarian look. The final touch came with a state-of-the-art Bang & Olufsen entertainment set to fit into a new teak Scandinavian wall unit. Before getting started, I called in a decorator to ask for suggestions, but he had nothing to add. My musician friends decided I had good taste and would have made an excellent interior decorator. They loved the new stereo.

The Foreign Language Days brought almost 1,500 students and teachers to our campus. A great deal of effort and time had been put into the preparations. My new secretary and I worked until late at night sorting brochures and pamphlets received from Germany into plastic bags bearing the German flag, to be given to the teachers. The speakers did a splendid job, and the students who won prizes for reciting poems were proud and happy. Activities such as language classes, film presentations, slide shows, and games took place throughout the main building. The German American National Congress had set up tables for serving coffee and cake to all. My colleague from the Bloomington campus, Professor Eberhard Reichmann, the head of West European Studies, gave one of his passionate lectures in the auditorium on German Day. He played German folk songs on his accordion, and the hall resonated with cheerful singing. In the evening, he brought life into my house by playing the piano at a party I had scheduled for the major contributors. Never before, with the exception of my big German Christmas party at the mall, had anything like it taken place on our campus. Strangely enough, Pretty Boy called it during the planning stages "an important collective response to departmental needs," but my new chair, probably still grieving his "fired" wife, did not utter a word about it in his evaluation at the end of 1980. The high-school teachers considered it a big success in their written evaluations, talked about the event years later, and begged for a repeat performance, but I received zero support from the old boys' club; you can guess why.

Before I knew it, I found myself getting ready for the summer abroad. I regretted having to turn down an invitation from Professor Baeumer of the University of Wisconsin to attend a National Endowment for the Humanities summer seminar. I was one of twelve Germanists invited, but was already committed to go to Bonn. I was also looking forward to going to Germany, because I had Bill Eldon, a doctoral candidate from Bloomington, coming along. He had assisted my colleague "the Nobleman" so reliably the summer before. –

Throughout the year, however, reports had trickled down that the Nobleman directed the program rather casually. He had taken off for an extended pleasure trip without much explanation, leaving Bill in charge of the group and neglecting to tell him where he could be reached. This behavior made me question his commitment to the program. There had also been complaints by students about his teaching in Bonn, as well as his rude behavior toward the conductor on a boat trip on the Rhine River, which almost ended in a fistfight. When I learned he had managed to secure a summer job at Bayer for his brother, a medical student in Strasbourg, by listing him as an IU student, I was upset. It was difficult to believe he could be so brazen as to falsify an official document. I realized it would be ill-advised for me to entrust the group to him in the future and that I would have to undertake measures to terminate his position in my department. It also became quite clear that in order to devote more time to research, unless I stopped running overseas programs altogether, I would have to come up with yet another alternative. I was determined to discuss my ideas with Mr. Knapp when in Bonn.

By then, the program enjoyed a fine reputation nationwide. I was leaning more toward accepting students from the Midwest, because they could more easily come to a personal interview. When Carlos E. Cavelier Lozano, from Bogotá, Colombia, called me from the University of Vermont, where he was pursuing a BA, to ask for an application, I tried to discourage him from applying, primarily because instead of the required four semesters of German, he had taken only one. He pleaded with me, assuring me that by May he would be caught up, and promised to spend many hours in the language lab and to do extra work. When Professor Scrace, my former friend and fellow graduate student from IU, recommended Carlos highly, I accepted him without an interview.

On May 13, 1980, as I entered the boarding area of Iceland Air in Chicago, I spotted the young man quickly. He stood alone in the center of the hall with a sign around his neck that displayed his name in bold black letters: Carlos Cavelier. He was about 5'7" and slender, with shiny black eyes and a full head of dangling black curls. He was of light complexion and, like the rest of the students, casually dressed. We walked straight toward each other, stretching out our hands: "Guten Tag Frau Dr. Beardsley." "Guten Tag Carlos." From that moment on, Carlos was the only student in the group who kept his promise to speak only German for the duration of the program.

After much pleading on my part, Edgerton Travel, in South Bend, had agreed to subsidize the bus fare for my group that year. I tried hard to keep the students awake during the scenic drive from Luxembourg to Bonn. We traveled along the Moselle and Rhine Rivers, which they had never seen, and I was always happy to hear an occasional "oh!" or "ah!" or "wie schön!" (how beautiful!). Helmut Rafalski, our capable liaison in Bonn, who jumped in as soon as the bus stopped, welcomed us. He loaded students and luggage into the cabs that transported them to their host families.

Bill Eldon was in charge of teaching the language skills, and I took over the culture section. The program was filled with even more activities than in previous years. While many field trips were required, other events, such as operas, some theater productions, and lectures, were optional. Since I was responsible for the culture sessions, I made it a point to attend as many of the optional events as possible. If no one else showed up, I could always count on Carlos. I have seldom enjoyed a student as much as I did this young man, whose favorite sport was soccer. He got up in the morning with the roosters, went jogging before going to early Mass, and always showed up in class extremely well prepared. Carlos was a real asset to the classes, always posing thought-provoking questions or raising social awareness, as when the students acted out what it would be like if Hitler had won the war. He was ambitious but modest and always careful not to draw attention to himself. At the university cafeteria, he often bought a bowl of soup for one mark, though he could easily have afforded a more costly meal, as he came from a privileged background. "I am a bourgeois, a comfortable-living member of the Colombian elite," he wrote in a letter to the students, answering their question about whether he had attended a Marxist school, which in part he had.

I admired Carlos for his social conscience: "While in high school I reacted to the socialist ideals of my professors . . . once out of high school, I reacted to the general environment, the bourgeoisie. . . . To see people so poor when you live so well, hurts, especially if you consider values of simplicity and humility as very high virtues. . . . I defend socialism as a means of understanding it, not of agreeing with it. Socialism is a mode of life of millions of people and we can neither condemn the society as a whole nor condemn their governments, because both of these imply that they should – radically – change their life styles, which will not happen because of the world's power distribution." Carlos was pursuing a double major in anthropology and sociology and was the director of the Anthropology of Vermont program, which fell under the umbrella of their Living and Learning Center.

Carlos and I arrived late for a performance of *The Idiot* by the Berliner Ballet, with Valery Panos and music by Shostakovich. We had no program. Only when the male dancer leaped onto the stage did we realize it could only be the great Rudolf

Nureyev, whom I remembered from the performance at the Marseille Opera House during my student year in Aix-en-Provence. – Carlos, a devout Catholic, and I went together to celebrate High Mass at the magnificent cathedral in Cologne, and listened in awe to the choir in the cathedral in Aachen, filled with treasures dating as far back as Charlemagne. We were equally inspired by the cathedral in Trier, where the services were officiated by the bishop we had greeted the day before in his gardens. Carlos and I were the only ones from the group who attended a lecture held in Spanish and German on the political situation in El Salvador, which featured representatives from the opposition to the junta. It was sponsored by a Catholic student society.

Berlin, which included a visit to the Wall, was exhilarating as always, and we appreciated the dinner invitation from the League of Friendship between Nations. I was as intent on keeping my connection with the GDR alive for future international activities as I was on keeping in touch with Bayer.

When Bayer invited our group for lectures on June 11, followed by the usual delicious lunch, I seized the opportunity to talk with Mr. Knapp about changes I had planned on making. It was becoming obvious to me that I could not continue to run the program in the same way for much longer. It was simply too time-consuming and too exhausting, physically and mentally, and left virtually no time for serious scholarship and for my book. On that day, June 11, 1980, Mr. Knapp was very understanding and suggested that the Carl Duisberg Gesellschaft (CDG) and Carl Duisberg Centers (CDC) would fit into my plans, thus laying the foundation for a new program that would begin in 1981. I paid another visit to the highly esteemed CEO of Bayer AG, Professor Dr. Gruenewald, who had heard about me and knew about my connection with the Beardsley family. It was a highly rewarding meeting. He vowed to give continued support to the program, and I left with great hopes for the future. Before returning to Bonn, I went to Cologne and cemented my plans during a meeting with the directors of the CDG and CDC.

The summer of 1980 was the last time I directed and taught the Bonn Program. It was the last time the program took place in Bonn and Berlin, the last time Mutti met us at the train in Hannover. It was not the last time I saw Carlos, who sent me pictures of Mutti and me and of the group years later. I wondered for a time if he followed the dreams he described in a letter: "I want Colombia not to be an industrial power in 100 years, as Brazil *will* be in 20. I believe in the idealistic back to nature, to producing food as did humans for thousands of years before oil (etc.) was taken into account. This is a fantasy, but just as theory can be applied, I have hope to bring this fantasy to life, to the breathing world." –

I was proud when Carlos earned an MBA from the John F. Kennedy School of Government at Harvard five years later, and happy for him when he told me of his marriage and later of the arrival of twin boys. I was not surprised to see him succeed further or to learn that at the young age of thirty, he was secretary general of

Colombia's Justice Department. In 1992 he sent me a copy of his newly published book, *Preludio a La Nueva Colombia* (Prelude to the New Colombia). After that, our lives went in different directions, although we recently reconnected. Carlos, now a father of four, still an enthusiastic soccer fan, and one of the leading dairy farmers in Colombia, continuously exerts much effort toward improving the living standards of underprivileged farmers. According to a Colombian I met in Mexico, Carlos is considered "one of the most important men" in South America.

A Mélange of Crumbling Relationships – Headaches in Academia – Writing in Self-Imposed Isolation – Visitors from Bamberg – Launching the Earn and Learn Program in Cologne

Upon my arrival in South Bend, I learned that Heinz, who had lost a kidney to cancer several years before, had succumbed to lung cancer only a few months after having won another dancing prize with Candy, the "china doll" for whom he had invested in a studio. They had competed in the spring in Blackpool, England, and won a couple of prizes, which I learned is not unusual, because the participants have to be rewarded if they are to continue pouring money into dancing lessons, expensive outfits, and all that goes with the territory. I was glad to hear that Anneliese, who had had decided to take lessons as well, had joined them with her dancing partner from Arizona and also won a prize. – But I was sad it all ended so quickly.

It seemed as though Anneliese's life were falling apart. When she returned from the hospital the day Heinz died, she found that her dog, a collie, had died the same day. At the funeral, her son informed her of the dissolution of his marriage – "seven years in hell," as he termed it. Blaming his father for much of whatever went wrong, he had changed his last name after first changing his first. He resented everything "Jewish," and called his mother by her first name instead of "Mother." He had moved into very humble living quarters out West, sold his car, stopped accepting money from home, no longer ate meat, grew a beard, and dressed down. Anneliese went through her own hell, because in going through Heinz's files, she kept finding love notes to the dancer. To cope with the pain, she increased her volunteer hours at the hospital, worked almost daily, including weekends, and accumulated over thirty thousand hours over the course of twenty years. She loved her work desperately. It became her lifeline. Occasionally, she took a trip to a mountainous country like Austria, Switzerland, or Alaska. Her big passion was playing the nickel slot machines at the casinos in the area or in Las Vegas, where she once hit the jackpot, winning almost $10,000. I told her to give it to the poor.

The first item on my agenda upon my return was the new proposal for and brochures to advertise the 1981 Earn and Learn at Bayer AG Program. The directors of the Carl Duisberg Association and the CDC had agreed to assist with the organization and teaching duties in Germany. In addition, they offered to channel funds from the German government to subsidize the program by way of fourteen scholarships of $1,500 each. Since we ran it as a noncredit program, the students needed money for flight and incidentals only. Nineteen students were given summer jobs at Bayer AG. Most of them started directly after the four weeks of intensive German at the CDC, where they attended classes with students mainly from underdeveloped countries. A select group of students, whose German skills were already good enough for them to hold down a job, started earlier. As the jobs paid handsomely, students were eager to land a position. I recall that one of my students had sold his car to obtain funds for the program. When he left Bayer, he had enough money to travel extensively throughout Europe. At one point, to save money, he slept in the desert somewhere in North Africa. I was impressed.

It seemed strange that given my contacts at Bayer AG, my old semi-family ties to Miles should end so definitively. Early in December, Bill Koerting, my former boss and friend, died – from emphysema, as I recall. He was a chain smoker, like Attorney James, and argued like him that we all had to die of something. A few months before, Doc's cousins, Ed and Walter Beardsley, the last giants from Miles, passed away as well; and I hoped Mrs. Koerting would understand why I could not attend the funeral. Ever since Doc passed away, I have avoided funerals and cemeteries.

During the fall semester, the Second International Conference on the Fantastic in the Arts, to be held on March 18–21, 1981, accepted my paper "E. T. A. Hoffmann's Fantasias: Animals and Their Masters," and I hoped my proposal for a special session on Hoffmann at the MLA convention in Houston, Texas, after Christmas would fall on receptive ears. I had a good panel with leading Germanists from IU–Bloomington, Dartmouth, Ohio State, UCLA–Davis, and the University of Calgary. I had no trouble organizing a lecture series with Professor Schaum of Notre Dame for Professor Segebrecht's forthcoming visit in March 1981 and was able to engage the PR director, Doloris Cogan, as speaker for the IUSB International Business Conference on November 7. My fundraising activities were fruitful again, though I very much resented being constantly turned down by the administration for funding of university-related activities. It seemed there was money for everything except foreign languages, which were always treated like stepchildren.

No matter how turbulent my life, I had always been glad to see Amadeus. With our busy schedules, we saw each other less and less, and our once-so-harmonious liaison began to crumble. Little by little, the youthful musician, consciously or subconsciously, began to alienate me by hinting at overnight liaisons with others and reproaching me for being old-fashioned because I refused to go to his apartment, join him in smoking pot, and participate in other sordid goings-on. I finally could endure it no longer and ended the affair by showing him the door, an act of high drama that resulted in his dumping my many gifts of clothing, mostly shirts I brought him from Europe, at my doorstep. Déjà vu – but with the roles reversed. Twenty years earlier, I had thrown the presents of Gable's clone back at him.

My relationship with the International String Quartet fell apart in concert with my relationship with Amadeus. I learned firsthand what the breakup of a quartet, which is not uncommon, is like. I tried my best to keep them together, knowing how beautifully they played. But their bickering and complaining about each other, coupled with their dissatisfaction with the Pompous Conductor, got to be destructive and almost unbearable. One, though playing with soul, was accused of making too many mistakes; another's playing was technically correct but without soul. The second violinist played better than the first, implying they should switch chairs – easier said than done, since they were husband and wife. Finally they convinced me, after many sleepless nights and after emptying many bottles of Scotch and brandy, that there was no alternative but to dissolve the partnership. The Japanese musician took advantage of the break. The wife learned to drive and brought a baby into the world. I ended up distancing myself from all four, because I could not trust any of them and ignored any and all attempts by them to contact me. I thought I did not hear right when I learned that all those dissonances had ended in harmony. They had accepted an offer at an elite university on the East Coast, where they stayed until all strings snapped and each one of them went to find his or her niche elsewhere.

(In retrospect, it strikes me as downright pathetic that only a couple of years ago the Pompous Conductor was given some sort of award for having brought the International String Quartet to the campus. It proved to me once more that the old boys' club continues to hold the power. During my tenure, I developed five different overseas summer programs that enabled some five hundred students to study in Germany, but I am convinced they would have bestowed a golden star upon me only if I were male. Coincidentally, in 2014 the female director of IU Overseas Study, Professor Kathleen Sidely, recognized my "pioneering efforts in taking IU students abroad before it was customary to do so." She thanked me for my vision of internships in particular, which I was ahead of the curve in creating decades before!)

The ordeal of the quartet's breakup was so harrowing and emotionally draining that for a very long time, I felt sick whenever I listened to classical music. I vowed never again to get closely involved with musicians, to be done with men, and to devote my life thenceforth to teaching and scholarship. – Yet, today, I cannot but once again treasure the memories of the music that filled my home and heart for several years. From time to time, I look at the beautiful silk fan Machie's mother handed to me when we all gathered at my home while her parents were visiting from Japan. I am told it is a rare act of kindness for a Japanese lady to offer her fan to the hostess.

The matter of terminating the Nobleman's tenure had been an extremely time-consuming and emotionally exhausting undertaking. Producing the falsified document finally convinced the administration to support my recommendation. After all those aggravations, I was in urgent need of peace and quiet. My decision was motivated not only by the need for self-preservation but perhaps even more so by my knowledge of other professors who had worked on a book for years without finishing. I was not about to join their ranks. I felt strongly that in order to be worthy of a full professorship, I needed a book with a scope beyond that of my dissertation.

As it was too late to apply for any major grants, I looked over my financial situation and decided to ask for a leave of absence without pay for the spring semester of 1981, which I was almost certain I would get, because it would save the university a sizeable amount of money. I was right; my request was granted. I had to attend to a few matters before the semester was over, and knew full well I could not isolate myself completely. There would be phone calls, meetings, etc. in connection with the new program; I would definitely need to tend to my duties at the conference, where I would chair a session in addition to giving my paper; and then there would be the visit from my friends the Segebrechts.

My new déjà-vu chairman, the Fly Trap, whose evaluation was otherwise acceptable, gave me grounds to be suspicious when I saw the following comment: "After being freed from the tensions and stress of the chairmanship, her relationship with her colleagues in the Department has improved. If this improvement is maintained, she can be a very valuable department member." He was obviously one of the complainers. I am sure he missed his compatriots and his marriage partner and was not about to let it be forgotten, even though he was not the author of the condemning comments. I wondered how long it would take him to bring his high-school teachers back into the department.

When a copy of my female colleague's administrator evaluation fell into my hands at one point during my tenure, I wondered what he and the rest of the top brass might have thought. Though her assessment and comments did not change the climate, it certainly made me feel warm at heart to read them:

During my academic career I have worked under a number of chairpersons, and I served in this capacity myself. Therefore I am quite cognizant that no chairperson is above criticism. If one wanted to be supercritical, minor faults could be found in almost every chairperson.

However, I believe it is the overall performance that must be considered as most important. What contributions did a chairperson make? How did he or she improve or at least try to strengthen the department?

Seen in the above light, I consider Dr. B.'s performance as chairperson to be superior. The conflicts, which did arise in the department, were of an academic nature, such as her efforts to upgrade the standards of the department and eliminate the differentials in quality among the various courses. Since I consider this effort to be of positive value, I would applaud it rather than criticize it.

Dr. B. has consistently fought for high standards. She insisted that the adjunct faculty in all the language divisions including Spanish be of the highest standard obtainable in the area. She rightly maintained that even full time personnel who do not hold a Ph.D. in the fields of language or literature should not be allowed to teach advanced literature courses.

Consequently in her stand for quality, she was bound to jolt the status quo and antagonize those who felt threatened by her attempts to improve the department.

Also one must acknowledge such innovative efforts as her inauguration of the Language Day Program, which was designed to recruit students for the future growth of IUSB and to improve community relations.

Finally I believe she has made a sincere effort to secure some equality in the allocation of salary merit increases. It is regrettable her supervisor did not heed her suggestions. I do not think his estimation was as fair as hers.

To the best of my knowledge Dr. B. has been efficient in communicating all information emanating from the administration to all members of the department. Consequently I am looking forward to seeing her serve again as a chairperson of the FL Department.

As soon as my calendar was clear, I got down to serious business. I wrote around the clock, turning off the telephone early in the morning and connecting it only when I had to make a call. I turned down all invitations to parties and dinners, except one at the home of my female colleague. I lived very meagerly, drove seldom, turned down the heat to 65 degrees, wore a suede leather vest lined with lamb's wool to keep warm, burned candles at night, and made logs out of newspapers soaked in water and dried over registers. I did not spend more than a total of $25 per month on food and gasoline and lived more frugally than during my student years. In the afternoon, I relaxed in a hot bubble bath, leaving a pad to write down ideas on the edge of the tub. My little house was so quiet a family of raccoons nested in my chimney.

Total immersion in the animal world of the German romantics agreed with me. I made good progress because I politely declined any and all invitations and seldom invited my German friend Darnelle, who had knitted a warm sweater for me out of gratitude for occasionally babysitting her young son, to the house. I felt sorry for the boy, because his parents were in the process of getting a divorce. I did not exactly enjoy listening to her tales, because I don't believe in breaking up the marriages of best friends, which seemed to be exactly what Darnelle had done. Though, in all fairness, Darnelle's friend had virtually offered her the husband, Darnelle's colleague and their tennis partner, on a silver platter when she expressed the hope that someone would take him off her hands. I did invite Darnelle, who had a PhD in English, to my home when my good friends the Segebrechts, from the University of Mainz, were visiting. She came to attend Professor Segebrecht's outstanding lecture on "E. T. A. Hoffmann in England," which he delivered in English before an audience comprising professors and students from IUSB, area colleges, and Notre Dame. – My students were also excited to meet the great Hoffmann scholar in person. I had spoken about him during my Hoffmann seminar, and his books were among those on reserve in the library. I was both happy and proud that I finally had a chance to reciprocate, because the Segebrechts had been hosting me at their various homes in Germany since 1973. It was wonderful conversing until late in the evening, reminiscing, exchanging ideas about our research projects, showing them the area when time permitted, and driving them for another lecture at the German Department on the Bloomington campus, where I was pleased to have him meet my former professors, who had become my colleagues, and my students, who all knew of him. Their visit was too short. The Segebrechts had already been to Texas, where Professor Segebrecht participated in the Romanticism Symposium at the University of Houston, and to Los Angeles, where he delivered a lecture at UCLA about "Brecht and Wedekind." When their plane lifted them away, I was both saddened and hopeful that they would not wait too long before visiting me again.

Soon after the Segebrechts left, I had to fly to Boca Raton to read my paper on Hoffmann and to chair a section entitled "Animals in Fantasy" at the Second International Conference on the Fantastic in the Arts, at Florida Atlantic University. Both my paper and the section were well received. I particularly enjoyed meeting new scholars and writers, such as Harlan Ellison, James Gunn, and Gene Wolfe, and I learned much about science fiction, a genre of literature about which I knew very little, if anything. Though the sun was shining in a blue sky, I barely got a glimpse of the famous Boca beach, because my manuscript at home missed me.

* * *

By the end of my leave, I had completed five hundred typed pages of my first draft. I had worked all summer and was pleased with my progress on all fronts. The first run of the new, no-credit Earn and Learn program in Germany had been successful, judging by comments and letters from students. I was ready to take it a step further by changing it in 1982 to a new overseas program for which the students would earn credit. I knew it would once more require getting approval from a whole chain of committees and administrators, since IU would no longer send along a professor to teach and supervise the program abroad. I had a good chance of getting it through, because one of my students, who had worked at Bayer after the Bonn Program, had received a Fulbright scholarship at the University of Trier and another had been accepted into IU's academic-year program in Hamburg for 1982. More importantly, a credit program so heavily subsidized by Bayer AG meant that tuition monies would fall into IU's coffers, and our institution would enjoy more recognition in the United States and abroad as well. By then, Pretty Boy had gone elsewhere and been replaced with "the Lemon," who squeezed me constantly not only to change the Bayer Program into a credit program, but to try to attract out-of-state students, because they paid double the in-state fee for tuition. It had taken me some time to figure out that making money is much too high a priority of universities in the United States.

The Nobleman had been given a year's notice by the university, which must have been very difficult for Pretty Boy, who had thought the world of him because he came from one of America's elite schools. Yet he could have saved him. No sooner had I disappeared to write than he applied for an assistantship to the chair of Arts and Sciences. Everybody chuckled behind his back, because the gossip line revealed that when asked about his managerial experience, he emphasized having been an apartment manager. – What bothered me personally was hearing through Bayer that the Nobleman's brother had weaseled his way into Bayer again in the summer, but was virtually kicked off the premises when he threw a fit because his job assignment did not measure up to his expectations. He seemed to think that he, the medical student, who apparently had trouble being accepted at a US medical school, was entitled to superior treatment. Having to clean the men's rooms did not exactly fit into that mold. Secretly, I thanked my Bayer friends for taking care of the matter so ingeniously.

With the Nobleman on his way out, we had to start all over again, looking for a replacement. About three hundred applicants had to be screened again – and I was not lacking for work, even though for the first time in years I was teaching a normal load. I had applied for a scholarship to finish my book, which unfortunately did not materialize. Determined to forge ahead and eager to finish, I applied a second time for a leave of absence without pay, which, since I was not neglecting anything besides teaching, was granted. I felt lucky, because a young man, a German from my hometown, Hannover, with a certificate in French, applied for a part-time position in German. They had just arrived from Germany, because his wife was pursuing a degree in international law at Notre Dame. I was able to hire him, though for insultingly low pay. He seemed taciturn and a bit stiff, but his German was impeccable; and since there were no senior literature classes scheduled for the spring semester of 1982, I felt confident my students would not be shortchanged. We had standardized the beginners' courses, so it would not be difficult to adhere to the outline. I would also be in a position to observe him during the fall semester.

Even though I did not have to be present in Cologne while the students were attending the intensive language course at the CDC prior to starting their jobs at Bayer, I felt it important to at least drop in briefly to make sure everything was under control. I met with the students after class, had discussions with the directors of the CDC and CDG, and followed up by visiting my Bayer friends in Leverkusen. To strengthen the ties, I treated three of the gentlemen to a luncheon at a rather classy restaurant on the Rhine River, which, I am sure, kept the momentum going.

1972–1984

The Padre Spins Another Tale – Catching Up with Mutti and Old Friends in Germany

I had promised the Padre a visit and a fishing excursion, so I stayed a few days in Bonn, just vacationing. I rented a car, and the Padre obtained tickets to Offenbach's opera *The Tales of Hoffmann*, which played at the Essen Opera. I had never been to Essen. Always having imagined it to be a "black" city in the heart of Germany's district of heavy industry, I was amazed that it was in fact rather green. There were beautifully landscaped parks throughout the city, and since the weather was perfect, the Padre suggested we visit the Krupp residence, Villa Hügel, where we spent some time admiring the famous art collections. Before going to the opera, we sat in the garden café, sipping a goblet of burgundy, which most likely accounted for my intense desire to sing along with the opera. I knew most of the arias by heart. Before continuing to Hannover to visit Mutti, as I tried to do once a year, the Padre and I went on one of our much-loved trout-fishing trips. He was eager to try out the new deluxe fishing rod I had sent him for his birthday. As usual, we had taken along a bottle of wine and cooking gear. The freshly fried trout, which he knew how to prepare so deliciously, never tasted better than alongside the creek where we caught them. – The Padre happily sang an old folk song about a mill on a stream. Being on his home turf, not far from the place of his birth, he simply could not contain himself any longer and had to spin one of his tales for me.

His dark and resonant voice always made me feel warm inside. Whenever his serious face lit up and he burst out laughing so hard that a hissing sound came through his teeth, I had to smile along with him. He always took great pleasure in spicing even his serious stories with a pinch of humor. It never occurred to me to question the truthfulness of his stories. They all rang so true. And when he promised that the story he was about to tell about the shepherd would be nothing but the truth, so help him God, how could I possibly doubt the words of this great preacher? What do you think? Imagine yourself sitting underneath a big oak tree, next to this wise, white-haired man, the trout stream rumbling nearby, just listening to him unfold his story:

I must tell you, there were some real characters at home in the Moselle Mountains – fascinating people. There was one in particular of whom I often think. He was a shepherd. He was old, but far from looking fragile. He was neither big nor small, but of medium build. I would not say that he looked well nourished, and am more inclined to call him haggard, even though two chubby red cheeks protruded above the weather-beaten beard. But those cheeks were precisely the reason why his small, dark, and sunken eyes looked a bit rascally when he smiled. Most of the time a curved, half-length pipe hung from the left corner of his mouth. I can still see him walking around in his dark-green double-breasted coat with the worn cape hanging loosely over his shoulders. He always carried a little hook-like scoop with his right hand, which was tied to a long staff. He used it to hold back obstinate sheep by hooking it around their hind legs.

Every day, at noon, you could see him stride along outside of the village. When he wanted to gather the animals around him, he did not summon them with his marshal-like voice, but simply put thumb and index finger against the tip of his tongue and whistled as loud as he could. His whistle was so shrill that the black shepherd dog, his constant companion, instantly pricked up his ears and, as if ordered by a high chief, set about driving the trotting sheep together.

There you have a rather detailed description of our shepherd. He looked just as one would imagine a shepherd; but appearances can be deceiving. He was not your usual shepherd. People were telling the strangest stories about him. He obviously possessed secret powers. He could cure deadly sick animals by feeding them a mash concocted of cow manure, sheep droppings, and herbs, while simultaneously uttering secret forms of prayer over them. His ministrations never once failed to have their effect. Even the day after the treatment, the cured beasts would move across the meadow in perfect health. In addition, the shepherd was a master of bloodletting, and understood how to pierce the bloated stomachs of cows with his sharp knife to deflate them.

One more. As you may have heard, people had to butcher secretly during World War I. They had to kill the pig in such a manner that the authorities would not find out. It occurred in the middle of the night. The art lay in killing the fattened pig in such a manner that it neither screamed nor screeched. Our shepherd knew how to slaughter hogs so that nobody could hear a sound. How he managed to do it and what kind of operation he resorted to, neither I nor anybody else in the village ever found out.

He was a true magician, our shepherd. I recall one incident which, to this very day, amazes and astounds me. Listen!

I must first confess that as a child, when I was eleven or twelve years old, I was quite a rascal. I do not want you to think, though, that I was the only one. There were three others, my closest friends Peter, Roland, and Seppel. Peter's father was in charge of the explosives used in a nearby quarry.

One day, Roland, who was visiting the village, had the clever idea of contriving an explosion with sparkling fireworks. Peter did not need much prodding. He was quick to offer to secretly secure, or steal, if you wish, a few handfuls of the blue granules of dynamite from his father's shed. As soon as we were in possession of the powder we agreed, after thinking about it, to stick the powder into an empty wine bottle and ignite it by throwing a burning match into the bottle. But every time the match slid through the bottleneck, it snuffed out. You must know that at that age we were a bit naïve when it came to physics. We realized eventually that our first attempt had been a failure and put our heads together to find a new solution. Seppel suggested we try a hole next to a root underneath a cherry tree in a nearby meadow. We stalked through the moist grass – it had rained the night before – as fast as we could and settled down underneath our cherry tree. Peter poured the powder into the hole. The experiment could start. We bent over the hole, tense and curious. I lit a match and threw it on top of the dynamite. It blew out as it fell down. Unthinking,

1972–1984

I left it on the powder, ignoring the glow, and tried to ignite the second match. Before I could throw it, the first match realized its original effect. A shiny blue flame shot into the air, a deafening sound followed – we recoiled. Seppel screamed in pain. We looked at each other, perplexed and scared. While Roland's, Peter's, and my hair and eyebrows were singed, we noticed severe burns all over Seppel's face. At that time we believed that putting something cold on something hot would soothe the pain. We ran to a nearby creek and put cold compresses on his face, which made him cry even louder. Helpless, suppressing our pain, we finally made our way home. Seppel was weeping softly. – Roland, Peter, and I had been successful in covering up at home. What had happened to the much more severely wounded Seppel, no one could find out. Seppel was absent from school the next day. We looked for him in vain for four long days. On the fifth day – we could not believe our eyes – Seppel appeared in class as though nothing had happened. His face showed neither a scar nor a trace of the burns. It was as though it all had been blown away. Curious and amazed, we asked him how that was possible. Quite casually, he answered, "The shepherd cured me – praying."

Whenever I visited Bonn, I stayed at Mutti Hoefer's house. I knew she liked to earn a few extra dollars. On the one hand, she was a bit stingy, always thinning the marmalade she served her guests for breakfast, but on the other, she enjoyed sharing with me a bottle of good Moselle wine, of which she stored a big supply in her cellar. She brought up a bottle of the best vintage the few times the Padre or another Jesuit stopped by. At times, her daughter, a dentist, married to one of Konrad Adenauer's physicians, came to pick us up for coffee and cake on the terrace of their beautiful villa in Godesberg, decorated with bright and lush flowers. I always tried to stop by their daughter's home in Cologne as well. She and her husband were also dentists and owned a stunning house in a posh suburb of Cologne. I found the winding staircase of mahogany particularly unique and beautiful. I enjoyed just sitting on their soft, navy-blue leather couch and looking out through thick sliding glass doors on the strikingly landscaped and, at night, illuminated terrace. Having no children, these two dentists, working tirelessly, favored patients with private health and dental insurance. With their large double practice, they could afford the most up-to-date dental equipment. I have not seen one like it since. The husband, owner of a grass-green Porsche and a fanatical race-car driver, must have spent fortunes on bodywork for his smashed cars. This time, I was glad to see that the marriage, which had been on the brink of a breakup, seemed to be mended.

The Padre had asked me to help the Jesuits buy a new couch set for the waiting room, to be used mostly by the Padre. I suggested a set upholstered with a black-and-white checkered pattern of coarsely woven wool, which they purchased on the spot, adding a glass-top cocktail table I had pointed out. The furniture was delivered just before I left, which meant I had a chance to try it out with the Padre. I don't remember ever visiting him in that room without him going to the wall cabinet, unlocking the door behind which the small refrigerator rested, and retrieving a bottle. The refrigerator was filled with the finest wines and brand-name liqueurs and brandy. Watching him open a bottle of golden Moselle, sample it, and pour it into the crystal wine glasses was like observing a sacred ritual. Whenever I left that room, for which one of my former Bonn students had made a flip-flop sign out of petit point which read *free* and *occupied*, I felt mildly tipsy.

I also felt tipsy each time Mutti performed her ritual, typically the minute I sat down in one of the rosé-colored couch chairs right after unloading my luggage. She always went to the kitchen, brought out a *piccolo* (small) bottle of chilled champagne, took two crystal champagne glasses out of the big oaken cabinet, and poured the bubbly. It was always foaming at the top, at the verge of overflowing. Mutti was already half-crying when I announced I could not stay very long. But we often spent a cozy evening at the home of Marianne, my old music teacher. She always went all out, serving a delicious dinner accompanied by a superb wine, followed by one of her chocolate crème desserts. It was fun talking about Sankt Ursula days. She sometimes brought up the time she slapped my face, which she never stopped feeling bad about. Each time she saw me, Marianne was full of compliments about my academic achievements and applauded my efforts on behalf of the students' international studies. I brought her up to date on the Padre, and thanked her wholeheartedly for looking after Mutti for me. She also asked if I had visited Sibby yet. When I said no, she seemed to smile. It so happened that Sibby's oldest daughter, a beauty just like her mother, abandoned by her father when she was a mere baby, lived in the next-door apartment with her boyfriend. They entertained Marianne all too frequently with screaming, crying, and whatever else accompanies battles between lovers. Marianne was forever lamenting how Sibby would feed her bad-luck stories just before raising the rent. I did tell Marianne when leaving that I planned to look in on Her Majesty, who lived right in my neighborhood, as you may recall.

Sibby knew I would visit her that evening. One of her lovely daughters greeted me at the door and told me her mother was upstairs in her bedroom, where I had no trouble spotting her. She was spread out on a light-blue velvet boudoir lounge, calling out in her sugary tone of voice, while batting her long black eyelashes over her seductive, watery blue eyes, "O Krimi, my sweet, how utterly lovely of you to visit me." Well, it was Sibby all right. She looked as slender as always. A strand of silver-gray hair amidst the black hair falling over one side of her face, and ending in soft locks on her shoulders, lent her a more sophisticated look, but contrasted strikingly with the shiny, bright-red silk kimono, which I thought looked a bit tacky. On the back of the embroidered kimono crawled a large serpent, dragon, or crocodile that glittered golden, light blue, yellow, and silver. The open kimono reached barely to her bony knees, had slits on both sides, and left in full view a black piece of lace, a nightie, held up by shoestring straps over her shoulders. She wore velvet Japanese slippers, plain and black, on pallid bare feet. Those parts of her body not covered were still chalk white and peppered with thousands of freckles. I stopped short of asking her if she had given up the massages with the famous Swan lotion. I was fascinated by her long neck, where an aquamarine in a richly ornate setting, triple the size of the one I bought in Rio, dangled down to her cleavage on a thin golden chain.

We talked about old schoolmates, and I sensed once more what I had felt at our class reunion shortly after I had finished my PhD. Although I generously treated the whole bunch for champagne, one of them, who was mother to two not very bright kids, had had the audacity to question the "legality" of my degree, implying I had bought it somewhere and hired a ghostwriter to produce my dissertation. Sibby, without coming right out and saying so, seemed a little jealous too. It appeared as though she totally forgot or ignored the fact that she failed the *Abitur* (qualifying exam for entrance to the university), when I reminded her of that calamity. I could have bet that her children as well as her friends thought she had passed with flying colors. She complained again about my not bringing any of her children to America and was upset when I told her Marianne had invited Mutti and me for dinner. I would have loved to tell her to treat our teacher and the good friend of her deceased father better, and to tell her I was glad I did not bring her overly dramatic daughter to America, but I bit my tongue and changed the subject to Amadeus. It was as though I had set an avalanche into motion. She started by bragging about her children, minimizing what seemed to me serious problems. She then talked about her son's friend – a teenage boy – Mario. I just sat and listened. I did not know what to say when she related in an exalted tone of voice how she had found this gorgeous boy, to whom she was so close, whom she adored passionately in each and every way – if you know what I mean – and whom she had taken into her heart and home. Just as she was about to send out the papers to adopt this boy, who allegedly embraced her with the same passion, he had vanished from this earth, never to be seen again by her or her children.

Mutti always shed many tears when she stood on the platform as the train pulled away, waving with a white handkerchief until I could see her no more.

Tying Up Loose Ends on Campus and Off – Starting New Projects at Home and Abroad

Back home, as I entered the door to the kitchen, a pretty sign, leaning against a bouquet of fresh flowers and reading "Welcome Home," stood in the center of the kitchen table, as was often the case when I returned from abroad. Next to it stood a freshly baked coffee cake. My good next-door neighbors, the Nurenbergs, who together with my cleaning lady looked after the house and garden whenever I was gone, had put it there. I was lucky to have ended up right next to them; we shared many happy hours together, more at their home than mine, because Helen, a petite brunette in her sixties and always smartly dressed, was a superb cook. Now and then, she surprised me with one of her lovely oil paintings, once of my house. She favored painting flowers and nature scenes. Her husband, Ziggi, a retired post inspector, was an excellent carpenter and gardener. Their lawn was always perfectly manicured. The couple was ceaselessly busy with volunteer work, be it at their church, delivering Meals on Wheels, or assisting the elderly with tax returns. They were good, compassionate people with whom I could share my joys and sorrows.

My other neighbor, who became a widow not long after I moved in, kept mostly to herself. At times, she let me take her grocery shopping, since she did not drive. Normally she had a cab driver on call, as she could not afford to be late for her hair appointments with her male hairdresser, who was irreplaceable. I saw her less and less as the bushes separating our properties grew higher. One day, I learned they found her dead on the floor. Rumor had it she died a millionaire.

In addition to my teaching assignments, I successfully raised enough outside funding to subsidize the new 1982 Learn and Earn program, which, in gratitude for the subsidies from the Carl Duisberg Association and Bayer AG, I named the IUSB/CDC–BAYER AG Study/Work Program. We attracted a group of good students. I was pleased to have completed another seventy pages of my manuscript, and in March 1982, I was again invited to chair a section at the International Conference on the Fantastic in the Arts. Since they had chosen my paper to be read, I accepted.

The crowds at the Oktoberfest held in my backyard were increasing from year to year. They all loved the German bratwurst, bought from a German butcher in Chicago, the imported German beer, and my German potato salad and sauerkraut, which I cooked for hours in advance. This year a new German major, Wade Johnson of Elkhart, had enrolled in my classes; he not only had an unusual gift for German, but also was a talented actor and a good pianist. He brought much life to the parties at my home, especially the annual Christmas parties, by playing the piano whenever we gathered to sing.

Anneliese had invited me to Phoenix, and I gladly accepted, because I liked the peaceful and sunny atmosphere for writing. However, I had to cut my visit short, because I had promised to be back to interview, screen, and observe the three candidates who were invited to the campus to teach German. In March, I took off again, this time for Boca Raton. A few weeks before the group that had signed up for my interim program in Germany would take off, they came to my house for a getting-acquainted and orientation session. I had chosen a former participant to accompany the group on my behalf, in case the students needed a liaison, and had a good feeling that I could send them to Berlin and Cologne without me and let the representative from the Carl Duisberg Society (CDS) take over for me. After all, I did drop in on them later in the summer, when I planned to consult with the CDC and CDG and Bayer prior to going to Bamberg.

The group was in good hands when I met them in Cologne. As soon as I had talked with the CDG and Bayer, I got on the train to Bamberg, visited the Segebrechts, and worked on my manuscript. It was good to discuss my progress with the expert. The Segebrechts loved to go for walks in the woods, and I was happy to join them.

While there, I also attended the Contemporary German Literature Colloquium at the university, and was invited by Wulf Segebrecht to readings by and discussions with two leading German authors, Gabriele Wohmann and K. Kinder. I also spent a few hours at the high school in Bamberg talking to an eager English class about German–American relations. As usual, I was amazed by their knowledge of the English language, and wished that American high-school students were equally good and motivated.

Mutti was a bit shortchanged this time – and I returned to the States just in time for the fall semester.

Toward the end of September, I received an unexpected phone call from a Professor Dr. Grüninger, who turned out to be a member of the board of directors of the CDG. He wanted to meet me personally to discuss the continued sponsorship of the program by the CDG and CDC as well as by the CDS, located in New York. Mrs. Cogan, PR director at Miles, was also present at the meeting. We got along superbly, and I received a green light for the 1983 program, which would be offered for IU credit.

When I found out that one of my former Bayer participants had been given a scholarship to participate in a three-week summer seminar at the university in Halle focusing on the language, literature, and culture of the GDR, with excursions to Dresden, Weimar, and Leipzig, I was thrilled that my connections with the East Germans were paying off for my students as well. During those times, my thoughts were especially with my friends in Poland, who were experiencing a dire hunger crisis. I filled many care packages with food and shipped them through a local church where the priest and most of the congregation were Polish. I wrote to Mutti to ask her to find out if it would be easier and faster to send packages from Germany, but unfortunately she was not feeling too well after being hospitalized for a short period of time. I was upset with my brother, who again neglected to inform me. His wife related the matter to me after the fact.

Back home, I was anxious to find a competent typist for my book manuscript. I was very discouraged after a couple of young women, both of whom had sworn they could handle the job, returned the first chapter full of typos and other mistakes; I had to let them go. I was also upset with the Fly Trap when I found out that over the summer, they had decided to eliminate the German position. Consequently, I could not hire either the young woman whom we had recommended or the other candidates who had been interviewed. I found his behavior utterly unprofessional – when the applicants called, they told me they had not even been afforded the courtesy of a letter informing them about the cancellation of the position.

In an attempt to do something for my students on the home campus, and especially for those unable to afford a summer abroad, I took them to the Huron Theater, in Chicago, to see a play we had read, Max Frisch's *Die Brandstifter* (The Firebugs).

Unfortunately, those riding with me arrived a bit late, because it was raining cats and dogs and I got lost on the freeway following another student driver. However, the lively discussions with the actors after the play made up for our being late. We stopped for a bite at the Heidelberg restaurant and returned home well after midnight, happy but tired. Because of the driving fiasco, I thereafter avoided driving to Chicago by myself.

I spent every free moment on my manuscript and supervised the typist closely. I had hired a new adjunct, a German teacher from Germany, who had married an American soldier and moved to our area. I bought a deluxe typewriter, a Royal, with a German keyboard and correction tape; and my adjunct started typing. Unfortunately, the process was rather slow. As she was from a village in the Rhine region, she had a tendency to change certain consonants from *s* to *t*, subconsciously, I believe. It was very annoying, but I was in no position to complain, because she was a far cry better than her predecessors, who had delayed the book's publication, and thus my promotion to full professor, by at least a year.

According to my records, it took close to four hundred hours each year to organize the Bayer Program. I felt the program was in good hands, but sent along a previous participant, a senior, to act as liaison between the German institutions and my students. The students returning from Germany had invariably profited immensely from the exposure. I was always pleased to observe their thought-provoking contributions in class after their return. I made sure to include the observations in my annual report, where I had made a habit of pointing out teaching innovations and changes.

We in the Foreign Languages Department were greatly disturbed when during the course of the semester, Arts and Sciences voted to change the required credit hours for all language courses from five to three credits. Students would from then on meet only twice a week for seventy-five minutes each time, which I considered pedagogically unsound. I addressed the matter in my evaluation as well, not that I ever expected the new requirement would be changed. The new chair of Arts and Sciences made no secret of having had a difficult time studying languages in college, which explained his lax attitude toward our curriculum. It did not take long for him to put pressure on me, via the Fly Trap, to lower my standards, which I stoically resisted.

The President's Council on International Programs once again awarded me a grant to defray travel expenses. I was rather busy that year reading papers at various conferences and universities, including the University of Wisconsin and Canada's McMaster University. In November, I was the keynote speaker at the Tercentennial Banquet at LaPorte High School celebrating three hundred years of German immigration to America. My topic was "Germany's Loss Is America's Gain – Friendship by Fate," and the address was later published in the German newspaper.

The same year, I had employed a landscaper and his son to perform some major landscaping in my yard and all around the house. Doc always said, "You pay for an education," and I most certainly did. Those two gold diggers, though doing an excellent job, took me to the cleaners to the tune of over $30,000. They worked in my yard for more than three months, custom built the garden table (for $500), and worked forever on the wooden fence, the decks, a round brick grill, etc. for hourly wages of $18 apiece. I did not have the courage to fire them, despite the frequent warnings of one of the subcontractors, and ended up just paying their bills as they were presented. At the end, I even opened a bottle of champagne on the deck and invited both to the Oktoberfest, because the wife of the son was majoring in German and enrolled in one of my courses.

With the end of my manuscript in sight, and because I always sought to expose students who were unable to visit Germany to a bit of German culture, I began in the fall semester of 1983 to plan another German Day, to be held on February 24, 1984. To ensure its success, my adjunct, Ingrid Hembrecht, and many of my students were anxious to pitch in. I was careful not to involve Darnelle, despite her German origin. I had distanced myself from her when it became obvious to me that she was taking advantage of my good nature, especially during my leave of absence. She asked me to babysit her son while she was off transporting her unemployed lover, a professor who did not get tenure, from the West Coast to the Midwest. As soon as he was in town, I began to hear from her only when she needed a babysitter – while she partied with colleagues for whom she had more criticism than praise. When she stopped by one sunny afternoon and jumped out of her car to show off a brand-new pair of sunglasses, to which she had simply helped herself in a department store, I decided to be polite and deal with her on a professional level only. It is difficult to maintain a relationship with someone for whom you have lost respect. I kept to myself and regretted ever having gone out of my way to promote her professionally. I shouldn't have been surprised, because I had met many opportunists in my lifetime.

Early in February 1984, I shipped the six-hundred-page manuscript *E. T. A. Hoffmanns Tierfiguren im Kontext der Romantik* (E. T. A. Hoffmann's Animal Characters in the Context of Romanticism) to my publisher in Bonn. Unfortunately, Mr. Grundmann Sr. had recently passed away, but his son, who took over, honored his father's commitment without question.

* * *

Ever since my first encounter with the German Democratic Republic, I had dreamed about integrating East Germany into my overseas program. I had mentioned it here and there when in East Berlin, as well as on our campus. The League was most receptive and offered to help as much as possible. The institutions in the West did not raise any objections, but would not be able to subsidize any activities in the GDR. The Overseas Studies director in Bloomington raised his eyebrows and could not see the point of taking the students behind the Iron Curtain. I argued long and hard, both verbally and in my proposal, and was elated when after hours of work, I received campus-wide approval. I had one of the most exciting overseas programs in the United States. It soon became the envy of many major universities. The new brochure advertised it as the "IUSB/CDC–BAYER AG Summer Program." Our itinerary would take us to Berlin, East and West, the GDR, Radolfzell (Lake Constance), and Leverkusen (Cologne). The emphasis would be on German culture, society, history, and language and on the workplace environment. Students would be required to hand in a twelve-page paper in German upon their return, which I would evaluate, together with the grades for their work at the CDC. The cost of the program would be minimal. If they budgeted right, students could come home with money in their pockets. I would personally be in charge of directing, organizing, screening, and grading.

With my manuscript in press and the new program well planned, I began to focus on the German Day to be held on February 24, 1984.

V *1984–1993*

Antonio

I have once again searched for an ideal spot out in nature, this time to tell you about a special man. I have found it along the endless strip of snow-white beaches running alongside the sparkling waters of the azure and turquoise Caribbean seas in Cancún, Mexico. I have discovered the perfect place to reminisce and write, a table in a secluded and elevated place in an open-air restaurant, sheltered by palapa. I am only twenty meters from the sea. The only audible sounds are the waves rolling across the sand of finely ground shells and splashing against a big rock, which I like to climb after my early-morning walk on the beach. From the top of the rock, I gaze exalted at the miraculously ever-changing phenomenon on the horizon, where in a clear sky the orange-golden globe emerges from the pristine sea, veiled by a few scattered clouds. I let the breeze play with my white-blond hair, which I gather in the back with a clip. It dries my skin, wet from walking through the waves. Out here, I feel once more as though I were outside of time and place.

As I stare from my table toward the sea, the ebbs and flows of my life sail through my mind like the seagulls dancing and darting back and forth above the waves or tripping across the immaculate sand. In the far distance, the sails of a lonely yacht are shining white against the blue sky, and as though out of nowhere, a blue-white paraglider cruises through the air before it descends slowly to the beach. Two honeymooners, their beautiful, slender, and tanned bodies shining with cocoa butter, are strolling along the beach holding hands and pausing for a kiss now and then. They are the stimulus I need to start writing.

I pause and ask myself, "Is it coincidence that I should just now, on February 24, 2001, exactly seventeen years later, reach the point in my memoirs where I will acquaint you with the last big love of my life, Antonio, whom I met for the first time on February 24, 1984, the thirtieth anniversary of my immigration to America? Was it coincidence that February 24 was the day of my planned German Day?"

February 24 – German Day – Thirty Years in America – Falling in Love Again

German Day focused on both Germanys, East and West. It was a team effort of the university, the German-American National Club, Miles Laboratories, and the students. Invited guests were area high-school students, their teachers, and interested people from the community. The chair of Arts and Sciences gave the welcoming address, and Raymond Johnson, vice president of Management and Information Services at Miles, was the keynote speaker. His topic was "99 and 1 Reasons to Learn German." Mr. Johnson was the father of Wade, my star student, and occasionally enrolled in my evening language classes himself. The German-American Club served open-faced sandwiches and beverages for all, and the students helped with the exhibits, the films on regional, cultural, and sporting aspects of both Germanys, and a film from Bayer to promote my program. We sang, played games, handed out prizes, and in the evening showed the film *M* by the famous German director Fritz Lang, with Peter Lorre starring in his first major role.

Much to my chagrin, I got terribly sick with strep throat the day before, so I had to rely heavily on the help of my adjunct instructors, who prepared the event superbly. I took antibiotics, and fortunately, by the time of the party, to which I had invited university administrators, colleagues, Mr. Johnson, and the PR director from Miles, I felt better. I was grateful for my good and impeccable housekeeper Shirley, the one positive thing that ever came my way through the chancellor. Everything was under control by the time the guests arrived.

I had told Doloris Cogan from Miles that she should feel free to bring as a guest her new assistant, who was also the archivist at Miles. She had spoken about the young historian, as she referred to him, in glowing terms and was eager for me to meet him. When she arrived with her guest, I was mildly surprised. He had the appearance and manner of someone of noble birth. He was over six feet tall and very slender, had a full head of very thick, dark-brown, slightly curly hair, and was dressed impeccably in a dark Italian-cut suit. The starched white cotton shirt and dark-red-and-blue necktie contrasted pleasingly with his handsome features, the almost square jaw, big, dark-brown eyes with long, thick eyelashes, well-sculpted eyebrows, and a tanned complexion. He seemed almost shy, was very polite, and when he smiled his teeth shone like a string of white pearls. The dimple in his chin gave him a gentle look, and whenever he batted his long eyelashes, one could not help being charmed. No sooner had Antonio been introduced than he offered to help with the drinks, went directly to the bar cabinet, and took over. As he handed me a cocktail, I noticed his long, slender hands and manicured fingernails. The few words we exchanged suggested an excellent education. A Renaissance man.

My party was, as always, a success. Doloris Cogan surprised me with a speech, addressing my achievements in the international arena, and handed me an American Eagle of Steuben crystal to commemorate my thirty-year anniversary. The guests began to leave after midnight. Doloris and her historian were the last to go. As soon as the door closed behind them, my thoughts took off in a different direction. I let Shirley clean up, excused myself, and went to bed, grateful that the day had been a success and that my throat seemed almost cured – without the magic of a shepherd.

A month later, I took off for St. Louis to participate in Washington University's seventh Symposium on German Literature, at which Goethe's narrative works would be addressed. Mike Lützeler, my old friend and fellow IU graduate student, had invited me to be a discussant for his lecture on Goethe's epic *Hermann and Dorothea*. It was an exciting conference and gave me an opportunity to get together not only with Mike and other top Germanists, but also with Lynne Tatlock, my first star student, as you will recall. By then, she had earned her PhD and been hired by Mike, who was chairman of the department. Upon my return, the chairman of the Department of Modern and Classical Languages at Notre Dame offered me a position, which I turned down for two reasons: In assessing feedback about their German course offerings, I realized I would be required to lower my standards considerably, which was out of the question, even at a considerably higher salary. Another consideration was my wanting to go up for full professorship in the fall. I did not think it wise to leave just at that point.

New Summer Program with Bayer AG, the CDG, and One Week in the GDR

We had accepted twenty good students for the new Bayer Program and landed at Tegel Airport, in West Berlin, on May 16, 1984.

With the help of the CDG, I had hired Yvonne Salazar, our new liaison, a vivacious, attractive woman with teaching experience in her early thirties, and fortunately a liberal.

She met us at the airport to take over. The students liked her instantly. Yvonne, knowing Berlin inside and out, took us to a few new places, such as the housing project, where the "alternatives" lived in communes. They were mostly students, struggling to cope with the housing and job shortage in Berlin. She also introduced us to the sector in Berlin where almost a million Turks, who came to Germany in search of jobs and better pay, had settled. They had introduced a totally foreign culture to the city, and often lived in apartments overflowing with people. It was easy to understand why the old-time Berliners were not thrilled about their presence. Yvonne walked with us to the housing sector in Oranienburg, where we saw how people lived at the turn of the century. It was interesting to see that in those apartment houses, the higher the floors, the smaller and narrower the windows. The apartments in the back looked down on small and gloomy courtyards and toward the gray facades of the opposite houses. It was depressing, to say the least.

A more uplifting excursion was the boat trip on the Wannsee and to Peacock Island, where hundreds of proud peacocks strutted through the park showing off their beautiful feathers. The students did not quite know how to react to a couple of transvestites sitting on the ferry. They were heavily made up, wearing blond and brunette wigs and dressed in almost offensively flamboyant clothes. I myself felt a bit embarrassed. The students loved the discotheques and the Schiller Theater Workshop, where they saw *Tucholsky in Rock*. They all welcomed the intermittent chats that Yvonne scheduled, at which they exchanged ideas and offered their reactions to what they experienced. It was quite exciting to have lunch in the cafeteria of the Reichstag after they saw the exhibit. Some felt the various lectures in German about questions relating to German history by representatives from the information center (as well as those by guides at the Reichstag) were rather challenging.

Yvonne, together with our liaison, the League for Friendship between Nations, had planned a day in East Berlin prior to spending the entire week in the GDR. The visit included the Brecht house and discussions with the representatives of the League about the development of the GDR, and it ended with a superb performance of Brecht's *Threepenny Opera* at the Berliner Ensemble. The last day in West Berlin was spent visiting sites and museums, which were a must, such as Charlottenburg Palace, the Belvedere Pavilion, and the Egyptian Museum. A common complaint was insufficient time to write their daily diary entries, one of the requirements of the course.

The day before our journey to the GDR, I became aware that several students had difficulty understanding the merit of visiting East Germany. I tried my best to explain to them what a unique opportunity it was to be exposed to socialism firsthand.

When we were ready to cross the border at Checkpoint Charlie, I became upset when, despite my having told them to leave all Western magazines and cassettes at home, I discovered that Wade was carrying a briefcase full of tapes, thus causing an unnecessary delay. He was lucky they did not confiscate them, though it would have served him right. The bus, furnished by the East Germans, awaited us with our guide, Connie, who was about twenty-five years old. It was not nearly as posh as the buses in the West, although it was superior to the rural buses I had ridden in Mexico and South America. I wanted the students to observe for themselves what life in East Germany was like.

In East Berlin they showed us much of what I had seen when at Humboldt University. We observed that they did not take us to the Wall, which we had seen on the Western side. I would have been upset had they skipped the Pergamon. When I told Connie that the wide red ribbons with such slogans as "The people work for the people," "May our German Democratic Republic live, our socialist fatherland," and "Successful path toward the well-being of the people" reminded me of the slogans of the Hitler era, she blushed. She kept silent when I suggested that the ribbons detracted from the aesthetic appearance of the often quite striking architecture of the buildings. We stayed the first night in a youth hotel in East Berlin. We gave the group time to roam around the center of the city before taking them up the big TV tower with the rotating restaurant, which is always a highlight. We were told on that day that our trip unfortunately had to be altered. Yvonne was furious, and though I was very disappointed, I tried to stay calm, because there was nothing we could do about it. Thus, instead of taking us to Leipzig and Dresden, they drove us north to Rostock, a seaport and university town on the Baltic Sea. We did stop at Potsdam, where we saw the sites I had visited when at Humboldt University.

I had not been to Rostock, and none of the students had ever been to this once-important Hanseatic city in West Pomerania, which previously had a population of about two hundred thousand. It is the largest German Baltic port, situated on the estuary of the Warnow and less than ten miles from the port of Warnemünde. It was badly damaged in 1942, when the British bombed the city, aiming heavily at Germany's largest aircraft factory, Heinkel. I get easily excited when I see ships and boats rocking with the waves, and love to look beyond the harbors out to the sea. – Unfortunately, I did not have an ocean view from my hotel room, but I got a good look at the Baltic when we took a rather short tour along the harbor and to the city the next day. On the way to the imposing Gothic church of St. Mary's, which was built in the fourteenth and fifteenth centuries and is known for its two Romanesque towers, the marvelous bronze font, and a curious clock, we noticed what I had observed in other East German cities. There were still, thirty years after the war, obvious traces of bombings everywhere.

Never having been to a shipping museum, I found it quite educational and interesting, but was more grateful for the ride on the following day, when we saw the hilly and fertile region for which Pomerania is known. It was soothing to ride through the peaceful and sparsely populated countryside, with its lakes and beach forests, as we made our way to the next stop, Kühlungsborn, a resort on the Baltic, where we had dinner on a big fishing boat in the harbor. As Rostock is known for the export of herring, we were served herring and different kinds of fish for supper. I, from Northern Germany, liked this, but several of my students made faces. I told the waitress that "Americans are rather spoiled when it comes to food." One of my female students got upset with me. She tried hard to convince me and all who could hear her that it was simply not true. If her German had been better, she might have swayed the waitress. Everybody had a good time after supper, as we danced until late at night. I imagine some had a slight hangover from the free beer the next morning, when the bus took us for an excursion to Schwerin, located on the southwest corner of the beautiful Lake of Schwerin, in the district of Mecklenburg. The main attraction, next to a tour of the somewhat depressed city, which was badly damaged during the Thirty Years' War, was a visit to the former ducal palace, built from 1844 to 1857 in French Renaissance style. It looked very picturesque, as it stood on a small, round island between the two lakes, Lake Schwerin and Lake Castle, with a bridge connecting the new palace with the older one.

Probably more exciting to many of the students was our free time in Schwerin, when we met a teacher with a couple of fifteen-year-old pupils on the square, who invited one of our students for an ice cream. They struck up a friendship and started corresponding regularly. It was almost sad when we had to say good-bye and return to Kühlungsborn. Yet, as soon as we entered the discotheque, it did not take long for most of them to strike up conversations with the East Germans. If any of my students were too shy, I found some eager beavers among the Germans to get involved in an exchange of questions and answers with the young Americans, who came from the land of plenty, a land they had only dreamed of.

Connie, our constant companion and able tour guide, arrived bright and early for our transport to the station, where we boarded a small train to another resort, Bad Doberan, known for its beaches and iron mud baths. – In Bad Doberan, we were taken to a huge and very impressive indoor pool where Olympic swimmers were trained. The pool, covered by a big glass dome, had a device which could be opened or closed to take advantage of the waters from the sea, which I found ingenious and intriguing. It was incredible to see that the GDR would spare no expense in its support of sports. Quietly, many of her citizens complained about it. –

Back in Kühlungsborn, we went sightseeing in the historic center of the town and were shown what is considered the most beautiful Baltic brick architecture in Northern Germany. I personally had been anxious to see it. It reminded me of the red-brick architecture in Hannover.

The heads of the Freie Deutsche Jugend (Free German Youth) had invited all of us to a meeting at their clubhouse to give our students an opportunity to meet with young men and women in their age group. My students did not like the presence of the older leaders, because they intimidated the younger members and functioned as psychological watchdogs, ensuring that no one deviated from their teachings, flavored by Marxist ideology. Yvonne, more outspoken than I at the time, got entangled in a heated argument about the propaganda they were feeding us. I myself viewed the encounter as an ideal example of what life under the regime was like. After the meeting, several students met up with a couple of the girls in a discotheque, where the exchange was more open, very enlightening, and so fascinating that several students exchanged addresses and corresponded with them long afterward.

We welcomed not having to change hotels every night, and the students were more satisfied with the accommodations than with the food. One student remarked that while in the GDR, we "lived like kings" in comparison to the citizens, with whom he genuinely sympathized.

We had time the next day to explore the town, which had a population of about ten thousand. I was saddened as I walked down the sidewalk along the boulevard to the beach. It looked as though bombs had torn the walks up not long before, and the gray stucco of the once-stately villas was peppered with cracks and small holes from gun and flak battles. The streets were empty, as were the beaches, where a few primitive and weather-beaten beach chairs with wooden frames and seats of white-and-blue-striped canvas, instead of the usual basket weave, stood scattered around. I connected with a couple of students who had never seen a beach chair, and I explained that I had seen them only on postcards. They planned to return later in the evening to try them out. One of the students had quite a scare when two soldiers stopped him on the beach, blinding him with a big floodlight. When he presented his passport, they told him he had better go home. The patrol was strict on the beach, because on occasion an East German would escape toward Denmark, swimming.

It was only natural that GDR citizens wanted to introduce us to places of which they were proud, which had been restored as well as possible, considering their shortage of funds for restorations. Thus, they also took us to Erfurt, which we would have reached faster had we adhered to our original plan (Leipzig–Dresden–Erfurt). The distance from Kühlungsborn to Erfurt was more like three hundred miles, and we spent the major portion of the day on the road, looking at Weimar, Leipzig, and Dresden from a distance. I tried to utilize the time by conversing with the students on the bus and eliciting their impressions. I was often surprised to realize how inflexible some of the students were when it came to digesting what they had seen. They had been indoctrinated so rigidly against anything and everything in the GDR that nothing could change their minds. Everything looked as gray as they had been told before they left. When I reminded them of the ongoing discrimination back home, the often deplorable living conditions among the underprivileged, the high unemployment rates, the crime, and the lack of health care for many of the poor and elderly, which was worse in the United States than anything they had encountered in the GDR, they avoided addressing the issue.

After the long bus ride, I did not blame the students for just strolling around downtown and ending up in a discotheque. There really was not much time to appreciate the restorations for which Erfurt was known or to spend time at the beautiful cathedral, which I had seen in 1978. Many had to finish their written reports for Yvonne, who was scheduled to head back to Berlin shortly after we boarded the train to Radolfzell, on Lake Constance, at 8:30 a.m.

There was not a single complaint about the guest families in Radolfzell, but several felt their placement tests at the CDC had not placed them high enough. The director, Dr. Becker, promised to look into it, and he straightened it out while I was still there. I had taken Mike Liffick for a second time to act as liaison between the Germans and the students. They were raving about Lake Constance, where they looked forward to spending four vacation-like weeks. The one big regret came when one of the students received a phone call from his girlfriend in the States, who informed him that she was pregnant with his child. He did the honorable thing, finishing the language course but withdrawing from the job at Bayer to fly home and marry the future mother of his child.

Finalizing the Manuscript in Bamberg – Operatic Intermezzo in Munich

On June 20, I took the train from Lake Constance to my beloved Bamberg. My good friends the Segebrechts had invited me to stay with them while Mr. Hahn, one of Wulf's doctoral candidates, assisted in going over the galley proofs of my manuscript. The time spent in this charming town in the land of Bavaria, dating back to before the year 1000, was as usual a special experience. – Though all three of us worked during the day, there was always time for a morning or afternoon stroll downtown. Now and then, I dropped in to listen in on one of the highly stimulating and engaging lectures by my favorite and much admired colleague, who had been called to Bamberg's university from Mainz a couple of years earlier. On the way back from the university to the Segebrechts' home, I preferred to walk along the Regnitz, a narrow river flowing into the Main River a few miles away, and rest on a bench to watch a family of ducks and a couple of white swans paddling back and forth, waiting for a piece of bread from a generous pedestrian. I was forever wondering what it would be like to live in one of those picturesque, half-timbered fisherman's houses on the bank of the river. I felt drawn to the masses of red and white geraniums and petunias hanging down from the flower boxes on the wooden balconies of these tiny, quaint houses in Klein Venedig (Little Venice), as the Bambergers refer to it.

Getting to Ezzo Straße, where the Segebrechts had just built their attractive all-white villa, involved a steep climb by my standards. The path was interspersed with a flight of stone steps. Each time I paused to look back and down over the red-tile rooftops of this gem of a town, which houses innumerable baroque treasures, I took a deep breath and could hardly believe that so much architectural beauty could have been preserved from medieval times in one spot. Before reaching the front door, I had to enter through a low iron gate to a garden in front of the house, which was filled with rich, dark-red, velvety roses. The path through the rose garden led a few steps upwards to another terrace filled with perennials of every imaginable color, arranged in such a way that each season would bring forth a new profusion of blossoms. Beyond the second section of flowers was the well-groomed lawn, flanked in the back, along the fence of the next villa, by hawthorn bushes, evergreens, and deciduous trees. To the right was a carefully planned vegetable garden. Not far from it stood a walnut tree, Ursel's pride and joy. Beyond the treetops and on the horizon lay Michael's Mountain, which featured a Benedictine monastery that had become a hospital. At night, I could sit and watch its inhabitants turn off the lights. Behind the hospital rose the rather unpretentious towers of St. Michael's Church, illuminated at night by a warm light. To the right I could see another church, Sankt Getreu. Its spires reached high above the rooftops of a clinic for nervous diseases, present even in Hoffmann's time. No matter in which direction I looked, architectural gems surrounded and inspired me.

What made the Segebrecht house so special was the flood of light inside, due to large windows and vaulted ceilings in the spacious entrance hall, which was also the library. The white walls were lined from top to bottom with books on white shelves reachable only by a bookshelf ladder. Big glass doors led from the living room to the terrace and from the dining room to the garden. Never before had I seen a stairway with big, thick glass panels and a white metal railing. The carpet throughout the house was light brown. A big and comfortable dark-brown sectional leather couch embraced a sizeable rectangular glass-top cocktail table on two sides. The set blended in elegantly with the cherrywood cabinets, which ran the length of an entire wall, and with the matching dining-room nook, located next to the entrance of a modern, all-white kitchen. I was occasionally present when the Segebrechts entertained colleagues, visiting authors, students, and friends in these rooms.

I always enjoyed listening to Bettina's piano playing, and her progress pleased me. She was growing into an attractive and very intelligent young woman, and she would soon graduate from high school and enter the university. I liked seeing her with her friends in one of Bamberg's many beer gardens, where Ursel and Wulf took me in the evening on occasion. Ursel and I liked looking at the many antique shops in Bamberg. She helped me locate a precious gilded baroque candlestick in one of the shops. Most weekends, Ursel planned walks in the woods, with a constant lookout for mushrooms. While walking, I tried to teach Wulf how to whistle on two fingers. Though he never mastered the art, he had much fun trying. Another favorite was a visit to the marvelous rococo rose garden adjacent to the New Palace. One Sunday afternoon, at a reception in the rose garden after an afternoon concert in the New Palace, I met Ralf Doering, a handsome blond-and-blue-eyed baritone singer. He turned out to be a recent dissident from East Germany, and like my uncle Artur, he had studied at the conservatory in Leipzig. One word led to another, and I asked him for his address, promising I would see what I could do for him back in the States. He had dreamed for years of "singing in the land of light and freedom." – On the last Sunday, I sat with my friends once more on the terrace, looking out on the garden, relishing Ursel's delicious fruit tart topped with rich whipped cream, which I can still taste today, and dreaming already about a forthcoming concert tour in America for the defected baritone.

My friends always took me to the train station when I departed; and they waved, like Mutti, until we could see each other no longer. – I left Mr. Hahn in charge of sending the galley proofs directly to my publisher. Before visiting Cologne and Leverkusen, I treated myself to a few days in Munich, from which I took a side trip to visit the magnificent and most significant baroque church in Wies, Bavaria. At the church, I met a friendly couple, the Kreuzes from Northern Germany. As there was no bus going to nearby Linderhof, they kindly took me along in their car to visit the flamboyant rococo castle, built by King Ludwig II in imitation of France's Sun King, Louis XIV. I found the castle overbearing, but was thankful for having seen it and even more grateful for having met the Kreuz couple, who took me back to Munich. They had a daughter in America, and we ended up corresponding for years.

I had never before spent any length of time in Munich, Bavaria's capital on the Isar River as well as the gateway to the Alps. I fell in love with Germany's richest and most colorful city as soon as I got off the train and walked through Karl's Gate, which, of the seven town gates from the fourteenth century, is one of the three that are still intact. It marks the beginning of the Old Town, the heart of the city, which instantly makes you feel happy, because you are continually in awe, no matter where you walk and look. Every house, church, or piece of architecture draws attention to itself. Be it the famous Church of our Lady, with its striking twin towers built in the fifteenth century in late Gothic style, the Old Town Hall from the late fifteenth century, or the recently built neo-Gothic hall, facing the Marienplatz, full of people most of the time and even more so when at 5:00 p.m. the chimes begin to play. Instantaneously, the tall, colorful figures in the tower start dancing and rotating to everybody's delight.

Munich offers so many architectural gems, and not only in baroque or rococo style, that I could not have seen them all had I stayed for weeks. I spent only a few hours in the old Pinakothek, which houses Europe's most impressive collection of paintings by the Old Masters. I saw the Wittelsbach Castle, the Residenz, and other places of interest, such as the university where Wulf Segebrecht had studied in the early 70s and collaborated with his esteemed professor, Dr. Walter Müller-Seidel, on the publication of the leading edition of E. T. A. Hoffmann's collected works. I skipped the beer cellar, where Hitler held the meetings that led to the putsch against the Bavarian authorities in 1923, and was glad that Munich, nearly half of which was destroyed during the war, had been restored so remarkably. Unlike other Americans, I had little interest in the great tourist attraction, the Hofbräuhaus, but in walking by I did look through the wide-open doors and saw a couple of hefty waitresses in their Bavarian dirndls plowing through the huge hall, with several mammoth beer steins in each hand, toward a round table on which a bunch of stout, red-faced Bavarians in leather pants were anxiously waiting to quench their thirst with a beer on that hot summer day.

Among the highlights of my visit were two outstanding performances, one at the opera festival of the Bayerische Staatsoper (Bavarian State Opera) and another at the theater of the elector, the Cuvilliés Theater. Though I knew I would not fit in dress-wise, I did not let it stop me from trying desperately to obtain tickets. I was lucky. A man outside the State Opera sold me a ticket for Wagner's *Tannhäuser* for a horrendous price, and a lady outside the Cuvilliés had a seat for Mozart's *Le nozze di Figaro* (The Marriage of Figaro). I sat in the orchestra both times, surrounded by Munich's most elegantly dressed patrons. I never saw so much damask, silk, and velvet, so many tuxedoes, so much gold and silver, so many pearls, diamonds, and tiaras all in one place. And the minute the first sounds of Wagner's opera reached my ears, I felt transported to a higher realm by the impressive performance. I thought nothing could surpass that experience, but the performance at the Cuvilliés did just that. The interior of the theater was splendidly rococo, with burgundy velvet, crimson damask, crystal chandeliers, golden embellishments on sky-blue vaulted ceilings, and light-blue curtains throughout. There could not have been a more fitting setting for Mozart's *Figaro*.

I was in great spirits – my book was forthcoming – and it did not take much to stimulate me to go on a shopping spree in Munich. I had not spent any money on clothes for some time, and since the exchange rate of three marks for a dollar was excellent, nothing could stop me from filling an additional suitcase with gorgeous designer and other fashionable clothes, such as I would never find in South Bend, Indiana, where I was about to start a new life.

Because I was in the mood, I continued shopping in Cologne after meeting with my program supporters and my student assistant, and even found a few choice pieces in Bonn, when dropping in on the Padre. I went on another spree with Mutti in Hannover. She loved to go shopping with her only daughter and always bought something for me that she liked when I tried it on. Leather was very "in," and I found a few special jackets and a coat in Hannover's fashionable stores, enough to last a lifetime. – Since I had my kitchen and bathroom spruced up soon after I finished my PhD, I offered to have Mutti's renovated, but she would not hear of it. She was full of praise for my professional achievements and surprised me when she insisted on taking me to her bank to sign certain papers to ensure that the proceeds she was accumulating in a savings account for me, the same as for my two brothers and her grandchildren, would in fact be passed on to me. It took a while for her to convince me to go, but I was glad I did when I saw how relieved she was after the documents were signed. I got the sense that, since the relationship between us siblings had vastly deteriorated, Mutti was uncertain as to what might happen should she become disabled.

Climactic Romantic Happenings – Multiple New Beginnings – Promotion to Full Professor

It was hot when I returned home in August. Having newly outfitted myself, I felt like a new person and decided it was high time to invest some money to bring my precious 1965 T-bird up to speed. Except for a few minor blemishes, the body still looked new. People occasionally stopped at a red light, rolled down their window, and asked what I wanted for it. I took it to Weiss Body Shop, which originally had been recommended by my former boss Bill Koerting, who claimed Weiss was the best around. They painted his Mercedes 460 SL after it was turned upside down, and he claimed you could not tell it had been damaged. Weiss had always taken care of my car. When I asked him to see what my twenty-year-old car needed – I was intent on keeping it at least five more years, or until it became an antique – Weiss checked it inside and out and informed me without mincing words that my car was rusting underneath. He added that it would be dangerous to drive and suggested that unless I had a double-car garage in which to store it, I should think about selling it. As I had no double-car garage, I had to part with my longtime friend. I traded it for a brand-new Mercedes-Benz 190 E, aka "the Baby."

Not Hitler's Child

For a long time, I had avoided buying a Mercedes or any other German-made car, always remembering the baby-blue Mercedes cabriolet which Anneliese had to leave behind with the Nazis. But I switched gears, because the 190 E was less pretentious and I knew it could last a long time – hopefully the rest of my life. Though by then I was fifty-two years old, I felt more like thirty, which was, I am sure, partly due to my predominantly young lovers, who always declared that nobody in the whole wide world would ever guess my real age. Unlike other women, who resort to the most ridiculous means and go to incredible lengths to hide their age, I made no secret of mine when asked.

* * *

Some distance from where I sit writing on the beach in Cancún, a woman is pulling a beach chair into the shade of a palm tree. As she stands up straight, I realize she is not as slender as I first thought. She is covering her heavily padded body down to the floppy thighs with an oversized white T-shirt. On the front and back are the printed black outlines of a brown bikini on a slender and sexy pink body, which from a distance looks so real that I was fooled by the camouflage at first. Never having seen the likes of it, I cannot help giggling.

* * *

A day or so after my brand-new, shiny Mercedes had been delivered, I accepted a dinner and theater invitation from Doloris Cogan, who lived in Elkhart. She reminded me that I could no longer hide behind my writing or a deteriorating car. I zoomed to Elkhart, feeling free as a bird and on top of the world. I enjoyed the fresh air blowing in through the open sunroof and felt chic in my newly acquired French pantsuit with tapered three-quarter-length legs and the fresh haircut from a salon in Hannover. It was late afternoon and sunny, and since I was wearing my high-heeled sandals, I almost stumbled over a throw rug as I handed the hostess a bottle of German wine. The glass-top table in her nicely furnished dining room was set for five. She had invited one of her assistants and his wife as well as Antonio D., the historian, who was late. I had almost forgotten him; the last time I saw him was on the 24th. Doloris, a divorcée and mother of three sons, was in her early sixties, colored her hair a dark copper red, wore too much rouge on her plump cheeks, and might have profited from a looser cut of the blue-and-white-patterned silk pantsuit, which looked tight over her big bosom. As she led the way downstairs to the bar room, decorated in white wicker furniture, I got a whiff of an obtrusive odor, a strange perfume. The entire room, as well as other rooms in her house, was full of mallard decoys, which looked a bit weird in the company of the white wicker elephant close to the bar, on which she rested the gin and tonic I had asked for.

Just as the hostess gave up waiting and asked us to sit down at the round table to eat, the doorbell rang and Antonio appeared, looking strikingly handsome with his dark-bronze tan, khaki-colored summer suit, and designer sunglasses. He could have passed as a movie star. He was late because he had lost track of time while polishing his beige Triumph cabriolet. Doloris offered to take us to the old theater in Bristol, Indiana, in her flashy and brand-new red Cadillac.

The play was a spirited performance of J. Kesselring's *Arsenic and Old Lace*. Doloris had asked me to sit to her left and Antonio to her right. During intermission, Tonio talked to me more animatedly than he had on the 24th. Being in the theater brought back memories of my drama-reading sessions in Bloomington. Ever since the Germans started to invade Elkhart, I had dreamed of finding a few suitable couples to start up another group. Since I wanted a break from research, this was the perfect time to look into it. I mentioned it to Tonio, who took to the idea like a lightning rod, offering to look into it at once. As I often do, I monopolized the conversation in the theater, talking about my exciting summer in Europe. At the end of the intermission, Tonio asked Doloris if she would mind switching seats with him so he could sit next to me, and she agreed. At the end of the play, nothing more was said about the reading sessions, and when I returned home, I did not dwell on the evening but focused on the new semester, which would involve both typical and new obligations.

* * *

A strong breeze is pushing the turquoise waves higher up on the beach; they intermittently crash against the gray rock below. Two seagulls, standing still on its top, spread their wings, sail across the blue waters in search of food, dip their heads down, and fly into the sun. As the waves recede, the foam dies down like that in a glass of champagne. A young, slender boy with curly black hair runs into the sea and darts into a high wave, where he disappears, momentarily reappears, and swims with big strokes in the blue waters like a big fish. Were he blond, I would compare his appearance to that of the young Tadzio, who fascinated the aging Aschenbach on the beach of the Lido in Thomas Mann's novelette Tod in Venedig (Death in Venice).

* * *

The first item on my agenda, once the fall semester started, was to get the dossier ready for my promotion to full professor. I had to make sure my book was in the publisher's hands. By then, I knew that since I was a woman, and of German birth, they would apply a double standard. I did not want to risk being told to postpone the promotion until they had the hard copy in front of them, even though none on the committee could have read or understood it and some male colleagues had been promoted to full professor without a single book in print. In Germany, you cannot even call yourself "Dr." unless your dissertation is published. I viewed this second book as my inaugural dissertation and applied strict German standards, or the standards of the Bloomington campus, if you wish. I went beyond the scope of the dissertation by addressing the function of animals in works by other German romanticists. Ultimately, I wanted to avoid the fate of several of my colleagues, who had tried up to three times to be promoted. One, after peddling his book manuscript all over the United States, finally landed a book deal with a publishing house in China. Many had to pay a hefty price for publication, and one, after spending a grant-funded year at Harvard writing a book about a topic relating to foreign policy in Russia, tried unsuccessfully for years to get the manuscript printed. One of the administrators published his second book by changing the title and a few lines of his published dissertation. I might have been given a professorship for my exceptional teaching and service record alone. I had a big file filled with excellent evaluations, solicited and unsolicited, from students and colleagues, and had a strong record of service due to my broad-ranging international activities, but since I always criticized promotions to full professorship for just service or teaching, I was not about to follow in the footsteps of those who received such promotions. I took great care not to ask a single colleague from my campus for a letter of support, and I listed as references the best in my field internationally and on the Bloomington campus. I asked one of my colleagues who had been promoted without a book in print to look through my dossier and tell me what he thought my chances were. A few days before I turned it in, he wrote the following letter:

It was quite an experience reading your dossier last night. Your achievements are really remarkable. Not only are you an extraordinary scholar, which I've always known, but your sense of commitment to teaching and students came out very clearly in those letters. You should have been at a better place, been paid what you're worth, and given the kind of recognition that you deserve and for which you – and the rest of us – hunger. But Indiana University is just not that way – least of all <u>this</u> place.

You should go through all levels in about twenty minutes. Keep plugging away – with your scholarship, with your teaching, with your endless assistance to your students that shows up in so many ways. You'll have the satisfaction of knowing that you're a thoroughly committed professional – <u>and</u> a caring person. There is no reason why the two cannot go together – although they often <u>don't</u> in this country.

I hope things go well for you this year – I'm sure they will. Try to ignore the fact, that others are scorched by the flame that still burns in you – because theirs has long since been extinguished. Keep that precious life force in you and don't let this place quench it – be glad that you're able to travel – keep things in perspective – which I can't do anymore.

I'd love to write a letter for you unsolicited and thought of it today but the way things are for me with some people it would be misunderstood. Just know that I'm always behind you, even though I'm usually so caught up in my own frustrations, worries, and fear that I seem far away. Good luck – and knock 'em dead!

I was very confident that my promotion would go through and was mighty glad that my colleague, A. Poinsatte, had taken over the chairmanship when the Fly Trap's term ended. I had also resolved to concentrate on creative writing for a change and to touch up some of my short stories for use in the classroom and possible publication. –

Toward the end of September, I was taken by surprise when Antonio called to inform me that he had found three German couples for the reading group, and I was a bit startled when he offered to team up with me. I was not sure his German was good enough, but abandoned my concern when he told me he had not only majored in German but also studied for a year at the university in Freiburg, Germany. I was impressed to find out later that he held a master's in English from Duke, where he had earned a Duke scholarship, and followed up with a PhD in classics from the University of North Carolina, in Chapel Hill. I could hardly believe it when I discovered that his dissertation, like my book that had just gone to the press, dealt with animals, specifically the medieval Latin animal story *Isengrimus*, based on Aesop's fables. His dissertation was entitled *The Cock-and-Fox Episodes of Isengrimus, Attributed to Simon of Ghent*.

Antonio and I spent hours on the phone getting acquainted, and after our first drama reading at my place, which we initiated with a couple bottles of champagne, he did not leave with the other couples. I did not object when he asked if he could sit with me on the couch. We talked until long after midnight, sipping more wine while I let him hold my hand.

By then, I knew the dissolution of his marriage had been finalized shortly after I met him on the 24th. His wife of twelve years, who had a PhD in English from Duke and a law degree from Notre Dame, had moved with his two children, a five-year-old boy and a three-year-old girl, to work for a law firm where she had clerked the previous summer. At the firm, she met another law-school graduate, whom she invited to move in with her and the children. As he talked about his children, it was clear he missed them very much; he claimed she had stolen them. I was a bit surprised when he told me he had initiated the divorce as a result of a major breakdown in communication. He felt fortunate to have been awarded joint custody. There was much bitterness in his voice, because he felt her first priority was her profession, and the children were left with him while she spent the summer clerking in Chicago and Cleveland. She seldom came home to spend the weekend with the family. He prided himself on having weaned and potty trained Liesl. I felt sorry for the children, but recalled the promise I had made to myself years before: the last thing I needed or wanted was a divorced man with children. I had once told Doloris Cogan in jest that what I needed was not a husband but a red-hot lover, but until then I had avoided any divorced man with children who showed the least interest in me. I kept reminding myself that after Amadeus, I had sworn to myself that I was through with men forever and would devote the rest of my life to my students, scholarship, and travel. I was seriously entertaining the thought of taking a trip around the world.

Antonio, priding himself on having some Native American as well as English and German blood running through his veins, had more sex appeal than any man I had ever met. Like Amadeus, he smoked, which did not bother me at all. – I hoped the difference in age would deter me from any serious entanglement. When I brought up my age, advising him to find someone his own age, he insisted that in his experience such women were boring, very self-centered, and interested mostly in their jobs and paying utility bills. Now and then, I did drive over to his townhouse, located on a pond and tastefully decorated with Scandinavian furniture. It was twenty minutes away, and I was admittedly a bit spellbound by this great entertainer and fascinating conversationalist. Antonio was brilliant and extremely well-read, wrote and had published poetry, was artistic, knew how to draw and paint, and was exceptionally knowledgeable about all kinds of music, classical in particular. He even played the piano – but could not hold a tune when singing. Antonio could talk about any subject. Although he did not share my religion, he shared my views on politics and had a definite knack for languages. He had studied Greek and German at the university, had picked up French while traveling throughout Europe as a student, and had learned Italian when he spent a summer as a paleographer dating manuscripts from the Middle Ages in a Benedictine monastery outside of Milano. His love of all things Italian contributed much, I am convinced, to his remarkable gourmet cooking skills. He always made pasta from scratch, and I had fun watching the process. Whenever I was invited for dinner, often together with others, he served a good wine and exotic hors d'oeuvres while the guests watched him cook. Tonio refused to be rushed. He always took his sweet time and had a tendency to be late, which he attributed to his being from the South. He favored a cookbook by Sophia Loren; and I was deeply touched when he spent almost an hour at the stove stirring the grain he had bought from a mill in order to follow Sophia's recipe for polenta, which he served me with a good Chardonnay after I returned home from a late class.

I knew enough about German wine, but noticed that Tonio favored French or California vintages. I asked him if he would do me the favor of going wine shopping with me before the next drama session, as I was no connoisseur. He suggested we might drive to Chicago, where he knew a good merchant, and stated that he would like to take me out to dinner while there. He felt it would probably be best to spend the night. The closer we came to Chicago, the more I worried, because I had no idea what Antonio had done about hotel reservations, and I was not quite ready to share a room. Before checking in at the Drake Hotel, located on Lake Michigan, we stopped to purchase a couple cases of wine. I had never stayed at the Drake and was impressed by its elegance, and by the way Antonio took over the minute we pulled up to the main entrance, where he turned the Mercedes over to the valet and supervised the transfer of our luggage. It was only when he walked up to the front desk and referred to the two rooms he had reserved that I was able to sigh with relief. Thank you, God! Antonio rose sky-high in my estimation. He was a real gentleman! – It was Saturday, and I had a beautiful lake-view room furnished with

English antiques, where I would feel at ease getting ready for my first big night out with my new friend in the romantic city of Chicago.

When Antonio picked me up at my room, he commented that I looked gorgeous. I explained that the black velvet knickers with wide gathered legs were the latest fashion in Europe, where I bought them at Liebe (Love), my favorite boutique in Hannover, together with the black-and-silver low-cut top and the black-lace stockings, which looked elegantly sexy due to the rose pattern and the black patent-leather slippers with high heels. I had held back with the jewelry, but put a drop of Calèche on my wrists and earlobes. I told Antonio that he looked great himself in his dark suit, white shirt, and silver-blue necktie and that I liked the Hermes cologne he was wearing.

Antonio had reserved a more or less secluded table in an elegant French restaurant, which we reached by taxi. The table was set with sterling-silver cutlery and gold-rimmed china on a white linen tablecloth. I felt uplifted when I noticed the sterling candleholder with two candles and a dark-red rose in a matching sterling vase. The waiter lit the candles and poured the Moët & Chandon champagne into the sparkling crystal goblets. Antonio tasted the champagne, looked at me with raised eyebrows, and asked if I too found the champagne a little off. I agreed, and the waiter brought a new bottle without question.

Antonio and I got into a deep discussion in which we psychoanalyzed, philosophized and mused, and touched each other's heart and soul. – I was amazed at the depth of his perception of my joys, fears, and anxieties. The longer we talked, the more I fell under his spell. We both seemed to have been transported into another sphere by the time we got back to the hotel, where he led us to his big suite, which was even more elegantly furnished than mine and which I had not yet seen. I entered as though it could not have been otherwise. We looked out of the big window at the illuminated buildings along Lake Shore Drive. The lake was black except for a few flickering lights from boats in the far distance. The lights in the suite were dimmed, and on the cocktail table stood a vase with a bouquet of dark-red roses. Music played softly in the background, and the candle next to the roses was flickering sensuously. – Antonio literally swept me off my feet and lowered me onto the soft silk comforter on the rich cherrywood bed – where I awoke in his arms in the morning, feeling exalted.

I could not recall ever having experienced a more romantic and enchanting first night of love. – After so many years, it seemed like the first time. We went to the Drake's seductive champagne brunch and took a stroll along the beach right across the street from the hotel. We both realized that our feelings surpassed our own expectations – we talked briefly about the difference in age, but refused to interrupt the trance just yet. Tonio checked out, but we lingered in an area to the side of the beautiful lobby, where we sat on a brocaded couch in a gilded frame next to the Steinway. We would have been alone were it not for the harp player, who was running her slender fingers over the strings of her golden instrument, bringing forth the most soul-touching and sensuous tones, which lost themselves in the leaves of the palm trees standing in big porcelain pots next to the pillars around us. We were sipping golden drops of wine, and paradise could not have lured us away from what was transpiring right there on earth.

* * *

The palms along the beach are waving their branches gracefully as the ocean breeze causes a gentle rustle, in concert with the birds chirping while they pause in a profusion of pink oleander blossoms. A proud peacock spreads his glistening blue-green feathers in the sun, while the hens, in their more modest attire, gather around their master.

* * *

From that day on, Tonio and I were almost inseparable. Either he came to my home or I to his. I felt as though I had been lifted from the ground on a fluffy pink cloud. The sensations were nothing but bliss and exaltation. Chicago, only ninety minutes away, became our city. We sampled its best hotels whenever the spirit moved us, took in theater performances, symphony concerts, and operas, dined in the best places, and discoed until the wee hours. Tonio had a friendship ring of sapphires and diamonds made for me, and I bought him a pair of art-deco lamps with flat amber glass bowls depicting nude dancing women. Toward Christmas, he went all out and took me to Bonwit Teller to buy a party dress. After I tried on several, he sided with the saleswoman and decided on a size six, designed by Jonathan Hitchcock. Both were convinced I looked like Jean Harlow in the bright-red, shiny silk dress with long, tapered sleeves. It was low-cut in the front, fitted in the waist, and accented with a triangular piece of black-and-silver pearl embroidery. The skirt flared out slightly and ended below the kneecaps. The red silk slippers matched exactly, and the art-deco necklace, made of huge red stones set in thick golden rings, did indeed look stunning with the matching earrings. I had never heard of the blond and sexy Jean Harlow. When Chicago was not convenient, we gave South Bend's crème de la crème a chance. – My head in the clouds, I lost a designer watch, which I had purchased on the Cours Mirabeau in Aix, at a discotheque in Chicago. The same night, Tonio lost his favorite silk robe, and we both kept losing house keys. Fortunately, our jobs were not too demanding at the time, and we could afford the luxury of soaring freely outside of time and place, all the time becoming even closer.

There were always special moments and new experiences, which we took as signs that the gods had brought us together. How often were we thinking exactly the same thoughts simultaneously? How often did we discover the same likes or dislikes, even in our daily lives? I thought it uncanny that we both owned the identical everyday dishes, Scandinavian furniture, and Bavarian wood carvings of putti, and many of the same German books.

Tonio introduced me to Chicago's Hamburger Hamlet one day. We were talking about German literature, and I asked him if he knew what was meant by *die blaue Blume* (the blue flower). He took a clean white paper placemat, chose a few crayons from a glass on the table, and sketched in no time at all the outlines of a lake with a young man lying in the grass on its shore, dreaming with the blue flower next to him. In black Gothic script, he labeled the painting "Heinrich von Ofterdingen," alluding to the title of Novalis's novel. I held back tears of joy – I had met someone who knew exactly what would go to the core of my being. Tonio could not have demonstrated the meaning of the blue flower – the symbol of German romanticism – in a more profound way than by illustrating a scene from the novel of this foremost German romanticist.

* * *

A strange thing has happened. A gentleman, his hair white from life and the sun, like mine, stopped at my table and said, "What are you doing, writing your life's history?" "Exactly," I exclaimed. "How exciting," he said and walked on. I am stunned – how could he have guessed?

Meeting Antonio's Children – First Pre-honeymoon – Captiva Island, Florida

Antonio and I were pleased that our friends had no trouble accepting us. We even collaborated and were effective in getting the PR heads at Miles to sponsor a German film series for the benefit of the general public, their employees, and our students. When Thanksgiving rolled around, it was Tonio's turn to pick up his children in Cleveland. He stopped by my place before he took off in his little Triumph, which he had parked on the street in front of my house. It was raining. When he came out and looked for his car, it was gone. The cute sports car had rolled down my hilly street backward and avoided several neighbors' yards, but did not miss that of the Jones at the corner of my street, where a tree finally stopped it and dented the rear bumper badly enough that it was not wise to drive it all the way to Cleveland. He had neglected to pull the hand break. I offered Tonio my Mercedes, which, after some coaxing, he accepted and took off.

I was a bit apprehensive about meeting the children. Tonio had made reservations for Thanksgiving dinner at Morris Inn, on the Notre Dame campus, which surprised me somewhat, considering that the university had terminated his position at the Medieval Institute under questionable circumstances, which, I assumed, had played a part in the breakup of the marriage. When he stopped at the house to pick me up, the children captivated me instantly. I found Liesl and Gustl absolutely darling. Gustl, who was five years old, was a stunning little boy who had a strong resemblance to his father, with long, very dark, thick brown hair, cut like a soup bowl by his mother to save money, so I was told. He had a big pair of shiny black eyes, bigger than my father's. He had a tanned complexion and a sparkling temperament.

The three-year-old Liesl was an adorable little girl, a bit on the plump side, which is probably why her mother called her "Pumpkin." Her hair was so long it hung down quite a bit over her shoulders. Her eyes were hazel. When she closed them, one simply could not fail to notice her unusual light-blue eyelids. Antonio continually pointed them out. Both children had dark, silky, long eyelashes, inherited from their father. Liesl was not as bubbly as Gustl. It was difficult to understand her at first. Although her babbling vaguely resembled a Southern drawl, Gustl, who spoke like an adult, translated for us what she wanted to say. Liesl had long ash-brown hair, and she clung to her "pinky" blanket for dear life, while sucking on her right index finger with stoic determination. It was squeaky clean.

My first test came when Liesl had to go to the bathroom and Tonio asked me if I would mind taking her. I had never helped a child in the bathroom, much less changed a diaper. Liesl impressed me. She was potty trained and knew exactly what to do by way of covering the seat with endless strips of tissue, which kept sliding, and washing her little hands afterward, pumping lots of soap out of the dispenser. I had to lift her so she could reach the soap and faucet. She was so loveable, and I could easily understand why Tonio put her on his lap at every opportunity.

I was quite excited after they dropped me off at home, and I decided right then and there that we should celebrate Christmas with the children before their mother picked them up on Sunday and took them back to Cleveland. Tonio was game, and we went on a shopping spree on Saturday afternoon. While the children were taking a nap after dinner, Tonio and I trimmed my artificial Christmas tree and spread out the gifts. Their eyes shone brightly, and they loved tearing up the wrapping. If Gustl had not thrown a fit because he had trouble waking up from his nap, the evening would have been perfect. Tonio explained that his son was prone to throwing fits and sometimes would bang his head very hard against the wall, a behavior Tonio said he copied from his mother. When he and his family were traveling in Italy on a research trip, Gustl thought nothing of throwing himself on the floor, screaming at the top of his lungs, and kicking his heels while the Italians stood by, admiring the cute *bambino* (little boy). Once, at age three, he fell into a well in Italy, which scared everybody at first. After he was safely retrieved, Tonio's ex-wife regretted not having taken a photo and wanted him to give a repeat performance. Since I knew nothing about raising children, all these stories sounded a bit strange to me. But I understood why Tonio wanted to see his children more frequently.

After the children left, Tonio came up with a plan for a post-Christmas vacation on Captiva Island, Florida. He wanted to spend Christmas with his mother and siblings in Northern Florida. I was committed to attending the MLA convention in Washington, D.C., until the 29th, when I would fly directly to Tampa, where Tonio would pick me up. He suggested we visit his mother for a couple of days and return from there to South Bend. I was concerned about winter travel in the little car, which seemed to spend more time in the garage than on the road, and finally convinced him to take my new car south. As I watched him take off in my baby Mercedes, I sensed he was mighty happy about the opportunity.

The moment the door closed behind Tonio, the phone rang. I could tell right away it was an overseas call and hoped it would not be Mutti, who had not been well for some time. At the other end was Erich, to whom I had not spoken in years. When he asked how I had been and mentioned rather en passant that his wife had died of cancer, I was almost speechless. I blurted out rather jubilantly that I felt great, that another book was in the press, and that I was madly in love with a most gorgeous young man. Erich was silent, and then he murmured something about being glad to hear it and hung up. It was the last time I heard from my red-hot lover from years before.

It was exciting to see the capital and many of my old friends and colleagues again at the MLA convention. Everybody was interested in hearing more about my new summer program. They thought it was great that I had gotten scholarships for several of my students to study for a few weeks in the GDR and that I had been personally invited to participate in the 1985 Poets' Workshop, to be held in conjunction with the 1985 American Association of Teachers of German meeting in New Hampshire. I invited a whole group of friends out for dinner the evening before I flew to Tampa. They included my dissertation advisor, Professor Weisstein, who had written a letter on my behalf regarding my promotion. In Tampa, Tonio awaited me at the airport, sporting a deep tan and looking like the twin brother of Aphrodite's Adonis.

It was dark outside, and it seemed he had driven for hours when he pulled into the legendary South Sea Plantation Resort, on the slender island of Captiva, which stretches north into the emerald waters of the Gulf of Mexico, boasts a two-mile private beach, and refers to itself as "the Tahiti of Florida." I was exhilarated when I saw the vast grounds. Spotlights illuminated the coconut palms, lush oleander bushes, and crimson hibiscus. Thick purple bougainvillea hung on the white stucco facades of the hotel units. Tonio parked in the back of our hotel unit and carried our luggage to our spacious room, decorated tastefully in Floridian style. He opened the sliding glass doors, which led to a big balcony. We stood a few moments, breathing in the ocean air and looking at the private beach, visible through the palm trees below. We had found a lovers' haven, where I knew instantly that we would spend a blissful holiday.

Tonio knew exactly how to create a special atmosphere. He had brought a Christmas present, artistically wrapped in a small white box, which he had placed under the light on the side table. Inside, I found a photo of a beautiful Chinese screen standing next to a black grand piano. The screen was a unique piece of art composed of four panels of wood decorated with pressed grasses, ferns, autumn leaves, and butterflies on a dark-yellow, lacquered background. Little birds sitting on branches were painted on it. He explained that he had it made for me by an artist friend in

Florida and that we would take it home on top of my car. I knew I would cherish it always.

Honeymooners sought out Captiva, the island where pirates and the Calusa Indians once roamed. It turned out to be a pre-honeymoon for me. I relished soaking up the sun on the white-sand beaches and searching for shells, of which we found some real beauties. I thought it was utterly romantic when Tonio pulled the mattress onto the balcony and we fell asleep while listening to the lullaby of the waves and gazing at the star-studded sky above us. Tonio demonstrated expert knowledge when he talked keenly about and pointed out the exotic species of flora and fauna in the Plantation Nature Preserve. I got excited when a huge alligator and a couple of turtles made their way through the swamps in the National Wildlife Refuge, and could have spent hours admiring the graceful pink flamingos.

I was thankful not to have to drive and immensely enjoyed riding along the coast and over to Sanibel as Tonio introduced me to regions of his beloved Florida, which I had not yet seen. He seemed to know his way around, and he took me to choice restaurants, where I sampled the most succulent seafood, including shrimp and soft-shell crab. The only disappointment was that a place to which he wanted to take me dancing on New Year's Eve was closed. Thus, I did not get a chance to wear the red dress, which, however, had already had its effect at a Christmas party in Elkhart, where Tonio became jealous of a man who had asked me to dance and who must have glanced at the upper part of my dress somewhat inappropriately.

We headed north on January 5 to a small town near Destin on the Gulf of Mexico, where Tonio's gray-haired mother, a tall and slender lady with dark-brown eyes just like Tonio's, welcomed me, thanking me right away for the table arrangement of flowers I had sent to her before leaving for D.C. Her large bungalow, big enough to board her family of five children, was inviting, friendly, and very neatly kept. It sat on a spacious lot with many beautiful flowers and vines, a well-kept lawn, and enough trees to provide ample shade on hot summer days.

The little time we spent with Tonio's mother did give me a chance to meet his oldest brother, who was obsessed with sports cars and showed us around his own very profitable and luxuriously furnished advertising agency. I also met his younger sister and her family. Unlike the other siblings, one of whom had a law degree and another, the older sister, a PhD in English, she had been content to be a housewife and raise a couple of boys and a girl. She had a strong interest in photography and, like her mother, was a devout Baptist. Everyone in the family had two things in common: they were extremely good-looking, and with the exception of the baby sister, who had eloped as a teenager with a busboy and whose marriage seemed to be on the rocks, they had been divorced: the mother twice, the oldest brother and Tonio once, and the lawyer and older sister three times each. I found all that a bit hard to digest, since there was no divorce in my immediate family, but tried not to judge. I liked Tonio's friend Diana, the artist who had crafted the screen, which we picked up and loaded on my car the night before we headed back home to snow-covered South Bend.

On the way home, Tonio filled me in on more family history. He mentioned he had also seen a girlfriend in his hometown whom he had met before me, a divorcée with a couple of children. He had told her about us over the phone, but felt he should explain to her in person. She had bought him a necktie for Christmas in the hope of rekindling the relationship. I felt sorry for her when Tonio told me that she shed many tears when she realized there was no chance. As soon as we arrived at my house, Tonio carried the screen inside and set it up next to my Knabe, the baby grand, not far from the window where the baroque candleholder from Bamberg stood.

Returning home refreshed and rejuvenated, I picked up what I had started a couple of months after my return from Bamberg. I initiated more phone calls to area universities and old friends on the East Coast with a penchant for music to test the market for Messrs. Doering and Grossmann, the dissidents from East Germany and Hungary who wanted to show off their talents in the good old United States. Before long, I was pleased to inform my artists that I had arranged ten concerts for them at various US colleges and other institutions for the month of October.

At this point, Antonio and I were actively involved, going from one house to another, reading German drama with several German executives from Miles, and coming up with other ideas to bring industry and the university closer together. We started the German Table at the Elkhart Elks Club and the German Film Festival at the Miles PR Center, where the Himmelhaus, a German-style grocery, served coffee, cake, and cookies free of charge.

On March 22, I was surprised and very pleased to receive a memo from the acting chairman of the Lundquist Fellow Selection Committee, which informed me that I had been nominated for the 1985 Eldy Lundquist Faculty Fellowship, which included a modest cash award of $3,000. Mr. Lundquist was a former Indiana senator, and I had occasionally enjoyed the privilege of speaking with him. He had shown a keen interest in my achievements in the international arena. As the German American Club continued to subsidize my overseas programs, I agreed to sit on their Steering Committee in Chicago (only because I hoped Antonio would drive me there if need be).

Because by then I had established a good relationship with Professor Dr. Grünewald, CEO of Bayer AG in Germany, I considered it imperative to meet the new CEO of Miles, who was the successor of Dr. Geks, with whom Antonio had enjoyed a superb relationship. Dr. Geks thought highly of Tonio's background in art, architecture, and history and had asked him along on a trip to Boston for an exclusive tour of the city. Since Professor Dr. Grünewald had encouraged me to get acquainted with the present head of Miles in order to see if the company could do more for us,

I called up Geks's replacement, who invited me to dinner at the Elcona Country Club. I thought it a bit strange that he did not want me to bring Antonio along, especially since he was part of Miles's PR Department. I did not pursue the matter and was surprised to see at his side a young, attractive woman, about Antonio's age, whom he introduced neither as an employee nor as his fiancée or wife. I had come up with a plan whereby young German Bayer employees would come to Miles during the summer not only to get acquainted with their American affiliate but also to receive instruction in English, history, or other subjects. While he felt they could not bring over Germans when they were letting Americans go, he did agree to buy one hundred tickets at $2 each for his employees to attend the Doering concert in the fall. Yet, when I later reminded him via his PR director, he seemed to have changed his mind. A few weeks after the meeting, his young live-in partner, who definitely, like many other women, had a weakness for Antonio, invited us both to the house, which looked rather gloomy, as I recall. She enjoyed asking for Tonio's input when selecting pieces of art to be presented to out-of-town VIPs and appeared to be envious of me. At least, I deduced as much when she quipped that she would buy herself a young lover when she reached my age.

In early spring, at about the time I had been awarded a full professorship, my book made its way into my hands. I decided to fly to the Big Apple for the Easter break to meet with my publisher, Herbert Grundmann Jr., in order to discuss the promotion of my book. I was thrilled when he informed me he had secured two excellent seats for the Broadway hit *Cats*. He had wanted to invite me because cats played a major role in Hoffmann's novel *Kater Murr* (Tomcat Murr). When I told him during the intermission of the spectacular musical for which my boyfriend and I were thinking of taking a trip to the Greek island of Crete in May, he recommended we stay at the Elounda Bay Hotel, which he considered the most desirable hotel in Crete.

I gave up the idea of asking the two newcomers to join our drama sessions as replacements for the Wittkuhns, who had been transferred to Pittsburgh, the new Miles headquarters. Instead, Antonio approached the Voepels, who had recently been transferred to Elkhart from Kansas City. Karl was a senior VP and his wife Renate a very attractive brunette with impeccable taste. She was a devout mother and housewife par excellence. They had three adult children. I met the Voepels when Tonio hosted our drama group at his place at the end of April. It started with bloodshed: just before the guests arrived, he broke a wine goblet while wiping it. The glass cut deep into his left hand, and a heavy stream of blood gushed out. I almost fainted – it reminded me of the time blood gushed from Mutti's head when the ax landed on her skull. One of the execs appeared at the door and dressed the wound right away; and when everybody set their lips to the filled goblets, smiles pervaded the room quickly. I passed the tray that held the folded pieces of paper with the names of the play's characters. A momentary silence was interrupted by exclamations of "oh!" "oh dear!" "ach nein!" "heaven forbid!" and "not me!" and a lot of chatter took over – which stopped abruptly the minute we got ready to start the reading. That evening, at the end of April, we read the comedy *Hauptmann von Köpenick* by Carl Zuckmayer, and we were fortunate to see the movie, starring the famous actor Heinz Rühmann, a couple of weeks later at the German Film Festival.

I was quite pleased that Antonio had been able to interest Miles in hosting the orientation session for the Bayer Program students from that point on. A number of students had to travel several hundred miles to attend, but all were impressed with the facilities, the welcome speeches by two of the leading PR executives, and the free lunch to which the company invited all of us. My orientation was followed by a Q&A session to which I had asked my star student, Wade Johnson, to come. I had chosen him to accompany the group because he had been a participant the year before. He was also mature, and his German was so outstanding the Germans thought he was one of them.

Antonio showed the students a film about the vast complexes of the Bayer company to give them an idea of what to expect, and he handed out packages of promotional material, including Miles products such as Alka-Seltzer and One A Day vitamins. In the middle of May, as soon as everything was under control and a few days after the group had taken off for Germany, Antonio and I flew directly to Heraklion, the capital of Crete, where we arrived after dark.

Second Pre-honeymoon – Crete, Greece

The trip to Crete, the birthplace of European civilization, was a lifelong dream come true, a dream that had intensified since my year abroad in Aix-en-Provence and my visit to Athens when cruising the Mediterranean in 1967. To visit Crete together with my Adonis was the ultimate. Crete was where the Minoans built palaces in Knossos and Phaistos, among other locations, between 2800 and 1150 BC.

Elounda Bay Hotel, not far from Agios Nikolaos, on the northeastern coast of Crete, stretched out at the foot of hilly and rugged terrain running down to the azure waters of the Aegean. The spotlights along the meandering path to our bungalow suite gave us a preview of the gardens filled with raspberry-colored bougainvillea, pink oleander at its peak, and clusters of wisteria adorning the white walls of semi-attached bungalows. Entering the bungalow was like stepping into a small fortress. The entrance resembled a Romanesque arch. The facade was of roughly hewn pinkish-brown stone. It was furnished in rustic Greek style. A vase filled with red tropical flowers stood underneath the warm light of a table lamp next to the couch, which was upholstered in handwoven cloth. A multicolored Turkish rug was spread out in the center of the room, and two steps led to the terrace at the edge of the rocky slope to the ocean. Across the waters, the green mountain ranges, which formed bays, were offset by the blue Mediterranean skies. Down below was a private beach of white sand, just right for sunbathing or taking shelter under blue and orange umbrellas.

Not Hitler's Child

At breakfast time, we walked through an enchanting park of flowering bushes and trees and sat on an outdoor terrace overlooking the blue sea, from which a gentle breeze came and caressed our radiant faces. Trellises with clinging roses separated tables from each other and gave us a sense of privacy. In this remote spot, created for lovers, we found once more our very own paradise.

Yet this piece of paradise came at an all-too-hefty price, especially since we had intended to explore the island instead of relaxing at the resort. After a couple of nights, we moved closer to town, where we found charming and easily affordable accommodations.

Antonio was an excellent guide. Though he had spent his research-related honeymoon on the Greek Isles, he had not been to Crete. As a classicist, he was superbly informed about Crete's history, mythology, architecture, and art. We decided to follow Doc's practice in Yucatán, and hired a driver and a car whenever we wanted to explore the island. It's the ideal way to travel when in love. – The gods smiled on us, and the sun was radiant in blue skies day after day. At night, the bright moon looked down on us from the star-studded heavens, and it mesmerized Tonio even more than me.

Nick, our driver, caught on quickly and fulfilled all our wishes. He took us to the more remote beaches whenever we wanted to cool off and swim, and he took naps in his big Mercedes until we returned. He drove through the rugged mountains and past grazing goats and sheep and introduced us to a tavern in a quaint village of four or five stone houses. Close by was a deciduous tree with a huge knotty trunk, more than ten feet in diameter, I am sure. We sat down at the inn's primitive table and drank a glass of raki with the villagers, who nodded a friendly welcome. Their faces were of dark-brown complexion and deeply wrinkled from labors in the field. They appeared to be a strong and proud people. A very old woman with a humped back, wearing a long black dress and a black scarf on her head, sat at a table close to a window, resting. The men sat around smoking long pipes and playing cards, as my grandfather used to. Not speaking any English, they smiled now and then and showed a few yellow-brown teeth when we communicated to them through gestures that we liked their raki. They waved when we said good-bye.

One day, our driver, who spoke some English, pointed out a place for us to eat in another village, where two small, square tables stood on the sidewalk next to the door of a very modest eating place. This reminded me of a spot Doc and I frequented in Yucatán. The table was partially covered by a piece of white cloth. Through the door, we could see the kitchen, where the woman was cooking. The chicken dish and the Cretan wine she served with it tasted wonderful. On another day, Nick drove quite a distance to Matala through a beautiful countryside of olive-tree groves interspersed with orange and lemon trees. He stopped right at the edge of a fisherman's pier, where two fishermen held up two big, freshly caught fish from which to choose before they cleaned and filleted them before our eyes. The cook, who served us a plate of tasty meze as soon as we arrived, stood ready to prepare the fish for us to eat right there at the table, on the bank of the Aegean. A small beach was below, so we could go for a swim as the food was being cooked. After cooling off, we savored the fish with a glass of wine while still in our bathing suits. It was a meal fit for a king.

A special treat was a visit to the mountain village Kritza, where we took pleasure in inspecting folk-art objects, ceramics, and woven fabrics and admired the natives in their traditional costumes in the forenoon, before driving to Vai, on the East Coast, for a swim at Europe's only natural palm beach. I have never seen a palm forest on a white-sand beach as strikingly beautiful and as peaceful as that of Vai. Not a single human being was to be spotted, as far as we could see. Nick insisted we go past the beach at Sitia before he dropped us off at another quaint café, where we had the best zadziki, of which I could have eaten a pound. The yogurt with honey for breakfast, as well as their Cretan goat cheese, cannot be matched anywhere. On the way from Vai to Sitia, directly along the Aegean, masses of raspberry-colored oleander bushes over ten feet high flanked the road. They were as thick and lush as any I have ever come across. The view, with the blue waters in the background, had to be captured. Nick stopped and took a picture of us two lovers, which we inscribed "outside of time and place."

Our long-anticipated visit to Knossos, the former capital of Crete, was an awesome experience. The prehistoric ruins of the imposing Palace of King Minos rest on the hill of Kefalas, near the Kairatos River. According to mythology, Minos was the son of Zeus and Europa. Walking among imposing ruins dating back to 1700 BC was an overwhelming experience. I was amazed at the vestiges of aesthetically striking architecture, the restored lightwell of the upper story of the West Wing, with its strong, wooden, Doric-like columns, and the replicas of frescoes, and even more at the Grand Staircase of the east wing, the Veranda of the Royal Guard. In the throne room, the high-backed gypsum chair of the king and a splendid processional frieze of many life-size figures caught my eye, such as the Cupbearer, representing religious ceremonies, and other well-preserved frescoes of women and dolphins. When looking at the complex architectural plan, with the diversity of wide flights of steps leading from one level to another in the palace, I understood how the comparison to a labyrinth came about.

Antonio and I visited the Herakleion Museum right afterward. It houses ancient objects from Knossos and others discovered at the most important archeological sites in Crete, like Phaistos, the Dictaean Cave ("the birthplace of Zeus"), and others. I was eager to see the objects, which my good friend and professor André Bourde, from Aix-en-Provence, had talked about, and was not disappointed when I spotted a rhyton (libation cup) in the shape of a bull's head, a dainty faience snake goddess, a jumping ivory acrobat, and the fresco of the graceful yet strong priest-king, all from Knossos. I told Antonio that he and the fresco could be brothers. I had always wanted to see the Phaistos Disc, and like Tonio, the paleographer, I marveled at the hieroglyphics imprinted on the plate in the seventeenth century BC. –

We purchased several reproductions of Cretan art objects at the shop of an artist located close to the museum, the most precious of which was a large pottery jar. Pebbles were painted at its foot, jumping dolphins on the body, and spraying bubbles on the top. Tonio also insisted I take home a selection of Greek clothes and a piece of colorful woven cloth for a skirt, and he took me to a furrier where he bargained long and hard over a white mink jacket, which we took after the owner agreed to throw in a dark-brown mink coverlet, which was to replace the white llama-fur spread, by then badly worn, which I had brought back from Cuzco, Peru.

At Nick's suggestion, we went to the plaza in front of a church after Sunday service to join the congregation as they danced in a big circle, showing off their Sunday garments handwoven from homespun yarn of the most vivid colors. After breakfast, he took us via the Lasithi Plateau, covered with a lush green carpet and real windmills and virtually encircled by mountains, to enter the sanctuary, the fabled birthplace of the almighty Zeus, the father of all the Olympian gods. There, in Mount Ida's massive form, between the horns (a symbol of power) of two mountain peaks, lies the Dictaean Cave, which we reached on foot after a twenty-minute climb on a narrow path, where we passed a mule loaded down with sacks of grain.

I will inject at this point a passage from a semi-autobiographical novel which Antonio and I began to coauthor after our return from Crete and which started at Elounda Bay.

From the size of the opening, overgrown with vines and laurel trees, one could not even guess at the huge vortex that lay beyond. As we descended the wooden steps into the half-light, darkness seemed to draw us down. The enveloping strangeness grew with each moist breath we took. Rugged walls glistened on all sides like a ruptured mass of veins and flesh. Mother Earth welcomed us with a clammy chill.

At the bottom of the steps we stopped and craned our necks upward. The opening had become a narrow slit. Mosses and ferns formed a dazzling fringe around its edge. Air escaping from the shaft coiled in white vapors.

After that, the path turned to slippery rock, and before continuing, we lit two candles. In their flickering light, we half walked, half slid to the bottom.

I explained that the large chamber at the base of the cave was an ancient temple of Zeus, known since Minoan times. The small room behind it was called the Nursery. Here, Rhea concealed the infant Zeus from his father Chronos and the young god was suckled by the giant goat, Almathea.

With the candle sputtering before us and our shadows lengthening behind us, we wound our way through the chambers of the cave and ascended into the clear, blue sky of the afternoon.

The descent into the cave, during which we saw the nursery and mantle of Zeus, which can be recognized in the various forms of stalactites that adorn the cave, made me understand why one would want to compare it to the cradle of Bethlehem, the birthplace of Christian civilization. The images of Chronos eating his children, the young successors to the Olympian throne, and of Rhea handing him a wrapped stone to swallow instead of her son, raced through my mind on the way back, and they continued to surface when I was on my way to visit Mutti in Hannover. Tonio flew to the States to meet his children, with whom he was anxious to spend the summer.

Back to Reality – Mutti Moves into a Nursing Home – The "Vultures" Come Out of Hiding

I arrived in Hannover on June 2, in the forenoon, looking forward to seeing Mutti. She had not been well since I last saw her, in the summer of 1984, but we had talked on the phone regularly until I went to Crete. I rang the doorbell many times. When Mutti did not open the door, I went to the good neighbors upstairs to ask if they knew of her whereabouts. They informed me that a couple of days earlier, late in the evening, they heard emergency staff breaking open the door to the apartment to rush Mutti to the hospital in an ambulance. It appeared that she had been lying for several days on the floor of the corridor, where she had fallen or collapsed and broken her pelvis. I was shocked; they let me call my brother from their apartment. My brother was extremely abrupt, refused to give me any details about what happened, and said with great determination, "She is going to die this time." I finally got him to give me the name of the hospital, but when I asked him for the key to Mutti's apartment, he refused and told me to find a place elsewhere.

I left my luggage with the neighbors, who told me they had observed that neither my brother, his wife, nor their three adult daughters seemed to look after Mutti regularly. I was both disgusted and upset. I took a cab to the Henriettenstift, the hospital where Mutti was, and when I walked into Mutti's room, which she shared with another patient, I was taken aback. When I hugged her, she did not seem to recognize me and asked about my husband. I was at a loss for what to do and tried repeatedly to explain who I was and where I came from, until little by little it seemed to dawn on her that I was her daughter. She tried to lift her hand, which I squeezed tightly, and I sighed with great relief when she whispered, "Oh, Christa, it's you." The lady in the other bed said something to the effect that Mutti had eagerly awaited my arrival. When I told the doctor what my brother had said, he shook his head and indicated that I should not give up hope. I asked him if I might look for the keys to my mother's apartment in her purse, and he did not object. I stayed for a couple of hours just holding Mutti's hand and telling her all sorts of things, and I knew that, at least at times, she understood what I was saying. I settled in at the apartment and informed my brother that the doctor had let me have the key. He left no doubt that he would rather I disappear and let Mutti pass on, but I assured him I would do my utmost to get her back on her feet.

It was about a twenty-minute walk from the apartment to the hospital. I walked back and forth twice a day, spending as much time as possible at Mutti's bedside. In no time at all, Mutti's physical strength improved, and she regained her spirits and her sense of humor. The other patients and nurses looked forward to my visits as well, and after a while I entertained them with stories about America and whatever I could pull out of my hat. Occasionally Mutti interrupted, pointing at me, her blue eyes shining with pride: "That's my daughter from America, and I have been there."

I had experienced virtually no contact with my nieces, including the oldest, whom I had treated to a vacation with me in America shortly after I earned my PhD. I was surprised when, a few days after my arrival, I found a note at the apartment door. It was a note from Angela and Heike expressing the wish to see me. I was genuinely pleased, called Angela, who by then was married, and told her I would love to invite her, her husband, her sister Heike, and her boyfriend, if she had one, to a nice restaurant for dinner. Her sister Astrid was not around. They all showed up, we spent a cheerful evening together, and I met with the girls the next day at the apartment to discuss family matters. They were extremely nice, but severely criticized their father. They accused him of heavy drinking, extreme greed, and clever manipulation. When Mutti had to be hospitalized for a couple of weeks in 1984, the first thing he looked for were all of the savings books which Mutti had over the years set up for herself and the children. She used to show them to me on my visits, because she was so proud to have saved so much from her modest pension. I finally understood why on my last visit, she had virtually demanded that my brother hand over my book to me and why she kept complaining that my brother had repeatedly ignored her pleas to return the other books, including her own.

In retrospect, it became clear that the girls were just buttering me up because they wanted something from me – and they succeeded. They were interested in inheriting certain items of furniture and china, and they knew that without a will, everything would be divided equally between the children. Nevertheless, I engaged an attorney and discussed the matter with Mutti, who agreed to sign a will according to which everybody's wish was recognized, or so I thought. After that, I never saw or heard from my nieces again.

My brother and his wife came to the hospital a few times to see what was happening with Mutti. When they saw that she was improving, they told me she needed to go into a "home" but that up to then she had refused to go. I reluctantly agreed, especially since it was clear that neither my brother nor his three daughters, for whom Mutti had again and again given up so much, were inclined to work out a plan to look after her. He kept complaining about Mutti's high telephone bills, which resulted from her constant overseas calls. I personally never discouraged her, because it was the only joy she had at that time in her life. – A year earlier, I had contacted a social worker to look in on Mutti and asked someone from her church to do the same, but obviously they turned out to be unreliable. Mutti, always thinking she could manage on her own, told them after a while she did not need them, and they stayed away.

Getting Mutti's consent to move her into a home was the hardest thing I have ever had to do. She finally agreed when I told her I had found a place with a balcony and flowers close to where she lived and where she used to visit old friends. She even seemed to look forward to it, because it was close to the lake, where she liked to go for walks, and only a couple of minutes to the stop from which she could take the streetcar to the beautiful cemetery, where she loved to visit Papa's grave, sit on a bench in the park, and chat with other visitors.

By the time I had to leave Mutti to go back to the States, via a short stop at Bayer AG, I was much relieved. Mutti was making great progress, and I knew she would adjust to her new home quickly, because she was an optimist and a fighter. However, only a few weeks after my return, I was informed by my brother that thenceforth I could reach Mutti at a home in a completely different part of town. They had not followed through with my arrangements, and had placed her in a facility run by nuns, where she shared a room with another lady. Since my brother was in charge, I was in no position to interfere and resigned myself to calling her as often as possible. She was always happy to hear my voice. Each time I asked how she was, she told me she felt so good she could dance a waltz with me.

In South Bend, I was looking forward to getting to know Antonio's children better. I was anxious to see their little faces when they opened the presents I purchased for them in Hannover's big toy store. Tonio had a swimming pool across from his townhouse, where they kicked and screamed while floating around or hanging on to an inflated swan or dolphin. I began to thoroughly enjoy Liesl and Gustl, and they seemed to take to me quickly.

I spent much time at Tonio's place, though we were discreet around the children in an effort not to overwhelm them with a new relationship in addition to their mother's, who had a live-in partner. When Gustl once told me it initially scared him when Howard moved in, I realized it was best to go slowly. I found what I thought was a reliable babysitter, the daughter of one of my older students. Though we learned from the children that she spent many hours on the phone with friends and though several household items mysteriously disappeared without explanation, Tonio did not feel free to make a fuss. Amy, on the other hand, explained that the children were at times rather rambunctious while Tonio was at work; but as soon as he walked in, they were little angels. I am sure they were not the only little actors in the world. One afternoon, Tonio asked me if I would mind babysitting Liesl, which I did not mind at all. I was in my den and naïvely believed Liesl could safely be left alone for a while, especially since she was playing nicely with her toys on the living-room carpet. Suddenly, I heard a big noise, but Liesl did not cry out. I rushed into the living room, where she was sitting on the floor. The Florida screen had tipped over and been stopped from falling on her by my Knabe piano. But my precious baroque candleholder lay on the carpet, broken into two pieces. When I said, "Oh, my candleholder," Liesl looked at me with her big brown eyes and simply said, "You can goo it." And she was right.

We kept the children busy all summer, going for rides, taking them to a movie or the county fair, where they could not get enough of the wildest rides, or packing the trunk full of swimming gear, floats, tubes, blankets, and a big picnic whenever we took off for the sand dunes on Lake Michigan, our favorite getaway. We went to the Episcopalian church in Bristol on Sundays, although Liesl was too young. She kept sliding around on the benches, keeping us from concentrating. Tonio once let them spend the night in his tent on the lawn bordering the terrace, but was a bit upset the next morning, when he discovered Gustl had broken the glass top of his cocktail table by pounding on it with a hammer. I had fun taking the two shopping, dressing up Liesl, and trying out different hairdos with her long hair, which she refused to have trimmed, not even an inch. Tonio, knowing their tastes best, took care of the cooking, but I gave it a try occasionally. Later, when I knew they especially liked my German eggs (medium boiled), which I dressed up with a Bavarian egg warmer, and the egg pancakes with sugar sprinkled on top, I began to surprise them with my breakfast on Sundays. I fixed that breakfast on the morning the mother and her partner picked them up. It was the weekend before Gustl's school started in Cleveland.

In the fall, I had a normal teaching load of three courses. In addition, my new friend Renate had offered to tutor interested students in German, free of charge. I could not have been more pleased. Her German was impeccable, as was her appearance. She was of an even temperament and had sufficient patience to tutor young adults, since she had children almost the same age. Several interested students began to meet with her on Tuesdays between 11:30 a.m. and 4:00 p.m. – It all started with her asking me to recommend a student who might be interested in tutoring her in English. As it turned out, she befriended a couple of the more mature students to the extent that they developed long-standing friendships. – The students praised her as a teacher and a person, and all of them showed up when Renate and her husband Karl invited my more advanced class to their beautiful home for a slide show about Germany. It gave my students an opportunity not only to get a glimpse of a home filled with artifacts and reminders of German culture, but also, and more importantly, to witness good old German hospitality at its best. Having found a new friend in Renate made it easier for me when, in the middle of September, I received a very short letter from my sister-in-law informing me in a matter-of-fact way that

Mutti had to undergo an urgent mastectomy, due to breast cancer. I received the letter ten days after the operation.

Hosting the Dissident Musicians from the GDR and Romania – Christmas in Florida

For the fall semester, I had agreed to sit on the steering committee of the Institute for German–American Relations in appreciation of their continued financial support of the various programs and activities I organized on our campus, including their commitment to helping promote the concert tour I had begun to orchestrate for the two defectors, Ralf Doering and Peter Grossmann, soon after my return from Bamberg, Germany, in 1984.

You may recall what the chairman of Arts and Sciences told one of my colleagues from the History Department early on during my tenure: "Christa-Maria is a dreamer." My colleague answered, "It's amazing how many of her dreams come true." Well, at that time, I never dreamed that one day I would come close to being an agent for two dissident artists from behind the Iron Curtain, a bass-baritone vocalist and a pianist, both in their early forties, and would arrange a concert tour in America for them. – Already during the summer, while Tonio was tending to his children, I began to plan for the tour in earnest. I pulled out all the stops, contacting every colleague, friend, and acquaintance at colleges and institutions in the East and Midwest who might be inclined to invite these two defectors for a token honorarium. The two did not have to be ashamed of their credentials: Ralf Doering, a bass-baritone, had studied voice at the School of Music in Leipzig. He defected in 1980, when he stayed in West Germany after a performance of Brahms's *German Requiem*, giving up his big villa and a lucrative career at the Leipzig Opera, where he had shared the stage with such great voices as Peter Schreier, Spas Wenkoff, Tomowa-Sintow, and Kiri Te Kanawa. Peter Grossmann, who had studied piano at the Bucharest Music Academy in Romania, had opted not to return to the East after a concert performance in Spain. His aspiration was to be the "best accompanist ever." He had been recognized for his outstanding performances as accompanist at the fifth and sixth International Tchaikovsky Competitions, in Moscow, and was also the winner of the sixth Robert Schumann International Competition for Pianists and Singers, held in Zwickau, East Germany. After numerous phone calls and volumes of correspondence, my efforts resulted in the scheduling of ten concerts between October 4 and October 26, for a total take of a mere $3,000, which may have been enough to pay for two plane tickets. Doering, suddenly and to my dismay, had decided to bring his teenage son, who had defected, to join his father on his journey to the New World, leaving his mother behind the Iron Curtain. Well, can you blame him? Of course, I then had to find accommodations for three instead of two men. My enthusiasm went so far that I encouraged Doering to apply for a teaching position at the School of Music in Bloomington, getting him in touch with Bill Christ, dean of the School of Music, whom I knew very well from sitting with him for years on the Overseas Studies Committee.

In an attempt to be perfect hosts for our visitors and to make it as cost-effective for them as possible, Tonio offered them his townhouse, which we stocked with food prior to picking them up at the Lyric Opera, where we had arranged for them to hear Placido Domingo in Verdi's *Othello* the day of their arrival. – We returned home late, dead tired. They seemed pleased to have a whole house to themselves. Doering determined right away that he and young Silvio – who behaved like a sissy, looked more like a girl than a boy, and had none of the handsomeness of his blond-and-blue-eyed father – wanted the master bedroom. Peter Grossmann was sent to the kids' room. I thought the arrangement a bit strange, because it meant father and teenage son had to share the same full-size bed. I guess it made things cozier for the two, because they seemed to kiss a lot. I am sure the pianist was happy to be in a separate room.

The next two weeks were packed with activities and chauffeuring the musicians around. I was flying high, as was always the case when I was surrounded by music – and America's audiences let them know their melodies could kindle a fire in the land of light and freedom. My university was not disappointed, and I held a party to which all who were invited came, including Gail Carson, a graduate of the New England Conservatory of Music, in Boston, who wrote a glowing review of their performance of Schubert's *Winterreise*. She even wrote about their little gig at my house, where they "delighted the party guests with humorous, playful renditions of Papageno's arias from the Mozart opera." Tonio and I loved it when Grossmann played the piano just for the two of us. He was indeed superb.

It felt good to have given the two defector musicians an opportunity to make their mark in America, after they had done so in Russia, Finland, Spain, France, Egypt, Poland, and the two Germanys. Both Tonio and I gave generously of our time. All their performances were a big hit and richly rewarded, if not with money, then with applause. We took them sightseeing at Lake Michigan and in Chicago, where I lost my purse and a pair of my favorite gold-filigree earrings, which Doc had given me in Yucatán. Before they took off in their rented car to head east, where concerts were scheduled at places including Connecticut College, the University of Rhode Island, and the University of Pittsburgh, I invited my guests and several of my seniors for dinner at a nice restaurant. As we chatted, the tenor bragged about an experience he had while living in his supposedly grandiose villa in East Germany. His whole face lit up when he entertained us with his story about the shortage of coal for heating his mansion. Instead of feeling guilty about robbing the children, he was proud of bribing the man responsible for delivering coal to a day-care facility to bring it to his house instead. I suddenly got very sick, was at the verge of fainting, and excused myself to get some air. I was deeply shocked to hear about his opportunistic behavior and felt myself so taken advantage of that as soon as they were out of the country, I broke off all correspondence, withdrew my support from at least Doering's career in the States, and regretted having spent almost $2,000 of my own money to help him, another opportunist, and his son. The visit ended on an even sourer note when they failed to show up for a concert in the East and missed several appointments with important agents, which I had set up, because they had preferred to go sightseeing. They rudely neglected to inform the parties or me of their whereabouts.

Their discourteous behavior was embarrassing to me, since only a month later, in connection with a meeting of the American Association of Teachers of German, Tonio and I attended a writer's workshop at Connecticut College, where we read from our novel in progress to students and faculty. We were quite pleased by the enthusiastic and positive reaction to our writing, and gladly agreed to join Professors Rita Terras and Marlis Zeller-Cambon, both from Connecticut College, as well as Peter Beicken from the University of Maryland and Lisa Kahn from the University of Texas, in starting a new writers' group. We decided to bring out an annual journal under the title *Literatur-Express*, in which German poems, German short stories, and translations of German poets would be published. All of the board members were German professors, most of whom were actively writing and publishing poems and short stories. My personal interest was fueled by Tonio's deep and ongoing fascination with poetry. He was forever creating new poems or rewriting old ones, and had published several before I did.

Shortly after our return, Mutti's big, heavy bookcase and a few dishes and crystal ware, which, with the help of my friends in Bamberg, I had shipped across the ocean, arrived at Tonio's townhouse. I had asked him for permission to set it up at his place, since I lacked the needed wall space for a big cabinet of carved oak. I was rather upset when the shipment came, because most of the pieces of china and glass, which appeared to have been packed very negligently, were broken. Fortunately, the cabinet, about six feet wide and six feet high, arrived intact, with the exception of a big scratch on one side panel. I was grateful that this family heirloom, in which Mutti stored books, china, silverware, and special treats for us children, had survived the bombs and was in my care to enjoy and treasure thenceforth.

The children were to spend Christmas vacation with their father, and I gladly agreed to Tonio's suggestion that we all spend the holidays with his mother in Florida. He felt it important for the children to see his mother, siblings, and cousins. He wanted to drive south in his newly purchased used Mercedes 190 Diesel, for which he had traded in his little Triumph when the costs of repairing it were simply not worth it. It was like having twin cars. His was champagne and mine was silver.

I felt wonderful, suddenly having two adorable children and a fabulous man to care for, and we played many car games on the way down and back. I even succeeded in helping Liesl gain her independence from her "pinky" baby blanket. She let it fly through the sunroof toward the pink clouds, where I told her it would be caught by the angels baking cookies in the rosy skies. – I retrieved it by pulling it in through the back window, wrapped it as a gift package, and asked her to keep it safe when I handed it to her a couple of years later.

The experience of spending Christmas morning with an American family was new to me. It was exciting to watch the children opening all the gifts and playing with each other, at times wildly, until it was bedtime. The Christmas dinner which Tonio's mother had prepared was traditional, with all the trimmings. She also served wine, though it was not in keeping with her Baptist faith.

I learned more about the family by listening and from what Tonio filled me in on while we drove home. There seemed to be some bitterness between him and his older brother, who, when Tonio's position at Notre Dame was abruptly terminated, had allegedly offered him a job in his advertising agency. Tonio had packed his car and driven down to Florida, where he waited in vain for a couple of weeks at his brother's house. When the brother never brought up the matter of a job, Tonio got into his car and drove back north. I felt sympathetic, because my own brothers had disappointed me repeatedly, to the point that I decided to distance myself. It was obvious that Tonio was content to live far away from Florida, even though his family kept saying he belonged in the South.

Right after New Year's Day, their mother and Howard came to pick up the children. Tonio and I spent our weekends writing our novel. On various occasions, Antonio talked about growing up in Georgia and Florida, and especially how his mother came to get an education. When it was his turn to be introduced into the novel, he rendered the following account, from which I will quote excerpts, because I cannot relate it as well:

Antonio's Story

I come from Boggy Bayou in the Florida Panhandle. It's a backwater off Choctawhatchee Bay, near Bowles, one of many crooked little half-salt-water, half-fresh bayous, like Cinco Bayou, and Gardiner's Bayou, and Rocky Bayou. They used to call it Nigger Bayou, not because of any black people there but because the water was so dark, but they stopped calling it that in the 1960s. The water was that way because of the big slash-pines and sand bluffs with magnolias overhanging the place.

I don't really come from Florida: I grew up there. I was born on Lookout Mountain. No one is quite sure whether it was in Alabama, Georgia or Tennessee. My family was on vacation with relatives, and I was delivered in the car, on the way to the hospital in Chattanooga, somewhere near Rock City. It was a huge, dark-blue, hump-backed kind of car called a Hudson, which stopped being made around 1950.

My family on my father's side came from County Line, Alabama, and my family on my mother's side came from Euteichas, Alabama, though it's no longer there, because they built a huge reservoir during the New Deal; and the courthouse is under water. We moved to Florida after the war, when I was four.

I don't believe in genealogy – neither as a discipline nor as anything you can do anything with – but a cousin of mine who runs a TV repair shop in Valdosta, Cousin Bunyan Votsnitt, compiled a family history several years ago showing that the first Ranson came over to Pennsylvania with William Penn. My mother was half Indian, and my father had some Cherokee Indian blood, too. That I know for a fact, although it was hushed up.

Well, the Indians – Cherokees and Creeks mostly, and some called Redwines – intermarried with the blacks. And no one wanted to admit to having any Negro blood, and still don't. Many of the early settlers were indentured servants or prisoners who moved across the state line from Georgia, and later proceeded across the line to Mississippi or Florida, in various states of domestication and gentrification.

My father's family was farther along in the gentrification process than my mother's, who were dirt-poor. My Mother and Daddy married for love – which in those days meant for looks, so as to have "well-bred" children. They produced seven of us. I was the next to the last, with four brothers and a sister in front of me and a sister behind me. Almost all of them are now on their second or third marriages, drive BMWs, and belong to yacht clubs and terrorize the city editor of the newspaper where they live.

In addition to Cherokee, there was Scotch and English and German in our family, which meant the houses were always immaculate, the green beans were boiled all day long, even children and babies drank coffee and tea, everyone smoked, and great emphasis was placed on family rituals, like the noon-day meal, which we called dinner, never "lunch." Also, Bible reading in a circle before bedtime... and Sunday afternoon drives in the Cadillac.

Mother's family brought a little welcome madness to it all. Her father was a woodcarver and fiddle-maker, and she grew up on Lookout Mountain, having to raise thirteen half-brothers and sisters after her mother, an Indian, or half-Indian, died from the influenza in 1919, and her father married a girl of fifteen.

They were, as I say, dirt-poor. Mother didn't have a pair of shoes until she was sixteen, and the family slept in beds like sardines. She must have been very beautiful, though, rather tall, Mongoloid cheekbones, dark hair and brown eyes. And intelligent, because she got a job taking care of old Mrs. Greencastle, the matriarch of a family with five boys who lived in what was called the White House in Valley Head, straight down the mountain from the Macs.

One day, after doing the dishes, she was sitting on the porch with one of the Greencastle boys, Uncle Jess, and he asked her, "Lilly, what do you want most in the world?"

"An education, Uncle Jess."

"Pray to the Lord, and you shall have it."

She hadn't been to school a day in her life, but she prayed. She had been to a revival at the Baptist church, and she knew how to do that.

The next week, Mrs. Greencastle took a couple of her boys up to Sunday ice-cream churning in Mentone, at the summer place of Mrs. Martha Barrymore, the philanthropist-friend, of the Thorpe railroad family. Mrs. Barrymore started a college on Stone Mountain near Atlanta, so young people we'd now call underprivileged children could go to school on full scholarship, while making furniture.

Mrs. Barrymore wore a pince-nez and had silvery hair, but was a tireless recruiter of Cinderellas, as well as being a fierce enemy of hookworms and podagra. She quickly learned about the mountain girl who wanted an education more than anything else in the world.

"Bring her to me," she said. They brought her. Mother became Mrs. Barrymore's lady's maid and worked her way through school at Barrymore College in about four years, which was amazing. There she met and married my father during the Depression.

So those are my parents. Daddy started a grocery store, and went away to the war in the Pacific. Mother broke eggs in a cake factory in Chattanooga during the war and raised children. When we moved to Florida it was supposed to be a definite step up, and very exciting. For one thing, we hired a maid.

The way it happened was, Daddy had our belongings packed by some cousins of his; and everybody fixed himself a suitcase, and then we all got into the great big Fleetwood, and Daddy drove over to the other side of the tracks. That's where the colored people, as we called them, lived. Daddy honked the horn, turned off the motor and some colored boys came over to his window.

"You got any sisters about fourteen, fifteen, sixteen, who want to live in Florida and be a maid?"

They ran off like a basketball squad and came back with Alatheah, one of their older sisters, about fifteen or sixteen. The deal was done in a moment – only, Alatheah said, "You better ass my granny."

"She not yo' granny," said one of the boys.

We were solemnly led to Granny, a plump colored lady who seemed to be everyone's grandmother, or great-grandmother, or great-great-, and claimed to be a hundred-and-thirty-two years old. Her husband was a mere eighty-nine. They were both sitting on the front porch. Snapping beans.

Anyway, Granny gave Alatheah her blessing, and she got her things together – no clothes or anything much, just a Bible she'd won in church and a cigar box full of hair berets and things – and she hopped into the car with us, and we drove down to Florida.

I grew up in a virtual wilderness, since ours was the only house on Boggy Bayou until the developments came in during the 1960s. Now the sky is darkened with condominiums. Our nearest neighbor was a woman with a hundred cats – Mrs. Early. Her house had no road to it, and she used to get in her motorboat and go to Pensacola for groceries, over forty miles away. Our house, too, fronted on the water – that was the front, not where the driveway was, which was the back. Right through the front yard where we planted mimosas was a footpath and horsepath that everyone said went back to the Indians. In the woods around us were possums and polecats and raccoons and deer and bobcats and – some said – bear. The man who built our house, a Civil War colonel, claimed to have killed a hundred and fifty bear the first year he settled there. The bayou itself had alligators and moccasins, and there were birds all over the place – eagles, chicken hawks, buzzards, flickers, woodpeckers, towhees, brown thrashers, blackbirds, mockingbirds, cardinals, whippoorwills, heron, ducks, grebes, and I don't remember what all. The bayou had shrimp, oysters, mullet, flounders, chofers, needlefish, sting rays, catfish . . . and even porpoises that would swim in from the Gulf of Mexico. As boys we used to scare a school of fish out of the water up onto the beach and catch them with our bare hands, the water was so crammed full. We also used to hitch rides on porpoises. Practically <u>lived</u> in the water. And camping! Sometimes we'd light off for days at a time, always living off the land, eating fish and shrimp and oysters and wild plums and grapes and blackberries and palmetto shoots. It was a boy's paradise.

There's not much more to tell about growing up there. I reckon I was the studious type. I slept in a hammock on the front porch (that is, the back porch) and remember reading books until the light faded and the whippoorwills started whistling. I read everything I could get my hands on. Built up a sizable library of remaindered books with their covers ripped off from Johnny's Newsstand in downtown Bowles. During the day, when I was not in school, I roamed the woods, mostly by myself, or went swimming, or went out in the row boat. It was not unusual for me to walk five or ten miles out into the woods, which I knew like the back of my hand. I learned to go very quickly and quietly, like an Indian, and still take things in. In later life, I noticed I could be traveling down the highway at sixty miles an hour and somehow manage to pick out a clump of air plants growing too far North or a hawk sitting on a dead branch.

I never wanted to grow up, and one of my clearest memories of a definite emotion was a sort of dread that came over me about twelve years old at having to become a teenager like my older brothers. The family encouraged me to stay little, though I shot up fairly quickly in size. When I was sixteen, six-feet-tall, I went away to college pretty much an emotional basket case. I could use big words all right, and I looked and dressed normal enough, but I was really pretty much incredibly immature emotionally.

Most of my thoughts were on one subject and one subject alone. Not sex, which would have been normal: God. Did he exist, and if he did, how could he leave the world in such a mess, and if he didn't, how come everybody kept pretending he did?

The college I went to was a Spanish brick renaissance affair surrounded by great big oak trees practically smothered with Spanish moss.

I burrowed into books and was going to be a biology major until I nearly flunked English in my freshman year; then I was determined to be an English major, until I took German and my professor made fun of my accent. Then I was hell-bent-for-leather to be a German major and go over to Germany on a student exchange. This I managed to do in my third year, not returning except to graduate. A lot of my classmates accused me of never having been to college because I was really only there two years before going away to Heidelberg, and even during those two years I was rather scarce around campus, not dating much or going to parties but studying a lot.

Suffice it to say I received an excellent, if somewhat lengthy and laborious, education. I changed majors, I changed schools, I changed graduate programs and I changed dissertation directors until I came right back to biology, where I had started, and obtained a Ph.D. in paleopathology from Johns Hopkins.

Friends or Foes? – Sexual Harassment on Campus – Summer Abroad Despite Gaddafi and Chernobyl

Antonio and I were very happy. We complemented each other in many ways and derived much enjoyment from our coauthorship. Through the process of writing and as a result of the semi-autographical nature of the novel, we learned much about each other, including our backgrounds, beliefs, and values, and our relationship continued to grow. We shared each other's job-related concerns and accomplishments, felt increasingly drawn toward each other, and spent more time together than apart, a development which did not go unnoticed among our friends and which brought to light some latent hostility – I became the envy of several of my female and even male colleagues, who with grimacing faces remarked how "radiant and young" I looked.

I accepted an invitation for lunch from the chancellor somewhat reluctantly. – I had kept my distance from him ever since that late afternoon a couple of years earlier, when the sky was dark with the blowing snow and he called me at home about an insignificant matter. The next thing I heard was his suggestion, made in a subdued tone of voice, that he would love to come over to my place; he added that we would have to be very discreet about it. I was speechless for a couple of seconds, not knowing how to react, but swiftly, without taking the bait, and acting as though I had not heard him, I changed the topic, excused myself, and hung up. My heart was racing, and I debated whether I should report the incident or perhaps tell his wife, whom I liked, but like other women in similar situations, I remained silent. Though the incident seemed quite harmless on the surface, I have never forgotten his "alluring" male voice and the word *discreet*, which left no doubt about his inappropriate intention. To compound the situation, enough rumors were circulating that his office had many a lurid tale to tell about all the hanky panky going on behind locked doors during or after parties in the university boardroom. Though it was against the law, I observed several professors on the fourth floor, where I had my windowless office, drinking secretly. If you recall, the professor who molested me in my office shortly after I had joined the faculty invaded my office on the fourth floor, on at least two occasions, to make a pass at me while under the influence. The atmosphere at the university was becoming increasingly unpleasant. I felt compelled to keep my office door shut.

Even today, the first day of spring in 2015, I am somewhat reluctant to emphasize the fact that I was sexually harassed on our campus, and I can fully appreciate why women in similar situations are afraid to come forward at the time the harassment takes place. Even some thirty years later, it takes guts to write it down. The anger is still there.

The chancellor felt he had not seen me in quite a while and invited me to lunch. He seemed to be interested in my overseas activities, but was probably much more interested in what I thought about the Prima Donna, who would become our chairman in 1986. By then, I knew the two were actually quite thick, a fact that had surprised me, because there were more than a few rumors floating around that the chancellor regretted having brought the Prima Donna to our campus. They were probably loyal to each other for religious reasons, as they were both Jewish. I did not hide what I thought of the Prima Donna, but was careful to give my criticism the proper intonation. The tone makes the music, if you know what I mean. – I thought this was a good time to tell the chancellor about Tonio and was blown away by his reaction to the news. Though he was impressed by all of Tonio's academic credentials as well as his poetic talent and other skills, I thought I did not hear right when he expressed regret because he had always hoped there would be "a chance for us." I thought it was impertinent and stupid for him, a married man, to advance such a thought, but smiled instead of blasting him. I was also embarrassed because the man was no Adonis. He was a couple of inches taller than I, had little hair left, and most of all excelled in being a weak leader, a criticism I had voiced on several occasions when he asked for my opinion about his annual addresses to the faculty. I don't recall how many drinks he had consumed, but was glad when it was time to go. After those comments, the inappropriate phone call in the winter gained even more significance.

The children spent the spring break with Tonio, which was around the time of Liesl's fifth birthday. Knowing how much she loved playing with My Little Ponies, I went all out in planning a birthday party for her, with a focus on the ponies. The Dainty Maid Bakery baked a big cake with pink and blue My Little Pony decorations. It looked lovely on the My Little Pony tablecloth, with matching napkins, cups, and plates. Liesl's big brown eyes were beaming. She took a deep breath to blow out all of the candles and succeeded the second time. Tonio played games with the youngsters in the kitchen and awarded the prizes we had bought, and I introduced a couple of games from my own childhood. I had no idea that children could be so much fun and that I would miss them – their parents picked them up much too soon.

One evening, after arriving later than usual at my house, Tonio, very upset, told me that his boss, Doloris, had taken him aside and tried her best to convince him that I had cleverly manipulated him into a close relationship by enticing him to coauthor the novel and by being nice to his children, all because I badly wanted a man and a ready-made family. I was somewhat surprised to discover she was really not my friend. I reiterated what I had told him before, that if he ever felt like rekindling his relationship with his ex-wife, if for no other reason than the benefit of his children, I would step aside and deal with it. In discussing the incident with a friend of mine, I learned what had been rumored in other circles, that is, that Doloris herself was simply jealous, because she had nursed a crush on Tonio ever since she took him under her wing, so to speak. I thought the idea rather far-fetched, since she was close to fifteen years my senior. She eventually resigned herself to the fact that she was powerless. We learned to coexist harmoniously until the "Ultra-Suede Queen," as Tonio and his friend the Episcopalian priest at Bristol used to refer to her, ceased being Tonio's boss. She was among the first to be edged out of her job into early retirement by her very German boss, S. S., who by then had tied the knot with the attractive young divorcée, with my friends Renate and Karl as witnesses.

I was disappointed when I was informed that one of my male colleagues, and not I, had been chosen to receive the Lundquist Fellowship, and I was even more disappointed when my salary increases were not what I had been led to believe, that is, at least a $1,000 extra annually for my rank of full professorship, especially since I continued to receive excellent student evaluations and was active in service and scholarship as well. By then, I had also been relieved of my chairmanship of the International Studies Committee and my membership on the Overseas Studies Committee, since I was absent more frequently as a result of my other international commitments and since I would take another sabbatical in the fall. I continued to serve on the Screening Committee for the Hamburg, Germany, program, which was important to me, since I liked to refer my Bayer students, as well as those who had earned a scholarship for the summer seminars in the GDR, to study for a year in Hamburg directly after they were finished in the GDR or were free to leave their job at Bayer.

Recruiting for the summer-abroad programs always took hours of time during the semester. Frequently, students who had committed themselves would unexpectedly cancel just around spring break, which necessitated my calling most of the campuses in the Midwest to drum up replacements. To keep the program going, it was important to fill the spots with the best possible students. At times, I spent the entire spring break recruiting, sometimes while sick in bed with the flu or bronchitis. It never again got as bad as in the spring of 1986, when the terrorist activities, with Gaddafi as the leader, were so threatening that many parents were afraid to send their youngsters abroad. I tried to assure them that though I could never guarantee a plane would not crash, even without terrorist involvement, I could also not guarantee that their son or daughter would not run in front of a car, that a train or bus they were on would not get in an accident, or that they would not get pregnant. To compound the problem, on April 26, the Chernobyl nuclear disaster occurred, killing those nearby and damaging food and crops worldwide. In the summer of 1986, over 50% of all programs abroad were cancelled nationwide. I finally went with seventeen brave students when the University of Michigan–Dearborn had heard of our program and sent four good participants. Four days before our departure, I attended an emergency meeting of all overseas directors called by the dean of Overseas Studies in Bloomington.

I took a deep breath when all eighteen of us boarded Iceland Air to fly across the big pond. – That year, I had been assured the trip from Berlin through East Germany would not be altered, but even though we paid for the journey up front in hard currency, we could never be 100% sure.

The Berlin and GDR portion of the program went off without a major hitch. The big bonus that summer in Berlin was the noticeable absence of tourists, for which we had Gaddafi to thank. It was in East Berlin, as I was walking with the students on the grand boulevard Unter den Linden, that I learned who Bobby Knight was. A couple of German students approached my students, who wore IU sweatshirts, to ask them about the basketball hero. Since I was not on the main campus and not at all interested in sports, I had no idea who he was. My students refused to believe I had not heard of the famous, or infamous, basketball coach.

That summer, fortunately, the GDR program would definitely take us south to Erfurt by way of Weimar, Buchenwald, and Dresden. As you will remember, I had visited those cities during my first visit to the GDR, in 1977. Our accommodations were not exactly first-class, and I was somewhat dismayed because, on a couple of nights, I had to share a very primitively furnished room, as well as shower spaces without curtains, with students. I wondered what those colleagues who accused me of using the program to get a paid visit to Germany would have said had they seen me at this place in the midst of these at times unruly young adults. I really had to control myself one day when, as I looked down into the courtyard of a second-rate youth hostel, I saw something resembling a huge mouse running toward a pile of garbage; the innkeeper explained that it was a rat. It was the first time I had seen a rat with my own eyes. Can you imagine what the reaction of the students would have been had I told them? The food menus included more vegetables this year as a result of the Chernobyl fallout. We were served white asparagus, which at that time was a rare treat in the GDR. I pointed out to the students that it might be risky to eat it, but we all enjoyed the delicacy.

It was also quite difficult for me, as a native of Germany, to deal with my students' reactions to our visit to the concentration camp in Buchenwald, which I had dreaded. I encouraged the students to vent their feelings afterward on the bus ride to Erfurt, when I asked each one of them to sit and talk to me. I was also pleased that another of my superior students, Sally Detlef, was able to come along, because I knew that she, like all the others before her, would not only benefit enormously from the experience, but would also set a good example for the rest of the group, once I left them in the care of the CDC in Radolfzell, on Lake Constance.

After the usual consultations with the director and staff, I hopped on the train to Bamberg to visit the Segebrechts for a few days. On the train, I read and reread the wonderful letters Tonio had sent me. They bore a distant similarity to Doc's letters, in that Tonio also injected quotes from poetry in English or German and on occasion switched over to German for a whole page. He conveyed how good he felt about us and how much he loved me, and I could hardly wait until he arrived at the Segebrechts on the following Saturday. He arrived soaking wet from a downpour. He had neglected to bring along an umbrella.

Third Pre-honeymoon – Italy

After having been hosted royally by my good friends, and after giving Antonio a quick introduction to my favorite baroque town, on Monday morning we boarded the early train to Italy, the land that for centuries has inspired the writers, painters, and composers who have set foot on her soil. We arrived in Venice, the seaport city on the Adriatic, which occupies one of the most remarkable sites in the world. Venice is like an island within a lagoon. It is linked with the mainland by a road and a rail causeway a couple of miles long.

Arriving by train in Venice is not your usual experience. It's an incredible feeling to step outside the Santa Lucia train station and see this magnetizing city as it rises out of the waters of the lagoon, enveloped by a bright blue sky and a soothingly quiet atmosphere and devoid of irritating traffic noise, fumes from cars, and this year, masses of tourists. I fell in love with Venetia at first sight and followed my Adonis, who had taken charge, onto the waterbus across the street from the station as though I were in a trance. The vaporetto transported us swiftly, passed gondolas and other water taxis, and provided us at the same time with a glorious overview of Venice's main architectural styles, from Byzantine and Gothic to Renaissance and late Renaissance. We passed long facades of historic places, such as residences, palaces (which are now hotels), churches, museums, public buildings, etc., before arriving at our *albergo*. The hotel was a brief walk from the launch and St. Mark's Square and was tastefully decorated in Venetian style. The friendly reception at the hotel left no doubt that our stay would be pleasant.

I loved traveling with Tonio, because instead of leading I could just follow. As a classicist, he was so well versed in Italian art and architecture, in Roman history and antiquity in general, that I was constantly amazed at his knowledge and ability to share it. We were once again fortunate to have perfect weather. The frequent rides on the Grand Canal, which divides the city into two parts, turned quickly into welcome occasions for sightseeing. By seeing the same scenes again and again, you get to know them so well you will never forget them. There was the Palazzo Nani Mocenigo, with its fifteenth-century Venetian Gothic architecture, the imposing Santa Maria della Salute (one of the so-called plague churches), and the skyline of the island of Giudecca, which features the magnificent sixteenth-century church San Giorgio Maggiore. It sits on its own island across the Canal de San Marco. From the top of its campanile, we had a superb view of Venice and its sixteenth-century courtyards.

Antonio knew how to find the most idyllic and romantic restaurants, and he studied the menus outside for the best-tasting antipasti, entrées, and wines. Having been to Venice previously, he insisted on our having a double espresso on St. Mark's Square the very first night. We sat at a table in front of one of the exclusive cafés that are part of the arched colonnade of shops, offices, and restaurants. We listened to violins playing sweet melodies from waltzes and operettas, and gazed exalted at the brilliantly floodlit Byzantine basilica of St. Mark, with its multiple ornate domes. The domineering campanile of St. Mark, Venice's patron saint, stands next to it. It is a square shaft of red brick, a popular spot around which hundreds of pigeons gather during the day to be fed by the tourists, most of whom want a snapshot with the birds to take home as a souvenir. We asked a vacationer to take a picture of us with the legendary Bridge of Sighs in the background and a gondola passing underneath. We enjoyed finding our way through the maze of narrow streets that lend Venice her singular charm.

Antonio made sure we spent extra time at the magnificent Doge's Palace to admire Venetian Gothic architecture in its prime and to view paintings by the great Italian masters. We marveled at the interior of St. Mark's Basilica, which used to be the doge's private church, and were overwhelmed by the richness of material, mosaic being the domineering decoration of the church. It reminded me vaguely of the mosques in Spain. We stood in awe at the Pala d'Oro, the retable of the high altar, where St. Mark's body lies. It is truly a goldsmith and jeweler's work of genius. We knew we would be back to spend more time at Venice's museums, the Accademia Art Gallery, and the Peggy Guggenheim Collection; and one afternoon we opted to check out the beach at the Lido, a fashionable seaport resort on an island southeast of Venice, and go for a swim. I was curious to see it, because I had read Thomas Mann's "Death in Venice" and wondered about the beach where the main character, Aschenbach, sat toward the end of his life, fascinated by young Tadzio. However, since I had been to the beaches in Florida, the Gulf of Mexico, the Copa Cabana, and others, the beach at the Lido did not impress me.

We had to cross the beautiful Ponte Rialto – the big bridge over the Grand Canal that connects the old Rialto of Venice with the island of San Marco – several times. It is also the main traffic route across the Grand Canal. Rialto was the ancient business quarter. One big arch supports two rows of attractive shops, facing the center, and two outer walkways. The view from the bridge over the Grand Canal is inspiring. One can easily understand why it is one of the many choice locations for artists. They sit or stand behind the balustrade, their easels holding a canvas or drawing paper, to apply their personal touch with brush or pencil while concentrating on capturing the canal, with the gondolas tied up alongside colorful facades of houses.

Tonio and I were fascinated by the many different masks popular at carnival time. We chose from among many moons, suns, stars, and jesters and acquired three or four good reproductions of those worn by the seventeenth-century troupes of Italian actors who performed commedia dell'arte. We then hopped on the vaporetto for our last stop, at another island, Murano, one of Venice's more than one hundred isles. The island is about one mile north of Venice and has been known since the thirteenth century as the center of glassmaking.

The island seemed almost deserted as we looked at the marvelous displays of the many artisan shops, all in one line and separated from the canal by a walkway. The visit was relaxing, and it was exciting to see the great variety of aesthetically refined pieces of glass, sculpted or blown. We had a chance to observe a glassmaker at work in his shop and realized what an extraordinary talent is involved in creating such exquisite pieces of glass art. I found the pieces in the Amanti Glass Gallery particularly inspiring, and would have happily carried home their Don Quichotte figurine or the pair Pantalone and Colombina, because they perfectly complemented the masks. I would not have minded taking home a dazzling chandelier of Venetian glass either, but was much pleased with two beautiful necklaces, one of octagonal blue and white crystal beads and another of white and pink glass blossoms, which Tonio wanted me to have. We found several cute glass animals for the children to put on the shelf in their room. – On the way to the hotel, we strolled once more across St. Mark's Square. We thought we should have counted the winged lions, symbols of St. Mark and the Republic of Venice, which we saw at so many places – above entrances to piazzas and on the facades of houses and towers – but we postponed it until our next visit.

We went to Florence via Ravenna because Antonio had read that it contains a wealth of early Christian art. Though the town itself lacks the romantic flavor of Venice and seems rather colorless, a look inside the churches reveals another dimension. Two sites in particular made the detour worthwhile, that is, San Apollinare in Classe (sixth century) and even more so the octagonal San Vitale (consecrated in 547 AD), in which the entire apse of the basilica is covered with Byzantine mosaics. The mosaics of the choir display a splendor of coloring and the magnificent garments of Emperor Justinian and Empress Theodora. They are remarkably effective, as are the marble mosaic pavements in some of the buildings. I felt uplifted by the light-blue and predominantly vivid colors of the mosaics covering all walls and the cupola in the mausoleum of Emperor Honorius's sister Galla Placidia (fifth century). The motifs depict the victory of life over death. We were both so enamored of the grayish-blue marble bowl of water with two doves sitting on the rim, one turning its head and the other drinking water, that we carried home a print of it. We stopped at the tombs of Theodoric and Dante Alighieri shortly before continuing our odyssey to Florence.

We arrived in Florence before daylight, to be overwhelmed by the marvelous architecture that awakens the senses at each turn and stands in stark contrast to the more austere architecture we had left behind in Ravenna. There are simply no superlatives that can fittingly describe Florence, the birthplace of the Renaissance. The world knows that the Italian province of Tuscany boasts more historical monuments than any other region in the world and that the most dazzling are in Florence. One could devote a lifetime to seeing and learning all about her many art and architectural treasures. How could one choose in a mere four days? Tonio had thought it all through before he took off to meet me. In a letter he sent to me in Radolfzell, he expressed what we must see in Florence:

We must be sure to see so many places in Florence – Orsanmichele, the Uffizi (one whole day), the Pitti Palace (half a day), Santa Croce, San Spirito, the Bargello (3 hours), Santissima Trinita, Santa Maria Novella, the Accademia, the University, the Musee Buonarrotti (early Michelangelos) and Ognisanti. It would also be nice to take an excursion (by bus or taxi) to the Tuscan countryside or to Siena. Siena is more beautiful than Florence. It poured all its magnificence into the Duomo, which the Florentines copied. Oh yes, I understand there are 200 shoe stores in Florence, something which should make your little itsy-bitsy heart leap. But the trick to seeing Florence is to arrange your schedule around the museum hours. You can shop after 5. And you can eat late, late, late.

We found another pleasant hotel not far from the Santa Maria Novella train station, where we arrived; and we visited Florence's main Dominican church right after an early breakfast the next morning. Santa Maria Novella was established in 1246 and was the first big church built in the new Italian Gothic style. Inside, it is very spacious, and I recall being moved by Brunelleschi's *Crucifix*. The church does not compete, however, with Santa Croce, headquarters of the rival Franciscan order, when it comes to the wealth of Trecento (fourteenth-century Italian) frescoes by Giotto, which we admired in two chapels and at Michelangelo's tomb. His nephew and heir, Leonardo Buonarotti, secretly moved his coffin and body to Florence, away from Rome, where the Pope had wanted him.

None of the other churches in Florence can rival the duomo (cathedral) of Santa Maria del Fiore (St. Mary of the Flower), on the Piazza del Duoma. The church's enormous ribbed dome was completed in the early fifteenth century, almost 150 years after it was begun in 1296. It was designed by the famous architect Filippo Brunelleschi and constructed entirely without centering. It is slightly larger even than the dome at St. Peter's in Rome.

As the great landmark of Florence, the dome, which is said to hold up to twenty thousand people, can be seen from miles away. I was struck by the peculiar striped appearance of the majestic structure, which is due to the decorative use of bands of white and gray-green marble, which was typical of Florence from the thirteenth to the fifteenth centuries and is attributed to Giotto, the renowned painter, sculptor, and architect. The almost three-hundred-foot-tall, rectangular-shaped bell tower next to the dome, also attributed to Giotto, is equally striking. It is covered with red, green, and white marble, and stands in contrast to the octagonal Romanesque baptistery of San Giovanni, located across the square from the dome and bell tower. The baptistery, which served as the cathedral until 1128, is much older than the del Fiore, which explains why its outer walls are decorated with mosaics.

It should come as no surprise that the great sculptor, painter, and poet Michelangelo, who lived in Florence during that period, was one of the artists who, working for the Medicis, decorated the cathedral. Because I had nursed a special interest in sculpture in the round ever since I became fascinated with it in Athens, I could not wait to see Michelangelo's *Florentine Pietà*, which he sculpted to grace his own tomb and smashed in a moment of impatience after having worked on it up to the time of his death. It now stands in the duomo. His student tried to repair and finish it, but the left leg of Christ is missing and his left arm is badly damaged. If I had trouble tearing myself away from that overwhelming sculpture, it was perhaps even more difficult for me to desert his strong and dynamic *David* in the Galleria dell'Accademia. I kept thinking about the *Apollo* in the Louvre and marveled at the gifts of these artists, who chiseled from blocks of marble masterpieces that would be revered eternally by mankind.

Fortunately, we did not live too far from the Piazza della Signoria to see the Uffizi Palace, which was used by the Medici government officials and now displays perhaps the greatest art collection in all of Europe. Every great Italian painter is displayed, but many other painters from Europe can be seen next to invaluable sculptures, drawings, etc. Here we saw the *Ognissanti Madonna* by Giotto di Bondone (1267–1337), the panel of *Madonna Enthroned* by Cimabue (1240–1302), and the panel of Simone Martini's *Annunciation* (1333). I had seen all of them in art books, but how awe-inspiring it was to see the originals.

We walked across the Ponte Vecchio (old bridge), which dates back to the Middle Ages. It spans the Arno at the point where the Uffizi runs down to the river and takes you to the Pitti Palace, on the other side. The bridge reminded me of the Rialto, in Venice. It too has many shops along its lower level, mostly selling artistic jewelry. I felt it lacked the charm of the Rialto, due to the upper level of apartment-like housing. – The Pitti Palace is the largest palace in Florence. It was started by a rival of the Medicis in the 1400s but taken over by the Medicis not long afterward. We looked at works by Raphael, Giorgione, and others and were curious about the Boboli Gardens, which slope steeply up the hillside. They consist of many parks with stone statuary and fountains and can be reached from the palace, because they were the Medici grand duke's old backyard and are considered to be among the largest and most splendid of Italian formal gardens. Had we had more time, we could have appreciated them more, because they are ideally located in the center of the city, providing a quick getaway from the often annoying noise of thousands of Vespas buzzing through the streets. Fortunately, the historic center is off-limits for parking.

Tonio made sure we stopped at the National Bargello Museum, built in 1255, to see Bellini's work. I'll never forget Ammannati's sensuous sculpture *Leda with Swan*, which reveals Michelangelo's influence, or the playful sculpture of *Bacchus* by Michelangelo himself. We saw the early works of Michelangelo at the Museo de Buonarotti, but unfortunately, we had no time to go for a ride into the Tuscan countryside and see the great dome in Sienna. I did have a chance to shop for a pair of shoes, but had to skip many churches and museums because we did not want to cut short our visit to Rome. We also had to miss an opera performance at the Teatro Verdi. While sipping a glass of Chianti with our tasty pasta dish outside a restaurant opposite the Teatro, we dreamed about returning some spring for the Maggio Musicale, when operas by Verdi and Wagner were said to dominate the repertoire.

We were grateful to have a window seat and a nice compartment on the train to Rome, and we thoroughly enjoyed passing through the lovely countryside. On the hillsides, groves of olive trees alternated with rows of grape vines or mulberry trees, and pines and cypresses lent the landscape its distinctly Italian beauty, which had inspired many a poet and painter.

The Hotel Raphael, where the cab let us out after our arrival in Rome, was an artist's dream as well. Cascades of ivy covered its outer walls, and the interior, with its objets d'art, gilded baroque cabinetry, Oriental rugs, antiques, and oil paintings, all reflecting fifteenth-century decor, lent the foyer a sophisticated ambiance so inviting that one could be content just to admire the art right there. It also included authentic ceramics and a Pablo Picasso original. On top of the seventy-room hotel was a rooftop garden café, from which we could see the Pantheon and the Cloisters of Bramante in the distance. The Parliament buildings, the Piazza Navona, and the Vatican were close by as well. – We felt like we had moved into a palace, as our room was tastefully decorated in precious antiques, and we decided to treat ourselves to a very special dinner on our first night together in the Eternal City. An inviting fire was burning gently in the fireplace as we were seated in the elegant restaurant of the hotel, where soft music played in the background. Tonio ordered an assortment of culinary delights à la carte, starting out with a most tender carpaccio and a red Châteauneuf-du-Pape. We ended the evening with a double espresso in the rooftop garden café, gazing down on the intoxicating, floodlit panorama of Renaissance Rome. During the night, we dreamed about this magnificent city, which was once the capital of the Roman Empire. It is now the capital of Italy, where the successor of St. Peter, the Pope, resides. We were ready to explore Rome early the next morning.

Though badly crumbled, the ruins of Titus's Coliseum, or amphitheater, which in the first century AD seated close to ninety thousand spectators, has enough Doric, Ionic, and Corinthian columns still standing to bear witness to its once magnificent composition. But the enormity of its size and function brought back the horror stories we were told as children by our religion teachers. When I closed my eyes, I envisioned brutal scenes of gladiators fighting each other, lions tearing apart the victims thrown into the arena, and the raging of fierce sea battles. When we later visited the catacombs outside the city and saw miles of fifth-century underground galleries with excavations in their sides for tombs or niches, in which humans hid or bones were piled up, the cruelties suffered by persecuted Christians and martyrs came to life for us with a new vividness. Being raised Catholic, I was perhaps even more sympathetic to their fate. While I found the little chapels and baptismals built underground heart-wrenching, I was stunned to see the size of the basilica in one of the catacombs. We could still see fine-looking paintings from the fourth century in the Catacombs of St. Sebastian. It was interesting to learn that the Jews too buried their dead there. I was thinking back to the time when we Germans had to celebrate Mass in secret to avoid being persecuted by the Nazis.

A more cheerful life was visualized in the Roman and Imperial fora, near the Arch of Constantine, which we admired from the Farnese Gardens above. We looked at a print to better imagine what a lively place it must have been when Romans shopped, assembled for public meetings, held tribunals, or discussed political developments. The Forum is badly ruined, in contrast to the imposing engineering marvel that is the Pantheon, temple of all gods, which was built by Agrippa between 27 BC and 14 AD but rebuilt by Hadrian around 126 AD. It is now the Church of Santa Maria della Rotonda and still a place of worship. Though it stands in a rather somber-looking neighborhood, once I stepped inside, it was simply awesome to stand and look up to the "eye," a wide opening to the sky in the top of the enormous dome, about 140 feet above the floor. It is the only source of light.

Antonio and I were hoping to get a view of the Pope officiating. Thus, on Sunday morning we walked down the Piazza San Pietro and looked in amazement toward the grandiose St. Peter's Basilica, the largest church in the world, created by such great sculptors, painters, and architects as Bramante, Michelangelo, Raphael, and Bernini. A portion of the square was fenced in for visitors attending Mass, and we could see only Jean Paul II's head from where we stood. It was nevertheless a momentous occasion for both of us, because I, being raised Catholic, and Tonio, a converted Episcopalian, knew the liturgy by heart and felt close as we bowed our heads in prayer to be blessed by the Holy Father on St. Peter's Square.

Antonio had called his friend Father M., the head of the Vatican Library, whom we were scheduled to meet after Mass. We walked almost reverently past the Swiss

Guards, who were dressed in their colorful uniforms designed by Michelangelo, and felt honored to be received with a warm welcome by Tonio's friend. He showed us into the library, pointed out several rare editions, especially to Tonio, and led us through a side door into the Sistine Chapel. It was a special privilege, because the ceiling was in the process of being restored in bright, living colors. Though some of Michelangelo's incredible frescoes were partially behind scaffolding, we were stunned by the intensity and power of the paintings of the Biblical stories, such as *The Creation*, *The Garden of Eden*, and *Noah and the Flood*. In the center is *The Creation of Adam*, and well above the altar is the enormous fresco of *The Final Judgment*. We were so overwhelmed by the great sculptor's work that, when leaving, we tried to clear our minds by walking through Bernini's Colonnade outside St. Peter's before going inside. This colonnade is referred to as "the arms of the Church embracing the world." I was stirred to sadness by Michelangelo's *Pietà*, which was protected by bulletproof glass. We never ceased to wonder at the treasures in this colossal house of God, and lingered in front of Bernini's magnificent black-and-gold baroque altar canopy, underneath which rests the tomb of St. Peter, the first pope. We walked over to Bernini's bronze chair of St. Peter and ended the visit by taking the elevator up to the dome for an unparalleled view of Rome. Up there, we felt close to heaven and to each other. As we stood, Tonio with his arm around me, we let a tourist take a photo of us with the forest of Roman domes in the background.

Filled with so many new impressions and a little tired, we located a table at a café on the Piazza Navona, where we sipped an iced coffee while being pleasantly refreshed by watching the splashing waters of another Bernini masterpiece, the monumental *Fountain of the Four Rivers*, with the Obelisk of Domitian in the center and the gigantic allegorical figures representing major rivers of the four continents. Tonio suggested we follow up with a stop at the sculptor's imposing *Triton Fountain* in the Piazza Barberini, in front of the *Fountain of Neptune*. The entire dramatic composition of the larger-than-life statues, the rocks, and the palace is itself a masterpiece of sculpture and architecture. One can easily understand how it would stimulate, among others, the great filmmaker Fellini, who focused on it in his *La Dolce Vita*. When you are next to it, the roar of the fountain makes you feel close to the sea.

We spent a forenoon in the Vatican Museum, not nearly enough time to do justice to the impressive collection of the great masters. Next, we looked down on the formal and empty Vatican gardens. No pope or clergyman wandered around reading his breviary or saying his rosary. There was more life in the vicinity of the ingenious *Fontana della Barcaccia* (Fountain of the Ugly Boat), spouting water at the bottom of Francesco De Sanctis's (1723–1726) Spanish Steps. I took my time when we climbed the twelve flights of steps of varying width up to the Piazza Trinità dei Monti, because how often does one get a chance to climb "the most romantic stairway in the world"? A perfect place for weddings, with the scenic Franciscan church Trinità dei Monti at the end of the ascent. The view from the piazza down on the palace of Via delle Carrozze, the church San Carlo al Corso, with the highest dome in Rome, and St. Peter's made the climb well worth the time. After making the ascent, one is not too far from the Piazza del Popolo and the Villa Borghese gardens, where the Romans go walking or take their children to play. – We did not stay long; instead, we found a romantic spot for our farewell dinner, and at bedtime, as he had done many times before, Tonio quizzed me about all we had seen and filled me in on the succession of emperors, whose names and dates he could recite from memory. It was hard to believe we were in the city where Julius Caesar, the great general and consul, reigned and that we had been on the Campo de' Fiori, where the Romans purchase their flowers today – and where centuries ago, just around the corner, Caesar was assassinated by Brutus.

The morning of our departure, we stopped at the big, circular Mausoleum of Augustus, not far from Italy's other big river, the Tiber, where we stood and looked through the glass that encases the grave of the first Roman emperor. We bade farewell to Bernini in the Basilica of Santa Maria Maggiore, where his tomb rests in the company of many other popes, and concluded our sojourn in Rome with a visit to Michelangelo's sculpture *Moses*, at St. Peter in Chains. Michelangelo was so impressed with his own creation that when finished, he called out, "Why won't you speak?"

I'll let Antonio sum up our trip by sharing some excerpts from a letter he wrote while crossing the Atlantic on the flight home:

What an absolutely marvelous two weeks we spent together! Time flew, and one barely even realized it was over when it came time to say good-bye in the Hannover airport. The triumphal progress through Italy could not have been planned better to take one to the heart of Italy. I will always recommend going to Italy straight after Germany – far better than from France or any other country – because one can best appreciate the contrasts that way – upright and laid-back, austere and luxurious, misty forests and sun-kissed landscapes. . . . We had a vacation jammed with new impressions and relatively free of any unpleasantness (I can only think of the noise in Rome and necessity of keeping one eye on the traffic always – we might have seen twice as much otherwise).

Thank you, honey pie, for being you – generous and loving and always game for the next thing. Much love, T.

Tonio had decided to fly back to the States from Hannover, where he had agreed to visit Mutti with me. I was glad to see that Mutti appeared to feel right at home in her new surroundings and apparently liked the lady with whom she shared a large, pleasant room. I noticed that Mutti's mind was wandering; she sporadically asked me who Tonio was, even though I had introduced him as my boyfriend. Whenever she asked, she looked first at me with her big, blue, questioning eyes and then at Tonio, a couple of heads taller than Mutti, who was suffering from osteoporosis. Tonio and I explained who he was again and again, but she kept on asking even as we sat at my old music teacher Marianne's coffee table. Marianne was completely taken by Tonio and could not get over my having found such a wonderful man, who was charming and ever so polite and caring vis-à-vis Mutti. After having said good-bye to Tonio, I stayed at a nearby hotel for a few days longer, and visited Mutti every day until it was time for me to take a train to Cologne, where I had scheduled meetings with Mrs. Hummerich of the CDG, the new Personnel director Mr. Rehbach, Professor Dr. Grünewald, and his successor, the new CEO of Bayer AG, Mr. Strenger. Mr. Fisher, also from Personnel, accompanied me to Mr. Strenger's office, because I had to pass through security to get to the top floor of the big Bayer building. Mr. Strenger greeted me in his well-lit and impressively big office. A large abstract painting by a contemporary artist covered one of the walls. Mr. Conrad, Professor Grünewald's former assistant, was present as well; and Mr. Strenger and I had a very lively and productive exchange of ideas. He assured me of Bayer's continued support, and when he encouraged me to feel free to ask for anything I wished, I mentioned that we were searching for subsidies to fund the first issue of *Literatur-Express*. Although he appeared to see no problem with my request, he suggested I contact the Miles Foundation in Elkhart, which he felt could do more for us. I felt wonderfully optimistic when we shook hands and said good-bye.

When I told Tonio about the visit, he was impressed, and he assured me that many at Bayer and Miles would be envious of the privilege being granted to me. Unfortunately, since Lem Beardsley was in charge of the Miles Foundation, and he and the board had little interest in helping us, I finally gave up trying.

I returned home on June 29, just in time to teach a course in the second summer session, which I had signed up for to boost my low income. I had asked one of my colleagues from St. Mary's to teach the first-session course, G101, and could hardly believe how poorly the group had been prepared. Finally, I got some feedback as to what had happened. My colleague and friend had put forth very little effort. Almost all of the students had earned an A, because he had allowed them to use the book when taking tests. I was furious and vowed never to let him teach for me again. After I had a similar experience with a colleague from Notre Dame, I stopped asking either of them.

Trials and Tribulations with the Ex, Stepchildren, and Other Adults – Engagement and Commitments

The children were already at Tonio's place when I arrived; but they spent more and more time at my house, where I took care of them while Tonio was at work. I prepared my guest room for them to sleep in whenever they spent the night. I taught a beginners' course twice a week in the evening and did not get home until 9:30 p.m. Tonio and I shared kitchen chores, depending on our schedules, and since I had Shirley in charge of cleaning, it all worked out rather well. I was curious to find out how well I could handle children, and was pleasantly surprised that we got along so well I felt like I belonged to a real family. I learned that the children were virtually raised by babysitters and, judging from their stories, that their mother slept until noon, or longer on weekends, leaving the hungry children to search the refrigerator for anything edible, typically uncooked hot dogs. My heart went out to them. I felt even sorrier for them when Liesl told me that when her mother's partner snored too loudly, she would come into the children's bedroom, take Liesl out of her bed, put her on the floor, and sleep in it herself. I could not understand how any mother could do that to her child. I saw to it that we rarely left the children with a babysitter and also found several nice children in the neighborhood for them to play with. We enjoyed playing croquet and other ball games with them in the backyard, and Gustl loved to climb the big maple tree via a rope ladder which I had bought for them. Liesl had a very hard time mastering the skill of climbing the tree and shed many tears in the process. Gustl had a special branch to sit on and enjoyed hiding in the tree or seeking refuge there when pouting.

As usual, the summer went by much too quickly. Tonio's ex-wife had complained about not being able to find a vacant hotel in which to spend the night when she came to pick up the children. Though her mother lived in South Bend, she had had a falling out with her and did not want her to know when she would be in town. Strangely enough, the grandmother never once tried to get in touch with the children. Though Tonio very much disliked his ex, I tried to convince him that in the interest of the children, it would be best for him to keep the lines of communication open, and that this time he should offer her and her husband the option of spending the night in his townhouse. He finally gave in, but warned me that in the end I would probably regret it.

Before the children were picked up at the end of the summer, I always took care to wash, iron, and neatly pack all of their clothes, including T-shirts, because I was shocked when I saw how messily their belongings were packed when they arrived. All of their clothing was carelessly packed and wrinkled, as though it had just come out of the dryer. It looked as neglected as the children themselves. I was embarrassed when some of my friends commented on it. – That summer, Tonio and I had gone all out and planned a farewell garden party for the kiddies. They wore the new outfits we brought home from Italy. Liesl looked adorable in her pink dress from Florence, with a pink flower in her hair, which was gathered in the back, and Gustl was proud of the new khaki shorts and the short white-and-orange shirt, also from Florence. They both had much fun decorating the yard with lanterns from Germany, setting up tables and a tape player, and putting a string over a big branch of the maple tree from which to dangle hot dogs, which the children had to bite off or into without the use of their hands. Tonio had borrowed a video camera and busily photographed the entire event. Liesl was so elated that she jumped up at one point, calling out to Tonio, "Papa, I love you." Whenever we watched that video, we anticipated Liesl's declaration of love.

All the kids had a ball, ate lots of hot dogs, cake, and ice cream, and showed off their prizes to their parents, and there was much screaming, and also crying, because Liesl was a poor loser when it came to playing musical chairs. Suddenly, without having made an announcement that they would come to the party, Tonio's ex and her husband, Howard, walked into the yard and greeted us distantly. I was surprised that the children, instead of running happily into their mother's arms, merely walked over and said something like "hi, Mom." She sat down, and without being asked, Howard, a homely man who was overweight, had red hair, was almost bald, and had a very squeaky voice, got involved in playing with the children to the extent that he dominated the scene by giving orders, making suggestions, etc., as though he were the host. I could see that Tonio was boiling inside, and I sat down with some friends. When the party came to an end, the uninvited and unwelcome couple informed us that they wanted to take the children with them that night to sleep at Tonio's townhouse. We, of course, had assumed and hoped the children would spend the last night with their father. Not wanting to make a fuss, I handed them the bag with the clothes, and without a word of thanks and hardly a good-bye from the children, they drove away. I never regretted having suggested they stay at Tonio's place more than I did that evening. The children left the glass figurines from Murano on the shelf in their room at Papa's house, presumably to play with them when they returned.

Out of kindness, I had placed a bottle of 4711 eau de cologne, which I had brought from Germany, on Tonio's bed for his ex-wife. They did not thank Tonio for letting them stay there, nor did she utter a word about the eau de cologne. My friend Christina, an MD from Germany and herself a mother of a handicapped child, without my soliciting any comments, said after the party that she had never seen a mother treat her children as "coldly" as that woman. I had noticed that when Liesl sat on her lap, instead of holding her adorable daughter close after not having seen her for more than ten weeks, she held Liesl away from her body, as though afraid the child would soil her dress, which was not even pretty. I remembered that I had seen her hold Liesl the same way in a photo when she was a baby, and it confirmed the opinion of one of my colleagues, who had shared an office with her at IUSB. She remarked that she had never seen a more "unmotherly" mother than her. When Liesl was still a baby, she would bring her to campus, put her on the floor, and never pick her up to cuddle or hold her. I began to believe what Tonio had often said: "She has ice water in her veins and a heart of stone."

As soon as I received all of the papers the students had to write in Germany, along with their grades from the CDC in Radolfzell, I corrected the papers, assigned grades, and returned papers and grades to the students. It was always rewarding to observe not only the progress the students made in German, but the even more significant progress they made in terms of maturity and independent and critical thinking.

Once I had tied up the loose ends at the university, I spent the sabbatical mainly organizing chronologically the hundreds of slides in my possession and the letters from Doc, Mutti, and friends, researching travel data, and filling many pads with the life experiences from which I would draw when writing the novel. Tonio helped, labeling and sorting all the slides into carousel trays. We spent much time discussing the outline and worked on the dialogue between the protagonists. Tonio used to type at the kitchen table on the portable typewriter he used in his student days, while I sat opposite him, helping with the composition of what he was typing. It was a stimulating but very exhausting task, which at the end of the day was rewarded with a dinner at a nearby restaurant or a meal Tonio whipped up himself. A bottle of wine restored our energy and enthusiasm. The process was much more involved than we had originally thought. We had to view all of the slides, photographs, etc. together. We changed the outline several times and had other major interruptions, as I had to continue recruiting students on a campus-wide basis for my Bayer Program and attend a meeting of the German Studies Association in Albuquerque, New Mexico, where we had an Editorial Board meeting for *Literatur-Express*. It was nice that Tonio came along. I joined him for one of his meetings in Indianapolis sponsored by the Indiana Historical Society, which coincided with a meeting of the Indiana German Heritage Society. It was just wonderful that we shared so many interests and that we met many new people and made new friends.

The beginning of the fall semester witnessed a major change at the university. Rumor had it that the old chancellor had been pressured into stepping down, partially due to his inability to break his drinking habit – he had crashed his car into a tree in a campus parking lot. A new chancellor, Daniel Cohen, had been chosen to take over. He was a chain-smoker, but tried hard to stop smoking by constantly chewing gum. I found it terribly annoying to have to watch and listen to the chewing whenever he addressed the faculty at meetings or gave formal addresses. He had a second wife, a blond German, who sold real estate. Both went all out to befriend the faculty, scheduling dinners for faculty and their spouses or friends over the course of one or two semesters. Tonio and I were among the first couples to be honored. Champagne flowed freely, and at one point, Mr. Cohen bent down and whispered into my ear, "I really like you." I smiled, shrugged my shoulders, and walked away. It is strange to remember, as I write about him twenty years later, that Daniel Cohen, after lengthy legal entanglements triggered by a sexual-harassment suit, was forced to step down as chancellor, suspended as a faculty member, and finally fired from his tenured position as well, a first for our university. In retrospect, his predecessor, also prone to engage in sexual harassment, should have been terminated as well.

The children came for Thanksgiving, and having started a tradition of celebrating Christmas at Thanksgiving whenever they could not be with us on the actual holiday, I put up my artificial German Christmas tree. Though they did not stay long, we thoroughly enjoyed having them with us, and we wished they lived closer so we could celebrate other special occasions together. They began to tell me more frequently that unless I were married to their father, we would not be a "real" family. They were obviously thinking of their mother, who had just gotten married to "Squeaky Voice."

On the evening of Mutti's birthday, December 3, Tonio and I were at his place. Changing the topic of conversation more or less out of the blue, he asked me if I would marry him. By that time, I had known and deeply loved Tonio for more than two years, had fallen in love with Liesl and Gustl, and was confident I could handle the responsibility. When I reminded him that I would someday be a little shriveled-up old lady, he assured me that since he knew how to take care of babies and children, he would know how to take care of me. I remembered that in a letter he had compared me to a child and my voice to that of a bird. Doc too had called me "Little One," and when I answered the phone, people often asked if my mother was home. Deep down, I also felt certain that Doc would have approved of Tonio, brilliant, charming, and always a gentleman, and I had learned from being married to Doc that age is less important than the heart and character. Though I was naturally aware of the age difference, I felt that unless people knew about it, they could not easily tell. Tonio seemed and acted older than he was, which also helped bridge the gap. He felt sure I would outlive him. As soon as I said yes, he got a bottle of champagne out of his refrigerator and shot the cork into the ceiling, and we drank the sparkling wine. We threw the glasses into the fire in the fireplace. Tonio asked when and where we should tie the knot, and I said, "July 4, 1989, in Venice, Italy." Tonio agreed, without questioning the plan's feasibility. We went back to my house to plan and to dream – and Tonio was ready to give up his townhouse and move in with me. We both considered the engagement a total commitment, and we wanted to share it with our friends at an official engagement party, with a proper announcement and all the trimmings, as soon as we could find a place to celebrate. There would be plenty of time before July 4 to plan the wedding in Venice. I also knew I would forfeit my VA benefits as soon as I remarried, but Tonio tossed that concern aside. He assured me I would not need the income, since he was climbing the ladder of success and would be able to take good care of me. I insisted on taking along the children, who would be older enough by then to get something out of the trip, instead of sending them to their grandmother in Florida, as Tonio suggested.

The timing was ideal, since I was still on sabbatical. I did not advertise my engagement among the faculty. As the children did not spend the holidays with Tonio, instead of my usual Christmas party for the students, we invited several members of our drama-reading group for dinner. After dessert, several guests begged Tonio to read us tarot cards. He had taken quite an interest in the art of reading tarot while in college in Florida, where he knew a fortune-teller. He was convinced the cards did not lie, because the woman had foretold the events of his life so correctly that when he learned again and again that she was right, he destroyed the paper on which she had written down the future events of his life. I never asked him why he tore up the paper. It was always scary when he read tarot. He turned off the radio and the lights, lit a few candles, and stood at the uncovered dining-room table, with the guests around it staring at the cards as he placed them in the middle of the table. His head was bent over the cards as he placed one after another on the stack. His black eyes took on a special glow, his dark, curly hair fell down to his forehead, and a great silence reigned throughout the house as he interpreted each card. He seemed like a Gypsy, and though I did not believe anything he foretold, the experience was magical, exciting, and a bit frightening. This time, my friend Renate asked Tonio to read her cards. Frighteningly, they foretold a grave event which was to take place in her life very soon. She did not say much after that and went home troubled. Only a few days later, she called to inform me that she had to fly home right away. Her mother had to be taken to the hospital and was in a coma. She kept referring to the cards. Unfortunately, she never again saw her mother alive.

Antonio and I left for New York just before Christmas, because the MLA convention was to be held from the 26th to the 28th, and we had an Editorial Board meeting for *Literatur-Express* during that time. Tonio and I were radiantly happy. He was wearing the Christmas gift I had surprised him with, a dark-brown leather jacket, lined with thick, dark-brown fur. He looked dashingly handsome, and we both smiled when at the book exhibit at the Sheraton Hotel (or the Hilton – I forget), someone approached Tonio and asked if he was Christopher Reeve. We spent a few glorious days in the Big Apple that rivaled those I spent there with Amadeus and even with Doc. Tonio was seriously inspecting the displays in the jewelry stores on Fifth Avenue, because he wanted to buy an engagement ring for me. I liked the idea of being consulted, and just loved the wide, Italian-made gold band with diamonds surrounding emerald-cut sapphires, which we chose at an exclusive shop. It matched nicely the friendship ring of diamonds and sapphires that Tonio had made for me at a shop in Chicago. I was so elated I decided to buy a long strand of pearls for myself at the same place. I insisted on paying for it myself, as I was still superstitious. "Pearls bring tears," as the German saying goes – and the pearls given to me by John Hauenstein had proved it true.

Upon our return, annual faculty reports were due, and I hastened to turn mine in. I was glad to include two favorable reviews of my last book, one in a German and another in a French periodical. I mentioned that Tonio and I had been asked to submit an excerpt from the novel to the Editorial Board of *Literatur-Express*. I wanted to show that I was making headway in the area of creative writing. In addition, I attached a copy of a letter from the chairman of the Division of Music, whose daughter I had taught prior to her attending courses in Vienna. He attributed her success in German to my teaching. The chairmanship of my good and always fair French colleague was coming to an end, and I was glad I had been able to come up for professorship under her reign.

I was a bit apprehensive when I found out that the Prima Donna would be in charge of the department next. I knew he had had it in for me since the salary issue came up during my chairmanship, but felt secure in that my record was almost impeccable. Or so I thought. I still felt that an individual neither holding a PhD in a foreign language nor teaching a regular load in the department he or she chaired was unacceptable as a chair, even an imposition. I also knew I had to resign myself to the situation, because I had no clout politically; and I never believed in playing that game. Believe me, the Prima Donna left no stone unturned when it came to academic politics. He knew how to infiltrate any and all old boys' groups, and even though behind the scenes nobody liked the man, I think they all tried their best not to antagonize him.

You can bet we did not invite the Prima Donna and his wife to our dance party in celebration of our engagement, which took place at the Knollwood Country Club at 8:00 p.m. on Saturday, March 7. Thanks to our friends the Voepels, who had a membership at the club, we were able to book it after a lengthy search. We had sent out folded invitations. On the cover was our photo from Crete, in which we stood in front of the pink oleander, with the blue Mediterranean sky behind us. The inscription, "Outside of Time and Place," appeared on the back of the folded invitation.

The round tables at the country club were decorated with pink tulips, white daisies, baby's breath, and delicate green asparagus twigs. In back of the big table, on which a great variety of culinary delights, including caviar, was enticingly arranged, stood a huge dolphin ice sculpture. Dozens of pink candles were flickering throughout the room and provided an intimate ambiance. We danced the night away with champagne and wine or whatever the guests desired. Everybody had a good time, including friends who had traveled far and colleagues, students, and administrators from area universities and industry. All contributed through their presence to turning the party into a special event. Several had assumed it was a wedding celebration. Unfortunately, Renate and Karl could not be present.

I had spent several hours at the beauty salon getting ready and earned much praise from Tonio, who himself looked gorgeous in his dark suit. He pinned a big white gardenia on the waist of my dark-green, long-sleeved Laura Ashley dress, of rich velvet. It was fitted in the waist, and the full gathered skirt, reaching to my ankles, flared out beautifully when I danced. When we were not dancing, we chatted or listened to the black singer's blues, accompanied by a pianist and percussionists.

The only fly in the ointment, if you will, was a gift from the Pompous Conductor and his wife, a tacky bouquet of fake purple irises, which was so insultingly cheap I put it in my trash can the minute I got home. I suppose it was meant to be a thank-you gesture for the extra effort I put into teaching his daughter enough German to get by in Austria.

At the party, the positive far outweighed the negative; and as I have shared an occasional letter from my friends with you, I will at this point inject excerpts from a letter written to us by Tonio's best friend and college chum, who had flown in from Kentucky for the party and spent a few days at our home.

I had such a wonderful time at your celebration of togetherness. . . . I really did enjoy myself, though, and will hold fast to the memories of meeting Christa . . . seeing Antonio surrounded by your friends there, and sharing a time in your charming and tastefully appointed home.

I regret, however, not being able to finish reading your book! I really liked it, and thought it began with bright, sure strokes. . . . I just want to finish it, now! So, <u>you</u> must finish it in order to afford me the opportunity to read it! Don't let me down on this; your public is <u>waiting</u>!

Let me say a word or two about Christa, Tonio. It is no mystery to me what you see in her, as they say. She shines, and radiates her shine to everyone around her. Her beauty both inside and out would be evident even to a blind man. And talk about an integrated character and presence! She seems to have great personal and cultural depth, made unintimidating by a charming modesty, and made accessible to others by a disarming honesty and a graceful manner that puts others immediately at ease. She is <u>super</u>, and you are one lucky sonuvabitch. Be nice to her! And thank you for inviting me up to meet her.

You truly do bring to me, as I am sure you do to many of your friends, a dimension of cultural breadth and refinement that is lacking otherwise. You are becoming our age's renaissance person, and I have an inkling that Christa is your equal in that regard, no mean feat. I'm proud to know you.

Have a grand time in France, and send us a postcard.

I was teaching an extra course again in the spring semester, and I was extremely pleased by the quality of students in my advanced literature course. The majority of the students had participated in the work-study program or spent a summer abroad in connection with the GDR program. One of my students earned a Grawemeyer Award as a result of having participated in the Bayer Program. Harvard, Princeton, and the University of Michigan asked about participation in my overseas programs as well as for guidance on developing such programs. When Sally Detlef informed me that the League for Friendship among Nations, in East Berlin, had offered her a summer fellowship, I was happy for her; and when I asked her to accompany the Bayer group that summer, she readily agreed. It was an ideal time for her, because she had been accepted to IU's French academic-year-abroad program in Strasbourg for 1987. She had also assisted with the planning of that year's program and was therefore well suited. She excelled so much in German during the summer that a director shooting a film in East Berlin thought she was a native. Tonio and I flew over to Germany with the students on May 15. Sally took off with the group to Berlin, and Tonio and I dropped in at Bayer. As they all knew about our engagement, they put us up at the fabulous Kasino. While I met with the Personnel Department, Tonio visited the PR Department in connection with his responsibilities at Miles.

Fourth Pre-honeymoon – Provence – Summer and Christmas with the Kiddies

We had rented a car, and after lunch we headed south toward France, where we looked forward to just taking it easy at a yet-unknown beach on the Côte d'Azur, in Provence. Tonio had never been to Provence, and I was eager for him to meet André Bourde and show him the region where I had spent my year abroad. We stopped at towns and places familiar to me, saw the magnificent papal residence in Avignon, my beloved Aix-en-Provence, Orange, and Arles, took in other sights on the way, and spent an exciting afternoon at André's very old, highly unique, and flamboyantly decorated stone house in Cavaillon. Villa Phocéenne, in Marseille, had been sold after the death of his beloved mother, my longtime friend. He invited us to an extravagant dinner party. The guests were seated at a long banquet table covered with a striking tablecloth – a piece of red-and-burgundy damask – and they were dressed in clothes more colorful than the cloth and the dishes and wines served. Unfortunately, we had to leave too soon, thus leaving behind a friend and his exotic guests and missing out not only on a highly stimulating conversation, but also on André's musical toast at the harpsichord, which always stood ready to beguile.

As we had no fixed destination, we stopped at places that looked enticing. At night, we searched for out-of-the-way lodgings in the charming Provençal countryside, and were always lucky to find places in remote villages where the locals dined and where cooks understood how to please our palate. As the tourists had not yet flooded the countryside and we both spoke French, we had our first pick and were excited that we could choose between two beautifully furnished mansions, Les Moulins de Paillas and Hôtel de Gigaro, right on the Mediterranean and close to the fashionable island resort Saint-Tropez. Our room in the Gigaro was spacious, with an oceanside balcony, and we spent our fourth dreamlike, paradisiacal pre-honeymoon at the French Riviera. We focused on just relaxing, swimming, sunbathing, or strolling along the beach, and since we had opted for the all-inclusive plan, we took our breakfast on the terrace next to the beach and dined in their tastefully decorated restaurant, from which we could look out on the blue waters of the Mediterranean as far as the eye could see. The cuisine was simply out of this world, as were the wines.

Our stay was all too short. Since we were at a more or less tucked-away location, we avoided museums and were content with an afternoon walk through nearby towns, including Arles, where Van Gogh lived and painted, and Saint-Tropez, where the rich and famous felt at home and maintained their luxurious villas. I had come to France with a mission, that is, to find a tiny "Megan" doll for Liesl's My Little

Pony collection. I had virtually combed the US toy stores for over a month, until the manufacturer told me Megan was no longer produced and was thus unavailable in the United States. But leave it to me: I found Megan in a small toy store on a narrow street in a quaint town in Provence after stopping at toy stores in too many towns to count. They had one Megan left on the shelf. I would have paid more than it was worth to get that little doll, which was only four inches tall. I was so happy I almost cried.

We checked in at the Königshof in Hannover, where we wanted to visit Mutti and take her out to celebrate our engagement. I continued my shopping spree for the children and bought toys I had always wished for but never received, because they were either unavailable due to the war or unaffordable for my parents. We took Mutti to a rather elegant restaurant at the Königshof, where we ordered a gourmet dinner. Mutti ordered quail eggs for the first time in her life. We sat next to a young couple and had a marvelous time, because Mutti was telling one joke after another and we could not stop laughing. We picked her up the next day to look for a new suit for Tonio. Mutti was happy to see us, but when I mentioned the good time we had the night before, she could not remember even having seen us. While Tonio was trying on suits and about to make a choice, Mutti, true to her usual self, began to criticize a minor wrinkle in the coat, at which point the salesman lowered the price so much that Tonio and I looked at each other in amazement, smiled, and finalized the deal at once.

Tonio wanted to take us out for lunch, but Mutti said she had just eaten. We knew it was not true and that she simply did not remember. It made me sad, but we took her anyhow, and she ate a big meal before we had to take her back to the home and say good-bye. There were always tears when parting, because I never knew if I would see her again when I walked out that door. I don't think she ever fully comprehended who Antonio was. A big consolation to me was that she never complained about the care she received. The nurse told me everybody liked listening to Mutti entertaining the patients by singing arias from their favorite operas. To get her started, all you had to do was mention a title. She sang clearly and in tune and always received well-deserved applause.

Tonio and I flew home together, and the children arrived not long afterward. As we had moved together and were officially engaged, we felt like a family. We told the children we wanted to have the wedding in Venice, Italy, and take them along, because we wanted them to be a part of the ceremony. I don't think they fully understood everything it involved, but they liked the fact that we were getting married. Our summer was filled with fun activities. We took out a membership at the Twyckenham Pool, within walking distance from my house. Tonio bought a baseball glove, ball, and bat to practice with his son in a nearby field, and we played badminton, croquet, and other games in the backyard after supper or on weekends. I enrolled Liesl in ballet, and just loved the days when mothers were permitted to watch the little dancers. Once, as she passed by dancing, she separated from the circle, ran toward me, threw her arms around me, said, "I love you," and rejoined the group. She looked adorable in her pink outfit with ruffles and the pink ballet shoes. I tried to be at the pool when Gustl, tanned to a dark bronze, participated in swim meets, because he was developing into an excellent swimmer. All the kids got excited when I yelled at the top of my lungs for him to go faster and whistled with my fingers when he reached the goal. No other parent could compete with me. We were glad there were nice children in the neighborhood to celebrate the Fourth of July with us. One of my students owned a couple of riding horses, and we all had a great time riding through the fields of their farm without toppling down. I felt warm inside when I tucked them in at night and sang a different German lullaby for each of them after Tonio had read them their bedtime stories and said, "Sleep tight, don't let the bedbugs bite." I could hardly hold back tears when, on a couple of occasions, Liesl put her arms around me and said, "I wish you were my real mom."

I never understood why the children's mother called so infrequently when they spent the summer with us. The few times she did call, I had to force the children to talk to her. When they did talk, they were so detached one might have thought they were talking to a stranger. When they received a postcard from their mother, it was written as if she were addressing high-school students, discussing historical facts, dates, and such. I thought she would be very pleased to hear the news that I had succeeded in getting Liesl, who was already in kindergarten, to stop sucking her index finger. I had done it by making up a rhyme in German – "Kein Fingerlein in dieses Mündelein" (no little finger in this little mouth) – which I recited each time the little pink finger moved toward her mouth. I warned her that the little finger would be worn down just like a sucker, and she looked at me in disbelief. No reaction from Ms. Ice Water. Tonio and the friends of mine who knew her were right – she was cold.

Of course, the children were not always little angels. I had several confrontations with Gustl, who was turning into a skillful little liar. He appeared to be proud of it, because he bragged that his mother had told him he would make a good lawyer. Being raised by two lawyers must have contributed to the fact that he used such terminology as "deposition" with ease. But he blew me away when, at the age of eight or nine, he asked me one evening about my will and went on to express the hope that since his mother never spent anything on them, he would get more when she died. Gustl displayed a vicious temper and great physical strength. One night, in a fit of anger, when his father was away on a business trip, he took hold of my ankle with such might I could not break away. On one or two occasions, Tonio felt rightly that the children had to be punished, even though it was several hours after the incident, that is, after he had come home from work. Each time, he grabbed the nice breadboard with a rooster painted on it, took the child out to the deck, and paddled his or her fanny a couple of times. Gustl, who first retaliated by mumbling something about "physical abuse," claimed later it did not hurt at all, but Liesl shed a few tears. Compared to my Papa's paddling with the carpet beater, this was nothing. Also, Tonio told me about the frequent whippings with a hazelnut stick administered by his mother, which caused red and blue streaks. They must have been extremely painful, because one day – when he was older – he grabbed hold of the cane, broke it in two, and told his mother to stop it at once. She never hit him again.

Never having had children of my own and not having been around them much, I was constantly observing them and making sure they played with children from families I knew. At times, they acted out of character, as on the day we were admiring our neighbor's newly acquired pet terrier. Liesl, without any provocation whatever, suddenly kicked the cute little dog in the stomach – I could not figure out what motivated her. The dog cried, Helen shook her head in disbelief, and when I asked Liesl why she had kicked him, she just looked at me with her big brown eyes as though she had done nothing wrong.

Antonio and I were concerned about the quality of the education the children, especially Gustl, received in Cleveland. I had observed that the schools' educational standards were gradually declining. The incoming freshmen were not nearly as well prepared as when I had started. More and more, language offerings at schools were being reduced or cancelled altogether, and unless the parents took a special interest in their children's education, their prospects for the future were dim. We had made a point of keeping in touch with the children by calling them frequently during the week, and we found that more often than not, the parents were not at home and had left the children in the care of a babysitter. Liesl once asked me to sing her a good-night song over the phone to remember me by. She almost never saw her mother anymore – only in the morning, when she braided her hair.

Several of the children's friends were attending a nearby private school with an excellent reputation, and Antonio and I thought it would be wonderful if the children stayed with us during the school year. Of course, it would complicate matters for the mother, since it would shift the obligation to her to keep them occupied during the summer. I always felt that the joint-custody arrangement had been very cleverly arranged. The children would be in school during the day, and in the summer they would be sent to the father, who also had a full-time job. I suggested to Tonio that just out of curiosity, even though there was no vacancy, I would like to have Gustl tested at the private school to see if he would qualify for admission. Gustl loved the classrooms and programs at Stanley Clark and was eager to learn about his scores, which were not at the top but would have been good enough had there been an opening. Well, we were dreaming, but we doubted that the mother, who of course was notified of the score results, would ever allow it. Even though Liesl usually had a rash when she arrived, it was not enough to prove that Tonio's ex was an unfit mother. Despite the fact that Tonio did not pay child support and inasmuch as I was the bursar in the family, I had figured out that his, or by then our, financial and emotional input exceeded by far that on the other side. I had further realized that

Tonio's and the children's anecdotes recounting the mother's miserliness were not exaggerated. Many of her recommendations come to mind, such as always using cold water in the washing machine, avoiding ironing clothes at all costs, never buying children's clothes that require dry cleaning, driving a car with a stick shift to save gasoline, taking your foot off the accelerator several hundred yards before stopping, turning off the stove a few minutes before the food was cooked, and saving corn that did not pop and using it again. She also suggested washing out Pampers and using them until they fell apart, not throwing away brown paper lunch bags until they were torn, not wasting leftover food from restaurants, helping yourself to extra plastic vegetable bags when shopping for produce, and taking your kids for a free lunch at Costco.

The children returned at the end of the summer, and it was life as usual for all.

Once again, I had taught during the second summer session to boost my income by 10%, and I was back to teaching an overload during the fall. I made sure we continued to work on the novel, which had been neglected over the summer. I was anxious to read the incoming papers from the Bayer group, and turned in the grades in a timely fashion. Except for a couple of sordid love affairs between students, Sally had not encountered any major disappointments. She had benefited much from the program in Weimar, and she continued her studies in Strasbourg directly after she finished at Bayer. I did not have to look for an assistant for 1988, as it was my turn again. The big event in the fall was the annual Oktoberfest, for which I had Tonio's help. And due to the connection with Miles/Bayer, we invited a much bigger crowd, including our drama group and a whole bunch of others from Miles. We had about ninety guests, who had a jolly good time, drank a barrel of German beer, ate lots of German bratwurst, sauerkraut, potato salad, etc., and did not leave until after midnight, after having sung many German songs, with me leading the singers at the top of my lungs until I was hoarse.

It was too bad that Professor Dr. Hänsel, from the Friedrich Schiller University at Jena, in the GDR, whom I had invited to give a slide lecture on Weimar (Buchenwald) to my students and talk about the pros and cons of socialism, could not come to the big festival.

I staged another "Christmas with a German Accent" event for my German students on campus; it featured German songs, stories, cookies, and candlelight. That year, the children were coming to spend the holidays. I invited the children's grandmother, but she declined. She probably had a bad conscience; she must have realized by then that I knew she was Tonio's former mother-in-law and that I had not forgotten how rudely she had treated me before I met him. Being a native of Austria and pursuing a science degree at IUSB, she had approached me to earn advanced credits in German. I recall her speaking highly about her son-in-law, a professor at Notre Dame, whom I did not know at the time, and other matters. It was obvious she had no trouble speaking German. I looked at the course offerings for the spring semester and suggested she enroll in a literature course, which I was sure would be enjoyable for her and would also reinforce her writing skills. She seemed to agree, but just before Christmas, she wrote a note informing me in a rather spiteful way that since I had suggested she take a literature course, she decided to take no German course at all. I had trouble understanding how someone who on the surface seemed rather friendly could be so uncivil – I had only tried to comply with her request. I was more upset, though, when I found out later she had managed to enroll in a German conversation course while I was on sabbatical. It was much too easy, but was very likely to guarantee her an A. The instructor told me, when I returned to campus, that the woman had made her life miserable by constantly interrupting her. From then on, I had her pegged as an opportunistic and devious person. Once I realized she was the mother of Tonio's ex, who had taken back her family name after the divorce, I had no trouble believing Tonio's stories about his "dreadful" mother-in-law. Small world!

Two months before Christmas, I had become intent on setting the mood for the children. I was excited that these two living Hänsel and Gretel children had come into my life! I wanted them to experience Christmas as I remembered it from my childhood. I sent them a letter from Santa asking for a wish list and gave them an Advent calendar to hang on a windowpane. I looked through every Christmas catalogue and cut out many colorful pictures of angels, Santa Clauses, Christmas ornaments, toys, etc., pasted them on white pieces of paper, printed little comments underneath the pictures, and sent them to Cleveland, never once receiving an acknowledgment or comment from the mother. Since there was little communication between the biological parents and stepparents, there was little feedback about anything we sent.

Before Tonio picked up the kiddies in Cleveland, we spent hours wrapping the gifts we had accumulated throughout the year, including Megan, and hid them in the attic. When he returned with the children, they rushed into their room, checking it for a gift or two, which I used to place on their bed as a welcome-home surprise. They felt comfortable very quickly, and Tonio and I were even more excited than they.

There was no way to hide the Christmas tree, which meant I had to break with tradition. We waited for the children and trimmed it together the night before Christmas Eve. They loved the ceremony. I had bought a colorful assortment of imported chocolate and marzipan ornaments in a German store in Chicago. They were eager to hang the chocolate bells, Santa Clauses, trees, angels, and cones wrapped in gold-silver, red, green, and blue aluminum foil on the tree. How hard they tried to make sure they looked pretty amidst the other multicolored ornaments. They searched hard for the perfect spot from which to hang their very own special ornament, which Santa brought them each year. Gustl had the honor of climbing the ladder to place the golden star on the top of the tree. Tonio combined wax candles from Germany with electric lights, but did not light either before Christmas Eve. All of the cookies I had baked and bought were arranged on colorful Christmas plates and distributed in the living- and dining-room area The gingerbread house, which Tonio and the children had built together, was awarded a special place in the center of the cherrywood cocktail table.

I asked the children to help set the table for our Christmas Eve supper in just the way I remembered it from home. I had the perfect nook for it. A carpenter from Hannover, Germany, had made a beautiful half-circle breakfast nook out of cherrywood to fit in the corner of my kitchen. I had accentuated the German ambiance by having a Roman shade made for the picture window next to the nook. The custom-made cushions on the bench were made from the same material. It was light-blue wool with a white-and-beige border, into which roses were woven. Above the oval table hung a round, bell-shaped lamp. Like the material for the shade and cushions, that for the lamp came from Bavaria. The shade consisted of beige, burlap-like material. The lamp diffused a warm light. It made everybody who sat at the table feel welcome. I had the nook built mainly for times when my students came over for a relaxing get-together with pizza and beer. They felt less inhibited when we gathered at that spot in the kitchen to chat in German. We watched Gustl light the candles in the apples, and after Tonio said grace, I placed the food on the table. Alas, both children made faces and refused to eat the sauerkraut and, in the end, had to be content with bratwurst, mashed potatoes, and applesauce.

I modified another German Christmas tradition. Instead of sending the children to take a nap after supper, I asked Tonio to take them for a drive to a subdivision in South Bend known for its beautiful displays of Christmas lights. Each year, the estates and homes competed against each other and poured small fortunes into an electric-Christmas-light spectacular. In their absence, I hurried up to the attic, retrieved the hidden gifts, and arranged them around the tree. Next, I lit twenty-four white wax candles on the tree, just as my papa had done, and then I turned out all the lights in the house. It was the signal for Tonio that Christmas Eve could begin.

They had to enter through the back door and the kitchen. Just as they arrived at the kitchen door, I called out and told them to follow me quickly outside to the backyard to see Christkind disappear like a star shooting up into the sky. I pointed to the star-studded heavens, and Liesl screamed, "There it is!" just as a bell rang inside the house. The children turned around and rushed toward the living room.

Their eyes shone brightly as they called out, "Oh!" Tonio made sure the children took turns opening the presents, and before they could play with the gifts, Tonio sat down at the piano, waited until I got out my violin, and played and sang a few Christmas songs with me. As it was snowing outside, Tonio thought it was too slippery to drive to the chapel in Bristol, thirty miles away.

Instead of a Christmas goose, we feasted on a duck, and the children even liked my red-cabbage dish and the apple cake I had baked à la Mutti.

Whenever the children came to visit for Christmas, they spent New Year's Eve with us. Categorically, we turned down any invitation from friends or colleagues in order to focus on the kiddies. Since they were virtually raised by babysitters, we tried to avoid leaving them with strangers. In Germany, we ate carp on New Year's Eve. Antonio and I started a tradition with lobster. Antonio, who was in charge of cooking, went shopping with the children so they could pick out the lobster from the tank in the store. It was served with drawn butter, salad, and baguettes. The children drank ginger ale and the adults champagne. We never had anything left over. The children were allowed to stay up until midnight. We made sure not to miss Times Square on TV, joined in on the countdown, made a lot of noise, and toasted with champagne. Gustl and Liesl got to drink out of mini champagne glasses. After the toast, we went outside. Feeling like a kid myself, I rolled around in the snow with the youngsters, and ended up lighting sparklers and a few firecrackers left over from the Fourth of July, all in accordance with my childhood memories from Kleine Düwelstraße. You can guess who liked the firecrackers and sparklers the most.

We hoped Tonio's ex would ask us to keep the children a bit longer, as she had done the previous year, when she and her companion vacationed in Australia. I had been spending a great deal of time helping Liesl practice vowels and consonants to improve her speech pattern. – But no such luck this year; they were right on schedule.

In the Christmas spirit, I invited Tonio's ex and her new husband for a cup of tea and cake served on my best china, which we had while the children showed off their gifts. Liesl put on her pretty fur jacket made of white rabbit, and Gustl paraded his brown leather jacket with a lamb-fur color, looking like a little pilot. They were very proud and fortunately did not notice the disapproving looks of the parents, who most likely commiserated with the animals from which the hides were taken. They sat, spoke little, and looked like sourpusses until they departed once more without a smile or a word of thanks. That was the last time I offered them tea. –

The Prima Donna Goes on the Offensive – The Berlin Wall and the GDR Start to Crumble – Child-Custody Troubles Continue

Faculty annual reports were due for 1987. I had a premonition that the Prima Donna, unlike his predecessor, would find something to complain about. I was glad to be able to report that an excerpt from our novel was appearing in print. To show I was serious about my creative writing, I had attended the Screenwriting A–Z seminar sponsored by the University of Wisconsin in Chicago, which resulted in our revising the first five chapters of the novel. We had completed the sixth. – I included a few unsolicited, highly complimentary notes from students to prove that my teaching skills had not deteriorated. I received these notes despite the fact that we had been forced to reduce our meetings with incoming freshmen enrolled in beginners' German courses from three or four to two times a week, that enrollment in German was slipping, and that more students were either withdrawing from courses or failing. – The Prima Donna called attention to these facts, and though he had high praise for my success in advanced courses – I was, according to him, "an academically demanding, careful and conscientious teacher" – he suggested that I resume the "systematic use of student evaluations as one way of gaining additional information regarding [my] approach and as a way of assessing means to reverse the decline."

I spent an entire weekend composing memos in an effort to enlighten the Prima Donna, who must have been aware that the decline in German (French was suffering from the same syndrome, though not as severely) was a nationwide trend and had nothing at all to do with my teaching. Many of my colleagues complained that schools and smaller colleges were either cutting back on German or eliminating it from their curriculum altogether. – I pointed out that since he was new as chairman, he was obviously unaware of the relevant factors. I called attention to the fact that the erratic nature of course offerings in German, which was due to budgetary constraints, resulted in courses being cancelled at the last minute, thus discouraging students from enrolling in German to begin with. I also mentioned that counselors discouraged incoming students from taking German because it was considered the hardest course on our campus. Moreover, there was a growing consensus among many of my colleagues from other disciplines that incoming freshmen were becoming increasingly less motivated. Many felt that since they paid for the course, they deserved at least a passing grade, no matter how poorly they performed. I suggested that the university stiffen its entrance requirements. – I explained that I had stopped systematically handing out evaluation forms in classes populated by students who had already evaluated me several times, and reminded the chair that I had consistently been promoted due to my teaching excellence. Professors from other disciplines had ceased to collect evaluations long before. I pointed out the good retention record in the advanced courses, which were ultimately important if we wanted to keep the German major alive. I quoted some passages from student evaluations, such as "we sure have a lot of homework, but so what – it's fun" and "I have been told that you are a tough professor, but that if I really wanted to learn German I should take Frau Beardsley." Another student made a similar comment: "I was almost afraid to enroll in your course, because I heard that you are very demanding, but I think now that it was much easier than I was led to believe." A student from a literature course wrote, "I look forward to the time and opportunity to once again take one of your literature classes. I enjoyed the small class sizes, opportunities for discussion, both at class and the informal reading sessions you had at your house, and your expertise and professional warmth and caring for your students. I have fond memories of all these things. Thank you for being such a fine teacher!"

I concluded my rebuttal by telling him that a number of students who withdrew at the beginning of the semester made comments to the effect that they were "not dropping the course because of my teaching, but rather because they cannot do the course justice, not having enough time to study." Having insufficient time to study was a major factor on our commuter campus all around. The majority of the students had to work to earn money for tuition. Many were married with children and preferred not to take a reduced course load, which would have left them more time to study. Everybody was in a rush to earn a degree and thus join the workforce and make money. I personally never encouraged a student to enroll in my courses unless I knew he or she had a chance to succeed. When I noticed early on that a student could not handle a course, I suggested they switch over to Spanish, which had a reputation among students of guaranteeing an easy A. The number of Spanish sections had increased by leaps and bounds over the years – and just recently, I heard that the German major is again in danger of being eliminated. I wonder why German-language enrollment has not improved since I left. Well, the Prima Donna conceded that "the decline in German enrollments may be attributable to a variety of factors . . . the dilemma might be characterized on the one hand by the perceived weakness in the caliber of many of our incoming students, and, on the other, by the desire to maintain high academic standards and expectations."

I had already been advised by the Fly Trap and the Lemon on a number of occasions to lower my academic standards. And there was the constant threat that I would lose my job, a threat which bordered on harassment. I already covered three fewer chapters than in previous semesters, so I refused to shrink my syllabus even more. I knew I was not unfair to my students. It was always my philosophy to be demanding as a teacher but fair in grading. If I saw at the end of the semester that a student had tried his or her very best, I would not flunk that student unless there was absolutely nothing to show. I also had an obligation to prepare my students for a potential German major and/or a transfer to the Bloomington campus. I observed what was happening in Spanish as a result of covering even fewer chapters. Although the students should have been prepared to handle a Spanish course in advanced writing or literature, they encountered major problems in such courses unless they were native speakers.

It did not come as much of a surprise that, for the second time, I did not receive the Senator Lundquist Fellowship. But since I am painting a picture of what goes on, often subtly and behind the scenes, in academia, I would like to enlighten you as to what went on behind the scenes in reference to my nomination for the fellowship. A few years later, when I had completely forgotten about the nomination, a file was sent to me that contained all of the confidential letters of recommendation that had been submitted on my behalf in connection with my promotion to full professor. In it was a letter from one of my colleagues from the History Department. I had no idea he had supported me and was rather touched when I read the following:

1984–1993

I can think of nobody more deserving, or as deserving, of the award than Prof. B.

Because she has her office among us historians on the fourth floor, I see Prof. B. almost daily, see the students who frequent her office, and often enjoy her conversation. She is a delightful presence, unfailingly energetic, committed to study and teaching, and abundantly helpful to both students and colleagues. She has gone far beyond the call of duty in creating special opportunities for IUSB students, particularly for study in Germany, and has often taken time to tell me about her research and ideas about teaching. I don't know of anyone who has accomplished so much while remaining such a devoted teacher and helpful colleague.

What shocked and disturbed me deeply, and still does as I look at the file almost twenty years later, were two comments scribbled in the margin, hardly legible. Next to the passage ending with "helpful to both students and colleagues," someone wrote "overstated," and next to the statement regarding "study in Germany," the person wrote "against all university rules." I would love to ask the party responsible for these comments to explain the second one, because it seems to imply that the overseas programs I developed and implemented over the years took place without the approval of our campus-wide committees and administrators, which is not only a lie, but unthinkable.

What is against all university rules is to return a file filled with confidential letters, including many written by international scholars and students, to the person on whose behalf they were written. Yet it was not the first time I observed such behavior in my department. I recall that when the Fly Trap took over the chairmanship from me, he turned over the dossier pertaining to our colleague's very precarious tenure case, which contained all the confidential letters of recommendation, including those that were not so flattering to him. No wonder the Spaniard disliked me.

Tonio and I were constantly planning ahead for the wedding in Venice, which was no small undertaking. It was essential to start early. Meanwhile, we were both busy with our jobs, I with an overload of four courses, including two advanced literature courses, and the usual preparation for the Bayer Program, which once again required my presence abroad. – But before I took off, the children were scheduled to visit again at Easter. I had a lot of fun buying German Easter eggs at my favorite store in Chicago and picking out Easter outfits for the children to wear to church in Bristol. Tonio and I had a great time coloring eggs with the kids, but I was in charge of hiding them in the yard and hanging the tiny egg baskets in the bushes. A big golden egg waited to be found in the bird feeder. Liesl, because she was shorter and thus closer to the ground, gathered more little treasures and moved much faster than Gustl, but in the end he felt rewarded when he discovered the golden egg. Since Tonio's ex was about six months pregnant and just waiting out the school year to follow her husband, whose job in Cleveland had been terminated, to the West Coast, I made the mistake of suggesting to Tonio that it would be nice if we saved her the long trip, deviated from the schedule, and drove the children to Cleveland ourselves, even though Tonio had just driven the long round-trip a week earlier.

I got another lesson in divorce behavior. If you think Ms. Ice Water would have been grateful, you have another thing coming. When we arrived, she stood in the door with a sinister look, barely greeting any of us, including the children. She complained about our being late, for which we apologized. Tonio explained that we had encountered car trouble on the speedway outside of Cleveland. There was no telephone nearby, and Tonio had proceeded slowly in the hope of arriving without ruining the motor. It was only when he asked her if he could call a service station and I asked if I could use the restroom and possibly borrow an aspirin that she let us enter and wait inside. Instead of engaging in a conversation, she went about her business, and the children vanished. Fortunately, the car trouble could be resolved within an hour or so. Once more, when we were ready to leave, there was not a word of thanks and a very meager good-bye from Ms. Ice Water. We returned home after midnight, after a five-hour drive.

Yet, being such a softy, and knowing how economical she was, when we learned about her impending move to the West Coast, I told her about a very reasonable red-eye flight. It was only when the children told me their mother mentioned I had given her a good tip that I knew she had taken advantage of my suggestion.

Getting a group of students together for the Bayer Program was more difficult this year, because after losing over half of the twenty students accepted by March 1, I was able to find replacements only as a result of making phone calls to places all over the country. But on May 12, 1988, I left with twenty-one students. It was my twelfth trip since the start of my summer-abroad programs in 1974.

New difficulties developed during the Berlin portion of the program. The tutor in Berlin had to be discharged and a substitute found, which was difficult to accomplish by phone and without a personal interview. Fortunately, the CDG helped me find a good replacement. The travel agent in the German Democratic Republic proved very lax in answering letters and phone calls. Mail was repeatedly sent to Bloomington or West Berlin instead of to me in South Bend. At times, the addressee's name was missing. Many mornings I had to get up before 5:00 to try to call East Berlin. The same East German touring organization arbitrarily altered the dates of our itinerary again after all other connections and arrangements had already been booked, with the result that I had to find a quick solution as to how and where twenty-one students would spend three extra days. With the help of personal contacts, and by drawing on a great deal of experience in this area, I saw to it that the program recovered smoothly. Many pitfalls were avoided; for example, the group might well have ended up stranded in a railroad station late at night had I not discovered that the wrong departure times had been booked for leaving East Germany. Luckily, I was in the habit of double checking all such arrangements, though, in this case, I had only a few hours in West Berlin to straighten matters out prior to entering East Germany.

Our venture started again in East Berlin with the usual sights. The last stop in the capital was in a building adjacent to the Brandenburg Gate, the Wall, and no-man's-land. We were ushered into a dark lecture hall, where a high-ranking officer in uniform with a chest covered in medals, tall, bald, and noticeably overweight, lectured about the poor relations between the two Germanys, attributing the blame to the West. At one point, he switched on the TV to show a video, which surprised me, because citizens in East Germany did not generally own videos at that time. The film focused on an East German border policeman who had reportedly been killed by Western border control from behind the Wall. I interrupted the lecturer and asked if he also had a video of several Western policemen having been shot by the East Germans and, more so, of the scores of citizens who had been shot as they risked their lives while climbing across barbed-wire fences and jumping out of windows in houses along the Wall in an attempt to escape to the West. I concluded by adding, in an admittedly flip tone of voice, that fortunately there would pretty soon no longer be a need to escape, because the Wall was reportedly going to come down. – For a split second, I believed the man would explode or have a heart attack. His face and bald head turned crimson red. He asked who had told me that, whereupon I fibbed, "Gorbachev!" He pulled himself together, stood very erect, and almost in a shouting voice proclaimed he would demonstrate, by showing the rest of his video, why Mr. Gorbachev would never make such a statement, why the Wall was the best thing that ever happened, why it never would and never must come down. He alluded to the fourteen-year-old girl who had murdered her father before escaping to West Berlin, where, so he claimed, she was illegally tried. When I defended the outcome of the trial, because my friend Hans Guenther, the attorney general, had been instrumental in saving the girl, he was speechless. We did not pay much attention to the rest of the film. My students were astonished that I could be so gutsy. Although the good-bye from the military host was frosty, to say the least, the incident triggered a lively discussion among the students. I am sure our host had not heard President Reagan's plea a year or so earlier: "Mr. Gorbachev, tear down this wall!" I began to wonder if they would invite us again the following year. It would not be my turn to go in 1989 – I would be on my honeymoon instead.

The rest of the trip in East Germany proceeded similarly to those in the past, except it included a new place, Meissen, where we were afforded a tour of the Meissen china factory, which all of us found exciting. We got to observe the workers at the various steps of creating the most beautiful pieces of china, which were unfortunately not for sale. Nobody, be they visitors or GDR citizens, could purchase it. All of it was shipped, just like the nutcrackers in Seiffen, to countries that paid hard currency. I was elated when the lady took a small, adorable angel's head that had broken off at its neck, put the trademark of two crossing swords on the broken piece, and handed it to me to keep as a souvenir.

I ventured off by myself for a short time in Meissen, curious to see what the side streets were like. The main street looked bad, but what I observed on the side streets was extremely disturbing. Of course, I had noticed in other towns that something was not right with socialism. Instead of improving the place, each time I came, the conditions had worsened. The infrastructure was crumbling before my eyes. The streets in Potsdam were probably in worse condition than those in Meissen. A glance behind the facades of the apartment houses revealed how badly the interior was in need of repair. It was obvious that socialism, as practiced in the GDR, was doomed to fail. Yet, even then, I foresaw no immediate change.

Although I had been more or less sympathetic toward their cause, I began to be more vocal in my criticism, which I am certain was reported to our hosts in Berlin. In Buchenwald, I excused myself again from viewing the documentary with the students. I could not take it anymore. I had also wondered at times if the phone calls I received at home without a response at the other end might have originated from the GDR. Someone at Bayer was sure I was being secretly monitored. They, of course, were not interested in my taking the students through the GDR, because like most West Germans, they never went there.

When it rains, it pours. On the way from Weimar to Erfurt, Julia felt rather sick. As soon as we had checked in at an appealing youth hostel, a former castle, I took her to the hospital, where the nurses and doctors treated us with great kindness. The doctor diagnosed her with mononucleosis and offered to hospitalize her at no cost. Admittedly, the facility did not look like the often state-of-the-art hospitals in America, but I certainly would not have hesitated to entrust myself to their care. Julia preferred to stay with us and, understandably, with her friends, even though she was deadly sick. Early in the morning, we continued by train, and we arrived in Radolfzell very late. Dr. Weber from the CDC and his staff took over, and had students transported to their lodgings in cabs. I went directly with Julia, who could barely make it, to the hospital, which was situated near a park on the outskirts of the town and looked very inviting. As soon as we entered and asked for the emergency room, they asked, "Who is going to pay?" It took over an hour to convince them that the student had insurance. Eventually they carted her off to a bed, and I fell into my own bed at the quaint hotel, dead tired. After numerous phone calls to the States and a flood of visits from fellow students, Julia, who from the beginning had struck me as a bit spoiled, constantly complaining about the food in the GDR and other petty matters, but never too tired to disco, even with mono, had calmed down enough for me to leave her in the capable hands of the director.

Julia was not the only problem child on this trip. Another female student, very attractive and heavily made-up, turned out to be a big rotten apple, refusing to speak a word of German whenever I addressed her, not even "Guten Morgen." The rest of the students urged me to send her home, but in the end I decided to give her a second chance, because she claimed to have no money and that her credit card was maxed out. She also had been highly recommended by my colleague from St. Mary's, whose student and babysitter she was. I later deeply regretted having admitted this girl. Instead of turning out to be the A student my friend and colleague had claimed she was, she gave me no choice but to flunk her, because her work at the CDC was inferior and the paper she had to write to earn credit never reached my desk. Instead, I learned from another student, who lived in the same house with her at Bayer, that she had many male visitors, one after another, climb in through her window, and thought nothing of engaging in improper entanglements with them in the presence of her roommates or letting them spend the night in the bed of a student who was away on a weekend trip. I should have guessed what I was in for the minute she arrived at the airport, dressed in a very sexy white suit with a long slit almost up to her navel and carrying a fancy white umbrella with lace fringes. After thirty minutes on the plane, she was already sipping champagne with a businessman and had managed to receive an invitation to connect with him in Cologne. When I asked her how her fiancé, whom she claimed to have waiting at Notre Dame, would feel about it, she laughed.

If you think my life has been boring, think again. The day before my departure from beautiful Lake Constance, Tonio's letter caught up with me:

Our favorite Nemesis slapped a court order on me and a summons to appear in "mediation" court tomorrow. . . . She went to a "mediator" and then to a circuit judge and told him that she was afraid I would <u>kidnap</u> the children! . . . She then waited until she thought we would be out of the country to serve the summons. She got the judge there to issue a restraining order that everything be maintained status quo according to our divorce decree and that if any modification be attempted it be done in the state of Oregon.

He explained that he had retained an attorney who asked for a continuance until Tonio returned to the States. He felt it was mainly a ploy on the part of his ex to change the jurisdiction. You may recall my fascination with legal matters, going back to my days at James & Hoff. I fell asleep wondering how it would all turn out.

I was glad to settle down in my compartment on the way to Cologne, where I had a meeting at Bayer AG with the director of Personnel, his staff, and the director of the American division of the CDG. Tonio and I were to meet there and had been invited again to stay at the Kasino, their hotel.

After Frankfurt, I got up to stretch my legs and walked through the aisle of the train. I could not believe my eyes when I spotted Tonio's head of curly hair, bent over a book. I pushed open the door to his compartment, we hugged and kissed, and he moved his luggage to my compartment. – I talked a mile a minute about my ordeals with the group, and when I was finished, he told me he had realized when it was time to board the plane that his passport had expired, which for some reason had passed unnoticed up to that point. Tonio brought me up to speed on the legal action and how "the Nemesis" had reacted to an "irate" phone call in which he had reiterated our desire to have the children spend the school year with us so they could get a better education. We decided that since there was nothing he could do about it, we should try to put it out of our minds and have a good time planning our fairy-tale wedding, an event which no doubt played a part in the ex's attack. She was jealous, which I could sympathize with, because I would have felt the same, especially since the children had reported that their mother's wedding had been a rather colorless event, no doubt partially due to the fact that she disliked the groom.

I alerted the appropriate people at Bayer about the student with mono and about another student, whose blood needed to be tested regularly. They foresaw no problem, since I had made them aware of the case prior to the student's acceptance into the program. Before I left, I thanked them warmly for their strong support, reiterated my desire to see the students placed in jobs related to their future careers, and raised certain concerns over environmental and safety issues, which they assured me I need not worry about. I recalled an incident whereby I received a phone call from a concerned mother in the middle of the night. Her son had asked for new underwear, because he had found holes in his boxers. He had neglected to wear the protective clothing furnished by Bayer to guard against contact with certain acids. –

We ended our meeting with lunch at the Kasino, to which Antonio, who was assisting with my program, was also invited. It was wonderful that he could take part in the overseas programs, which I had taken much pride in developing over the years.

Cologne is right around the corner from Bonn, and I had contacted the Padre to tell him we would stop by and invite him for a glass of wine on the way to Italy. I wanted to introduce him to Tonio and invite him to the wedding. – Tonio liked the Padre, and vice versa. They had much to talk about, considering Tonio's background as a classicist and his experiences as a paleographer in various monasteries in Italy, not to mention his friendship with Father M. at the Vatican Library. As expected, the Padre was the conversationalist par excellence. I was not sure what he really thought of my marrying Tonio, because I did not ask him – I most certainly was old enough to decide for myself. I suspect he regretted that there would be no more hikes and fishing adventures. When he expressed doubt regarding his ability to come to Venice, citing his failing eyesight, I speculated that the real reason was that, in marrying Tonio, a divorced man, outside the Catholic Church, I would henceforth live in sin and upon my death go straight to hell. Since reading Dante's *Inferno*, I had always thought (somewhat facetiously) that the more interesting people were in hell and that there would be much to discuss and dispute, which would be more exciting than listening eternally to harp music among the angels in heaven.

Wedding Plans in Venice, Italy – Problematic Students

After having delivered the Padre safe and sound to his doorstep, we hopped on the train to Venice and shared the first-class compartment with a nice gentleman. Tonio was reading. Keyed up from all the meetings at Bayer and our visit with the

Padre, I grasped the first opportunity to strike up a conversation with the gentleman. As it turned out, he was the chief engineer of the new railroad that was in the process of being built and that would start operating in one or two years. It was much talked about, because it would be the fastest train in Europe. He was on the way to Munich for a meeting. Tonio was always surprised about the very interesting people I met because I was not afraid to speak to strangers. – It passed the time until Munich, where he got off. Before we knew it, the train stopped in my favorite city: Venezia.

My friend Ute Schott, from the CDG in New York, had recommended a pensione on the Giudecca Canal, close to a vaporetto stop and not far from Santa Maria della Salute. This church was built in gratitude to the Virgin for ending the Black Death. We had a spacious room, furnished nicely, though not elegantly, and a wonderful view of the canal and the skyline of Venice on the opposite side. – The first item on our agenda was to find a church and a priest. We looked inside Santa Maria della Salute, which would have been a wonderful place for a grandiose wedding, with the many steps leading up to the portals; but this was not at all realistic. The church was much too large and magnificent for our presumably small group of guests. I had also forgotten that this church was out of the question for the simple reason that I, a Catholic, in marrying Tonio, a divorced Episcopalian male, could not be married in a Catholic church. –

St. George's, an Anglican church, was the only Episcopalian branch in Venice. We found Father Baar, an American, at home after his siesta, and had no problem engaging his assistance. The church's calendar was free on July 4, 1989. Looking forward to the big event, he invited us for tea and to meet his wife and took us to look at the church. By comparison to Santa Maria della Salute, St. George's was small and narrow. We liked both the frieze of putti all around the walls close to the ceiling and the columns, which were set about ten feet apart and integrated into the walls. They introduced an air of height, accentuated by the arched windows that let in much light. We saw that the church, if decorated with an abundance of flowers, green trees, and candles, had the potential to play host to a festive occasion. We had a good idea as to what we wanted and headed straight to the florist nearby, who was recommended by Father Baar. The florist, who spoke better French than English, tried his best to get the order straight, and when we left him after exchanging addresses and phone numbers, we decided to find a romantic restaurant and carry on planning and dreaming over a plate of pasta and a bottle of Chianti.

Father Baar had scheduled a meeting with Christina Thoresby, the organist, a tall, haggard, long-nosed, antiquated lady – compliments to Venice from the Church of England. The lady was dressed in a light, very old-fashioned, floor-length, coffee-brown coat, complemented by an ancient straw hat with a wide rim of the same color, covering her thin gray hair, twisted into a bun. She looked and acted like a character out of a Charles Dickens novel. Her large brown handbag must have served her for more than half a century. We had no idea how well she played the organ, but she was highly interested in the entire affair and assured us there was nothing to worry about. Indeed, she turned out to be a rather pleasant character. Not at all stingy with gossip, she walked us through some of the streets of Venice, pointing out which person of noble birth lived or was still holding out in this or that degenerating palace. She insisted we must not miss her dear friend Peggy Guggenheim's collection and must admire the Klees, Kandinskies, Picassos, Chagalls, Dalís, and such, which, of course, we eventually did. We suspected she would ascertain whether we followed her advice. She also tipped us off to a very romantic garden restaurant, located not too far from the church, with trellises overflowing with bunches of red princess roses. After talking to the manager and checking out the menu, we decided it would be ideal for us. We could always go inside, should it rain.

The organist-spinster had also recommended a pensione for the wedding party, which we promised to look at after investigating other possibilities. We had fun looking at the luxurious hotels along the Grand Canal. We asked to be shown the bridal suites in the five-star Hotel Bauer, located at an enchanting corner of the Grand Canal, and were impressed by the magnificence of the suites and the richness of the interior, all furnished in invaluable antiques, and I wondered quietly if I could fall asleep at night in the midst of such splendor. Antonio suggested we dine at the Bauer, where we sat on the terrace behind a balustrade of flower boxes bursting with pink, draping geraniums, and watched the setting sun disappear behind the Santa Maria della Salute across the canal. The water was lapping gently against the gondolas below, and in the distance a gondolier was singing to the lovers in his black boat as they glided through the night among the palaces, whose lights slithered mysteriously, like golden snakes, along the black surface of the canal. We decided we would wait until the wedding and go to the church in grand style in the golden gondola. Tonio and I decided that one or two nights with Gustl and Liesl at the Bauer at a cost of several thousand dollars was not worth the risk, because the children might unintentionally break a vase or some other priceless artifact. –

We were in an exploratory mood and simply could not pass up the legendary Palazzo Pisani Gritti, where we indulged in a mouthwatering piece of torte and a cup of mocha in Italy's oldest café, dating back to the sixteenth century. The splendor of the Gritti Palace hotel surpassed that of the Bauer, and as we sipped the café, served in delicate bone-china cups, we felt almost like the kings and queens, prime ministers and presidents, who had sat there before us.

Venice was not overrun with tourists, as we had feared; but it was a good idea to check out the Pensione Accademia, located in the center of the city, and the district of Dorsoduro in advance of the wedding. We fell instantly in love with the big villa and its setting of twisting informal gardens leading to a canal. It sat tucked away behind an iron gate and had all the allure of a Sleeping Beauty castle. The facades were covered with flowering and vivid green vines. Masses of pink oleander bushes crowded the flaking stucco facade and reached as high as the stone balustrade of the balcony on the first floor. Stone benches sat in intimate places, flanked by roses or flowering shrubs. Here and there a statuette accentuated the grounds.

As we stepped inside, we were stunned by the luxurious interior of the spacious foyer, furnished in classic Venetian style with rich wood paneling, gold-framed mirrors, Oriental carpets, antique chairs, brocaded loveseats, and sparkling chandeliers throughout. It still reflected the character of the Russian embassy it once housed. How blessed we felt to have found our very own fairy-tale spot in the middle of Venice.

Tonio reserved six double rooms for our wedding party and asked for recommendations for nearby hotels in which the other guests could stay in case all of the remaining twenty rooms were booked.

You can imagine how thrilled we were. One major task lay ahead of us: music! A fairy-tale wedding without music is unthinkable. We asked for directions to the Conservatorio di Musica Benedetto Marcello, which was not so hard to find, since it was directly on St. Mark's Square. We opened the big door leading to the interior of this awe-inspiring palace, built in the sixteenth century by the powerful Pisani family. I felt even smaller when Tonio and I walked up the wide stairway in the hope of finding someone who could enlighten us as to whom to ask to find a quartet to play on July 4, 1989. As we looked around the huge vaulted hall, with the sun shining through its tall windows and massive wooden doors leading to rooms behind which the unknown was looming, the door in the center opened unexpectedly, and out came a young man with dark hair and glasses. We walked up to him and told him about our wish. He turned out to be Stefano Zanchetta, a violin instructor at the conservatory as well as a violinist with the renowned chamber-music orchestra I Solisti Veneti. By the time we said our good-byes, he had assured us of securing a quartet from the chamber ensemble to play for us during the wedding ceremony, the reception, and the dinner. Tonio was to mail suggestions for a program a few months in advance. We were blissfully happy and continued to fantasize and chart our course as we rested, drinking a glass of Venetian wine with a gourmet pizza in a restaurant around the corner from St. Mark's Square.

Leaving Venice well satisfied, we took the train to Bolzano (South Tyrol), where we planned to stop briefly in order to locate the ideal place for our honeymoon with the kiddies. We wanted to imitate the Austrian von Trapp family from our favorite family musical, *The Sound of Music*. The children used to compare me to Fräulein Maria whenever we sang her songs. We soon found the ideal place, the Hotel Icaro, a brand-new, twenty-room, mountain-lodge-type hotel built on the highest alpine plateau of Europe, the Seiser Alm. It seemed made for honeymooners with children. Flowering meadows surrounded this family-owned jewel of the Dolomites. Here, Gustl could roam and Liesl could gather the prettiest wildflowers to make into a wreath for her head. How peaceful and quiet it was – no cars were allowed. The 360-degree panorama, with a distant view of the rugged Dolomites, the El Dorado of mountain clusters, and the valleys covered with carpets of nature, was as picture-perfect as the mountain scenes in the musical. When we noticed two children, a boy and a girl about the age of our children, playing next to the house, we told the owners, Mr. and Mrs. Sattler, to reserve two adjoining rooms with balconies and choice views for the following July.

The next morning, the train sped north toward Mutti in Hannover. As usual, we took her, together with my good friend Marianne, for coffee and cake at the outdoor restaurant on the Maschsee, where Mutti had so often enjoyed sitting on a bench watching us children throw pebbles into the lake or feed bread crumbs to a family of white swans. We knew she was only kidding when she told us she would jump into the lake if we did not stop fighting. I was sad when I realized she still did not really know who Tonio was, because she asked the same question as before and explained repeatedly to Tonio that she was the youngest of seven children. As in a refrain, Tonio, untiring, answered, "The youngest and the best," whereupon she replied, "Oh, they were all good." Marianne could not get over what a charming, warm, and considerate partner I had found, and was impressed that Tonio always supported my mother when walking up or down stairs.

I was anxious for Tonio to meet Sibby in person. Although I did not inform her of the fact, she played a major part in our novel. She was exuberant as always when she heard my "sweet voice" and immediately suggested taking us out for dinner at her favorite restaurant, where she knew the cook personally and guaranteed he would whip up one of his specialties. She asked whether we would mind if her teenage daughter tagged along, but she must have known we would not object.

Sibby took us to the restaurant in her Mercedes, using every trick in the book to flirt with Tonio, just as I had expected, and we were secretly amused that she never gave up, even while we dined at the Golden Goose. The Goose was an intimate but classy restaurant, and the meal her friend concocted was indeed superb; but even more superb was Sibby's coup, in which she somehow managed to have the bill for the dinner to which she had invited us, presumably to celebrate our engagement, end up in front of Tonio, who, gentleman that he was, pulled the American Express card from his wallet and, without blinking an eye, paid the bill. When Sibby and I were alone for a few minutes, she raved about Tonio, his good looks, intelligence, and manners. One minute she talked about our age difference and the next about how she could not get over how young I looked. She advised me that not a soul would notice if I didn't tell. – When I asked her about Franz, she talked nonstop, saying he often spent a few days and nights with her, usually after a bout with the bottle, but always returned to his wife and kids. For the umpteenth time, she reported in dramatic terms that she had unsuccessfully tried to take her life by turning on the gas stove but that fortunately, or unfortunately, one of her children found her just in time. – She dropped us off at the hotel, where we said our good-byes. But that was not the end of the evening at the Golden Goose. When Tonio looked at the credit-card receipt from the restaurant, he noticed someone had changed the figures by adding an additional $30 to his 20% tip. The Golden Goose had laid a "golden egg" in the true sense of the term. On the flight home, as we discussed the guest list for the wedding, we agreed that Sibby would not be invited. –

We were still anxious about Tonio's passport and sighed with relief when we successfully passed through customs in Chicago. Neither the American nor the German and Italian controllers noticed the expiration date.

We had been home just a few days when the children arrived by plane from the West Coast, despite the fact that the mother had accused Tonio of intended kidnapping. You can be sure her legal action brought with it a flood of erratic telephone conversations between her, Squeaky Voice, and Tonio as well as their and Tonio's attorneys. At times Tonio asked me to deal not only with his ex and Squeaky Voice, but even with their attorney, who at one point revealed to me that the ex had said she was glad Tonio was going to marry me. I found that strange, because when Tonio first announced he had decided to remarry, she advised him never to do so. – I had disliked Squeaky Voice ever since the day they crashed the garden party and could understand why, at one point during the custody ordeal, Tonio almost flipped out because Squeaky Voice refused to call the children to the telephone. Tonio was so upset he contacted the police, who showed up at his ex's house to make sure the children were all right. During the shouting matches, I sometimes left the room and crawled under the bedcovers until it was all over.

I am certain Ms. Ice Water took great pleasure in making our lives miserable, and in forcing us to eventually spend over $4,000 on legal fees, just to maintain the status quo. She knew full well that we never, even in our wildest dreams, would consider keeping the children with us against their mother's wish. Of course, the fact that they had moved to the West Coast did not simplify the situation. We tried hard to keep the children out of the squabbles. It was difficult, especially for Tonio, who now and then talked about how nice it would be if Gustl could attend Stanley Clark. He did point out that in a couple of years, Gustl could decide for himself where he preferred to live.

Not long after the children had arrived, the birth of their stepsister was announced, which resulted in Liesl's reverting back to toddler behavior. She crawled around the floor like a baby for a week or so, but was all right when the photographs of the baby arrived. – The summer went fast and was filled with games and with swimming at the community pool or in Lake Michigan. We bought bikes for both children, and Tonio took Gustl on his first camping trip on Lake Michigan before the children flew back to the West Coast.

The fall semester brought with it preparations for new courses. We ran into difficulties due to budget constraints, in response to which I had to rent videos not available in the National Television System Committee's American standard. It was a real nuisance to transport my personal multisystem back and forth to avoid being restricted to showing only videos available in the United States. In addition, the Prima Donna had put a limit on the pages I could copy each semester on the Xerox machine (I must have been the only faculty member so restricted), and when I complained, he suggested I charge the students for the copies. I considered that extremely unfair to my students. – I was very excited about a senior seminar, "Masterpieces of German Prose," involving literature from East and West Germany, in which I planned to treat selected works by East German authors, studied through films based on their writings.

I had very good students that semester, including two from Austria and two from Germany, which guaranteed lively class discussions. – We were like a big family. Since Tonio was a superb gourmet cook, we began inviting the upper-level majors to our house for dinner once each semester. One of the students, a native German, appeared with a huge bouquet of beautiful flowers, which I will never forget. In retrospect, it seems that she hoped the bouquet would guarantee her an A for every course she took thenceforth. When that did not happen, she changed her major and finally dropped out altogether. – Though married for the second time, with two children, she had a definite penchant for Tonio, which I observed when she kissed him on the lips, just like that. But, understandably, she was not the only student who was unhappy about receiving a B. Another native German, who expected an A simply because she spoke the language better than she wrote it, rang my doorbell one day, complaining that I had not recommended her for an achievement award in German. I explained to her that speaking the language does not guarantee you an A in a literature course. Those native German students who were disappointed when they received a B or even a B+ had never attended a high school in Germany. In contrast, those native Germans who had made the *Abitur* were, with one exception, straight-A students, and several earned a PhD in German.

I experienced a big disappointment with a very bright student from an Eastern Bloc country who, after much effort on my part – I pulled strings in addition to channeling financial support to her from a small scholarship fund – finally became eligible to participate in my Bayer Program. Regretfully, she behaved all too irresponsibly by failing to turn in the required paper by the deadline. After numerous fruitless reminders, I had no choice but to flunk her. She continued to sink as time went on, missing too many classes and exams, and after a while, her frequent tears failed to improve her grade. She complained – and thus provided the administration with a reason to go after me. By then I had learned to protect myself. In questionable cases, I photocopied papers and poorly written exams just in case I needed documentation. Fortunately I had to resort to such documentation only once. I found out later that the dissenter from the East had a reputation on campus for missing classes frequently and for trying to sweet talk herself out of sticky situations. I always felt saddened when a promising student slowly, before my eyes, slid downhill. I was even more saddened when I discovered that one of my students had blatantly deceived his parents by changing to Bs the low grades on the transcript sent by the registrar. The situation was extremely disturbing, since I knew the parents. After agonizing over whether to inform them, and after seeking advice from others, I finally told them, which unleashed a major family crisis.

Another very intelligent and attractive student, who pursued a double major in French and German, handed in a late paper in connection with a culture course. It was so well written that Tonio vowed it was plagiarized. That interested me, because the student herself had told me the Prima Donna accused her of plagiarizing a French paper. Unable to prove it, I gave the student a passing grade. Later, I learned that the same girl turned up in Germany at Bayer's doorstep (she had been there as a participant the previous year) and asked for a job, despite the fact that she had been informed by Bayer, myself, and the Carl Duisberg people that there was no job available for her that summer. I found her behavior extremely impertinent and could never understand why Bayer did not send her packing, unless the fellow with whom she had an affair the year before helped her to get in. She also expected to receive better treatment than she got, despite the fact that many times she came to class unprepared and was consistently late handing in term papers. I was not surprised when it came to my attention that she referred to me as an ogress, and I am sure she was not the only one. – There were others who tried to get away with plagiarizing. One student at the fourth-semester level handed in an essay that appeared to have been copied from the jacket of a record. I told him that if he could write this well at the fourth-semester level, he should be enrolled in senior-level courses. He had to rewrite the paper in my office while I was present. He did not like it. His face turned red as a tomato when he saw the many mistakes he had made. This deceiver was actually quite bright. He was majoring in French and was also a close friend of Brigit, one of my German majors who had participated in the Bonn Program together with Harry.

Harry, a bright, respectful, successful, and gentle young man, who used to water my flowers when I was conducting the overseas program, called one day after having graduated and asked to see me at home. He was rather sad when he confided in me, because he lacked the courage to tell his parents, that he was gay. It was my first encounter with a gay student. As it turned out, he had liked Brigit very much – but she gradually realized she was a lesbian. I was glad to know Harry felt he could confide in me, but was sorry his dream to raise a family one day would not be realized. He eventually introduced me to his partner, a pleasant young man, but I never found out how Harry's very religious and conservative, but kind, family reacted to the news. I sensed they would be overwhelmed at first but would learn to understand. – Maybe the two even raised a family.

In 1988, Sally Detlef was elated when she was accepted to the Heart of Germany Exchange Program at the Free University of Berlin, to which another German major, the more mature Liz, divorcée and mother of seven children, had been accepted a year earlier. Liz and her sister Regan had benefited noticeably from regular tutorial sessions with Renate, not only because their language skills improved, but also because they became good friends.

I was very much pleased when Miles asked me to refer former Bayer Program participants for possible employment, and I was grateful when Bayer offered more summer jobs for students who spoke German well enough to work without first going through the language training at Lake Constance. It meant the students could earn very good money while furthering their German-language skills. The professor in charge of the German course offerings at the Kokomo campus asked for my advice in connection with introductory and intermediate courses and was grateful for the outlines, syllabi, and course objectives with which I furnished him.

The considerable effort put forth by the administration to attract students from all walks of life to our commuter campus brought a gentleman about thirty years my senior, and almost a head shorter than I, to my office door. He was born in Düsseldorf, Germany, in 1901. I was not quite sure what he wanted when he first approached me, but was a bit worried that he was hoping for something I was not inclined to give. He had experienced a most colorful, yet tragic, past, which he was summing up in an autobiographical sketch that he prefaced as follows:

I dreamed of the day I could attend college and attain a degree. Because I was handicapped by the lack of funds, I had to postpone this dream. . . . Then came the Nazi assault when homes were destroyed (including ours). The Jewish people were mistreated and sent to concentration camps. My late wife was beaten and for many years to come, suffered and required constant doctor's care. I had to take on three extra jobs to pay for the doctor and medication. After the death of my first wife, there was a void I had to fill; and, at long last, I applied for admittance to IUSB.

I vaguely identified with his fate and, mainly out of pity, accepted his occasional invitations to lunch or his home, where he gave me a sampling of his singing voice, which, considering his age, was quite good. As a tenor, he had received extensive voice training in Germany from renowned opera singers, yet was unable to follow a regular career as a result of the impending threats from the Nazis. The tenor was an old-school gentleman who always greeted me by kissing my hand, brought boxes of chocolate candy, and spoke and wrote nineteenth-century German almost perfectly. – He was very well-read and able to discuss certain plays by Goethe and Schiller intelligently. As a singer, he had developed a special liking for Heinrich Heine's *Book of Songs* and prided himself on owning the collected works of the German literary giants. – He eventually enrolled in my literature course, which I thought would be a snap for him, but unfortunately, due to much sickness, he was absent more frequently than he was present. He had also found a new wife. With much perseverance, and as a result of my treating him more or less like a student of an individual reading course, he finished and eventually earned the much-desired BA, accompanied by much fanfare and a banquet. I was unable to attend, because I was on the way to Germany with my students.

The tenor also brought his new bride to the Oktoberfest and the Christmas party at our residence. At the parties, any unpleasantness that had occurred during the semester was forgotten, as was the case when Tonio and I met with students for a beer on Fridays at our newly established German table at the Oaken Bucket.

Gustl and Liesl flew in again from the West Coast for Thanksgiving and were getting used to being supervised by the red-capped stewardesses. They loved it when I greeted them with a box filled with fresh, chocolate-coated dunking doughnuts, which I picked up on the way to the airport, and they always ran to their room to look for the presents awaiting them on their pillows. We celebrated Christmas just as we had before, and talked much about the forthcoming wedding in Venice, for which we had begun preparations early to make sure all our ducks were in a row. We introduced the children to our good friends – the Englesburgers, the Martins, Father Minnix, and the Connors – all of whom would be invited. Gustl and Liesl were somewhat uncomprehending when we told them how fortunate we had been to find Francesca, Gigi Connor's sister, who lived in Venice and who had promised to orchestrate the big event in Venezia herself to make sure it all unfolded smoothly. I told them about the Seiser Alm, the mountains, the meadows, and the children they would play with, and before they fell asleep I sang their favorite good-night song, "Edelweiss" from *The Sound of Music*. When they returned in June, we would go shopping for our wedding attire.

When the children were gone, we usually spent a quieter Christmas at home or with friends and worked on the novel, which had been neglected somewhat due to my untypically demanding course preparations as well as having to teach three courses at night. We had been in touch with a West German publishing house, Verlag für Angewandte Wissenschaften, which had expressed an interest in reading the manuscript.

The Prima Donna's Kiss of Death

In preparing my annual report, which I knew would once more be scrutinized by the Prima Donna, I took great care to include everything pertinent and ended up with a report over nine pages long. I pointed out that I hosted the director of the Carl Duisberg Association, who came to our campus from Germany specifically for a meeting with Chancellor Cohen, myself, and others, and that I defrayed the expenses using personal funds. I restrained from criticizing the chancellor for reneging on the dinner invitation he had made, even though at the time I thought it was extremely unwise, petty, and rude, considering the enormous benefits, financial and otherwise, our students derived from the Bayer and CDG connection. I also urged the university to purchase a multisystem video monitor and recorder, and I went into great detail about all of the courses I had taught during the academic year. I furnished solicited student evaluations from all my courses, including those associated with the Bayer Program, and saw no reason for concern. Yet, because I knew that if you want to find something to complain about, you can, I decided to attach all the unsolicited comments offered by students in the form of thank-you cards and letters. They are so outstanding that when reading them today, I get teary-eyed. As had been the case so many times before, a student commented that he or she "learned more in [my] class than in a lot of other ones." A student from a beginners' course wrote, "I will be continuing German next semester and will try harder and hopefully do better! – Thanks for everything – if I had any other professor I would have never lasted for even one week!"

Even though I had furnished extensive explanations for why students dropped the beginners' courses, the Prima Donna still blamed *me* for the admittedly noticeable rate of attrition. The year before, he faulted me for not collecting solicited evaluations. When I tried to appease him this time, he pointed out that "the system of solicited student course evaluations used at the end of each semester produces primarily evaluations from those who have succeeded in the courses; those students who have previously failed and/or withdrawn are not present to submit evaluations. Thus, student evaluations submitted in such circumstances need to be interpreted in context." I cannot recall one instance during my career as a professor in which a colleague's *nonexisting* evaluations were called into question. – He did point out that I did an "excellent job teaching the superior students" and that "the majors and minors are provided with a rigorous and rewarding program."

I was glad this was the last time the Prima Donna would evaluate me. His chairmanship ended with the spring semester. Yet, to satisfy my own curiosity, I performed a survey on student attrition in my service courses, which showed that only 8% of matriculating students had dropped out for reasons over which the instructor had control. The survey was based on an individual knowledge of each student and the student's career at IUSB.

The spring semester kept me busy with teaching, committee work on the home and Bloomington campuses, and everything connected with the 1989 Bayer Program, which I did not have to attend.

Virtually out of the blue, the second week in March, the Prima Donna's kiss of death arrived in my mailbox. It was getting-even time, I felt sure, for having dared to give him a low increase in salary when I was acting chairman. It was also proof that my longtime suspicion about his dislike for me was well-founded. Looking back, I still wonder if he unleashed his anger toward me in his memo because I was a native of Germany. His memo was one and a half pages long and addressed to the chairman of Arts and Sciences, with copies to me and the dean of faculty. It was written in the most hostile, inflammatory, and abusive tone imaginable, accusing me of constantly harassing and attacking colleagues in the department, challenging decisions by administrators, going repeatedly over their heads, ignoring or avoiding them altogether, overspending, writing too many memos (especially the one in which I pointed out his use of discriminatory language toward me), and being the primary reason why nobody wanted to chair the department. He noted that he had observed me throughout his sixteen years on campus and wanted to put all of this down before his term ended so that it would be considered when salary decisions were made.

I was utterly stunned, partly because I could not believe that any man would abuse his power so vehemently and be so vicious on paper. I would have been ashamed to compose such a document, not to mention put it in the mail. It was a compilation of vastly inflated, twisted facts and outright lies. Of course, he must have sensed that I had lost respect for him long before and that I was not the only one on campus who harbored an intense dislike for him, as an anonymous evaluation of his administrative skills that made its way into my possession will attest:

I have never encountered an administrator who is so hungry for power. . . . He wants to have all authority over everything, and is usually only willing to accept advice which agrees with his preconceived opinions. He attends many meetings of faculty committees, and when he disagrees with opinions being expressed he will at times sit making awful faces, implying that those speaking are complete idiots, and at other times intervene so forcefully as to quell all other comment. Often he is correct, but at times he is not.

[He] is apparently completely unwilling to accept faculty authority in any matter, even those clearly specified to be primarily faculty concerns in the new IU constitution. Rather than working with the Academic Senate he attempts to establish new procedures and structures to circumvent it.

Indeed, much of his criticism of me could have been directed at himself. In addition to his partial position, there were only four full-time professors in the department. He must not have known that two of them had approached me and suggested I take over the chairmanship after his term ended. His buddy the Fly Trap was not one of them. It is true, as I have previously mentioned, that I had several confrontations with the Fly Trap. What I have not mentioned was a confrontation at a departmental meeting at which the Prima Donna was not present. When I brought up the matter of my low salary, reminding the Fly Trap of my rank and also that I had been promoted to associate professor even prior to being tenured, he responded, "You were only promoted because you are a woman." I was so devastated at the time that I went home and cried. It seemed that everything I had worked so hard for was wiped out in a single moment. I have not forgotten it to this day. When I questioned my comparatively low increase in salary on another occasion, he said, "If you don't like it, why don't you leave?" In that climate, I had learned over the years to avoid those who had hurt me and, outside of meetings, to speak with them rarely.

Not Hitler's Child

Though I was only speculating, I knew the Prima Donna was furious when one of the French majors who had agreed to attend McGill University for a summer term, an arrangement he had made with the university, changed her mind at the last minute and enrolled in my Bayer Program instead. This left him without anybody to send in her place. Last but not least, much professional jealousy was involved. My outstanding student evaluations must have irritated him. He was also envious of my overseas programs, so much so that while chairman of our department, he was instrumental in calling for a review of the program by a committee on our campus. I also suspect that as a non-PhD in French, he felt insecure professionally and disliked female professionals in particular. The way he treated my female French colleague was unconscionable.

I wondered about the timing of his memo. He knew I was getting ready for my wedding in Venice, which must have irked him. I would not have put it past him to hope to put a damper on my plans. He by no means looked healthy. Though I never knew exactly what was meant by the term, I thought he looked like "death warmed over," a bit gray-green, like dry spinach leaves. – Regardless, I rose above his kiss of death, tucked the memo in my briefcase, and derived much relief from sharing its contents with a number of my colleagues on the fourth floor and others whom I ran into. They shook their heads in disbelief and advised me to consider the source, ignore it, and get on with my life. When I spoke with the dean, who, as everybody knew, had no use for the short-term predecessor, I left his office knowing he would just let it rest. – The memo was written on March 6, 1989. On March 16, I forwarded to the chairman of Arts and Sciences a memo to which I attached a copy of a note I received from my beginners' class students: "Für Mutter Beardsley! Wir lieben Sie!" (For Mother Beardsley! We love you!). I told him I wanted to share this special occasion in my teaching career with him and asked him to add it to my file. On Valentine's Day a student had knocked at the classroom door and delivered a dozen carnations with the card. Later that day, a Valentine's balloon was delivered and, together with a card from another beginners' class, kept with the secretary. Very few of my colleagues on campus, if any, ever received valentines from their students. I sent a copy of the memo to the Prima Donna. Although he remained silent, the chair of Arts and Sciences responded to me as follows:

I want to thank you for sharing with me the appreciation recently shown by your students. There is no doubt in anyone's mind that you have built up a strong, loyal, and talented group of students genuinely interested in German. This is not easy to accomplish, and I commend you for that.

I was pleased to see that he sent a copy of his memo to the Prima Donna. It was my "good-bye kiss" to him under my old name.

As we would not see the children until June, Antonio and I decided to throw a big, splashy party, partially in honor of Ute Schott's visit. Ms. Schott was the assistant to the director of the CDS in New York. She had come to participate in the screening of the applicants for the 1989 Bayer Program. We pulled out all the stops. Tonio, through his brother in Florida, ordered a barrel of jumbo shrimp and a large shipment of raw oysters, which would be flown to South Bend. We hired two waitresses, a bartender, and a pianist. You can bet that everybody talked about the bash for a long time, even after we were married. We invited all our friends and colleagues and several administrators from IU and Miles, omitting my archenemies.

The Wedding Date Draws Closer

After the party, we focused on our wedding. Tonio, drawing on his artistic and paleographic expertise, crafted each invitation in the form of a beautifully handwritten letter on parchment-like paper, which we sent to all our friends and most of his family, although we knew that only those who could afford it would be able to attend. He also wrote to Mr. Zanchetta at the Conservatoria in Venice and asked specifically for a piece by Charles Ives, the American composer, since we were to marry on Independence Day. Tonio also dealt with Francesca and all parties in Venice, while I was in charge of travel, attire, and the children. I had come up with the bright idea, to which Tonio agreed enthusiastically, that we return on the *Queen Elizabeth II*. I knew the children would just love it. After all, the von Trapp family came to America on a ship.

At the beginning of April, Tonio went with me to Chicago to look for a diamond. He had thoroughly studied the art of choosing the best color and the most flawless gem, and ended up acquiring a beautiful, clear-blue, two-carat diamond in a Tiffany setting from a reputable jeweler. Tonio picked it up a couple of weeks later together with the certificate. He put the diamond, which also happened to be my birthstone, on my finger over a glass of champagne on my birthday in the cozy ambiance of the well-known Carriage House restaurant, before dinner was served. It was the fieriest diamond I had owned up to that point and definitely made the statement Tonio intended it to make. I loved it and still do.

I taught two courses during the first summer session, one a beginners' course and the other "Oral German for Teachers," in which I introduced a new element. With Tonio's help, we had acquired a video recording of the miniseries *Väter und Söhne* (Fathers and Sons), which had been broadcast in Germany and brought to Miles for the company's employees. It was a portrayal of the rise and fall of IG Farben coupled with historical developments from World War I until after World War II, as well as a depiction of the strengths, weaknesses, and intrigues of the family. I used the recordings, along with other material and grammar exercises, as a stimulus for class discussions and was impressed by the results. I had wanted to teach mainly to boost our travel and wedding budget, which, as you can guess, amounted to a small fortune.

My friend Donna Harlan, without my asking her, had volunteered to be my matron of honor, and I lacked the courage to tell her I had intended to ask one of my students who was planning to come to the wedding while at Bayer AG. Moreover, instead of asking Donna, I asked my good friend Renate to go shopping for a wedding dress with me. We went to the fashionable Jacobson's, in Kalamazoo, Michigan, and decided on a beautiful ivory-colored dress. The skirt was made of thin layers of chiffon, which flared out like tulip leaves toward the ankles. I could not have found a more fitting gown. The bodice up to the neckline and the long, tapered sleeves were of Venetian lace. We chose a cap embroidered with tiny white pearls on chiffon, and found a pouch-like bag and pumps with high heels, which matched perfectly. The sleeves and the long back of the dress, which featured a fitted waistline, were accented by a long row of tiny covered buttons. I asked the lady to hold for us an adorable, closely matching long dress for Liesl. It was lace over pink taffeta. I knew she would love the pink ribbon around the waist. Yes, my sweet little flower girl would look like a princess.

The children arrived on schedule, and as so many times before, as soon as evening set in, they rushed into the backyard with a jar, covered by a lid with holes, to catch lightning bugs, which they did not have on the West Coast. Tonio often grilled hamburgers, and they never failed to ask for chocolate ice cream if given a choice. I saw to it that the cookie jar was filled with chocolate-chip cookies, and wondered how long it would take Gustl to be up to his trick of asking me if I would like him to bring me a cookie, mainly to be in a position to get one for himself.

Soon after the children's arrival, we drove to Kalamazoo for shopping. Liesl tried on the lace dress, observed herself in the big mirror with big, shiny eyes, and then turned around, looked at me, and said, "You really want to buy this for me?" When I told her, "Yes, if you like it," she threw both arms around my neck and called out, "Oh, thank you!" It was a successful shopping trip all around. Gustl looked most handsome in his black blazer with silver-gray pants, white shirt, and black-and-white necktie, all by Pierre Cardin. We bought the black shoes half a size too big, because he was growing so fast. Tonio had ordered his wedding tux, which would be ready to be picked up just before our departure on June 28.

Prelude to the Wedding in Venice

Tonio and I had to get married legally in the States first, which meant the ceremony in Venice would be a celebration, similar to the custom in Europe. Thus, we had asked Father George if he would perform the service in the little church in Bristol, Indiana, on June 24, which also happened to be my name day. He agreed with pleasure, and Tonio and I were as happy as we could be, because all our plans had unfolded without a hitch.

A couple of days before June 24, Tonio's older sister called him and, before hanging up, asked him to call me to the phone. I do not recall exactly everything she said, but I have never forgotten that she told me in no uncertain terms that I was not welcome in their family. I was speechless and did not understand why, after having known about our wedding for almost three years, she had never, when we saw her in person or spoke to her on the phone, uttered a single word of displeasure about our plans. – I remained silent, said good-bye, and told Tonio what she had said. He was upset, told me something to the effect that she was most likely drunk, which was not unusual for her, and elaborated about her unhappy state, in that she was already on her third marriage and probably not very happy either, because her third husband – so rumor had it – wanted to move with her to Mexico in the wake of his shady dealings with the labor union in Chicago. (I never quite knew what that was all about.) – I discussed her warning with her mother and Father George, and they too advised me not to give it another thought. I was never very fond of her anyhow, especially after Tonio had told me about the promiscuous life she had led, even in her teens. Tonio and I thought it rather strange that she had insisted that he never ask her divorced boyfriend, whom she married in England a year or so after our engagement, if we could spend a night at his penthouse, which overlooked the lake in Chicago. Actually, it would have been nice of him to make the offer himself, since we had offered them our house if they ever desired to spend some time there when we were out of town.

While I asked my friend Renate to be a witness, Antonio asked his friend Job. We swore everybody to secrecy, and not even the children knew about it. – June 24 was a Saturday filled with sunshine. It was exactly five years and four months after Tonio and I had met, on February 24, 1984. – The Episcopal chapel was radiant from the rays of the golden sun, which shone gloriously through the colorful windows and played upon the ornate golden candlesticks on the altar holding big, lit candles. Arrangements of pink and white flowers rested on the altar, ready for Sunday Mass. The ceremony in front of the altar was simple, beautiful, memorable, and binding. It felt good to have our close friends on our side, and we wished Renate could come along to Venice, since Job and Father George would be there.

We were ready to go on June 28, marriage certificate in hand, passports stamped with visas, suitcases for everyone crammed full, and clothing bags holding our wedding outfits. British Airways set down in the morning at Heathrow, in London. Fortunately, the black London cab that looked like a huge rectangular box was bulky enough to hold all four of us as well as our belongings. Not so fortunate was the hectic ride to Victoria Station, where we had to catch the train to Dover. The cab driver was yelling and screaming at the top of his lungs, in British jargon, incomprehensible to me, at a truck, which blocked the road while the driver unloaded milk cans or such. He finally got results, sped toward Victoria at a forbidden tempo, and dumped all of us at the entrance steps to the overwhelmingly large station, a landmark of English Gothic architecture. With the help of a porter, we made our way through this largest and busiest of stations and hopped on the train in the nick of time. We were off to catch the hovercraft, which would take us across the channel to Boulogne, France.

The hovercraft was a unique first experience for all of us. As we did not have a car, we walked aboard and settled into an airline-style seat. As soon as the hatches were closed, the four-thousand-horsepower gas turbines started up, and we felt and watched the air fill the rubber skirts beneath the craft. Moments later, huge propellers sent the craft blasting across the English Channel at about sixty miles per hour. The children had a pop and Tonio a coffee. When we approached the French coast, the hovercraft, instead of slowing down, continued to speed ahead in a surge of spray, which was a bit scary, but it made a smooth transition from water to land before settling on the concrete pad of the hoverport. The ride across the channel is the fastest connection between England and France. We were excited and quite anxious not to miss the train to Paris, but at the baggage claim I realized I had left the bag with Liesl's and my wedding gown on the craft. I ran back, yelled, "Please wait!" and retrieved the gowns before it headed back to England.

Suitcases in hand, we had to hurry again and navigate a bumpy railroad track to catch the train that would transport us to our final destination: Venice.

In Paris, at the Gare de Lyon, another beautiful work of architecture, built at the turn of the century, we finally had time to catch our breath. I had made first-class reservations on an overnight train, because I thought the children might enjoy spending a night in a sleeper. They were quite excited, as they could not remember ever having slept in a bed on a train. We woke up early enough to see the Swiss mountains, and when stopping in Verona, we looked out the window and chatted with a German filmmaking crew. They were shooting a movie on the platform. I spoke with the actor, supposedly well-known, but not to me.

Our arrival on June 30 at the Venezia Santa Lucia station and the transfer via waterbus to the Accademia was another new adventure for the children. The flowers in the gardens and along the facades were in full bloom. The children loved the palatial ambiance and were happy about their large rooms, located across the hall from ours. – We tried to get a good night of rest, because for the next three days, we would be busy making preparations and welcoming guests. It was difficult to give equal time to everybody. In the evening, we sat in the elegantly furnished hall outside of our rooms, sipping wine, chatting, and talking as the guests trickled in from various countries, including Germany, Austria, Turkey, Costa Rica, and the United States. I did not want to believe it, but during the night, we could hear heavy rain splashing against our big windows. It had never rained when we visited Venice before. Why now? Unable to control the weather, we had to submit. Though it rained intermittently for the next three days, it did not stop us from getting ready. We were relieved when Sally and her boyfriend arrived to help with Liesl and Gustl. The children were even happier when Tonio's best man arrived with his family from Costa Rica. They teamed up with little Annie and Bob very quickly to explore the secret stairways and the basement of this old palace and former Russian embassy. All the adults were very helpful and took the children along for some sightseeing and to feed the pigeons on St. Mark's Square. As though it were not enough that it rained every now and then, on the night of July 3 we had a torrential downpour, so fierce that all the thunder and lightning made it difficult for me to sleep. I was also worried about Tonio, who had met with the male guests at Harry's Bar for a sort of bachelor party. When he finally appeared, soaking wet, talking about the rain and the party, I was amused when he told me he had overheard a group of people in the bar talking about the American wedding and voicing their amazement that I Solisti Veneti would be playing. They commented that not even the Venetians could get I Solisti Veneti to play for them.

We met with Father Baar and the organist-spinster, Ms. Thoresby, at the church the day before the wedding to go over the details of the ceremony. We took along Donna, Bob, the children, and Father George, who would officiate as the second priest. At one point – I don't remember exactly why – Tonio thought it might not be a good idea after all to include Gustl as ring bearer in the wedding. Gustl was shattered – he had been looking forward to being in the wedding so much. After I finally convinced his father that he simply could not make such a last-minute change, Gustl was in and happy. – I found it rather strange that Father Baar complained that the church would virtually burst with flowers and asked if we could reduce the amount, but he let it go when I told him I loved lots of flowers.

Fairy-Tale Wedding in Venice on the Fourth of July

Francesca had scheduled an appointment for me at 9:00 a.m. at the most exclusive salon in Venice. The wedding was set for 4:00 p.m. To put a damper on our day, the vaporetto (water taxi) drivers had decided to go on strike, which meant we had to walk everywhere. The master of the salon was awaiting me with a staff of three beauticians. There was no other customer in the salon. I had let my hair grow, and he recommended that he freshen up the color to a rich golden blond. I knew it would be a long procedure, but let them do whatever they saw fit, including a facial, manicure, etc. We arrived at the Accademia about an hour and a half before the start of the wedding. Antonio was a nervous wreck, because they had been looking all over the place for the ring and me. – There was also the big question of whether the golden gondola, that is, the wedding gondola, would be available to take my attendants – Donna, Bettina, Liesl, Anny, her mother Susan, and Francesca – and me to the church. Bruno, the chief gondolier, was afraid the rain would ruin the gondola. If it were unavailable, we would have to walk to the church, since the vaporetto drivers were on strike.

Then a miracle happened! As Donna was busy buttoning the little buttons on the back of my gown, and Francesca fastening on Liesl's shiny, long hair the wreath of dainty greens and white baby's breath with pink and white sweetheart roses, the sun pushed through the clouds and beamed through the large windows. At that moment, someone announced the gondola was coming from farther up the Rio San Trovaso and approaching the landing at the Accademia. While the men were walking to church, we were gliding along the canals and underneath the bridges of Venice, guided by two gondoliers dressed in white linen suits and white-and-red-striped shirts. The gondolier in the front had a decorative rectangular piece of red linen with gold stripes hanging down to his left knee from underneath his jacket; the one in the back wore the linen on his right side. He stood on a rich red Oriental runner, which was draped over the aft of the gondola. It accented the luxuriousness of the golden gondola seats. They were like thrones, with carvings of gilded nymphs, angels, and sphinxes. Reverend Baar awaited us at the San Vio landing dressed in his magnificent mantle, brocaded with gold on crimson damask. He offered his hand to help me up the broad stone steps to the sidewalk leading to the church entrance. I was holding my bridal bouquet, a masterpiece of the most beautiful snow-white stephanotis and pink sweetheart roses.

St. George's was probably never before decorated so magnificently. At the end of each bench were draped large bouquets of pink stargazer and white lilies with baby's breath on soft cushions of green, flanking the aisle. Ms. Thoresby's festive organ prelude signaled the opening beat for Tonio to start walking down the aisle with Gustl, holding the lacy, heart-shaped cushion on which the ring rested, with Donna following him. Liesl, pretty as a princess, carefully strewed rose pedals from a basket on the runner while Bob accompanied me toward the altar. It was like a dream when Bob walked me to the altar, where Tonio awaited me, smiling and looking ever so handsome in his long, contoured black jacket, a gardenia in his lapel, the striped dark-gray trousers, dressy white wing-collared shirt, silver-gray vest, and matching ascot. We were virtually embedded in masses of flowers. The Communion bench was solidly covered with white and pink blossoms, on both sides of the altar stood palm trees and green bushes, and on the altar itself, between the tall, golden candlesticks, stood four arrangements over three feet high of radiant pink stargazer lilies with pink and white larkspurs, white daisies, and baby's breath. Both priests participated in the rite of holy matrimony. Father George sealed the vows while Father Baar recited the text. As though invited, the sun suddenly broke through the windows even more radiantly, played upon the gold in the vestments of the priests, and let the ring that Antonio placed on my finger sparkle.

The I Solisti Veneti quartet was on the balcony in the back of the church, where the organ was located. They awaited Ms. Thoresby's cue for the beginning of the nuptial Mass. Our young musicians played so brilliantly and sensitively that I felt transported to an even higher sphere – from the moment the first sound reached my ears until the last one lost itself in space. Their music elevated the unfolding of the Mass to a higher level. They had chosen selections from two of Mozart's divertimenti for string quartet, K. 176, in D major, and K. 178, in F major, and to commemorate the Fourth of July, they played the first movement of Charles Ives's first quartet.

The entire ceremony lasted about an hour and a half. When we went to the vestibule to sign the parish registry of St. George's, Reverend Baar showed us a page in the same registry commemorating the visit of Charles and Diana, the Prince and Princess of Wales. I found the entry ever so exhilarating and thought about Diana's storybook wedding. Our wedding in Venice seemed like a fairy tale to us too, especially when my Adonis and I stepped into the gondola, and our guests, who had congratulated us so warmly outside the church on the Campo San Vio square, stood at the quay waving at us happily and restraining Liesl, who almost fell into the canal because she wanted to come along for the ride. They cheered on as Bruno, one of the gondoliers, pushed the gondola away from the landing, smiled as we kissed and I smelled Tonio's gardenia, and followed us with their eyes as we glided away from the San Vio for a nuptial promenade toward the Grand Canal. On the way, as we passed underneath bridges, onlookers waved down toward us, calling out, "Felicitationes! Felicitationes!" They waved until we arrived at the Zattere, a big raft on the canal in front of the well-known Linea d'Ombra piano bar, where Francesca had prearranged the reception. Tables and chairs and the buffet were set up on the raft, which rewarded us with a grandiose view of the Pool of St. Mark on one side and the skyline of Giudecca on the other. A Cunard ocean liner had dropped anchor close to Giudecca, as though welcoming us in advance to our forthcoming ocean voyage on the *QE2*.

Our professional photographers had stayed with the other guests, who were walking through the streets of Venice carrying the lush bouquets of flowers from the pews. Our illustrious friend, the youthful Padre Dr. Emmanuel Longin von Moederndorff, related to the House of Thurn and Taxis in Austria and a friend of Ingeborg Guenther from Berlin, looked rather amusing as he paraded through the streets with the flowers on top of his panama hat. The guests met in front of my favorite church, Santa Maria della Salute, from which they proceeded to the reception and placed the bouquets on the tables. A few others, including Dr. Geks, Tonio's former boss, who had flown in from his vacation spot in Turkey, had engaged a gondola for the ride. We had about forty-five guests, of all ages, and at the reception, though the sky was overcast, we finally had more time to talk to each other over champagne and caviar and a wonderful buffet of culinary delights, Venetian and American, such as smoked turkey breast.

I took much pleasure in presenting each of my bridal attendants with a special gift: for the adults, a sugar bowl and creamer set in silver, with the wedding date engraved on the tray, and for the children, porcelain figurines, all beautifully wrapped by Francesca, who looked gorgeous in her blue-and-pink chiffon dress and the wide-brimmed, royal-blue straw hat. She had also prepared a big basket filled with *regali* (presents) for all the guests. It is a Venetian custom to present each guest with a gift, which in our case was six or seven big sugar-coated almonds, wrapped in a white, netlike gauze pouch tied with pink ribbons, twigs of dainty pink flowers, and a tag showing pink roses and the wedding date. Tonio took care of the male counterparts.

I was especially pleased that my good friend Bettina had been able to come to Venice, and I regretted that her parents were unable to make it. The Kreuzers, whom I had met in 1984 at the Wieskirche, were there, as was my former professor Ferdinand Piedmont and his wife. The Engelsburgers had brought along their son. – An ancient countess congratulated us from a window above the restaurant, and Tonio sent up a glass of champagne to her. Liesl almost threw a fit on the walk when we asked her to hand back my bridal bouquet, which she had caught. When I tossed it again, it ended up in Sally's hands.

Our musicians went inside to play, and the beautiful room with wood-paneled ceiling and walls resounded when they played a trio sonata by Giuseppe Tartini; we were stirred by the adagio movement of the same composer's Violin Concerto in G Major. I thanked the players, the second violinist Glauco Bergtagnin, the violist Donna Lorenzo, the cellist Antonio Viero, and especially Stefano Zanchetta, many times. I would like to thank Mr. Zanchetta once more as I think about him at this particular moment in time. –

Only a few weeks earlier, thanks to the Internet, I was able to locate Mr. Zanchetta, who was on a concert tour in Japan with I Solisti Filarmonici Italiani, and received from him by e-mail some of the program notes as well as the names of the other musicians, which I had forgotten. I am happy to elaborate that Mr. Zanchetta, who is now the father of twins, has raced up the ladder of success in the international music world. He has to date performed as soloist with such renowned chamber orchestras as I Solisti Veneti, I Nuovi Virtuosi di Roma, and I Solisti Italiani in over 1,500 concerts all over the world.

We were so glad when the quartet met up with us again and played at our wedding dinner at the rustic Poste Vecie, which Francesca had engaged because the restaurant we had found a year earlier was closed. Poste Vecie claims to be the oldest restaurant in Venice, dating to the sixteenth century. It is next to the Rialto fish market. It was indeed a truly Venetian place, and we only regretted not being able to feast in their romantic garden restaurant. It looked like rain, so they had set their big, round tables for eight, covered with pink damask tablecloths, in the wood-paneled dining room. In the center of each table sat a bowl filled with white daisies, a lit candle, and little German and American flags. The decor was fitting for the occasion. Francesca had chosen the place because it is known for its outstanding Venetian cuisine and for observing the finest culinary traditions of the Serenissima Republic. It was simply out of this world. They served an array of fish and meat appetizers like fried prawns and carpaccio risotto to please everybody's taste, and followed with a choice of consommés and pasta and fish entrées, as well as a beef Wellington more delicious than any I had ever tasted. Their wines were superb, and the wedding cake, the *dolce nuziale*, was so sensuously and deliciously fluffy it melted in your mouth. I can still taste it: a wonderful tiramisu.

The evening was special not only because of the music, food, and atmosphere, but more so because of all the friends who had traveled from so far to be with us on this memorable occasion. And they too felt good. Some who were there, especially the women, were touched to the point of tears by a moving speech in which Tonio drew a parallel between me and Martha Washington, who was widowed at the young age of twenty-five, left with two children, and taken on by her husband George when he married her in 1759, thirty years prior to becoming the first American president. Tonio's speech incited Father Emmanuel to an impromptu speech about "taking off," which was followed by a special toast to the bride by the best man.

The buoyant atmosphere was interrupted by the disappearance of Bob's seven-year-old son Evan, who had quarreled with the other children and run away. Fortunately, Tonio and Bob found him hiding in a dark corner of the fish market. The guests were unaware of the incident, but it was a signal that it was time to end the evening and put the children to bed.

I was deeply moved, and oh so happy, when back at the Accademia, Antonio pulled out his romantic wand and transformed our special, last night in our Sleeping Beauty castle in Venezia into an experience that will never cease to linger in my memory.

Honeymoon in Tyrol – Home via Germany and England on the *QE2*

The sun was shining the next morning, causing the masses of pink flowers in the boxes on the balconies to look even more vivid than the day before. We shared breakfast with our guests at the Accademia, I went around thanking everybody for the precious gifts and for having graced us with their presence, and before noon a vaporetto, back in service, picked us up to take us to the train station. We were on our way to the Seiser Alm, with a planned stopover in Merano. Bob and his family were with us on the same train as far as Verona, where we bid them farewell as they proceeded on their long journey to Egypt to cruise the Nile.

Marianne Schirduan loved Merano so much that each year she spent her summer vacation there. We spent a few hours in the city, where East and South meet. We saw snowcapped mountains in the far background and slender, waving palms lining the river, which flowed past the palatial Kurhaus and its romantic rotunda, and hoped to be able to listen to a concert sometime, because Merano is known for hosting the great orchestras of the world. We had a dish of ice cream in a sidewalk café on the famous river promenade, bordered by parks and gardens full of flowers, and bought an adorable dirndl for Liesl in the shady medieval shopping arcades. Gustl did not want a pair of lederhosen.

Toward the late afternoon, the cab dropped us off at Icaro, on top of the Seiser Alm, where the Sattlers welcomed us warmly and showed us to our rooms, tastefully furnished in Tyrolean-style oak furniture and blue-and-white handwoven curtains.

Down comforters lay on the beds, just as I had expected. A pair of glass-paneled doors opened to the balcony of solid wood, which offered a magnificent panorama of the mountains, with the Schlern predominating. Vast meadows sprinkled with red, blue, white, and yellow flowers were spread out like carpets all the way from the Icaro to the mountains. Here and there, you could see clusters of evergreen trees. From the balustrade of the balcony hung flower boxes thick with bright-red geraniums – all of it was picture-perfect and ready for us to act out our *Sound of Music* dream.

Our days at Icaro were filled with sunshine, happiness, and laughter. Gustl explored the meadows and came upon a wood-carver in a cottage, whom he befriended. The wood-carver showed him how to carve a figure; and later, we bought for Gustl a St. Christopher holding a lantern, for ourselves angels holding candles, and for Liesl an angel's head with a dispenser for holy water, to be attached to the wall in her bedroom. We hiked to take the cable car up to the immense alpine rose gardens, where we looked in vain for edelweiss but found quite a few royal-blue enzian flowers. Gustl and Liesl got along splendidly with the Sattler children, a boy and a girl. We were relieved that they played so well together, despite the fact that Gustl and Liesl spoke hardly a word of German and no Italian, unlike the Sattlers, who, like all Tyroleans, spoke both. Once or twice, the Sattlers took all their guests to an inn in a nearby village for a fondue outing, where they also served fried potatoes, of which Gustl could not have enough. We enjoyed strolling through the small mountain villages in the area and always looked forward to the tasty meals and desserts that the Sattlers, along with Grandma Sattler, prepared for the guests. Grandma baked a mocha-crème birthday cake for Tonio that tasted almost as delicious as the wedding cake. If you have had a half-inclusive plan in Europe, you know that their breakfasts are so rich, plentiful, and tempting in choices that you can skip a regular meal at lunchtime.

A couple of days after our arrival at Icaro, Ingeborg Guenther and Father Emmanuel caught up with us. She introduced him as her nephew and loyal travel companion, since she had taken him on worldwide trips for the last few years. They stayed a couple of nights, which gave us time to chat and get to know Emmanuel, and when they left, we issued them an open invitation to America, which they assured us they would eventually accept.

When it was time to leave, Tonio made sure we got on the right car at the station in Bolzano. We had reserved a sleeper to Hannover, where we wanted to visit Mutti for a couple of days on the way to England. We sat ready in our seats, with the luggage stacked high in the luggage racks above us. Tony had laid the sturdy luggage cart on top of a suitcase. The train moved, connecting our car to another one with a jolt. At that moment, the luggage cart above us tumbled down, and one of the wheels landed on the top of my head, inflicting terrible pain. I was in shock; Tonio jumped from his seat, put his arms around me, and was very worried. He asked me if I could see or felt dizzy and how badly it hurt, and asked the conductor to bring some ice for the bump on my head. Gustl was sympathetic and attentive. Liesl just said, "It doesn't bleed," and that was it. With the exception of the shock and a throbbing pain in my head, I felt all right. I tried hard to talk about other things, yet was a bit concerned about possible aftereffects.

We checked into the Louiesenhof, close to the railroad station in the center of Hannover, on Friday, which, in addition to visiting Mutti, gave us a day and a half to do some shopping, show the children where my house had been bombed, and take them to the formal gardens of Herrenhausen, where the huge fountain shoots over one hundred feet into the sky. We let them run through the labyrinth of hedges where I used to play when my parents took us to the gardens on holidays. I took Liesl to Karstadt, a toy store, where she picked out a big doll with blue eyes and blond, curly hair. She insisted on taking the doll along on our visit to Marianne, who had invited all of us, including Mutti, whom we picked up on the way, to her apartment for coffee and cake. It was wonderful to be together; and I forgot about my head, which seemed to be all right. Liesl sat on Mutti's lap and showed off her new doll, deciding right then and there to name her "Maria," after Mutti. Mutti smiled and felt honored, and as always when surrounded by her family, seemed just like her old self, singing, telling her favorite stories, and quoting a proverb whenever it fit into the conversation.

I don't think she quite comprehended that I had gotten married, but she could certainly see I was very happy. As usual, it was sad when we said good-bye at the senior citizens' home. I promised to call her soon and was grateful to Marianne for looking in on her. – Mutti could no longer come to the train station, thus missing our departure for Calais via Cologne, where we had a layover long enough for me to show the children the magnificent cathedral, which is directly opposite the railroad station.

This time, we sped across the channel from Calais to Dover in a hydroplane instead of a hovercraft. It too lifts partially from the water, thereby decreasing the resistance and increasing the speed. It did not take very long, maybe thirty minutes. The rental car was ready for us, but we decided to exchange it for a larger one, because we had trouble finding room for all of our luggage. We left Dover in the early afternoon. Tonio had to get used to driving on the left side of the street, which we found a bit amusing at first. Never having been in England, I was amazed by the loveliness of the countryside and the similarity between the old towns and those in certain regions of Germany. We drove southeast along the coast until sunset and found a couple of rooms at the quaint Mermaid Inn, located in the small tourist resort and port town Rye, in East Sussex. Most of the half-timbered houses date back to the fifteenth century. They are very well-kept and, with the flowering gardens and climbing rose bushes in front of them, look very charming and picturesque. Our rooms had very small windows and such low ceilings that Tonio could easily bump his head. They were also very dark and reminded me of my grandparents' place. Yet, at that point, I did not care, because as the evening was approaching, I had begun to feel very sick and feverish from a sudden cold. All the stores were closed, and Tonio finally obtained some tablets from the innkeeper. I went to bed and let the three go out to eat without me. In the morning, we found a drugstore and thus more medicine. We looked at Lamb House (house of the novelist Henry James), saw the Ypres Tower, and stopped briefly at the twelfth-century Church of St. Mary, which was closed. The continuing drive to Southampton along the coast was lovely, and by the time we reached the *Queen Elizabeth II*, I felt better.

It was quite a sight to see the famed ship in dock at the English port. It is the flagship of Cunard Lines, Britain's maritime fleet, which had broken records for over thirty years. The *Titanic* had begun her maiden voyage from the same port twenty years prior to the date of my birthday in 1912! The *QE2*, with thirteen decks and the ability to hold 1,741 passengers and a crew of 1,004, is 963 feet long and weighs 70,327 tons. She boasts very graceful lines, which are highlighted by its navy-blue hull. This floating city is most deserving of the surname "Grande Dame of the Oceans." We were impressed by the elegance of the ship's interior and found our outside cabin, which we shared as a family, quite spacious and comfortable. As soon as we settled in, we went to explore the ship, inside and out, and watched as some of the passengers arrived in big limousines and the crew transferred their very impressive trunks, hatboxes, and such to the ship. Those were first-class passengers, no doubt.

The ship sounded its horn for takeoff, and we looked for the children to summon them up to the deck as we left the port. A band was playing the national hymn, "God Save the Queen," but we could not find Gustl. Tonio started to search for him frantically, and we notified the ship authorities, who looked everywhere. I tried to keep calm, but was afraid he might have walked down the gangway to the pier. – As the ship was leaving the harbor and as Tonio, beside himself, was on the verge of tears, an officer appeared on deck with Gustl. He had found him in the game room playing Nintendo. We were furious and utterly disappointed that he had spoiled the departure for all of us. I felt that a memorable punishment was in order and decreed the Nintendo Room off-limits to him for the remainder of the voyage. A flood of tears and exclamations revealed that he hated the trip because for once he could have played Nintendo to his heart's content free of charge. I found out later that it was not easy to enforce the punishment without ruining the trip for myself. I tried my best, but after a while everybody quieted down and we all took advantage of the variety of activities the ship had to offer.

After the Gustl ordeal, Tonio began to feel sick and had to lie down. He was totally stressed out, it seemed, but did get up for dinner at the elegant Mauretania restaurant, where we had most of our meals. The *QE2* had a reputation for superb cuisine, and having been on different cruises since, I can vouch for the excellency. We liked our waiters, who served us everything our hearts desired. A new and beautifully presented menu was handed to us at each meal. In addition, a large, oval-shaped buffet greeted us in the center of the restaurant. It presented an artistic and colorful display of exotic appetizers, fruits, cheeses, desserts – you name it – just in case the rich selection on the menu had left something out.

Liesl and I had enjoyed getting dressed for dinner, since it was a rather elegant affair. Yet it was not as lavish as at the Queens Grill, where the first-class passengers dined. – As we had a table to ourselves, I tried hard to teach the children certain table manners, and by the end I was pleased to see it had not all been in vain. – Since Antonio felt under the weather, he missed out on some of the superb entertainment, and Gustl and I danced up a storm one night when Tonio went to lie down. Liesl joined the children's group. They painted and made keyrings and other souvenirs. A highlight of the trip was the talent show in the big lounge toward the end of the ship. Liesl dressed up as Princess Elizabeth. She wore the lace dress from the wedding and my beaded cap on her hair, which we curled. She won a silver Queen Elizabeth medal for her performance. Gustl, who was quite a good little actor and not at all bashful, wore his Pierre Cardin suit with a borrowed hat and earned a big round of applause when he danced and lip-synched "When the Saints Go Marching In." Tonio and I sang behind the curtain in front of which the band was playing. Gustl's prize was a bright-red umbrella with *QE2* on it in white. The talent show was the ideal finish for our family wedding adventure. – We knew that when the cruise director bid us farewell, we had pulled off our *Sound of Music* gig. As we walked off the ship, she called out, "There goes the singing family!"

It was hot and sultry in New York on that Sunday morning, the 23rd of July. We knew the chocolates in the box the waiter had given Liesl on the last day would melt into a messy pap. Our flight to South Bend would not take off until the afternoon. I had reserved tickets for a boat tour of New York Harbor, which in retrospect was a bad idea, since the children were not ready for it and too tired to appreciate all the sights. It was pleasant to be on the water, but no one was in the mood to wait in line to ride up to the Statue of Liberty or to walk on the hot pavement in New York City. The city could be tolerated only by seeking shelter in an air-conditioned restaurant and by allowing the children to run up to every fountain, take off their sandals, and hold their bare feet in the water. It was just too much of a good thing. We were glad when we returned home at dusk, safe and sound, and could cool off with lemonade on our deck at the house on Southeast Drive. We were a real family – all with the same name, since I had taken on Tonio's family name.

Married Life with Tonio and the Children – The Fall of the Berlin Wall and a New Summer Program

The children were anxious to call their mother, because even though she had their itinerary, complete with phone numbers, she never once tried to contact them. It did not surprise me; she called rarely when they spent the summer with us. Tonio insisted that I have my head checked to make sure the luggage cart had not caused any injuries. Fortunately, the CT scan turned out negative and we did not have to worry. – We found a special place in our home for the gifts our friends had given us in Venice and for those sent by friends and family who were unable to come. We loved the huge bouquet of stargazer lilies the Piedmonts sent soon after we returned home, and we anxiously awaited the wedding album Tonio had bought in Venice and left with the photographer and his partner and companion Ornella. Finally, Francesca informed us that the delay was due to his having taken ill. – Therefore, we doubly appreciated the album of beautiful photographs of Venice and the wedding, which Father George had given us shortly after his return to the States.

The children's departure meant it was time for Tonio and me to get back to work. – Being actually married was wonderful; it was so nice to have Tonio waiting for me at home when I taught late. He always turned on the outside lights, greeted me with a kiss, and had dinner waiting for me, and after dinner we discussed the trials and tribulations of the day over a glass of wine. We had a wonderful circle of friends, with whom we got together almost every other weekend, either at their homes or ours, and felt we had no reason whatever to complain. It took a while for me to get used to my new name, but I did not regret the change at all.

Finally, the oversized photo album arrived from Venice. It was inside a white felt bag with the inscription *Le idée di Ornella* and was truly a wedding album the likes of which neither of us nor any of our friends had ever seen. The photographs, many of which were 12" x 12", were simply out of this world, and they recaptured our fairy-tale wedding in every way. – Tonio and I looked at the pictures and reminisced about the events and the guests. Whenever I saw a picture of Father Baar and the spinster, I remembered what Tonio had told me at the Seiser Alm. Father Baar had asked for a check of over $1,000 for himself and a second one of $500 for the spinster, who had played but one hymn. I thought of Mephistopheles in Goethe's *Faust I*, who said, "The church has a big stomach." I used to associate his words with the Catholic Church, but discovered in Italy that the Episcopalians are just as hungry. (I was glad Tonio had insisted on making the check out to their foundation.)

At the university, contrary to the Prima Donna's proclamation that no one would be found to chair the department, we had a new chairman, the Spaniard, whose tenure had been disputed a few years earlier. He was appointed despite the fact that, during the tenure negotiations, the committee had decided to circumvent his chairing the department, should the situation arise in the future. He was proud to have been given a chance. I felt, despite my previous reservations, that anybody was better than the Prima Donna or the Fly Trap.

After a review of the Bayer Program conducted by a special committee on our campus, which by all indications was set into motion by the Prima Donna primarily to find something to criticize, I discussed the program with the CDS in New York and decided to change it to a noncredit program. Many letters in support of the program had been sent, but as the committee was slow in making a decision, the CDS and I relieved the committee of their mission by simply pulling the rug out from under them. I also reached an agreement with the CDS to split the fees they collected from students 50/50, in view of the fact that I was responsible for recruiting the students and for the organizational tasks in the United States. Of course, the change meant my campus would no longer profit from the program. Students no longer had to pay tuition, which for out-of-state students was exorbitant anyhow. I had become increasingly disturbed when the chair of Arts and Sciences pressured me to accept more out-of-state participants.

The students liked the new Learn and Earn program. They would still attend the subsidized intensive German course in Cologne and work for Bayer, thus earning more money than before. We eliminated the Berlin and GDR portion of the program and no longer required a paper or assigned grades for credit. Strangely enough, no one at my campus ever openly complained about it, and I was pleased. As it turned out, Bayer AG, generous as always, had taken up the practice of sponsoring an all-expenses-paid, long-weekend trip to Berlin in addition to a boat trip with dinner and dancing on the Rhine River. The company flew the students to Berlin and even gave them a generous amount of cash to spend on their holiday.

It was a mild day on November 9 – the day CNN reported that the Wall at East Berlin was being opened. Busy with the wedding, and out of the country, I had not paid much attention to what had already started: in July, many refugees had gathered in German missions in East Berlin, Budapest, and Prague. By September, fifty thousand refugees had fled by way of Hungary. On October 7, the fortieth anniversary of the GDR, the number of protests increased. On October 9, the famous Monday demonstration, with more than one hundred thousand people, erupted in Leipzig. On October 18, Erich Honecker was removed from office, intensifying the avalanche that no East German official wanted to, dared to, or would have been able to stop. On November 4, the largest demonstration in the history of Berlin took place. On November 7, the East German government resigned, and on November 9, the Wall fell. Its construction had begun on August 13, 1961.

I was standing in the kitchen, in front of the small TV. – At first I felt numb, and then tears started rolling down my cheeks, first slowly, then freely. I was glued to the TV that weekend, watching the fall of the Wall, where only a year before I had stood with my students and provoked the East German in uniform by saying, "I heard the Wall is coming down." I was just bluffing in May 1988, never dreaming it would happen, at least not so soon. – I watched with the world as millions of East Germans and others rushed toward Berlin, flooding the roads with their little Trabis to get a real look at West Berlin, to purchase a piece of Western merchandise, to drink a glass of West Berlin beer, or to see and be present at such an historic event. The flood peaked on Saturday, November 11, when they began tearing down the rather brittle Wall with giant drills amidst a jubilant chaos of people waving, celebrating, holding hands, and dancing. Germans were united – crying, laughing, kissing, embracing, and climbing up the Wall in front of the Brandenburg Gate, where the German flag, with black, red, and gold stripes, fluttered victoriously in the back of the chariot. Champagne flowed freely, musicians played triumphantly, and the tumultuous atmosphere subsided only gradually. In the end, the entire Wall was carried and sold off bit by bit. Friends from Bayer AG even brought a piece for me when they visited me in the States.

The minute the Wall started falling, the phone rang, and the local TV and radio stations asked to interview me. They arrived with cameras, microphones, and tape recorders. I gave them an account of my observations over the years, and voiced my skepticism regarding the confidence expressed by the West, that within a mere ten years the situation would be normalized and Germany's unification intact. Even if the infrastructure could be restored in ten years, I was doubtful that the psychological barriers, which had been in place over a period of more than four decades, could be torn down so quickly.

Tonio and I celebrated the changes in my program and the fall of the Berlin Wall when in the Big Apple for a short trip over Thanksgiving. Ute Schott had helped us secure a reservation at the fabulous restaurant Régine, of which, at that time, there were two others, one in Paris and the other in LA. – The place was incredibly swanky. When the cab drove up, the entire street was lined with stretch limousines and their chauffeurs. The restaurant was dimly lit. Each table offered a private setting, in that it was separated from the neighboring tables by ivory silk screens against which stood a big vase with an arrangement of lush red and white tropical flowers. The white-gloved waiters were so quiet they seemed invisible. Each course was a masterpiece in the presentation of exquisite cuisine, and the wine was superb. – Thick, soundproof glass doors opened to an exotic discotheque where a small, sexy band excited the dancing partners. The floor was a round piece of solid glass, but moving and floating. Blue, green, red, purple, and yellow lights rotated and flashed underneath the floor and rushed back and forth on the encircling walls. Tonio and I had never experienced dancing on a floor or in an environment such as this, frequented by New York's *haute volée*, known politicians, actors, and industrialists. As we were leaving, I tried to recognize this or that guest, which was difficult, because several were wearing sunglasses. We knew this was a once-in-a-lifetime experience and that we would never again splurge as we did at New York City's Régine.

A Real Family Christmas

December 25, 1989, was our first Christmas as a real family, and I was probably more excited than even the children, though I must admit that Tonio, too, loved preparing for their arrival. We had secured tickets for *The Nutcracker* in Chicago and made reservations at the Palmer House. We had bought fancy clothes for the children to wear to the theater, because we had no idea what they would look like when they got off the plane. For Gustl we found a pair of navy-blue pants, a white shirt, a necktie, and a red cardigan and for Liesl a red velvet dress with white lace embroidered with red flowers. I was sure she would love the white tights with little red hearts and the pretty bow for her hair, which had grown so long it hung below her waist. I had told the children to be sure to ask their mother to send along a pair of good shoes to wear to *The Nutcracker*. We were reluctant to buy shoes without first having the children try them on.

The plane was late. It was snowing. I will never forget what they looked like when they got off the plane. I was shocked to see that Liesl was wearing worn-out moccasins, which used to be pink, and Gustl's sneakers did not look any better. They had not brought a second pair. We hurried through the traffic to McCormick's Place. The children changed into their new clothes in the restrooms, but wore the old shoes. We arrived at our seats just in time. The beauty of the ballet and the music soon let me forget the shoes. The children were spellbound and bedazzled by the music, the dancers, and the magic that unfolded on the stage. I had started sending Liesl to ballet lessons a couple of years earlier, and Gustl was taking lessons on the West Coast. I hoped that eventually they too would dance in a *Nutcracker* performance.

The children enjoyed room service the next morning. It was snowing outside. We went shopping for shoes to wear at Christmas, and all of us were thrilled at the sight of the thousands and thousands of sparkling lights in the trees in the Windy City. We marveled at the animated fairy-tale scenes at Neiman Marcus and rewarded a Salvation Army man, who was standing near Marshall Field's jingling his bell, by throwing coins into his bucket. Snowflakes clung like tiny white feathers to our hats and coats as we took a walk down the sparkling Magnificent Mile before we all drove home.

To make this Christmas more special than the last one, we had gone overboard with gifts as well. Tonio and I had gone shopping at Marshall Field's, in Chicago, and bought a deluxe doll mansion, made in Sweden, for Liesl, and an electric train set by the German manufacturer Maerklin for Gustl. I had hunted through many catalogues and stores looking for dolls, furniture, etc. for Liesl's house and looked just as hard for trains and parts for Gustl's train set. I commissioned my cleaning lady to sew for Liesl's Maria the most exquisite wardrobe any doll has ever owned. The garments were made from velvet, silks, taffeta, fur, etc. And a carpenter made a poster bed with a canopy of light-blue cotton covered with white ruffled lace for the doll. I had also started a collection of Steiff puppets from Germany and found a puppet theater in Chicago.

The night before we picked up Gustl and Liesl in Chicago, Tonio and I had spent hours wrapping each gift separately on the mahogany dining-room table. Both house and train came with an elaborate array of extras. For the house, we had gotten an entire family of little dolls of several generations, together with cats and dogs. The state-of-the-art furnishings for the six or seven rooms, which included Oriental carpets, were as luxurious as you can imagine. We had found a baby grand, an aquarium, a fireplace, table lamps and chandeliers, a color TV, a Christmas tree with electric lights, a computer, dishes, flowers for tables, and geraniums in window boxes. These items would certainly excite any child or adult. Next to the horse in the stall, there was room for a white Mercedes-Benz. Both Antonio and I were Mercedes-Benz lovers. I owned one in silver, and Tonio's was gold.

Gustl's train set came with a handsome assortment of tracks, switches, train stations, several machines to fire up, sleeping and dining cars, and wagons to transport a diversity of goods and passengers. For the train station, we had bought little half-timbered house kits, a village and church, and other buildings, which had to be assembled. We simply had to get the bushes, evergreen trees, and tiny figures in bathing suits to spruce up the landscape. We enjoyed collecting as much as we liked, wrapping each tiny box in which we embedded the treasures. Antonio was in charge of wrapping and labeling. It was indeed a labor of love. We kept imagining how the kiddies would react to all those little miracles and could hardly wait to watch them open the gifts I had hidden, again, in the attic. We all had as much fun trimming the tree and following our now-customary Christmas ritual as we did in 1987.

Remembering the children's dislike of sauerkraut, and having observed how much they liked fondue in Tyrol, I asked them to place the glazed, dark-red fondue plates on our Christmas Eve dinner table and agreed to let Gustl light the fondue burner while Tonio and I were busy with other chores. Everything seemed so peaceful. Yet, all of a sudden, a flame shot to the ceiling. It came right from the cushion on the bench next to which Gustl usually sat. He must have spilled some lighter fluid on the cushion and accidentally dropped a burning match on the spot, thus igniting the spill. We were momentarily upset, but quickly extinguished the flame and prevented a bigger fire. A hole was burned into the cushion, and a large black spot remains on the bench as a constant reminder of the scare. – We should have realized that Gustl, like other boys, had an obsession with fire and matches. He felt compelled to light every candle he could lay his hands on and strike matches just for the fun of it. He went wild when his father allowed him to ignite firecrackers.

The Christmas Eve excitement outshone the fire scare quickly. The children said grace. Soft Christmas music was playing in the living room as we dunked bread and apple pieces into the cheese sauce. We all enjoyed the tasty morsels, and harmony was restored for the evening to proceed.

I set up the gifts while Papa and the kiddies were out looking at Christmas lights. When they returned and saw the tree with the lit candles and gazed upon the mountain of Santa's surprises, their big brown eyes beamed with excitement. But since they were getting older, I had dreamed up a little prelude to the evening. They first had to dress for the occasion. Gustl put on his nutcracker outfit, red cardigan, and black pants, and Liesl slipped on the costume she had wished for. She truly looked like a sweet angel in the white gown with transparent, silver, sparkling wings and a halo on her long and shiny hair. While Antonio played the piano, Liesl, carrying a long, white, burning candle, marched slowly alongside the dining-room table toward the lighted tree singing "We Wish You a Merry Christmas" sweetly and ever so softly. She sat down on a stool next to the tree. Gustl sat on the floor next to the Nativity scene, a gift from Mutti, and began to read the Christmas story from the Bible. Liesl sang a bit out of tune, and Gustl skipped a line now and then. When the performance was finished, they got the go-ahead to open the presents, alternating with each other. It was so wonderful to watch them look at the new toys and hear them ask us for help setting up the train and the dollhouse. Now and then they took a break to eat the cookies, chocolates, and marzipan, but the gingerbread house was left intact – until one of their little friends took a bite out of it on Christmas Day. I cracked nuts. The whole family was happy and content, and we drove to Bristol to celebrate Midnight Mass at the little chapel where Tonio and I had been married on June 24, prior to the big celebration on July 4 in Venice.

It was snowing on the way to the Episcopal chapel, but the roads were not too slippery. The church was filled with parishioners. Luckily, this meant that there was not much room for the kiddies to slide back and forth on the benches, which was one of their favorite pastimes. It was a traditional Christmas Eve service. Antonio and I sang the hymns together just as Mutti and I had. I had to hold back tears. I felt like part of a real family. After wishing each other a merry Christmas at the end of the Mass and saying hello to Father George, we drove home. The children fell asleep on the way. Antonio had to carry Liesl to bed.

On Christmas Day, I cooked the traditional German Christmas goose, which both children liked. They were also fond of my sheet cake covered with apples, almonds, and sugar. We set up the train on the dining-room table, which kept them busy all day. At night, they put on their first puppet-theater performance for us, and when it was time to go to bed, we tucked them in, covering them with the down comforters. I had to sing a song for Liesl and one for Gustl. Liesl begged for Flies's lullaby "Sleep, My Little Prince, Go to Sleep," and Gustl asked for Brahms's Lullaby.

All of us were looking forward to our traditional New Year's Eve lobster feast. We let the youngsters take a sip of champagne at the end of the Times Square countdown and went out into the snow to set off a few firecrackers, much to the children's delight. Both ran around the front yard with sparklers while Tonio and I made sure they did not get hurt. All too soon, they were on the plane home, which for us meant it was time to return to work.

Affirmative-Action Hassles Start – Tonio and I Visit Reunited Germany

After lengthy and serious discussions conducted over the previous month, I reconsidered my situation at the university, which, thanks to the Prima Donna's hostile behavior, had brought my usual interest in scholarship to the point of stagnation. I felt compelled to take some sort of action. In addition, I had been urged on numerous occasions to take some action by several of my female colleagues, and by none more ardently than my matron of honor, Donna Harlan. She felt I had nothing to lose in fighting back, because I was a full professor, could afford it financially, and had my husband's support. She pointed out, as others had, the many hurdles that had been put in my way and that it was obvious I was vastly underpaid in comparison to males, not only in my department but across the university. After going to the library and obtaining a copy of the salary list, Tonio and I agreed to do something about it. From Adrian Ringuette, the retired main counsel at Miles, Tonio had obtained the name of a top attorney at Bingham Summers Welsh & Spilman, in Indianapolis. On January 2, Tonio drove with me to Indianapolis, where we met with the senior partners, G. Moss and W. Adams, to discuss my options for possible action against the university. They laid out the pros and cons and emphasized the difficulty inherent in such an action and the lack of a guarantee that they would be successful. We left after a two-hour conference, and I advised them that I would furnish any and all pertinent documents and information that would help them evaluate the foundation for legal action. I assured them that, until given further notice, I would discuss with no one what took place at their office. Tonio and I both felt relieved to have taken this step and decided that even if I would be unable to affect a change financially, it would be psychologically beneficial to call attention to what was going on and let a third party deal with the situation. I felt as though a big weight had been lifted from my shoulders.

I handed in my annual report in a timely fashion, attaching evaluations as required. Two of my students received honors awards for German, and another one had earned a PhD at the main campus. I had also been effective in helping my adjunct instructor Thomas Ahrens get accepted to the PhD program in Bloomington without his being required to take certain prerequisites. Since from then on the Bayer Program was no longer under the umbrella of the university, though I still considered my input a form of service to the students, I informed them that as of that date, our campus had reaped a profit (after expenses from tuition, up to $18,000), that approximately two hundred students had participated in the Bayer Program, and that a total of approximately $180,000 of grants-in-aid from the Federal Government of Germany had benefited participating students since the program's inception less than ten years before. – I further pointed out that I had personally taught all twenty-two German courses listed in the university bulletin, with the exception of G403, German Literature to 1770, plus others not listed, and had successfully maintained both the service courses and the German sequence leading to a major in that language.

The new chairman evaluated me fairly, and it felt good not to have to write a rebuttal – but for some reason, someone upstairs decided not to let him serve out his term and, without asking, replaced him with the Fly Trap.

On February 2, 1990, the attorney assigned to my case, after having reviewed the documents I had forwarded to him, came to the following conclusion:

It is clear that that during the past ten to twelve years, the working relationship between the members of your department has been very uncooperative. This negative work environment has manifested itself in many different ways, including department meetings, which ranged from open hostility to the point of having no meetings at all during the past semester, critical evaluations by department members, which engendered vituperative responses, and a general lack of respect among members of the department for some of their colleagues.

Although it is obvious, it bears repeating that neither the legal system nor lawyers can make people like or respect each other. From all indications, the working environment among the members of your department has been intolerable for many years, as it is unlikely that this law firm can say or do anything on your behalf to improve that overall environment.

However, in reviewing the materials we received from you, it appears to me that there are grounds for making a formal complaint of salary discrimination to the campus affirmative action officer and, if necessary, the appeal procedures within the Academic Handbook. I believe the most appropriate way to bring such a complaint would be in the form of a comprehensive "letter brief" setting forth all of the pertinent facts and arguments in support of your position. Our objective would be to convince the University that for over ten years your salary has been maintained at inequitably low levels in comparison with your male counterparts, that your salary should be elevated immediately to achieve at least general parity with the male professors in the department, and that you should be remunerated for the salary discrepancy which has existed for so many years.

I must emphasize, however, that although I believe there is merit to your claim, I can make no assurances that we will accomplish any of the desired objectives. Convincing employers that salary discrimination exists and should be remedied is never easy, even in the clearest cases of discrimination. Your situation is complicated by a number of factors, including the length of time this discrepancy has gone unaddressed, and the unique backgrounds and responsibilities of the male professors in your department with whom we would be making the comparison. The University will undoubtedly point to numerous factors other than your sex in attempting to justify the salary discrepancy.

I agreed with his finding, but although I was fully aware of the uncertainty of the outcome, I instructed my attorney, whose rate at that time was $150 an hour, to go ahead. On June 21, 1990, after several revisions, the letter, which was more than twenty pages long, was sent to the Affirmative Action Office. I decided to let others worry about it. Whenever a document or a relevant incident presented itself, I just dropped the attorneys a quick note, tucked the document in an envelope, and put it in the mail and out of my mind.

While all this legal work was going on, I was immersed in teaching, which was always rewarding, and even therapeutic. The culture course required several revisions and video additions due to the fall of the Wall; but the Goethe seminar, one of my favorites, had attracted top students, and many times we simply could not stop our discussion when the two and a half hours were up. When possible, I had also shown film adaptations of plays we had read, which enriched the experience greatly. Each time we interpreted and analyzed the works of that great man, I discovered something new. When I came home at night after an evening of Goethe, I always felt stimulated. While I was working on an article, in addition to reworking the novel, of which we had completed ten chapters, I also participated in several community events by way of lectures and other obligations, such as service on committees on both campuses as well as the overseas program. My nose was kept to the grindstone. Tonio and I were both working when the children spent their spring break with us. But we made certain we had a good time with them whenever time permitted. Tonio went with them to the movies, or they picked out their favorites at the video store. Tonio always made caramel popcorn, which they favored. The week was gone before we knew it.

Tonio and I attended various parties, including one thrown by Donna, to which faculty as well as the ex-chancellor and his wife were invited. It was an evening I will never forget, because as it went on, I observed the ex-chancellor motionless and slouched back in an easy chair, totally despondent, his mouth and eyes open. His wife had already left, because as everybody there knew, she objected to drinking. I called attention to the chancellor and someone shook him. He came to and muttered a few words, which left no doubt that he was badly intoxicated. – Tonio suggested we take him with us to sober him up and then take him home. We sat him down on the couch, and after he drank a few cups of strong coffee, he began to talk. – At one point during the conversation, when Tonio was in the kitchen, he turned to me and said he was sorry I had married Tonio because he had hoped to have a chance with me. I thought I did not hear right, shook my head, and figured he was still intoxicated, but I also remembered the phone call during which he asked to come over. Tonio later told me that the chancellor had questioned him as to why he had wanted to marry me. When I filled Tonio in on his previous inappropriate comments, he shook his head.

1984–1993

In the middle of April, I received a phone call from the CDS in New York; they asked me to arrange a meeting in South Bend for the director of the Robert Bosch Foundation. He wanted to meet with community leaders and certain faculty members from IU and Notre Dame in an effort to recruit graduate students from law and business schools in the Midwest for a year-abroad program that would prepare them for leadership positions in government and industry. It sounded like an excellent opportunity, and it was commendable that they were branching out to our region, having up to then focused mainly on elite schools in the East. Tonio and I arranged for and successfully hosted an appropriate party at our house. Among our guests were colleagues from Political Science, History, and the School of Business, as well as a diverse group of leaders from the community, the press, broadcasting, etc. We also sent a brochure to the attorneys in Indianapolis in case they knew of someone.

Since our return from Italy, Tonio and I had been busy looking at houses to buy, because, as the children were getting older, we needed more space. We liked our place very much because it was in a good neighborhood, only a five-minute drive to the university and a thirty-minute commute to Elkhart for Tonio. Most of all, we liked the backyard, which was very secluded and beautifully landscaped. We finally decided to stay in our house and look into the feasibility of adding an entire floor – that is, two bedrooms, a full bath, a library/den, and a family/entertainment room – and of doubling the garage. We located a reputable contractor and a fine architect, and by spring they started tearing up the concrete floor in the garage, a foot thick, with heavy drills and big noises and so much dust I could hardly stand it. I was glad Tonio and I had an excuse to get out, because we had booked a flight with the Bayer group for May 5. Tonio had never been to East Germany and was curious to see at least some of it.

After I turned the students over to the Carl Duisberg representative in Cologne, Tonio and I were again put up at the Kasino, and I had my usual meetings with all parties involved in the program. I also got to meet Ms. Pieps, who was responsible for all the foreign students working at Bayer. She also arranged the various outings for them. We were treated royally as usual.

I had arranged for a meeting with the Padre in Bonn, and we invited him out to dinner not far from the Rhine River. I had been eager for him to meet us as a married couple, and he was happy to see us. We drove toward Berlin in our rented car. We were surprised that we were stopped; it turned out that all Americans had to present a passport. – We spent a day in the reunited city. Tonio was overwhelmed at the huge KDW (Shopping Center of the West) and took many pictures of the rather eclectic displays of foods, meats, cold cuts, delicatessen, fish, and fowl from places around the world, including packages with 1,800 grams of caviar for almost $5,000. He got carried away with the colorful fish from the Indian Ocean, doves, pigeons, pheasants, hens, and quail, with bear, boar, and buffalo ham, and whatever else you can think of. Of course, he took pictures like mad on the streets of Berlin of whatever struck him as unusual. He could not get enough of the Pergamon Museum, my favorite, or of the Gemäldegallerie, in Dahlem, Berlin. He filled many pages with photographs of works of the great masters, such as Correggio's *Leda and the Swan*, Botticelli's *Mary with Child and Singing Angels*, and El Greco's *Mater Dolorosa*. All of them turned out well. Before we proceeded to the Chinese theater cutouts, the primitive art, the Aztec warrior god, the Incan masks, and an oceanic totem fascinated him.

We arrived late in Potsdam, where my friend Susanne, the former archivist from the Goethe and Schiller Archive in Weimar, lived with her much younger husband, an anesthesiologist, and their absolutely adorable little daughter, Claudia, who had the most beautiful curly golden hair and big brown eyes. A major attraction was Juergen's brand-new yellow Trabi, which, much to his chagrin, after he had waited for it for thirteen years, arrived a month after the Wall had caved in, when everybody wanted to own a car from the West. He let Tonio drive the little box, which he likened to driving a mower. It was nice to see my friend again, whom I had visited on occasion when in East Germany with my students and who had kept me apprised very carefully of how they viewed their situation in the GDR. Though they seemed glad that the Wall had come down, they did point out the remaining discrepancies in salaries, housing, education, etc. –

I was surprised to see that the streets in Potsdam were torn up badly, and I noticed that since my last visit a few years earlier, the place had deteriorated even more. Tonio wanted to see the places in Potsdam I had visited and talked about, and we even went to Dresden via Weimar so he could observe what had been rebuilt and restored since 1945 – and what was still in ruins.

Impromptu Detour to Childhood Places

As I had talked much about the tyrant Uncle Adolf from Bad Helmstedt, and about Villa Glück Auf, I suggested we drive to visit the childhood villa, where we spent time before moving to the one in V., the nightmare we had to endure for seven long years. I filled Tonio in regarding the tyrant's demise. For years, he was so demented he did not recognize his own children, not to mention his wife, who refrained from sending him to a home mostly because she did not want to part with some of his wealth. Nobody could understand how she could tolerate him, especially when she reported that he went to bed every night with an ax under his pillow. – The stately villa stood only a few yards removed from the former border, which consisted of barbed-wire fences flanking no-man's-land. Although it had been opened for access to the next village, it was still very much covered with trees and shrubs. We had no desire to drive in that direction, so we turned and continued toward Hannover by way of Hildesheim.

Hildesheim dates back to the eighth century. It is located on the Innerste River, which also flows through Mutti's home village, Giesen. The town was also close to where Maria, my old Sankt Ursula chum, used to live. I was tempted to look her up after having lost contact with her not long after Doc and I took her along on our 12,000-mile trip in 1956. Everybody knew the Vollmers, who were big farmers, and when Tonio drove into the cobblestone courtyard and stopped in front of the ancient red-brick farmhouse, we felt a bit strange at first. But there was no reason for hesitation, because when Maria's older sister recognized me, she asked us in and offered us a cup of coffee, and we chatted for a while about old times. Unfortunately, Maria was out of town.

It was raining cats and dogs that Pentecost Sunday, and Maria's sister offered to show us a few places in Hildesheim. She kindly furnished us with umbrellas. – Of course, Mutti, who lived only five miles away from the town, had taken us many times as children, especially to the oldest church, the cathedral of the Roman Catholic diocese, which dated back to the tenth or eleventh century, to show us the magnificent bronze Bernward Doors, the Christussäule (Christ's pillar), and the baptismal fonts. Each time we stopped at the Thousand-Year Rose, which still blooms above the east choir of the cathedral, we never failed to note the wooden Knochenhaueramtshaus (butchers' guildhouse). Bombs had destroyed the landmark in 1945, and I had not seen it since it had been rebuilt in its original form. Both Tonio and I were impressed, not only by the restored butchers' guildhouse, but also by the restoration of the remaining houses on the square, especially the hand-painted facade of the Wedekindhaus.

We had to drive through Mutti's village on our way to visit her in Hannover. I had not been there since I turned my back on those who treated us so inhumanly during the war. Mutti, from time to time, mentioned in her letters that someone had died, married, or had children. But as nobody ever tried to look me up – or, from what I could gather, ever bothered to pay Mutti a single visit, even though she lived only thirty minutes away by car and in the past had worked hard for them whenever she visited her homestead – I had no desire to revisit the past. Yet I could not resist taking a look at the village, and Tonio was game.

I was shocked by the transformation that had taken place. The cobblestone street going through the center of the village, which once held three hundred inhabitants, had been topped with asphalt. Right at the beginning, it led directly into a big truck yard filled almost to capacity with 18-wheeler monstrosities. They stood parallel to where my grandfather's half-timbered house used to be, which was replaced by a modern one-family home with gray stucco facades, but no flowering garden. They used to grow pretty flowers in back of the brown picket fences. More asphalt, a bakery, and a grocery store replaced two additional neighboring houses that Mutti and I used to visit. An office building stood not far away from the big barn that previously stored grandfather's farm machines. There was no trace of horse and cart, of chickens and pigs. Gone also was the storage place for the coal grandfather used to sell. Gone was the pump where we helped to fetch water, gone the idyllic charm of the village of my childhood. Also gone were Aunt Stingy and her sinister husband, to whom grandfather had left the homestead and business, from which they built their truck empire. They in turn left it to their last son, because the two born earlier had died at an early age. We refrained from knocking at the doors to the house where my cousin Clemens supposedly lived, and drove back to the Ernst Inn, the tavern directly at the town's entrance. It was only a few meters from the truck court, which could be viewed from the hotel rooms the Ernst had added. My grandfather used to play cards at the inn after Sunday Mass. It was obvious that while the economic miracle had brutally wiped out the quaint ambiance of the village, it had benefited these villagers big time, at least monetarily.

Tonio and I entered the inn, intending to call my relatives on the phone. The place had been remodeled. When I asked the person I thought was the proprietor if he knew Niele's number and if I might use the phone, he seemed to recognize me. He turned out to be the Neverbee's nephew, Johann, who had been forbidden to talk to or visit Mutti and me at the Croft after Doc had passed away. He was just there for a beer, but I told him I would like to talk to him a bit more. I called my relatives' number and a boy's voice answered. I introduced myself, and when he told me his parents were out of town, I asked him to come over to the Ernst and meet my husband and me. He sounded quite excited, and he appeared at the inn within minutes. He was quite tall for a twelve-year-old and had reddish-blond hair and blue eyes. He had had no idea I existed and was thrilled to discover having a distant cousin in America. We asked him to invite his brother Clemens, about fifteen years his senior, to join us, and it did not take long for his brother, tall, blond, blue eyed, and rather handsome, to arrive.

We talked and got acquainted and were happy to have connected after so much time had passed. Aunt Stingy and her husband had both succumbed to cancer, and it seemed that their grandmother had been the driving force behind the truck business, which consisted of approximately thirty-two big semis. Their Aunt Trudis had married a man who was connected with the Cultural Ministry in Bonn. They had two daughters. One was studying medicine and the other Germanic languages and literature. My cousin was an English teacher. Tonio fetched our album with the wedding pictures, and they were quite impressed at what they saw. When we left for Hannover, Frank promised to visit us at the hotel on Pentecost Sunday with his sister Simone, who was a student at the University of Goettingen. – Tonio and I were pleased to have taken the initiative. They made a good impression – after all, they were twice removed from Aunt Stingy, their grandmother. When Frank came with his sister Simone, a strikingly beautiful young woman in her early twenties, we spent a few animated hours in the restaurant at the Louisenhof; and when we said our good-byes, we promised to write to each other.

As always, Mutti was happy to see us, though her mind was wandering more, it seemed. She still asked who Tonio was. I was upset that I did not see the picture we had sent her for Christmas on the wall. Tonio had arranged family snapshots in one large frame for Mutti to enjoy. I checked her room and eventually found it hidden underneath a stack of sweaters in the closet. I then knew my brother had removed it from the wall and hidden it. – I hung it back on the wall and hoped it would not disappear after I left. I asked my friend Marianne, when we went for coffee and cake, as always, to stay on the lookout for the pictures when she stopped by at Mutti's. – We avoided Sibby, who was still treating Marianne rather shabbily.

We returned home in time for me to teach a course during the first summer session. The bright-red tulips mixed in with white narcissuses and golden daffodils were blooming cheerfully in the backyard, undisturbed by what was going on with the remodeling. Our house looked as though a hurricane had gone through it. The garage was torn up, and a big red truck was parked in front of it, getting ready to pour concrete. Half of the yard was full of lumber, and several men were tearing off the old roof. They had a good view of the redbud tree, which was bursting with blossoms. – It was amazing how fast they worked. The upper floor was erected, the Kohler bathroom was ready to be installed, and the beautiful custom-built stairway of rose-colored hardwood, imported from the Amazon by our friends the Butuses, was about to be delivered.

Traveling along the Mississippi to New Orleans and along the Gulf of Mexico to Florida with the Children

I was not quite finished with the first summer session when Gustl and Liesl arrived after another hassle with their mother over plane tickets. – I am sure there are thousands of divorced parents who have to contend with similar aggravations. I swear, whenever it was our turn to arrange for the kids' travel, our Nemesis could have won a prize for setting up road blocks for us at each step of the way. She refused to be inconvenienced, which would have meant getting up before noon to take the children to the airport. The schedule was never acceptable. However, when it was her turn, she expected us to abide by her terms, even when it meant having to pick them up very early in the morning in Chicago, which involved a three-hour drive. It got so bad that Tonio was unable to deal with her, and I was tempted to give up many times. The problem was compounded when I tried to take advantage of frequent-flyer rewards. It took years for her to finally sign up for them. Considering that she was a lawyer and supposedly very bright, I decided over the years that she was definitely lacking in natural intelligence.

Can you imagine her reaction when we surprised Liesl for her birthday with a yellow-white cockatiel? It was named Pretty Boy, after the cockatiel Tonio had as a boy. – We had it delivered in its cage together with anything and everything that would make the bird and Liesl happy. Ms. Ice Water's first reaction was "who is going to take care of the bird when the children are with their father?" I assured her they were welcome to bring the bird with them. I ordered the appropriate carrying cage for transporting the pet and made arrangements with the airlines for its travel, which was not exactly without complications, since I could expect no cooperation from the mother. – Thus, when the children got off the plane and we saw Liesl carrying Pretty Boy with her, we were tickled pink to see them. The bird was entertaining, but we had to keep an eye on it to make sure it didn't fly away.

As we did not want to subject the children and ourselves to the ongoing construction for the duration of their visit, as soon as I was done with the second summer session, we decided to trust our contractor Overberg, his architect, and his foreman, Bernie, to proceed without us. We wanted to take the children to Florida for a reunion with Tonio's family, which was long overdue, and asked our good neighbor Helen, who loved animals, to take care of Pretty Boy while we drove south along the grand Mississippi River to New Orleans, from which we would continue along the Gulf of Mexico to the family reunion, east of Pensacola.

We first headed south toward Bloomington, to show the children the campus of my alma mater, where we spent a couple of hours giving them a tour. They stuck their feet in the *Showalter Fountain* to cool off, looked up at the big globe in Ballantine Hall, where I attended most of my classes, and thought the Musical Arts Center was quite neat and "humongous." I thought it would be great if they went to college in Bloomington. They did not say much when we drove by the very humble apartment where I lived during my student years.

We stopped for lunch on the way to New Harmony, the small town that in 1814 attracted a communal religious group from Germany, known as the Rappites or Utopian Society, because they were looking for a utopia in the wooded hills of Southwestern Indiana. – Tonio and I had been to New Harmony to spend a weekend together with Father George a couple of years earlier, and as it was on the way, we wanted the children to see the simple wooden structures of these separatists. Ralph Schwarz, a well-known architect from the East Coast and a friend of Tonio, had only recently restored these structures to their original state. Ralph had also worked with Tonio and supervised the renovation of the Century Center at Miles, which was completed in time for their big centennial celebration, where I had been a guest in 1984, prior to dating Tonio. We took Gustl and Liesl through the red-brick Owen House from 1830, now a museum of the decorative arts of the 1830s and 1840s; and they liked the round, snow-white Athenaeum Museum, built by the renowned architect Richard Alan Meier in 1974, located high above, on the bank of the Wabash River and the outskirts of the peaceful little town. This town has attracted explorers, intellectuals, and artists from around the world.

Knowing it would get hotter the farther south we drove, we filled our cooler with cold beverages and ice to keep the food we had packed for picnics on the way from spoiling. Tonio had suggested we avoid chain restaurants and hotels and search out mom-and-pop motels and family-type restaurants to get a taste of genuine Southern and Cajun cuisine. We got excited when we arrived in Cairo, in Southern Illinois, and saw the meeting place of the two magnificent rivers, the Ohio and the Mississippi. Cairo is also known as "Little Egypt," because of its location at the confluence of the two rivers, which reminded the settlers of the location of the Egyptian capital on the Nile. As soon as we located a low spot along the bank of the Mississippi, we waded in the water of this awesome waterway, almost 2,500 miles long. If you add the Missouri, the length grows to over 4,200 miles.

Driving into the small town of New Madrid, Missouri, on the west side of the Mississippi, we noticed right away that the people were in a state of anxiety. They were preparing for a flood of cameramen, who were moving in to cover a major earthquake that was expected to take place. I had no idea that the fault system which goes through the area produces approximately three hundred events per year and that in 1811 this tiny town had experienced a major earthquake and was indeed susceptible to others. Fortunately, the quake expected later that year never surfaced. – We checked out the local historical museum and stuck our feet in the big Mississippi, before admiring it and a couple of monstrous barges from the Riverview Observation Deck. A short distance from town, we found an inviting picnic table alongside a forest, where a medium-sized dog came out of the bushes to beg for food. It was a skinny, light-brown, obviously homeless mutt. The children fed him all our bread, and they became friends so quickly it was difficult to leave behind poor Toots, as Gustl named him.

We picked up the Natchez Trace Parkway in Mississippi. Not well versed in American history, I was told that the Natchez Trace is considered the oldest road in the world, that Native Americans, called Mississippians, built it as early as 8000 BC and used it for traveling, trading, and hunting. – The Trace led us to historic Port Gibson, where in 1863 the most decisive battles of the American Civil War were fought. A few miles north was the Vicksburg fortress, which guarded the Mississippi. When it was surrendered on July 4, 1963, together with the fall of Port Hudson, it resulted in giving the North undisputed control of the Mississippi River. – In Port Gibson, Tonio pointed toward the huge, golden finger of God on top of a church steeple. I found it somewhat comical, as I had seen weather vanes or crucifixes on steeples but never God's golden finger. What seemed equally strange was the presence of a Moorish church in Port Gibson. But I reminded myself that hundreds of denominations have taken root in America.

As we drove from Port Gibson through Mississippi, vast cotton fields passed by on both sides of the road. The children and I asked Tonio to stop so we could pick a few cotton balls, just as I had done in Georgia when Doc took Maria and me on the long trip in 1956. Tonio took a side road to stop at a hill covered with grass, an Indian mound presumably several thousand years old. Back on the Trace, Tonio got a speeding ticket from a trooper, who appeared out of nowhere on this deserted, though beautifully paved, road. I could not get over the endless miles of hilly countryside, where trees and bushes, as well as the ground, were covered with suffocating and eerie kudzu vines, which Tonio claimed could not be eradicated. The tall trees resembled ruins of castles, and I wanted to keep my distance from the region's vegetation, for fear it might entrap me and keep me as one of its phantoms in this ghostlike landscape.

Tonio had told me about the beautiful antebellum mansions built in the 1800s by the many millionaire cotton kings, and left unscathed by the Civil War, that we were about to see in Natchez. Natchez, the oldest settlement along the Mississippi River, is named after a tribe of prehistoric Indians, whose massacre in 1729 was the bloodiest in US history. With its rich antebellum cotton culture, post–Civil War decline, and modern industrialization, Natchez can be considered rather symbolic of the South.

All four of us marveled at the fabulous Georgian and Victorian mansions. They boasted ornate wrought-iron fences, painted black or white, behind which lush green lawns, bushes, and flowering shrubs set off the white houses, whose strong pillars and columns supported the roof overhanging the gallery, on which big rocking chairs stood waiting for you to sit and enjoy the breeze.

We had a chance to feel what it is like at Rosedown, a stunning Georgian-style plantation house with gardens on 3,500 acres of land, located on the Great River Road in St. Francisville, Louisiana. Daniel Turnbull, who derived his wealth from cotton, sugarcane, and indigo, built the house in 1835. It was fascinating to see once again how European culture and art had impacted Americans who had the means to travel. Turnbull and his wife Martha, of the Barrow Dynasty in West Feliciana Parish, had filled their mansion with artifacts from around the world, arranged their gardens in the image of seventeenth-century French-style gardens as seen in Versailles, and placed many statues from Italy and France on the formal grounds. Taking full advantage of their access to the river, on which they transported their goods to New Orleans, instead of returning the boats and barges empty, they brought back their imported treasures. They even brought in camellias, azaleas, sacred cedar of Japan, and other exotic Oriental flora, which we admired as we walked through the park, where a gazebo stood not far removed from the former slave quarters. After a tour of the mansion, we sat on the gallery, taking a break in the big rocking chairs and looking down the long, wide path, lined with huge live oaks, that led up to the impressive white entrance, reminiscent of the Brandenburg Gate. Tonio took a special picture of Liesl, who sat on the steps to the gallery in her pretty white dress with a ruffled, light-blue, polka-dotted skirt, imitating a Southern belle by saying, with a distinct Southern accent, "I declare!"

A peaceful and mysterious elegance surrounds these white mansions filled with antiques. They shimmer through the branches and knotty stems of live oaks over one hundred years old, draped with moss. It is not uncommon to find a plantation house where you can take a ghost tour. Instead of taking such a tour, Antonio drove up to the St. Francisville Inn, a Victorian-style bed and breakfast, built in 1878, embellished with three steep, flamboyant gables, and nestled in a grove of moss-covered live oaks. Here, where John James Audubon had lived and worked, we were going to spend the night. Liesl and I were ecstatic, because we each got to sleep in a canopy bed. Hurrah!

Breakfast was served in the charming, red-brick courtyard. In the center stood an octagonal stone fountain with a statue of a maiden carrying a jug on her right shoulder. Before we left, Antonio asked Liesl to sit on the rim of the fountain for a picture.

It looked like rain as we drove into New Orleans, also called "the Crescent City" because it is situated along a bend in the river. I had fond memories of New Orleans from my last visit in 1956, with Doc. Tonio was successful in locating a nice hotel in the Vieux Carré (French Quarter), around the corner from Bourbon Street. We were starving, so we dropped our luggage and went to hunt for the highly recommended Felix's Restaurant and Oyster Bar, on Bourbon Street. However, the rain suddenly poured down in buckets. There was no place to seek shelter, so we took off our sandals and proceeded barefoot. The water was splashing in all directions, and when we entered Felix's, we were soaking wet. By the time we finished our various seafood dishes, which were as delicious as we had been told, we were dry and in the mood to see what Bourbon Street might have in store for us.

Luckily, a jazz band, consisting of a combination of younger and older players, trumpets, drums, a trombone, and a saxophone, was playing up a storm, which lifted our spirits at once. I picked up the rhythm and could have danced in the street if someone had been willing to join in. They were fantastic. What rhythm! I hated to leave, but since we could spend only one night in New Orleans, Tonio urged us to explore the French Quarter and admire the different facades, with their attractive wrought-iron railings and trim on the balconies. I enjoyed watching the mix of people, including the Cajun cowboy who walked in front of me and the many different nationalities that hurried or strolled through the narrow streets. The children were mesmerized by Mike, a clown on Jackson Square, who played tricks with a bunch of balloons while whistling. We talked with him, as he appeared to be a bit lonesome, and we could not get him off our minds even when back at the hotel and during supper, which included the best blackened catfish ever. Tonio drew a good sketch of him in the photo album, since we were out of film at the time.

The sun was shining the next day, when we explored the city for more sights and ended our sojourn with a horse-and-buggy ride, starting at Jackson Square and taking us past a few fine houses on St. Peter Street, adorned with the most striking cast-iron lacework we had seen in the city. Tonio took a picture of Gustl leaning against the famous cast-iron fence surrounding the square, where a statue of Andrew Jackson stood. In 1815, he had commanded the armed forces that prevented the British invasion of New Orleans. Opposite is the St. Louis Cathedral, first built in 1788, which makes it the oldest cathedral in the United States – but if you come from Europe, it seems quite new.

Grandmother was happy to see us, and especially Gustl and Liesl, when we drove up in the late afternoon just to say hello. Through Tonio's brother, the lawyer, who looked more like Clark Gable than the boyfriend I had thrown out because he was married, we had rented a condo on the Emerald Coast, not far from Fort Walton Beach. The brother was on his fourth marriage, which looked as though it might last, because in the meantime he had turned into a somewhat obsessed Christian. He had taken the beachfront condo and left us the one facing another building.

The days were filled with swimming in the Gulf of Mexico, even though the water was really too warm, which might have accounted for the occasional jellyfish left behind on the beach by the gentle waves. Tonio took off now and then for photo shoots of dunes, sea oats, and other plant species along the beach, while Liesl and I found out how scary it can be to step into quicksand. The boys could not get enough of paddling around in the kayak or floating on air mattresses. Liesl was terribly disappointed when her little cousin, Amalia, screamed to high heaven when Liesl asked her to spend the night in our condo. The little girl, with her dark-brown curls, snub nose, and Southern drawl, would have been more adorable if she had not been so utterly spoiled by her mother, who changed her outfits, pretty as they were, three or four times a day. I suspected her pretty mother was secretly hoping her doll would marry a prince or someone who came close to royalty. Suffice it to say, there were no princes on that beach.

The male cousins entertained themselves by staging water battles and flying the big kite Gustl had brought along, and one day they went canoeing on Juniper Creek with their fathers, Aunt Jude, and Amalia. It was humid and blistering hot, which was reason enough for Liesl and me to stay behind. When they returned, they claimed to have had a great time, feeling like Indians, and devoured pizzas before flopping down on their bellies, side by side, on the pulled-out hideaway bed to watch TV until they fell asleep.

The family reunion, attended by the rest of Tonio's siblings, with their respective spouses and children, was lively as always, and everybody contributed when it was time to cook. Tonio bought all the drinks, the lawyer grilled the fish, the youngest sister brought a cake, and the older one made a salad. We talked much about the wedding in Venice and our trip to the Alps and the journey home across the Atlantic. We thanked them once more for the pretty quilt they had collectively given us, but I kept quiet about the butcher knife the lawyer had sent, which we had considered a strange gift. In Germany, giving a knife as a present is definitely taboo, because it is presumed to "cut apart" the friendship. Our wedding album made the rounds, and I could not help but notice that Tonio's older sister, the one who had told me I was not welcome in her family, never looked at a single picture, even though she sat on the couch with her husband, who took quite an interest because his hobby was photography. She was drinking wine, and everybody knew about her tendency to overindulge.

Tonio and I took off one day, leaving the children with his younger sister, whom I very much liked. She always treated me kindly. He had scheduled a meeting to discuss a Miles diabetes exhibit with Dr. Sam Eichold, founder of and contributor to the Eichold-Heustis Medical Museum of the University of Alabama–Mobile. This was to be displayed in 1991 at the Providence Hospital in support of the Providence Diabetes Center's educational program. Dr. Eichold, a retired MD, had invited us for lunch, and afterward he gave us a tour of the museum. It suddenly occurred to me that it was the perfect place for Doc's many surgical and other instruments from World War I, including related documents and memorabilia that I had in my possession. Dr. Eichold was more than receptive to my suggestion that I donate the items to his museum, and before we left, he assured me that he would have a special cabinet built and arrange for a very distinctive display.

On the way to his beautiful Southern-style mansion, furnished with priceless antiques, Dr. Eichold drove us past the port, where several big cargo ships had docked, and he gleamed with pride when pointing out a number of handsomely restored antebellum estates. He then stopped in front of one house in a run-down section of the city, which we could have bought for the sum of one dollar. It would have taken close to a million to restore it to its former beauty. –

I must admit, if it were not for the heat, I would not have minded living in the South. Whenever I had been there, either with Doc or, as was more frequently the case, with Tonio, I was impressed by the complete absence of anxiety or urgency. The waiters in the restaurants and the personnel in the hotels, usually African-Americans, were genteel, refined, and noticeably polite. It was a relaxing ambiance, and I always felt genuinely welcome.

Tonio used a different route to drive north, taking us cross-country at times, so that we could appreciate the hilly and scenic countryside and the often strikingly poor towns with too many crumbling structures. I remember a church that had been turned into an auto-parts store and the tin-roof-covered mountain cabins with old, vinyl-covered couches on the front porch. It was reminiscent of the shacks on the back roads of Michigan that housed the patients Doc treated for free. The wood structure of St. Seppels, an Episcopal church, on the mountain in Mentone, Alabama, resembled a barn, except for the three gables and a crucifix on top. The wood was so weather beaten that one feared it would soon collapse if not cared for constantly.

The children enjoyed their ride through DeSoto State Park on a little train, as well as the fountain that falls over one hundred feet from the outlet of De Soto Lake. I would have liked to see a wedding at the humble and very rustic Mentone Wedding Chapel. Unfortunately, we found that all of the churches were closed when we tried the doors. On our way to Nashville, Tennessee, Tonio scheduled a picnic in the Noccalula Botanical Gardens in Gadsden, Alabama, where we saw Noccalula Falls. When we stopped for a break in the capital of Tennessee, we did not even try to gain entrance into the Grand Ole Opry. The sun seemed to beat down on us even more, and we sought out the shade when searching for a restaurant to have a bite to eat. Glad to get back into the air-conditioned car, we were by then anxious to return home, where it would hopefully be cooler. We spent the night at a hotel in New Albany, Indiana, where we talked about our many experiences and realized we all had acquired a deep tan, most of all Tonio and Gustl, who could roast in the hottest sun all day long. Liesl kept talking about the restaurant, where the waiter would pass by the tables and throw rolls to whomever wanted one. We could not remember the restaurant's name, but it was also the place where the children had their first barbeque, which was so good it became one of their favorite foods.

New Addition to Our House – First Sign of Tonio's Temper

It was raining in South Bend when we returned home. The house looked as though ghosts had taken possession during our absence. Blue plastic sheets were draped alongside a portion of the yet-unfinished spaces of the upstairs construction. The house was dark when we entered, and we were too tired to go on an inspection tour. I was surprised, though, by a big hole in the ceiling of my den, but I had to wait until the next day to discover that Jim, the contractor's young son, who could not work unless the radio was blaring, had stepped through the ceiling. In the morning, we found that water had leaked into the living room, which meant replacing the grass-cloth wall covering. We were nevertheless glad to be home, because it was definitely advisable that we be present to watch and render advice as the construction proceeded.

The children were happy to play with their friends at the pool, and they never complained about the mess. They did not really know how to react to a postcard their mother had written from the San Juan Islands, in the state of Washington, because with the exception of her greeting, she wrote exclusively about historical events, dates, and buildings, which was as usual over their heads. I think she changed her tone a bit after I warned her during a telephone conversation that unless she communicated with the children at their level, she would risk losing them.

As soon as the cedar shingles were up, Antonio, who had decided to paint the house himself, inside and out, regularly changed into his painting clothes after supper. Unless we had plans for activities with the children, he was busy crawling around on the scaffolding and staining the shingles dark brown. He got Gustl engaged in the process, but it soon became obvious that he lacked the proper coordination. – As the children would have their own bedrooms, we took them to Ethan Allen, where they could select their beds, mattresses, fancy covers, the colors and carpets for their rooms, and whatever else their little hearts desired. – Packing the children's suitcases for their return to their mother's house, especially compared to the packing for the wedding trip, was no big deal, because to keep the clothes neat, I had decided to store the outfits I had bought in their closets at our house. They did not object at all.

Toward the fall, the addition was complete, so we could start furnishing and put on the final touches. Tonio and I enjoyed hunting for antique lamps, mirrors, and chests, and once the house had experienced a major renovation throughout, we sat back and were mighty proud of our accomplishment. We felt it had all been worth it, the major expense as well as the work, even though at one point the work brought me to the verge of collapse. That day, Tonio decided to stay home from work to deal with the construction crew. The next day, I was ready to continue.

In an effort to create a certain German ambiance in the house, we had brought home from our last trip to Germany brass door handles with key locks, drapes, and cartons of very heavy cobalt-blue tiles for a stove that would sit in the new library/office/entertainment room, which had a cathedral ceiling. Antonio designed the rather sizeable stove, and a man in the business of building them, after a long and not hassle-free process, delivered the masterpiece, which weighed about half a ton. Together with three other men, and just in time for Christmas, he struggled to take it upstairs without scratching our prized stairway. When it was placed on the gray slate foundation, it already looked nice, but when Antonio hung a big acrylic painting of Greta Garbo, in royal blue, red, and white, on the white wall behind the black chimney pipe that ended high in the vaulted ceiling, it looked aesthetically stunning. The painting was a gift from his friend. Tonio wrote a poem to accompany it with the title "The Classic Garbo."

We fired up the stove as soon as it was ready, learning in a hurry that it did not take much to heat the room, which quickly became our favorite. As they were more contemporary in design and, with three large windows, very light, we brought up the Scandinavian wall-unit shelves, along with the Bang & Olufsen entertainment center and the white couch set with the glass cocktail table.

We had fun hanging pictures, including a Venetian scene in aqua that we brought from Venice and a sketch by Christoph Meckel, a wedding gift from the Segebrechts, who were good friends of Meckel. On the shelf, which almost reached the white-painted cathedral ceiling, Tonio placed the art-deco piece given to us as a wedding gift by good friends who had left the Kibbutz in Israel to join the business world in America. It was an urn-like vase of pink cracked glass on a metal tripod stand. On the shelf below stood a cloisonné urn from China.

It was getting late, and both Tonio and I were sipping a glass of brandy while arranging knickknacks. We had received a beautiful, tall, all-white Royal Doulton bridal-pair figurine from Karl and Renate, which I thought would look perfect in the company of a white dancing girl that belonged to Tonio. Suddenly, instead of placing the white pair on the shelf, Tonio hurled it onto the newly laid ipe wood floor, close to where I was sitting, and shouted, "I never liked this!" The figurine broke into a thousand pieces, leaving a deep scar on the floor – a constant reminder of this first outburst of his inexplicable anger. All I could say was "I liked the figurine – why would you do this?" Rather en passant, I muttered that breaking it could have symbolic implications for our marriage. Antonio ignored my comment and continued placing art objects on the shelf. I cried to myself out of fear or shock, or perhaps both. How could I ever explain to our good friends what happened to the lovely wedding gift? When they finally asked, I said it was broken when we were remodeling.

At about that time, I was disappointed to find out that my original attorney had left the firm and that a new one had been assigned to my affirmative-action case. Though he seemed competent, it was necessary for him to get acquainted with the case before proceeding. Following his advice, I had filed a charge of discrimination in the Indianapolis District Office (EEOC) on September 5, 1990. By then, I was sure my archenemies, given the way they were avoiding eye contact with me, knew what was going on. –

On October 3, the day of Germany's reunification, we staged an Oktoberfest that surpassed all previous ones. More than a hundred guests filed in. Many were curious about the new addition. Mrs. Koerting, who by then was in her nineties, came with her son Richard, Antonio's new boss, and almost broke her foot stumbling over a step to the deck. I never quite understood why, when I told her Father George would marry us, she felt compelled to announce that he was gay. Father George was among our guests as always. We had just learned that he had a major problem with alcohol and planned to go to Hazelwood for treatment. My friend Renate was puzzled when, unexpectedly, he put forth a great deal of effort to convince her to teach him German. Even the Schauters showed up, though Tonio had had quite a dispute with them at some social function, when the ultra-German VP from Miles arrogantly proclaimed that "all Americans are stupid." He was one of those who took sadistic pleasure in axing employees. It goes without saying that he was disliked by everybody, including his superiors, who regretted ever having gone out of their way to import him to Elkhart and promote him. I could never understand how his wife, a robust Brunhild type, could put up with a man who was obviously a womanizer. Though Chancellor Cohen and his German wife had intended to come, they did not show, perhaps because of my legal action, but who knows why? He had commended my Bayer Program in his mission study, but he never displayed my two book publications in the cabinet he had made to show off faculty publications, probably because nobody read German well enough to understand them.

In view of what was going on, I was more than pleased when on November 26, 1990, a report on alumni revealed that the IUSB German program had a greater number of majors than either French or Spanish. I wondered what the Prima Donna and the Fly Trap would have to say about it. After I referred to it in my annual report, the Fly Trap, in his very tame evaluation, ignored it, just as he ignored the fact that I had found twenty-three summer jobs in Germany for my students. He did reference the fact that I had given a TV interview regarding the reunification.

It felt like Christmas again on Thanksgiving, because the kiddies were coming. The house was ready for them, and so were we. We trimmed the tree together, and as we now had a stairway, we wound a garland with red bows around the railing. On the new mantelpiece above the fireplace, which matched the muiracatiara wood of the stairway, we placed another garland with little angels. Above the mantel hung an oil painting, the *Lacemaker's House in Bruge*, my wedding present to Antonio. It was by an Indiana artist, H. G. Davisson, who was born on April 14 (Doc's birthday) in 1866.

The children loved running up and down the stairway, on which we had placed a wool runner with an Oriental design. When Gustl slid and almost hurt himself, however, we ordered them to walk slowly.

Gustl tried out the crawl space in the attic, which was accessible through a little door, and made plans to invite his friend for a sleepover and to play chess. Liesl called her friend from across the street to show off her room and her dolls. They sat in the window seat on the Laura Ashley cushions that matched the ruffled comforter on her sleigh bed. – We never had much time when they came at Thanksgiving, but father and son set up the train on the big board that Bernie had made, which filled the entire den. The two spent hours in the garage building a Matterhorn and surrounded the mountain with village houses, a church, and trees. Once the train was running, the entire family was mesmerized by it. Liesl even left her dollhouse and Maria unattended. She looked so pretty in the multicolored skirt I had knitted for her, similar to the one Mutti had made for me years before, that when she stood next to the piano playing a song on the violin, which she had brought along, I almost cried. She assured me she would continue with piano lessons, which she and Gustl had started in South Bend a couple years earlier. While Liesl had joined the school orchestra, Gustl played the trombone in a band. We were always glad to hear that both had continued with dancing.

It started to snow after the children left, and we got busy putting up Christmas lights in the snow-covered evergreen trees outside and a wreath with lights on the red-brick wall of the chimney. Our home looked inviting and cozy when our dinner guests arrived. A fire was crackling in the fireplace, and we were glad we could take our guests upstairs to sit and chat over a cheerful after-dinner drink with a fire burning in our tile stove, which earned much praise from everybody. Everything had turned out just as we dreamed it would. We had spared no expense, and we were confident that we would live, work, and create here in peace, harmony, and happiness forever.

In Chicago, Andrew Lloyd Webber's *The Phantom of the Opera*, which we had not yet seen, was playing, though Tonio and I had on many occasions frequented the Lyric Opera, where at one time we had season tickets. Together with our friends the Voepels and Hagenbergs (Mr. Hagenberg was another VP from Miles), we planned to see *The Phantom* on New Year's Eve and made reservations at the Palmer House. We all dressed in our best clothes, showed off our minks, and had a delicious dinner before attending a most memorable performance of the musical. When we returned to the Palmer House, it was full of celebrating guests and others, some not so sober, seeking shelter from the windy weather on the streets. We found a secluded table at which to chat and sip a drink, and we toasted the new year feeling happy and content. I was not so happy when the Hagenbergs, both heavy smokers, succeeded in getting Tonio, who had tried hard to quit, to accept a cigarette. Despite my plea not to tempt him again, they ignored me and offered him more. Back in our room, Tonio assured me it was just a "social smoke," and fortunately he did not start to smoke again, as I had feared he might.

Jet-Setting to London – Shattered Friendship

On January 2, 1991, Tonio walked into the kitchen after work and asked if I would be game for a quick, extended-weekend trip to London for a mere $650, including airfare and a hotel room for two. It meant leaving on the evening of the 3rd and returning on Sunday the 7th. How could I refuse such an offer, since I had seen nothing but a web of crowded streets in London when riding in a cab from Heathrow to Victoria Station a year earlier? It did not take long to pack – and I even contacted the publishing house Faber and Faber and felt extremely fortunate to get a commitment from one of their editors to meet with us on a Friday afternoon, even though almost everybody took off early for the weekend. –

I felt like a jet-setter. Chicago to London went faster than Chicago to Frankfurt. We arrived at our Best Western hotel, which featured Scandinavian decor and was not far from the heart of the city, in the late afternoon. Antonio, who had attended a minisession in London during his freshman year, knew just which tube or double-decker bus to take in order to introduce me to the most important landmarks on our whirlwind, yet deluxe, tour of London, which, much to our surprise, was rain free. Each and every famous building I saw, be it the Houses of Parliament, where we listened to Big Ben strike, or Buckingham Palace, where we tried in vain to get a glimpse of a member of the royal family, impressed me. We took a double-decker bus to Trafalgar Square, and we had tickets for the Donmar Warehouse theater, on Earlham Street, where we saw Steven Sondheim's musical *Into the Woods* later that evening. On Friday afternoon, we met with the editor at Faber and Faber, the well-known publishing house where the works of T. S. Eliot, Jean Cocteau, James Joyce, Tom Stoppard, and numerous prizewinning authors had been published. We were asked to send a two-page synopsis and several pages of sample text, and we were pretty excited that they were interested enough to bother to read a sampling of our novel in progress.

On Saturday, Tonio was convinced I would love strolling down Portobello Road, the famous antique market near Notting Hill Gate. He was right; I enjoyed looking at the many galleries, antique stores, and exotic vendors' boutiques selling goods from India, Morocco, and other such places. We discovered several unique antique treasures and a stunning pair of designer silver earrings. Portobello was more rewarding to me personally than our visit to Harrods, where Tonio purchased an unusual candlestick, to be used as a base for his desk lamp. Harrods, with all the Christmas lights inside and out, did look magical at dusk, and I got excited when I spotted a huge Laura Ashley store on the same street, where I bought an adorable dress for Liesl at a very good price. – There was not much time to appreciate the famous exhibits in the British Museum, but we vowed to return someday. On Sunday, we took a last tour through the main part of London on a double-decker bus. We passed Trafalgar Square and the London Tower and stood in awe in front of Westminster Abbey, where the most splendid coronations, weddings, and grand ceremonies take place. Unfortunately, we did not have enough time to stay until the end of the service, because our plane to the States departed in the early afternoon. It returned us to South Bend after supper.

I had filed my annual report prior to leaving and wondered what the Fly Trap would say; he had, I am sure, anxiously agreed to be acting chairman after they terminated the Spaniard's chairmanship one year early. In view of the fact that the affirmative-action matter was in progress, I was curious to see his evaluation. I knew they would be more careful at this point, because the Fly Trap, in charge of scheduling classrooms, had the audacity to schedule all of my classes, instead of on campus as usual, in a nearby high-school building the university made use of. It would have entailed the major inconvenience of walking across a very busy street, which would be particularly difficult at night. I told my friend Donna about it, and she mentioned it to the ex-chancellor at lunch; the same afternoon, the Fly Trap informed me that he had moved the classes to a campus location. – His evaluation was carefully worded. He did mention that I did not send any student evaluations, which was correct, because the Spaniard, to whom the evaluations were delivered by the student who collected them, never turned them over to me. He also "encouraged" me to participate more actively in university activities, which puzzled me, because I had just filed a lengthy report listing thirty-seven university-related activities in which I had acted as participant or founder over the years. By comparison, my colleagues, including the Fly Trap, listed one each.

I got busy preparing for my classes, especially a senior seminar on works of German romanticism, which I looked forward to, as it was my favorite period. I had several superb students, one of whom had just been accepted to the PhD program at the University of Michigan. I was back to teaching twelve credit hours that semester, which meant an overload of three credits. I spruced up "Oral German for Teachers" through the use of newspaper and magazine articles that reflected the changes in Germany since the fall of the Wall. There was not much time for scholarship, I admit. I was due for a sabbatical in the fall of 1992 and was optimistic that we would then finish the novel in progress. I needed – as I always did when working on books for publication – a block of uninterrupted time.

In mid-January, in the evening, I was talking with Liesl on the phone. The TV volume was low when Peter Arnett reported on CNN that a massive air offensive to liberate Kuwait had just started. I told Liesl to turn on the TV. Scud missiles were sailing through the dark sky. It was incredible to witness live warfare from my own living room.

Antonio and I were much concerned about the well-being of a friend who had just left to visit her son and friends in Israel. We were told that Iraq had fired short-range Scud missiles at Israel, hitting apartment buildings around Tel Aviv and Haifa. We were relieved when her husband reported that his wife was fine and that she would return in a few weeks.

Tonio's mother had wanted to visit us in our new house, and she arrived while Operation Desert Storm was raging. She felt rather sick as soon as she got off the plane. We took her straight to Liesl's new bedroom, where she recuperated quickly. I am not sure if all of her praying helped, if it was the tender loving care we gave her, or both. She met several of our friends for dinner at a local restaurant, but only stayed a week. I tried hard to get to know her a little better, but it was impossible to develop closeness with her. She was very attractive, quite a lady, but completely devoid of what Mutti had so much of – motherly warmth. Antonio had warned me that she was a fanatical Baptist, made a habit of listening to the Bible preachers on TV, was a generous donor to all of their causes, and would constantly try to convert me, which was true. I was taken aback when, during a conversation I had with her, I expressed the regret that because of the age difference, I would probably have to leave Tonio behind somewhere along the road, and she responded, rather bluntly, that she was sure he would not be alone for long.

If Tonio's mother seemed blunt by comparison with my own mother, she was a lamb compared to Tonio's former mother-in-law, who, as you may recall, had a few years earlier written me a nasty note at Christmas concerning her refusal to enroll in a literature course. During a telephone conversation with her, around the time the Nemesis had accused Tonio of intended kidnapping, I pleaded with her to intervene for the sake of the children, suggesting it was time for her to bury the hatchet. I can still hear her scream, "Then I'll bury the hatchet in Tonio's neck!" That was the last time I tried to negotiate with her. It was no use. Judging by what the children told us, their grandmother held that when they were with us, it was tantamount to their being in la-la land. From then on, we referred to her only as "the Hatchet Woman." Suffice it to say that she did not like her second son-in-law either. We never asked her what she thought of her daughter's change in religion, from Episcopalian to Catholicism, a move to which Tonio objected when Ms. Ice Water sought an annulment of their marriage. He wrote several letters to the bishop, but what would have been impossible during my time in Germany was no problem in the States, which was especially the case, a clergyman informed me, if you helped out with a hefty contribution of hard cash. Remember the Goethe quote about the "big stomach" of the church?

A couple weeks after Tonio's mother had left and thanked us many times, we sighed with relief when our friend Jessica returned safe and sound from Israel. Tonio and I accepted an invitation for dinner at the home of one of our mutual friends, to which the Englesburgers were also invited. We toasted with wine, enjoyed the food, and as the evening advanced, got engaged in a heated discussion about Desert Storm and the horrors of war. It so happened that before Tonio and I left for the dinner, my friend Wulf Segebrecht, who had a visiting professorship at Penn State University, had talked with me on the phone, and we had both expressed our disgust and frustration over the war atrocities in the West Bank as well as in Kuwait and Iraq. I told our friends how sorry I felt for the innocent civilians who were being massacred in the process. At that, my Israeli friend's face turned red. She jumped up from her chair and yelled at me across the table, accusing me of having made an anti-Semitic statement. Stunned, I pointed out that the victims were, after all, human beings, at which point she shouted back that they were not human. I was speechless, and I turned to Father George, who had just returned from Hazelton, and asked him if he agreed that Arabs and Iraqis were not human beings and not created by God as the equals of everyone else. His face turned red, and he stuttered, "I don't want to get into that." – I remembered that Wulf had reminded me that it happened to be the anniversary of the bombing of Dresden on February 14, 1945. I was so hurt and irritated by my friend's accusation that I was quick to draw a parallel, in which I pointed out that the Arab civilians were as innocent as the thousands of mothers and children of Dresden who were killed shortly before the end of World War II, forty-six years ago, to be exact; but, I added a bit sarcastically, she probably thought they deserved it since they were all little Nazis – ergo not humans.

I was very disappointed and deeply offended by Jessica, who I thought was one of my best friends, and Antonio and I decided that under the circumstances, this so-called friend should never again be invited to our house. I almost regretted having gone out of my way on Jessica's behalf by writing a very strong letter of recommendation for her that helped her gain admission to the university. I had obviously misjudged her. I was so sure that both she and her husband, who admitted to Tonio that he was embarrassed by her behavior, knew how I felt about the Holocaust. We had had numerous in-depth discussions about that period in time. They knew I had endured a major falling out with relatives and immediate family members as a result of strong feelings and divergent opinions about the Hitler era. – I began to wonder if their friendship was genuine.

A few days after the incident, Antonio took their art-deco vase off the shelf, went outside, and smashed it on the pavement. He swept the shattered glass into a dustpan, emptied it into a plastic bag, wrote a long letter to the wife, dropped it into the bag, and vowed to hang it on the doorknob outside her husband's office door. I pleaded with him not to go to such an extreme. The relevance of broken glass on November 9, 1938, briefly came to mind. Ironically, the wedding gifts from two people who had witnessed our vows on June 24 in the chapel in Bristol, one a German and the other a Jew, were shattered.

I began to feel bitter in the following days, telling myself it did not mean a thing that I had been so anxious to become an American citizen at the earliest possible moment after my immigration in 1959. It did not matter that I had denounced my German citizenship before an American judge. It did not matter that in my German-culture courses, I had criticized the Nazi crimes repeatedly, because as a German professor I felt it was my responsibility to keep the horrors alive so they would never occur again. Sadly, I resigned myself to the belief that the stigma of my German heritage would always be remembered, be it consciously or subconsciously, by both Jews and others. I was always recognized as a German, despite my constant protestations that I was American. The incident also alerted me that I must henceforth be aware of discrimination against me personally. It seems strange that it took me forty years to admit to myself that I would continue to feel ashamed of the crimes the Germans had committed. However, I would not share the guilt regarding their actions against the Jews, actions that began to surface in the Nazi era when I was six years old.

The falling out with my friends coincided with my participation in two conferences held on our campus. One was on the reunification of Germany. I shared the panel with colleagues from the Departments of Economics, History, and Sociology. The sociologist Dr. Janusz Mucha, a visiting professor from the University of Nikolaja Koernika, in Torun, Poland, impressed me quite a bit. I was quick to accept his invitation to participate, together with Professor Penikis, a colleague from Political Science and a native of Latvia, in another conference to be hosted by the Departments of Sociology and History. The title of this conference, which would take place on February 23, was "History in Fast Forward." It was to cover the changes in East-Central Europe and their impact on South Bend, in particular on the ethnic communities (Polish, German, Baltic, Hungarian, Ukrainian, and Yugoslavian). I was eager to share with my colleagues and the audience my experiences in and observations of the former GDR, now referred to as "the new federal states of Germany," from the previous thirteen years.

In my memoirs, I have revealed my thoughts and opinions regarding the developments in the former GDR. I emphasized during our discussions that I agreed with the renowned writer Christa Wolf, who on October 8, 1989, stated that the preservation of certain traditions – revolutionary traditions – could be vital for both

German states, and who had identified both positive and negative aspects of socialism. I further quoted Lafontaine, the candidate for the SPD, or Social Democrats, who said on October 3, 1990, the day that commemorates German reunification, that "German unity is not completed, it is only begun." I reiterated the importance of breaking down the psychological barriers, because it would otherwise be a long time until we witnessed a united Germany in the true sense of the term. Yet, as my East German friends had assured me, they were full of hope and confident that it could only get better.

It turned out to be a good meeting, and I immensely enjoyed sharing the panel discussions with Janusz Mucha. After the conference, we talked more about my experiences in the former East Germany and the summer seminar I had attended at Humboldt University, in East Berlin. Tonio and I invited Mucha and his wife for dinner several times, because they were not only excellent conversationalists, but also sincere and genuine people. They were like Dr. Valdivia-Cano from Peru, virtually ignored by his Spanish colleagues, who were responsible for inviting him to our campus in the first place. Antonio and I sought out visitors from abroad. Getting to know them opened up parts of the world that up to then had been more or less foreign to us.

Toward the end of the spring semester, on a Friday evening, when I was expecting Tonio's return from a business trip to Chicago, he called to ask me to pick him up at the tollbooth entrance. When I arrived, he was standing not far from the booth, where someone had dropped him off. His Mercedes was not there. Outside of Chicago, near Gary, Indiana, an 18-wheeler had rear-ended him and totaled his car. We knew that had he not been in a Mercedes, he would not have emerged from the accident so safely, and possibly not at all. He was in shock, and for several weeks he had to wear a collar because of bad whiplash. To add to his anxiety, he had endured a scary experience when trying to cash a check at a check-cashing booth in downtown Gary. He was surrounded by a bunch of questionable characters who – so he feared – planned to jump him the minute he cashed the check. Tonio was too stressed out to deal with the insurance agents. I was glad to help, especially since I was better at controlling my emotions when dealing with such matters. Tonio was glad I took care of the hassles. After a few days of rest at home, he was back to work as usual.

Tenth-Anniversary Celebration of the Bayer Program in Leverkusen

My Learn and Earn program with Bayer was flourishing, with thirty-nine summer jobs and twenty-five study grants. It was the tenth anniversary of our partnership with Bayer AG and the CDS. –

Tonio, still suffering mildly from whiplash related to the accident, which also entailed many trips to the dentist, did come along on a short trip to Germany, starting with a visit to Mutti, who was very upbeat whenever she saw me but still could not place Antonio, even though he was always so nice to her. We spent the customary evening with Mutti at Marianne's place and stayed the next night in Giesen, thirty minutes by car from Hannover, where we got to know my cousin and his wife, who were more hospitable than the old folks. It was good to see the three children, with whom we had been corresponding and occasionally speaking on the phone. In the spirit of fairness, we had promised my cousin Trudis, with whom I had exchanged letters and talked on the phone a couple of times, that we would look in on them in Euskirchen after the meeting with Bayer AG.

Tonio and I had been invited once again to stay at Bayer's Kasino, and when I met with Pieps the next morning, she asked if I had brought along a more formal dress and went on to announce that Bayer had planned a special ten-year anniversary party for me, to celebrate the existence of the Bayer Program. I was completely surprised and could only say how grateful I was to be honored in such a way. The celebration took place in one of Bayer's private, wood-paneled dining rooms at the pharma complex. A long and heavy mahogany banquet table had been set for about twenty people. Beautiful white bone china with cobalt-blue and gold rims was arranged on a rich white damask tablecloth with matching napkins. Shiny crystal goblets for red and white wines waited to be filled, and the heavy sterling-silver dinnerware boasted of the company's wealth. At the head of each plate stood a white porcelain scroll on which the menu was written in black script. In the center stood an elegant sterling bowl filled with fresh white and pink long-stemmed roses. Two tall sterling candleholders with three arms each stood on either side of the flowers.

All the guests were in some way connected with our program, and some occupied the upper echelon of management at Bayer and the Carl Duisberg Association. When Tonio and I entered, they were already standing close to the entrance of the room, chatting and sipping champagne. Everybody's head turned when we walked in and Pieps greeted us. A waiter approached us right away to offer us a glass of champagne from the silver tray. What a wonderful surprise! Tonio and I were glad to have brought along an appropriate dress and a dark suit. – Just as we all were seated, the door opened and Hans Knapp, the director of Personnel, who ten years before had been instrumental in offering his assistance with furthering the program and saving it from being abandoned, walked in and came to greet me. Everybody's face lit up, because they had not been sure he could make it. I was deeply moved to see him. He came directly from the hospital, still weakened from a cancer treatment. During the course of the dinner, many toasts and speeches were given, mostly pointing to my efforts on behalf of furthering German–American relations. I reciprocated by expressing my gratitude, particularly to Mr. Knapp and those most closely involved with structuring the program, for their interest and generosity. – The surprise at Bayer was without doubt a high point in my professional career. I still rejoice whenever I look at the beautiful vase presented to me at the event. It is a replica of a vase from the Römisch-Germanisches Museum, in Cologne. It stands in my china cabinet, close to the menu that rested in front of each guest's plate. It was painted in black letters on a porcelain scroll; Mr. Fisher had let me take it as a souvenir.

My cousin Trudis, who lived not far from Cologne, had invited us for cake and coffee at their impeccably clean and polished home, decorated in contemporary furniture with glass surfaces galore. As is to be expected from a true German housewife, she had gone all out and set a beautiful table with her best china. She served fruit tarts and buttercream cakes with all the trimmings, especially lots of whipped cream. Their pride and joy was a garden, accessible through sliding glass doors. I have rarely encountered a small piece of land crammed so full of well-arranged perennials, vegetables, fruit-bearing bushes, and fruit trees – and without a single visible weed. It was best to admire the garden from the terrace if you did not want to risk stepping on a posy or pea.

I told them in detail about the party at Bayer, to which they did not have much to say, and I felt all along that the conversation was somewhat constrained. Trudis, with her squinting eyes and rather harsh voice, reminded me of her mother, Aunt Stingy. She most certainly had brought her daughters up to be proper. They were both "noticeably intelligent" and "wunderkinder," according to Frank, who did not have much use for the entire clan, I gathered. I thought it was admirable that the younger one played the piano and studied Germanic languages and English at the University of Freiburg, Antonio's alma mater, and that the older daughter played the violin and studied medicine. When she told us she had plans to come to Delaware at the end of the summer to participate in an internship, we were quick to encourage her to arrive a bit earlier and spend a week with us. She seemed to like the idea.

Both girls, as well as the parents, were totally smitten with Antonio – not only his looks, but his intelligence and noblesse. Trudis made what I thought was a snide remark, stressing that instead of going for a PhD, she had opted to raise children. She did not pursue the topic when I told her about my friend Jocelyn, who had earned a PhD as a widow with three young children. I would not have been surprised if she had asked me, as some of my boarding-school chums did, if I had my dissertation written by a ghostwriter. Be that as it may, we spent a pleasant afternoon together. Tonio and I thought her husband, who had a doctorate in agriculture and a rather high position with the government in Bonn, was a bit on the quiet side. We felt a little sorry for him, because he was definitely under his wife's thumb. When saying good-bye, we told them we would love to have them visit us, and it seemed as though they might take us up on it, especially Kirsten, the medical student.

I started teaching my summer-session course right after we returned from Germany. Since my salary was still low, and to keep up with bills from my attorney and other extraordinary expenses in connection with the house renovations, I had signed up to teach courses during both sessions. The children arrived when the first session was almost over, and they were ready to try out Papa's new car. It was another used Mercedes, but instead of a diesel it was a 190E, also champagne, which was nice because I still drove my silver Mercedes, which looked like new.

Gustl and Liesl took full advantage of going swimming and playing with their friends, who came over to our place, and vice versa, and they had fun entertaining us by dancing, playing their instruments, and talking at the dinner table about their art classes and day camp. When the weather permitted, we ate outside on the deck. – I had started them out with piano lessons from Mrs. Rusk, who had an excellent reputation. While Liesl was pretty good about practicing, it was a constant hassle with Gustl, even though he was, in my opinion, more musical than his sister. Liesl's playing was more technically correct, while Gustl's was more sensitive. My big disappointment was that they progressed very slowly, even though Ms. Ice Water finally bought an upright piano for $500 or so. It always sounded out of tune when Liesl played a piece for me over the phone. Their teacher was a teenager, who charged $7 to teach the two for half an hour each. Of course, there was Liesl's violin and Gustl's trombone. It was several years before they finally had private lessons for those instruments. I was always upset that little effort was spent along those lines. After a while, I gave up trying.

We decided rather on the spur of the moment, when Tonio's work schedule opened up, to take a few extra days off work for a trip up north. Ever since the completion of the bridge across the Straits of Mackinac – in 1957, just before Doc died – I had wanted to see it. We all agreed that a trip along Lake Michigan to see Mackinac Island would be fun. Gustl and Liesl had never been that far along the shore of Lake Michigan, and though it was quite a stretch, we were anxious to get to the island, although we would have to take a ferry and leave our car behind.

Since it was a weekend in the middle of the summer, the crowds on the island were almost unbearable. When we found out that we would be charged $5 each just to sit on the famous porch of the Grand Hotel, considered the "world's largest summer hotel since 1887," we lost interest. After all, we had had the pleasure at Rosedown Plantation only a year before. To make the entire stay on the crowded island even worse, there was a constant downpour of heavy rain. It's not much fun to be dripping wet while visiting the sights at Fort Mackinac and looking at canons used during the War of Independence, or to be all muddy while seeing the field where the battle between the British and Americans was fought. There was hardly enough time for a horse-and-buggy ride, which took us back to the ferry, and thus to the car at Mackinaw City, earlier than we had planned.

The rain did not stop us from admiring the bridge, which spans five miles of open water, linking Michigan's Lower Peninsula with the Upper Peninsula. It has a local reputation as "man's greatest engineering and construction achievement." We drove home along the west side of Lake Michigan, that is, through Wisconsin, which I remembered from my trip with Doc and Auntie Hazel in 1954. It was not one of our more memorable vacations.

Tonio's mother had been asking us to send Gustl down for a week, and we complied. When he returned, his reports were rather mixed. He complained about how tight his grandmother had been, expecting him to pay for his own lunch at a restaurant as well as for a movie ticket. When she complained to me on the phone that we did not send enough spending money with him, I was rather upset. I could not understand why a grandmother who invites her ten-year-old grandson for a vacation would expect the child to defray such expenses. I guess the rumor that she held on to her pennies was true. I had already suspected it when she once sent us one-eighth of a self-baked fruitcake for Christmas.

The children were still with us when we had an international potluck garden party for my summer-school students, to which everybody contributed a dish. I had always hoped our children would express the desire for me to teach them some German and was very pleased when Liesl expressed an interest. I was amazed at how quickly she grasped the grammar and completed her written exercises. Unfortunately, her enthusiasm tapered off, and it stopped altogether when she was back in school, where she took French. Like so many other schools in the country, hers did not offer German; and I was certain that if we offered to pay for a tutor, Ms. Ice Water would not encourage the children.

Sadly enough, a casualty occurred late one afternoon. Liesl had put her cockatiel in its cage on the garden table, forgetting to close the door. When we noticed the cage was empty, we were all upset and immediately started to hunt for Pretty Boy in the trees, bushes, and yards and on rooftops all over our neighborhood, alerting everybody. When it got dark, we were forced to stop and went to bed sad. We looked again the next day, but the bird had flown the coop. We hoped a hungry cat hadn't snatched him up. His disappearance coincided almost exactly with the death of one of our two goldfish, named after Tonio and me, but to this day I do not know which one lay belly up in the glass globe. I think Liesl gave them too much food. Well, we stored Pretty Boy's carrying case and the cage in the attic and never asked about the reaction of the Nemesis.

It was nice that the children had not yet left when Kirsten, who had accepted our invitation, arrived from Germany. We tried our best to make her visit a pleasant one, showing her all our area had to offer, including Lake Michigan and the Amish in and around Goshen. Tonio also took her to Chicago, where they combed the city for a T-shirt for her new boyfriend, a medical student. We had given her a twenty-dollar bill for that purpose, yet she returned empty-handed. Something was wrong with each and every T-shirt. It was then that I realized how extremely critical this young woman was. She looked just as sinister as her mother and her grandmother, Aunt Stingy. I cannot remember hearing her utter a single word of praise. Even when she was in Delaware, she had nothing but criticism for America,

Americans, and everything American. Actually, she reminded me of my younger brother's wife, another German. I did not invite her back. It was too stressful.

The affirmative-action complaint was moving slowly. I had sent the attorney numerous documents, such as information regarding those males with whose work he wanted to compare mine. Tonio was of great help with the typing, and we spent hours responding to accusations, especially those of the Prima Donna. I researched the publication records of my male colleagues, which was not difficult since no one had much to show. – I was very pleased with the long, detailed letter my attorney had sent to the chair of our Affirmative Action Committee, which convincingly refuted the accusations and cited numerous acts of discrimination against me, in particular by the Prima Donna and the Fly Trap, as well as the noticeable discrepancy in salary, which amounted to a difference of 30% to 50%. He ended by adducing legal precedents and asking for a fair amount in damages. It felt good just to have someone from the outside share my point of view. If nothing else, the grievances had been aired and those accused would have to deal with them. The case was moving along very slowly, and when everybody was on vacation during the summer, it slowed to a halt.

Downsizing at Bayer AG and Miles Gains Momentum – Visitors from Bayer and Berlin

In September, Tonio's firm, Miles, made an extraordinary announcement: it had been taken over by its parent company, Bayer USA, housed in Pittsburgh. Certain discussions suggested that Tonio might have to go to Germany, but they decided he should remain pro tempore in Elkhart and receive a promotion to annual-report and site-communications manager. I would have gladly taken off to follow him, no matter where.

Tonio and I had revised the novel a couple of times to make the form of all the chapters consistent with the altered overall concept, style, and point of view. We were optimistic that we were on the right track, because already in February we had received a letter from the senior literary editor at Faber and Faber, who pronounced the manuscript "highly literate . . . though not right for this list" and encouraged us to concentrate on finishing it for further submission. I attached a copy of the letter to my request for a sabbatical in the fall semester of 1992. Toward the end of November, my attorney gave me a draft of a long letter he planned to send to the EEOC, which he asked me to critique.

Though I tried hard not to let the lack of support from my supervisors bother me, I admit I found it difficult, with my heavy workload, to sit down and be creative. The thought that for years I had gone far beyond the call of duty professionally without being fairly rewarded was nagging at me. It was also getting increasingly difficult for Tonio and me to find time to write together. I was busy as usual with teaching an overload of courses and with the overseas program and committee work, and Tonio, who had been promoted, put in more hours at work and traveled extensively in connection with the writing of the company's annual report. We were both ecstatic when the International Association of Business Communicators notified Antonio that his annual report had won him the Silver Quill Award of Excellence.

Our friends Pieps and Peck from Bayer AG had decided to accept our long-standing invitation and join us for that year's Oktoberfest. We were glad to finally have an opportunity to reciprocate for all their valuable assistance with the students at Bayer and for making all our visits to Leverkusen memorable. They brought with them a piece of the Berlin Wall and several unique Oktoberfest posters from Munich, which we attached to the entrance door on the big day. – They loved every minute of their stay, the new house, the over 120 guests, several of whom they knew through Bayer, and the German beer, bratwurst, and sauerkraut – and they participated in the passionate singing, which lasted until well after midnight. I was always equipped with enough handout sheets to allow everybody to sing along. The Germans were impressed by our efforts to keep alive a part of German culture in America. As they bid us farewell, we were certain they had not regretted crossing the Atlantic.

No sooner was the Bayer couple gone than we turned our attention to planning another grandiose party for our expected guests from Germany and Austria: Ingeborg Guenther, widow of the deceased attorney general of Berlin, and her young travel companion, Dr. Emmanuel Longin von Moederndorff, OSB. They would cross the Atlantic on the *QE2*, stopping first to visit the Padre's very affluent relatives in New Jersey, and fly into South Bend by the end of November. Tonio had drawn on his outstanding penmanship and formulated a classy invitation to a cocktail party in honor of our aristocratic guests. We engaged a trio – violin, cello, and piano – from the Division of Music at Notre Dame and hired a bartender and waitresses, who dressed in black and white. Our guests, in fancy attire, were in a fabulous party mood as soon as they entered and heard the pianist playing Viennese waltzes. I invited Germans and Americans, even the new chair of Arts and Sciences, but ignored the ex-chancellor, who by then, in a state of total intoxication, had smashed his car into a tree, broken many bones, and was fortunate to get away with a long recovery. Several of our Venetian guests had met Ingeborg and Emmanuel at the wedding in Venice (Donna, Father George, and the Piedmonts had been able to come), and it was almost like a reunion.

We talked with our guests until late at night and invited a few of my students over for pizza so they could listen to Ingeborg's stories. It was that evening that I observed how protective Ingeborg was of her young friend, especially when he showed a special interest in one of my attractive female students. Tonio, the classicist, and Emmanuel, the theologian, hit it off especially well, since they both knew several of the same monasteries in Tyrol, Austria, and Bolzano, Italy. Father George invited all of us for a delectable dinner served in his luxuriously furnished home in

Elkhart, full of antiques, of course. Unfortunately, we did not meet his close friend Bob Beardsley, Walter Beardsley's adopted son. Bob, much to Walter's dismay, as he once told me, did not produce any heirs since he was gay. Bob's presence would have been interesting for Emmanuel, as he was homosexual himself. I heard the adopted son had made quite a fuss when his father did not bequeath several valuable paintings to him, but they ended up in his possession after a legal hassle. When we visited, Bob was at his castle somewhere on the coast of Portugal. Father George insisted we visit the Ruthmere Mansion, of which he was the curator, and which had been refurbished between 1969 and 1973 by the Beardsley Foundation, under the direction of Robert, the great-great-grandson of A. R. and Elizabeth Beardsley. The impressive Beaux-Arts mansion, with its French furnishings and fine art, is always a good place to visit, particularly when a musical event takes place in one of the lower rooms. It was of particular interest to me because the original owners were related to Doc.

We used to refer to Emmanuel as "the Baron" because of his noble birth and demeanor. Although I had asked him to smoke his cigarillos outside or in the garage, I caught him smoking repeatedly in the library upstairs after breakfast. He sat in a couch chair next to the tile stove, wearing his shiny, silver-gray silk robe; a big, black, dangling crucifix that rested on his hairless chest, together with his pale face and skinny body, gave him an air of anemia. He probably would have caught pneumonia had I insisted on his smoking outside. He was a bit squeamish. Whenever I asked him if he would like an egg for breakfast, he declined politely. But each time, Ingeborg added that if I boiled it for him, he would eat it. When I told her to feel free to take care of his special needs, she retreated from the kitchen. – When the pair left and expressed the hope that we would visit them soon, I wondered if it would ever happen. The many times I had been in Berlin, either alone or with Tonio, not once had we been invited to Madame Guenther's home.

We tried to get our Christmas cards out before the children came, and Tonio composed one of his witty newsletters. Since it was signed by both of us, I will take the liberty of quoting a few of his "predictions." Our friend from Peru, who was also the editor of a local paper, liked them so much he published them:

1991 has been such an eventful period that I'm moved to offer a round of predictions for next year:

1. The sun will come up one day and no one will <u>read</u> anymore.

2. The Dead Sea Scrolls will be proved to be the ancient equivalent of a <u>chain letter</u>.

3. Washington, D.C., will become a <u>theme park</u>. I know I predicted this last year, but Congress couldn't decide on a theme. A resolution is now close. It will be a Media Circus, complete with civics classes à la <u>Jeopardy</u> and a chance to have your photo taken standing next to a cardboard George Bush.

4. People will get sick of diets and going to the gym.

5. American women will demonstrate their growing anger toward the male establishment by adopting frilly fashions that emphasize their figure, neck, bosom, earlobes, legs, cheekbones, and belly buttons.

6. Men will retaliate by pointedly not noticing . . . elevating sexual relations to an unheralded level of reticence and steamy new possibilities.

7. Elizabeth Taylor will have plastic surgery and emerge looking like Michael Jackson!

8. An English publisher will put the sum of all human knowledge on a laserdisc.

9. Television will become even more inane than it is.

10. Israel will make peace with the rest of the world, but people will not be thrilled at the prospect of moving the United Nations to Tel Aviv.

It was also the year Anita Hill spoke out against Judge Thomas's appointment to the Supreme Court. The hearings kept us both stuck in front of the TV, scratching our heads.

Gustl and Liesl had so much enjoyed the overnight stay at the Palmer House two years before that we decided to fly them into Chicago for Christmas again this year. Both loved the Palmer House, where we took a few lovely photos of them in front of the huge Christmas tree in the center of the foyer. It was decorated rather elegantly with big rosé, silver, and bronze-colored ornaments. We took the two along Randolph Street at night to see how the department stores tried to outdo each other with Christmas lights, decorations, fairy-tale and winter-wonderland window displays, and carols. We talked until late at night, ordered breakfast to the room, and had a barrel of fun going Christmas shopping with the kiddies, who were at that point eleven and thirteen years old and growing quickly. Each got to pick out a new fancy outfit. Liesl could not wait to put on her dress, a shiny, black taffeta skirt with a blousy, white organza top and long sleeves. A bright-red rose at the collar matched the wide red belt. We bought red tights and a red bow for her hair to complete the outfit. She loved to dress up, and I enjoyed watching her. The red velvet Laura Ashley dress from London looked adorable on her. Gustl also looked attractive in black pants and the new red cardigan. –

Christmas in our new house was wonderful. The Christmas lights in the newly planted evergreen tree in the front yard looked even more inviting because the children had lined the flagstone path and steps leading to the front door with lanterns. We had a surprise visitor, Wade Johnson, my former student, who stayed for Christmas dinner and got to admire Gustl's train set. On Christmas Day, we set up two card tables in the new addition, where Tonio and I each put together a puzzle with one of the children while a warm fire glowed in the stove. Liesl finally agreed to have her hair shortened by a couple of inches for New Year's Eve, which was thrilling as always, especially when the firecrackers were going off in the front yard, where Tonio and the children had erected a snowman almost six feet high, as tall as Gustl. After setting off the firecrackers, we sat around the kitchen table and took turns pouring molten lead into a bowl of ice-cold water to read each other's futures from the strange forms that took shape. It is an old New Year's Eve custom in Germany. Everybody guarded the silvery shapes like a treasure and took them along when we retreated upstairs, where a cozy fire burned in our new blue stove. – Tonio told the children to turn off the lights, and lit a candle on the cocktail table so we could see the tarot cards he had promised to read. Suffice it to say that I am not superstitious and brushed aside the thorny and torturous future that Antonio unfolded before our eyes when it was my turn. Thorns and daggers predominated. Now, as I look back, I have to admit that there was some truth in what Tonio foresaw – because when I read my evaluation by the acting chair, I discovered that more daggers were in fact pointed at me. He had no connection whatever to languages and was also assistant to the newly hired chair of Arts and Sciences, a woman from the outside. This acting chair had already irritated me during the semester; he sent a memo reprimanding me for not having used the campus phone to call several universities in the state. I could have saved the university $29, which was true. The fact of the matter was that I had been unable to connect, and as the matters were urgent, I resorted to the outside connection. The phones were another bone of contention, in that for a long time, while both the Fly Trap and the Prima Donna enjoyed the privilege of their private lines, my female French colleague and I had to share a phone. I received numerous long-distance calls. Whenever people attempting to call me reached my colleague first, they were forced to call back, which meant an additional expense to them. After a while, I instructed everybody to call me at home.

His evaluation was the briefest I ever received, yet he accused me wrongly of "not posting regular office hours." Not only were they posted to the left of my office door, but they were also listed on my course syllabi, which I distributed to the students at the beginning of the semester.

I know these are not major offenses, but if, over time, you notice a pattern of being singled out, these slights take on a deeper meaning. My attorney felt that the university discriminated against both women faculty in the department by "dumping" obsolete computers in our offices while the males were furnished with more recent models. The fact that the evaluator had to question the pedagogical basis of running my literature seminar for two and a half hours once a week instead of one and a quarter hours twice a week was proof enough that he had no idea what he was talking about. It surprised me that he totally ignored my report on the tenth anniversary at Bayer. A recently divorced mathematician, he obviously needed a target for his frustrations, though he did have a baby on the way with his new wife, a student. Some of my friends insinuated that many of the males resented me for having led such a spectacular life and for always being upbeat.

Escalation of Discrimination – Sojourns in San Francisco and Germany

The deathblow came on February 24, 1992, from the Lemon, who had made his way (no doubt with the help of support letters from the Prima Donna and others) to the position of vice chancellor to Dan Cohen (who has recently been fired for sexual harassment). It was payback time. The Lemon, doubtless with the support of Cohen, in what my attorney later referred to "as a nearly unprecedented decision,' ignored the committee's recommendation of approval and denied my request for a one-semester sabbatical. Devastated, I talked immediately with the new dean, who had the impression that the request was denied because I had not finished the book – for which I had received only a single one-semester sabbatical. He had ignored the fact that in order to complete my last, four-hundred-page publication, I had to take two one-semester leaves without pay in addition to a one-semester sabbatical. – Looking back, I should have listened to several of his colleagues in the History Department, who had criticized his publication record, especially the book that earned him full professorship. They claimed he should never have earned full professorship for it because it was so similar to his dissertation. The titles were almost identical. The first was *Black Tennessee* and the second *Blacks in Tennessee*. His first book was 320 pages long and the second a mere 124. When I compared his record to mine, a question that came to mind was, Why did it take him seven years compared to my three to get his dissertation published? Obviously, he had to make many changes, whereas I had to make none.

I was a bit optimistic after my meeting with the new dean, who wrote a memo I hoped would, together with my attorney's arguments, change the Lemon's mind.

My attorney pointed out, in what I considered to be a very convincing five-page letter, the double standard applied in my case. Referring to the Prima Donna's still-unfinished coauthored work, which had been in progress for ten years, he stated that he was "already listing it as a credit in promotional materials." He argued that "male professors are credited and rewarded in advance for publications, [and] female professors are pressed for 'progress' and 'productivity.'" He concluded by challenging the committee to investigate the charge that one of my male colleagues "used his most recent sabbatical to renovate his basement."

I could go on and on about the many pages of disputes my attorney had previously listed, including the fact that the Prima Donna, though claiming to be a French professor, never produced a single article, much less a book, on a literary subject, that his scholarship was entirely in other disciplines, history and audiovisual studies (education), and that he had not published one word in French, his supposed area of concentration. He also pointed out that the Fly Trap's two brochures of poetry, which represented the entirety of his publications, were published by a Miami-area backroom publishing operation run by Cuban-refugee friends of his, whereas my books were published by a reputable international publisher in a series of scholarly monographs subscribed to by every research library in the world. He had previously made the defendants aware of the Prima Donna's catalogue of translations of French historical documents, which was published in typewritten, mimeographed form by "IUSB Press," an imprint that seems to have been invented for the occasion, as IUSB had no press. He did not mention that the native French students in his classes had produced the translations as exercises.

The hearing would take place before the Affirmative Action Committee on our campus shortly after the children departed after spending a brief but happy spring break with us. The chancellor had appointed both the chair and the committee members. I had the option of going before the committee alone, that is, without legal representation. By that time, after investing in several hundred hours of legal fees, I felt it was better to ask my attorney to fly up and represent me. Of course, this meant the university's legal counsel would come up from the main campus. When the meeting started, I was made aware of the procedure, which precluded me from getting involved directly with the proceedings. The committee members were required to direct yet another appointee to present their questions to the respective attorney, who read their question to the person who was interviewed. It was a highly bizarre situation in which everything seemed filtered and not quite real. The Fly Trap had already retired, and not one person on the committee had any idea about my field of study. In addition, since nobody was sworn in, the entire hearing lacked the expected aura of justice. – It lasted several hours, and when Tonio and I took the attorney out for dinner before he flew back, we had no idea what they would decide.

Meanwhile, my attorney was still communicating with the EEOC representative, who had not made a single attempt to meet with me personally. He talked to me only on the phone, infrequently and always briefly, which I found rather strange. I also had the feeling that he had no idea what my profession was about. His English was not exactly perfect. It struck me as equally strange that my best friend and matron of honor, Donna, who for months had egged me on to take legal action, and whom I had made aware that the EEOC officer would contact her, probably by phone, set her answering machine from that point on to engage at the phone's first ring. It was clear that she screened each incoming call. She never talked to the EEOC official. In view of her reputation as the prime gossiper on campus and having observed her, on occasion, go out to lunch with the ex-chancellor after viciously criticizing him to me, I suddenly realized the mistake I had made in singling her out as my confidante. I have reason to believe she used me all along to milk me about my case only so she could pass the information on to her former boss, even though he had, with the help of his friend the Prima Donna, demoted her. I wonder what he would say now if he knew that during the course of the proceedings, she informed me that he had said, "Chris does not need the money." – Only years later did I realize it was my confidante who must have told the chancellor my father was SS, which was not true. I had told her he was SA (a Brownshirt).

About that time, the Michiana Fiction Writers contacted me and asked if I would agree to a public reading of a chapter from our book in progress, *Between Two Worlds*. I readily accepted, and the reading was announced in the local newspapers. The response to my reading on May 4 was enthusiastic. I was grateful for the group's constructive criticism.

I was glad Tonio was able to join me, because he was very busy with Dick Beal, a dwarf and the voice of the dancing Speedy, the popular trademark used to promote Alka-Seltzer for years. The tiny guy, a little over three feet tall, was in town for Alka-Seltzer Week. This commemorated the sixtieth anniversary of Alka-Seltzer, the famous fizzing remedy made of aspirin, sodium bicarbonate, and citric acid. He was also in Elkhart to autograph his recently published book, *Think Big*. I happily accepted an invitation to a dinner given by the company, represented by several of its top executives, in his honor. Years before, when I worked at Miles, I had brought home a little rubber Speedy for Mutti. It stood for a long time on her kitchen shelf.

After the anniversary, on May 22, Tonio had to fly to San Francisco for a PR conference and asked me to come along. I was elated at the prospect of seeing the beloved city, which I had first visited with Doc and my friend Maria in 1956, for a second time. – Riding in a cab through the rich valleys to the heart of San Francisco, a major Pacific port and the gateway to the Orient, reminded me how very German the hilly terrain looks, all covered with meadows and trees. Tonio had reservations at the Marriott, near Union Square, which features an exclusive shopping district. It was also the place of the conference. Whenever time permitted, we left the building to roam the city. As it turned out, we had more free time than when I was there with Doc.

Tonio, the expert tour guide, took me up to Nob Hill, where I admired the mansions, which bear witness to the opulence of the nineteenth century and which survived the fires and earthquakes that plagued this beautiful city. Tonio just had to take a peek at and a photo of the lovely lobby in the classy Fairmont Hotel before we took the glass elevator to the top-floor restaurant, which offered a great view of the city. Having a penchant for vibrant flowers, I could not resist asking a pedestrian in Pacific Heights to take a photo of us in front of a huge, lush, raspberry-red bougainvillea vine overhanging a white stucco wall protecting a stately mansion. The view from Pacific Heights down to the sea was overwhelming. I had not previously been to the Presidio, a US military base, where we walked down Lovers Lane, flanked by tall eucalyptus trees. The Palace of Fine Arts, with its Greco-Romanesque rotunda with Corinthian colonnades, was not far from the Presidio. – Our ride in the cable car reminded us of the lift on the Seiser Alm, though looking down on a busy street bears little resemblance to gazing down on the valleys in the Dolomites.

A cable car also took us down to Fisherman's Wharf, where the two of us dined in a romantic restaurant, from which we watched the sun set in the Pacific Ocean. After dinner, we made our way through Chinatown, picking up a kimono for Liesl and Chinese slippers for Gustl. I found it of interest that this district was home to the largest urban population of Chinese people outside of China. – We stopped at Pier 39, one of the most popular tourist spots in the United States. It was quite crowded, but it would be worse on June 6, when the twelfth-annual Street Performers Festival was to start. Just to buy frozen yogurt involved a long wait. Yet it was worth seeing the colorful displays of fruit stands and vendors, as well as the kite shop, where the kites were so flamboyant that Tonio just had to take a snapshot. Wherever we visited, he always had an eye for the unusual. He was fascinated by and took many pictures of eye-catching window displays at upscale bookstores, Christian Dior, Bang & Olufsen, Victoria's Secret, a showplace for Jaguars, and antique stores – and he even snapped a photo of a big elevator sign reading "THIS CAR UP."

The city's big attraction is at Pier 39, where the sea lions, attracted by the great number of herrings, rest on the docks. They have come in during the winter ever since the 1989 Loma Prieta earthquake. At first, there were between ten and fifty, but now up to nine hundred surface and stay until the summer. Almost motionless, they loaf around on long wooden floats, not far removed from the piers of exclusive yachts, always at the ready to sail. – At Pier 39, we also took a brief bay cruise on the Blue & Gold Fleet and admired the skyline of the Marina and Embarcadero, which looks even more spectacular at night, when it is illuminated. The boat went underneath the San Francisco–Oakland Bay Bridge, and we admired this incredible structure, spanning four and a half miles of Pacific waters. In the distance was the Cow Palace, where rodeos and other big events took place; but of greater interest to me was Alcatraz Island, in San Francisco Bay, which the fleet encircled in order to give us a good look at the former federal prison, which sat high up on the rock. The former inhabitants were surrounded by an abyss of water on all sides.

The Golden Gate Bridge, where I lost my glasses in 1956, again took my breath away, even though, at a length of a little over one and a half miles, it is much shorter than the Bay Bridge. The cables holding the suspension bridge and its rusty red color lend it a certain grace. When you consider that the steel wires used in the cables of the bridge are long enough to circle the earth three times, it is pretty amazing. We took the car and drove across the bridge to spend half a day at the Muir Woods National Monument, named after the famous conservationist John Muir, to whom we owe the establishment of Yosemite National Park, among other public lands. Just as I was in awe of the *Sequoia sempervirens* trees when driving along the West Coast, so was I astounded when stretching my neck to look up at these coastal redwood trees, some of which are 350 feet high and the oldest of which go back over two thousand years. Walking through the groves of these gigantic trees, I felt as though I were in a huge Gothic cathedral, its colossal pillars supporting the dome of heaven. We were happy in Muir Woods, straying on a hidden path, playing on a narrow footbridge, finding our balance while crossing a creek on a fallen tree, and having our picture taken while sitting next to a giant rock at the foot of a massive sequoia.

It was our last day in San Francisco. Tonio suggested we dine in the fine restaurant on the top floor of the Hyatt Regency, where we had an ocean-view table overlooking the Bay Bridge, the Terminal Tower, and the Embarcadero skyline, surrounded by the blue waters of the Pacific. We agreed with John McGloin that these two bridges are "symphonies in steel."

On the flight home, Tonio talked about the conference and the people he had met. I had been introduced to several of them at the welcoming party. The mood among them was somewhat mixed inasmuch as there was an overriding concern among the attendants about the sluggish economy and the effects of corporate downsizing. Antonio had talked about it before. At Miles as well as its parent company, Bayer, the process of either letting employees go or urging them into early retirement had started several years before. The working environment was bleaker; employees had to take on additional duties when coworkers were fired or squeezed out. Gradually, those remaining, even vice presidents, began to feel uneasy and tried to prepare themselves for possibly being the next to go. However, Tonio was optimistic that his head was not on the chopping block.

Back home, we had to shift gears and get ready for our trip to Germany. Tonio was by then a part of the Bayer Program. We had screened applicants at Miles in early March and had held the orientation again at our residence at the end of April. Tonio was also coming along with us to Germany. We met the students at the O'Hare terminal on May 30, excited and nervous as always. They all looked their best, with fresh haircuts, new casual clothes, and sweatshirts advertising their home campus, and they were anxious to fly to the Old World, which would be so new for them. Tonio continued as our official photographer at the terminal. He had already assembled a few nice prints at orientation time.

We arrived at the airport in Cologne on time, and the Carl Duisberg representatives took over. Tonio and I had been invited to stay at Bayer's Kasino; and when I met with Pieps the next morning, she presented me with a typed program listing meetings and activities for the two days of our stay.

Pieps and her husband Peck rolled out the red carpet for us, including a regular sightseeing tour of Cologne and of the new additions at Bayer. Their personal friend Monsignor Weber gave us a private tour of the cathedral. I had visited it many times before, but it seemed as though I were seeing it for the first time. He took us below and showed us the Roman sewer, which was a first for both Tonio and me. We had not seen Dr. Geks since the wedding, and he invited us to meet him in the afternoon at his elegant villa on the Rhine, with a breathtaking view of the Petersberg. After the war, it had been a favorite meeting place for high-ranking politicians, who gathered there to make decisions concerning Germany's future. He definitely favored white, black, and glass in his home, which contrasted strikingly with the bright red and yellow tulips that greeted us at the entrance to the house. The stunning villa was furnished in contemporary Italian designer pieces that projected an air of sleek elegance and contrasted noticeably with the quaint atmosphere of the Wine Cellar restaurant in the Kasino, where we ended the evening with a superb steak tartare and an exceptional goblet of wine.

The wine the Padre ordered in Bonn, when we took him out for lunch along the Rhine River, was equally as fine and made us feel good. We were pleased to see each other still healthy, though the Padre seemed to have shrunk a bit. We also invited my cousin Trudis and her family for dinner at a restaurant on the Rhine, and finally met Kristen's boyfriend. He was not much taller than the Padre, but he was very shy and blushed easily. – After having seen those dear to us, we drove northward to Duderstadt, the place where I spent five happy years after the war studying and playing tricks on the nuns at Sankt Ursula. I had to show it to Tonio, especially since it played an important role in the autobiographical section of the novel. Tonio thought I had described the place to him rather well, but unlike me, he did not feel hesitant about entering the school, which still looked sinister. Mater Ursula was long dead, along with several others, but Sister Dorothea, though shrunk to dwarf size, was all smiles and full of praise for all my academic accomplishments, since I was one of the few graduates from their school who had made it up to professor. When we left, she insisted that from then on she would make sure I received the annual publication *Ursula-Schiff*, which I never received before. I really did not care.

We drove along Main Street to look at the half-timbered houses, the old cathedrals, City Hall, and the ancient residence of the head of the church, which I had visited often. Since we were so close to Gieboldehausen, the town where I was born, Tonio wanted to take a look at the place, which I left when still in diapers. As both the courthouse and the house of my birth, formerly adjacent to it, were gone, we looked at a so-called castle, a timber structure with a steep roof covered with dark-gray slate, which did not look like a castle to me, but rather like a big, rectangular house with a high roof. The seventeenth-century church where I was baptized was being renovated. We could take a peek, but only through the entrance door.

Our next stop was Sankt Pankratius, in Giesen, the church where Mutti was baptized and liked to sing. It was ancient and surrounded by the cemetery where all of Mutti's ancestors, as well as her parents, two older brothers, several of their children, and others I have spoken of herein, were buried. It bordered directly on the backyard of the big, new red-brick house my cousin Clemens was almost finished building. When Tonio and I paid our respects to the dead, I observed right away a definite favoritism. The richer the dead or their heirs, the bigger and more impressive the graves. I noticed that the graves of my grandparents and those of Lisa, my favorite aunt, and her daughter Elisabeth were already eliminated, while those of Clemens's older brothers, who died years before they did, were still there.

My relatives hosted us generously, and at one point Clemens took off with Tonio to go to a nearby inn for his weekend drinking bout, from which he always needed to be driven home. We talked a lot about family, present and past, including those we visited when in Cologne. I noticed that not much had changed since I left; the backstabbing was as vicious as ever. I am glad I was not around when they raked me over the coals. The new house had to be shown off. A villager had told us it was the biggest and most expensive house in the village, costing about one million marks. It was built like a fortress, and you can be certain it will stand there for generations to come without cracking, unless bombs or an earthquake hit it. The floors and stairways inside were marble and wood throughout, the rooms spacious, and the windows large – and the dog had free range of the whole place, including a spot on the kitchen bench when she desired it. In the basement bathroom next to the big party hall was a fixture for males only, which I had never seen in a private home before. – You would not have to worry about not hearing your alarm clock in the morning, because the bell tower was only 150 feet away – and the bells did not have a damper.

My cousin's wife gave me a tour of the village and proudly pointed out all the houses they had purchased or built to rent. I think there were twelve or thirteen, fewer than the thirty-eight or so semis they owned a year earlier. To be sure, I was impressed. I wondered why they had so little ground around their new mansion, but they explained that they preferred to build another apartment house on the adjacent lot to increase their rental income. I think they loved being close to other houses so they could look straight into their neighbors' living quarters, something like quality control, if you know what I mean. My cousin's favorite pastime was a nightly visit to a nearby forest to search for an unsuspecting deer with binoculars. After killing it, he would cut out its liver and heart immediately. His wife fried and served them to the hunter while they were still fresh.

When we told Mutti the next day that we had visited her nephew, she said it was so nice, even though they never visited her and my cousin's children did not even know what she looked like. – I thought Mutti looked much better when we saw her. I felt numb, though, when the nurse whispered into my ear that she was bloated from "old-age cancer." She added that the course of the disease is very slow. It was harder this time to say good-bye, though Mutti, as always, did not complain. She did not know who had removed our pictures again. That's just how it was.

Overture to Tonio's Relocation in Pittsburgh

I was glad not to have signed up for summer teaching, because I had anticipated working more on the novel, which I hoped would be completed by the end of the year. I had made arrangements for a substitute for my courses, at a cost to the university of $3,000 for the entire semester. I had been able to avoid scheduling an advanced literature course, which would have required a PhD and thus been more costly. As the legal matter was still under consideration by the EEOC, and as the Lemon, supported by his loyal committee, had not changed his mind, when I returned from Europe I decided to sit out the summer and enjoy the children. There were exciting decisions being made concerning Tonio's position at Miles. He had earned his second promotion that year, and they had decided to move him to the new headquarters in Pittsburgh in 1993.

As soon as the children got off the plane, we told them the good news and that, at the end of July, we would all be flown to Pittsburgh in the company jet to see if we would like it and to get a feel for the housing market. But first, we wanted to go on a family vacation to Sleepy Hollow, where Liesl and I had spent a lovely weekend the previous summer. Ever since the Loesers had taken me there in the early 60s, I had spent several wonderfully relaxing and fun-filled weekends at the park-like resort. Whenever I had wanted to get away, I took off for the shores of Lake Michigan. As you will recall, I once took my brother and his family, and another time I teamed up with my college friend Rita to take a break from studying.

Our art-deco-style cabin was close to a white-sand beach more than one thousand feet long and stood opposite the very big, glass-walled pool. There were many youngsters for Gustl and Liesl to play with, and the recreation director knew how to keep the little folks entertained. The Fourth of July celebration on the beach turned out to be a great success all around, especially the fireworks! We all developed a tan as dark as Oreo cookies, even Liesl. On rainy days we played monopoly and poker inside, and when the sun came out we went biking, drove to the nearby go-carts for a spin, or crawled onto the inflated air mattress and rubber boat to be rocked by the waves. Tonio was the self-appointed chef and concocted many a delicious meal, taking advantage of the grill next to the cabin and the open markets nearby. We simply had to go to the smoked-fish place and select a few pieces to take home when we were ready and the children had bid farewell to their newfound friends.

The day we were scheduled to board the Miles jet at the Elkhart Airport was filled with anticipation. We all dressed appropriately for this important visit, which would initiate a major turn in all our lives, a move to a big city in a new state, which had a positive ring to it. Liesl wore the bright-red miniskirt and the white top with the big red ladybug that I had brought from Germany, and Gustl, who was much taller than I, looked handsome in his blue-green shorts and white-and-green-patterned short-sleeved shirt. We took enough snapshots of the interior and exterior of the plane to fill a few pages of a photo album, and we eventually settled in at a fine hotel in Pittsburgh, the name of which I have forgotten. Tonio and I were wined and dined by the heads of PR, while the children had room service at the hotel. We spent a whole day with a realtor looking at houses and getting a feel for the area, but did not find anything that appealed to us.

Miles's big concern was whether I would be willing to leave my tenured position at the university and join Tonio. I made sure they understood I would do everything in my power to come along. Neither Tonio nor I believed in commuter marriages. In addition to flying all over the country in connection with the writing of the next annual report, he had been traveling back and forth between Pittsburgh and Elkhart quite a bit over the last few months. It was not the kind of life either of us was anxious to pursue forever. We looked at several residential areas before we flew home and had no doubt we would find a house where we could be very happy. Of course, the thought of having to sell our home, on which we had spent so much time, thought, and love, and on which the paint was barely dry, filled us, perhaps me even more than Tonio, with sadness.

Toward the middle of August, Tonio was getting sick with a bad cold, or so we thought. No over-the-counter drug or home remedy seemed to help, and I was extremely worried when, one night, he was burning hot and had difficulty breathing. I told the children to be good while I took Papa to the hospital. The doctor in the emergency room quickly diagnosed Tonio with severe pneumonia. He administered a heavy dose of antibiotics and told Tonio rather bluntly that he must stop smoking at once. Tonio vowed to stay away from then on from what my grandfather used to refer to as "coffin nails." He was well aware that his father had died of lung cancer. It took almost four weeks for Tonio to get back to work.

No sooner did Tonio feel better than it was my turn to come down with something – a case of acute bronchitis. I don't recall ever having been so sick. I was extremely disappointed that the drawn-out affirmative-action dispute looked as though it might go on forever, with no relief in sight. In addition, the final reason given by the Lemon for denying my request for a sabbatical was "lack of funds." I found it impossible to believe, since it would cost the university no more than $3,000 for an adjunct to teach the service courses. What depressed me even more was the fact that I had saved them not only thousands of dollars over the years by teaching at least twelve three-credit-hour courses for free, but also approximately $40,000 by taking my leaves without pay. Meanwhile, Tonio was enduring much stress as a result of the new obligations, which included speech writing for the extremely demanding and much-feared new CEO of Bayer USA.

The big positive on the horizon was my new chairman and the new dean, who had not been around when I started the complaint process. My doctor urged a sick leave, because she realized I was physically and emotionally unable to teach. Under normal circumstances, if a sick leave extended beyond six weeks, the university reduced the remaining weeks of the semester by 50%. I knew that one of my male colleagues, in a similar situation, was fully compensated for the entire semester, and I was curious to find out what they would do in my case. I was happy when my new chairman, who showed me great respect, was able to secure the sick leave with full compensation. He argued correctly that it would not benefit the students to have a new instructor after six weeks. He also recognized that the funds were available to compensate both of us. It proved to me once more that I had been singled out by the Lemon for personal reasons. – At that time I was sick of fighting. I followed my doctor's orders and even agreed to seek some counseling, which turned out to have a positive effect, because the woman who counseled me understood well what was going on at the university. She had had her own experiences. It was just good to air my frustrations to a sympathetic professional.

In October, Miles informed Tonio that we should start preparing seriously for the move to Pittsburgh. The news was not unexpected, and I talked to my chairman about taking a leave of absence instead of quitting my job. It was important that I not lose the pension plan I had paid into for so many years. It was the one advantage of working for IU; they did have an excellent retirement plan. I knew of another male professor who had negotiated an early retirement without losing the plan, so I was optimistic.

We got the ball rolling with a letter to the university on October 22, 1992, and knowing that this might be our last autumn in the Michiana (Michigan–Indiana) region, we took advantage of what it had to offer. Tonio had received two complimentary tickets to a Notre Dame–Brigham Young football game on October 24. The last time I had been to a live game, also at Notre Dame, was with Doc in 1957. I had completely forgotten all the pomp that accompanies these games, and was fascinated by the tailgate parties, the acrobatics of the cheerleaders, and the colorful performances of the bands. – A ride through the wine country on the dinner train on October 31, which started in Paw Paw, Michigan, was special not only because we enjoyed Karl and Renate's company, but also because the food and wine were as palatable as the fall leaves in the countryside were radiant.

The fall leaves were still clinging to the trees when we went for a second house-hunting trip to Pittsburgh on November 14. After looking at numerous homes in preferred subdivisions, we found a brand-new gray-and-white beauty in Fox Chapel, which we were tempted to buy, though for a very high price. After lengthy deliberations, I began to fear that the location, far out on several acres of woods and down in a concave spot, could create problems in the winter, when it might be difficult to get up the driveway, which was covered with gravel, from the garage.

When our agent drove up another driveway and parked the car close to the entrance of a beautiful two-story yellow-brick colonial on half an acre of beautifully landscaped grounds with mature deciduous and evergreen trees, we fell in love with the twenty-year-old manor immediately. It was just perfect, with five bedrooms and three bathrooms, a two-car garage, a family room, a big kitchen, a formal dining room, elegant outdoor-lighting fixtures, and a state-of-the-art forty-foot swimming pool. Most importantly, because the owner, an artist, had a grand piano, there would be a spot for my Knabe. The windows were large and let in much sunshine. I could already envision a cozy fire in the fireplace in the family room with the snow falling outside on Cohasset Lane.

Tonio closed the deal soon after we returned home; and when the children arrived for their Thanksgiving-Christmas, after we had completed our ritual, feasted, and toasted with a glass of champagne, we looked at the pictures of what would be our new house. They seemed happy and sad at the same time, because we all had just gotten used to, and dearly loved, our house in Indiana. We emphasized the lovely neighborhood and the big swimming pool, which even had a waterslide. There was also a large fenced-in area for a dog that Tonio was looking forward to. The children did not complain that the flight from the West Coast would be a couple of hours longer. The Nemesis had once again sent the lawyers after us, because she suddenly wanted us to pass on to her the frequent-flyer rewards I had collected for the children's travel. We hoped she would stop creating these ridiculous legal hassles.

By November 29, I still had not heard anything from the university regarding my request for a leave of absence. I could not think of a single reason why they would want to deny the request, because it would, even at my low salary, be financially advantageous to them. I wrote another memo, and while I waited for the response, we readied ourselves to fly once more to Pittsburgh, to meet with the realtor and sign the contract on December 12, or thereabouts. It was the same day we had been invited by Dr. Schreiber, the head of the PR division, for a Christmas party.

Pittsburgh was covered in a thick blanket of snow and ice when the realtor chauffeured us to our future home to sign the contract. Loaded with the ice from a fierce storm the night before, the trees glistened like crystal. The house looked like a fairytale castle nestled amidst the snow-laden trees. When the Schreibers, who lived in a tastefully decorated English Tudor home in an exclusive neighborhood, greeted us at their door, we were eager to tell them about our find. I could not stop talking as they gave us a tour of their own stately house and as we stood near the fireplace and exchanged pleasantries with Tonio's future colleagues. We were excited to get acquainted and were confident about finding new friends, like the Cohens or the Wittkuhns and Wentzels from our drama-reading group, who had preceded us.

Tonio and I were flying high. He had received his second promotion in a year. His older brother, owner of the art-deco advertising agency, after having declared bankruptcy, had survived coronary bypass surgery and turned vegetarian, while the not-so-nice sister had gone into hiding with her shady husband. They inhabited a self-constructed fortress in the mountains of Mexico in order to raise fierce black dogs. I was about to be liberated from the stress and tension at the university, though I must say, I had learned to develop a new attitude of self-confidence. The minute I entered the university complex, I would take a deep breath, and I walked through the corridors with my head held high, always smiling and greeting colleagues, students, and janitors with a big smile – everyone except the Prima Donna. I have never forgotten the day I was alone with him in the elevator, going up. I could have stalled and let him go alone, but I walked right in, my snub nose in the air. He was about my size, and without either of us uttering a single word, I looked straight through him, as though he were not even standing there. It was so strange; I was amazed at my own detachment. I also promised myself that the next time the pesky English professor pushed his way into my office half-drunk, I would report him.

Tonio and I Cruise the Caribbean at Christmas: Antigua, Dominica, Saint Lucia, Saint Vincent, Bequia, Martinique, and Montserrat

While Tonio was taking care of his obligations at work, I started packing for our planned cruise in the Caribbean on the *Renaissance III*, which started from Antigua, in the Lesser Antilles, located in the Leeward Islands, about 250 miles southeast of Puerto Rico. It was our Christmas getaway without the children, who were not coming that year. Though Tonio had been in Barbados for a business conference earlier that year, neither of us had ever visited these islands in the Caribbean. Given my penchant for all things exotic and tropical, I was very much looking forward to our adventure. And we were not disappointed. Indeed, we really lucked out in finding the Yepton Beach Resort, where we had reservations for a pre- and postcruise stay.

The attractive native, who chauffeured us in her jeep from the Saint John Airport to the resort, impressed me with her perfect English. She explained that it was only in 1981 that the island gained its independence from the West Indies Associated States of Britain. She also claimed to know 25,000 people by name or sight. It was dark and warm, though not humid, when we arrived at the Last Resort, tucked away in the northwest corner of Antigua. The lights along the path to the rooms shone on huge masses of my favorite flowers: blazing bougainvillea, desert roses, and hibiscus. There were coconut palms, banana trees, oleander bushes, frangipani, lady of the night, and an array of the lushest tropical flowers throughout these gardens of almost forty acres. A paradise welcomed us once more.

We had a spacious room with a balcony looking down on a silvery white-sand beach, where we could stroll along the edge of the turquoise waters of Hog John Bay. We would even find a shady spot underneath one of the palm trees that lined the beach and reached up higher than our balcony. They must have had a storm not long before, because a couple of coconut palms had fallen. Their branches were being washed back and forth by the gentle waves, while some roots were still anchored in the sand. Tonio and I skipped the sightseeing in Saint John and instead spent the few days swimming, sunbathing, and sipping tropical drinks. We also went shopping for more clothes for the cruise. He bought several gorgeous bathing suits for me. One came with a matching pareo. It was a shiny ivory color with a pattern of silver and gold glittering seashells, aqua corals, and red starfish hanging in a fisherman's net. This outfit earned more compliments from the guests than any piece of clothing I had ever owned.

We loved eating our meals at the open-air Patio Caribe restaurant, with a view of the freshwater pool and a gentle breeze from the sea. It was so romantic to sit at tables close to bougainvillea vines, crotons, and lemon trees and to watch the colorful birds hop around and coo in the branches or pick up a couple of crumbs from the white linen tablecloths at breakfast. At night we fell asleep listening to the soothing singsong of tree frogs and crickets. The owner was a friendly Canadian who introduced us to his cook and general purchasing agent, Louie, who had a well-rounded shape and the nicest smile. Her background could not have been more exotic. The forty-five-year-old was part Dutch, part African-American, part Chinese (grandmother), part Creole, and part Indian (subcontinental). She was from Trinidad, and prepared meals so delicious we were tempted to come back sometime in the future.

On Saturday, December 19, we boarded the luxurious, Italian-built *Renaissance III*. With only 4,500 gross register tonnage and a guest capacity of one hundred, she was smaller than the *Renaissance I*, but was just as elegant as the French liner. The walls in our spacious deluxe suite and those in corridors and other public areas were paneled with highly polished hardwoods and trimmed with gleaming brass. Our suite had two large ocean-view windows, and the entire wall behind the king-size bed was covered by a mirror. The couch and chairs were upholstered in light-brown suede, and the bathroom was all marble and gold. On the glass cocktail table stood an ice bucket with a complimentary bottle of champagne, which we enjoyed after we returned from another short shopping spree in the port shops.

Tonio wanted to buy a couple of Christmas presents for me prior to sailing. We walked directly to the shops across the street from the ship and looked at the display windows of Little Switzerland, the well-known jewelry chain that you find in so many port towns. It did not take too long, and Tonio, who always enjoyed surprising me with special gifts of jewelry, agreed to purchase the items we picked out and that I had refrained from buying for myself: a heavy, chain-like necklace, a bracelet band, and a wristwatch, all in eighteen-karat gold. I bought an unpretentious emerald ring for Liesl for her next birthday. They gave us a big, bright-red umbrella with *Little Switzerland* printed on it in white, just like the one Gustl received on the *QE2*.

Back in our cabin, we freshened up, popped open the bottle of champagne, and watched the sun set in Antigua Bay. Another honeymoon started – this time without the kiddies.

Since it was a Christmas cruise with only fifty-eight passengers, it meant that with a crew of sixty-seven, we were treated like royalty. – The ambiance of the ship was tantamount to that of a private yacht. I personally preferred to converse with the European staff when possible. And by the time we left, we had gotten to know some of them almost as well as our fellow passengers. It goes without saying that the food was superb. The entertainment was as exciting as the itinerary: Antigua, Dominica, Saint Lucia, Saint Vincent, Bequia, Martinique, Montserrat, and back to Antigua.

Dominica, the British Windward Island also called "Sunday Island," had something mystical and intoxicating about it. We took off from Portsmouth on the jeep safari, which took us through the dense tropical rainforest that blankets the rugged mountain slopes. We passed rare and delicate orchids, liana, and rubber trees in which here and there a purple-winged sisserou or a red-necked or Jacquot parrot injected a splash of color. Tonio and I were struck by the harmony in which people lived with nature – even poisonous snakes, about which we were warned – and with one another. In Dominica, the least-developed place we saw, the people in the outlying regions own no property, use little tobacco or drugs, and live outdoors except when they sleep in tiny, shack-like houses. They buy few groceries, picking whatever fruit they want wherever they like. If the bananas on long stalks are too cumbersome to carry, the women will gracefully, like caryatids, balance them on their heads. I had not observed women wash their clothes in a river since my vacation with Doc in Yucatán. The inhabitants led a carefree life, working about as much as they liked and the way they liked. It was not uncommon for the fathers of babies born to unwed mothers to be held responsible. However, the villagers took care of and provided for one another.

We could hardly believe it when, on the way back to the port, when it was already getting dark, the jeep stopped to pick up a bunch of women and girls walking toward the next village to go dancing. There were maybe five empty seats in the jeep, but fifteen girls piled in and miraculously found seats on each other's laps or on the floor. One of them, an attractive blond, was the daughter of the coconut-plantation owner, who spent half the year in Toronto, but she fit right in with the natives.

Our next port was Castries, capital of the very picturesque and mountainous island Saint Lucia, in the British Windward Islands, which consists almost wholly of volcanic rock. It has a large, almost landlocked harbor, surrounded by hills. As the *R3* docked, the white, crescent-shaped beach at the edge of the emerald sea and at the foot of the rocky hills, with posh resorts built right into the tropical terrain, looked enticing enough for an extended vacation. But we had only a forenoon, and we opted to go snorkeling. It was an experience I had not yet had, and with Tonio, the expert swimmer from Florida, at my side, intermittently taking my hand to pull me to a special sight, I was not afraid, even though I was not exactly an Olympic swimmer. A new, wondrous world of marine life opened up in the crystal-clear waters not far from Castries. To observe the multicolored fish swimming in schools around, above, or between red, yellow, or gray coral reefs and brightly colored sponges, or to follow a lone beauty dashing through waving weeds, mingling with other brilliant sea life, and quickly passing a slowly moving sea turtle, was unforgettable.

Tonio spotted Bagshaws on the pier and could not leave the tempting store without buying a colorful array of souvenirs made of fabrics silk-screened by hand, pure Belgian linens, and fine Egyptian cottons. I had an opportunity to show off the beautiful linen skirt with a tropical flower design he bought for me while still on the ship. The conversation at lunch was full of snorkeling anecdotes, but the talk shifted at sunset, when we cruised Soufrière Bay, gasping at the spectacular view of the Soufrière volcano and the two cone-shaped Pitons, the Gros and Petit, each over two thousand feet high, while sipping tequila sunsets on deck.

We spent a full day and a night at Saint Vincent, another British Windward island and part of the Grenadines. It is a comparatively small island (eighteen miles long and twelve miles wide), and many call it "Breadfruit Island," because it was the first in the Caribbean to be planted with the bumpy-skinned vegetable, brought on the *Bounty* from Tahiti by the legendary Captain Bligh, which accounts for its being called "the Tahiti of the Caribbean." It all takes on a special meaning for me as I write about the Emerald Island, because only nine months ago, in December 2000, I took a cruise around Tahiti, tasted breadfruit on Bora Bora, and saw the suspenseful movie *Mutiny on the Bounty* right where it was shot.

We rode through the tropical countryside of this gem in the sea, in the center of which towers another semi-active volcano, which is responsible for the shimmering black-sand beaches of the Atlantic coast. As we passed the women's penitentiary, we asked the driver about crime. He reported that only three prisoners inhabit the prison in this rather picturesque setting. They were incarcerated because they killed their husbands. "But," he explained, "if a man commits murder, we just kill 'em."

All cruises have a theme night on which the guests dress accordingly. On the 22nd, the dress code was Caribbean casual, with shoes. Tonio and I pulled out our new white outfits. Tonio wore his white pants and a bright-colored shirt, and I debuted the long white skirt, over which I wore the new pareo, tied diagonally around the waist. We both had a dark tan, which contrasted nicely with the gold jewelry Tonio had given me. The fiesta started at poolside with Caribbean rum punch. A steel band with great rhythm came on board and entertained us well. They even let me try out their drums and other percussion instruments before they had to leave the ship again. The gala dinner that followed was first-rate, and by the time all the guests gathered and relaxed in the chairs and couches of the luxurious lounge for dancing and partying, everybody was in the best of moods. By then everybody knew everybody. Tonio went around with his camera taking pictures. They came in handy when he described several passengers in our customary Christmas newsletter, which I take the liberty of passing on to you. He had a real flair for it:

The first we met, champagne in hand upon boarding, were a New York travel agent and companion. One or the other had been married to several Italian noblemen (serially).

Then we met an ex-construction-company owner <u>olim</u> salmon-boat-operator <u>nunc</u> retired professor from Eugene, Oregon, 80 if a day, with his Parisian professor-wife, who assured us she had brought along her Molière, "not just for tax reasons." We did see her reading by the pool and making lots of notes. She told us she loved the students and could not stand her colleagues. C'est la vie.

Among the other passengers were a California cattle rancher and his wife, who works for Charles Schwab; a Dallas family, the man in the oil business, the woman a director of MBAs, with two children, a boy and a girl; two certified snobs from Cape Cod with a presidential name . . . and a whole raft of Pittsburgh folk – three cabins' worth, some apparently from the Alcoa or Westinghouse hive, now happy as June bugs in golf heaven in Myrtle Beach.

And there were the Canadian smoke-detector manufacturers, Texan surgeons for the massively obese (700-plus pounds) dipsomaniacs, rakish waiters, voluptuous stewardesses, lascivious officers, Russian émigré intellectuals and voluptuous Syrian Jewish widows dressed in black spandex and gold lamé by Henri Bendel and trying out rich new Mexican husbands. Oh, and I forgot, The Addams family was on board. Have you read Katherine Anne Porter's <u>Ship of Fools</u>?

The *R3* dropped anchor in Friendship Bay, Bequia, a mere seven square miles, in the morning. Bequia is a part of Saint Vincent's string of the Grenadine Islands, so called because these islands are strung like a necklace of precious stones and an abundance of wild passion-fruit flowers, known among the French as grenadine. As the tender took us to the white-sand beach not far from the Friendship Bay Hotel, I was reminded of the palm-tree beach at Vai, on Crete. I was glad to see the palms, because the prospect of roasting in the sun without shade for almost a day would have forced me to spend more time on the hotel grounds instead of close to the blue waters. Tonio soaked up more of the sun than I did. I went by myself on a snorkeling venture, because the water was so shallow I did not even need a vest. Tonio, who had received scuba-diving instructions on the boat, went off into deeper waters. We had lunch on the beach, where the crew had set up a tasty barbeque. We could easily have overeaten, since there is always an overabundance of mouthwatering cuisine on a cruise. It takes tremendous self-discipline to practice moderation. My motto: I eat to live; I do not live to eat!

We showed up again for breakfast on the morning of Christmas Eve. It was served when we anchored in the Fort-de-France on Martinique, the southernmost island of the French West Indies. It is easy to understand why the hilly and mountainous island is also called "the Island of Flowers," because there are blossoms everywhere on bushes and trees, and the poinsettias grew taller than I. We had only half a day, and as I was anxious to try out my French, Tonio and I just walked along the streets of the capital, where the palm trees are often taller than the buildings, taking in the French ambiance and buying a bottle of duty-free French perfume and an assortment of postcards of tropical plants and scenes by a local artist.

We dressed up for the big Christmas Eve buffet, prepared by the Austrian chef Karl-Heinz, and sat with the oil man, his very beautiful wife, who always wore the most striking jewelry, and their two children, about Gustl and Liesl's age. Their children's Christmas present was the cruise. And while they did not complain, I would bet a few other surprises were awaiting them the next morning. Tonio and I thought it was great that most everybody joined in when the trio played Christmas carols in the lounge. It was my first Christmas Eve on the open waters of the Caribbean.

The ship was sailing north to Montserrat, in the Leeward Islands, named after the famous mountain near Barcelona, which I had visited while studying in France in 1967. The pear-shaped volcanic island still shows traces of its colonization by Irish settlers. I found it curious that the surname of this place is "the *Other* Emerald Island." The ship anchored at Plymouth Harbor at noon on Christmas Day. – When we returned from breakfast to change for another excursion, a surprise awaited us in our cabin in the form of a handwritten invitation:

The Captain / Fabio Cella / cordially invites you / to join him at his table for / dinner this evening / December 25th in the / restaurant at / 8:00 p.m.

Never before had either of us been invited to a captain's dinner, and while we were about to set out on the rugged path of our excursion, we wondered why we had been singled out for such an honor. I soon forgot about the captain, however, because I had to be careful not to slip or fall as the path became increasingly steep and rugged. I was relieved when the slight pain I had noticed in my chest, but was careful not to advertise, was gone as soon as the path went through the more shady jungle and rubber-tree area. It was quite an adventure; we stopped to look into a simmering volcano, admired colored rocks and minerals, and crawled around the ruins of a plantation house. Tonio tried his best to catch my hat when it sailed down the mountain slopes. – Someone mentioned that among other celebrities, Paul McCartney, Elton John, and Stevie Wonder liked to vacation on the island, and I wondered if they ever ventured out this way.

Just when we thought it was smooth sailing for the rest of the hike, a rubber boat appeared and transported our rather small group of the physically fit across a bay to put us ashore at an even wilder, but very humid and moist, jungle path. Already, in the distance, we heard the roar of the horseshoe-shaped Great Alps waterfall, which cascades over rocky cliffs more than seventy feet high into a crystal-clear mountain pool. Tonio and I put on our bathing suits, slipped into the pond, and stood, arm in arm, underneath the frosty mists that showered over us. In this paradisiacal setting, they felt like manna from heaven.

The hike back to the ship went more quickly, and we had ample time to get dolled up for Captain Cella's dinner, which turned out to be memorable because it was not only Christmas Day, but also our last supper on the *R3*. The flowers in the dining room were mostly red and white poinsettias, and soft Christmas music filled the room. Everybody's eyes were shining, and "Merry Christmas" wishes abounded. The captain greeted us at his table. We were joined by the sophisticated but somewhat fragile-looking couple from New England with the presidential last name and by the tall, strong, blue-eyed, and very healthy-looking California rancher and his stunning broker wife, who could have passed as his sister. If the New Englanders were a bit quiet, it was perhaps because the rest of us made up for it. The captain found it "fantástico" that Tonio and I had gotten married in Venice, and as everybody at the round table had traveled worldwide, there was enough to talk about. I myself was in awe of the cattle rancher, who owned thousands of acres which he claimed it would take a man on a horse man a whole day to cross; without a horse, a human being needed a jeep to keep track of the herds. I was impressed that the wife was herself an achiever in high finance; she held a top position at one of the leading investment firms in the country.

The dinner ended with a choice of desserts, including Sachertorte, which resembled a piece of art, being surrounded by chocolate-cream outlines of butterfly wings. I watched Tonio try his luck for a short time in the casino. As neither of us believed in gambling away hard-earned dollars, we joined the guests in the lounge and, deciding to do something about all those calories, danced on the slick parquet on the now badly rocking ship. I slipped and Tonio caught me. I felt nauseated, and my concerned husband escorted me to the cabin just in time.

Our farewells in Antigua were enforced by an occasional "let's stay in touch." We knew we would see the New Englanders again at the Yepton Beach Resort, where we would spend a few extra days and which we had recommended to them as well. I could not help noticing the many pieces of luggage piled up next to Lolita, the Syrian from Mexico, and her (approximately) sixth husband while they awaited a cab on the pier. How could one forget this woman, who had had several face- and body lifts, wore a different set of ultrafashionable clothes and bathing suits each time she made an appearance, flashed her jewels during the day and more so at night, and made sure her companion replenished all the oil on her body as soon as the last application had soaked in? The poor guy was massaging and tending to her eternally, and toward the end of the journey, he looked so worn down that I suspected he was ready to discard the propped-up doll, if not right away, then certainly before she could talk him into another cruise. She, like most of us, was well-advised to lose a few pounds as soon as possible, which Tonio and I resolved to do right after New Year's Day.

Tonio banged out that year's belated Christmas newsletter on December 31, and his predictions for 1993 were as follows:

Before issuing the predictions for 1993, I would like to point out that eight of the 10 I promulgated last year came true, including the transformation of Washington, DC, into a theme park. I see the White House is scheduled to appear on "Lifestyles of the Rich and Famous."

1. Queen Elizabeth will be mugged on the streets of London by one of her own subjects, and it will be revealed that the royal purse contained Kleenex, and a tin of headache pills.

2. Clinton will get the economy going again by reorganizing the Bureau of Labor Statistics.

3. The State of Israel will officially change its name but no one will be allowed to say it.

4. Helmut Schmidt will burst.

5. A professor at Duke University will publish a book on the persecution of sexlessness in our society.

6. IBM will split into six autonomous companies so it can lay off more employees than it has and hire them back as consultants.

7. The sun will come up one day and no one will read anymore. (Predicted last year, admittedly.)

8. Twelve million Californians will experience what newspapers term a hysterical earthquake.

9. Television will sink to new depths of fatuity.

10. Lawyers will hire public relations professionals to address their negative image and the two parties will bill each other.

Tonio was commuting between Pittsburgh and South Bend weekly to manage obligations at his office in Elkhart and his office in Pittsburgh and to visit plants requiring his presence in connection with the writing of the annual report. There were many deadlines to meet, and he was under extreme stress. He had also been given responsibility for writing the speeches for the new CEO and at times went way beyond the call of duty, as when he translated into German a lengthy speech to be delivered in Germany. The CEO was mercilessly demanding, I thought. One Friday afternoon, when Tonio was ready to fly home for the weekend, the courier delivered a message to his hotel: the CEO wanted a speech. When Tonio inquired whether Monday morning would be OK, he was told the CEO wanted it on his desk by noon on Saturday. Under these circumstances, we were very much looking forward to moving to Pittsburgh by the end of the spring semester.

At the university, I continued with teaching and the Bayer Program preparations as usual, and it was an incredible relief to finally receive a highly complimentary evaluation, this one from my new chairman. For the first time since my French female colleague had been chairperson, I felt that someone – who came from the outside, no less – had treated me fairly. He termed my teaching "outstanding," my service "very good," and my scholarship during the one semester I was not on sick leave "weak," which was accurate. I had reworked several of my short stories, which would eventually become part of our novel. – Dr. Romero and his wife, as well as the new dean of Arts and Sciences, joined us for dinner on a few occasions. Tonio and my chairman got along very well, meeting occasionally for lunch. I had clued him in on the affirmative-action developments, with which he sympathized, and informed him that since I was at that point asking for a leave of absence, I had instructed my attorney not to go ahead with the lawsuit that he had suggested. The EEOC still had not made a decision. I was ready to sign the letter asking for my leave of absence, effective May 1993.

VI *1993–1995*

1993–1995

The Corporate Undertaker Buries Tonio Half-Alive – Tonio's Fascination with Native Americans Awakens – Our Lives Spiral Downwards – Mutti Dies

It was Wednesday, February 24, exactly nine years after I had met Tonio, one year after I had received the deathblow from the Lemon, and one week before we were scheduled to finalize the purchase of our dream house in Pittsburgh. It was snowing outside. I was working at Tonio's desk in the library upstairs in the middle of the day when the phone rang. It was Tonio. He asked me if I was sitting down, which I confirmed. He told me without much ado that he had just been told his position had been terminated, effective immediately. He then asked if I had already signed the letter asking for the leave. When I said "not yet," he seemed relieved. I pulled myself together quickly. In a flash, I remembered that according to Tonio, his former marriage had started to unravel when he lost his previous job at the university. I told him he should be glad the stress was over and that there was no need to worry. We certainly could make it on my salary and would have more time to finish our novel. I asked what would happen with the house, since we had made a down payment of earnest money, and he assured me it would not be a problem, since the company agreed to purchase the house and then resell it. They had also agreed to give him at least nine months of severance pay and provide outplacement services for him in Pittsburgh, which meant continued commuting, with associated benefits. –

I immediately called my chairman to inform him of the change in my plans and that I would stay on at the university after all. He foresaw no problems and was very sympathetic. – I was anxious for Tonio to come home. When I saw him, he was very downcast and bitter. He could not understand how, after two promotions in one year, after being wined, dined, and flown back and forth, and after having encouraged me to give up my tenured position, this could happen. They couldn't have cared less that he had a calendar filled two months in advance with travel, meetings, and speeches to write and was finalizing the annual report for printing.

Over a glass of wine, Tonio told me about a strange feeling he experienced when it happened. It took place in a room on the top floor of the Mellon Bank, in Pittsburgh, where he had been ordered by an official of the company to wait for someone. The visibility through a massive wall of windows was almost nil. A snowstorm was raging outside. When a man in a dark suit entered and told him, at great length, what to expect, Tonio was overcome by a feeling that this man was essentially a corporate undertaker.

Tonio tossed and turned during the night, complaining about nightmares, always linked to that fateful day. We talked and talked, went over and over what might have triggered the action, but in the end there was nothing anybody could do to change it. Every man, even when he has witnessed a deteriorating work atmosphere for months, believes it will never happen to him, that *he* is immune. Gradually, we realized he was not the only victim of downsizing. The outplacement offices were filled with managers, VPs, and others higher up. Several of our good friends in Germany and the States had had to retire early, and heads had rolled at Miles and all over the country for quite a while before Tonio was laid off.

Tonio took it personally, wondering whether it had something to do with his being "too professorial," as his boss sometimes called him, or with his having made an off-the-cuff remark to an interviewer from a business journal about the often "hectic" life of his CEO. If you are forty-two years old, intellectually brilliant, creative, and handsome, your ego gets bruised easily. It gets bruised even more if you have had a similar experience that led to a breakdown in your marriage only ten years before. I myself had never experienced losing a job and never had a problem finding one. I told Tonio that we could have a wonderful life, even if he decided to stay home and turn to writing. We often referred to our remodeled house as a "writer's cottage." I strove hard not to let him see how very sorry I felt for him and did my best not to let it get us down. But when I noticed he was in no mood to continue writing our novel, I felt it was good that he continued to commute to Pittsburgh once a week to talk to the consultant assigned to him for the outplacement process. Tonio and his consultant had something in common. Both had Native Americans among their ancestors.

When Tonio came home from his first outplacement meeting, he wore a new pair of black, thick-rimmed glasses for which he paid $400. He seemed to think it would be good to adopt a new image while looking for a new job. Considering our altered financial situation, I was a bit surprised by the expense, but did not make too much of it. – On February 24, Tonio was let go.

On the evening of March 5, while Tonio was in Pittsburgh, I received a phone call from my younger brother in Detroit, from whom I had not heard in years. He stated simply, "I just want you to know that your mother died yesterday." I was numb and asked him if he knew when the funeral would be; he believed it was in two days. When I asked if he would fly over for the funeral, he answered no – because she was already gone. I told him about Tonio's recent loss of his job, to which he responded very unsympathetically, saying something like "there are many like that walking the streets in Detroit." He told me how well he was doing, having bought a big house in Grosse Point with high taxes. But our conversation ended in the usual deadlock and the realization that nothing had changed and never would.

Tonio wanted me to go to the funeral, which was very complicated, both job- and timewise. I called the funeral home and the priest in charge of the patients at the home where Mutti had stayed. I asked for a two-day delay of the funeral. They assured me it would not be a problem. I asked Tonio to persuade my older brother in Germany to go along with the delay, but the answer was no. Father Tukay talked to me at length and suggested that since Mutti, who had died in her sleep, was gone, we should come in May, when we could stay at his house; he would hold a special service for her in his church. I felt better, thanked him, and called my cousin's daughter Simone, who was engaged in an internship at Volkswagen in Detroit. I informed her of Mutti's death, but told her it would be all right if she spent the weekend with us, as we had planned when she arrived in Detroit a few weeks earlier.

It was refreshing to see Simone again, young, beautiful, bright, ambitious, and eager to graduate from the University of Goettingen with a degree in economics. It was her first visit to our home, and to America, and the three of us spent a wonderful weekend in Chicago, where we introduced her to barbequed ribs. It was a refreshing change for both Tonio and me. We asked her to come back for Easter and bring a friend, which she promised to do.

While Tonio was occupied with finding a new job, I was busy with teaching and getting the information out to my new Bayer group, which the CDS, Tonio, and I had screened in Indianapolis. Tonio was still being treated by a dentist for a problem stemming from the accident in the spring of 1992. He had not yet received an insurance settlement from the driver who rear-ended his Mercedes, and he eventually had to turn the matter over to an attorney in Chicago.

A week after Simone visited, I was reading the Sunday edition of the *Chicago Tribune* and stumbled upon an article about Native American Educational Services (NAES) College in Chicago. I had never heard of the place, but thought the article might interest Tonio, since it was the only independent, Native-owned, and Native-controlled college in the country, focusing on tribal knowledge, community service, community development, and leadership. Tonio read it immediately with great interest. They were trying to strengthen the institution and attract more Native American students. I recall that he wrote a letter to the college soon after reading the article, but I did not pay much attention to it, as I had to get ready for the children's arrival for their spring break. The children, I am sure, enjoyed their stay, despite their father's loss of a job, and may even have been a bit happy that we were able to stay in our house. Unfortunately, I was teaching and Tonio had to take a trip to Pittsburgh while the children visited. Liesl made the big decision to have a major haircut at the age of twelve, which everybody liked, including her friends back home.

It seemed like the children had just left when Simone arrived from Detroit on the Saturday before Easter. When she noticed the huge bouquet of two dozen dark-red long-stemmed roses on the piano, Tonio could not resist telling her, despite my protestations, that it was my birthday. Tonio had made reservations at the lovely Checkerberry Inn, near Goshen, Indiana, on Easter Sunday. Simone and her German friend Christian, who joined us on Sunday morning, just loved the place, with its country-style decor, and the food was outstanding. It turned out to be a good Easter, and I was sorry to see them leave so soon.

On April 17, Tonio and I, together with the representative from the CDS in New York, held the annual orientation for the Bayer Program students at our house. We asked a former participant to attend, answer the many questions, and present a list of dos and don'ts, and we handed out relevant material and information. All the students were excited, and they got acquainted, picked a future roommate, and enjoyed the refreshments.

Tonio and I had decided to use the time off to take advantage of some of the many frequent-flyer miles we had accumulated. We booked a long-weekend flight to Charleston, South Carolina, on May 8 and a two-week flight for Germany and Ireland, which would leave on May 25. Tonio was eager to take a trip to Ireland in order to check out some of his European – that is, non–Native American – ancestors in connection with his new and surprisingly strong interest in family history. He had become rather eager to trace his roots, or so it appeared to me, since the day he established contact with NAES College.

Ireland was not exactly at the top of my list, but as these were not the happiest times, I thought it might be good for both of us to get away for a couple of weeks. Most of all, the good Father Tukay had arranged to hold a special service for Mutti in his parish church, Sankt Elisabeth, on Friday, May 28. – I also needed to look in at Bayer AG in Leverkusen to make sure the students were taken care of.

Gustl Runs Away from His Mother – The Charleston Dilemma

Just when I thought all the ducks were in a row, on the evening of April 18, a Monday, I called Gustl from my den simply to chat and see how he and Liesl were getting along, just as I had so many times before. Gustl announced in a rather excited tone of voice that he was going to run away from home. I was stunned, called Tonio to the phone, handed him the receiver, and sat down on the couch. Tonio asked his son where he was going to run to, and said that if he did not know, he had better run to him. The discussion that transpired over the next hour or so between Gustl, his mother, and Tonio resulted in Tonio's persuading the airlines to issue Gustl a one-way ticket for a red-eye flight for the same evening from the West Coast to South Bend, Indiana.

I hardly slept during the night. So many thoughts and fears were racing through my head. Why did Tonio fail to consult me on such a major decision? Granted, we had wanted both children to live with us for a long time, but had finally decided that it was too late for Gustl, who was almost fifteen years old. If I had been consulted, I most certainly would have tried my best to convince Gustl to stay with this mother at least until the end of the current school year. The children were scheduled to come for the summer on June 18 anyhow. I could not understand how the mother could just give in to her son's whims and put him on a plane to fly three thousand miles in the middle of the night. Tonio explained that Gustl's mother's refusal to purchase a BB gun, as well as another, bigger water gun, had triggered the crisis. Gustl said it was "the last straw." While I sympathized with her decision, Tonio felt that any boy Gustl's age should own a BB gun. I cried silently, but put a positive spin on the situation when discussing the move with Tonio.

As Gustl's grades had gotten worse, I pointed out to Tonio that since he was unemployed, he could devote a great deal of time to tutoring Gustl, supervising his homework, and enjoying his company. I took a deep breath and promised myself I would be a more caring mother to the poor boy than his biological mother had been. I would prepare his breakfast, pack his school lunch, send him off to school in the morning, and await him with a snack when he came home. Being busy with my own lectures and night classes, it would be difficult for me to assist with his homework, and I knew I would be unable to help him with math.

Tonio wanted to pick up Gustl at the airport without me. He arrived with his mother's big burgundy suitcase the next morning around 7:30. The suitcase was very heavy, because she had urged Gustl to pack as much as he could so he would not bother her with requests to mail his things. He carried the bright-red boom box we had once given him for Christmas.

Father and son had already had breakfast by the time they came home. It was obvious that Tonio was happy to finally have his son under his wing. They took the luggage up to Gustl's room, and before I had a chance to talk to Gustl, the two took off again. They returned a couple of hours later. Gustl was the proud owner of a BB gun that had to be tried out promptly in our backyard, as though it were the natural thing to do. I personally – ever since my childhood experience in V., when the German tried to shoot me because they thought I was a Pole – cringed at the sight of guns, let alone the sound of their shots. I knew it was fruitless for me to object in any way, and I learned to tolerate the loud, hour-long shooting sessions outside.

We enjoyed taking Gustl shopping for school clothes. Anything he wanted by way of clothing, he got. He had enough casual clothes to compete with any of his peers. Tall, dark, and handsome as he was, the girls would cluster around him like hens around their "cocky" rooster.

Tonio had thought it advisable to schedule a session for Gustl with a family counselor, who, according to Tonio, concluded that the situation was a typical case of a mother "dumping her son at the father's doorstep."

Judging by Gustl's oral reports, school was great, and when I asked Tonio to make sure he checked Gustl's homework, I observed him glancing at it and saying it was OK. Gustl, who seemed to know all the material and to understand it better than we did, did not ask for help. Being new at raising a teenager, and always being a bit reluctant to criticize a stepson, I too took him at his word, though I should have remembered that in the past he had not always been honest. In the art of persuasion and manipulation, he had become almost as masterful as his sister, who a few years later prided herself on being able to get people to do whatever she wanted them to.

Tonio and I were confronted with a major decision, that is, what to do with Gustl during our planned trip to Charleston, South Carolina, and Europe. We finally decided that while we could ask one of my seniors to stay with the boy during our weekend trip to Charleston, we really should take him with us on our trip abroad, even though it meant a sizeable increase in expenses and flying on different airlines. I suggested that, out of fairness, we take Liesl along as well. After we had easily gotten approval from her teachers for an early departure from school, the Nemesis, despite the fact that Liesl was an all-A student, refused to let her join in on what would certainly be an educational trip. –

Liesl was scheduled to play in a youth orchestra, in which she played second violin. Even when Liesl tried her best, and no matter how hard she tried, she rarely played an entire melody or sound in tune. It sounded scratchy. Sadly enough, I doubt she could tell the difference. She may have improved a bit later, when her mother finally broke down and engaged a teacher for her. It also helped a little when I sent her, at $25 for half an hour, to one of our better violin teachers at the university. But if practice is not kept up, teaching will not do much good.

I was disappointed that Liesl could not join us, because it would have been nice for her to meet my relatives, our friends at Bayer, and Father Tukay, all of whom had graciously assured us that it would be all right to bring Gustl along.

My student Heidi agreed readily to stay with Gustl while Tonio and I flew to Charleston. We had reservations at the Rutledge Victorian Guest House, a bed-and-breakfast in the historic district, right next to a beautiful park full of bright flowers.

The inn's promotional materials boasted that "time had stood still" there, and it must have, because both of us were somewhat disappointed. Our room was comparatively small, the wallpaper and curtains looked a bit tacky, and the furniture was neither antique nor valuable. The room was named "Abigale," after a girl, and breakfast was served on a small table at the foot of the steep stairs. It consisted of an assortment of muffins next to a coffeemaker and a pitcher of orange juice. Just help yourself. Well, you had the luxury of sitting on the wraparound porch in a weather-beaten rocking chair and enjoying your muffin with a cup of weak coffee while looking across the street at another house of Italianate architecture offset by white columns. We were tempted to change hotels, but stayed because it was good enough for a few nights.

Charleston is a picturesque city that reminded me of Mobile, Alabama. It is located on a peninsula between the estuaries of the Cooper and Ashley Rivers and a long bay that leads to the Atlantic Ocean. Tonio, the ideal tour guide, knew just which mansions to take me to; they were fine examples of such architectural styles as Georgian Colonial, late Victorian, Queen Anne, Spanish Colonial, and Renaissance. One simply cannot, nor does one want to, see each and every mansion in two days. I liked the Heyward-Washington House, with its formal garden from the late eighteenth century, where Thomas Heyward Jr., signatory of the Declaration of Independence, lived, and where George Washington once lodged for a week or so. It was a three-story brick mansion, decorated with elegant furniture from the same period. The Joseph Manigault House, an example of Robert Adam architecture from 1803, struck my fancy as well. I would have liked to be served at the dining-room table in the room that ends in a concave curve on one side. The Roper House, at 9 East Battery, with red-brick and white Doric columns, was so striking that I for one will never forget it.

It was scorching hot when Tonio and I went to Sunday Mass at St. Michael's Episcopal Church, which somewhat resembles London's St. Martin-in-the-Fields. It is the oldest church in Charleston, according to the parishioners with whom we mingled after the service. We sought out the shade to talk with the charming folks and were tempted to follow their advice. They strongly encouraged Tonio to apply for a position at the College of Charleston, where we witnessed a commencement service the same afternoon. The suggestion was not out of place, since Tonio was seriously considering positions at universities, national archives, and such, as they came to his attention.

Toward evening, we strolled over to Waterfront Park, walked along the water's edge on the promenade lined with royal palms, and sat down on a bench to watch the water splash in the fountain. It was a replica of a big pineapple, cut in half, and an ocean of raspberry-pink petunias surrounded it. It happened to be Mother's Day, and Tonio took me out to a nice restaurant and thanked me, as he had so many times, for being such a good mother to his children. He used to refer to me as their "real mom," which always touched me deeply. I will never forget when Gustl told me, "You are better than my mom."

The day before we returned home, I gave Tonio some time to check out a few places on his own. I had trouble enduring the blistering heat, in the 90s, and was relieved when we returned to a somewhat cooler climate in Northern Indiana. – I was not at all relieved when we saw Gustl's report card, which contrary to what he had led us to believe, was quite bad. Realizing that changing schools was probably partially to blame, Tonio talked to him briefly and contacted Father George, who had been the Episcopal chaplain at Howe Military Academy, about two hours from South Bend, to determine what would be involved in enrolling Gustl at Howe for the next school year.

Something had to be done, because we observed a change in Gustl's attitude the minute we questioned his performance at school. He was much taller and stronger than I, and he treated me disrespectfully. Once, I asked him to pick up from the floor in his closet a leather jacket my friend Renate had given him, and he quipped, "I like it there." When I looked at him angrily, he bent down, looked me in the face, and said, "Hit me, come on and hit me!" The image of my father hitting me with the carpet beater flashed through my mind. I was tempted for a second to comply, but braced myself, told his father about it in the next room, and was perplexed when he said I should have hit him.

Given that Tonio was looking for a job while I was teaching, it was difficult to raise an occasionally hostile stepson, and I realized it would become more difficult when Tonio was away from home. Unless I could quit my job, which under the circumstances was out of the question, I feared I would eventually fail. I did not dare to ask Gustl to stop the daily shooting binges in the backyard. It was so annoying. The minute he started, the neighbor's dog began barking and jumping up against the fence in concert with the shots, until his owner put up a double fence. Tonio, still elated that he had his son, refrained from criticism most of the time.

A few days before our departure to Germany, Tonio went to Chicago, where he had a meeting with the people at NAES College to discuss his designing a pamphlet promoting the institution. He was quite excited about it – and I observed that as the interest in his Native American background intensified, he was gradually drifting away from me. His reading interests shifted almost exclusively to Native American literature. I supported him, though cautiously, because I was afraid – I don't know exactly why – that he might get sidetracked from looking for a real job.

In view of the trip, Tonio had gotten permission from Gustl's teacher for him to leave school two weeks early. During the discussion, he discovered, much to his dismay, that his son had not turned out to be as "nice and perfect" as we had hoped. To put it bluntly, the teacher told him that Gustl had made her life "miserable, a living hell" and that he liked to be the center of attention, especially when it came to the girls. She confirmed my opinion that his handwriting was extremely poor, as was his spelling, and she highly recommended that we send him to Howe, because he needed discipline and direction in his life. She agreed to write a letter of recommendation, which would be ready for us to take to Howe upon our return from Europe. Gustl did not take kindly to the idea, despite the fact that one of the reasons he had given for running away was that he expected better schooling in Indiana.

The Three Donizettis in Germany and Ireland

Father Dr. Tukay had prepared a warm welcome for us in Hannover, and his housekeeper, Sister Hanna, served tasty German meals and delicious cakes. The High Mass service for Mutti was special. I was grateful our good friend Marianne had been able to join us. We all sang together, listened to Father Tukay's moving sermon, and took Communion side by side. Tonio and I invited everyone to a good dinner at a nearby restaurant, where we reminisced about Mutti and got better acquainted with the good Father, who had moved to Hannover from Poland after the fall of the Wall. Gustl had excused himself and gone with a young man from the parish to attend the commencement services at the high school. He gave an enthusiastic report about the party that followed the ceremonies. Everybody wanted to monopolize the handsome American, who looked much older than he was.

On Saturday morning, Father Tukay took me aside and suggested that I invite my brother and his wife over for coffee and cake in the afternoon. He felt it was a real shame that our relationship had fallen apart, and wanted to try to bring us back together now that Mutti was gone. My first instinct was to express my regrets and assure him that it would be fruitless and, as always when I had reached out, painful. I did not want to go through such a stressful ordeal ever again and felt it better to just let it rest. He persisted, and I finally agreed to let him call my brother, who lived twenty minutes away. My brother answered the phone. Father Tukay explained why he would like to invite him and his wife to his home. My brother cut off the conversation with an emphatic no. It was the last time I allowed others to attempt to reestablish on my behalf a relationship that was fundamentally unsatisfactory.

The same afternoon, Father Tukay took us to the cemetery to offer flowers and say a prayer at Mutti's and Papa's graves. Tonio removed the ribbon from the wilted wreath still at the gravesite, bidding farewell from the four of us. – Germans love to promenade and sit on benches in cemeteries when visiting gravesites, a custom I had intensely disliked ever since Doc passed away. As we walked back to the gate of the cemetery, I recalled the story Mutti, who frequently visited the cemetery, told me a few years before she passed away. I found it quite amusing. She had wanted to bring flowers to my father's grave in the big, park-like cemetery but was unable to find it. It was getting dark. She sat down on a bench to rest when a woman came along. Mutti told her she could not find her husband's grave, handed her the flowers, and asked the woman to put them there in her stead. She felt it really did not matter on whose grave they ended up.

Before leaving, I spoke with the gardener about maintenance for the grave. He informed me that my brother had taken care of it.

* * *

On Monday morning, before driving me to Giesen to visit my relatives, Father Tukay took me to the bank, where he had arranged through one of his parishioner friends to close out the savings account Mutti had set aside for me. I knew it would come in handy, especially if Tonio did not soon find a job. – Both Tonio and Gustl had come along. While Tonio waited in a chair in the lobby, Gustl stood close to me at the bank counter, scrutinizing, to my great annoyance, every transaction that took place. As so often, whether for the sake of keeping the peace or for fear of driving him away, I kept quiet.

When we stayed for a couple of days with my cousin in Giesen, young Frank took Gustl to another party, where once more he was the center of attention. As the Germans are not very strict about teenagers drinking beer, I am sure he did not abstain. – We were glad to see the two boys getting along, because Frank, about Gustl's age, was scheduled to visit us right after we got back. Tonio wanted to take the boys south for a major camping trip.

Like Frank's parents, my Euskirchener relatives outdid themselves in preparing a delicious supper for us. I was a bit surprised when they told us they had made reservations for us at a nearby hotel. Our hotel room was so tacky, with purple wall coverings and a mirrored ceiling and wall, that it could have been a brothel. Tonio was even more taken aback in the morning, when the man at the counter presented him with a large bill, which we had assumed our host would take care of. I was not surprised, since it was perfectly in line with the genes of her mother, Aunt Stingy. In all the excitement, Tonio left his camera behind at their place, but fortunately it caught up with us at Bayer AG, which was only twenty miles or so away.

Bayer AG and the Kasino impressed Gustl, just as it impressed us when we stayed there for the first time. He loved the German dinner at the wine cellar, where he became so overconfident that he gave our hosts a sampling of his attitude. I felt compelled to remind him of his table manners. The incident ended with him leaving the table, and Tonio was not very pleased with the way I had handled it. – Fortunately, Gustl was well-behaved when we took him along to Düsseldorf, where I had a meeting with the appropriate representative to discuss the possibility of additional summer jobs at Henkel AG. He and his wife had invited us to their lovely home, a remodeled half-timbered house that was several hundred years old. It was unique in that they had preserved the quaint charm inside and on the grounds but had combined it with modern architectural improvements and facilities. The very attractive hostess served coffee and cake in a grotto-like setting, and when we left, it seemed we had made new friends.

We took off the next day for London, and continued to Dublin, Ireland, on the same plane. Gustl had flown to Germany on another flight, because he did not have a frequent-flyer ticket. – Tonio, despite the afternoon traffic in Dublin, adjusted rather quickly to driving on the left side of the road. I would have been a nervous wreck, especially with Gustl's constant commentary. To keep our costs down, we decided to stay in bed-and-breakfast lodgings. The streets were virtually lined with vacancies, and we found a hospitable abode rather quickly. Gustl, without being asked by either his father or me, acted as though he were the person in charge when it came to choosing a room. I was careful not to put him in his place. In all fairness, he was always quick to assist with the luggage.

We took off on our seven-day whirlwind trip right after a typical Irish breakfast, which never failed to include some kind of salty fish. Tonio wanted to get away from the city and primarily explore the countryside of the Emerald Isle. Green it was, no doubt about it, and the rain fortunately stayed away until the latter part of the trip. We drove for miles on roads flanked by fieldstone fences overgrown with green vines. These hedgerows were too high for me to look over from the compact car. Only when there was a break in the rows or when we stopped the car to get out could I see the green-and-gold valleys on which sheep grazed peacefully. The small houses with flower boxes hanging in front of the windows seemed peaceful as well. The large hills were rounded and turfed and provided a soothing panorama. I loved riding through the occasional green tunnel formed by trees arching overhead, which was reminiscent of the forests back home.

We were lucky to find a small farmhouse early on. Its only vacancy was one large room with two beds and a cot. The room was not ideal, but the family was so kind that we felt immediately at home. The big attraction was a son Gustl's age. They hit it off instantly. We gave Gustl permission to go with his new Irish friend to the village and meet more friends. – We did not hear Gustl return, but I realized in the morning by his nasty disposition that they must have had too much Guinness, which Gustl drank in response to pressure from his somewhat older peers.

We all were cheerful when driving through the countryside of the remote Ring of Kerry, with its blue lakes and striking seascapes. I was elated when, in Killarney National Park, we encountered masses of deep-purple rhododendrons as tall as trees, clinging to the hilly terrain amidst lush mosses, ferns, and fields of tropical fuchsia. I found it hard to believe that these beautiful and ornate rhododendrons, so hard to grow in my own backyard, were here considered invasive, similar to kudzu in the Southern United States. We stopped the car to admire one of the gigantic pink bushes. Gustl ran down the embankment to get close, only to get stuck in a swamp and soak his sneakers.

Gustl was bitten by the castle bug as soon as he encountered his first, a ruin he explored immediately by first descending into a deep, dark space and then climbing as high as he could. After that, he was constantly on the lookout for more castles, and Tonio was more prone to humor his whims than I, who had seen many castles, often more elaborate than the ones here, during my travels in Europe. Actually, by this point, the trip had turned into one tailored to Gustl's desires. – Yes, we did end up at the famous and very touristy Blarney Castle, built out of solid limestone and dating back to 1446. It is situated not far from Cork, the town from whose harbor ships departed full of famine immigrants to Ellis Island in the middle of the nineteenth century. – We waited in a long line to lie on our backs, lean our heads backwards, and kiss the underside of the Blarney Stone. All three of us gained the privilege of telling lies, or the "gift of the gab," for seven years. I do not lie when I tell you now, after my seven years have long since expired, that the castle walls are in places eighteen feet thick.

I personally found more charming the Norman tower Thoor Ballylee, part of a ruined castle that William Butler Yeats bought from his friend, the dramatist Lady

Gregory, and converted into his summer house, near Coole, Galway. We climbed the tower, which became the central symbol of his late work, looked out the window behind the desk where Yeats wrote, and understood why the idyllic spot in this serene countryside inspired him to create what is considered his best work. I remarked on the distinct physical resemblance between the modernist poet and Tonio, at which my husband, also a writer of poetry, smiled. I had dreamed of a writer's cottage such as the one we found at the nearby lake, but knew it would always be a dream.

Dreamlike, out of a shroud of mist and rain, the black Cliffs of Moher emerged in the distance. For a length of about six miles, the black sheets of rock rose seven hundred feet out of the Atlantic. It was an eerie sight, and if ghosts had appeared somewhere out of the cliffs, it would have seemed perfectly natural. The cliffs were named after Mothar, a ruined promontory fort, which was demolished during the Napoleonic Wars. Gustl did climb the signal tower after crawling around on the slippery cliffs, where Tonio had taken a risky picture of him.

By then, it was raining cats and dogs. I sought shelter in the car, partially to avoid the rain, partially to hide my tears. I felt emotionally worn out by "Earl Know-It-All" and sighed with relief when Tonio suggested we go out to dinner without him. I needed the break more than I had realized. I thought how much more enjoyable the trip would have been had we – as originally planned – traveled through Ireland alone.

Tonio drove across extremely treacherous mountain roads before heading back to Dublin, via Belfast. The roads went along rugged cliffs and were so narrow and steep at times that one could not see approaching cars. We prayed that in that deserted countryside, where here and there a black or white mountain sheep chewed on a sparse cluster of grass, no vehicle would attempt to pass. Gustl asked us to stop so he could fetch a piece of wool hanging on a scrawny shrub along the road. On the way down, in this rather stony region, there were no hedgerows, and the houses in the villages that we passed were rather small and simple by comparison to houses in German villages. – We did not pause in Belfast, especially since we had to pass through a thorough security checkpoint at the city's outskirts, but we stopped in a couple of towns on the way so Tonio could get information from town officials about the records of his Irish ancestors, who he knew had immigrated to the States long ago.

About forty miles northwest of Dublin, we paused to see what was left of the ancient Kells High Crosses, decorated with biblical scenes and dating back to the ninth century. Of the same age is the round, ninety-foot-high stone tower and the House of Kells, a hilltop monastery where brethren sought refuge from the hit-and-run attacks of the Vikings.

1993–1995

On the way to the airport, Tonio drove through the streets of Dublin just long enough to give us an overview, because we had to return the car and catch our flight to London. Our suitcases had gotten heavier, because we had been just as tempted as thousands of tourists before us and stopped at one of the big Blarney Woollen Mills that dominate many Irish towns. We too stocked up on Irish linen and woolen sweaters, and we purchased a beautiful Royal Tara bone-china vase, hand-painted in light Irish green, of course.

We spent two nights in a luxurious suite at one of the Marriott hotels in London, which, thanks to frequent-flyer rewards, did not cost us a dime. Gustl got at least a taste of London. I believe nobody was more anxious to return to our own home and beds than I. I freely admit that of the many trips I have taken to exciting places around the world, Ireland remains at the bottom of my list. But this can most likely be attributed to the stressful nature of the journey, due largely to Gustl's argumentative attitude about where to stay, what to eat, what to see, and whether he could sit in the front of the car (which meant I saw little), etc. Those of you with opinionated teenage sons or stepsons understand what I mean. If I had to do it again, I would stay home, even if it meant missing out on going to the moon.

There was little time to rest when we returned home late on June 13. Our calendar was full. Frank would arrive from Germany on June 15. The next day, we had an appointment for Gustl at Culver Military Academy at 1:00 p.m. On June 17, we were scheduled for an interview at Howe at 9:00 a.m. Liesl would arrive for the summer on June 19, and on June 21 the "guys" wanted to leave for their camping trip.

Frank stayed home to sleep while Tonio and I went to Culver Military Academy, which seemed like a dream school for any youngster. The recently completed, state-of-the-art library, not to mention the grounds on a lake, where one could take riding lessons or go sailing, were especially impressive. The school was for the very affluent, to which the tuition, rivaling the cost of a reputable private college on the East Coast, attested. The admissions director tried her best to lure Gustl to the school, where the military component was said to be less rigorous than at Howe. – Howe was smaller, very nice, and well maintained, and the social environment was more military and presumably more strongly oriented toward discipline. The headmaster, a history instructor, was serious, not at all persuasive, and very matter-of-fact. Frank had come along, and as we were given the tour of the campus – including the soccer field, tennis courts, gym (which had a pool and a basketball court), theater, library, chapel, and barracks where the cadets were quartered – he looked a bit pale and shook his head in disbelief that anybody would be sent to such a place. I was surprised. From what he had told me about his father and what I had observed, he was as strict and at times as angry as they come. He was Aunt Stingy and Uncle Hanne's son, after all. At Howe, we spoke to a few cadets who were happy, but judging by the absence of Gustl's usual exuberance, I gathered that he was not exactly crazy about the prospect of becoming a cadet. Tonio and I agreed that although it would be just what the boy needed, we would not force him to go. We postponed our decision until after the camping trip.

Tonio, Frank, and Gustl Go Camping, Tracking American Indian Ancestors Down South to Key West – Tonio's Temper Escalates

Liesl was happy to see her brother again and told me she would never run away from home, which I understood full well. We both worked hard to help the boys get ready for their trip and took care of last-minute shopping at Sam's. Frank was amazed at my willingness to put so much time and effort into helping them. On Monday morning, the Mercedes was loaded to the hilt, with the newly acquired camping gear on the roof, and we took a quick snapshot in the driveway. Tonio and the boys then rolled down the hill on the way to Dillon State Park, near Zanesville, Ohio, where they wanted to pitch their tent in time for an ongoing festival. The next morning, they were scheduled to drive to Washington, D.C.; from there, they would head south to follow the Indian trails and visit places connected to Tonio's ancestors.

Liesl had missed out on our trip to Ireland and could not join the campers, but Tonio had made reservations for us at the charming Marquesa Hotel, in the southernmost city of the United States, Key West, Florida. We flew down on the 26th and were very happy with our newly decorated hotel, right in the historic district of the city. Our room was furnished impeccably in early American antiques. From the gallery outside our room, we looked down on a beautiful patio with a swimming pool. Surrounding the pool were high, white stucco walls, to which masses of bougainvillea vines, hibiscus, and other tropical plants were clinging.

Liesl and I explored the town, with its thousands of T-shirt and souvenir shops, dined leisurely, and ate more shrimp dishes than we ever had before. Because it was too hot to sunbathe on the beach, we preferred to cool off in the pool, which Liesl virtually monopolized. A guest named it after her. – At sunset, we strolled over to the pier, where a variety of performers entertained us, such as clowns, musicians, and a man freeing himself from heavy chains wound around his body from head to toe. We were thrilled to spot a big school of the most colorful tropical fish – just by looking into the water from the pier's edge.

When the boys arrived on schedule three days later, we thanked them many times for the beautifully handcrafted gifts of Indian jewelry and a handwoven blanket they had bought for us when they visited the council house of the Cherokee tribe. They raved about the show *Unto These Hills*, which they saw while camping on the riverside at Camp Cherokee.

We ordered the best pizza ever, or so the boys claimed – it was topped with pieces of barbequed chicken. We visited the Spanish Colonial mansion in which, between

1931 and 1961, the Nobel Prize winner Ernest Hemingway wrote his best works, including my favorite, *For Whom the Bell Tolls*. It sits in a tranquil spot, surrounded by big trees and a large, fenced-in garden. We did not go inside. I was not too keen on the idea, because I preferred to avoid the more than fifty descendants of Hemingway's cats, six-toed ones among them, that roamed the place. Being allergic to cats, I admired the mansion from the outside.

The children could hardly wait to arrive in Orlando, where we had reservations at Disney's Fantasy World Club Villas. But we had one more stop on the way. Because Frank had never been snorkeling, Tonio had made reservations at the Hop-Inn Guest House, in Marathon. He took the boys on a boating and snorkeling trip, while Liesl and I relaxed on the beach outside our cabin. – The seating in Tonio's baby Mercedes would have been even tighter had Liesl and I been as big and tall as the guys. We were lucky the air conditioning did not break down as we cruised along on the highway that connects the Keys with long bridges over vast expanses of water. We were about 150 miles from Miami, but only about ninety miles from Cuba.

We all liked the Fantasy World Club Villas, close to the Epcot Center and Walt Disney World, where Tonio had made reservations for three nights. In no time at all, we settled in and felt satisfied with our rooms, and our three musketeers tested the three large pools on the grounds, one right across from the villa. Tonio and I sipped a glass of wine, well deserved after the long trip, before starting with supper. – Following the advice of many, we stood at the impressive entrance to the Epcot Center before the gate opened the next morning. With Gustl's help, we combed the center thoroughly, soaking up all of the excitement that this fabulous and wondrous center has to offer. We returned to the hotel exhausted from our journey into this paradise for young and old, and Tonio and I decided to allow the children to explore Walt Disney World's Magic Kingdom the next day on their own. While they were in fairy-tale country, we created our own, starting with a bottle of champagne . . .

Tonio went all out preparing a dinner of Southern fried chicken, mashed potatoes, corn, biscuits, and salad, followed by ice cream. It was as good as or better than his spaghetti with meatballs the night before. He opened a bottle of red wine for us. The children drank Coke. – While we were washing the dishes, Tonio complained about the poor service. They had neither emptied the trash cans outside nor replenished the towels. We called the front desk; they promised to see to it at once, and I forgot about it. –

It was late in the evening. Gustl, Liesl, Frank, and I were watching TV in our pajamas when Tonio stormed through the entrance door, went straight to the kitchen of our resort suite, and grabbed the forty-gallon trash can, filled to the brim with corn husks, chicken bones, lettuce leaves, spaghetti, pop cans, paper napkins, etc. A half-emptied glass of red wine fell to the floor and broke, and the wine spilled like blood on the white tile surface. Tonio ignored it and ran out the door, clutching the trash can. When he returned, he said he had dumped all the trash into the swimming pool. It was July 3, and the resort was booked full for the holiday weekend.

I saw the spaghetti, corn husks, chicken bones, flakes of mashed potato, limp napkins, and empty pop cans floating in and settling at the bottom of the light-blue pool – never before had I been so horrified. My stomach was cramping; I felt sick and hot. It took every ounce of willpower not to cry or get angry. I was so embarrassed. What would the children and my cousin think, and what would happen, if the hotel management connected this irresponsible act to us? They could sue us for the damages, an expense that would have been a great burden, because Tonio had been without a job since the termination of his position in February. Tonio would have been the logical suspect. According to Frank, who had been present, Tonio "flipped out" when confronting the management at the front desk about the poor service. He was so enraged they called the police.

I was not a good swimmer and did not know how to dive, so I was unable to clean the pool. I tried to put a humorous spin on it and pleaded with Gustl and Frank to put on their bathing trunks and fish out the garbage from the pool before it was noticed. Fortunately, after an hour or so, they had cleaned the pool quite well, without being seen. Tonio was in bed, furious, accusing me of being a "traitor" because I asked the boys to clean up the mess and threatening to do it all over again. Fortunately, he fell asleep. – Neither Tonio, nor I, nor the children spoke of the incident for a long time. When we arrived at Tonio's mother's place toward evening on July 4, our fourth wedding anniversary, everything seemed completely forgotten. When I asked Frank about it years later, he did not even remember it.

Meeting Tonio's family again was nice, especially for the children, who got to play and talk to their cousins. We spent a day at the beach and got to know Tonio's niece better, who was quite pretty and very talkative. The boys liked her, but Liesl and I kept looking at each other, wondering how this nineteen- or twenty-year-old girl in her last month of pregnancy could have chosen to wear such a tight and short bathing suit. We thought she looked obscene or grotesque, or both. I knew what my father would have done to me if he had seen me dressed in such a way. She was proud of her clientele, being a manicurist, and was looking forward to being a mother. – After her grandmother expressed her concern that it was uncertain whether the biological father of the child was the last boyfriend, who was the love of her life, or the man who had just married her, I felt a bit dizzy and was glad once more that we lived far away from Florida. –

The boys were excited to discover an unloaded rifle under their grandmother's hideaway couch with which to tease her. They also giggled behind her back when they observed her religious fanaticism and her obsession with TV preachers. Though she was very hospitable, it was difficult to elicit any kind of practical advice from her. The answer was always "pray and take the Lord into your heart." When I told her about Tonio's recent fascination with his Native American background, the recommendation she advanced was "pray and help Tonio get back to the Lord; Tonio is no Indian."

I could have prayed day and night, but Tonio was not inclined to abandon his fixation. He was elated when Frank presented him with a book on Indians on his birthday. It was the day on which the boys returned from their camping trip – the day after they had explored Mammoth Cave National Park, in Kentucky. The three had gone on the potentially awesome Discovery Tour, which, however, turned into a big disappointment for Tonio. Instead of staying close to his father in the cave to bond with him, as Tonio had hoped, Gustl remained far ahead and at the side of the guide throughout the tour. To top it off, not only had he forgotten his father's birthday until we reminded him when he got home, but the card he gave Tonio was addressed to "Tonio" instead of "Papa." I lent him money to go downtown and buy his father a birthday gift. It took the totally crushed father quite a while to make up with his son, Earl Know-It-All.

I was back to teaching a summer course two nights each week, and Frank had eight more days until he took off for Germany. We were all glad to return to our routines, because Frank and Gustl were no longer the best of friends. Gustl called Frank a "sissy," claiming that on the trip he had behaved rather "girlishly." One morning, when the boys were eating breakfast at a table near their big tent, a raccoon surprised them. Frank screamed, jumped up on the table, and looked on aghast as the raccoon devoured the entire loaf of bread within a minute. Frank was doubly disappointed because he just "loved" the soft white bread, so different from the gray pumpernickel in Germany. Indeed, during his last week with us, he munched on the bread incessantly. Gustl had some basis for comparing him to a girl, because he preferred to cling to me, and he even cleaned the entire kitchen one day instead of joining the boys and girls at the pool. He did like the beach and the towering dunes on Lake Michigan and would have preferred to spend more time at the lake, even though his skin was so fair he turned red as a lobster in no time at all. –

Frank had filled two suitcases with jeans, denim jackets, sneakers, T-shirts, and bottles of sweet-smelling eau de cologne for himself and his friends. Liesl had frequently noted how rich he was, having enough money to buy so many things – but nobody cried when he boarded the plane on the 18th. He faxed a nice thank-you letter after he had returned home, but his parents never uttered a word of appreciation to us for having taken their son on a trip to see America.

Tonio flew to Pittsburgh to meet with his outplacement counselor to discuss the possibility of working for NAES College, should they – as it seemed they might – offer him a position. Gustl had landed a little job helping out at the community pool, where he was still on the swim team. When his father returned from Pittsburgh, he told him about his plan to spend a few weeks with his mother on the West Coast before school started. He was not at all willing to go to Howe but very much in favor of going to our public high school, with all his buddies from the pool. He hoped to play his trombone in the school's band.

When he had suggested visiting his mother not long after he had run away, we did not discourage him. But when he brought it up again, and after we had observed the boy over the summer, it seemed incomprehensible to both of us that he wanted to return to his mother so soon after he had run away. After all, he had insisted that he had had it with her. It was obvious that Tonio was not happy about his son's wish.

Something in Tonio was brewing. On Sunday evening after dinner, he usually had a bottle of wine. Gradually Tonio replaced the liter bottle with a double bottle, which on weekends he started drinking in the early afternoon. On one occasion, like a flash of lightning, Antonio's destructive temper kicked in even more furiously than it had in Orlando. It was late and dark outside. He screamed at Gustl, telling him that if he went back to his mother, he did not ever want to see him again. He stormed into Gustl's room, which we had decorated with so much love, emptied the glass shelves of all of Gustl's childhood treasures, and threw them on the floor. He hurled a photo in a glass frame against the bedpost. Broken glass lay scattered on the red carpet. He ripped the pages off Gustl's *The Far Side* calendar, which he cherished so much, tore the bedding off his bed, and to top it off, grabbed Gustl's precious bright-red radio and flung it with great force onto the hardwood floor in the corridor, where it broke into many pieces. Still raging, he picked up the big canvas suitcase, which Gustl's mother had loaned him, and defaced it with a black marker by putting several Jewish stars on it, presumably because she was Jewish. It was useless to try to stop him. He went downstairs to look for Gustl, who was hiding in my den. Antonio grabbed him, pulled him to the back entrance, told him to get out, and locked the doors behind him.

Liesl and I were in a state of shock. She kept asking, "Why is Papa so mean? Why is Papa doing this?" Tonio sat on the couch in the living room silently, sipping a glass of brandy. After a while, Liesl and I began to look for Gustl outside. Every time we unlocked the doors, Tonio rushed up and locked them again. We finally found Gustl on the side deck, cowering in a corner next to a big flower box. He had covered himself with a blanket. Liesl and I told him to come inside and go to bed. We tried for a long time to erase the marks on the suitcase. No use! When Tonio came to bed, I pretended to be asleep.

All night long, thoughts raced through my head in search of a solution to this seemingly insurmountable problem. I had gradually become aware that I was in many ways psychologically stronger than Tonio, just as Mutti was vis-à-vis my father. I did not want to be the stronger one, because I had hoped Tonio would be a rock in my life, like Doc. I was tired of being strong again and again, but I had no choice and arrived at a decision.

Gustl was already at the pool when Tonio sat down at the breakfast table. Whenever possible, he slept in, asking me to take messages for him, which I did reluctantly, especially when it sounded as though someone wanted to talk to him about a possible job or when his mother called before 7:00 a.m. because of the lower rates. – I told Tonio that he would never forgive himself if he sent his son home under the threat of never wanting to see him again. I suggested that I call the headmaster at Howe once more and ask if we could come again and allow Gustl to spend more time alone on the campus, which would give him a better opportunity to talk to cadets. I also assured Tonio that I would be willing to use the small inheritance from Mutti to pay for tuition and fees. It would have been just enough to cover all costs for the first year. Tonio thanked me for being so generous, but I knew that if Gustl stayed with us during the school year, I might not survive it. The headmaster looked forward to seeing us at 2:00 p.m. that afternoon.

When Gustl returned from the pool, I asked him to come into the living room, where I, without Tonio, informed him of our decision. I also told him I would be unable to assist him with certain homework and that, with Tonio being gone quite a bit, he would be much better off at a school where his life would be more strongly regimented and where he would enjoy being among peers. I reminded him that a major reason for his coming to Indiana had been to go to a better school and that the headmaster had told him the tests he had taken indicated clearly that he could excel academically. I told him about my own boarding-school experiences, and Gustl readily agreed to give it another try. All of us, including Liesl, dressed as though we were going to Sunday Mass and appeared punctually at Howe to drop off Gustl. As Tonio, Liesl, and I drove off, we watched Gustl walk away with two or three cadets. When we returned, Gustl greeted us enthusiastically and informed us he would really like to go to Howe after all.

Gustl Enrolls at Howe Military Academy – Tonio Works at NAES College and Moves to Chicago

Tonio and I were relieved, and we went out to a nice dinner in Sturgis, Michigan. Gustl talked about the cadets, who must have convinced him that life at Howe was not as bad as it sounded and that it was actually a lot of fun. Liesl was content to stay in her school at home, even though it meant being separated from her big brother. –

Gustl's mother was not at all pleased at the prospect of her son's enrollment at a military school, and she made clear at the outset that she would not contribute a penny. – I took care of all the paperwork, and joined Antonio in signing a contract as cosponsor of the finances, as though I were Gustl's biological mother. – Gustl, who was anxious to make some money, applied for and was successful in getting a job husking corn in the fields. It was a physically demanding job, and we were glad he stuck it out, because several of the boys did not last very long.

Tonio took every free minute he had, night and day, to work on his genealogy, to the point that our evenings together were rare. The pamphlet he had designed for the college had turned out well, and the president of the college, a woman, had scheduled a meeting with him on a Wednesday afternoon in the last week of July to discuss a position as dean or assistant dean, if I recall correctly. – He returned that evening after having spent almost five hours on the road, only to be stood up by her. I was quite upset and reiterated what I had told him ever since he expressed an interest in the place, that is, to help the college on a voluntary basis but keep his eye out for a position either at a bigger university or one that corresponded better to his education and experience.

He drove back to Chicago and met with the president two days later, but spent a few hours doing genealogy research at the National Archives before the meeting. It was essential that he substantiate his Native American ancestry if he was to be gainfully employed by the college, which I understood to be funded entirely by the US government.

At this point, Tonio spent one or two days every week at the National Archives in Chicago, often leaving very early in the morning and assuming I would take care of the children. At the end of August, he decided to take the college up on their offer of a position, though it meant taking a salary cut of about 50%. We had just enrolled Gustl in boarding school, and since I was responsible for paying all the bills, I feared we would have to eliminate certain extravagances, especially liquor. I was also suspicious of the college's offer, which was not exactly forthright, and sensed that Tonio too had his doubts, even though he vowed repeatedly that they were as good as their word. Why then did they repeatedly put him off when he reminded them that they still owed him the money for the pamphlet he had designed? –

One evening, when he went to the bedroom to change after returning from Chicago, I followed him and asked, as I had before, if the college had paid him. Tonio turned red in the face and glared at me wildly – soon, my face was burning and my head spinning, and my body sank down on the carpet. Little by little, I digested what had happened. I had experienced a flashback from my childhood, when I wept as I saw my angry father treat Mutti the same way. – I began to cry when Tonio had gone upstairs to his computer. After a while, I followed him. The children came from their rooms when I stood across from him at his desk – still weeping, questioning him – "Why?" When the children realized what had happened, they looked at me in disbelief. Tonio took hold of my left hand and twisted my left ring finger so hard I cried out in pain, begging him to stop. He would not stop; I feared my finger would be totally crushed. When the children did not try to stop him, out of desperation, I grasped the address book on his desk and hit him over the head with it until he stopped. – Strangely enough, at just that moment, the phone rang. I answered, and Tonio's older brother was on the line. When I told him what had just happened, all he said was that we should see a counselor. Not a word to console me or calm me down. My finger hurt and was blue and purple for almost two weeks, and a tingling sensation remains today. I have not played my violin since.

Tonio did not apologize, because he probably felt I had deserved to be punished. You want to forget what took place, but once it has happened, you never can – never. I did not tell my best friend or Tonio's mother, who would have advised me to "pray to the Lord." We did not go to a counselor.

And life went on . . .

I forgave Tonio just as Mutti had forgiven my father, attributing his erratic behavior to stress, confusion, and insecurity and perhaps to some sort of despair. I knew the man I married would have been incapable of this kind of domestic abuse. This was not the gentleman Tonio considered himself to be. However, I convinced myself that once he found a good job, everything would be fine.

All the errands and tasks related to getting Gustl ready for boarding school kept me busy, as did dinner invitations from friends and my new chairman and his wife. Tonio was virtually buried behind his computer. He spent hours on the phone tracking down distant relatives and other sources in an effort to further his genealogy, to the point that I both began to resent his obsession and tried to take an interest in it. I gave him my library card. He checked out mountains of books relating to Native American culture and history, which he read until late at night. He would not be disturbed, and I stayed downstairs in my den when I was not with the children. They were not in favor of their father's penchant for the Indians but, understandably, did not interfere.

Tonio did take Gustl on a three-day camping trip on the dunes of Lake Michigan. Shortly thereafter, we dropped him off at Howe, where he moved in right away. When we gave him a big good-bye hug in front of his building, we were confident that he was in good hands. – Tonio and I sat down on a bench on the grounds near the church, where he put his arm around me and said it was the happiest day of his life. – We obtained special permission from the school to surprise Gustl on his birthday a couple of weeks later, when we spent two hours with him in the evening. He thanked me for the birthday cake I had ordered for his barracks and assured us he liked the place a lot.

At the university, I was busy with the beginning of the semester, teaching a full load as well as taking on two students on an individual basis and taking care of matters relating to the Bayer Program. I also decided to neither sue nor start a class-action procedure against the university, which I had been considering for two years. Those were the options the EEOC had spelled out in their letter of August 25. I was pleased with the new chairman, and I engaged in a rigorous recruiting effort, something which, deep down, I resented doing; but I knew it could result in boosting enrollment for the German major. I met with twenty-two promising candidates personally in my office, and to appease my institution, I attached a detailed report on each and every one of them to my annual report.

Tonio got involved with his Native American students, who were mostly older and required much individual attention. If I recall correctly, there were fewer than twenty enrolled in the entire college, which resembled more a big barracks than a university. Tonio's biggest complaint pertained to constantly having to call students at home to make sure they would show up for classes. Deep down, I felt sorry for him, but was careful not to share my feelings. Yet I could not help making a catty remark on occasion, as I did once or twice when referring to his colleague as "the Squaw." After he told me in a rather angry tone that it was a derogatory term, I stopped using it. I sensed the job did not meet Tonio's expectations, but he put in a great deal of time and effort and was determined to make it a success. He was commuting to Chicago by car or train on a daily basis, as were hundreds of other people who worked in Chicago. On the side, he continued to network in search of another job.

Two weeks into the semester, Tonio broached the subject of a small apartment in Chicago. Commuting would be difficult in the winter and on days when he had night classes. I was not thrilled about the idea, thinking immediately about the added expense and greater separation, but realized it was probably the sensible approach. I even suggested it might be convenient to have a flat in the Windy City, where we could spend weekends and take advantage of cultural events. I sized up the contents of our house and was sure we could find plenty of household items and furnish a small apartment without spending too much money. We searched the *Chicago Tribune* for ads, and before I knew it, Tonio informed me he had made a deposit for a place into which he would move the following Monday. I was very disappointed that he had again ignored my input. It was too late. I went about gathering pots, pans, dishes, blankets, etc. with which to furnish his new apartment.

He stayed in Chicago during the week and came home on weekends. I was happy we had planned the annual Oktoberfest for October 9 and that Father Tukay, from Hannover, was coming to visit with his friend Father Willibald. Gustl was on leave as well. It was the first time he experienced the Oktoberfest, of which he had heard so much. About seventy-five guests arrived. Gustl's good friend Andy came with his parents and grandparents, the Butuses. I was not happy when Gustl told me later that his friend had almost passed out from drinking too much. Tonio did come home during the week to help entertain the two priests, and he drove them to Chicago to show them the city and his new apartment. While they were in South Bend, Tonio got a call from a headhunter that led to an interview with Sara Lee, in Chicago. Unfortunately it did not work out. Tonio blamed it on the fact that in the letter thanking them for the interview, he had added an *h* to *Sara*. Well, we never found out. – The priests had a ball at a big Oktoberfest hosted by the son of our friends the Butuses outside of Niles, Michigan. The son was in the process of building a sensational house in the woods. It was strong as a fortress, boasted at least eight thousand square feet, and had every state-of-the-art convenience and gadget imaginable. It was not yet finished, but we all could see what it would look like. All the woodwork would use woods imported from the rainforest. I had never seen so much food and drink, and neither had the priests, who had their fill of the roasted pig, lamb, turkey, ham, bratwurst, and much more. I was afraid Father Willibald, already very overweight, would keel over any minute.

We were disappointed that Tonio, still not feeling well, did not join us when Father Willibald sat down at the piano. We sang German songs and arias together until it was time to go to bed. The priests wanted to surprise Gustl at his school the next day, because it was time for them to fly back to Germany. – If they had been able to stay a few extra days, we would have taken them with us to the first grand affair at Howe, Founder's Day. Watching Gustl, who had earned a partial scholarship for playing the trombone, march and play in his uniform was a special treat. He looked so proud and handsome, and he was liked by his peers and the teachers, including the headmaster. The instructors were full of praise for Gustl's progress, and they confirmed what we had learned from the news releases the school sent us regularly. In almost no time at all, Gustl had blossomed academically, earning an almost straight-A record, with high marks for his character. He excelled in rifle shooting, held his own on the soccer team, and was sought after as an actor for school plays. We had reason to dance at the grand ball in the evening, where parents appeared in their party best.

The rest of the fall semester was packed full of travel for Tonio. He still flew to Pittsburgh on occasion, had meetings with the attorney in connection with his car accident (an issue that had yet to be settled), was under the care of a dentist, attended powwows on several weekends, and flew to Mobile, Alabama, to attend a Native American convention and workshop in Montgomery. Although Tonio had continued to wear his good business suits when he started at the college, after a few weeks he began to wear only blue jeans to better fit in.

The college still had not paid him, which began to trouble me when Tonio's severance payments stopped and when I saw the high Visa bills listing charges for computer software and Native American goods from upscale catalogs. – Not only was I very frustrated by Tonio's failure to discuss these purchases with me, but there was no need for dishes with a native American design, a thick Indian blanket with a wrought-iron stand, couch pillows, antique snowshoes, woven rugs, big plants, a large bust of an Indian chief, and other purchases. Tonio kept referring to his severance pay.

Holiday in Cancún, Mexico – Tonio Breaks with the Indians in Chicago and Lashes Out at Me

I must admit, a trip I had planned was not essential either, and perhaps a bit selfish on my part. But due to the frequent powwows Tonio attended on weekends, we spent less and less time together. I missed spending leisure time with my husband. Thus, I was very happy, and even surprised, when Tonio, who had previously exhibited no desire to go to Mexico, was suddenly in favor of flying to Cancún together over the Thanksgiving break. The children would be with their mother, and if we used frequent-flyer rewards, the flight and five nights at the five-star Westin Regina Resort would not cost us a thing.

Cancún, having been discovered only twenty years earlier, did not exist as a vacation destination when Doc and I honeymooned on the Yucatán peninsula. Tonio and I looked out the window as our plane approached the small airport. We were startled by the panoramic miracle below. No wonder the sweeping stretch of white sand along this graceful peninsula, cuddled by the crystal-clear turquoise waters of the Caribbean, was favored by Mayan kings over one thousand years ago.

We felt like newlyweds as the cab stopped to let us out in front of the luxury hotel, which featured modern Mexican architecture and was enhanced by palm trees, oleander, hibiscus, and sparkling fountains. Entering the spacious lobby, adorned with works by Mexican contemporary and folk artists, we felt transported into another realm, and it was exciting to step into our spacious room. Vibrant blues, yellows, and pinks were the colors that, in combination with the handcrafted Yucatán furniture, projected a distinct, cheerful Mexican ambiance. From the big balcony, separated by sliding glass doors from the room, we looked down on the calm sapphire waters and the pristine beach adjacent to the hotel grounds. A gentle breeze ruffled the fanlike leaves of the coconut palms. We slipped into our bathing trunks, hurried downstairs, and walked hand in hand across the snow-white, limestone-based sand known for staying cool even on the hottest days. We looked back at the disappearing footprints in the wet sand and forward toward the natural reef of Punta Nizuc. We went for a swim in the soothing waves, with graceful seagulls coasting by, and ended the day with a superb Italian dinner at one of the resort's exotic patio restaurants overlooking Nichupte Lagoon, where the setting of the sun, at that very moment, seemed unparalleled.

Tonio's fascination with Cancún intensified when we took a bus tour to the Mayan ruins at Chichén Itzá, still well preserved, which we climbed together, just as I had with Doc over four decades before. I could hardly believe the masses of tourists, swarming around like ants on their hill, and remembered how much more quiet and peaceful it had been way back then. Now there was a big hotel and a huge restaurant, where we had lunch and watched two Mayan children perform a dance before checking out the souvenirs. Tonio was looking for little peace pipes, beads, and feathers with which to craft Indian mementoes for his students. He had invited a group for Thanksgiving dinner at his apartment in Chicago the day after our return on the 30th.

Tonio and I spent the rest of our vacation sunbathing and taking the bus, which, for a mere 50 cents, took passengers to any of the numerous stops in the legendary hotel zone. We enjoyed visiting the very glitzy Plaza Caracol, the mall where the rich and famous spent their money. I was very excited to spot a handsome young pianist playing a grand piano superbly in the mall. He told us his parents were from Russia and that he hoped to earn enough money to go back and to study piano in Paris. He played for almost an hour – any piece of classical music we suggested. It was great, and we gladly rewarded him.

On another day, Tonio haggled with the Mayan vendors at the bazaars and flea market downtown. We got into an argument over yet more Indian mementoes, which he simply had to have, but he calmed down later on, when we met a well-educated Mayan Indian who had been to Europe and spoke several languages, including German. He had been selling his handmade crafts at the Plaza Kukulcan, a mall. Tonio contemplated how he could help the man sell his pieces in the States. – I myself, having had some distance from the situation in Chicago and realizing that Tonio's mind was made up to make a go of it, was beginning to mellow, and considered that once I retired, we could sell the house and move closer to Tonio's place of work, Chicago.

One evening, while eating at one of the restaurants in the Plaza Kukulcan, where the gray marble floors shone like mirrors, we were handed a coupon for a free breakfast at the Cancún Sunset Club. We accepted the treat, called, and were picked up in a cab the next morning. The exuberant hombre took us to an exotic Mexican resort, where we ate while listening to and questioning the salesman. After spending more than three hours with him, bedazzled by the tastefully decorated rooms in the not-yet-completed hotel of over two hundred rooms, and even more so by the view directly from the bed onto the impeccably white beach with the lapping turquoise waves under a cobalt sky, we had committed our hearts and pocketbook in exchange for thirty weeks of vacation spread out over a number of years. They threw in three maintenance-free bonus weeks to spend in our truly deluxe presidential suite, which was closer to the beach than the rooms at the Westin Regina. Our champagne glasses were kept full all the while, and as soon as the deal was closed, another bottle was presented to us, accompanied by their shrill "felicitaciones."

On the flight home, we mused about taking the children to our new vacation spot, which was only a four-hour flight away and, in the long run, affordable, since we could prepare our meals in the suite. I talked about it with my seminar students after class, and they thought it was great.

Tonio drove to Chicago early in the morning, after spending almost all night crafting souvenirs for his students. On the way, he had picked up a turkey and other food for his dinner. He called me in the evening on December 1 to tell me the dinner never took place. In the morning, I gathered that he had brought up the matter of compensation. Though a check had reached him, it was lacking substantially. As their argument led nowhere, Tonio went to his office, picked up his computer, typewriter, books, and records, and quit on the spot. – I was dumbfounded, but careful not to say I told you so. I knew he must have reached his limit if he was willing to offend the Native Americans. One of his much older students joined Tonio for dinner to discuss the situation with him. They had become friends. Star was a true Indian, who had lived and been gainfully employed in Alaska, where he ended up losing everything while taking care of a wife with cancer. Although sober, he was an alcoholic, and he still hoped to reclaim a tract of land in Alaska.

I was bewildered by the turn of events. On the one hand, I felt sorry for Tonio, and on the other, I hoped he would terminate the six-month lease he had signed with the assurance that an earlier cancellation would not create a problem. I also wished we had not invested in the vacation place. On the way to the university the next morning, I was contemplating how to get out of the contract, even though we had arranged to spread out the monthly payments. – It was a gloomy morning on December 2 when, deep in thought, I stopped briefly, as I had a thousand times before, at a familiar intersection. Out of nowhere, a car rammed into my baby Mercedes on the passenger side, pushing me sideways across the intersection and into the stop sign, which bent and slowed my car down enough to bring it to a stop a few inches away from a white frame house at the corner. I was in shock – squeezed between the seat and the door until someone came to free me. The owner rushed out of her house to make sure it was not damaged. The car was totaled. I told the police I thought it was my fault, though in retrospect, I realized it was more likely the fault of the student, who was late for class. Someone called my secretary, instructed her to cancel my classes, and asked her to take me home, which was only a few minutes away.

A friend insisted on having me examined at the hospital, where I learned that, thanks to the strong frame of my Mercedes, I got away with big, black-and-blue bruises and aching bones. I called Tonio to tell him what happened and that it was not necessary for him to come home since he would be back the next day anyhow. I had no class until Monday and handled matters with the insurance agent – the towing of my car, etc. – mostly from my bedside. By the time Tonio came home, everything, except the replacement for my car, had been taken care of.

On December 10, Tonio and I appeared before the attorney in Chicago, who took the deposition relating to Tonio's accident in 1992. I saw for the first time his somewhat dark efficiency apartment, located in a former hotel. It was decorated with all his Native American objects. Tonio appreciated their spa and security system, because he had noticed some drug addicts in the neighborhood. He also rented space for his car in a guarded lot around the corner.

It was on the same weekend that my old friend Dele Jaeger celebrated her eightieth birthday, which it was impossible for us to attend. I sent her a nice gift, knowing full well that she considered one's birthday the most important day of the year, a belief I never shared. I still try my best to avoid telling friends when my own birthday is – and to automatically forget theirs, no matter how frequently they call my attention to it. I have no calendar in which I register birthdays, which are in my mind reserved for children. I know full well that others think I am nuts in this respect, and they are entitled to their opinion, as I am to mine. I believe celebrating a birthday is tantamount to celebrating that one is a year closer to death. I can do without it. Doc used to say, "I am not afraid of dying, but why be in a hurry about it?"

Tonio, to my knowledge, never returned to the college and blatantly ignored their calls, as they had his in the past. Instead, he filed a detailed complaint with the workers' compensation authorities, which after a number of months yielded results in his favor.

Christmastime was once again upon us. It was the children's turn to spend the holidays with us. Liesl, who was doing very well in school, flew in from the West Coast, and Tonio picked up Gustl at Howe. The children were then both in their teens and no longer believed in Santa Claus. Liesl had brought her violin and Gustl his trombone, and we all sounded much better when we played "O Tannenbaum" and "We Wish You a Merry Christmas." The presents were of a different nature. We had brought a beautiful chess set from Cancún for Gustl, and Liesl loved her red wool coat and other presents she had wished for. Along with his sister, Gustl opened the presents his mother had sent. Liesl made it her business to add together what the pair of slippers, a book, and two T-shirts had cost, and she announced in a matter-of-fact tone of voice that Mom had spent no more and no less than $27.50 on Gustl's gifts. I thought her behavior strange, and thought it equally strange that Tonio got rather upset about a very tacky clock, made of highly lacquered wood, sent along for Gustl by the step-grandparents. I loved the golden hoop earrings Tonio had found to match the jewelry from Antigua, and he liked the collapsible easel of light-colored wood, as well as the paper, paint, crayons, and brushes, with which I surprised him. I had seen some of his sketches and was convinced that my poet, when inspired, would be very creative with the brush as well.

Right after Christmas, it was remarkably cold outside. We had planned to spend a few days with the children at Tonio's apartment, to go window-shopping and maybe take in a show in the Windy City. The day before, the children and I were in a jovial mood, still in our robes, and Tonio, as often when he did not have to go to work or attend a meeting, could not get out of bed. He had pulled the pillow over his head to block out the noise the children and I made in the house. I knew he had been awake, because the glass of orange juice I had brought to his bedside ever since we had been together, rain or shine, was empty. He knew that when the children were home, I liked having the whole family around the breakfast table and always prepared their favorites, German pancakes or French toast. Tonio made American pancakes or waffles. We always had bacon, eggs, fruit, and juices.

It was about 10:00 a.m., and Tonio still had not joined us. Even Gustl was up. I went to the bedroom. As he was not budging, I began to pull back the down comforter, begging him to get up and reminding him that it was late and we were waiting. – As though stung by a tarantula, he jumped out of bed in his red Christmas pajamas, looked at me with catlike eyes, pushed me onto the bed, ran into the kitchen, and returned to the bedroom carrying a heavy pitcher; before I knew what was happening, he poured a half gallon of ice-cold water over my head and body. Not knowing how to react with the children in the house, whether to cry or to laugh, I swallowed my pride and uttered something like "what is wrong with you, and how could you do this?" I dried off, wrung the water out of the sheets, and aired out the mattress and the comforter. Thirty minutes later, we all sat together more or less quietly, and ate our breakfast. I was hoping the children would think it was a joke.

That same afternoon, Tonio told us to pack our things for the trip to Chicago. He wanted to leave the next morning and be back before New Year's Eve. Though I felt better, I kept thinking about the ice water. The children were already sitting around the kitchen table, not far from the stove, where I was putting the final touches on dinner. I decided to serve a bowl of chicken noodle soup, which the children liked. I opened the can with the can opener affixed to the cabinet located behind Tonio's seat. I do not know why, but as I passed behind Tonio, I stopped, held the opened can above his head, and teasingly said, "How would you like it if I poured the contents of this can over *your* head?" To actually do it would have been totally out of the question for me. Out of respect for Tonio, I would not have done it, especially in front of his children – and I did not believe in wasting good food and knew I would have to clean up the mess. Tonio was obviously in no mood to be teased in this way. It was too late. He grabbed my arm with the can and slapped me so hard on the cheek that Gustl straightened up in his seat, saying, "Oh!" Liesl just looked on with big eyes. I don't remember what happened to the soup can. They probably ate it, as there were no spills to be cleaned up. The next thing I recall was that he grabbed me by the shoulders and pushed me backward to the door leading to the hallway to the master bedroom, all the while raising his right index finger, commanding me furiously to go to my room, where I sat in a corner in the fetal position, crying until no tears were left.

When I heard the three laughing and playing games upstairs, I could not bear it any longer. I gathered every ounce of strength I had left and told Tonio to leave the house before night. The children could stay with me if they so wished. I went back to the bedroom – still in shock – and Gustl and Liesl came to look in on me a couple of times, asking if I was sure I did not want to come with them to Chicago.

Deep down, I knew they preferred to be alone with their father. An hour later, I heard the garage door close. I was alone. —

After that incident, I had to talk to someone. I knew it would be fruitless to speak to his family; I also knew that none of my relatives in Germany would understand. Frank had told me how much he despised his own father for the terrible way in which he had seen him treat his mother, whom he had very often found crying. Though he did not say anything about physical abuse, judging by my cousin's weekend drinking binges, I could easily guess the rest. When I talked to my friend Renate the next day, I confided in her what had happened and what had already taken place in the summer. She expressed her concern and said that Tonio, ever since he took the apartment, had been distant and did not love me anymore. I explained that he was not acting rationally, that he was hurting and certainly not the man I had married, and that all would be well again in time. I told her that one does not desert a man when he is down, which I considered a cop-out. It helped just to talk to a friend, but ultimately I had to make a decision about what was best for all of us, not just me. Tonio called a couple of days later to ask if they could come back home, saying he wanted to try once more. I told him it was all right. When I felt the need to at least mention to the children what had happened, I asked Gustl in the kitchen what he would have done if his stepfather had treated his mother the same way. He answered, "Everybody deserves to be hit now and then." Liesl stared at her brother, her mouth wide open.

And life went on . . .

New Year's Eve was not as happy as before, and my tarot cards foretold gloom and doom. We spent long hours putting puzzles together. Liesl's was a picture of tropical fish. She liked it so much that she asked her father to glue it onto a piece of cardboard so she could take it home and hang it on the wall in her room. When Tonio tried to pick it up, it tore, and it was damaged so badly that Liesl screamed at the top of her lungs. Tonio took Gustl back to Howe, where he was welcomed by his peers and anxious to dive right back in.

I was pleased with my new chairman's evaluation. He seemed impressed by my Bayer Program, which was still going strong without the university's blessing, and praised my teaching. He recognized my continued involvement as treasurer of the literary journal, where we had published another excerpt from our novel. Much to my regret, ever since Tonio had become fixated on his genealogy, he stopped working with me on the book.

I was sad and disappointed that Tonio decided against canceling his lease. He insisted that he would have a better chance of finding a job by using Chicago as his networking headquarters. I had trouble understanding his reasoning, because many of our friends who had lost their jobs were operating from their homes. I knew deep down that the overriding factors for Tonio were the apartment's proximity to the National Archives, access to his new and updated computer, which he had taken with him, and the fact that I was out of his hair when he was in the city. Even when he did come home for the weekend, he spent hours on the phone tracking down information for his genealogy. At times he was excited about having located a distant relative, but at other times he was so upset he could hardly sleep. By chance, I had overheard him talking to his brother about one of his twin stepsisters, with whom he had not had contact in years. It appeared that his father had abused one of the daughters so badly she eventually changed her family name. Both brothers, who had lived with the father when young, and his mother refused to believe the story.

Tonio had always been more of a night person, but this tendency had become extreme. Many times, I pleaded with him in vain that it was way after midnight and time to come to bed. I began to resent his infatuation with the genealogy, but when I complained, he said I should be glad he was not a womanizer.

Researching Native American Ancestry in Atlanta – Vacationing on Grand Cayman Islands in the Caribbean – Tonio Abandons the Native Americans in Chicago

Early in January, Tonio informed me rather bluntly that he would drive down to Atlanta, Georgia, to conduct research for his genealogy, and continue from there to Eight Mile, Alabama, to meet a distant relative, whose daughter was also working on a genealogy. I was not very pleased about his plan, but was quick to ask if he would mind if I came along and helped, since the semester had not yet started. Tonio did not object, and we took off for Atlanta, where I had not been since I went with Doc in 1957. I hardly recognized the city, but we did little during the two days except sit in the Atlanta-Fulton Public Library, not far from the impressive City Hall, looking at numerous microfilms and record books. We saw the Martin Luther King Jr. National Historic Site only from a distance. I did squeeze in a hair appointment before visiting Tonio's relatives. It was a Saturday, and I had made the appointment by phone. Tonio dropped me off at the street corner where the beauty parlor was supposed to be located. I told him I would walk back and meet him at the library after I was finished. I found the parlor, but was startled when I saw nothing but African-American men through the window. I did go inside, and all heads turned my way. I asked about the beauty parlor, and a man, smiling, told me to go through to the back. About six African-American women were either having their hair done or busy taking care of a customer. When I mentioned that I had called, a lady answered kindly that it was OK and asked me to sit down and wait. – It was the first time I observed how the hair of African-American women is straightened. It was a time-consuming process, as strands of hair were clamped between two hot irons that were pulled down. I enjoyed talking to the women, and had the best shampoo ever. Tonio thought I looked great, and so did his relatives in Eight Mile, Alabama, whom I told about my experience.

Tonio's relations lived way out in the sticks. Several pieces of broken-down farm machinery stood around the yard. They owned a humble bungalow that felt very cozy inside, especially as I had come down with a bad cold. His aunt pampered me with hot tea and put me to bed with warm covers while the three sat around the kitchen table, on which she had earlier served a tasty country-style supper. I never felt as welcome when visiting Tonio's immediate family, and was glad to have gotten to know these kind people. They were very sympathetic about our situation, and when I confided in his aunt about what had transpired, she encouraged me to hang in there. Before we drove home, she gave us some of her homemade marmalade to take along. I corresponded with her after we returned.

Tonio went back to Chicago and I back to teaching, trying hard to smile and put a positive spin on our commuter marriage, which was hard to explain to my colleagues and friends, who questioned why Tonio could not work just as well at home. I sometimes told them it was actually nice to have some time to myself during the week and that he came home on weekends and whenever we had special plans. During the winter, I picked him up at the South Shore train station.

One Friday night, I picked him up because he had promised to drive me to Indianapolis the next morning to screen students for the Bayer Program. We had to leave at about 7:00 a.m., but no matter how gently I tried to awaken Tonio, he would not budge. I presumed he had been drinking too much the night before and finally left without him. I was quite sad, and my CDS friend noticed immediately that I was not my usual self. In addition, with the downsizing in progress at Bayer AG, they had reduced the jobs and scholarships for our program to fifteen. It was out of my control. But I wondered quietly if it had anything to do with Tonio losing his job. I did learn that they gave ten more places to the person in Pittsburgh who was in charge of internships for American engineering students. When I entered the house in the evening, Tonio apologized for not having come along and had dinner waiting for me.

I learned not to dwell on disappointments. Besides, we would soon be off on another trip. Again with the help of frequent-flyer miles and a bonus week the Cancún Sunset Club had given to us toward a stay at a resort, I had made reservations for my spring break on Grand Cayman Island, in the British West Indies. It is the largest of a group of three islands in the Caribbean, about 150 miles south of Cuba. Judging by the brochure, it looked very enticing, and I hoped it would be as nice as Cancún.

Tonio and I loved the spacious one-bedroom suite at the Indies Suites resort. It was cheerfully decorated with rattan furniture, and it had a patio enhanced with tropical plants that looked out to a Jacuzzi in a large pool, with a cabana bar at the far end of a long courtyard. The resort was across the road from a beautiful stretch of the well-known Seven Mile Beach.

Sunshine, blue waters, and a cobalt sky always lift my spirits. I felt rather daring and suggested to Tonio that we rent bikes to go grocery shopping. I had not sat on a bike in forty years, but since the low-lying island was virtually flat, I was certain it would be all right. I rode around the parking lot of the resort a couple of times, and off we went to the store, about a mile away. We loaded vegetables and groceries into the baskets mounted in front of the handlebars, and drove back on the left-hand side of the more or less busy street, Tonio in front of me. As we approached the intersection where we would cross the street, I heeded his signal to slow down and started breaking. The groceries in my basket began sliding toward the left. I lost my balance and crashed, my bare left knee striking the sandy shoulder of the street. The groceries lay spread out next to the bike. Tonio, concerned, rushed to my side and helped me up, across the street, and into the lounge of the resort, where he secured ointments and bandages, which he wrapped around my knee after having cleaned the bleeding wound as much as possible in our suite. I assured Tonio, who kept blaming himself, that it was not his fault at all and that I was sure it was nothing to worry about.

Much to my dismay, the pain kept increasing, to the point that any attempt at walking was excruciating. I felt terribly sorry for spoiling the vacation for Tonio. He was very attentive, dressing the wound every day, and did his best to cheer me up. We sat at the beach and agreed that, with all the seaweed on the sand, it was not at all as nice as the beach in Cancún. Tonio ventured out every now and then to go snorkeling and served a delicious gourmet dinner every night. I waded in the gentle waves on the beach in the hope that the salt water would hasten the healing of the wound. But I stayed in the room or on the patio when Tonio ventured out to the district of West Bay to see Hell, which received its name in the early 1930s when an official visitor from England took a shot at a bird among the large patch of pointy black rocks, missed, and said, "Oh, hell." It sounded rather tacky, and even tackier was the name of the gift shop, Devil's Hangout, from which Tonio brought a postcard portraying a red devil, almost like the one on his tarot cards.

Tonio checked out Georgetown, the capital, with its big banks, while I tried my best to draw a picture with crayons for Liesl. But when Tonio took to his brush and easel, which we had brought along, I felt right away that given some time, he would produce a painting worthy of hanging on a wall in our house.

I was determined to go snorkeling at least once at Grand Cayman, so well-known for its underwater scenery and the best scuba diving in the Caribbean. We both joined a group of visitors for the resort's farewell sunset cruise. It turned out to be the highlight of our vacation. The guides were extremely helpful and the people jovial, and it was downright sensational to see a huge swarm of stingrays all in one spot and tame enough that you could momentarily lift them out of the water with your own hands. The guide dove and came up with big conchs to prepare a conch relish, which looked better than it tasted. I was happy when he handed me a conch shell to take home as a souvenir. As we sailed back to shore, watching the sun set and tasting one of the resort's rum fruit drinks, I almost forgot about my knee. When we returned to the States, in time for the children's spring break, the whole family came along to the doctor, who, after an X-ray, determined I had a hairline fracture in my kneecap and put my leg in a cast. He recommended I stay off of it as much as possible, which unfortunately I neglected to do.

I was much relieved when Tonio's lease expired and, with Gustl's help, he moved back home. Even though he remained buried behind his computer, I was so happy I decided to throw him a big welcome-home party, to which I invited all our friends in order to show them that Tonio and I were still together. – I scheduled the party a week after the orientation for the Bayer students, which Tonio and I, together with the CDS representative, conducted at our house as in previous years.

Full of Hope for a New Beginning in Princeton, New Jersey

Not long after I had invited our friends, Tonio was summoned to the headquarters of Educational Testing Service, in Princeton, New Jersey, for an interview regarding a position as director of PR. The first interview went so well they skipped the second. They were very anxious to have him aboard, because they had screened six hundred applicants over the course of the year. Just before the party, Tonio had been offered and had accepted the appointment at ETS, the world leader in standardized testing and professional accreditation, and he was scheduled to fly to Princeton to discuss specifics on the Monday after our celebration.

We now had two reasons to celebrate the end of an old era and the beginning of a new one. You can rest assured that I went all out with preparations. Thus, when Tonio announced on the day before the party, while I was very busy cleaning and getting ready, that he had invited his Indian friend Star from Chicago, offering him one of the children's rooms for an overnight stay, I was stunned. – I thought I had misunderstood him, because he never said a word about the visitor when we discussed the guest list. We had always made sure we agreed on who would be invited. Tonio also knew that when I was busy hosting a party, I felt quite uneasy having strangers in the house. It was also possible that his friend would not feel at ease at this particular party, where people would be well-dressed. Star, his long gray hair always greased and poorly groomed, came across as a person who economized with water. In fact, Tonio had told me he had been evicted from his sister's apartment because he had collected a dead duck in a park, put it in a plastic bag, and hung it on a doorknob in the basement. He was a pack rat who lived out of a big old car, filled with junk and books. His sister, an alcoholic, though still employed at a bar, had thrown him out many times before, as had the rest of his family. I understood from Tonio that Star's entire family, like many Native Americans, had fallen victim to alcoholism. I felt he would simply not fit in with the rest of our guests, and begged Tonio to at least find another accommodation for him for the night. I was grateful when Tonio booked a room for him at a nearby motel, The Wooden Indian, which under the circumstances might sound ironic.

The party turned out well, and Star occupied himself by entertaining the younger crowd. At one point, I suddenly noticed a strange odor and smoke coming from the dining room. Star was burning certain herbs or weeds, perhaps sage, in a big oyster shell and performing an Indian ritual. While it did not bother me, my younger friend Patty, who suffers from severe allergic and asthmatic attacks, told me she felt sick from the odor, excused herself, and went home.

Tonio picked up Star at The Wooden Indian for breakfast, but instead of taking off for Chicago afterward, he was still at our home in the late afternoon, when his sister called from Chicago. She had gotten it into her head to come to South Bend that evening – why, I never found out. Tonio had to fly to Princeton in the morning, the party mess still had to be cleaned up, and there were important matters to discuss. I don't remember how I finally succeeded in convincing Tonio not to let the sister come – whom Star supposedly detested, and whom I had never seen or talked to before – and to send Star on his way.

No sooner was our farewell party over than I started planning for the annual Mother's Day Ball at Howe Military Academy, in which the Nemesis, who never once visited her son at the school, had shown no interest. Gustl, who did not have a girlfriend, either at the school, where dating was forbidden, or back on the West Coast, finally came up with the idea of asking Annie to be his date. She was the daughter of Tonio's best man – Gustl had befriended her at our wedding in Venice five years earlier. We discussed the idea with Annie's parents, who lived in Costa Rica. They talked with Annie, and to make a long story short, Tonio and I picked up the beautiful, intelligent, vivacious, and very talented young lady at the airport a day before the ball. She had brought two dresses from which to choose, and Tonio had bought for me a stunning George F. Couture original at Jacobson's, the store where I had found my wedding dress.

Gustl was thrilled with Annie. He turned out to be the envy of all the cadets. He presented her with a wrist corsage of sweetheart roses and had a dark-red rose for me. The gesture touched my heart as much as the corsage of white gardenias Tonio pinned on my dress. We all had a grand time dancing, chatting, and going to church the next day. We had lunch at a restaurant of the youngsters' choosing, and left some time for the two to walk in the park before we had to say goodbye. Annie needed to return to Costa Rica before missing too much school. Everybody thanked me for making a dream come true.

The week before Tonio started his job, he hitched a U-Haul to his Camry, and we both headed to Plainsboro to furnish the makeshift apartment his company had secured for him.

Before going house hunting the next day, a Sunday, Tonio and I had to return the U-Haul. We were driving slowly along a major street when suddenly the U-Haul was coasting alongside our car, all by its lonesome self. We stopped the car, jumped out, and luckily stopped the trailer in the nick of time. Fortunately, the street was free of traffic.

Tonio thought it might be exciting to buy an old Victorian house in a neighboring town in Pennsylvania, but he changed his mind quickly after we saw the interior of this historic jewel. We walked through the house, up and down the many flights of heavily worn, carpeted stairs, looked into many wallpapered rooms, and tested the squeaky boards on the porch. I eventually had to leave the house; my eyes were itching and red, because at least ten meowing cats, darlings of the owner, were constantly underfoot. We quickly realized that insofar as Tonio was much less skilled with the hammer than with the pen, we would have to invest almost as much in repairs as we would in the price of the house itself, which was way beyond our means. – We took this overpriced and run-down antique off our list and continued our search.

The sun was shining in a blue sky when the realtor stopped in front of the villa on a small hill, surrounded by blossoming fruit trees, white rhododendron bushes, both pink and evergreen azaleas, and blue spruces on a manicured lawn. As she unlocked the wide, double-panel glass doors to the almost new house in Primrose Circle, a subdivision about eight minutes from Princeton, we stepped into an atrium with a large skylight. The floor was covered with terra-cotta tiles. It was an ideal place for our hibiscus and other tropical plants. A second double-panel glass door with brass trim opened into the house, which had vaulted ceilings that rose to the second floor. The stairway, covered with a plush white carpet, ended in a half-circle balustrade on the second floor, from which one looked down on hardwood floors covering the wide, open corridor, a spacious den with bow windows and a mirrored wet bar, the sunken living room, and the chandeliers in the corridor and dining room. Recessed lighting and recessed speakers were mounted in the ceilings throughout the house. Above the living room were two big skylights, through which the trees in the woods bordering the property were visible. A broad window that reached from one end of the living room to the other, and high up toward the vaulted ceiling, opened the view to the woods. It was as though one could walk right into the small forest.

There was a perfect spot next to the windows for my baby grand, the Knabe. Opposite were French doors, which opened to a double deck covering the entire back of the house. From the open corridor, you entered the long and spacious kitchen and family room. The floors were covered with the same terra-cotta tile as the atrium. The state-of-the-art kitchen counters and island were covered with off-white, hand-painted tiles depicting herbs and vegetables. Fluorescent lighting fixtures, mounted underneath the white oak cabinets, illuminated the tiles at night. A garden window was installed over the sink, letting in daylight for a cheerful atmosphere. Between the kitchen and family room was a space with a bow window for our half-circle cherrywood breakfast table. The owners had left a ceramic ceiling lamp, ideal for the table. The fireplace and mantel in the family room would be perfect for our Scandinavian entertainment center. An entire wall of windows and French doors opened from the family room to the double-deck patio, on which a big Weber grill stood. The full basement could eventually be finished and could house our wood-burning stove. –

It was love at first sight, a place in which to start all over, a new beginning in an Ivy League university town, next door to both New York City, the ultimate cultural center, and idyllic countryside. Its owner, the CEO of a corporation, who kept his red Porsche in the garage and had another home in Martha's Vineyard, had seldom inhabited the two-year-old house. It was a place where we could happily retire. The developer maintained the grounds for a fee that included access to tennis courts and a swimming pool in a scenic setting, not far from a pond where Canada geese liked to stay. We were worried another prospective buyer, who had just looked at the house, would snatch it away. An hour later, we made an offer, handed the realtor a check for earnest money, and asked her to join us for a bite to eat.

We were getting increasingly excited about moving to Princeton – so different from the anticipated move to Pittsburgh. Though I never said anything, deep down I wondered why Tonio's new boss had not asked him to introduce me, especially since, according to Tonio, he had shown much interest in me. An old bachelor with a taste for the arts, he liked to keep Tonio in his office well after work hours, talking to him about literature, movies, and music, even on days when he knew I had come to spend the weekend and was anxious for Tonio to come home.

The question of terminating my position with the university had become more acute, especially since ETS did not look too kindly upon Tonio commuting. Though my chairman cautioned us not to be too quick to sell the house and move, Tonio had convinced me that once he was hired, moving to Princeton would be the only option. "They bury their employees on their own grounds," he quipped. When I asked him about the notification he had received regarding a three-month trial period, he explained that such trial periods were for employees of lower rank. I went ahead and composed a letter to the dean in which I expressed my concern for the students, vowed to assist in a smooth transition, and asked respectfully for a two-year leave without pay and for a reply by June 1.

The dean wrote back a month later to inform me that my request was being processed. Without hesitation, I signed a letter composed by the university stating that my decision to leave was irrevocable, that I was ineligible to return to my faculty position, and that I released the university from any claim or cause of action related to my employment prior to that date. I realized then that they still feared I might take legal action.

I was eager to get out of South Bend and away from the university, where the incoming freshmen were getting lazier and were at times downright insulting, always complaining about too much homework. Except for advanced classes and seminars, teaching was no longer enjoyable. To compound the problem, the adjunct instructor whom I had recommended when on sick leave had turned out to be ill-equipped to teach university-level classes. Although she was probably a good high-school teacher, she categorically ignored my instructions. She was unable to keep up with the syllabus for beginners' courses. As a result, her students were unable to perform at the level I required for the next semester. It would have taken a couple of years to straighten out the discrepancy.

Though I was pleased with my new chairman, I was anxious to take leave of a place where a handful of administrators had caused me so much grief. I also observed that the zoo-like atmosphere of the department would not go away any time soon. The new chairman had already encountered problems with my old male colleague and the new one. The Prima Donna, who had been highly in favor of him in the beginning, soon found fault with him. He finally had his fill and left for greener pastures. I am confident my letter of recommendation helped him secure the new position.

Tonio and I had long agreed that a commuter marriage was not for us. I began to realize that Tonio needed me at his side when, shortly after he had moved into the Plainsboro apartment, he called me one night complaining about the police, who had issued a summons for him to appear in court. It seemed that when programming his phone, he accidentally dialed 911, whereupon a policeman appeared at his apartment door. When Tonio apologized for the mistake, the officer left. But when Tonio made the same mistake a moment later and the police reappeared, it must have triggered an altercation, aggravated by the fact that Tonio was drinking wine and also, I presume, by the sight of the many liquor cartons in the apartment, which were full of books waiting to be unpacked. – To compound the problem, a report about the incident, giving Tonio's name, had been in the local paper. I felt scared and worried, not only because we had to hire an attorney, but also because Tonio was obviously drinking more and more, especially when alone. I had almost forgotten what Frank told me about Tonio's passing out, dead drunk, on their camping trip when they spent a night at an old friend's cottage in Fairview, North Carolina. At the time, I thought it was nice that they could visit Anne, who had suffered much – her daughter was murdered in her apartment during college, and after the tragedy, her marriage broke up.

Tonio, Liesl, and I had planned to attend the wedding of my cousin's oldest son in Germany, in the absence of Gustl, who, we agreed, could spend the summer on the West Coast, where he had landed a good summer job at a day-care center. We had enough frequent-flyer miles to cover our fare. When Tonio, at the time he was hired, had asked his new boss for a day or two off to attend the wedding, he turned him down flat. Tonio told him to forget he had asked.

Liesl and I Frolic at Our First German Wedding in Giesen, Germany

Early in June, after having taken care of all the mortgage papers for the new house, and after putting our pretty house up for sale when we had received the go-ahead from the university, Liesl and I crossed the Atlantic and landed in Hannover, where we spent a few lovely days at Father Heinrich's residence. Sister Johanna spoiled us with her fine cooking.

Father Heinrich was kind enough to drive us to the town of Celle, founded in the middle of the thirteenth century, where Liesl and I saw the many outstanding half-timbered houses built between the sixteenth and eighteenth centuries. I had never been there. It was the town where my father had had his first job at the court, prior to being transferred to Gieboldehausen, where I was born. Father Heinrich also drove us to Sankt Ursula, in Duderstadt, so Liesl could see the convent school and the town where I spent four years of my life after the war. Unfortunately, the place was under construction. Gaining some time as a result, we returned to Hannover by way of V. to get a good look at Uncle Adolf's mansion, where we had spent seven years under his tyranny. I don't know if Liesl, who is always careful about expressing her feelings, appreciated seeing the places where I lived during my childhood, about which I had told the children many stories. – I didn't know if she would really appreciate the Niele wedding. Father Willibald, who had driven us on behalf of Father Heinrich, left quickly after dropping us off.

I thought it was a bit unusual that my relatives, who greeted us at the door of their new house, did not ask the Father and his housekeeper to come inside for a cold drink or a cup of coffee. Liesl, on the other hand, found it downright grotesque that stuffed and mounted animals occupied every corner of the house: the mounted deer heads and antlers on the walls, the pheasant on the buffet, the red and silver foxes with their fluffy tails on the couch and armchairs. Whispering in my ear, she asked why there were so many dead animals. I explained that my cousin was a hunter who was very proud of his achievements. I told her that although I too felt sorry for the poor creatures, we had to be tolerant and simply ignore them. –

Liesl was well-liked by my relatives, of whom she had met several in the States. However, she was as bewildered as I by the big eve-of-the-wedding shindig, at which the entire village, customers from all over Lower Saxony, friends, relatives, and my cousin's buddies from the Fire Department – in short, no fewer than three hundred guests – appeared, ready to party until dawn. It was raining cats and dogs, but nothing stopped the crowd from smashing big boxes full of new and old china, glasses, and flowerpots with much gusto on the pavement in the courtyard, where the more than thirty semis usually parked. Everybody watched while the bride and groom swept together the broken pieces and carted them away in big cardboard boxes. All this for the sake of good luck in their marriage and as a lead-up to the bash in the huge hall, normally used for storing and repairing semis. The hall had been cleared and the walls draped in red velvet, borrowed and hung by a future brother-in-law who worked in the theater's carpentry in Hildesheim. From the lofty ceiling, big crystal chandeliers, also from the theater, hung suspended. Many long rows of wooden tables and benches had been set up and a large space kept clear for a band and dancing.

As we entered, Liesl and I took in the array of drinks on offer: wine, schnapps, whiskey, soft drinks, several kinds of beer from barrels, and more. A wide variety of appetizers was set up on tables, and for the main feast they had big kettles filled with roasted piglets and beef, as well as platters and bowls full of potatoes, salads, vegetables, etc. It was simply overwhelming. Liesl and I chatted and got acquainted with other guests, several of whom recognized me instantly as Mutti's daughter even though they had never seen me before. I danced many a dance with a villager who paid me many compliments, despite the fact that my leg was still hurting.

We had a lot of fun, but I thought it was peculiar that neither my cousin Klemens, with his oversized beer belly, nor Trudis's husband danced a single dance with me, if for no other reason than to be polite. I was probably too American or too worldly, or their wives were the jealous type, which would have been ridiculous. The evening ended on a more upbeat note for Liesl, who got to meet a nice-looking young man, Christian, a year older and a few inches taller than she. They took to each other in no time at all. Both made big eyes when the delicious sheet cakes were served. I was elated that Liesl had found someone to talk to. They got by with broken French and broken English. She did not see him again until after the church wedding, which was preceded by a civil ceremony in the mayor's office on Saturday.

Only family members were invited to the municipal ceremony. My cousin made a big fuss before we marched down the village street. He swore he would neither walk out nor go to the church wedding if the bride insisted on keeping her maiden name. I thought it was a bit late for that, and wondered why he had not thrown a fit a few weeks earlier, when his son's fiancée moved into their future house on the premises of the truck park. I also wondered what my cousin's father, Uncle Hannes, would have said. After all, he had treated me like a prostitute when, at the age of twenty, I showed up at his house with lipstick and a permanent, yet with my virginity fully intact, and had barred me from entering. This bride was not even Catholic and was an outsider in this ultraconservative Catholic village. She was not only Protestant but came from the big city, Berlin, and smoked. She "sinned" secretly, because, according to Frank, his father had threatened to kill his own children if he ever caught them smoking.

There was no reason to worry. At the legal ceremony, I observed that the minute they were joined in marriage, the bride whispered to her sister that she had made a great catch. Apparently, it had never entered her mind to keep her last name. I also believe my cousin Trudis would not have minded had she kept her old name, because she liked the newcomer even less than the rest of her family. – I did not even want to think about what they all thought of me, mingling with the very villagers who had produced the Neverbees, who had lured me to America with a care package in 1954 and smeared my name here and abroad when I married Doc. Regardless, the instant that food, wine, and beverages were served, the mood shifted toward a more conciliatory one.

While we were getting dressed for the big event at the church, I worried that the low-cut dress I had worn at the Mother's Day Ball would be frowned upon by my villager relatives as too daring. It was made of emerald, fully pleated silk and had a full-length skirt with a long slit on the left side. Its most prominent feature was huge, puffed-up short sleeves with layered, gold-rimmed ruffles. In Hannover, following the advice of Father Heinrich, I had already decreased the length of the slit, but I subtracted another couple of inches before risking an appearance in the village church. My spike-heeled pumps were studded with silver and white beads. The young people loved my outfit, and the bride's mother, from Berlin, could not stop raving about it, but the middle-aged generation, especially my female cousin, who wore a navy-blue pantsuit that Frank thought looked like pajamas, collectively raised its eyebrows. My cousin also disapproved of Liesl's light cotton dress, which had a pink, white, and blue floral design and a flaring skirt and ruffles. It was cut low enough that we had to stitch in cups to prevent people from looking down to her bellybutton. I had brought it from Jacobson's, because there was no time to go shopping before flying over. Liesl adored it. She made big eyes and shook her head when nasty Trudis said I had talked Liesl into wearing it. Liesl asked why so many of the Germans opted to wear dark and black dresses – what they wore at funerals – to a wedding. She was not present when I caught Trudis in our room going through Simone's closet to check out her black taffeta Laura Ashley dress. She was searching for the price tag, which I found disgusting. Considering she was Aunt Stingy's daughter, I should have expected it.

On the wedding day, all turned their heads when the bride entered the baroque church. She looked beautiful in her low-cut, shimmering, lacy white dress with a trailing, gathered full-length skirt. A big taffeta bow was attached below the waist in the back, and a narrow, sparkling band across her forehead held the gathered veil. She did not wear any myrtle, the symbol of virginity, but carried an elongated arrangement of draping dark-red and white roses, which matched the rose the groom wore in the lapel of his black wedding suit. He was tall, blond, blue eyed, and very handsome. A guitarist and a singer enhanced the ceremony. In the absence of a High Mass, and compared to ours in Venice, the ceremony was brief.

When the wedding party left the church, the big bells were ringing, and before the newlyweds could step into the horse-drawn carriage, they had to saw into two pieces a big log blocking their way at the entrance gate to the churchyard. Many villagers were gathered to watch them, and the children came running to gather the coins the groom hurled toward them.

Another delectable meal awaited us at Ernst, the inn where I first met the cousin who was just married. The banquet tables were set with rich china and silverware, and the three-tiered wedding cake seemed whiter in front of a cluster of bright-red balloons. I sat across from Trudis, who was embarrassing her daughter's friend by referring to him as her son-in-law, even though no engagement announcement or any reference to it had yet been made. Since he was studying medicine like her daughter and was the son of a physician, it would according to her standards be a marriage made in heaven, despite the fact that he was not Catholic. The poor balding guy turned crimson red, and everybody, especially Klemens Sr.'s children, felt sorry for him, because he was constantly being pushed around by the ogress. – I happily talked about Tonio and his new job and sent around pictures of the dream house in Princeton. They all made big eyes but were careful not to say anything nice. Of course, the Germans hold our houses in low esteem, likening them to matchboxes the slightest wind could blow away.

There was more food to come that evening. A German-style supper of the most delectable cold cuts, salads, meats, and desserts awaited us after we had a couple of hours to relax and look at the presents, the value of which Trudis estimated and compared immediately, especially when it came to mine. Fortunately for the bride, nobody else must have noticed as she smoked a cigarette in her white gown outside the back entrance. I wondered whether all hell would have broken loose had her father-in-law spotted her. It was probably a blessing that the more intellectual opposition had had the wisdom, or audacity, simply to drive off with their offspring instead of staying behind and chatting with the low-IQ relatives. – The Klemens clan, that is, the trucker family, was upset that they left, and trashed them until it was time for supper, the grand finale.

Liesl and I had never witnessed wedding traditions such as those that unfolded before us once the dancing resumed. Bride and groom wore old-fashioned white nightcaps and oversized, white, long-sleeved nightshirts over their wedding outfits and danced beneath a tent of wide purple ribbons tied to a stake, held up by a guest in the center of the room. Other guests, standing in a circle, held up the ends of the ribbons. I do not know what the meaning was, but perhaps it was to depict a heaven protecting the dancing couple.

This ritual was followed by one in which Liesl won the prize, much to the disgust of Trudis's daughter. All the single girls held a thin white veil and, when given the signal, tore at it. Liesl ended up with the biggest piece, which meant she, the youngest, instead of the eager Kirsten, was next in line to marry. Kirsten insisted on repeating the ritual until she ended up with a bigger piece. So much for competition and envy on my side of the family. – On Sunday morning, I was almost glad to observe that the Protestant boyfriend ignored the big push and did not attend Mass. Every time the portal opened, heads turned in anticipation and drooped when he failed to appear. He had gone running with the dog instead.

The days before our flight home were special. Liesl's boyfriend picked her up to go biking and to join his family's outing to the big fair, where Christian, whose father played the organ on Sundays, played the flute, marching in a band. They went on rides, won prizes, ate German bratwurst, and had a jolly good time. At night or early in the morning, Liesl came into my bed to tell me everything about her new friend. We were never again so close, and it was a sheer joy for me to observe her first crush on a young boy. She remarked how polite and kind he was, and they exchanged addresses and snapshots, vowing to write to each other. She wished we did not have to leave so soon, and upon returning to the States, she could not wait to find a little stuffed elephant to send him for his upcoming birthday. –

At home, I was greeted by a long letter Tonio had faxed. I wish to share a few excerpts with you:

Not a day has gone by that I haven't missed you, written you a letter in my head, wanted to tell you something, thanked the good Lord for you. So many things to share! At least and at last, I will commit some of my feelings and impressions about Princeton to paper so you will have mail from me to read when you return and so they will not go unrecorded.

My foremost feeling is one of newness and awe. How many times do we get the chance to wipe clean the slate of life and start over! It is exhilarating beyond words to work in a place where what people see is what they get and where I bring zero baggage to the situation. I am shocked and amazed that people accept me at face value and that they even appear to like me and seek me out. Existence at Miles (ugh, how it hurts) had become that of the leper. I remember Cary Grant answering an interviewer's question as to how he could lead such a charmed life with the statement, "I made up the character of Cary Grant as someone I simply always wanted to be." So do I feel every day at ETS. I am making it up as I go and having one hell of a good time.

I've been concentrating on my job. Have done little else. Went to the Princeton University Library both of the last two Saturdays all day.

....

I do get lonely and overwhelmed by all the new experiences. True confession time. I'm probably not as bad as the reservation Indians who arrived in Chicago back in the days of federal relocation and got lost, but it is bewildering to a degree, all the highways and noise and rush-rush-rush. I'm glad I have a six cylinder car to get out of the way of all those greedy people in BMWs en route to New York to make pots of money. If you don't get out of their way they'll run you over. They might run you over anyway. So if I have a vice, it is holing up in my apartment and calling people long distance. The phone bill is likely to be a whopper. At least I'm not chasing women or hanging out in bars.

Call me borderline schizophrenic or worse, but I cannot escape the frequent feeling (it comes at the end of a good, satisfying day at work) that there is something afoot in my life. A plan. It began in Chicago when I felt good and alone and at peace. "Alles war ausgeruht, wie es im Rilkeschen Spruch heisst" [everything is rested, as Rilke writes]. I reached a similar point after my first marriage and end of my teaching career in 1982, when I hit bottom, so to speak, and discovered what I described at the time as a philosophy of "applied intelligence" to guide me in all affairs. Much has progressed since then and though I am not eager or voluble in talking about it, I am obedient to a spirituality that informs and infiltrates all I do or say. Sometimes I have experienced it as a sensible burning of the ears and audible imperative. Other times I have questioned that presence with a silent "Who are you" and received differing answers (but always an answer). Many times the spirit world has behaved in a tricky, teasing or comical way. I have discussed it with no one.

I'll provide you with one, slightly risible to be sure, example. Dreams. I will have a dream in which I am left with the feeling that I entered. I don't want to say I entered the spirit world, but rather that the spirit world took over ME and entered MY body. I sensed that the spirit, whatever or whoever it was, got a real kick out of it. Not that the spirit accomplished any great thing or delivered any pressing message to the sub lunar world or anything. My overwhelming impression afterwards was the spirit took a kind of joy ride using my corporeal presence and kinship and genetic statement as a vehicle to have fun and remember, fleetingly, what it was like to inhabit a fleshly form. It made me grateful that my poor, abused physique had been the receptacle, and that the paltry string of circumstances I have managed to turn into an individual social and geographical existence had appealed sufficiently to that disembodied influence to enter and enjoy.

Always and ever, of course, the question: whereto? "Quo adusque. O mea anima?" Your ears may burn on occasion, or you may shoot a silent thought and see someone's antennae prick up, but why? And to what purpose? Just for the otherworldly thrill? I think not.

It all comes down to spirituality. Through that long night of the soul in Chicago, I did learn one thing. I learned that all things have life. Spirituality is something you do every minute you live, not a compartment of life you activate on Sunday or only dressed in church clothes or not when needed. Religion is not an act you put on, a ceremony you enact to get to heaven or stay right with God. The whole environment is a living complex worthy of constant respect – rocks, trees and things. Rolled round in earth's diurnal course, as Wordsworth says, social protocols, forms of politeness, tradition, etiquette, even history, which is nothing but honesty and persuasion, and especially the future, which is nothing but responsibility and managing expectations. The Cherokee venerated geographical formations (the hills that held the bones of ancestors) as living things. Our Western materialistic society worships cash in the bank as something to be captured and sealed away from harm or any change, the deadest thing imaginable, a superstitious and fetish-like blind adoration.

....

I cannot close without telling you how very much I am in love with you, whether I do a good job of conveying this or not. It is true. You are my one and only true love, forever and always, in all ways, and one day I will become unencumbered and eloquent and make you more sensible of that inside me.

Yours with much, much love.

In this letter, he also expressed his concerns regarding our and especially my responsibility in raising the children, Gustl in particular. He spoke of his own and my somewhat strained relation with his mother and siblings. – I was both touched and bewildered by the letter and wanted to cry, not knowing why. It was late when I called Tonio to tell him we were back. I thanked him for his letter, but I fell asleep as soon as I went to bed.

Early Clouds on the Horizon in Princeton – Lightning Strikes, Then Hits – Tonio Returns to Outplacement – He Seeks Solace at the Sweat Lodge – Wrestling with the Pain of Loneliness

Liesl and I made sure the house would look inviting whenever the realtor came to show it, and I was relieved when the second party made an acceptable offer to buy, though for $70,000 less than what we had put into it when remodeling. They got the bargain of the century inasmuch as the house was vastly improved for the location. That settled, we looked forward to our visit with Liesl's father, whom she had not yet seen that summer.

Our plane was late that Thursday, three days before July 4, our wedding anniversary. Tonio had just arrived at the gate when we deplaned. I immediately sensed that something was dreadfully wrong. Instead of giving us a hello kiss, he looked at me, seeming totally crushed. He said, "I am late, the sh—t just hit the fan, I'm smoking again." He was holding a burning Benson & Hedges cigarette. – I was speechless, had a piercing pain in my stomach, and felt very hot. Tonio filled me in about what happened, trying not to arouse Liesl's attention. He spoke German and English as he told me that his new boss, of whom he had spoken in glowing terms after returning with him from a visit to New York City, had called him to his office and, for three hours straight, read him the riot act, so to speak. He allowed him to leave only after Tonio was psychologically utterly drained. – It was clear that the midterm review of his job was less than satisfactory, yet there was still time to improve. –

From that day forward, a new cloud of stress hovered over our lives, a cloud we tried to ignore in the hope that it would eventually disappear on the horizon. – The evening of our arrival, Tonio had confided in Liesl that he had a surprise in store for me. Liesl let the cat out of the bag – or the puppy, rather. Her father had made a deposit for a terrier and had plans for us to pick it up in a town on the coast on Saturday. I did not want to believe it, yet when a woman called, while Tonio was at work, to confirm the appointment, I knew it was true.

Liesl and I agreed that to bring a puppy into the chaos of moving, when we would be busy supervising the packing of dozens of boxes, was unthinkable and completely impractical. I knew I could not handle the additional burden, physically or emotionally. Not to mention that, with the exception of little Nelly, killed by Uncle Adolf a couple of days after he came to us during my childhood, I had never owned, been around, raised, or house-trained a puppy. Liesl, who had had unpleasant experiences with a stray dog Gustl brought home on the West Coast, was not eager to be burdened with a puppy either. – I had previously agreed that eventually, after having settled in, the whole family, Gustl included, could go out and look for a dog.

I could not believe Tonio would spring this on me. He had it all worked out and wanted me to take the puppy back to South Bend, never realizing that special arrangements had to be made with the airlines. All day long, Liesl and I plotted about how to talk her father out of it when he got home. When the lady called back the same afternoon, I hinted that she should not be disappointed if the deal fell through. When Tonio arrived, we had a lengthy debate in which I asserted that this was the worst possible time to acquire a pet. I thought I had convinced him. I had also discovered he would have to pay an additional $250 each month for rent if he decided to keep the puppy in Plainsboro. And who would look after it when he was at work or visiting us on weekends?

It was raining cats and dogs the next day. I was relieved the matter of the puppy was settled. We decided to show Liesl the Atlantic Ocean and the beach, hoping the rain would stop. After showing Liesl the new house, we drove east. The closer we came to the ocean, the more the downpour increased. Liesl looked at me guardedly. All of a sudden, Tonio stopped at a trailer. I knew instantly what he was up to. He wanted me to see the little dog after all. I was incensed and refused to enter the trailer, but gave in at last. I did not want to look at the puppies, knowing full well that once I had seen them, I might change my mind. Tonio was playing with the dogs in the pen. I kept my distance, all the while trying to convince Tonio that I was neither able nor willing to train a dog during this chaotic time, when I was in charge of everything having to do with a major move. When nothing else seemed to sink in, I told the lady that I could not guarantee the little dog would survive the move without the needed care, that I would give her whatever it cost to keep the puppy, and that we might be able to come back in the future. The lady reacted as I had hoped. She turned to Tonio and told him she did not want his wife to have the dog. The drive home would have proceeded in utter silence were it not for Tonio turning toward me halfway home and saying, "You can be glad I am not throwing you out of the car."

Not Hitler's Child

A week later, Liesl was busy decorating our house one last time, for Tonio's birthday. We were both disappointed when he informed us something had come up at work and he could not come home after all. We were doubly sad, because we had invited a number of my students for a good-bye party. Two students from the Music Department at Bethel College had volunteered to sing. It was the last time one of my musically gifted German students played my Knabe piano before it was moved, a couple of weeks later, to Primrose Circle in Princeton, New Jersey.

I called all my friends to say farewell once more, but refrained from contacting my matron of honor, who had betrayed me so badly. Since I had dropped all legal action against the university, which she had so ardently encouraged, she put forth much effort to regain my friendship by sending me gifts in the mail and even stringing balloons outside my office door. But once I get burned badly, I retreat forever. It's my way of self-protection.

Liesl and I worked many days packing books into boxes dropped off by the movers, who informed us they would be responsible for everything except the books. Together, Tonio and I owned an extensive library, and by the time we were finished, we had filled over one hundred boxes. – The day the forty-foot moving van stopped in the driveway, Tonio, again, did not show, because he had been unable to get out of Newark due to thunderstorms. We were grateful that my good old friend Patti, the one with the allergies, whom I had known when Doc was still alive, brought us lunch, thus forcing us to take a break. In the absence of Tonio, who had wanted to assist in cleaning the house before the new occupants arrived, Liesl and I handled the job ourselves. We swept, wiped, mopped, and scrubbed until dark, and I was so exhausted that when we arrived at the hotel to spend the night, I realized I had left my purse, along with my billfold and IDs, at the house. When I arrived at the hotel after yet another trip, I wanted to cry.

Tonio arrived the next day toward noon when all was done, but he was present to turn the keys over to the realtor. I had received a letter from Dan Cohen granting my leave without pay and told Tonio we had the green light and that I would apply for early Social Security to boost our income until my pension from the university started, in 1996. We went out for a nice dinner at The Grill before flying together to our new home on the East Coast, still worn out.

The sun was blistering hot when Tonio opened the door to our dream house in the late afternoon. Since he had moved in as soon as the purchase was finalized, most of the household items from the temporary apartment, including dishes, kitchenware, a card table, chairs, and a mattress, had been placed. We threw some laundry into the washing machine, and Tonio volunteered to make pizza. He had opened a bottle of red wine. I set the table and asked Liesl to check the laundry. When I sat down at the table, Antonio asked Liesl to check the pizza, which was in fact ready. Liesl complained that she could not do two things at once. Then, out of the blue, Tonio flew into a rage, shouted that I had no idea about raising children, and

I don't remember what else. Everything happened like lightning. He slid the big butcher knife, a wedding gift from his lawyer brother, under a piece of pizza on the stove and balanced it as he moved toward my plate. Instead of sliding the pizza onto the plate, he suddenly pointed the knife very close to my face and instantaneously brought it down on the plate with a bang. The plate broke into many pieces, which fell on my lap and shattered on the terra-cotta floor. In shock, I stuttered, "Oh, Antonio, that nice new plate, why are you doing this?" He shouted that I had never liked those plates anyhow. – These were the dishes with the Native American motif and were among the objects he had accumulated without my consent when he moved to Chicago. I did like the design, but not the unnecessary expense at a time when our financial situation was becoming more and more strained. – Once enraged, Tonio could not be stopped. He went to the kitchen cabinet and started smashing one piece after another of the entire set of dishes for four, throwing them the full length of the kitchen and family room in the direction of the windowfront, where they stopped sliding. In the midst of the rage and the shattering dishes, Liesl started crying, saying it was all her fault and that she was sorry. Seeing that he had not stopped, she ran for cover in the basement. Afraid to move, I sat still in my chair, speechless, in shock, traumatized, frozen. I thought of the O. J. Simpson crime, which had just happened. After all of the dishes were shattered, Tonio stormed out of the house and sped away in the car.

Liesl was my first concern. I called her out of the basement and put my arms around her. Trembling, she asked repeatedly why Papa was doing these awful things and urged me repeatedly to talk to someone. I told her to wait a moment while I cleaned up the broken dishes, which needed to be done before the movers arrived early in the morning. In the absence of a broom, I took a towel, pushed the pile of fragments onto a piece of cardboard, and emptied it into the trash can in the garage.

To distract Liesl and myself, I suggested we go upstairs, put on a bathing suit, and christen the beautiful double Whirlpool in the master bathroom. It was a spacious bathroom with vaulted ceilings. You walked right into it from the master bedroom. There were no doors, except for the one that led to the shower and restroom. The Whirlpool sat in the corner between a pair of washbasins. Shiny ivory marble tiles, just like those on the lavatory counters and floor, framed it. Above it were two skylights and two garden windows through which you could see the trees of the forest. Behind the counters were wall-to-wall mirrors, a feature that resembled the walk-in-closet doors in the three bedrooms.

The whirling water felt soothing, but Liesl was restless, and we got out before long. We lay down on the mattress on the white-carpeted floor in the master bedroom. Outside, the thunder and lightning began. I held Liesl close, as I always did when she crept into my bed during thunderstorms. We were silently waiting for the phone to ring or for Antonio to drive his car into the garage. We fell asleep waiting.

Antonio never came home that night. I rose early the next morning and let Liesl sleep. When I entered the kitchen and family room, I stopped abruptly. The entire windowfront resembled a spiderweb. The sun, unable to penetrate, turned it into a wall of silver, glistening, cracked glass, reminiscent of the art-deco vase Tonio broke three years earlier. The cracks were so substantial I could not see the deck or the forest. A small, round opening in the glass resembled a bullet hole, or a small hole in a windshield caused by a stone. I was devastated. I heard the moving van outside, opened the door, and explained that a chair had fallen into the window and caused the damage. An hour later, Tonio walked in, looked at the damage, shrugged his shoulders as though it were nothing, called a glass-repair shop, changed into a suit, went to work, and left Liesl and me to manage the movers. He never uttered a word about his actions the night before, and neither did Liesl or I. I was afraid to unleash another outburst – or something new and even worse.

Breaking glass and objects dear to others simply to relieve anger and frustration was an obsession Antonio shared with many Germans. To this day, just before they get married, they engage in what I have always considered insane, almost barbaric behavior, and as I noted in connection with my cousin's wedding, they do it all for the sake of luck. With the many divorces taking place, one wonders why they keep the custom alive.

Instead of a new and wonderful beginning – which we had been looking forward to since Antonio's fabulous new job first brought us to this ultimate dream town – a silent fear began to take possession of my soul. It seemed that the destructiveness I had just experienced for the third time since Tonio had bonded with the Native Americans was another stage in the breakup of our marriage, which ten years earlier had started in the most romantic way imaginable. When we got engaged, we threw our champagne glasses into the fireplace, convinced the bliss of romance would last forever.

And life went on . . .

Competing with my fears was the stronger force of denial, denial that it would get worse, and a renewed conviction that I could make things right. I opted again not to dwell on the incident and to forgive and at least try to forget the broken glass. But what happened that night is as impossible to forget as the broken glass I saw as a child the morning after Crystal Night.

When you deeply love a person, you look deep inside to understand what could have triggered such unusual behavior. I saw a husband afraid of being crushed again after an extreme high, a man at a loss for what to do or where to turn. I too was afraid, afraid for him, for myself, for what was to come. –

To push back the fear, I, more eagerly than Tonio, proceeded with the activities typically involved with moving into a new home. We arranged furniture, placed plants, hung curtains and pictures to beautify our wonderful house, and set about unpacking hundreds of boxes. Our good friends the Voepels surprised us with an exquisite arrangement of orchids, which I placed in the center of the cocktail table, just where the sun beaming through the skylights would shine on it. – I was concerned that Liesl had spent little time with her father that summer, and both of us hoped he would take us on drives to check out the countryside and the beach and to look for a little elephant before it was time for her to leave. It pleased me that Tonio asked Liesl to help him decorate his office, but when she reported that he had decked out the entire place with his Native American crafts, I worried, wishing he had waited until his job was secure. My fears came to a head when Tonio, on a Saturday afternoon, a mere week after we had moved in, announced while unpacking the crystal that he would have to leave soon and pick up Star, his Indian friend from Chicago, at the train station in Trenton, and take him to his apartment, still under lease with ETS.

At that point, I completely lost it. All my pent-up emotions were unleashed. It was the only time in my life that I cried and screamed at Tonio or another human being with such anger and despair. I leaned over the balustrade upstairs, yelling that I could bear it no longer. I asked how he could break his promise that when he left Chicago it would be the end of the Indians and that he had said good-bye to Star forever. – I warned him not to bring the man into or near our house, that he would not be welcome. I questioned his sanity – why would he bring Star to Princeton at a time when his job was on the line, and what would they think if they saw the two together in restaurants or walking along the sidewalks? How could he do this to me without first discussing it, or to Liesl, who had hardly spent any time with him? Tonio continued unpacking glasses silently. I went to our bedroom sobbing, nearly beside myself, thinking I was losing my mind. Completely helpless, I watched Tonio change clothes in the bedroom and heard the garage door close with a bang. When I finally pulled myself together to fix a meal for Liesl, we turned on the TV and watched the Simpson trial.

A couple weeks later, I found the copy of a check for $90 that Tonio had sent to Star to pay for his train ticket from Chicago. I never saw Star, and I talked to him on the phone only once, when he called my attention to the danger of alcohol without mentioning Tonio's name. I learned from Tonio that his friend liked walking around Plainsboro, where he made the acquaintance of other semi- or "wannabe" Indians, as Tonio referred to some of them.

And life went on . . .

It was a Friday. We had taken Liesl to the airport, planning to grill a couple of steaks when we returned and to spend our first evening alone in the new house. I had longed so fervently for a relaxed evening with Tonio and intended to make it special. Our lawn furniture stood on the deck, which looked directly into the little forest, where dogwood trees blossomed in the spring. Our bright-red hibiscus bushes were thriving, and the birds were singing. A perfect night lay ahead, or so I thought. But it was not meant to be.

I was getting ready to set the table on the deck when Tonio stated in a rather resolute voice that he had plans to go to a circle meeting with Star that night. Surprised, I reminded him of our plans for the evening, but realized quickly that he would not change his mind.

I have never felt more alone than I did that first night in the big house. I sat waiting in my car in the garage and then went back to bed, listening for the garage door. I fell asleep crying. Tonio came home at 1:30 a.m. I heard him moving pots and pans around in the kitchen before he came to bed. He took off again the next morning to go to a sweat lodge, with a pot of beans he had soaked during the night and cooked in the morning. He returned Sunday morning at 2:00 a.m. His clothes and shoes were covered with mud. I asked if he would join me for a service at the Episcopal church in Princeton. We had talked about joining the church when we attended a service prior to moving. When he did not respond, I knew he was not interested. –

I was optimistic that a visit from Simone, who was to arrive at the beginning of September, would be good for both of us. She would not stay long, but even a week would be a welcome change. Our house looked even nicer since we had acquired two Oriental rugs, one for the living and the other for the dining room. I was looking forward to having someone to talk to, and when we picked Simone up at the airport in Newark, it seemed like old times. She loved the new house, and Tonio helped cook. We picked up a couple of lobsters one day, because Simone had never tasted one.

One Saturday, Tonio drove with us to Philadelphia, located on a peninsula between the Delaware and Schuylkill Rivers and less than two hours from Princeton. I was glad to finally visit the city where Doc had earned his MD at the famous Jefferson Medical School. – Tonio led us straight to Independence National Historical Park, where we were in awe when setting foot in the old state house, now Independence Hall, dating back to 1732. The impressive red-brick structure is said to have been the colonies' grandest public building when it was built. Entering the building felt like stepping into a sanctuary, even though the interior is by no means sumptuous, but rather simple. To be aware that such documents as the Declaration of Independence (in 1776) and the US Constitution (thirteen years later) were drafted and adopted in these halls is like a religious experience, for here is the birthplace of the United States of America. – Gripping as well was the moment I stood in front of the Liberty Bell, the international symbol of freedom that originally rang in the steeple of Independence Hall. Unfortunately, the 2,080-pound bell cracked twice, had to be replaced by a new one, and now rests silently in a shelter on the ground.

On the way back to the car, we walked through the tree-lined cobblestone streets of Society Hill and admired the blend of seventeenth- and eighteenth-century townhouses, interspersed with new ones and accented by pocket gardens and parks. The picturesque ambiance was so inviting that we all agreed it was a place where we would not mind living. – But we returned to Princeton. One day, Simone took a train to Washington, D.C., and she returned excited. The two of us had many a conversation about Tonio's precarious job situation, and Simone was sensitive enough to observe his dramatic mood swings. She understood even less than I did his fascination with everything Native American and thought it might just be a phase men go through at Tonio's age. I was surprised when she asked me if she could smoke in the house, but did not have the courage to require her to go out on the deck or into the garage. Tonio had adopted the habit of smoking outside. He was glad to share a smoke indoors with a smoking partner.

Soon after Simone had left, Tonio's position was terminated without severance pay, but ETS guaranteed outplacement services for both of us. It was as though the sky had fallen in. Tonio wrote a long letter to his employer in the hope of getting at least some financial retribution, if not for him, then for me, since I had given up my position at the university. I suggested he ask them to turn over the amount it would cost them for my outplacement services, since it would be impossible to find a position of full professorship in German in the area universities, where budgets were being cut, especially in foreign languages. It was to no avail. In a way, I found it strange that they questioned Tonio as to whether he really was a Native American, but considering his demeanor and conduct, it was not surprising.

Thus, here we were – in a brand-new home with big mortgage payments, in a region where the cost of living was at least triple that in the Midwest. Unemployment compensation was negligible, and to add to our financial stress, Tonio was informed that the unemployment benefits he had collected in Indiana were illegal. Someone had made a mistake, and an immediate reimbursement of thousands of dollars was requested. – My monthly income was less than $900. I felt a pain in my stomach and was scared. Gustl was still in boarding school and always needed something for school or outings and the like. I stopped driving my car and canceled my car insurance, as well as all subscriptions for papers, magazines, etc., drastically reduced telephone calls to out-of-town friends, and spent a minimum on groceries. If I had learned one thing during hard times after the war and during my student years, it was how to get by with little. We had already decided to strike any kind of liquor from our shopping list, because Tonio had realized that due to his Native American roots, he was more vulnerable to liquor. He did not stop smoking and, much to my sorrow, started smoking a more expensive brand of cigarettes. On the package was an Indian head. He claimed Native Americans believed tobacco was sacred.

Tonio went to the outplacement offices regularly, rewrote his résumé for the umpteenth time, tried, upon the advice of his counselor, to take on a new image (I forget what), began to network again, this time in the New York area, and landed an interview now and then, only to be rejected. – I could not bring myself to spend much time at the outplacement headquarters, sitting in one of those three-foot stalls assigned to their unemployed clients, calling around to find a job. I found them degrading and downright inhuman. I did go a few times to place phone calls overseas and to friends, just to give the outplacement people an excuse to collect their probably exorbitant fee from the companies that had fired their clients. They also assisted with the rewriting of my résumé. When I showed it to a top-ranking senior vice president with a law degree from IU, who had been looking for a new job for almost two years, he was impressed, which did not help me. He thought it was inexcusable for Tonio's company to have let us move so quickly and to urge me to quit my job at the university.

Spending time at the outplacement office was depressing, because all the job seekers looked depressed, even when they tried to hide it. The IU graduate, a man in his late forties, was forced to take his children out of school and would soon have to sell his three-garage mansion; and his wife was as depressed as he was. He feared she was sick.

My Bayer Program had run its course for the last time, and I decided to use my expertise along those lines to create a new program. What better place than Princeton, where all the headquarters of the big German and Swiss companies were located? I met with the chair of the German Department at Princeton, who was very interested, as was the chair at Ryder, and I spoke with Hoechst, BASF, Siemens, and Hoffmann-La Roche, who were unanimously impressed to hear about my programs and the fact that during my tenure as a professor, I had sent close to five hundred American students to study and/or work in Germany. But the companies were unable to commit themselves, because they already had similar programs in place or were reluctant, in view of the high unemployment rate in Europe, to start new ones. Tonio, who previously had vowed that he would take care of me and that I did not need a job, wanted me to apply for an opening at a boutique, selling dresses. I just could not bring myself to do it.

I met several of our neighbors at Primrose Circle. They were very sympathetic and invited me occasionally for a luncheon or game party in their state-of-the-art homes. Each one looked more pretentious than the next. The majority of the owners were retired and had exchanged their big estates for life in a maintenance-free community. What I saw here topped many of the homes I had seen in the past, as their furnishings seemed to have been transported directly from the showroom of an upscale furniture store into their new showplaces. Our neighbors liked the Oriental style, and their house had a Japanese flair throughout. Of course, everybody had to outdo the Joneses next door, even here. The big thing was the house models, of which there were three. The Winston model was the top. When conversing with the ladies, it was all about millions, exotic travel, second homes in Martha's Vineyard, Hilton Head, Boca Raton, Florida, or some island in the Caribbean in which to spend the winter. One had over fifty signature basketballs in a specially built illuminated glass cabinet, which sat center stage in a spacious and glitzy party room downstairs. Another neighbor spoke about a surprise party to which her husband was flying in many guests from all over to celebrate her sixtieth birthday on a big yacht hired for the day, from which they would view the New York City skyline while dining at night. –

As I write today – September 11, 2001 – that memorable skyline has been dramatically altered. The proud twin towers of the World Trade Center and a portion of the Pentagon in Washington, D.C., were destroyed by brazen terrorist attacks, killing close to three thousand innocent civilians; and the towers are no more. –

A third neighbor had ended up all by herself in a Wilson model next door to ours, after her husband of forty years exchanged her for a much younger woman. She kept mostly to herself and had a chauffeur, and when I finally talked to her, I learned she was still in therapy, trying to cope with the tragedy in her life. Everybody, even though it was completely uncalled for, had a gardener planting more and new flowers, shrubs, and trees, just to distinguish their home from the others. All houses were of light-gray wood with stone. I described them as giving the impression of socialism in the midst of capitalism. If left behind in such an environment, I would wilt quickly.

And I felt alone as the days went by. A few times, Tonio was kind enough to take me for a ride in the lovely countryside. We went to Washington Crossing State Park, on the Delaware, to see historic buildings from the eighteenth and nineteenth centuries. We loved strolling down the crowded streets in the picturesque and quaint town of New Hope, across the state line in Pennsylvania. It is an antique collectors' paradise. Always in search for something Native American, Tonio stumbled upon a very handsome Indian, the owner of a crafts shop, who invited both of us to a meeting. I was anxious to go, but when the time came, Tonio went without me.

I also asked him to take me along to a sweat lodge one day so I could better understand what it was all about. I had read that the experience aims to purify the mind, body, spirit, and heart, and that one is expected to approach a ceremony with respect, sincerity, humility, and the ability to listen and slow down, and I could not understand why Tonio felt I would not fit in. Later, when I met a couple of his new friends, who were all chain smokers, I lost interest somewhat. One guy, "the Medicine Man," did not look Indian at all but more like a person who lived on the edge of society. He did wear a small leather pouch around his neck, and his few strands of long gray hair hung in a ponytail over his shoulders and back. I learned he was a dentist but not very successful, because like others in the group, he had succumbed to alcohol in the past.

The dentist lived with a strikingly beautiful woman, who looked more Indian than the rest of the group, but also smoked heavily. Tonio spent much time at the dentist's modest home in the evenings. I began to resent them, not necessarily because of their beliefs, but because not only did they alienate Tonio from me, but like their companions, they had failed in their respective professions and were in no position to help my husband. I gathered from talking to the Medicine Man, who was constantly in trouble with the law, that he had stopped drinking and most likely had been instrumental in getting Tonio to stay away from alcohol. If that was the case, I was grateful, and I was also relieved that he insisted, when at a point of desperation I asked how native Americans felt about physical abuse of their wives, that such behavior was totally unacceptable. As soon as he sensed I was talking about Tonio, he became angry and vowed to have a serious talk with my husband. – A year or so later, the dentist committed suicide.

Trying to Mend the Cracks with the Help of Dr. Alice and Her Husband, the General

Tonio resented my having confided in his friend, but at that point I was so desperate that I had to talk to someone who I hoped would have some influence. – I also agreed reluctantly when Tonio suggested we seek counseling. I was afraid that seeing a counselor would only be the first step toward the dissolution of our marriage and furthermore a sign of failure, that is, of being unable to work out the problem by ourselves. I did not believe in divorce and agreed mainly because I hoped it might help Tonio curb his anger. I asked the realtor, whom we had both befriended, for a recommendation. After we spent an hour with the counselor, he informed us that he had not yet received his license, which meant my insurance, which fortunately covered both of us, would not cover the fee. Therefore, we had to find someone else. He recommended, among others, a licensed psychologist with a PhD. – The first time we met Dr. Alice Goodloe Whipple, I knew that if anyone could help, she would be the one. I personally related to her not only because she was a woman, but also because she too had earned her doctorate, even later in life than I had, and like me had married a widower connected with the US Army, a retired brigadier general.

The moment Tonio parked the car in front of the stately white frame house with green shutters, sitting back from the road on a one-acre lot and projecting an ambiance of elegance and peaceful charm due to the mature trees and shrubs on the grounds, I knew I would feel welcome. As soon as we rang the bell, the kind general, whose light-brown hair and short mustache were graying, opened the door and, with a big smile, welcomed us inside. A pair of dark-brown English springer spaniels flanked him. While ordering them to behave, he asked us to take a seat until his wife arrived. It was getting dark outside, and the light of a table lamp on an antique table in the entrance foyer shone warmly on the Chippendale chairs, covered with red velvet. The chairs used to belong to his grandmother. They stood at each side of an antique table and opposite a second one, on which I saw a vase filled with a bouquet of flowers and a sampling of books. While we were getting acquainted with the kind general, his charming wife, her big blue eyes beaming, held out her hand, greeting us with the friendliest voice. You could not help but feel drawn to her. Her short white hair was softly curled. Like her husband's, her clothing resembled English fashions, as is customary among true Princetonians. I noticed that she had a slender shape and was a little taller than I. We followed her into her office, a big living room furnished with beautiful antique furniture, paintings, vases, warm lights, and Oriental carpets that reminded me vaguely of the Croft.

Alice Whipple, who originally pursued a degree in theology but in later years earned a PhD in psychology from SUNY, counseled us together and at times alone. We did not mind it, because it gave both of us a chance to chat with her husband, whom we simply called "the General," in his library. Tonio discussed with him an array of topics, including historical events related to Native Americans. – This sophisticated gentleman, raised as a youngster on a Louisiana sugarcane plantation, had enjoyed the privilege of an impressive education. While at West Point, he was awarded the Rhodes Scholarship, and for three years he studied economics, politics, and philosophy at Oxford, where he earned an MA prior to obtaining a graduate degree in civil engineering from Princeton, where he later held a visiting lectureship in water resources.

Occasionally, the General and I conversed in French, which he spoke fluently. During World War II, he had been a colonel and the chief logistical planner on the staff of General Eisenhower. Later he had lived in France, in charge of other assignments. We also spoke German with each other after he related to me his personal involvement in the decisions pertaining to the division of Germany in his role as secretary general on the staff of General Lucius Clay in Berlin. I found it incredible that here, in Princeton, New Jersey, I would meet a man who had played such a decisive role in the rebirth of the country where I was born and raised, at the time I was in boarding school at Sankt Ursula. General Whipple discusses the event in his yet-unpublished, highly absorbing, and historically enlightening autobiography, in a passage I would like to share with my readers:

It was of course provided in the basic agreement that Germany would be demilitarized, and demobilization of her armed forces was to proceed rapidly. As regards higher policy, Secretary of the Treasury Morgenthau had devised a proposal for the elimination of Germany's industrial power, and reduction of her to the status of a "pastoral nation." This would have made her a very poor nation indeed; as her arable soil is limited and her population great, especially after the Russians sent us most of the German populations from the expanded Poland. This proposal of Morgenthau's had been initialed by Roosevelt and Churchill at the Quebec conference. Although Roosevelt was now gone, Morgenthau was still a powerful secretary of the treasury. Moreover, one of his men was to be chief of the finance division of OMGUS.

Germany had been devastated by the war destruction and bombing, divided by the occupying powers, and subjected to inflation and to shortages of everything needed. Personally, I felt strongly that we needed to help the Germans. My chance came a month or so later, when Clay asked me to prepare, for his signature, the first of a monthly series of reports on the occupation. I included material prepared by the various division chiefs, and then added a paragraph of my own. It said in effect that it was entirely unnecessary to exact any more reparations or take economic measures to reduce Germany's war-making capacity. On the contrary, it was going to be desirable to help the Germans economically in order to facilitate their transition to an orderly and democratic society.

When I brought this first report in to General Clay, he first said "Why is this report in final form? Why not in draft?" "It's to save time if you approve it." "Suppose I want to change it?" "My secretary is standing by if you do." "It's six o'clock now." "Yes sir, but she is ready." He read on, then suddenly frowned and pointed at my bit about helping the Germans. "Where did this paragraph come from? Who wrote it?" "I did, sir." "What made you think I would want to say that?" "It seemed to me implied by some of the other things you said. Besides, I think it's right." "Humph." He read it all through a second time, then signed his name and told me it was a very good report. Apparently this report created quite a lot of interest in Washington, and in effect it began to be applied. From this time on, it was tacitly understood, at least by most of us, that we were there to help the Germans. It was almost a year later, in September 1946, when the secretary of state officially announced a relatively benevolent U.S. policy for Germany.

I found it of equally great interest that at the time of his retirement from the Army, General Clay was instrumental in getting Whipple, then a colonel, back in touch with the Army Corps of Engineers, where over the years in his capacity as chief engineer and author of monographs and more than one hundred articles, he was held in the highest esteem for his many major contributions to the development and management of water supply and water resources in the United States. He has received numerous awards, distinctions, and a formal commendation from the president of the United States. His latest award was the Lifetime Award–Water Resources and the Environment, which he received from the American Society of Civil Engineers at the age of ninety-two.

The sessions with Dr. Whipple took on an increased importance. I looked forward to each visit because it meant Tonio and I would spend time together, for which I yearned in my increasingly lonely existence. Dr. Whipple gave us books to read, the first of which was John Gray's *Men Are from Mars, Women Are from Venus*. I tried to read it together with Tonio, but he leafed through it quickly on his own and zeroed in on the concept that men like to hide in their caves. It seemed to justify his withdrawal from me, and little effort was spent following the advice of our counselor. She suggested we spend some time together each day either by taking a walk after supper or watching a video, that we try to talk for at least a couple of minutes about something cheerful, and that we give each other a hug in the morning. We adhered to her recipe quite regularly at first, but as time went on, we did so more sporadically and only when I took the initiative. I will never forget the evening when, after dinner in the kitchen, I suggested we chat for a couple of minutes. I asked Tonio if he wanted to start. He nodded and I waited. But he did not utter a single word. He stared out the window toward the forest, and underneath the table his right foot twisted nervously. His face was flushed. He was unable to bring out a single word. I was dazed and felt infinitely sorry for him. Finally, I began to talk about something insignificant to break the great silence. I was not sure whether he was really unable to think of something or just did not want to participate. It was a total breakdown in communication. I learned that it is impossible to rekindle a relationship in the absence of genuine feelings on both sides.

Tonio had a den on the first floor that any man would dream of having. There was a large bay window, a big desk, and a leather chair as well as a state-of-the-art computer and even a small TV on a shelf next to the wet bar. A red upholstered Scandinavian armchair stood in front of his desk, and all of his books sat on glass shelves mounted from top to bottom on two wide walls. A lush green houseplant near the flight of windows accentuated the room. – The big negative was the absence of a door. He had made it clear many times that he could not stand the fact that I could just walk in or type on the computer during the day, when he was at outplacement. He knew I used the computer only to type, because we did not have access to the Internet and I was computer-illiterate at the time. All of the rooms downstairs, with the exception of the lavatory, were open. As a result, I often retreated to the master bedroom, where we had a loveseat and a TV, and where I would not bother him. – Every morning, he slept until almost 10:00 unless he had an appointment with the outplacement people. I still brought a glass of orange juice to his bedside, served breakfast, had dinner ready when he came home, and made sure the house was picked up and clean and the laundry washed. He reminded me a couple of times that he was about to run out of clean socks. – On occasion, I asked him to make a pizza, and he also pitched in when I asked him to assist with some of the housecleaning chores.

Although I adhered to the same routine as before, our relationship entered a state of almost silent coexistence. Almost, but not totally – there were times when he was loving and considerate and times when he was so withdrawn I did not dare to come close. Tonio communicated with me less and less.

The children were to come to Princeton over Thanksgiving. First Liesl, and then, just before she left, Gustl. They were together for a few days, and though I had been looking forward to their visit, it turned out to be a painful occasion for me, as most of the time Tonio went out with his children or played with them alone. I felt alienated. What had already started in South Bend at Christmas continued: Tonio and the children ganged up on and at times ridiculed me. I sensed that Tonio, instead of treating me as his equal or the mother of his children, as he had for years, had begun to deal with me as though I were a child. The children must have sensed it. Gustl grew increasingly hostile and completely ignored my plea to practice restraint in view of our tight financial situation and to refrain from asking his father to buy unnecessary things for him to take back to school. His father would not deny his son anything, and he had no objection to his shooting the BB gun in the small forest bordering on our property whenever he felt like it, which was a lot. Thus, it came as no big surprise when Gustl excelled on the school's rifle team.

Tonio sprung another surprise on me the day before Thanksgiving. He announced he had invited a friend and his wife for dinner. He had met the laid-off attorney at the outplacement firm. I was not pleased, but did what I was expected to do. I cooked my standby dish of beef roulades, set a festive table, and earned compliments from all – and more importantly, the mood was temporarily harmonious. I was not too impressed by the attorney, who openly criticized his wife at the table. From what I observed of his legal skills, I was not surprised that he was let go. He was in the process of establishing an office at his residence, which sounded sensible; but he would have to wait a long time for me to seek his advice.

Gustl had not yet been to the coast, and I asked Tonio if we could go for a ride to Atlantic City. I was curious to take a peek at Trump's billion-dollar-plus showpiece, the Taj Mahal, and see how it compared to the casinos in Las Vegas and Monaco. I thought Gustl too might enjoy the outing. I was also anxious for us to get out of the house. It was a beautiful ride through the Garden State and along the coastline, but when we arrived in Atlantic City, it was cloudy, the sea was rough, and the beach along the boardwalk not very clean. – Tonio let Gustl and me out of the car, long enough for us to run up the many steps of the replica of the Indian Mausoleum and get a glimpse of the insanely presumptuous interior. It was a myriad of the gaudiest colors and over-the-top designs, more flashy and opulent than I had imagined. We opened the doors and immediately saw hundreds of slot machines in the midst of so much blinding glitz, accompanied by so much noise from the machines as clattering tokens poured into buckets, that I turned on my heels and we both rushed back to the car. I felt sick and vowed to never again step into that casino.

With the children's departure, the loneliness set in once more; the sweat lodges, the circle meetings, and the work on the genealogy pulled Tonio away from me again. In the morning, he sat in his car in the garage, the leather seat reclined, smoking and staring at the wall in front of him. On moonlit nights, he smoked on the reclined lawn chair on the deck, staring into the full moon and listening to the voices of the spirits in the forest. He was extremely upset with me one evening. It was a day after he had returned from a sweat lodge way after midnight and spoke on the phone with the dentist at the bottom of the stairway beneath the vaulted ceiling. Tonio spoke so loudly I could hardly miss what he said. At one point, he spoke excitedly about the old woman he had encountered deep in the woods. It was pitch dark, and he had lost his way back to the car. He saw her coming out of the bushes, and she pointed him in the right direction. He assured the dentist she was a good spirit and that without her guidance he would have been lost. – Not knowing much about the spirits and their function in the lives of Native Americans, I thought I did not hear him correctly. It sounded like something out of a fairy tale. I asked if he was now communicating with spirits. He got angry and told me the conversation had not been for my ears.

The matter of the spirits upset me. I realized later I could have approached it more diplomatically. Nevertheless, at the time, I tried to understand Tonio's way of thinking, and in a discussion with him asked if his communicating with spirits might be similar to the concept of romanticism in which animals are endowed with a soul and with voices, as in fairy tales. Furthermore, as a Catholic, I was aware of many faithful hearing the voice of God or being spoken to by saints. But when he refused to look at it from those perspectives, I dropped the subject. I was still in denial, still trying desperately to stop him from drifting more and more into a world which was admittedly foreign to me, a world which is difficult to enter in the absence of someone loving and understanding to guide you. Even though I felt deserted and rejected, I kept looking for ways to hang on.

A Shimmer of Hope in Cancún – Heading toward the Final Breakdown

I had, without much trouble, gotten Tonio to agree to spend two weeks in Cancún just before Christmas. It would be the first vacation at our newly acquired executive suite after we had successfully negotiated a more favorable term. We split up the time between the Sunset Lagoon and the Royal Sunset. I had again secured frequent-flyer tickets, and since we would use a maintenance-free bonus week, fourteen days would cost us very little. We had wanted to take Liesl along, since she missed out on the trip to Ireland. I made all necessary arrangements for her to meet us in Cancún. But, again, the Nemesis put a stop to it, and we went alone.

When the van picked us up at the airport and we drove through the hotel zone, bordered by palm trees, oleander, and the usual tropical bushes and trees, I felt optimistic that the time in the Caribbean would be soothing and healing. – We knew what to expect and were pleased with the accommodations at the Sunset Lagoon, where we were to spend the first week. But in the middle of the night, we were aroused by loud sounds of hammers. Tonio, who had an extremely low tolerance for any noise at night or in the morning, got very upset, called the front desk, complained loudly, and gained thirty minutes of calm. Then it started again. The next day, Tonio complained again, but when the noise continued the second night, we insisted on being moved to the Royal Sunset Hotel, directly on the beach and the Caribbean. It was much quieter, though even here, where they were still in the finishing stages of the construction, an occasional drilling or pounding was heard. But the location of the room was the ultimate. When I woke up in the early morning, I could observe the most magnificent sunrises directly from my bed. Sliding glass doors led to the balcony. I was ecstatic, but was afraid to awaken Tonio, who had read until late and resented being roused. How I would have loved for him to witness those magnificent sunrises. Each moment, a new and awe-inspiring panorama unfolded on the horizon, where sea and sky touch.

The turquoise ocean and the immaculately white shoreline were lovely. Tonio, as always, roasted in the sun for hours, and I sought out the shade under the thatched roof umbrella most of the time. I walked along the beach, played in the waves, and swam, usually alone. Tonio swam with me or joined me for a walk along the beach maybe once. He had brought the easel, and when I asked him to paint a picture for me of the scene from our window, he surprised me with a beautiful aquarelle, artistically more striking than anything he had created before.

We had not yet seen several of the ruins and decided to rent a Volkswagen Bug to explore Cobá and Tulum. – The Cobá ruins, part of a large ancient Mayan city from about 750 AD, were mostly unrestored and hidden away in the jungle, with the exception of the ball court and Nohoch Mul, a very large pyramid. It is believed that, with over six thousand structures spread out over thirty square miles, and housing about fifty thousand Maya, it was the largest of all Mayan cities. After walking a while through the jungle, we found the towering pyramid particularly fascinating. We were virtually alone, and I stayed behind on a bench and watched Tonio climb the 120 very steep steps. When he reached the top, two women surfaced and talked with him. I found it hard to believe, but I could clearly understand every word they said. Nobody had pointed out that the acoustics were so perfect here, and Tonio seriously considered writing an article for *National Geographic*.

On the way home to Cancún, we stopped at Tulum, a thirteenth-century commercial trading port, considered the most important archeological site on Mexico's Caribbean coast. The beauty of the site struck me. The sun was setting, and it seemed like a phantom out of a dream. Ocean cliffs protect it on one side, and on the other, a stone wall shields the site. There is a small, private beach, which seemed like a jewel at the foot of the daunting ruins of the temple and fortress known as El Castillo. Unfortunately, the site was about to be closed, and we could not take advantage of all it had to offer, but we did enter the Temple of the Frescoes to see the mural honoring the diving god, the most important god in Tulum. A visitor pointed out the stucco masks that decorated the corners of the temple.

The last night, we looked for the Russian pianist in the Coracal Plaza Mall. We listened to his music as a final farewell. – The next day, when we were about to move our suitcases outside our rooms, I noticed our luggage cart was missing. The bellboy had obviously left it behind in the cab that drove us from Club Lagoon to the Royal Sunset. I was upset and started to question the bellboy, who blamed me personally for not removing it from the trunk of the cab. When I told Tonio the bellboy blamed me, he almost flipped out – to the point that I was extremely embarrassed. He complained loudly to the management and others in positions of authority and ended up yelling at the bellboy, asking him to apologize to me for accusing me and demanding reimbursement for the cost of the cart. He calmed down only after the poor guy had pulled out of his pocket a stack of dollar bills from tips and counted thirty-five of them into the palm of Tonio's hand. Though I was on the one hand touched by Tonio's sudden display of chivalry toward me, I tried to tell him not to go so far. I feared he would not stop, because I remembered when he had flipped out not only in Orlando, but previously, when he missed a business flight on which I had come along. At that time, he blamed the airline representative at the gate for not holding up the plane until we arrived. He was banging his umbrella on the counter so fiercely that I had trouble getting him to stop and convincing him it was not her fault.

Some twenty years later, the same bellboy was still there. He was quite surprised when I handed him a generous tip despite the fact that I had not asked for his help with my luggage. I felt so relieved.

We returned home on Christmas Eve, and of course, no decorations were up. I pleaded with Tonio to help me wind the garland around the balustrade and trim it with red bows and tiny white Christmas lights. I wanted to light it as we sat down for Christmas dinner in our beautiful dining room, for which I intended to roast a duck. – Tonio searched in vain for a bird on Christmas Day. We were lucky to locate a restaurant nearby, where we were served a tasty meal in a cozy atmosphere.

Tonio had also agreed to attend a New Year's Eve concert at Lincoln Center, where Kurt Masur, from the former East Germany, conducted the New York Symphony Orchestra. It was wonderful. They played waltzes by Johann Strauss, operetta arias from Léhar, and melodies from Richard Strauss's *Rosenkavalier*. The audience was enthusiastic, cheered, and gave a prolonged standing ovation, and I had a hard time tearing myself away. It rained cats and dogs, and we decided to forego Times Square, because of the many warnings we had received from Princetonians and New Yorkers. They said it would take hours to get out of the city, not to mention the strong possibility of being robbed.

We returned home not long after midnight, and called the children to wish them a happy New Year. I hoped so much, given the evening filled with music – just like old times – that we would be together that night. But Tonio, who had mentioned he wanted to go to the lodge to meet with his circle and watch the sunrise, was determined to leave despite my pleas and the downpour of rain. It was still close to the December solstice. He had been careful not to miss the equinox meeting on September 22. I told him I too would love to watch the sunrise and asked if we could do it out on our deck. – Without saying a word, he put on his old clothes, and when I heard the garage door close, I broke down and cried. I felt like a bird locked up in a huge golden cage. – He returned the next morning disappointed. The sky was overcast. Not a single one of his friends had shown up.

In January, I filed my annual report for 1994. It was brief, for I had taught only during the spring semester. My new chairman's evaluation was fair and balanced.

He emphasized my effectiveness as a teacher, my commitment to the students and the overseas program, and my office as treasurer of *Trans-Lit*. It was the last evaluation, signifying the end of my twenty-two years with the university.

Tonio's mood swings continued, but appeared to subside for a while after he had seen a psychiatrist a couple of times. He seemed to think Tonio's problem started with the termination of his job at Miles, and that he was physically exhausted from the stress that had increased continuously ever since. I myself had a session with the psychiatrist and found his insight that I had to cope with a lot rather telling. He drew a number of circles on a piece of paper, and in the circles he wrote all the examples of what I had given up in an attempt to sustain the marriage. He called attention to my diminished commitment to scholarship in exchange for caring for Tonio's children, to my having relinquished my tenured position and thus my main source of income, to my giving up my house at a substantial loss as well as my eligibility for VA benefits from my former marriage, and to my contributing substantially from my personal assets to enhance and maintain our standard of living. In short, he suggested I had become so subservient to my husband that I had lost my prior identity. I remembered overhearing Tonio talking on the phone to his older sister about me. He assumed that since nobody in New Jersey knew who I was, I felt like nobody. Tonio was at least partially correct. I had given up my former name, the name for which I was known in the academic community. When we left the doctor's office, he predicted that Dr. Alice, the psychotherapist, would have her hands full with us.

My friends were unaware of what was taking place, as was Tonio's mother. I wrote her a long letter in early January, telling her about our beautiful house, how wonderful it would be for the children to go biking and swimming and to play tennis or basketball, and how convenient it would be for Tonio, should he find a job in New York City. The bus stopped right at the entrance to our subdivision. I told her we were confident Tonio would find a job soon, but that we would have to economize until he did. I did not hide the fact that we had been on an emotional rollercoaster and that it would take much effort, goodwill, and faith and many prayers to survive. I also wrote about a meeting sponsored by the Episcopal church, to which we both went, where we met many jobless men and women. I told her about their bad-luck stories and assured her that even though we were the only couple with both partners unemployed, we had much to be thankful for. I asked her not to worry, assuring her that the children were both well and that we were in touch with them regularly, and closed by asking her to give my best to all her family and to pray for us. A few weeks later, she sent us a little book with prayers.

Not long after I had written to Tonio's mother, he sprang yet another surprise on me. He informed me that he was considering opening his own PR business. It was obvious that nobody wanted him and that there was no longer a place for him as an employee in the corporate world. He had come to that conclusion after receiving advice from another unemployed PR person. She was a divorcée with two adult children; her ex was a professor at Rutgers.

I felt a stinging pain in my stomach. I knew it would be hard to reason with Tonio. He had long ceased to listen to my advice, always accusing me of wanting to control his life. Frightened, I wrote him a long letter pointing out that his behavior had been impetuous ever since the loss of his position with Miles and calling his later actions a mistake. I asked him to think the matter through before he acted. I feared the added financial burden would be too much to shoulder at that time. – I knew Tonio had no business sense, and cautiously reminded him that when it came to dealing with lawyers, bankers, and bureaucracy in general, he had always preferred to pass the reins to me. I reminded him of our joint bank accounts, credit cards, etc. and that since we would be jointly responsible, I should have been consulted. I told him he was too stressed out and that if he did not stay on top of the situation, or if for some reason the partnership did not work out, the consequences could be catastrophic. I ended by telling him how deeply I loved him, asking him to discuss the matter with me, and reminding him that in a successful marriage nothing is more important than communication, communication, communication.

Tonio did talk to me, but was in no way inclined to change his mind. He was dead set against my suggestion that he start working from his office at home, as others in our neighborhood did, to keep costs down. He seemed to listen to my advice to make sure his partner picked up her share of the expenses whenever he advanced any funds. She had also told Tonio she did not want me involved in the partnership, which was fine with me, since I had no intention of getting involved. I made up my mind to stay out of the venture altogether. I also informed Tonio that I was not willing to withdraw any more funds from my personal investments to help with the new undertaking and that he should contribute his share to pay for the other monthly bills. He did not object, and told me he would withdraw the money from his pension fund; and despite my warning him that he could not use the term *Inc.* unless he formed a corporation, he went ahead with plans for a firm, incorporating the name of an Indian tribe.

Anxious to forge ahead, he and his partner rented office space, purchased new furniture, and ordered stationery, business cards, and everything needed to equip a state-of-the-art facility, including a costly sign, which the person renting out the office space objected to for some reason. To fit into the Native American mold, Tonio began to let his hair grow and exchanged his glasses for contact lenses.

When Liesl arrived to spend the spring break with us, Tonio presented both of us with a card showing that we were members of the Hawk Clan of the Southeastern Cherokee Confederacy, whose reservation is located near Albany, Georgia. He told us he had chosen "Wildcat" for his Indian name and suggested we think of names for ourselves. The card had been sent to him from "Chief Rattlesnake." The name of his wife was "Strawberry." I was speechless. He had never asked if I wanted to become a member of the clan. While I was inclined to humor him, because I thought it was a little funny, Liesl said outright that she did not want another name. – Tonio had obviously been in touch with the chief; I found a thank-you note to Tonio scrawled in pencil and peppered with spelling mistakes. It was most likely the son. He thanked Tonio for the $10 or $20 he had sent to him. I did not mind Tonio helping a poor child, but knew he had not sent a birthday gift to Liesl. What did bother me was the copy of a bill from a flower shop, which showed a charge of $90 for two dozen red roses that were sent to his psychologist friend and former teacher – with a card signed "Love."

It was good having Liesl around for a short while, and I was pleased when Tonio took us both to Philadelphia, where I got a better look at Thomas Jefferson University, formerly Jefferson Medical College. I suggested we treat Liesl to a belated birthday lunch at the famous, early-nineteenth-century Bookbinders Restaurant, which Doc had repeatedly praised and had hoped to take me to someday.

Gustl arrived when Liesl was just about to leave, and unfortunately, despite a congenial beginning, it did not take long for us to lock horns. His room was next to ours, and the walls were too thin to block out the sounds of his radio. It was so loud I could not sleep. I finally went to his room and asked him to turn the radio off, which he refused to do, because he needed the noise to sleep. When I asked Tonio to talk to his son, he turned onto his other side, claiming it did not bother him. – The next day, when I was listening to classical music, Gustl and I got into a heated debate about classical music, pop, and rock 'n' roll. It ended with Tonio giving in to Gustl, who changed the channel to rap, or whatever it was. –

The children were scheduled to spend the summer with us, and I called all over trying to find a summer job for Gustl close enough to be reached by bike or bus. He showed very little interest, and I finally gave up trying. He had just obtained his temporary driver's license, and it was only natural that Tonio would take his son for a spin. I was hoping and praying they would not have an accident, which would have meant an astronomical increase in insurance premiums. – Gustl was extremely confrontational, and I hoped to surprise him and let him drive the two of us toward the coast the next day.

Just as I was about to apprise Gustl of my plans, Tonio informed me that Gustl would spend the day alone in the woods, in a teepee, to communicate with nature, I believe, or something to that effect. I warned that it looked like rain, but Tonio put a piece of dry bread and a container with water in a bag for his son, and into the woods they went. When Tonio picked his son up toward evening, he took a bowl of bean soup along. – Gustl was rather withdrawn after that, probably blaming me. I had a feeling it was not his idea of a vacation. I actually felt sorry for the kid. When it was time to take Gustl to the airport, Tonio did not want me to come along. I told him I just needed to get out of the house and insisted on coming along for the ride. I had grown accustomed to sitting in the back when Gustl came. He sat next to his father and enjoyed the privilege of listening to whatever music he chose. There was little communication, though I kept on trying. Gustl hardly said good-bye to me, but at least I got out of the house for a couple of hours.

Tonio spent most of his free time in the evening behind the computer. As soon as his office was functional, he sought refuge in his new cave each night after supper, and worked fiercely on his genealogy. He made it quite clear he did not want to be disturbed, and I tried hard to abide. It became a problem when, late one night, Gustl called from school, wanting me to fax him permission immediately to spend the weekend with another cadet. I told him his father was not at home and did not want me to disturb him at the office. I tried to explain to him that since we did not know the boy or his parents, his father should first talk with them about the invitation. I let him know I was sorry but that there was nothing I could do. He might try calling his father himself, I said, or he would just have to wait. He started screaming at me at the top of his lungs, insisting that I just did not want him to have a good time. He was filled with more hostility and hatred than I had ever seen in him. I was afraid he would awaken everybody on his floor and hung up.

With the exception of our counselor, whom I did not want to take advantage of by calling whenever I felt depressed or lonely, I had no close friends in Princeton. On occasion, a young woman in her early twenties, a graduate of Sarah Lawrence College and a patient of Dr. Alice, visited me. She was going through a divorce with a man from Turkey and had free room and board at the residence of the Johnson & Johnson family in exchange for dog walking. My heart went out to her. In addition to the problems with her husband, her father had recently passed away and her mother had just fallen apart. She squandered her money by filling her house with stray dogs and homeless male teenagers. – Needing to hear human voices, I spent much time watching TV, and was excessively interested in the Simpson trial. And, as I had used soap operas as an escape mechanism when Doc passed away and when writing my dissertation, I started taping the programs during the day and watched them or portions thereof at night, until I fell asleep. I always awakened when I heard the garage door open, but never let on that I was awake when Tonio came to bed.

Three weeks after Tonio opened the office, what I had dreaded occurred. His partner quit before the corporation, which his attorney friend helped him form, was registered. Thus, when the attorney and his wife invited us for a grill dinner at their house to celebrate the new corporation, Tonio was alone. My heart went out to him, and I carefully hinted that I would not mind helping him out at his office, answering the telephone and taking care of other related matters. He said he could handle it by himself.

At about that time, when the dogwood trees and the shrubs and fruit trees around the house and all around Princeton were in full bloom, Tonio, standing in the kitchen, informed me in a rather detached tone of voice that he would leave me as soon as he could afford it. I sat on the couch in the family room. He told me he no longer had feelings for me, could help me neither with my problems nor if I were sick, and could no longer invest in our relationship. In his mind, he had left me a long time before.

I felt numb at first, then hot, and begged him not to leave me, not after all I had done for him and the children. I reminded him of everything I had given up to follow him to Princeton – my job, my house, my name, a great deal of my assets, my pension from Doc, etc. – and that I had devoted my entire inheritance from Mutti to the tuition for Gustl's school. I accused him of having used me to take care of his children just long enough for them to become college aged, of discarding me now that I had outlived my usefulness. I argued that he had promised twice before God to stay with me until death do us part and had promised he would never again go through a divorce. He had assured me repeatedly of his deep love and loyalty and had vowed to take care of me. I broke down crying, saying I had no place to go. Then, in a last desperate attempt to hang on, I promised to do anything he wanted me to – let him smoke in the house, move to some island, go to a reservation, anywhere – and swore I loved him. I had gotten more desperate as I spoke, and I began to lose it when I noticed that Tonio, who never uttered a word, had pushed the button on his portable tape recorder, which he had put on the island counter in the kitchen.

Under the circumstances, I could no longer be without a car and needed my insurance reinstated. I also noticed that my driver's license had expired. Tonio dropped me at the bureau and left to pick me up later. In a state of emotional exhaustion, I took my driver's test and flunked. I had never before flunked a test and was devastated. It turned out that I had not looked at the instruction book carefully and ignored the different laws in New Jersey. I went back a few days later and passed.

Tonio's youngest sister in Florida was to marry for the second time. I asked to come along, but he wanted to go alone. I purchased a gift, secured a frequent-flyer ticket for him, took him to the airport, and picked him up when he returned. It never occurred to me to discourage him from going. – On the way home from the airport, I tried again to reason with him, reminding him of what this would do to the children, but I gathered that his family must have supported his decision. After all, each one of them had been divorced at least once. – I found it strange that his sister thanked me in a note for letting him come to her wedding.

And – life went on . . .

At times, I wished I could be angry and courageous enough to throw Tonio out of the house. I just could not do it. I was utterly confused, and always looked forward to my sessions with Dr. Alice. She was always kind, understanding, and sensitive to the situation and tirelessly tried to lead me to understand and accept what was really going on. She encouraged me to pamper myself. Thus, I tried to relax at night in the Whirlpool. She also helped me realize I should think of myself while I still was able to and that I should look out for myself emotionally and financially.

Tonio discontinued coming to the sessions with me, which made it easier for me to ask the General, Dr. Alice's husband, for advice regarding legal and financial matters. Tonio kept insisting that we procure a property settlement and split our finances, which I had been reluctant to agree to, because it meant a definite step toward a divorce. I was still hoping for a turnaround. – With the help of Dr. Alice, I finally realized there was no chance that Tonio, who was getting more deeply involved with the Indians, would change his mind. He had told me on several occasions that it was not my fault, but that we came from two very different cultures.

It was hard for me to comprehend how the man I fell in love with, and who so often told me he loved that I was "so American," had made a 180-degree turnaround and complained that I was "so German." When we got married, he vowed never to go through a divorce again, promising that he was basically a very loyal man and that he would take care of me. Now, he reminded me that I told him when we got married that if he ever wanted to get out of the marriage, I would let him go. It was true; it was what Doc had told me. Hence, I decided to let him go. I asked him how many more times he would do this to a woman, and he said as many times as was necessary.

I was determined to work toward an amicable dissolution of our marriage. I let him stay in the house, continued to cook dinner, washed his clothes, and took orange juice to his bedside even after he had moved into Gustl's room because he thought it would be best. In turn, Tonio helped to cook occasionally, brought home a carton of my favorite ice cream, and felt free to sunbathe on the deck on weekends. Yet on most weekends, he went on hikes with a couple of his friends from the sweat lodge. – One day, he had thrown his laundry into the washing machine before he left for his office. When it stopped, I set about putting the clothes into the dryer. I heard a clinking sound, looked at the button of the drum, and saw Tonio's wedding ring. It had obviously fallen out of his jeans pocket. When he came home in the evening, I showed him the ring. He took it, said nothing, walked to his den, opened the drawer to his desk – the same drawer where he kept the ring from his first marriage – and tossed it in.

One night, after Tonio had gone to bed right after returning from another long hike, I heard him groaning. I got up and opened the door to his room. He lay in bed coughing up blood. I was concerned, and he seemed glad I was there. I brought him a cup of tea with honey and medicine and stayed at his side until he felt better. I still felt sorry for him, because I had a gut feeling he was not well. – Now and then he asked me why I was so nice to him. Each time, I answered that I loved him.

Gustl had expressed the wish to work in Michigan that summer to be close to his friend, and he wondered if I could talk to the friend's parents. He had visited them a couple of times for the weekend. They agreed, and Gustl was happy there. He knew his father and I were breaking up, but never mentioned it to our friends. About eight weeks into the summer, Tonio came home and asked how I would feel about letting Gustl go to Brazil with his friend instead of spending the rest of the summer with his mother. When he told me he would have to pay for the plane ticket, I found it hard to believe that he would even entertain the thought, considering our financial constraints.

I was looking forward to Liesl's arrival for the summer, although I knew it might be difficult on all of us under the circumstances. Meanwhile, Tonio and I had decided to engage the attorney who handled the purchase of the house to draw up the property-settlement agreement. Tonio let me handle the matter. He had agreed to sign the house over to me in exchange for my agreeing to pay all of our remaining debts. I had told him that since I did not want the divorce, I would not pay for any fees or costs relating thereto. He did not object.

I was all set to go with Tonio to pick up Liesl at the airport in Newark. I had gotten dressed for the occasion and even bought the traditional doughnuts for her. But Tonio wanted to go alone so he could tell her about our breakup on the way home. I was distraught and sad, and went upstairs to go to bed, crying and realizing that as a mere stepmother, even though I had given all I could to be a mother to Liesl, I would have no rights whatever after the breakup.

Liesl came to my bedside when they arrived. I gave her a hug and wished her a good night. The next morning, when I explained to her that I did not want this, she assured me that she knew. – Living together under one roof almost like old times was stressful, and I felt a bit relieved when Tonio decided to go south with Liesl for a three-week vacation, to trace the footsteps of their Native American ancestors and to visit Tonio's mother and family. Still, I asked if I could come along, but it was out of the question. I stayed behind and worked out the settlement with Mike, which was ready to be signed when they returned.

Liesl and I were grocery shopping when I suddenly took so ill with stomach pains that I had to sit down on a bench in the store before I was able to drive home. I went upstairs to rest, and Liesl brought me a glass of water and an aspirin. She kept asking me if I was all right, and wondered why her father, whom we told what happened when we came home, had not once come upstairs to see how I felt. I had forgotten he had informed me that he could no longer help me if and when I got sick. On my birthday, he brought home a cell phone, which he suggested I keep in my car for emergencies. I appreciated the gesture, but considering our tight financial situation, I was glad I could return it without incurring any charges.

I suggested that it would be nice for Liesl to spend a week in New York City to visit her maternal grandmother, the Hatchet Woman, and her recently divorced uncle. But before she left, I took her to Dr. Alice. I thought it might be beneficial to Liesl to meet and talk with her. Dr. Alice explained that the separation, the second the child had experienced, did not mean she and I could not remain very close friends. She gave several examples of similar circumstances in which stepmother and stepdaughter had become best friends after a divorce. I was glad I had taken Liesl. – Tonio drove his daughter to the big city, dropped her off at her grandmother's door, waited in the car until she made contact, and drove away.

VII *1995–2000*

1995–2000

In Search of a New Haven in Bloomington, Indiana, a Music Lovers' Paradise

I had to decide what to do and where to go, because it would be difficult for me both to afford the property in Princeton and to maintain the lifestyle I had grown accustomed to. Years before, I had planned to retire to Bloomington, Indiana, not only because I had friends there, but with the presence of the world-renowned School of Music, it would be a place where I knew I could be content. I remembered the Meadowood Retirement Community, where many professors retired and where I might one day want to go. After discussing it with my old friend Dele, I took her up on her invitation to come and spend a few days visiting and looking at houses.

I was aware that I was an emotional wreck, unable to hold back tears, even when strangers, including a woman on the plane, asked me about my husband. I don't think I ever shed so many tears for such a long time in my entire life. It was a bit comforting to find out, at a support group Dr. Alice took me to one evening, that other women had the same problem, especially one who was left behind with two little children and another whose husband had left her for a younger woman whom she knew.

It was wonderful seeing Dele again after almost four years. Though she was as resolute and vibrant as ever, her physique had been noticeably altered due to severe osteoporosis. She walked with a cane. – I also saw Rita, who had called me a few times in Princeton and organized a Kaffeeklatsch (gossip circle) for old friends. She was suffering from hip problems, and Karla, who never phoned, had also aged noticeably. Ever since I had known her, she was sick with something. This time, she was complaining about pains in her arm. Her shoulders were bent and her skin looked like parchment paper. I tried to ignore that she was not as elated to see me as Dele, who had become her closest friend. I was in agreement with Tonio, who called her a very bitter person, and with those who could not understand what Dele possibly saw in the sinister Karla.

I did not see a house for sale in Bloomington that I really liked, but knew, when I returned to Princeton, that Bloomington would be the place to go. I urged my friend Rita to come for a short visit while I still was in Princeton. When she could not come, I invited Heidi, my former student, with whom I had stayed in touch, and who had never been to Princeton. She did not hesitate, and we had a good time visiting the picturesque towns in the area. We also ventured out to the coast on a sunny Sunday. I was lucky the police did not issue a traffic violation when I failed to stop for a pedestrian who had one foot in the street, intending to walk to the other side.

Tonio, who seemed to be eager for me to get out of Princeton, offered to put an ad in the paper. I told him I needed time and that I felt he was jerking me around, but I decided not long after his offer to go ahead with the ad. Property values were beginning to slide, partly because they planned to open the main road for trucks from a nearby quarry. I wanted to sell the house myself to save the broker's fee and made sure the place looked inviting at all times.

While focusing on the sale of my house, I offered to proofread the manuscript of Tonio's 465-page genealogy, the printing of which he financed by withdrawing almost $20,000 from his pension fund, which I considered another impulsive decision on his part. Instead of printing five hundred copies at once, I would have started with fewer copies and proceeded with more only when I knew the book would sell. It was no longer my concern. – At the end of August, he presented me with "the very first copy, hot off the press," inscribed with his appreciation and thanks.

When Tonio told me he was looking at houses in which he could both establish his office and rent out a room, I knew at once that without my backing him and without collateral, no bank in the world would lend him the money. I found it irresponsible of the realtor, who knew about our situation and who had led me to believe she was a real friend, to even encourage him. When the banks did not come through for Tonio, he was angry, blamed the realtor, was through with her, and rented a small efficiency apartment nearby. He asked his "Indian" friends to help him move.

They, including the dentist and his wife, drove up with a truck and a van, carried out the boxes I had filled with everything I could find of what Tonio had brought into the marriage, disassembled Gustl's bed, Tonio's desk, and the rest of his belongings, and loaded it all onto the truck. I stood by all the while, crying. I then pulled myself together and told one of the sympathetic friends how all of this started and how hard it was. I cautioned him not to do all the heavy work alone but to ask Tonio to come inside and help. The narcissist stood outside, a bright-red cowboy scarf tied across his forehead and taming his long, dark, curly hair. He was chatting, laughing, and spreading photographs of himself all over the hood of the truck. He asked the dentist couple to help him choose a photo with which to promote his business in a news release. As they finished loading, I asked Tonio what he had done to feed his friends. He had not thought about it, and I suggested he order a couple of pizzas. I set the table for them in the breakfast nook. While eating and jesting, Tonio put on a CD with classical music. They teased him about it, and he changed it to a recording of Native American chants. He took off without saying good-bye.

I had agreed to let Tonio come and go, and I let him keep the house key and use the washing machine and dryer as needed. But I got mad when, one day in the forenoon when I was upstairs, I heard Tonio and Gustl walk into the house, talking and throwing laundry into the washing machine. I had no idea Gustl was in town to visit his father and had not spoken to him since the night he screamed at me, for which he never apologized. I had told Tonio I did not want his son ever to enter my house again. Going through a divorce and dealing with a hostile stepson was too much for me to deal with. The two made no attempt to say hello and left with the washer running. I was furious and not about to either transfer the wash into the dryer or put in the next load of dirty laundry, which they had dropped in front of the machine. They had obviously assumed that I, as I had for so many years, would finish the entire load for them and have it ready to go when they returned. How could they be so callous and think I would be so stupid!?

Later, in the afternoon, when I was again upstairs, I heard the two come to pick up the laundry. Tonio expressed surprise that the washer had not been emptied and that the rest of the laundry was still standing there. Still irritated, I called down from the balustrade, told Gustl he was no longer welcome in my house, and retreated to the bedroom. I heard the garage door close, and when I came downstairs, the laundry was gone. – About six weeks later, I received a letter from Gustl, addressed in red. I assumed it was an apology for the screaming event six months or so earlier. I was certain he had written the letter upon his father's request. He once told the children they should always apologize, even if they did not mean it. I did not want to get roped in again and be subjected to more hostility and rejection in the future. I could not and did not have to take it anymore. I put the letter in my desk drawer, where it still is today, unopened. Whenever I think of Gustl, his words "everybody deserves to be hit now and then" flash across my mind.

It was not long after the washer incident that a handsome couple, the first to look at the home, indicated that they were seriously interested. The husband was an attorney, and they took their time to make a serious offer even after I had lowered the asking price. But they ended up purchasing our dream house for a price several thousand dollars less than what we had paid for it. It was the third time I had sold a house and was by then used to taking a loss. It was better to accept an offer than to hold on and pour more money into the place as time went on. Moreover, I was eager to leave and start a new life.

I turned everything over to my attorney and flew once more to Bloomington to undertake a serious house-hunting spree, with the kind assistance of my friend Dele, who very much enjoyed driving around and looking at houses. My friend Rita thought I might really like her friend Loreley's Tudor house, but, with the exception of a large family room and a nice backyard, it was definitely not my style. I hated to disappoint her friend, whose husband hardly uttered a sentence while we were there, but Dele explained that he was always very quiet. When I was on the verge of despair because I had found nothing I really liked, and considered renting a place while I had a house built on a lot of my choice, the realtor showed me a home that had just come on the market and had not yet been advertised or shown. I fell in love with the red-brick ranch-style house, to be advertised as "elegant and charming," and so did my friends. It was built and owned by a contractor who was in the process of developing an upscale subdivision, not quite as stately as Princeton Walk but designed on the same principle. I had looked at a model, and the builder tried hard to persuade me to invest in one of the new homes rather than buying his former residence.

But after some reflection, I did opt for his custom-built house in Sycamore Knolls. It was a combination of the Croft, Southeast Drive, and Primrose Circle. I liked the privacy of its location on a half-acre lot adjacent to a narrow forest, and its one-floor construction would be ideal for my retirement years. I always wanted a red-brick house. The tan cedar siding in the back and on the garage lent it a certain warmth. It sat back on the lot, and three square brick posts with brass-trimmed lanterns that provided an elegant ambiance, especially at night, flanked the stone walk to the front entrance. The house looked like the ideal place in which to entertain, and all of my furniture would find a place; the Knabe and Mutti's oak cabinet could stand in the music room, the SABA hi-fi from Doc in the library, and the tile stove on the screened-in porch, which I envisioned as a future winter garden. The interior of the house was well-lit, and another major selling point was the red-brick see-through fireplace, exactly the kind I had always wanted. Even the cherrywood breakfast nook had a fitting place in front of the big kitchen window. The fact that the place had been newly decorated and landscaped was an added bonus.

Back in Princeton, I told my friends Dr. Alice and the General about it. I made an offer of $5,000 less than the list price on September 30, but the owner refused to come down more than $1,500. And when the General advised me to grab it before it was gone, I accepted; on October 1, we had a deal. My friend Rita kindly offered to monitor the inspection, and everything proceeded smoothly and quickly. I had to turn over the house in Princeton by November 1 and could move into my house in Bloomington on the 4th. –

For the first time in a while, I was happy and optimistic. I had found a place to look forward to. Being by then an expert in the moving department, I quickly negotiated with a company and was able to hire them for $5,000 less than the move to Princeton had cost us. Yet I had at that point donated almost two-thirds of my library to Ryder and Princeton and truckloads of household goods, clothing, knickknacks, and whatever else to the Vietnam Veterans. – I spent many late nights packing boxes, and left only a few valuable antiques to be wrapped by the movers. As Tonio was completely uninterested in any of the children's belongings, telling me to just throw them all away or give them to Goodwill, I began sorting out their drawers and closets and filled boxes and suitcases with their favorite things, hoping Tonio would safeguard them for his children.

It was late in the afternoon, the day before the loading of the moving van was scheduled. I was so exhausted I feared I would collapse. I was waiting for Tonio, who had promised to dismantle all the bookshelves, cover the nail holes in the walls, and help clean the house when it was time for me to move. When he did not come, I got the ladder and started taking down the many glass shelves and brass brackets from the walls myself. – He finally showed up late, but did manage to fill all the nail holes. He returned the next forenoon after the forty-foot van was loaded full and had pulled out of the driveway. Tonio swept and mopped the floors and helped load my car. As we said good-bye, I gave him one of the signed bowls I had inherited from Doc, for which he had asked. It was from Arizona, hand-painted by a Native American. He offered to drive ahead to show me the way toward the Pennsylvania toll road. I told him I was OK. He gave me a kiss and told me that someday I would understand why it had to be this way.

The day before, I felt sad when I bade farewell to my special friends Dr. Alice and the General. Once I decided to drive to Bloomington, the General even provided me with road maps from the AAA. I had to give myself a real push to drive, because I was not certain I would be emotionally strong enough. I was at first tempted to have the car transported by the movers, but when I learned of the cost, I made up my mind that I just had to drive. And as I look back, I am convinced that due to Dr. Alice's tireless encouragement and her assurance that I should be glad to get out of the relationship, coupled with the General's strong support and advice in business matters, I slowly regained the strength and self-confidence I had almost completely lost. I had disliked it intensely when Tonio kept telling me how tough and strong I was. Often, I had just wanted to crawl into a hole and never come out. When I felt his way, I would sit silently for hours, stare out the window, and think back to my happiness with Doc, who became my anchor. And somehow life just went on and something inside, like a flame, though almost extinguished, flickered or surfaced and pushed me into the future the way a river flows toward the ocean.

Once I was headed west on the main highway, I drove fast in the Mercedes, which Tonio had signed over to me because he preferred the Camry, which was newer and bigger. Actually, we did not quarrel about who got what, and the attorney had mentioned that Tonio instructed him to handle the marriage dissolution as smoothly as possible. – I was glad I had the baby Mercedes. It was like going back in time – I had fallen in love with Tonio after I had just acquired my new Mercedes. Thus, I was in a way back where I started.

I began to feel freer and more optimistic as I sped along, reflecting on what had just ended and on what lay ahead. I still mulled over Tonio's words, wondering why he had said on one occasion that he needed the hiatus and would not rule out the possibility of falling in love with me all over again. I believed him when he insisted it had nothing to do with my age and reiterated that it was not my fault. Deep down, I knew that if and when he remarried, it would be to a Native American. I stopped at a motel at the midway point, called my friend Dele, and arrived at her house in Bloomington in the late afternoon on November 2. I felt good – and proud of having driven 740 miles in twelve hours.

The movers unloaded everything on Saturday, November 4, and, with a few minor claims left to settle, I was ready to start unpacking the boxes I had just spent weeks packing. It was the fourth time in eighteen months I had unpacked; I swore this would be the last time I moved. –

The day I moved in, an old friend and colleague, Thomas Ahrens, from my hometown, Hannover, whom I had helped get into the PhD program for German in Bloomington, came over and introduced me to his new wife, who was also pursuing a PhD. Both were working on their dissertations. I was grateful when they pitched in and helped with a few items, and I promised to have them over for dinner as soon as I saw my way clear.

Between unpacking boxes, arranging furniture, and making lists of what was needed to be comfortable, I was flooded with daily phone calls from friends and invitations to luncheons, dinners, Kaffeeklatsches, movies, and lectures at the university or the Meadowood Retirement Community. I hardly had time to think. Of course, there were my other friends in the States and abroad who were pleased about the positive change in my life.

The gods were smiling on me again. Ten days after my arrival, Indiana University celebrated the initiation of the fabulous state-of-the-art Bess Meshulam Simon Music Library and Recital Center. Kurt Masur, whom Tonio and I had heard on New Year's Eve at Lincoln Center in New York City, was guest conductor of the IU Philharmonic Orchestra. They played Wagner's overture to *Tannhäuser* and Mahler's Symphony no. 1. In a gala ceremony at the Musical Arts Center, Masur was awarded an honorary doctorate degree, his fifth. For the first time in years, I felt I was truly a part of our great Indiana University.

I had gone to the concert with Karla, whom I had viewed as the dark cloud on the horizon when I decided to move to Bloomington. However, I had made up my mind to give her a chance after all those years, especially since she was a close friend to Dele and Rita. We had a good time at the concert and the grand reception, where we were tempted by the most delicious pastries and even stood in line to congratulate the great Masur and ask for his autograph. I got the distinct feeling that he did not like autographing programs when he turned to his host and said in German that this was the part he disliked the most. I was glad the many music students did not understand what he said. But there is no denying he is a sensational conductor.

I became aware of how much I had missed music when, on the next day, Karla and I went to a special concert in the brand-new Auer Hall. The eighteen-year-old freshman cellist Mark Kosower played, accompanied by Hie-Yon Choi, a young Korean pianist. The minute he started playing, I sat up straight in my seat and said to myself, "Here plays the second Yo-Yo Ma." As I listened breathlessly, a string snapped. He went to replace it, and then he and his accompanist captivated the audience anew and earned a long standing ovation.

During all these festivities, I ran into several of my former professors. One of the first was Professor Remak, who was as omnipresent as always, though a little bent. Professors Banta and Johnson and Piedmont were ardent music and theater lovers and apt to surface anywhere. All were surprised and happy to greet me, but I detected they felt a bit awkward too. After all, I had returned under less than ideal circumstances; but I could not have come to a better place to reestablish my life. I subscribed promptly to the "Prelude," a leaflet which appears monthly. It lists numerous free recitals and concerts as well as four operas from which to choose each semester. You can hear music of all kinds, including great jazz, from midday to midnight. It's a music lovers' paradise.

One week after I had moved in, Tonio called one evening to make sure I arrived safely and was settling in. He was very friendly and felt quite talkative. He complained about his sweat-lodge friends, who had turned on him ever since Gustl's last visit. He had taken him to a sweat lodge, where Gustl supposedly mixed hashish into the sacred herbs during a ritual and wreaked havoc. It was an act tantamount to sacrilege, and the dentist threatened to sue Tonio. I found the story amusing, and wondered how he could have gotten hold of the drug at a school with such strict antidrug and antismoking rules. Tonio also told me that as of November 11, Gustl, whose grades had dropped badly, was back with his mother. Even though she had agreed to pay the school's fees, she never did, regardless of the many times they warned her and asked Gustl why his mother refused to pay. They finally threw him out and told him not to come back. It seemed just like her. I could not understand how a mother could act so irresponsibly, and thanked God I did not have to deal with Ms. Ice Water anymore.

Tonio also complained extensively about his business as well as everything and everybody else in Princeton, including the police, who seemed to watch him. He had trouble getting his company off the ground, his genealogy was not selling as well as he had hoped, and he had trouble paying the rent and his bills. When I reminded him that I had expressed my concern early on, he called me a "wise woman." He had decided to move to Nashville, Tennessee, where he was sure to fare better, and added that it was only a five-hour drive from Bloomington. I was suddenly afraid that one day he would show up at my door and wondered what he must look like, with his hair now hanging down to his shoulders. I told him I too had my problems, because I had damaged my car when I backed out of my driveway to follow Dele to a restaurant where we wanted to eat together. I had been in a hurry, and scraped the full length of my car along the three-foot-high red-brick wall bordering the west side of my long driveway. I drove so fast that I saw sparks flying.

I felt sorry for Liesl, who wrote that she missed me. Tonio did not want the children to visit him at Christmas, because he had no room or money, and even though she earned a six-figure salary, the mother would not pay for the children to visit their father. But the children did not complain.

On December 1, Heidi came to Bloomington for a visit. She was anxious to see my house and was kind enough to help me hang several paintings. I showed her around Bloomington, and we talked about our forthcoming trip to Cancún, which, much to Dele's regret, meant I would again not be around to celebrate her birthday. – I never met anybody who liked being celebrated more than Dele. It seemed that as soon as her birthday had passed, she thought about her next one. She never let me forget that I did not show up for her eightieth. I made sure to leave a present for her, mainly as a thank-you for hosting me and driving me around while house hunting. I bought her a VCR, which she did not have, and which I knew would come in handy when her grandchildren visited and when she wanted to tape her favorite soap opera while out lunching with her friends.

As a thank-you gesture, I had invited Heidi to come with me to Cancún. I hoped she would at least visit the ruins at Chichén Itzá while we were there. I was disappointed when she showed no interest in the ruins or other sites and that she seemed afraid of the Mexicans. Instead, she basked in the sun every minute it shone. She was almost black when it was time to return. I learned I would have to be careful about choosing travel companions in the future.

Shortly after I returned from Cancún, Tonio called to inform me of his relocation to Nashville, Tennessee, where he had engaged an attorney to file for divorce. Since I knew it would happen, I had no words left to say and no tears left to shed when Tonio told me he had started the process.

As soon as Karla learned about the divorce, she was adamant that I hire an attorney in Bloomington. She was obviously comparing what had taken place in her own divorce to mine. No matter how often I assured her that I had an airtight property-settlement agreement and had gained ample experience with such matters during my seven years as a legal secretary, she would not stop. Just to end the annoyance, I saw an attorney and showed him the agreement, and he confirmed what I already knew; there was nothing wrong with it. His bill was $75.

I did not put up a Christmas tree, but hung a few strands of lights in a tree in front of the house. On Christmas Eve, when Dele was with her children and grandchildren in Washington, D.C., Karla and I attended a candlelight service in a Lutheran church. I had trouble singing because it brought tears to my eyes, just as I had trouble holding back tears when I went Christmas shopping for Liesl and Klemens's son Moritz, who was born exactly nine months after the wedding. The candles reminded me of happier times. Karla, who criticized me for not controlling my feelings, came back with me to my place, where we had German Christmas cookies and chocolates while a fire was burning in the fireplace. I lit the candles in the arrangement the Piedmonts had dropped off at my place.

Christmas Day turned out to be unusually exciting. One of Karla's friends, who had emigrated from Russia years before, invited us for dinner. They owned a very large house deep in the woods. The moment I entered the kitchen, I couldn't believe my eyes. A fat pig of about two hundred pounds lay on the kitchen floor near the back door, snorting. I mused over the pink mass of fat for a minute or so and joined the rest of the twenty or more guests in the dining room. As we sat around the long table, filled with many colorful and tasty dishes, and a turkey bigger than I had ever seen, the pig suddenly pushed through the door, wobbled inside, and flopped down in front of the large fireplace just like a cat or dog. This pet belonged to the sister of the hostess. She and her husband had brought it together with their two children in their car all the way from Ohio. They seemed surprised at the size of the hog themselves. When they acquired it as a pet, they never considered that it might grow so much. I was glad I did not have to share a car seat with the pig on the way home and often wondered if it would eventually be slaughtered.

After dinner, I asked everybody to come and watch me concoct my famous *Krambambuli*. The blue flames licked the rum-drenched sugar cone lying across Mutti's copper bowl. When the last drop had fallen into the hot red wine, everybody held out their cups to be filled and to toast. All got excited, and I promised to pass on my recipe to the host. It felt good to be among a cheerful crowd. I was grateful to be invited to another dinner, hosted by the Piedmonts a couple of days later, when Dele, Rita, and her invalid husband had left for Florida. Karla got sick at the last minute, but wanted to catch up with them right after the new year.

Adjusting to Old and New Friends – A Musical Wunderkind Strikes a Chord – Antonio Lowers the Boom – Marriage-Dissolution Woes

While I was still settling in, Dele had introduced me to her young Korean friend, Hie-Yon Choi, a concert pianist who had studied at the *Musikhochschule* in Berlin, where she met the renowned Hungarian pianist György Sebők, who in turn encouraged her to study in Bloomington. She was the pianist who had accompanied Mark Kosower. I had come down with a very bad cold. Not in the mood to cook a New Year's Eve dinner, I invited Hie-Yon and Karla out to a restaurant, telling them to order anything they liked. Hie-Yon chose something special, but Karla behaved rather strangely. She asked for broccoli soup, and when I was presented with the bill, she insisted on paying for her soup; I felt almost insulted, and Hie-Yon remarked that Karla was a very complicated person.

We went to my place after dinner, and I was elated when Hie-Yon sat down at the piano to play. I was glad I had it tuned just before Christmas. She played so beautifully and sang hymns so movingly that tears came to my eyes. It was the first time I heard my Knabe in my new house. Hie-Yon and I sang a few Christmas songs together, and I thanked her profoundly for playing for us. I could not help but notice that Karla, who was bent over her ever-present needlework counting stitches, neither smiled nor sang nor uttered a single thank-you. We talked about our background in music, and Karla was still disturbed about having earned a C- in music appreciation in Germany. I kept my comments to myself, but sensed immediately that she did not have a musical bone in her bony body. She was still the sourpuss I remembered.

Neither Karla nor Hie-Yon cared to ring in the new year, and they left early. I did not mind waiting for the big moment by myself, because I had followed Dr. Alice's advice and done something to "pamper myself." Tired of squinting at small TV screens, I had bought a state-of-the-art Mitsubishi thirty-five-inch TV. It had found the perfect spot in my library, where I watched New Year's Eve unfold in all its excitement in Times Square.

Before Karla took off for Florida, she got in a few digs. I did not quite understand why. But not long after I had arrived and put forth every effort to blend in with the German clique, she opened old wounds by reminding me of the man she had hooked up with after I had thrown him out and after I had left. She mentioned that he was an alcoholic and that I had written a letter to his wife, which was not true. If so, I never mailed it. She found fault with me for suddenly being "so nice" to my old friend Dele's grandchildren, just because I had sent along a few gifts for them. When she had assured me, previously, that presents do not make friendships, I knew she resented my having given Dele the VCR. Thus, the cloud on the horizon that I had dreaded all along was slowly thickening. Still, I sought to excuse her comments, attributing them to old age. – She also did not approve of my having picked up Hie-Yon very early one morning to take her to a prayer meeting at the Lutheran church. Granted, the roads were slippery and icy, and I had trouble getting into the spirit of the meeting since only five members were present, but it had been my decision and was of no concern to her. Regardless, I did find out at the prayer meeting that such a ritual, that is, openly communicating with God, was definitely not for me. I tried to explain to Hie-Yon, a very devout Christian, who had meant well, that if I were to rejoin a church, it would most likely be the Catholic Church, even though I disagreed with much of its teaching. – I believe Karla was envious of my relationship with the young musicians. It was clear that she was jealous when Hie-Yon invited just Dele and me for a Korean meal at her apartment.

When Karla had taken off for Florida, I felt relieved. I enjoyed looking out the window on my snow-covered woods and was ecstatic when a couple of deer ran across the white grounds and disappeared behind the trees. I talked to my friend Renate, who had moved to Kansas City to be close to her grown children. Anneliese, in Arizona, was happy that she was at least on talking terms with her son Kermit, who unfortunately to this day has not been able to bring himself to visit his mother, now in a home for the elderly. Dr. Alice and the General were always anxious to get a progress report. They were both doing well, the practice was growing, and the General was actively involved in consulting, writing a book, and giving lectures, all at the young age of eighty-seven, and to stay fit, he jogged every day and played tennis twice a week with men who were anywhere from ten to forty years his junior. I was faxing letters to my relatives, Father Heinrich, the Segebrechts, Bettina, and Pieps and Peck in Germany, and it felt good to know they were always interested in hearing the latest. All of them advised me to make a clean break with Tonio and his children. I had already stricken Gustl from my list, but I could not bring myself to desert Liesl.

When the clique returned from Florida, Karla continued with her teaching job in a college about fifty miles away. She worked practically for free. While I was glad to be away from the pressure and deteriorating standard at colleges, she thrived on teaching; and when I listened to her describe her method and the material she covered, I knew she would not have lasted had she taught for me. However, in talking with her, I did gain more insight into how low the standards were at different universities. I doubt any of her seniors even tried to earn a PhD, else I would have heard about it. When the invitations for coffee circles and dinners were forthcoming from old and new friends, I went, even to Karla's house, where I always felt tense and was afraid I would break something when helping with the dishes. Every pot and piece of china had to be handled just so. She did not believe in dishwashers or clothes dryers. She ironed the bedsheets and everything that came from the washer. She was still afraid to stay alone at night, but I never asked her to spend a night at my house as I had during my student years.

Karla talked about the many times she had taken care of Rita's husband – some fifteen years earlier, he had a major stroke in connection with a drinking bout. They had removed part of his brain, including the portion that stored math, German vocabulary, and other intellectual ballast. Rita had convinced everybody that if they read and talked to him every day, his memory would improve. Therapists, as well as Dele and Karla, tried their best, but shook their heads when I asked if it had helped. They did it mostly for Rita, whom, in view of the deplorable way he had treated her before the stroke, they called a "saint" because of her patience. When I finally saw him again after so many years, judging by his handshake, he seemed as strong as a horse. I was among Rita's friends who never liked him. Several had issued strong warnings before she got married, but she thought she could change his habits nonetheless. Curiously enough, he was nicer than when he had all of his brain.

I was hoping they would not ask me to keep him entertained, but, hypocritically, I did offer to help if necessary. Karla had nothing good to say about him and repeatedly emphasized how glad we should be not to have such a rock hanging around our necks. I knew how Dele felt. Whenever his name came up, she said like a robot, "I never understood why Rita married him." In response, I always suggested that she ask Rita herself, but I doubt she ever did. To be honest, I was a bit jealous that Rita still had a husband to care for. She obviously felt it was her duty to care for him. We were raised like that in Germany. With such a big difference in age, it could happen to others, especially me. When I was married to Doc, I would have given anything to take care of him, and I am sure Rita's good friend Loreley, the war bride, would have sacrificed much to have her husband still around. A month or so before they were going to move into their new condo, he lay dead beside her, despite the fact that he was several years younger. She displayed a big photo of her hero on the piano with a bouquet of fresh flowers next to it. I can understand why she loved this man, who against his parents' objections married a German with a child born out of wedlock. She always reminded me of my good friend from boarding school who was shunned by society when she found herself in a similar situation. She should have looked for an American soldier and come to America!

Dele, who lived not far from me, was always looking for a reason to get out of her rather depressing house, and she came over to visit and have supper with me several times a week. I tried out Mutti's standard recipes on her. She praised each and every one and even joined me for a very light drink of Scotch and water. She was from Northern Germany and used to similar dishes. Dele no longer liked to cook, and I never liked driving around at night. I also did not want to get roped into going out for lunch with the same group almost every other day, and it took a while for me to get the message across without offending them. Dele often stayed after dinner to watch a show or a recorded soap opera on my big-screen TV, and joined the group I invited over to watch the twelve-part video from Germany *Väter und Söhne* (Fathers and Sons), the same video my German majors used to practice conversation. Our German senior group always had a good time, except for two who criticized everything, Karla and another German.

Whenever I invited Dele over for dinner, she suggested I ask Karla too, even when I would have preferred not to cook for three. Most of the time, she had not yet returned from school, and I was secretly relieved when she could not make it. She used to call me every night, talking for hours. Almost without exception, she was able to upset me whenever we interacted. I don't remember how many times she questioned my having bought such a big house, a house much bigger than theirs, or why I had to drive such an expensive car, a Mercedes, or why I needed to have a screened-in porch, or whatever else. Yet she did bring over flowers every now and then. Each time, I wished she had not done it. I told Dele and my friend Renate about Karla's repeated attacks, and Renate wondered why Dele never spoke to Karla about it. At times, I felt so bad I almost regretted having moved to Bloomington. – I was glad she did not tag along when Dele and I looked for a leather couch for my library. They say two is company and three is a crowd, and it is often true.

* * *

"Time heals all wounds" is another saying. I certainly had enough experience to know it was generally true. The big question is, How much time? – All those get-togethers with the senior citizens did not simply wipe the slate clean. Time and time again, I burst out in tears or felt depressed, especially after Tonio had called or when friends and acquaintances kept asking if I had heard from Tonio and what I had heard from him, even after I had begged them not to do so. Nobody needed to ask, because unlike others who try to hide their past, even by lying, I have always been quite communicative and truthful when talking about events in my life. I have learned that one way or the other, the truth will eventually emerge. Karla went so far as to mention the name of her therapist, a nun who lived in Indianapolis and whom she had seen or was seeing secretly. I was confident that I could manage on my own, and often substituted the word *sad* for *depressed*, which in my case was more accurate. I never took any medicine for clinical depression, and believe the term is used rather loosely. I also saw nothing wrong with seeing a therapist, provided there was a need for it.

I experienced a whole range of feelings when I held Tonio's "Dissolution of Marriage Agreement" in my hands. I felt numb and sad, but not really angry, as well as a bit stunned and relieved when I noticed that Tonio had actually changed his name by adding that of a wild African beast to it and changed his race to "American Indian." I noticed right away that he signed it on January 24, because the 24th had taken on a special meaning. I kept my promise, went directly to a notary public, signed it on February 14, Valentine's Day, and returned it promptly, pointing out that they had neglected to change my name back to what it was. Dele had come along to the notary, and I invited her to a café downtown for a cup of coffee and a scrumptious piece of cake with whipped cream.

Three days later, I received Tonio's letter together with copies of the 1995 tax return. He thanked me for tending to the agreement in a timely fashion and said the dissolution would be final within sixty days, if I did not contest it. He seemed to feel better. His book was beginning to sell and would soon be available over the Internet. He had picked up a promising client, a *Grand Ole Opry*-style show in Nashville, and had found a good friend, a Cherokee Indian. He was proud that Chief Rattlesnake had appointed him regional chief for Tennessee. Some man named Standing Bear had taken over for him in New York and New Jersey. He also sent a phone number where he could be reached, which I was determined to use only in case of an emergency. I thought it a bit strange that he sent along a photo of himself standing at a lake bordered by a forest. He wore blue jeans; his wavy hair had grown longer. He was smiling and holding a cigarette. Tonio was still a thriving narcissist.

Though I never once encouraged him to do so, Tonio called now and then, late in the evening, usually when he had something disturbing to pass on. Little by little, I learned he had left the few nice pieces of furniture behind in the apartment in Princeton to pay for the rent he owed. He also mentioned that he was glad to get out of the place, especially after the landlady had shared with him the ghastly details of how her husband had hanged himself in the room where Tonio stayed. He also wished he could wipe clean the entire period when Gustl had "slid downhill" again. I was not too surprised when he blurted out that the medicine-man dentist in Princeton had committed suicide, but wondered how things might have turned out for us had he ended his life a few years earlier, thus missing the opportunity to interfere in our marriage. When I inquired whether he had found an American Indian woman, he answered, "Noooo!" – I was always upset when he called and had a hard time going to sleep afterward, but was not quite at the point of telling him to stop calling. In the back of my mind, I sensed that as long as the agreement was not finalized, I might still need to contact him. Once the line of communication was broken off, I would have to go through an attorney, which would be costly. – Even though my pension from the university had started in January, I did not want to squander it on legal fees. Besides, I still had to pay the debts I had assumed.

On February 24, forty-two years after my immigration to America, the phone rang, and what a surprise! The Padre, now eighty-six years old, called me from Germany. It was the first time he had called in all the years I had known him. I was pleased to hear that his health was relatively stable, but felt sorry for him that he had to undergo another laser intervention to boost his deteriorating eyesight. He said he had seen the disaster with Tonio coming and urged me to make a decisive break. I thought to myself how times had changed. In years past, no priest would have advised me to break my marriage vows. It was good to hear from the Padre, because I could never understand why Father George, who had been a constant guest at our home and flown all the way to Venice to marry us, never once called me back when I told him what was happening to Tonio and me. Maybe alcohol was to blame. The same cloud of silence cloaked the rest of our Elkhart friends, who never missed a party. Like most of my friends, especially the Segebrechts and their daughter Bettina, who was studying law and with whom I had reconnected, the Padre wanted me to come to Germany and visit. It was too soon for me. – The Segebrechts even suggested I might want to return to Germany altogether. That was out of the question! I love America and will stay until the day I die.

I was excited when I woke up on March 20 to find my house nearly covered by a blanket of snow, almost three feet deep. The landscape was a winter wonderland. The branches were coated with glittering ice. Several had broken off because the heavy snow weighed them down. Fortunately, most of my trees were spared, but many fruit trees in the neighborhood were destroyed. – Thanks to the snowplow that had barricaded my driveway with a snow wall almost four feet high and too heavy for me to tackle, my car was stuck in the garage for several days. For more than two days, 36,000 people, including me, were without electricity. It was very cold, and I was almost out of wood for the fireplace. Yet I roasted a potato and hot dogs before I crawled under the covers, a wool cap on my head. Just when the last piece of wood was reduced to ashes, a private snow remover came by and plowed me out. I guess I could have followed my neighbor's example. She put all the candles she could locate in her bathroom around the rim of the tub to keep warm, but at that time I had not met any of the neighbors.

I don't know why, but I always had a penchant for nature's frolics. This time was no different. Only two weeks later, at Easter, I had the joy of watching four deer stopping by. They first cleaned out the bird feeder and then attempted to nibble on my daffodils, but ran away when they did not like the taste. They might have eaten the pink and white blossoms on the dogwood trees in my forest had they been able to reach the branches.

I forgot to ask Tonio if dogwood trees and spring flowers were growing on his eighteen-acre tract of land in central Tennessee, which he had purchased with the money he had left in his company savings plan. The land was an old Yuchi Indian site, and was a way station on the original Natchez Trace. But I questioned the wisdom of spending the rest of his savings on a piece of vacant land. It was no longer my business. What did concern me was Liesl. I told him I was disappointed that she had not acknowledged my birthday package. I had put forth a special effort to add something on behalf of her father, because I doubted he would send her a gift and perhaps would even forget to congratulate her. In the past I had made sure he did not forget. Tonio had sent me copies of all his poems, and I had included for Liesl the one he had written for her when she was born. I had also enclosed some of her mementos, which I had safeguarded for her.

I was eager to tell Tonio about the good things that were happening in Bloomington. I had more wildlife than I could remember ever having before, and more importantly, I had just been out to lunch with Hie-Yon. Dele had invited me along to take her out for lunch. When I arrived at Dele's house, she had fallen and injured her nose and was unable to go. She appreciated my offer to take the student on her behalf. As luck, or the good gods, wanted it, at this particular luncheon, Hie-Yon, who had sensed my love for music when she played at my house on New Year's Eve, asked me if I would be interested in hosting Schubertiades at my house starting in the fall semester. As you will recall, I always had a faiblesse for house music, and I told her I would love it. She suggested we combine the concerts with readings of poetry or prose from the period and recommended that I ask a colleague from the German Department to lead the discussions. She promised to take care of the programs and secure the artists. I was ecstatic!

By April 15, I had to file my income-tax return, which was more complicated than usual, but manageable. Compared to what hit me two weeks later, it was child's play. – I received a letter from Tonio that set me back emotionally more than any conversation I had had with him since I left Princeton.

He started by expressing the hope that I was over the flu and feeling better. The next paragraph addressed his correspondence with the IRS, which he enclosed. Our 1993 tax return was being audited, and he had advised the IRS that I would handle the matter since I had been responsible for keeping track of receipts. He advised them that his wife would prefer to appear in person rather than handling the audit by mail. I was in shock, but read on only to find out what I had assumed.

The divorce was finalized on Monday, April 22, and he pointed out that "all went troublefree."

The following paragraph shocked me as well. He announced that on the same day our divorce came through, he and a country singer-songwriter with two albums out were married in a civil ceremony. She was his age and of Creek, Ute, and German ancestry, and they were very happy. They had met in September at a Rutgers conference.

He finished with a plea for "disposable money" to be used to build a small cabin on his land, very "rude and humble, one-room," costing about $6,600. Also, he stated that if I could find it in my heart to buy back the Davisson oil painting I gave him as a wedding gift, the money would be most useful to him at that time.

By that point, I was boiling and felt faint at the same time. Our 1993 tax return was extremely complex, because it was the year Tonio lost his job, worked in Chicago, took many research trips in connection with his genealogy, etc., and he had not kept any records documenting his business miles. He had known about the audit for over a month and not uttered a word about it. I wanted to cry, but could not. – I suddenly realized he must have moved out of the house at the time he met the singer and had deceived me all those months. I knew then why he had moved to Nashville and wanted to build a cabin and why he was always so nice on the phone. I was not about to send him the $2,000 I spent for the painting, and simply ignored the request.

I had a hard time understanding how Tonio, who loved Billie Holiday and the blues but could not stand country music, could marry a country singer. On another level, I was relieved he had someone to take care of him in case he took sick. I had been so afraid that one day he would show up at my door asking for help. He no longer had health insurance, and I gathered from phone conversations that nobody in his family was inclined to help him. I also knew that, once again, he had acted impulsively. I did not envy the woman. – I felt sorry for Liesl, whom he had not told about his marriage plans. When she found out, she not only opposed it but was mad at her father because he had forgotten her birthday.

I was so struck by Tonio's letter that I was unable to tell anybody in Bloomington about it right away, but I sent a copy to Dr. Alice and the General, who were stunned. Instead of calling the IRS, I sat and stared out of the window for days. After I finally pulled myself together, I told my friends, but played the matter down. I had been audited on other occasions and came out ahead. Deep down, I knew it would be a major undertaking to sort through Tonio's receipts all by myself. As soon as the IRS kindly agreed to an extension, I felt better, went to the garage, pushed out my newly purchased Toro lawn mower, turned on the electric switch, and spent an hour mowing my lawn.

I liked being outdoors and took Dele up on her offer to go for rides to nearby Nashville or through Brown County State Park to admire the abundance of redbud and dogwood trees. I equally enjoyed going out to Rita's cozy cottage, located in the middle of a forest and at the edge of a ravine. The forest was full of spring flowers, bluebells in particular, and the dogwood trees were enchanting. I gladly helped her out by keeping her husband company one day when she was at work. Never having spent any time alone with him, and not really knowing how handicapped he was, I took along the big photo album of our Venetian wedding. Judging by his laudatory comments, there was no doubt that he thoroughly enjoyed the pictures, the likes of which he had never seen. There was also no doubt that his mind was not nearly as bad as I had been told, because we talked about the forthcoming elections and in particular about Senator Dole, whom he favored. Lastly, there was no doubt that he suddenly looked at me somewhat deviously and, before I knew it, pinched my right breast. I doubted no longer what I had been reluctant to believe when Rita's friends told me about his womanizing past, but I did not tell Rita about the incident. Most likely, being one of those wives who always look the other way, she would have accused me of dreaming.

About two weeks before the end of the semester, Karla had a mild heart attack and was hospitalized for a few days. I virtually had to force myself to pay her a visit, because I tried to avoid hospitals ever since Doc passed away. I called "the Thistle," the owner of the flower shop who was named for her prickly tongue, to ask her to send a little arrangement to Karla. She asked whether I would mind if she sent it from the two of us. I told her to go ahead and let me know how much I owed her. I was a bit curious, because Dele, each time the Thistle's name came up, added her refrain: "She has good taste, but overcharges." I realized what Dele was talking about when I received a bill for $24 for two dwarf-sized begonias in a small redwood planter, and I wondered who would be naïve enough to pay $48 for something that cost her no more than $5, and was aesthetically boring. I apologized to Karla, who was feeling better, for the measly plants and made up my mind never again to buy flowers at that shop.

Karla's heart attack was the message she needed to stop working. As soon as she decided to capitulate, I notified my friend Thomas Ahrens, tipping him off that there might be at least a part-time job for him. I told him to hurry up and finish his dissertation, on which he had worked for years, and apply. He was offered a half-time position and was happy about it. I never could understand how anybody could spend so much time writing and rewriting a dissertation. His second wife was just as slow, and I have no idea if she ever finished.

Ever since the divorce was finalized, I experienced more frequently than before stomach pains accompanied by acute nausea, similar to the attacks I had had in Princeton, where they were diagnosed as heartburn. I finally went to the doctor, and after I was subjected to every test imaginable, including swallowing a "snake," he located a bunch of small stones in my gall bladder and suggested, though it was not an emergency, that they be removed as soon as possible. He attributed the problem at least partially to the stressful times I had been through, and put me on a fatless diet up to the time of the laparoscopic cholecystectomy, aka the "buttonhole procedure." He guaranteed I would be out of the hospital in one day, which was longer than I had ever spent in such a facility. The operation was scheduled for July 8.

I spent long hours sorting through boxes filled with receipts and recorded Tonio's numerous trips and related expenses in a ledger. On June 18, I went with my boxes to the IRS and spent five harrowing hours with the representative, a masculine-looking female. When I was free to go, I felt I had been through the wringer, but was ever so relieved and waited anxiously for the final report.

I was glad the doctors had not forbidden me to mow my lawn, because one day in June, after my audit, while mowing, I finally got to know a couple of my neighbors. A tall, blue-eyed man waved hello from his riding mower. I waved back, and we both stopped our machines. He introduced himself with a German name, and when I told him I was born, raised, and partially educated in Germany, his face lit up. He invited me right away to come over, meet his wife, and share a bottle of German wine, which he happened to have handy. His wife was an attractive brunette. They were both in their late fifties and rented houses to students. We hit it off right away, and even exchanged a few German phrases. The wife, part German and part Native American, was a designer of knitwear, specializing in American Indian designs for a leading magazine and dying wool with natural colors. She was in the process of writing a book about her hobby and was interested in what I had to say about Tonio's "identity crisis." I asked if they too liked the deer wandering through our backyards and if they had seen the pair of adorable fawns with the white spots playing on my lawn. They warned me not to plant tulips or roses, because the deer would eat them for dessert. I spent almost three hours at their lovely home getting acquainted and admiring the many designer sweaters she had knitted, and promised to reciprocate with a German meal in the not-too-distant future. – It was almost like having found a substitute for my good neighbors of some twenty years in South Bend, the Nurenbergs.

A week before my operation, three days before our Venetian wedding anniversary, Tonio called. He had heard about the forthcoming operation from Liesl and wanted to wish me luck. He never inquired as to what kind of operation it was but asked immediately about the money for the painting. I bombarded him with all the details surrounding the audit, which he treated like a big joke. I told him that until I knew what the back taxes would be, I could not give a dime. He asked for a down payment of $100. When I referred him to his wife, who most certainly would love to support him, he was silent, and then murmured that they were not married. He accused the woman of being a scam artist, claiming the marriage had been a hoax and that the marriage license had never been registered. He called her a drug addict and said she had thrown him out of the house, dumped the few pieces of clothing that he had left into the garbage can, and to top things off, called the police, who threw him off the property. He told me he had no real place to stay, slept here and there, and was urgently in need of money. When I advised him to ask his mother, his very rich sister in Mexico, or his brothers, he insisted on first asking his creditors. Contrary to what he had told me before, his business had not in fact taken off. And he had begun to advertise Indian jewelry on the Internet. At that point, I felt sick, because I knew it would lead to nothing. When he informed me that he had a partner, I suggested he ask him. But when he said that the partner was penniless as well, I ran out of ideas. I enumerated all the expenses I had incurred, such as hospital bills and paying down our mutual debts. He asked me not to tell his children about his situation. He had not yet informed them of what happened. I ended up mailing him the $50 the insurance company had sent to reimburse him for a dental claim and begged him in the letter to stop telling me about his personal and financial problems, because I had trouble taking care of myself. I wanted to live out my life in peace. – One of my friends called him "crazy"; another said the last wife did exactly what I should have done years before. And my friend Bettina thought the Tonio story was so bizarre that she suggested I write a best seller.

Just when I hoped he would be taken care of by someone else, I had to be afraid again that he would show up in Bloomington. Dele warned me not to open the door should he show up and not to give him another dime, or even think of taking him back, under any circumstance. I had to be strong and avoid being manipulated by him again. He knew I had always had a soft spot when it came to being compassionate.

I was invited to spend the Fourth of July with my long-lost friend, former student, now divorcée, and colleague Heide. Her mother was visiting from Germany, and we all met at the little house out in the country where her daughter and son-in-law, both teachers, resided. It was great seeing her again, this time as an accomplished professor at a nearby college. We did not mention it, but I suspected that our mutual former professor, for several years her partner, who on the previous Fourth of July had committed suicide by putting a bullet in his head, was on her mind as much as my own wedding anniversary was on mine. Mother, daughter, and granddaughter had prepared very tasty Fourth of July dishes, and the son-in-law proudly pointed out all the pieces of furniture and improvements he had contributed to their idyllic home. My friend still had a flair for fashion, but was, like her mother and Tonio, still addicted to cigarettes, obviously the reason why her complexion was a pale gray. When I left, all wished me good luck for the operation.

I was all set for the operation a day in advance, when I had to undergo the preparatory stages. They asked me whom to notify in case something went wrong. I felt strange about this, because I was not about to burden anybody, and just told them to call 1-800-GOTT, address: Paradise. When I came home, I mowed the lawn. – At

5:30 the next morning, I was awakened by a grunting noise outside my bedroom window. I looked through the shade, and a huge buck with antlers was grazing about two feet away. I could not have wished for a more cheerful good-luck wish. Dele insisted on accompanying me to the hospital.

The anesthesiologist said good-bye, and about forty-five minutes later, the operation had been concluded very successfully. When I came to, I asked the doctor why he had brought me back into this desolate world. He smiled. Later, I told the nurses that death cannot be all that bad, and that it is actually nice to no longer worry about how to get through the next day and to be able to sleep peacefully and tight. They wondered if I might be kidding, but I was not. –

I had sent word to all of my friends not to visit me, but I finally let Dele come, because she kept insisting. By then, I had learned that the clique thrived on sympathy, which Dele was a master at imparting. It was Karla's as well as Rita's greatest remedy. They liked to provoke sympathy and had a dire need to be pitied.

I was in great spirits in the hospital, and had much fun chatting with the nurses. I had their full attention as well as that of my roommate. They all wanted to hear the Tonio story. The patient in my room, who had come in deadly sick, suddenly perked up while listening to me, and when her husband called, she told him she would call him back as soon as she had listened to the rest of my story. –

Dr. Jesseph was wonderful and charming. I cannot vouch as to whether he is the best at the hospital, but I had no complaints. When he finally came to give me the good news – which I had guessed the day before, when the nurses said they thought I could go home a few hours after the operation – I told him to sit down on my bed and hold my hand so I could thank him properly. He blushed and seemed a little embarrassed. I gave him the *Spiegel* magazine Rita had given me, so he could read the article that explained the buttonhole procedure he had performed on me. He spoke a little German, and I told him the magazine was his to keep.

Rita came to take me home, and the nurses on my floor told me they wished all patients were like me and that I could come back anytime. I was still resting in bed when the doorbell rang and a florist delivered a stunning arrangement of flowers from Dr. Alice and the General.

When the report from the IRS arrived, it turned out that though I had more receipts than needed, Tonio had made a mistake on the tax return. After everything was said and done, and after they audited the return for 1994 on which he had made the same mistake, I ended up paying $2,000 out of pocket, the equivalent of the price of Tonio's oil painting, and also of his share of the amount, which he had promised to pay, but didn't. I just wanted to be done with the matter, and when he called to give me a new address care of a certain "Two White Feathers," he almost got angry with me because I could not help giggling. He said it was impolite to laugh about someone else's name. The white feathers reminded me of the dream catchers Tonio had made for his Indian students in Chicago. They were also on the peace pipe he had given me as a good-bye memento.

Because more and more of my friends and relatives in Germany had acquired fax machines, greetings arrived from all over. Bettina and I engaged in an intensive fax correspondence. Like her mother, who wrote the most informative and colorful letters, Bettina kept me thoroughly informed about her law-school exams and her boyfriend, Constantin, also a law student. I enjoyed Ursel's letters, because she occasionally brought me up to date about events related to the latest developments in contemporary German literature, and about literature prizes awarded to renowned German authors. She also kept me informed about Germany's economy. At that time, the unemployment rate had skyrocketed, as it had in the States. The Segebrechts were hoping their daughter would find a position to her liking once the exams lay behind her.

I was interested in learning more about Bettina's first love, the well-read Constantin, who sounded a bit exotic, and not only because of his Italian birth. When I first learned about him, he had just lost his mother, leaving behind the father, a rather well-educated man, in a physically and mentally dire condition; he was in need of the son's care. To compound the tragedy, with the passing of his wife, who shared with her husband an excessive compassion for dogs, he was left with about fifty canines roaming the halls of their eighteenth-century manor, located on the outskirts of a charming village outside of Regensburg, next to the cemetery where his mother had been laid to rest. No wonder he failed a law exam at that time. – Bettina, always an A student, passed her exams. I was happy to congratulate our new attorney and eager to meet Constantin. I invited both to visit me soon.

For Simone, who had fallen madly in love with Jens, a young man from Hildesheim, the future heir of the Koch luggage stores, 1996 seemed to be an important year. Jens was a sports fanatic with a thirst for expensive wines and travel. I wondered what her grandparents would have said had they known he was without any religion because he did not want to pay church taxes. He sounded like a nice enough guy to me, but I regretted that, unlike Simone, who had graduated from Goettingen, he had not attended a university.

Never in my life had I been to the hospital as frequently as I had since my arrival in Bloomington. Rita called me one morning in the middle of August to inform me, halfway crying, that her husband had tried to kill himself. While she was taking their son, who had visited from the West Coast, to the airport, he had "slit his throat from ear to ear," she said. Fortunately, one of her friends had walked in on him and called an ambulance, which took him to the emergency room. She asked me not to tell anybody, because she was fearful of what people would say about him, and I assured her my lips were sealed. Before the day was over, several of her friends had been eager to tell me what happened. I went with Rita to the hospital in the evening. They let him come out into the corridor from behind locked doors, which was a new experience for me. I was rather surprised when I did not see any sign of a cut, or even a Band-Aid, on his throat. A day later, I asked Rita to show me the knife he used. It was a dinner knife with a very dull blade and round tip, impossible to slit your throat with. I realized it was most likely another attempt to manipulate his wife, or as several friends explained, to punish her for having left him behind when taking their son, with whom he always had a poor relationship, to the airport. Rita insisted she could never again leave him alone, an intention she abandoned very quickly.

I observed that Rita had a tendency to overdramatize situations, and little by little I learned to ignore her complaints as well as Karla's, also a master in seeking pity. Sometimes, I thought one was trying to outscore the other. No sooner was the Lester calamity forgotten than Karla was back in the hospital because she was losing blood, possibly due to cancer. She had enough visitors and sympathizers to give her the boost she hungered for, but it was not cancer.

The Music Starts: Schubertiades

I decided it was high time to get more involved with young people. Having gotten to know Hie-Yon better through the planning of the Schubertiades, I was glad to assist her with a couple of translations of letters for competitions, though she spoke German very well. I also drove her around in search of a used car, and appreciated her introducing me to Eva Mengelkoch, another German pianist. I invited her over for dinner, and we discussed the dissertation she was writing for a doctor of music degree. – Meanwhile, I had also reestablished contact with my good friends the Challifours, who invited me for dinner. Amber, who still looked the same as she did twenty-five years before, was teaching French and German at a private high school in Indianapolis, and John had advanced to full professor of math and physics at IU. Two of their sons, Ryan and Collin, were still in college, and Trevor, who was finished, had just found a bride. Unfortunately, I was unable to accept their invitation to a garden party to celebrate their engagement. I had invited five of the six Schubertiade musicians who were to perform that semester to dinner on my screened-in porch.

The dinner for the musicians was delightful. They were lively, chatting about music, performances, great musicians, and their professors, about Germany, Denmark, Korea, and Taiwan, about forthcoming recitals, competitions, joys, and fears. We had a real love feast. All of them followed Hie-Yon to my Knabe in the music room and gave me and each other a taste of their superb talents, a taste of what to expect in the next few months.

Eva Mengelkoch had been a little reserved, because she was not feeling so well, but she blossomed the next day, when she agreed to play in an impromptu house concert to which I had invited the newly engaged couple and their parents. – I had not seen Trevor since the time his parents stopped by in South Bend with their three boys on the way to a camping trip at Lake Michigan. He had become tall and handsome, had found a good position with a financial institution in Minneapolis, and had a very attractive blond, blue-eyed Swedish bride, Katie, who was in her last year of college. – I had invited them for dessert, and after Eva had played a Schubert sonata so beautifully that we were all entranced, I served cream puffs and coffee as well as a fruit salad with whipped cream. The young pair was elated, and the parents and I were thrilled to be together after so many years, and toasted the two with a glass of French champagne.

Getting ready for the first Schubertiade, which would take place on Friday, September 20, was time-consuming but very exciting. I had found the most fitting invitation for the first event: a black-and-white keyboard across which lay a dark-red rose. The stamps on the envelopes depicted a rose as well. Ferdinand Piedmont helped with the guest list. It included friends, neighbors, renowned pianists, singers, former opera divas, several of my German professors, businessmen from the community, students from the School of Music, others studying German or other disciplines, and friends of friends – in short, music enthusiasts. I had listed the Waldorfs and the von Steins, whom I had met at coffee circles, even though they were not my first choice. I had no idea these couples were on my colleague's blacklist, the Waldorfs because she had not invited him and his wife to a couple of house concerts at her million-dollar mansion and the von Steins because they never greeted them in church. Also, the Thistle had had a bad experience with one of them when von Stein ordered a houseplant, which the husband refused to pay for when it arrived. – Thus, I took them off my guest list, much to Dele's dismay. We mailed out forty invitations and kept our fingers crossed that at least one-third would come. Ferdinand had agreed to act as MC, and the Thistle offered to provide flowers for the buffet table.

In addition to my own party planning, I felt obliged to attend all those birthday get-togethers that I was not really crazy about, but knew they would never forgive me, especially Dele, if I came up with an excuse. I tried my best to fit in and invited the whole clique, including Karla's step-niece and her husband, out to dinner. At the same time, Rita had gone ahead with the purchase of a condo two houses away from her friend Loreley, at the location where I had almost ended up, and I was glad I had found my more secluded place. I was sure the gods had once more looked out for me. Rita, who liked to rally each and every available female friend, with the exception of Loreley, around her, expected us to be ready to pitch in and husband-sit Lester. She roped in my services a couple of times after the pinching incident. He liked to sit on my porch to watch the birds and the wildlife and liked my pot roast so well he had seconds. –

Shortly after they had moved into the big new house, I stopped to drop off a plant, I believe. I had more errands to run for my party and was about to jump back into my car when Rita virtually demanded I take Lester for a walk, imploring me not to let him out of my sight. I did not have the courage to tell her I had no time and agreed just to walk with him around the settlement. The next thing I knew, Lester was sitting in the front passenger seat with the seatbelt tightened. Rita had disappeared into the house, and I decided to take him for a short ride instead.

When I stopped at the gate to the settlement to turn onto the road, Lester unfastened his seatbelt and said he wanted to get out. I told him he could not do that, because his wife had instructed me not to let him walk by himself. He insisted it was all right and opened the door, and when I told him to close it so I could turn and drive him back home, his face got red. He lifted his arm to strike my face; I quickly tilted my head to get out of his reach. I was dumbfounded, unable to stop him from getting out. I pulled my car over to the curb, got out, and asked him to come back into the car.

Lester had sat down on someone's lawn next to the sidewalk, refused to budge, and told me to go on and that he did not need me to walk home. Not knowing what to do, I was afraid I would be blamed if he fell. According to Rita, he had fallen before. And even though he never incurred any major breaks, at least compared to Dele, whose bones were much more brittle, I turned around and drove back to Rita's house to tell her what happened and that I was unable to get him back into the car. When I told her he had tried to hit me, she laughed. In leaving, I let her know she was welcome to that man and that I had had it. I was still upset when I came home and remembered right away the last time Tonio had lashed out at me. It's a behavior one never forgets.

From that day on, I knew Rita was still covering for her husband. I made up my mind that the next time she asked me to take care of poor Lester, I would find an excuse not to. I should not have been surprised when a couple of days later, Rita implied that dear Lester had denied what happened. – Right after the incident took place, I related it to Dele and Karla, who shook their heads in disbelief, because he had never attempted to physically abuse them. They thought his behavior was unacceptable, but would ignore it, as Dele had ignored Lester's insistence years before that he would never again set foot in her house. Well, what can you do with someone who has only two-thirds of a brain? It could happen to me! If I ever felt sorry for the guy, I stopped right then and there, and was secretly hoping he would refuse to ever set foot in my house again. What a circus! How lucky I had been to find a means of transcending such human follies: music.

Hie-Yon's first Schubertiade evening, Friday, September 20, had arrived. Everything was ready. The piano had been freshly tuned, the programs and biographies printed, and the chairs set up so each guest would have a good view of the artist. The house radiated a festive atmosphere inside and out. – The entrance hall extended into the music room with a direct view of the piano. Both rooms were cast in a warm red hue coming from the dark-red, quilt-pattern satin glass lamp, an antique from the Croft. It stood on Doc's favorite English game table in the foyer, together with two golden baroque angels holding candles.

To the right of the piano stood an antique candle table, holding a silver three-tier candleholder with white candles, burning. Across the keyboard lay a dark-red, velvety long-stemmed rose. The music room opened directly into the dining room, where a stunning centerpiece sat on the mahogany dining-room table. Ferdinand's wife had arranged delicate Dendrobium orchids: they draped down from the four horns of plenty of the antique Vaseline glass epergne, illuminated by two burning candles.

The guests were dressed quite elegantly, and I greeted them with an exotic, nonalcoholic fruit punch, which they sipped while getting acquainted in the library, where a cozy fire was burning in the fireplace. – At 8:30 p.m., Ferdinand began with an introduction to the concept of a Schubertiade, spiced by a couple of anecdotes. He followed up by introducing the artist. She had come earlier to rehearse a few movements and mentally prepare herself in my den.

When Hie-Yon walked up to the piano, the audience was instantly captivated by her demeanor and appearance. She wore a full, long skirt of black taffeta with a border of slim white stripes. Her soft white silk blouse had full and long gathered sleeves and a round collar. A fitted black vest with delicate white embroidery accented her fine, swan-white profile. Her thick and long jet-black hair was held together in the back by a big black velvet bow.

Hie-Yon's appearance transported us back into Schubert's time and set the mood for her performance of Franz Schubert's Impromptu, op. 90, no. 3, followed by his Piano Sonata in B-flat Major, D. 960. She was fully engrossed in her music, played brilliantly and with great depth, and touched all of us deeply. The audience rose to their feet and applauded enthusiastically, and when she bowed in front of the piano for a third time, I congratulated her with a big hug, handed her the long-stemmed red rose, and had to hold back tears of joy.

On this memorable evening, the gifted young artist set the stage for other Schubertiades to follow. She was then already well on her way to joining the ranks of great pianists. As I write, she holds a prominent position as professor of music at Seoul National University, South Korea, and continues to enthrall audiences with her concerts worldwide.

When the applause had ceased and the guests stood in line to congratulate the artist, a couple of men poured French champagne into the crystal bowls and flutes, and others helped to carry the food from the kitchen to the dining-room table. I was glad to have kept the antique dishes from the Croft. They looked so festive. Doc's favorite was the big, oblong Limoges fish platter decorated with hand-painted seashells, on which I served thinly sliced smoked-salmon fillets garnished with an arrangement of colorful vegetables. The rest of the foods were spread on gold-rimmed Limoges china platters.

My guests chatted, laughed, snacked, and drank until almost midnight, and a few lingered over a brandy or liquor. Most of the visitors accompanied their good nights with hugs and praises. Hie-Yon, who drank no alcohol, had to leave early because she was departing soon for a concert tour. I thanked her profoundly, and we knew we would stay in touch. I was hoping Father Heinrich, whom I had told about her forthcoming visit to Germany, would be able to arrange an impromptu concert for her in Hannover.

I was grateful that Ferdinand's wife, my friend Amber, and a couple of kind "elves" had stacked the dishes and put away the folding chairs; but as soon as I had taken care of the leftovers, I went to bed, not caring one bit what the place looked like. When I woke up in the morning at 7:00 or so, a peek into the kitchen was enough for me to turn around and crawl back into my cozy bed.

With welcome interruptions from guests who called to express their thanks once more, including Rita, who had come with Lester, I spent the next few days recuperating mentally and physically and putting my house in order; and before I knew it, it was time to start all over again for the next Schubertiade. The time in between was filled with more birthday gossip parties, a concert by Itzhak Perlman, Mozart's *Don Giovanni*, and outstanding recitals at both Auer and Ford Halls in the new Music Library.

Evenings were spent in the Law Library researching the laws related to my claim against the Veterans Administration for reinstatement of the pension I lost when I married Tonio. It seemed I had been fighting with the Veterans Administration all my life. This time, I went at it with a vengeance, claiming that since the law in effect at the time I remarried held that in case of termination of the marriage the pension could be reinstated, the grandfather rule should apply. I pulled out all the stops, documented the developments of my case by going back to Doc's death in 1957, referenced relevant verteran-related laws as well as the pension law in Germany, after discussing the matter with my lawyer friend Bettina, and even found a recent precedent in the *Herald Times*, which reported a case in Alabama in which a Confederate widow's pension had been reinstated after her husband died, whom she had married after her first husband, a veteran, had died. She was widowed at the age of twenty-one with a young son and married the eighty-two-year-old Confederate private W. J. Martin in 1927. Thanks to my legal experience from working for attorney James, I put together a document of seven pages which my good friend the General found to be well argued, and I sent it all the way to Washington, D.C.

I put my legal disputes out of my mind while waiting. I knew full well that the wheels of justice grind slowly. What better remedy is there than music to transcend all earthly woes? And music filled my house with another evening of Schubert, four weeks after Hie-Yon had set the stage. A stunning young mezzo-soprano, Lisa van der Ploeg, captured our hearts and souls in an hour of Schubert's lieder (songs). The songs were arranged by motifs of love, night, and death. Lisa, raised in Denmark, was a student of the renowned soprano Costanza Cuccaro. Her extraordinary talent was evident the moment she began to sing. Her voice was full and warm. She sang with much sensitivity and passion, such as I had not personally heard with such force (or should I say volume) in my home. She could not have chosen a better accompanist than Eva Mengelkoch, Professor Leonard Hokanson's doctoral student, whom I already knew. – I was so moved by Lisa's warm personality and singing that I made a point to be present at the forthcoming Metropolitan Opera Regional Competition at the Musical Arts Center, where I sat all day listening to twenty-eight of the best vocalists in our fine School of Music. They sang nothing but arias from the most familiar operas. I was as elated as her handsome husband Brad when Lisa was chosen as one of the three prizewinners. Subsequently, she was chosen to sing the role of Carmen in the Merola program of the San Francisco Opera. The birth of twin boys appears to have slowed her down, but not enough to stop her from performing in the Western states. She recently received a rave review for her role as Madame Flora in Menotti's *The Medium*, when she made her Cinnabar Theater debut in Petaluma, California. Lisa also sang Amneris in *Aida* and Azucena in *Il Trovatore* ("a spine-tingling performance") as well as witch and mother in *Hänsel and Gretel* with the Intermountain Opera in Montana.

It usually took me a while to calm down after the excitement of the Schubertiades. The guest list was growing, and so was my social life. It was a good feeling to walk into a recital hall and meet many of my guests and the students who had performed at my home. I began to make a point of attending their recitals, not only because I knew I would be in for a treat but also to show my support. And without fail, each and every one of them was happy to see me come, applaud, and congratulate. –

In my effort to become self-sufficient, when I needed kindling for my fireplace I bought a small saw, which I used in my little forest to saw a few branches that had broken off during the ice storms. I realized I was not as strong as I used to be, and noticed a pain in my chest when I climbed the embankment too quickly. The pain felt like the one I had felt when hiking in the Caribbean, but not as severe as the pain I had felt the day I returned with Liesl from the wedding in Germany. That day, we were running through the endless United terminal in Chicago to catch a flight. I was carrying a heavy piece of luggage. Liesl was way ahead of me. The pain in my chest was so bad I thought I would break down. I had to sit down and no longer cared if we missed the plane. – I had learned to ignore the chest pain, which surfaced rarely and only when I exerted myself. – In Bloomington, after getting used to the hospital and having met my health-insurance deductible for the removal of the gall bladder, I decided to mention the pain at my next checkup in December.

The third Schubertiade of the fall semester was scheduled for November 15, before Thanksgiving, and I was very anxious to hear Sabine Simon, who was, like Hie-Yon, a student of the now late György Sebők. She had aroused my attention instantly when I heard her play a movement of a Beethoven piano sonata on the evening the artists tried out my Knabe at the welcome dinner. She played with amazing confidence, sensitivity, and introspection. She touched my soul. I was not surprised that major orchestras in Berlin, Dresden, Leipzig, and other parts of the world had asked her to perform with them in spite of her youth. Besides being an outstanding pianist, Sabine had an entrancing personality. She was humble, gently smiling, and nearly angelic, with an almost transparent complexion and light-blue eyes. Tall and slender, she wore her dark-brown hair artistically gathered in the back. Sabine enthralled audiences when she stepped onto the concert stage. At the November 15 Schubertiade, she bedazzled our audience with four Impromptus, op. 142, by Schubert during the first half of the program. The dashing young Mexican Arturo Nieto-Dorantes, another one of Professor Sebők's international prize–winning wunderkinder, joined her in the second half. The two pianists impressed the audience with Schubert's Fantasy for Piano for Four Hands in F Minor, D. 940, followed by his Introduction and Variations for Piano for Four Hands in B-flat Major, op. 82, no. 2. No doubts remained, judging by the enthusiastic applause and the great praise showered on both, that Sabine and Arturo were well on their way to stardom. We all hoped they would return for more performances and take us along on the way.

I felt like I was in music heaven. Sabine, together with a handsome couple from Zurich, Switzerland – Danielle, a soprano, and her husband Jeffery Byers, a baritone – as well as the charming Mexican pianist Arturo Nieto-Dorantes and the American Linda Lamkin, an accomplished flutist and doctoral student, had accepted my invitation for Thanksgiving dinner. The Byers also brought their two handsome young boys and helped with the cooking. The highlight of the evening took place in the music room, where all four musicians played and sang to their hearts' content. I had just heard Jeffery sing Don Giovanni at the Musical Arts Center. It was like a dream to hear him and his wife sing Mozart in my very own house. When Danielle sang one of the Queen of the Night's arias from *Die Zauberflöte*, I was overwhelmed. The singers greatly benefited from Arturo's knowledge of the opera repertoire. Both his parents were singers at the Mexico City Opera. On this Thanksgiving Day, my musical children brought the roof down.

Before Danielle and Jeffery left that evening, they once more expressed their wish to perform in a Schubertiade sometime soon. I explained that Hie-Yon was responsible for the program and promised to see what I could do. When after several attempts I was unable to reach Hie-Yon, I told the eager singers it might be all right if, after the intermission at the December 6 Schubertiade, we added a couple of Mozart arias and Christmas songs, during which the audience could join in. They were excited, and I did not give it another thought, because the following week two days before the house concert, I had a doctor's appointment to check my heart.

I never expected that anything would be wrong with my heart, but was a bit concerned when the EKG showed an irregularity. The doctor insisted on a follow-up with the cardiologist Dr. Henrich, which was scheduled three days after the concert. The concert kept me very busy, especially since I had to put up a thousand lights in trees and bushes around the house and decorate the interior with scores of candles and Christmas ornaments.

Although we might have thought we had heard the crème de la crème, all of us were in for another climax. Hie-Yon had succeeded in persuading the young cellist and star student of János Starker, our famous cellist and Grammy award winner, to take part – this was none other than Mark Kosower, who had excited me already at the inauguration concert for the Music Library. I was thrilled to learn that others had compared Mark to Yo-Yo Ma. It was incredible that he would play for us here. Hie-Yon and Mark played Schubert's Arpeggione for Cello and Piano, and you can rest assured that the guests were on the edge of their seats and showered the two with their applause and bravos. Though the Introduction and Variations for Flute and Piano, D. 802, and the Schubert lieder arranged for flute and piano by T. Boehm, played by Linda Lamkin and Gloria Lin, were beautiful, it was difficult to surpass Mark's Arpeggione.

In retrospect, I can understand why Hie-Yon was upset with me for having allowed the Byers to sing Mozart and Christmas songs on an evening reserved for Schubert, yet the evening was without doubt an all-around success, and so was the *Krambambuli* I served in the spirit of the Christmas season.

Three days later, at 7:00 a.m., I registered at the hospital. The procedure was more involved than I had anticipated. In keeping with what comes natural to me, I tried to look at it from a comical point of view. As I lay on the examination table waiting for the catheter and stent to be pumped into the artery, I asked the doctor, who was almost as handsome as Tonio, if he could possibly play some Mozart and was surprised when he said, "No problem." I was not sure he was serious when he claimed not to like Mozart because he was too repetitive. He asked if I wanted to watch my heart and the arteries in the monitor, and I turned my head to see. He called the nurse to show her my "strong heart," but soon came to a spot that hurt so badly I alerted him. When he was about to finish poking around my arteries, I asked him if the machine in the back of the room was printing out my bill simultaneously. He said, "You are right." Judging by the long list of items charged, he was not kidding.

Back in his office, he drew a picture of my arteries and pointed out that the major one exhibited 50% blockage, which was not fatal, but something to be watched. The rest of the arteries were clear. He told me to lose a few pounds, which I considered odd because I did not think I was that heavy. But I made up my mind to follow his orders. I also thought that if it took sixty-five years for one artery to clog up by half, I had many more years until it reached the 100% mark. I also realized that all those dinners and coffee parties, not to mention the buffets, were major contributing factors. I certainly did not want to look like a fat matron.

However, it was too late to cancel the big coffee party, which I had vowed to give in honor of Dele's birthday at least once during my and her lifetime. I had told her to invite whomever she wished; and on December 12, though I was still pretty shaky, twelve senior female guests, some of whom were curious to inspect my house, sat around the tastefully decorated dining-room table, eager to taste the cakes I had personally managed to bake without burning something. Dele had included Mrs. Waldorf, Mrs. von Stein, and the Thistle. Von Stein never showed. Even though she had been pressuring me to show her my house, she had forgotten. The Thistle got busy in her shop, but I think she did not show for the reasons I cited above. Dele's friend Dicke was right: the Waldorf woman held her skirt together with a safety pin, because buttonhole and button were too far apart. She was always on a diet, but the longer she talked about it, the more her stomach and buttocks inflated. She got so red in the face when she spoke that I thought she might keel over any minute. She was one of those women who are all fake, saying things with much conviction but not meaning them. I did not invite her or Mrs. von Stein back.

Dele was mighty grateful for the event and never again complained that I had missed her eightieth-birthday celebration. It was the first and last birthday party I ever hosted at my home. Just imagine if, in addition to the monthly house concerts and other holiday events, I felt obliged to throw numerous birthday parties, which I didn't like anyhow. I would not have had time to do anything else, and worse, would have quickly regained not only the twelve pounds I managed to lose but also the chest pain.

Changes in Lifestyle and Friendships – Visiting Family and Friends in Germany

I started watching my diet seriously the day I landed in Cancún, two days after the birthday party. The week on the beach was lovely, and I was glad I had come by myself. I had not realized it, but the heart exam had rendered me rather weak. I tired easily and decided to take it easy. I enjoyed not having anybody around who would complain, boss me around, or need to be accommodated. I could not help but think back to the times when I had come to the Royal Sunset with Antonio, and at times I was overcome with sadness. However, the emerald waters have a magic that cheers me up and splashes away gloomy memories. – I met another German woman at the hotel. She was from Saskatchewan, Canada, and she became a clinging vine. She got on my nerves, speaking to me in German so faulty I started correcting her in the hope that she would disappear. It was useless; she always popped up out of nowhere, and even tracked me down when I had sought shelter at a shady spot behind a huge rock on the beach. –

I walked for hours in the hotel zone, exploring the magnificent hotels. They are like palaces; each one is more luxurious than the next. Their lobbies boast exotic gardens with tropical flora as well as palms and banana trees intermingled with hibiscus, oleander, and fountains. I always found a secluded spot in which to relax with some papaya or pineapple juice or a piña colada before I continued my hotel odyssey. I carried my Spanish–English dictionary and practiced Spanish with the bellboys, maids, and merchants. The Russian pianist was again at the glitzy Coracal Plaza, and I listened to him play. I told him about my Schubertiades, and he was most envious, because he had heard much about our School of Music. He himself was hoping to save enough money to study piano in Paris.

The week in Cancún went by fast, and I was happy to return home. It was snowing, and I got out my fake Christmas tree, knowing full well the Germans would raise their eyebrows, especially Dele, the Thistle, and her husband, who also did not like my kitchen drapes; but I did not care. – I had sent a big Christmas package to Liesl and was glad she liked all the goodies. She had decided not to visit her father, who lived in the one-room cabin he had built with the help of a few Indians in Tennessee. When Tonio told me how desolate the place was and how he was struggling to make ends meet, I felt sorry for him. He had invited Liesl to visit, hoping against hope that the mother would pay for the flight, but Liesl had already committed herself to go cross-country skiing in Oregon with her family. I was hoping she would visit me in the summer after I returned from Germany.

The day after Christmas, Karla called in the morning to ask if she could stop by sometime in the forenoon and drop off a Christmas gift for me. I really did not want anything, but to be polite and to avoid feeling guilty, I too had picked up a little gift for her, and I told her to come on over. I waited for about an hour. She did not show, but called to ask if she could come a bit later. She wanted to lie down and rest first. Since we had not planned to meet for lunch or such, it did not matter when she came. Shortly after she had hung up, I received a call from my next-door neighbor, a petite widow with a Polish name, the spelling of which I keep forgetting, whose husband died of a mysterious disease and who was a neat freak, like Karla. She wanted to show me a few of her latest rubber stamps, of which she owned over three hundred. She made pretty cards for all occasions. It's a solution, if you do not know how to draw. They were cute but a bit tacky. I told her I was waiting for my friend Karla, whereupon she suggested I leave a note at the entrance door telling her where I was. She had a cup of tea and cookies waiting. I tried to call Karla to see if she had left, but the phone was busy. – While admiring the latest rubber-stamp creations, watching the widow spend more time cleaning the stamps than creating cards, and eating a couple of cookies, I was also on the lookout for Karla. I did not see her, nor did she come to pick me up. I called her from my neighbor's place, and when there was no answer, I went home, the note still on the door. – I called Karla again to ask why she did not come. When she recognized my voice, she started screaming at me furiously, accusing me of causing her to fall in front of my house because I was not there when she arrived. She claimed to have broken a rib and to have gone to the emergency room to have herself X-rayed – and that she had pain so excruciating she could not stand it. She couldn't talk to me any longer and had to lie down. She hung up before I could say anything. I called Rita to see what she knew about the fall, and the instant she heard my voice, she yelled, "Yes, it is all your fault!" – I knew Karla had planned to invite Dele and her sons, who were in town, out to dinner, and I was sorry she was obviously not well enough to go through with the invitation. But Rita explained that the X-rays were all right and Karla was on the way to meet her guests at the restaurant. At that point, I was furious and deeply hurt. I found it hard to believe that a friend would lie so blatantly in an attempt to make me feel guilty. What hurt even more was that both Rita and Dele believed her and never bothered to call me.

The clique was leaving for Florida in a few days, and I made a point of stopping by at Dele's house to set the record straight. I told her that if she happened to talk to Karla, she should tell her I had no desire to speak to her. – Right after they arrived in Florida, Karla suffered her second heart attack and immediately blamed me for causing it. At that point, I thought she had lost her marbles. Rita called me in tears, imploring me to send Karla, who had had such a hard youth, a get-well card. I thought about it for a few days, and despite the fact that I knew the hard-luck story about her youth was ridiculous, because she had always bragged that her youth was so much better than mine, I sent her a postcard with the portrait of a saint, and composed a wish to the effect that she should find the same inner strength. – She chartered a plane to fly her to the hospital in Bloomington.

I made it clear to all that Karla was thenceforth no longer welcome in my home and that in the future I would not accept invitations to any event to which she was invited. I thanked my guardian angel for giving me the perfect excuse not to ever again have to tolerate Ms. Sourpuss, who was a dissonant presence also at the Schubertiades. My friends kept insisting that Karla was just very jealous of me. Nobody dared to argue when I explained that after what I had been through the last two years, I was well-advised to keep my distance from harmful influences, including green-eyed monsters. – Inherent in that break was a crack in my friendship with Dele and Rita, who had unduly pressured me. I fully understood that they would not desert their longtime friend, if for no other reason than out of gratitude for her having spent hours tutoring Lester or for her having showered them, as she did her doctors, with flowers and embroidered doilies. I did not expect or even desire it. In fact, I hoped to remain friendly toward the two, but no longer felt obligated to either one of them in any way.

1995–2000

To celebrate the hiatus, I decided on the spur of the moment to invite some of my good neighbors, including the Challifours and the Beyerles, to come over and ring in the new year with me. We had a great party with noisemakers and glittering hats, good food and champagne. It peaked when Jeff and Danielle sang the Papageno-and-Papagena duet from Mozart's *Magic Flute*. The only one who complained about not having been invited was Dele.

A bad icestorm ushered in the month of January, but I did not let it stop me from talking to various contractors, seeking bids to transform my four-hundred-square-foot screened-in porch into a winter garden. Also, I was anxious to have my tile wood-burning stove hooked up and ready in time for the fall weather. The year – 1997 – marked Schubert's two hundredth birthday, and I tried hard to find commemorative coins to give to the artists as a thank-you gesture after their performance. But since the price of gold coins was out of my reach, I hoped I would find something on my forthcoming and long-overdue trip to Germany. My friends wanted to see me and vice versa. Thanks to frequent-flyer miles, I secured a free flight.

Linda Lampkin, the doctoral candidate and flutist from Colorado, had graciously volunteered to organize the three programs for the spring semester. As promised, on January 31, Jeff and Danielle, accompanied by Arturo, captivated the audience with an all-Mozart repertoire – one can never hear enough Mozart – and we called this particular concert series "Mozartiades." I was particularly moved when Jeff Beyerle sang "Das Veilchen." It took me back to the time when my music teacher Marianne introduced that lovely song in class. Not much later, I sang it, accompanied by either my father or my "first love," Hans.

As we had hoped, Mark Kosower, who had really enjoyed the first time he played, made another appearance. He brought along his sister Paula, who had studied with János Starker before Mark arrived. She was the principal cellist of the IU Symphony Orchestra, and she played brilliantly. Thus, we definitely had two top cellists performing on February 28. Arturo accompanied Mark in the Adagio from Mozart's Clarinet Concerto in A Major, the Sonata for Two Celli in B-flat Major, and the Rondo from the *Haffner* Serenade in D Major, transcribed for cello and piano. After the intermission, Arturo amazed us with two sparkling Mozart piano sonatas, the first in B-flat major and the second in A major.

A week before I took off for Germany, on April 4, 1997, I hosted the third house concert of the season, which emphasized Mozart and Schumann. We were grateful to Arturo for filling in at the last minute for Leela Breithaupt, a highly accomplished flutist, who had received a last-minute call to play with the Indianapolis Symphony. Arturo never disappointed us at the piano – and we were fully satisfied when Lisa and Eva touched our hearts with Schumann's song cycle *Frauenliebe und -leben*.

Getting ready for the homeland is not as easy as you might think, especially if you are making the rounds. I spent forever looking for appropriate gifts, and ended up filling an entire suitcase with toys, blue jeans, books, and souvenirs from Mexico. My new neighbors had kindly promised to look after my house, the flowers, and the deer. I could not have wished for better neighbors. The landlord couple had walked over for dinner or a glass of wine when we were snowed in. I admired the wife, who had taken a little girl from an underprivileged household under her wing as a "big sister." My next-door neighbors, the Overlys, were as nice as could be. They had recently returned from a two-year stay in Malaysia, where Norm had been in charge of closing down the IU program just before the commencement of his retirement, which, curiously enough, coincided with my own. We got along superbly, and I was amazed to discover that he and his wife Jeanne had been missionaries in Hiroshima, Japan, years before. I respected them for actually having done something that once upon a time the Padre had talked me out of. I too had signed up to join a mission to help the victims of the atom bomb in Hiroshima, and ended up in America instead. – I also looked up to them for their outstanding contributions to the community. The Overlys stood ready to help the underprivileged, victims of AIDS, and the sick and elderly, to deliver Meals on Wheels, to donate their time at the local Middle Way House, or to help build houses and cook meals for Habitat for Humanity. They organized fundraisers for their church, where Norm sang in the choir and delivered sermons when the minister was out of town. My neighbors were true Good Samaritans, pillars in the academic and local community, always lending a helping hand to their aging friends and always there for their four children, two of whom were adopted African-Americans. Norm, former president of the World Council for Curriculum and Instruction, never failed to be among the friends who gathered when the time came to pour champagne at the Schubertiades. I guarantee that unlike another husband of a friend, he never pulled a disappearing act and left his wife wondering where he might be.

On April 19, my plane landed in Hannover on time, and Father Heinrich waved at me through the glass wall at customs. It was a cheerful hello. He introduced me right away to Herbert Jansen, a friend from his parish and a retired director of a vocational school, recently widowed. We chatted all the way to Father Heinrich's residence, where his housekeeper, Sister Johanna, greeted me warmly. She had set the table, which was ready for us, including Mr. Jansen, to enjoy her fabulous cuisine. Mr. Jansen was invited again for supper and stayed late watching TV and drinking too many bottles from Father Heinrich's wine cellar. I watched my intake of alcohol, because I was ready to retire sooner than the gentlemen wanted me to. Father Heinrich kept hinting that his friend had taken an instant liking to me, and did his best to encourage me to strike up a serious friendship with the gent and, if marriage was out of the question, to consider him as a future travel companion. I was careful what I joked about, but did accept a luncheon invitation from the jovial, silver-haired suitor, who was about my size, for my favorite dish, herring. I also agreed to join him for dinner after Sunday Mass at one of Hannover's choice restaurants, because Father Heinrich and Sister Johanna were included.

This cavalier also accompanied me on a rainy morning to the Hochschule für Musik und Theater and introduced me to the president of the school, Dr. Becker, a devout Catholic, member and organist of Father Heinrich's parish. When he picked me up an hour later, I could report that I had had a most promising conversation with the president and his assistant, Professor Richardson, an American mezzo-soprano and former Merola prizewinner. Their idea of having my wunderkinder perform at the forthcoming Expo 2000 in Hannover was brilliant. Who would have guessed that forty years after I had so fervently wished my father would enroll me in this school, I might have a chance to strike up an alliance with them and further my young musical friends' careers?

My cousin's oldest son, Klemens, came to pick me up in Hannover to spend a couple of days with my relatives, in particular to see their little son Moritz for the first time. He was the spitting image of his grandfather, very blond and blue eyed. Everybody was most kind and hospitable and fed me well with the traditional pork, beef, and venison roasts, soups, rich baked cakes, and mountains of whipped and ice cream. I had to watch my intake to avoid clogging up my artery again. – I fell into bed in the bedroom in their huge built-out basement, which had windows and a bathroom across the corridor. Down there I felt very safe, although the atmosphere was rather sinister and reminded me of bunkers. The house was built with walls so thick it would stand for centuries. Next to my bedstand were tabloid magazines galore, and although I never would have thought of spending a penny for a single one of them, I got caught up on all the sex scandals, murders, sinful liaisons, divorces, etc. of Hollywood's and Europe's movie stars, as well as on the world's royal families.

I had been looking forward to meeting the gorgeous redhead Simone again, and it felt good to hug her at the train station and to see her tastefully decorated apartment in Bremen, where she had found a good job with Succhard. She showered me with chocolate, and I treated her to dinner in a quaint and cozy wine restaurant. We had so much to talk about that we had not finished when it was time to go to bed. Simone was head over heels in love with her friend Jens, and was forever listening for the phone to ring.

I looked around the neighborhood in Bremen while she was at work, and even when she was ready to drive back to Giesen with me in the early afternoon that Saturday, I felt there had not been enough time to talk.

The minute we arrived at her parents' home, Simone's focus was on her boyfriend, and before I knew it she was off to Hildesheim to spend the night with loverboy. – Meanwhile, her mother and I had time to catch up, and it did not take long for me to deduce that the mother was not at all pleased about this Jens. She would have preferred a former boyfriend, and was hoping that one of these days Simone would somehow realize she deserved better.

Lisa, with her dog Hanna in the front seat, drove me around the village. She pointed out the dozen or more modest apartment houses her family had built, and made sure I would remember which house would go to which of the three children once the parents were dead. On Sunday, Simone appeared early to bake two wonderful cakes, because Jens was invited to join us so I could get to know him. He was rather nice and would have been handsome were it not for a few crooked teeth. He was fairly bright and spoke English well, because he had spent some time in California. Lisa and I kept looking at each other, because the lovers seemed glued together not only at the hips but at their lips. I thought it was tasteless and impolite behavior and never would have expected it from Simone, who also went to school with the Ursulines.

I was offended when their big, bad-smelling dog crawled next to me at the coffee table, angling for a piece of fruit tart, and I understood why Jens pushed the boisterous canine under the table several times. He was careful that nobody watched him, as the women and Frank, I am sure, would have pitied the dog and disliked the boyfriend more than they already did had they witnessed his behavior. When I asked Frank how often their pet was washed with soap and water, he looked at me as though I were crazy and said, "Never." No wonder, I thought, that a flea had bitten me one night. I was a good girl, though, and my lips remained sealed.

My lips also remained sealed when, one evening, my cousin returned from his deer watch in a nearby forest with a dead deer in his trunk. He hung it in the garage, dressed and skinned it, and was exalted because he had not shot one in months. He handed his wife a stainless-steel bowl containing a bloody mess of heart and liver, and asked her to fry it for him, the victorious hunter, right away. I left the kitchen, thinking about my precious deer feeding near my house, and the thought of eating the deer's heart and liver was repulsive. I was glad I was spared that particular meal. I enjoyed it more when my cousin took us to the old hangout Zur scharfen Ecke (At the Sharp Corner), where we sat around thick wooden tables in a quaint atmosphere and could order anything we wanted. My cousin, used to drinking beer on weekends until he could not stand up straight, was true to his reputation, and I was glad he asked Lisa to drive us home when the time was ripe. – It was close to Hitler's birthday, and from listening to some of my cousin's old-timer friends, I was afraid they would start singing songs from the Third Reich. Rumor had it that some old timers were still in the habit of secretly celebrating the Führer's birthday. I was careful to steer clear of that topic, remembering full well the disputes I had had with my father, but I was also secretly saddened, because I sensed that this environment was not for me, relatives or not.

I had not been in Cologne and at Bayer since 1993. Peck greeted me at the train station. He had not changed at all. The four days with Pieps and her husband were sheer fun. Their tiny yet elegantly furnished Bayer apartment looked as inviting as it did the last time I was there with Tonio. The Kasino hotel and its wine-cellar restaurant had maintained its old charm and superb cuisine. They gave me the red-carpet treatment, wined and dined me in the area's choice restaurants, introduced me to a new exhibit at the Konrad Adenauer Foundation, and on a Saturday morning insisted on taking me to Düsseldorf, where, for the first time, I got an introduction to the capital of Nordrhein Westfalen, in the smokestack heart of Germany's industrial Ruhr region.

The weather was perfect as we strolled along the broad Königsallee (King's Boulevard), where parks abound. It is easy to understand why this city, where you see women parading up and down the "Kö" in their most recent designer clothes, is compared to Paris and is home to many who belong to the fashion industry's who's who. I was overwhelmed by the opulence evident not only in the shops in the Kö Gallerie and Kö Center, but wherever you looked. The antique stores were filled with rare pieces, be they furniture, silver, china, or other treasures from around the world, and the fur shops and fashion houses displayed their top designs. My friends invited me to a unique restaurant on a side street, where I ordered a gourmet pizza and a glass of Cabernet before we returned to Cologne. The next morning we attended a High Mass, with all the pomp and circumstance, in the Cologne Cathedral.

My friends had also been kind enough to arrange a meeting for me with the Padre and offered to drive me to Bonn to see him. – He took me into his arms the minute he entered the room and was visibly moved, as was I. When we were alone, he did not waste a minute before questioning me about what happened with Tonio. He asked for a step-by-step account. His hearing had noticeably deteriorated, which may have accounted for his extremely loud voice. When he asked me point blank if I had truly loved Tonio, I felt strange and assured the Padre I would never have married him had it been otherwise. Suddenly, I just wanted to leave. I felt as though I were before an inquisition. I got up and said my friends were waiting to take me back. It was the last time I saw or spoke with the Padre. As I think back, I don't know what provoked him to treat me in such a way. I suspect he was troubled by the fact that I had not come alone. Thenceforth, I kept my distance. May he rest in peace.

To see the Segebrechts in my much-loved Bavarian town Bamberg was as exhilarating as always. We talked late into the night. Bettina came home on a Friday just in time for Ursel's supreme pizza. For Saturday, Ursel had planned a family pilgrimage. Her younger sister Mausi arrived with her family in two cars, one of which was a brand-new Mercedes cabriolet, which Bettina and her cousin got to drive. Thus, a caravan of three cars took off for a lovely drive through the scenic countryside to visit the Franciscan monastery with its rococo basilica, the pilgrimage church Vierzehnheiligen (Fourteen Auxiliary Saints), built between 1743 and 1772 by the famed architect of the late baroque and rococo style, Johann Balthasar Neumann. I had never seen it before and felt uplifted as soon as I sighted the undulating facade flanked by bell towers with onion domes and steeples, looking down on the valley, with its meadows and forests along the Main River. The style of the basilica's interior was rococo, and one could spend hours studying the elaborate frescoes, gilded carvings, all fourteen sculpted saints, and the powerful organ and altars, as well as the baptismal font that adorned the interior.

I was delighted when, on Sunday, Ursel announced we were invited to stop in and say hello to the Leupolds, Ursel's younger sister Hansi, and her husband, when visiting Rothenburg, Ursel's place of birth. I had been in Rothenburg years before, when her mother was still alive. On the way, we said hello to her eighty-seven-year-old Aunt Sophie, who looked very fit, and stopped at the gravesite of Ursel's parents. The Leupolds were most hospitable, and led us right away to their elegantly furnished dining room, where a delicious strawberry cake was waiting for us in the center of a round table. The Leupolds, both employed by the regional school system, had traveled much. Hansi was also a gifted painter of aquarelles, but I was particularly intrigued by their very striking home. They had completely remodeled an old half-timbered house by adding modern touches in such an artistic way that the medieval flair was preserved and highlighted by glass panels and recessed lighting. In the foyer, floodlights illuminated tall houseplants and a fountain, thus giving light and life to an otherwise dark corner. I had never seen anything like it. Most of all, a certain glow pervaded the home throughout, and it occupied my mind as we drove back to Bamberg, where my friends had to get ready for the next day. –

Ursel, who held a PhD in German, had a heavy load, teaching seniors French and German at the Kaiser Heinrich Gymnasium, where Bettina made her *Abitur*. Wulf wanted to put a few finishing touches on a university lecture about ballad poetry, which I looked forward to attending. It never failed: the moment Professor Segebrecht stepped behind the lectern, the students stopped talking, and from beginning to end, their professor had them and all who listened under his spell.

As coincidence would have it, the same day I attended Wulf's lecture, I went to a meeting of the E. T. A. Hoffmann Society. When the members gathered later for a glass of wine, it felt like it did years before, when Hans Guenther, Wulf Segebrecht, and I used to congregate and sip wine until the wee hours. – Wulf, as was to be expected, was by then celebrated as one of the most eminent German literary critics. And it came as no surprise when he was given, just recently, the prestigious Frankfurter Anthologie Gedichte und Interpretationen (Frankfurter Anthology Poetry and Interpretations) prize by the highly acclaimed Polish-born German literary critic Marcel Reich-Ranicki.

I had some free time to roam around Bamberg to look for tokens to bring back for my Schubertiade performers. Also, in my constant drive to help promote my wunderkinder, I explored the area along the Regnitz River where the Bamberger

Symphoniker had five years earlier erected their state-of-the-art concert hall, the Sinfonie an der Regnitz. I was lucky to find the new director, Francis Hunter, in his office, and was grateful when he granted me an audience right on the spot. We talked for more than thirty minutes about our music school, about János Starker, who had a CD out with the Bamberger Symphoniker, and about Mark Kosower, Lisa van der Ploeg, Sabine Simon, and Hie-Yon Choi, all in an effort to interest Mr. Hunter enough to bring one or all of them to perform with his symphony in the future. He seemed interested, and I promised to forward a sampling of their recordings.

Before I left, Mr. Hunter took me on a tour of the house. As soon as I had bid the director good-bye, I heard the sound of music in the distance, and went in that direction. David Stahl, music director of the Charleston Symphony Orchestra, was in rehearsal with the Bamberger Symphony, which he was scheduled to guest conduct. I climbed up on the stage to introduce myself during intermission, and could not wait to tell my friends about my venture. – I could not have hoped for a more fitting send-off from the town where E. T. A. Hoffmann himself had been music director and had been inspired to generate his best creations. – In Bamberg, I also came up with the idea of presenting my wunderkinder back home with a bust of Schubert to commemorate their contributions to our Schubertiades, and before I continued my blitz-tour, I packed a dozen little Schuberts into my suitcase.

Bettina had been anxious for me to visit her in Regensburg, and she took me along in her car. The time was all too short, because I had to return by train the same day, leaving at about 11:00 p.m. But we did squeeze in enough for me to get an idea of what life in that picturesque town was like. Here, Bettina had spent several years studying law at the university, and she was still busy with exams in addition to her part-time position with a law firm. She was proud of her lofted efficiency apartment with a balcony overlooking a park near the Danube, and would have liked to acquire a little rabbit similar to the one she had for years as a child, but Constantin kept persuading her otherwise. She was so happy to see me, and I was moved to see her sit opposite me, tears streaming down her cheeks, tears of joy. Bettina had also arranged a brief meeting on the grounds of the university to introduce me to her best friend, Christiane, who was specializing in law dealing with child abuse.

I easily understood why Bettina had fallen in love with this well-preserved Romanesque and Gothic city, known as the "medieval wonder of Germany," and why she dreamed of owning an apartment someday in a refurbished patrician house. We walked through the narrow cobblestone streets past architectural marvels, churches, and other historical monuments, and paused to admire the pure German Gothicism of Regensburg Cathedral, dedicated to St. Peter, the construction of which began in the late thirteenth century and was completed in 1634. It was where the famous Regensburger Domspatzen (Sparrows of Regensburg) had their start. We climbed the steps to the fourteenth-century Town Hall and walked in awe through the extensive hall occupied by the first German parliament, the seat of the everlasting Imperial Diet from the seventeenth to the nineteenth century. – When in Regensburg, it is a must to taste the special hot dogs served at the oldest hot-dog stand, Wurstküche, along the Danube River. We sat at a table next to the river and the Roman-built Stone Bridge, Germany's oldest, constructed between 1135 and 1146. The sausages were just as mouthwatering as expected.

We had to hurry, because the handsome and very charming Constantin, Bettina's boyfriend, expected us at the Schloss of the Princes of Thurn and Taxis, who made their fortune as imperial postmasters of the Holy Roman Empire and, in 1809, converted the conventual buildings of the abbey church of Emmeran into a palace. Constantin had a part-time job at the castle, and as the place was about to close, he took us directly across the courtyard to the well-preserved cloisters of the oldest abbey church in Germany, built in the thirteenth century. The cloister was remarkably well-preserved and truly a major achievement of Gothic architecture. I was disappointed that the big iron gates to the crypt where the ancestors of the House of Thurn and Taxis were put to rest were closed, but I thought it was cool that Constantin, who turned out to be a very knowledgeable and well-read young man, pointed to an open window in the castle and explained that Princess Gloria, the very young widow of Prince Johannes, who had recently passed away, was at home. – My whirlwind trip to Regensburg ended much too soon, especially since I genuinely enjoyed getting to know the vivacious Constantin at an Italian restaurant over pasta and Chianti. He promised to stay in touch and visit me in America, with or without Bettina, in the not-too-distant future. *Arrivederci*, Constantin . . .

Back in Bamberg, though my friends had sat at their desks until late at night, Ursel insisted on taking me to the train station the next day at noon. Wulf was at the university, or so we thought – all of a sudden, a couple of minutes before the train began to move, he rushed up to the platform and into the compartment to wish me a personal bon voyage. We waved until we could see each other no more.

Seeing my relatives again was like culture shock. Lisa picked me up at the station, and I had to get readjusted to the truckers' surroundings. Frank was home from the hospital out in the country, where he had stayed in a cozy private suite for a respiratory problem, which, from what I could observe, had been blown way out of proportion just so he could extend his "vacation" in the scenic surroundings and cash in on 100 marks of pocket money each day. He was at liberty to come home for visits during the day to see his friends, if they were unable to visit him there. – So much for Germany's social conscience.

It was Pentecost weekend, and the young people had plans for outings. Klemens Jr. asked if I would like to join them on a weekend trip with little Moritz, but I tactfully declined. I was totally exhausted from the many stops, and felt I had done my duty a week earlier by taking their precious toddler on a daily walk through the village to church, not realizing what I was getting myself into. They all thought "visiting Jesus" with the aunt from America was so wonderful. I was well aware that they were glad someone took the little rascal off their hands. The boy was cute, but most obstinate. He had a fascination with the baby lambs, goats, and chickens we stopped to see at every step on the way to Jesus, whose name he learned to utter rather well. All were convinced it would one day earn him a higher place in heaven.

I myself was forced into a liaison with a baby lamb my cousin had brought home because its mother had died when giving birth. Lisa successfully trained the "Bambi" to suck milk from the bottle, and before I knew what was happening, I was feeding the little scoundrel myself. I went so far as to crawl into the stall, pitch-dark and barely big enough for me to sit in, to feed the lamb, while forever pushing aside that dreadfully smelly mutt who jumped into the stall with me, constantly licking the lamb at its bare pink spots, who knows why. It was not my best moment, and though everybody thought I was just great because I dared not complain, I sighed with relief when I was free to brush off the straw and leave behind a task I had performed with the utmost reluctance.

It so happened that Simone's birthday fell into that period of time, and I was surprised nobody said anything about a party. I knew how important birthdays are to the Germans. Just after I had arrived, Moritz had had a birthday and was showered with gifts, and then came his mother's. I was reminded by Frank, I do not know how many times, to give her a gift, as though I would commit a crime if I did not give her another present in addition to the one I had brought for her when I arrived. – I kept asking why there was no party for Simone, and they eventually did organize a family get-together in the backyard to toast their daughter, joined by her boyfriend. I was glad to see her once more before I returned to the States a couple of days later. I was somewhat disappointed that Simone did not seem too excited about an old silver-dollar coin from Doc's collection that a jeweler had framed and made into a necklace for her.

I ran into a problem finding someone to take me to the airport the next morning. Frank probably thought he had done his duty by hauling to the airport an adjustable table, which I had bought for my winter garden, so it could be shipped home. Simone had plans with loverboy, and my cousin kept mum since he liked to sleep in. Finally, when I said I would take a cab, Klemens Jr. came through for me. I wondered what Frank or Simone would have thought had I found an excuse not to take them to the airport when they visited us in the States. My cousin hardly spoke more than ten sentences with me during my stay and never showed his face the morning I bid his wife Lisa farewell. I had a gut feeling she was glad to see me leave. When she noticed I was shedding a few tears, she laughed.

On the plane back to the States, I remembered Lisa's mocking remarks about my marriages to Doc and Tonio, and knew it would be difficult to develop a genuine relationship with the folks in that place in the boondocks, with whom I had nothing but some drops of blood in common. I did not even appreciate my cousin's hunting skills, remembering Doc's dislike for deer killers. I would be upset if someone shot the fawns in my own backyard. – I wondered how many more barrels of beer or big bowls filled with rich Italian ice cream Lisa would bring home for her husband to gobble down, and how long it would take for him to suffer another heart attack. Yet I decided to be silent. I liked Simone and Klemens Jr., who had taken me to the airport, and I had invited Frank to visit me soon. He did have some admirable qualities in that he opted to care for the elderly instead of joining Germany's compulsory military. Remembering his reaction when he went with us to Howe Military Academy, I am convinced he was afraid of discipline. I resolved to continue sending them birthday and Christmas packages and to overlook the fact that my own cousin never once sent a personal note. I even wondered if he knew how to write.

Exploring Southern Indiana with Liesl prior to Her Visit to Panther, Her Metamorphosed Native American Father

Back home, I hardly had time to relax from my whirlwind tour of good old Germany, which was more stressful than any trip I had ever taken. It seemed that every night I went to bed exhausted, more from talking and being afraid to say the wrong thing than anything else. There were perhaps too many changes of scenery, too many mentalities to adjust to. I knew that on my next trip I would not visit more than two places. – I had barely closed the front door of my house when the phone rang: Liesl was anxious to visit me for a few weeks provided I paid for the flight, which I agreed to do by using frequent-flyer rewards. Her father had no money, and her mother was as stingy as before. To add to my stress, Liesl missed her father, and I ended up routing the trip in such a way that she would pass through Nashville, Tennessee, the city closest to the single-room cabin where her father coexisted with nature.

When Liesl arrived on June 18, the builders, who had started right after my return, had made good progress with my winter garden. They had also assembled my adjustable table, which arrived from Germany a day after me and which I was unable to put together. All my friends were envious, especially Dele, who wished she could find one like it in the States. – Liesl and I got along very well after not having seen each other for two years. She had grown into a slender, attractive young woman. She had learned how to drive, and I gladly let her drive my baby Mercedes whenever she wanted. We traveled around Southern Indiana and drove along the winding and picturesque highway toward Nashville, the quaint, presently rather touristic little town where artists liked to settle, but stopped on the way at the T. C. Steele State Historic Site. Liesl had not heard of T. C. Steele, the Hoosier Impressionist artist. She was an excellent cross-country runner and seemed to prefer running through the hilly terrain of the site instead of lingering in front of the paintings in the painter's studio or admiring his Brown County home. I wished she could see the fields overflowing with narcissuses and daffodils in the spring.

Liesl was as surprised as I had been, when one of my neighbors had taken me for a ride, to find out that two Benedictine monasteries, St. Meinrad Archabbey and Monastery Immaculate Conception, are located in Southern Indiana. Built between the end of the nineteenth and the beginning of the twentieth century, they are by comparison to German monasteries rather young, but I like to impress my visitors with the fine examples of architecture. – Americans and most Europeans enjoy a picnic or walk through our Spring Mill State Park to get a hint of how the Pilgrims who settled in Southern Indiana lived. They never fail to be amazed when we stroll through downtown Columbus, known for its architectural quality and innovation. It boasts buildings designed by, among others, I. M. Pei, the Saarinens, Pelli, Meier, and Roche. There are exceptional renovated and restored Victorian buildings and award-winning streets in this historic downtown. On a hot day I like to cool off while lunching in a restaurant in the enclosed downtown mall, The Commons, where the world-famous clanking sculpture *Chaos I* never fails to intrigue me. –

I promised Liesl to take her another time to see the incredible Marengo Cave, one of many in Indiana, but also wanted her to catch sight of the $30-million restoration project in progress at the West Baden Springs Hotel. At the turn of the century, upper-crust health seekers and high rollers from all over America sought the hotel out. The mineral springs and black-tie gambling casinos attracted them. Two hundred feet in diameter and 130 feet high, its atrium was once the largest free-span dome in the United States. The architectural miracle was ultimately a victim of the market crash in 1929 – Bill and Gayle Cook, owners of the Bloomington-based medical equipment manufacturer, who are known for numerous restorations of historic buildings in Bloomington, funded the restoration. – Liesl and I opted to lunch at the Beechwood Inn, in an atmosphere of turn-of-the-century elegance. But for dessert, we climbed the many steps to the presumptuous French Lick Hotel to lick an ice-cream cone in the plush but somewhat deteriorating lobby of the hotel, known for hosting Democratic conventions.

Liesl was more prone to voicing discontent than contentedness. On a sunny Sunday my friend Loreley, decked out from ears to neck to fingers and wrists with chunky pieces of silver jewelry, invited us to the Indianapolis Museum of Art to view their exhibit *A Celebration of Watercolors*, which focused on Joseph Mallord William Turner's paintings. Liesl was noticeably quiet for the entire trip. We had a lovely brunch in the delightful restaurant in the gardens of the museum before viewing the exhibit. We did not stay long, because Liesl's rather skimpy outfit, though attractive, was too flimsy to protect her against the air conditioning, which was cold enough to freeze any enthusiasm. She was ready to leave rather sooner than later.

Fortunately, Liesl was happier when we got ready for our first Fourth of July neighborhood potluck barbeque, for which I had invited about thirty guests. Liesl had taken on the task of decorating the big winter garden, which was not yet finished, but far enough along to utilize for the bash. I was amazed by how talented Liesl was in creating a setting; when she was finished, using up yards of red, blue, and white ribbons, flags, balloons, and lanterns, she earned many a compliment for the atmosphere she had generated. – Several Schubertiade guests had come, including Sabine and Arturo, who toward the end sat down at the piano and got us excited, especially Liesl, who thought Arturo was so handsome. Everybody pronounced the party a great success after we had finished the event by blasting a few fireworks into the black sky before everybody left, some more or less tipsy, some sober. Liesl and I reminisced a while. Tonio had called in the forenoon to talk to her, and I was a little surprised that he remembered our Venetian wedding from eight years before.

It felt good having Liesl all to myself, and I tried my best to keep her entertained, taking her out to eat in good restaurants downtown or on campus and on a trip to Indianapolis to visit the splashy Circle Centre Mall and the upscale Keystone Crossing Mall. We looked into the Hard Rock Cafe but decided to have our big hamburgers at another place. When we returned after dark, we realized we had locked ourselves out of the house, but we were saved when Liesl crawled through the bedroom window to let me in.

Liesl had four more days until it was time to get on the bus to visit her father, who promised to pick her up after the nine-hour ride to Nashville, Tennessee. If you think those travel arrangements went without a hitch, think again. I felt that as a matter of principle, and since I had paid for Liesl's round-trip flight, one of her biological parents should pay the $50 for the bus ride. Tonio, who had promised to pay, was completely broke, living in his shelter on $40 a month, which he made from renting his beautiful Camry to a woman on a nearby reservation. When I heard the story, I almost got sick to my stomach and suggested Liesl ask her mother, a full partner in a law firm who made a large salary. I was sure she would come through for Liesl, and I could hardly believe it when Liesl told me her mother had put her on the plane with only $10 in her billfold. Liesl, who agreed with me that her mother should pay for the fare, called her. But when she did not budge after Liesl pleaded with her for at least twenty minutes, I felt so sorry for the poor kid that I told her to hang up. I could no longer endure the torture and told Liesl not to worry – I would take care of the ticket, and when I put her, together with the violin she had brought along, on the bus, I gave her another fifty-dollar bill to spend on food when she was with her father. I was disgusted with the mother, and remembered what Tonio had said all along, that she had a rock for a heart and ice water running through her veins. I then regretted having once opened up to her after the divorce had gone through. I had talked to her about Tonio's abusive tendencies and at the same time alerted her to Gustl's opinion that everybody deserves to be hit now and then. I felt a mother should know what goes on in her child's mind. She reacted with silence, but Liesl told me that when his mother asked him about the statement, Gustl denied having made it. But because Liesl had heard him, she spoke up and told her mother he was lying. I suppose a mother wants to believe her son – I have known other mothers who have fallen into the same trap. I don't know why I was surprised; the few times she called while Liesl was visiting, she never once inquired how I was or whether we were having a good time or such, but immediately asked to speak to Liesl.

Poor Liesl was in for quite an experience in her father's humble cabin in the woods, miles away from Nashville, Tennessee. Though she did not complain, I sensed that it must not have been easy to observe her Papa's new way of life. She was concerned about his extreme loss of weight. Although 6'2", he weighed barely over 120 pounds. They ate spaghetti most of the time, but he ate little so Liesl could have more. There were a couple of cats to catch the mice, and the dog had died because Tonio could not afford to pay for treatment when he got sick. They had to fetch water from a nearby stream, and in the absence of plumbing, bathed in a lake close to the cabin. Tonio's hair was quite long and stringy, and he dyed it black to cover the gray, but when the sun bleached it, it had a reddish cast. Liesl, whom he had long wanted to acquaint with her Indian heritage, must have gotten quite an education when he introduced her at the reservation. She said that Papa lived much better than they. He had had an old truck to get around in, which broke down. Gustl had once sent him some money to get it fixed, but it did not last. Whenever he and Liesl needed transportation, a woman from the reservation drove them, as on the day when Liesl had to go to the airport to fly back to the West Coast. When I heard all that, I could not help but remember what the General had said about Tonio soon after he had met him. He said that Tonio was on his way to self-destruction.

Tonio had dropped Liesl off at the Nashville airport in time for her flight at 4:30 p.m. and left. At 8:30 p.m. Liesl called. Her flight had been cancelled because of thunderstorms. They had put her up in an economy hotel. She had less than $5 left. She went to a pay phone to call her mother, who did not help her by offering to wire money, but reminded her to collect all receipts so she could later collect. She did not know where to reach her father, because he had no phone, so she called me, knowing, as she said, that I would take care of her. I spent about two hours on the phone to find out what they had done to reschedule Liesl's flight and made sure she had enough money, knew how to get to the airport in the morning, and could manage until she got home. Most of all, I tried to calm her down and just chat, because she kept saying it was the first time she had ever stayed in a place all by herself. Neither Tonio nor her mother ever called to inquire about their daughter. But Liesl let me know when she was safe.

The summer of 1997 was about as hot and humid as I could remember. The temperature frequently hovered around 110 degrees Fahrenheit. I kept the carpenters' glasses filled with ice water while they were remodeling, and instructed them where to make changes and improvements as they went along. I was mighty pleased with the finished product by the end of September and was anxiously awaiting delivery of the rattan furniture in time for the Oktoberfest, for which I had invited my friends Pieps and Peck and their young friend Maxi, whom I had met when visiting in Cologne. She was to arrive later.

The time prior to the Cologners' arrival was filled with more musical delights. Eva Mengelkoch and her Japanese friend, Yoka, came to practice several days in a row for a violin competition in Berlin. Eva asked me if I would host a dress rehearsal for the two, so that several of her friends, including Joshua Bell's parents and Leonard and Lou Newman, all active participants in Bloomington's Friends of Music, could come and render their constructive criticism, and I did not have the heart to refuse. On September 5 about twenty guests came to listen to the young artists' lovely performance, followed by a buffet and champagne. I personally enjoyed meeting more music lovers, and they were most appreciative of my contribution to the local music scene. I added them to my Schubertiade guest list, and made sure they were invited to the Oktoberfest as well.

The Japanese violinist did not earn a prize in Berlin, but for the next Schubertiade, on September 26, three international prizewinners brought the house down once again. Sabine Simon started the evening with J. S. Bach's Partita in D Major, which was followed by Igor Stravinsky's *Suite Italienne*, played by Hie-Yon Choi and Mark Kosower. It could not have been surpassed. The evening was special also because my former fellow student, Mike Lützeler, having been awarded the Rosa May Distinguished University Professorship in the Humanities, was in town for a guest lecture, and thoroughly enjoyed the evening. He brought me up to date on my former student, assistant, and friend Lynne Tatlock. She too had climbed high on the ladder of success. She was happily remarried, chaired the German Department at Washington University, had been elected president of the American Association of Teachers of German, and had recently been installed as the Hortense and Tobias Lewin Distinguished Professor in the Humanities at the same university. He promised to give her my best and assure her that I would call her soon. He was pleased to hear I was still on the board of the former *Literatur-Express* publication, which we had renamed *Trans-Lit*, and asked to say hello to Peter Beicken, who had taken over as editor when Rita Terras retired. Meeting old friends and acquaintances in a setting tantamount to musical paradise would have had a positive impact on anybody's psyche.

Strange Company from Cologne – New Neighbors – So-Called Friends – Tonio's Apology

I was flying high when I picked up my friends from Cologne on October 9. They too were full of energy. We ate, talked, and drank until late at night. I kept replenishing my German beer and wine supply, and was quite aware of their gourmet tastes, a fact that I, being the marginal cook I am, had dreaded all along, and even announced to them in advance. They had assured me repeatedly not to worry about my cooking skills, that they were not fussy at all. Well, I worried anyhow, and almost panicked when, on one of the first nights, I served pasta with a homemade sauce and Parmesan cheese, together with a salad everybody used to rave about. But Pieps asked if the sauce came from a can and claimed the pasta was not genuine Italian, that neither the olive oil nor the parmesan cheese was what they were used to, and that the salad was lacking in I don't remember what. My good neighbor Madrean, one of Bloomington's top nurse practitioners, who due to her many international commitments as a keynote speaker had a very busy schedule, had baked for my guests a truly American delicacy, a key lime pie, out of the goodness of her heart. I was so embarrassed. My guests made fun of the "mush" and refused even to taste a piece. Peck announced right then and there that he never ate cake, which meant I had wasted my time baking a simple pound cake to have on hand, just in case. I was devastated, but felt relieved that they found no fault with the eggs, cheeses, butter, marmalade, and sourdough bread I had bought at a reputable local bakery. They ate so many loaves of that bread during their ten-day stay that Pieps, who was constantly making fun of overweight Americans, would have won a prize herself by the time she went home. She had to buy a corset to reduce her boxlike body by an inch or so. Her face became so red when she drank all that beer that I feared she would burst any minute.

Suffice it to say that these two Germans made me nervous from day one. They must have thought I was stupid when I took a wrong exit on the way to pick up their friend Maxi at the airport in Indianapolis. – I am sure they sensed my insecurity, which climaxed one day when we had gotten our signals crossed. I had dropped the three off in front of the Musical Arts Center for an opera on campus, after having pointed out my old student hangout, Nick's, on the other side of the campus. I told them I would pick them up at the MAC at 5:00 p.m., which gave me time to prepare a cold supper in compliance with their suggestion: cheese, butter, baguettes, wine, and a fruit salad for dessert. When I returned to the MAC, they were not there. I drove around looking for a while, and then parked illegally in front of the MAC and waited for more than thirty minutes. Finally, I drove home and waited for the phone to ring. When it did, Pieps asked when I would pick them up and complained that they had been waiting. I told them I had been there, as planned – and then it dawned on me that they had been waiting at Nick's instead of the MAC. I should have guessed they would be hanging out at the tavern drinking beer instead of touring our beautiful campus. Suffice it to say that Peck was very upset with me and insisted on taking a cab, which I knew at that particular time of day would take a while. When they arrived, I got chewed out some more, but I did not defend myself, because with that type of German, it's better to just shut up. Anyhow, the guests are always right. I believe the wine and the fire I had made in the fireplace played its part in calming them down.

I had been quietly upset when I took them to Nashville, which I admit is a tourist spot, but was offended when Pieps did not even want to look inside a store where mountain instruments and other typical American crafted artifacts are displayed.

They also refused to have lunch at the Hobnail, a popular old-fashioned restaurant where the food is always outstanding. They did not like the decor, but in retrospect, the fact that no beer was served might have turned them off. No doubt that was the reason why I ended up driving for thirty more minutes to take them to lunch at The Commons in Columbus. But, as expected, they also snubbed their noses at what Columbus had to offer. What do you think they had to say when I invited them to Donizetti's *Don Pasquale*, to give them a sampling of our outstanding opera productions? I should have saved the expense and effort. They hardly applauded, voiced no opinion, and kept debating whether there might be a similar building at their Cologne University of Music. I guarantee there is nothing like it at any music school in Europe or America. – I was almost glad our Indian summer was not at its prime when they were here and that instead they were blessed by a lot of rain, something that should have made them feel right at home; in Cologne and Northern Germany, the rain never seems to stop. It's one of the reasons – as you can now see – why I left Germany. Actually, the Cologners were almost as bossy as Karla and the Thistle, the flower shop proprietress, also from Cologne.

A couple of days later, when even the West Baden Springs architectural wonder, with its two-hundred-foot dome, had failed to impress them, I just turned over my car keys again, so they were free to drive around by themselves as long as they desired. And if they decided to take Maxi, who had arrived a few days before the Oktoberfest, to lunch again at the Beechwood Inn, fifty miles away, where they liked the beer more than the dome across the street, I couldn't care less.

Eighty guests had promised to come to the Oktoberfest in response to my neighbor Ann's nicely designed flyer, which advertised German beer, sauerkraut, potato salad, and bratwurst from a German butcher in Indianapolis, which my good friend Amber had been kind enough to pick up for me.

While I was thinking out loud about how I prepare the sauerkraut, which I have made for enough Oktoberfests in South Bend to know that everybody likes it, Pieps started giving me her version of how to make it, or better yet, why not just buy it ready-made from a barrel? It took a while to stop her from butting in, and I finally persuaded them to go sightseeing with Maxi. Maxi was a young, very attractive divorcée, who kept boasting about her job with Bayer AG, where she was in charge of firing employees in overseas plants in the ongoing downsizing process. She gave Pieps many opportunities to ignore my plea not to talk about Tonio, whom they had thought the world of. They could not let it go, and when I grilled T-bone steaks for them, they could not resist the temptation to point out that those Tonio had prepared on their visit to South Bend were better than mine. I guarantee, during their ten-day visit, there was little if anything I said that was not in some way negated or criticized. You cannot imagine how tempted I was to tell them what Tonio had said about a barely edible meal they once served us at their home. – I don't remember how many times they virtually decreed that I should cut off all relations with Liesl.

By the time the three Cologners returned from their outing, I was finished with my twenty-five pounds of sauerkraut, which I had hidden in my garage. You could not smell a trace of sauerkraut in any corner of the house. – My guests dressed for the Oktoberfest as though they were attending a banquet. It did not take long for the festival to get underway, and everybody had a great time. Norm and John pitched in when I started grilling the bratwurst, and the landlord recommended the many varieties of imported German and Dutch beers he had contributed to the festival. The sauerkraut and bratwurst earned the highest praise even from the Germans. The Cologners had brought a couple of unique Oktoberfest posters from Munich, which I had displayed at the doors, and everybody remarked how special they were.

When my colleague Eberhard Reichmann, former Hitler Youth and now professor emeritus, sat down at the piano and played a medley of German folk songs and operetta arias, everybody was in high spirits. I distributed sheets with the lyrics so we could all sing along. A couple of my German friends cautioned me to watch the somewhat tipsy pianist, who had a tendency to drift into songs from the Third Reich, but the danger was eliminated when Leonard and Lou, both Jewish, took over the piano and, together with the accordion played by Amber, continued until late at night. Pieps was so happy she started to dance, and my only fear was that she would go right through the floor and end up in my crawl space. I had not had the place checked for termites. It would have confirmed what they thought of my house, which they loved so much. For the price they paid for a small condo that they rented out in Germany, they could have bought three houses as large as mine. I wondered why they were content to stay squeezed, all their lives, into a four-room apartment in which there was no room to sit in the kitchen. Maybe they wanted to condition themselves to casket measurements.

The three had to leave early in the morning, but even at breakfast they repeatedly poked fun at American kitsch, a figurine of a piglet, I believe, that they had bought as a souvenir for someone back home. They did not leave a minute too soon, and I did not even argue when they insisted on taking a limo. There would not have been enough room in my car for their wardrobes and the loaves of bread which they had taken along because they could not live without it. Maybe they had planned to picnic in Chicago, where I had found a most reasonable hotel for them. Though, when I had suggested earlier we go for a picnic in Spring Hill, they looked at me as though I were demented, because in Germany, they quipped, only the Turks go on picnics. When they bade me farewell, inviting me to visit them the following year in Cologne, I just smiled and hoped they would find a cheap room for Maxi, who until they left had not found a room in which to stay. When Peck suggested they put a cot for her in their room, Pieps's head swelled red and she drew the line. I never quite understood their relationship triangle. –

I was so glad the coast was clear by October 24, when the next Schubertiade rolled around. Sabine, who had taken over the organizing of the programs, had lined up four new students: her boyfriend, the Venezuelan clarinetist Gorgias Sanchez, student of Howard Klug and Mark Friedman, pianist Daniel Rubenstein, violinist Mirjam Tschopp, from Germany, and violinist Margie Sakira Harley, from Costa Rica, student of Miriam Fried. They performed works by Brahms, Chausson, and Khachaturian. – Sabine proudly announced the release of her second CD.

There seemed to be no end to parties, and just when I had decided to sit out Thanksgiving, I received three invitations from friends and accepted the one from the Overlys, who invited me first. I also knew that Jeanne, who must be the most motherly mom and grandmother I ever encountered, was as good a cook as her husband. I offered to contribute an apple cake, and when I rang the doorbell, all of their children, who had come from as far as Japan and the East Coast, were already having a good time in the family room. I was surprised that little Jermard, their adopted daughter's grandson, whom I had at first thought to be a girl because of a full head of black curls, was eager to say grace and did it so movingly. With over twenty-five dishes, each more delicious than the next, it was truly the most memorable Thanksgiving feast I had ever been a part of. One of the main dishes was a mouthwatering crown roast of pork prepared by Norm. It looked so good that it was almost a pity to slice it down. It felt wonderful to sit with such a large group of family and friends around a splendidly set banquet table. As the Overlys had lived in Japan and Malaysia, their beautiful china and wine goblets added to the Asian atmosphere that was so inviting throughout their big home.

Bloomington Christmas parties abounded. The next activity on my social calendar was a glitzy event at Loreley the war bride's new house, the place where she settled after years of making her fortune by selling real estate and chocolate at the local mall. That same weekend I had invited my former star student Sally Detlef and her new husband. She had located me after a while, and I was anxious to see her. It was nice of Loreley to let me bring them along, because she knows how to entertain majestically. I wondered what my young friends would think of Loreley's house. She surpasses my own penchant for accumulating things, to the point of being obsessed. She hoards anything and everything, old or new, glitzy or dull, colorful or gray, glassy or tinny, pottery or plastic. Her house is stuffed so full of silver, crystal, china, tin, glass, pottery, pictures, paintings, valuables next to not-so-valuables, cute and tacky knickknacks mixed in with precious and kitschy figurines. Crystal and glass chandeliers compete with ceramic candelabras hanging from the ceiling or affixed to the walls – wherever there is a spot big enough. There is not an empty surface to be found, be it on floors covered with red Orientals or walls on which pictures, paintings, and photos compete with tiles and bright-colored glass pendants suspended on windows. Any visible chest, console, table, or stand is covered with mementos, and each time I go there I discover a thousand more pieces, little, medium, or big, that I missed the time before. I would not be surprised if someday she opened a store selling bric-a-brac. –

Loreley loves to exhibit what is hers, including her jewelry, real and fake. And she does not stop there. Her behavior on one occasion was so outlandish that it is hard for me to describe – it was unlike anything I had ever witnessed. (The actions of my boarding-school friend Sibby might have come close.) I will never forget the day I entered Loreley's bedroom, which contained a huge collection of silver brushes, combs, mirrors, candleholders, lamps, trays, icons, and countless whatnots. She rested on her four-poster cherry bed like a somewhat ailing queen on clouds of shiny and flowery silk sheets, pillows, and comforters. Next to it hung a round glass tray, three feet in diameter. So many glass and crystal figurines were displayed on the disk that it took her almost as long to keep them sparkling as her silver, which took her fourteen days to polish. She lay in the voluptuous bed, made up so heavily that, were it not for her cheerful chatter, one might have thought she wore a mask. Although her neckline revealed her true age, her face always looked exactly the same. Even today, there is never a hint that she has just returned for the fourth or fifth time from another attempt by her favorite doctor to sew, clamp, glue, switch, replace, or rethread a couple of arteries from toe to shoulder that were threatening to stop functioning properly at any time, especially if an installed pump were to stop doing its job.

I sat in a chair between bed and suspended glass shelf when the pivotal moment occurred, and contrary to my heavy protestations that I did not want to see her wounds, or whatever it was she had to reveal from underneath her negligee, she sat up in bed, almost simultaneously tossed aside the flowery cover, pulled up her white, lacy negligee, spread apart both well-shaped legs, and barely missed the glass disk with her pink, manicured toe. All of this in the hope that I would be in awe of all the blue-green discolorations of her flesh, the over thirty stitches that looked like a zipper, starting at the very end of her, pardon me, floppy thighs. I tried not to look at the damage, because I was convinced that, if she could have guessed what I really thought, she would have thought twice. She would have realized that in revealing what she did so proudly, she left those of us who had to endure the embarrassing indiscretion with no need to further speculate about our friend's age, which she so desperately tried to hide.

Be that as it may, Loreley's party was an outright success, because she had spiced it up with a piano player and an accomplished baritone, Ray Fellmann, from the music school. To everybody's delight, I succeeded in persuading him to sing a few operetta arias, thus drowning out the somewhat tinny sounds of the baby grand, badly in need of an overhaul. It was time to leave; I thanked our hostess, suggested she give her musician a rose from the vase next to her deceased hero, and pitied the poor man who had passed away all too soon.

We left to have some time to ourselves before the young couple drove back to Sally's parents' home. The Detlefs had been frequent guests at our home up north, and were among those lingering after most guests had left. Her mother had been among my female colleagues, not to mention friends, who had offered ardent critiques of the administration. She had been tireless in encouraging me to file a complaint. I told Sally I could not understand why her mother never once tried to contact me in Princeton, even after I had sent her a long letter confiding to her the problems with Tonio. I stopped myself from inviting them to come down to a Schubertiade, but was elated when my former French colleague and her husband once drove down to share the music event with us. –

My favorite neighbors, the Overlys, rarely missed a Schubertiade and always trimmed their house and the bushes, as I did mine, with thousands of tiny lights, which looked so inviting when the guests arrived. At the Schubertiade on December 12, the new dean of the music school, David Woods, and his assistant, Ted Yungclas, who was his partner, honored us with their presence. – The artists, Arturo among them, were especially excited when Sabine told them the dean had promised to come. The program, with Schubert, Brahms, and Chopin compositions, was sure to please all. Sabine introduced her new and multitalented friend, the very young Brazilian pianist Fernando Araujo. He began to play the piano and compose at age seven, and sang the Third Spirit in Mozart's *Magic Flute* when he was twelve years old. When Fernando played compositions for piano by Brahms and Chopin, he had just started studying with the world-renowned Menahem Pressler. Fernando stood out not only because of his talent but also for his looks. A full head of brown curls framed his handsome face, and contrasted pleasingly with the white shirt with blousy long sleeves. Some insisted he looked like a young Beethoven, and others compared him to Mozart. There was no dispute about his musicality and his charm. I was disappointed that the dean and his partner left without much of a good-bye. He had to fly out of town the next morning to some fundraising event. It obviously did not help much, because only two years after he had arrived on our stage, the School of Music ended up heavily in the red. He was encouraged to resign, and left for new and more harmonious surroundings.

I had considered the December Schubertiade to be my Christmas, and was looking forward to some peaceful solitude in my home. Ever since my winter garden was finished, I found it to be an ideal place to look out to the seven-foot-tall A-frame birdhouse next to the deer-feeding station and observe the colorful and diversified wildlife that came ever so close. – I could not help but pat myself on the back for having caught and successfully avoided an overcharge of $4,000 by the contractor for my favorite room. My thoughts returned swiftly to Mark Kosower and the time in September when he came a couple of hours before the concert to practice. I told him to go into the winter garden and closed the glass door to the library. He was practicing ferociously, and suddenly I heard a big bang. One of the strings on his cello had snapped. It was the second time I had witnessed the breaking of his cello strings. I was excited and asked if I might keep the string as a souvenir. Mark smiled and said I was welcome to it. – Thinking about broken strings reminded me of a strange occurrence at one of Hie-Yon's piano recitals I attended with Dele in Auer Hall. A string broke while she was playing the Steinway. She finished the entire concert with one string missing, and it sounded a bit tinny whenever she depressed that particular key. Dele, who sat next to me, never noticed the change, and she wondered if it was due to a weakening of her hearing capabilities.

While I was reflecting, the phone rang, and at the other end was Wade Johnson, with whom I had lost contact for several years. I was very excited. The last time I heard from him, he told me that, because of his excellent German skills, Coca-Cola had transferred him for a six-month stay from Atlanta, Georgia, to Vienna, Austria, where he was in charge of computers. He had had difficulty locating me, because I had moved around and changed my name. Hearing his voice was the best Christmas present I could have wished for. He was living in Heidelberg, Germany, and wanted to thank me for having taught him German so well that the corporate giant had fulfilled a longtime dream and sent him for a couple of years to Heidelberg, where the Germans were so impressed with his German that they refused to believe he was an American. We spoke for a long time and promised not to wait until next Christmas to talk again. I am pleased to add that I recently received an invitation to come to his wedding; he had found the "love of his life," a German bride.

I felt most fortunate to have such a loyal young friend, and wondered why my cousin's daughters could not have turned out more genuine and sincere, especially Gunild, who had earned a stipend for teaching an introductory German course at Yale for a year, but never contacted me; and instead of accepting my invitation for Thanksgiving, she crossed the Atlantic to see her fiancé the second time since her arrival in September. Disappointed, I felt the stipend would have been better placed with a student seriously interested in spending the year learning American customs and culture firsthand. What a shame to pass up the many opportunities. Like her sister before her, and some other Germans I know, she had nothing but complaints to voice. I was optimistic that when Bettina, who at that point had a good position as an attorney with the AFZ (Social Security Agency), finally came to visit, it would be a pleasant stay.

Two days before Christmas, I found a handwritten letter from Tonio in my mailbox. I was tempted not to open it, but curiosity got the upper hand, and I was glad it did. It is important enough to share with you and include in my memoirs:

Dear ——,

You're probably not overjoyed to hear from me but please read on.

Remember how your mother used to say never to let the sun go down on your anger? I have wanted to write you this letter for months and months. Decided tonight not to let the year end without writing to you.

Where to begin? I'd like to ask your forgiveness for a number of things. You know what they are. When I gave up alcohol – in May of last year – I began to see my behavior towards you (and others) in a clearer and clearer light. Many of the things I did and said to you are truly horrifying to me now. Great Spirit doesn't ask us to do penance or anything, just to ask forgiveness and <u>change</u>. So I am asking your forgiveness and hoping you will see from this letter that I do "own" my mistakes and have learned from them to do better.

On the positive side, I would like to say that we had a successful marriage – until the end. You were marvelous with Gustl and Liesl, and most affectionate and supportive towards me. Our relationship was a bold sort of experiment. There was 18 years between us and a world of difference in our backgrounds and upbringing. I have many happy memories, as I trust you do as well. It is to both our credit that we lived so well, had so many friends and acquaintances, traveled practically everywhere and enjoyed ourselves to the fullest. Thank you for giving and sharing so generously! My spirit will always dance in your heart! No one else on this earth will ever know what a wonderful woman you are – though I am sure many will suspect it!

As for me, I am very happy here in Middle Tennessee and quite proud of my accomplishments (thankful might be a better word for it). By some miracle I was able to buy land that turned out to be an old, old Yuchi Indian site – a waystation on the original Natchez Trace. I have managed to build a log cabin and become self-sufficient, living on $40 a month. I've learned about carpentry, cutting wood, using solar energy, fishing and lake management, herbal medicine and wild food sources, plumbing and PVC, tinwork, hunting and hide processing, junking, salvage and reuse of materials, barter, growing vegetables, auto repair and woodcraft. Most importantly – and central to everything else – I've learned a lot about the world of spirit.

Hope you have a good Christmas and here's sending you my best wishes for a happy, healthy 1998!

Yours, in peace,

It was a considerate gesture on Tonio's part to write the letter, and I knew it was intended as a sign of closure of another era in his life. Somehow, a part of the Tonio I had fallen in love with seemed to resurface. It did not really matter that I forgave him – which, in my heart, I had done quite a while before – because I also felt much pity and could not grasp how a man of such unique intelligence and charm, who had climbed so high so fast, could alter his identity and way of life so dramatically, so quickly. He did not ask me to forget, because he too knew that life teaches us that memories are forever, the good and the bad and even the ones that may seem quite insignificant to the person who caused them. There are people who are capable of suppressing even crimes to the point of believing they never happened. Unfortunately or fortunately, I do not fit into that mold. I still think back to the letter Tonio wrote in June 1994 referring to his borderline schizophrenic tendencies, and I wonder even today if he was correct in his self-assessment.

My spirit will always dance in your heart were the words in his last letter that touched me most profoundly. They flickered for a while and inspired me to get ready for my New Year's Eve party, which was turning into a tradition, just like the Schubertiades, the Fourth of July, and the Oktoberfest celebrations. –

More Schubertiades – Music Lovers – Miracle of High Tech: Doc's Return

At each soiree, new musical friends joined in. They included former professors who had become colleagues, such as the Goethe specialist Peter Boerner, whose latest edition of the RoRoRo series on Goethe had just come out in color, and his wife, Nancy, who had completed her doctorate as a librarian, the hardliner Albrecht Holschuh, with whom I sat for years on the International Studies Committee, and Henry Remak, who in his advanced years was as active in the academic theater as ever, having added an occasional performance on our opera stage to his repertoire. The vivacious and elegant Nelda Christ, now widow of Dean Christ, both of whom sat with me on the International Studies Committee, graced us with her presence on occasion. Dele, who hardly ever missed a performance, was a constant reminder of my favorite professor, Hans Jaeger. It was like old times.

Thanks to the Schubertiaden, I met and learned to admire and very much like another couple, the Bayerles. Professor Bayerle is an exemplary professor of a rather esoteric discipline, Ural-Altaic languages, always engaged in research, even in his retirement, by way of delivering lectures, directing dissertations, and teaching graduate students on our campus and in Hungary, his native country. He and his wife, Telle, from Finland, are among my favorite guests. Telle, a graduate of the Juilliard School, was for years a brilliant, strikingly beautiful, international prizewinning pianist. She tempered her performance career with the arrival of their sons. Both Telle and her husband are endowed with the true understanding and sensitivity necessary to appreciating and valuing in all its depth a piece of music and the artist performing it. My musicians always looked forward to their presence and sought out Telle's reaction after their performance.

Telle Bayerle was not the only professional among my guests. I was always delighted when my more recent friend Harriet Karlsond and her husband George Calder could come. He was the former conductor of the symphony orchestra in Giessen, Germany, and assistant to Dean Webb in the School of Music. I was much pleased to learn that Harriet had been engaged for years as a leading soprano at the opera in my hometown, Hannover – the very same opera to which my father had taken me so often as a child, as early as I can remember. This was the stage where I had sung in the Niedersachsen Chor (Choir of Lower Saxony) just before I emigrated, and where Sibby's father and Marianne had sung on occasion.

With more and more guests coming through my doors, it was unavoidable that a discordant one would surface now and again, such as the pushy Herrings and the assertive Snappers, who tended to squeeze ahead of the young artists at the buffet table only to engage them afterward in endless conversations, thus making it difficult for other guests to get to know the performers. When Snapper's wife alerted me, somewhat naïvely, I thought, that her husband and Horatio Herring were in the habit of teaming up to get a free lunch at receptions following lectures on campus, I was dumbfounded and wondered if music was the main motivation for them to come to my house. Some of us speculated about why the Snappers seldom arrived together. My friend Dele had trouble understanding how Rubin, a professor in his prime, had so much free time to attend the many recitals on campus when her own husband had been spending his evenings researching, writing, and publishing books up to the day he died. I assured her that deadwood professors were as common on our campus as on others, but joked that maybe someday there would be another publication on the shelves of our library from Snapper, perhaps postmortem.

At the 1997 New Year's Eve party, Regina Musica again reigned supreme at the Knabe, thanks to Lou Newman's potpourri of melodies from America's most popular musicals. Afterward, I was too wound up to go to bed. I put a couple of logs in the fireplace and the tile stove, sat, looked at the deer-feeding station where everything was quiet, and reminisced about all I had experienced the previous year. I had no regrets and was grateful for getting to know so many young and gifted people, and was a bit saddened that up to then I had not received a single reply to the long follow-up letters I had written to Germany after our meetings. Neither the music schools in Hannover and Cologne nor the Bamberger Symphoniker acknowledged receipt of my letters. But then again, Expo 2000 was still a couple of years away, and I was hoping that Hannover, even though its music school was of much lesser prestige than ours, might still come through for my wunderkinder one day.

My friend Renate once sent me a card with a quote from John Burrow with which I identify: "The longer I live, the more my mind dwells upon the beauty and the wonder of the world." Those who read my memoirs will notice that, from the early stages of my life, I have had a drive to travel and see the world, a drive that has persisted and even intensified. – One of the benefits I derived from my marriage to Tonio was Cancún. Once I had ventured to the crystalline white beaches and marveled at the turquoise waters, the emerald jungle, and the mysterious Mayan temples, I was smitten, drawn to it. I just had to close my eyes and dwell on the beauty of this wonder of the world and was anxious to return. And on January 23, off I went for two weeks in the sun to take in the miracles of the ever-changing sea, the rising and setting sun, and the waves, dancing or storming, crawling or splashing ashore. Sometimes, I find a seashell that holds the sound of the sea, which calls me daily – every hour, every minute, and every second – until it is time to say *adiós*; but I promise to be back and be captivated all over again.

My visits to Cancún are never exactly the same, because in the afternoons, I sometimes take the bus to the malls and look for souvenirs or gifts to take home for friends or for babies that have been or are expected to be born. My cousin Klemens Jr. now has two boys to his credit, and several of my neighbors have become grandmothers as well. This time, I was fascinated while watching a silversmith make a dozen sterling napkin rings for me, and spent hours looking for a silver pendant for Lisa, who expressed an interest in a silver coin pendant like Simone's. I eventually settled for a silver disk embossed with ancient Mayan script to surprise her with. I took along a smaller one to keep with other gifts in my "treasure chest" for future occasions, even a possible birthday. When four or five weeks had passed after my cousin's wife should have received the surprise, she still had not acknowledged receiving it. I inquired via fax and finally learned that she "loved" it. It was too late. I stopped sending gifts to those who failed to acknowledge them, no matter how insignificant.

This year, I gave myself a spontaneous birthday present. Spontaneous, because Arturo called to confide that he felt a bit depressed because he had just had his last final exam before graduating and had also broken up with his girlfriend, the very pretty horn player. I asked him if he was free and in the mood to go for a ride in the country, inviting him to dinner at the Beechwood Inn in French Lick, where he had never been. He accepted enthusiastically, and the late afternoon and evening turned out to be just wonderful. As we approached French Lick, it was like driving beneath a canopy of dark-pink lace. The road was flanked by redbud trees in their prime. Their bud-studded branches reached across the road like arches, and with the shimmer of the setting sun on the opening buds, it was awesome. Arturo's spirits had lifted, and as we toasted each other at the inn with a glass of wine, I could not resist telling him it just so happened to be my birthday.

Three spring-semester Schubertiaden attracted new artists and new guests, and I was very impressed with Martina Arroyo, the much-celebrated soprano who had come to Bloomington from the Metropolitan Opera in New York City. She had performed in the biggest opera houses around the globe, and as a teacher, she sent many a talented student to follow in her footsteps. One of her protégés, the twenty-five-year-old tenor Johan Weigel, from Sweden, performed songs by Schubert and Brahms on April 24; and a few days earlier Madame Arroyo and her husband came along for the dress rehearsal. Johan was much looking forward to singing in the chorus of the Bayreuther Festspiele that summer, and I recall Martina advising the budding tenor, while we chatted over a cup of coffee, to be careful not to stress his young voice too much. It is not uncommon for opera companies to lure young singers to attempt very demanding roles. They are flattered by the recognition and ignore the fact that they can easily ruin their voices.

The Liederabend festival was another highlight. The Hungarian soprano Mariana Zvetkova, also a student of Madame Arroyo, as well as the winner of many prizes, including the Queen Elisabeth International Voice Competition, startled us with Richard Strauss's *Four Last Songs*, followed by Mark Kosower and his sister Paula, who played cello duos by Béla Bartok and the Suite for Two Cellos by Popper. Credit should also go to the young French pianist Ludovic Frochot, student of Menahem Pressler and winner of many international prizes, who so sensitively accompanied the singers.

I was still busy cleaning up after the soiree when the director of development from the School of Music called, informing me that she had received an e-mail from a Wayne R. Beardsley, who was trying to get in touch with me. I was completely dumbfounded, told her that this must be my late husband's grandson, and requested that she forward a copy of the e-mail he sent to her. When I received the e-mail, it appeared that W. R. Beardsley had found my name in the *Directory of Endowed Funds* while surfing the Web. It had been forty years since I last saw Wayne. After Doc passed away, I soon lost track of his daughter and daughter-in-law, and they had assumed I went back to Germany after I sold the Croft. – Once, when starting to work on the novel, Tonio and I had driven to Jones, Michigan, to find out where the grandsons might be. The owner of an inn told me he had heard that Wayne was the captain of a ship somewhere on the East Coast, which was not much to go by. I gave up my search, but often felt, especially when going through the ordeal with Tonio in Princeton, that it would be nice to know where and how they were.

When I held the e-mail in my hand and read that Wayne wanted me to know he was pleased to learn I was interested in music and that he and his wife loved music as well, it warmed my heart. I ignored the rather wicked remarks of two of my so-called German friends, who immediately warned me that the New Yorkers were only interested in my money. I wrote a brief letter to Wayne and his wife Diane, telling them how excited I was and what I had been up to. – I shared the startling news with many friends, and they found the story amazing. For some reason my relatives in Germany abstained from any comment. Even Tonio, who called at about that time, was happy for me, despite the fact that his own situation seemed to have deteriorated even further. Another poor woman with several children, one on a dialysis machine, had taken him in. I refrained from probing, because I did not want to be upset.

Sunday, May 10, was Mother's Day, and Arturo's parents, the opera singers from Mexico City, had come to attend the graduation ceremonies a day earlier. I was sad to see the charming Arturo leave. He was, whenever he came, most attentive, and always gave me a big hug and a kiss on the cheek. I invited him, together with his parents, as well as Sabine and her boyfriend Fernando, for brunch at the Tudor Room on our campus, so they could eat to their heart's content. I was very touched when Arturo handed me a bouquet of spring flowers, enthusiastically wishing me a happy Mother's Day. We had such a good time at the brunch that I asked all of them to come to my house, where we popped open a bottle of champagne in the winter garden. I enjoyed listening to the fascinating opera-related anecdotes Arturo's parents had to tell, but thought to myself that Sabine and Fernando might pipe down the kissing, which reminded me of Simone and Jens; but no such luck. While we sat talking and laughing, they smooched until sundown, when we all had to bid each other farewell.

A couple of weeks after my musical children had left, I received the anxiously awaited reply from Wayne. In broad strokes, he brought me up to date about the main events that had shaped his life since we last saw each other. I was delighted to hear that he had two sons, eighteen and nineteen years old. Eric, the youngest, was about to graduate from high school, and Peter was just finishing his freshman year at Amherst College. I had something in common with his wife, a French teacher who had spent her junior year in France, and was pleased that Wayne had moved up the ladder of success. He had become a VP at one of America's leading financial institutions in New York City, not far from where they lived. He told me about his last visit to the Croft. His impressions were similar to mine: after the fire, the place, though rebuilt, had taken on a rather eerie look. – He confirmed what the man in Jones had told me, that he owned a sailboat, a photo of which a friend looked up on the Internet and printed out for me. And I saw the beautiful yacht *Vertigo* sailing in all its glory. It was not hard to guess that he spent much time sailing on Long Island Sound, since they owned a house within walking distance.

His act of discovering me was extraordinary. In his letter, Wayne put it rather succinctly: "It was really the Internet, as well as music, that put us in touch." Since he was in charge of global systems operations, it did not come as much of a surprise that he had come upon an Internet reference to my book about E. T. A. Hoffmann, which, as he later told me, he found while browsing in a university library in New Zealand. – He and his wife were indeed great music lovers, and took advantage of the music lovers' heaven that is New York City. They reciprocated my desire to stay in touch, and I felt moved when I read that they would like to meet me personally. – I thought about Doc a great deal and talked about him even more when Wayne and I finally conversed, endlessly, over the phone. I could have sworn Doc played a part in bringing this high-tech miracle about.

Liesl and I Go Theater Hopping in Ontario, Canada

I could not wait to tell Liesl that she would visit in June. Tonio had succeeded once more in manipulating me into funding a round-trip ticket for her, which also included a detour from Bloomington to Florida, for which Tonio promised to pay. He wanted her to spend the Fourth of July and his birthday with him and his family. According to a letter I received from his mother before Liesl arrived, he was staying with his brother and trying to resume a more civilized existence. He was teaching part-time at a community college. What surprised me more about his mother's letter was her sudden impulse – I am sure she was persuaded by her son – to thank me for making it possible for Liesl to visit them in Florida, but also for all I had done for Gustl and Liesl and for trying so hard to keep my marriage to Tonio together. She explained her silence of almost three years with having had a gall-bladder and hernia operation in the summer of 1995, and ended with "God bless you." I never understood why she would not send her grandchildren a plane ticket to visit her. Strange woman.

Four days after Liesl's arrival we took off for our theater-hopping trip in Ontario, Canada. Liesl had a good grasp of the theater, since her mother, with a PhD in English literature, had taken the children to many productions and also sent Liesl to a Shakespeare festival on the West Coast. Her mother had readily agreed to the venture when I suggested it. We took turns driving, spent the night in a motel northeast of Cleveland, and arrived in the small and very pretty village of Niagara-on-the-Lake (Ontario) by noon. We stayed at Apple Tree, a bed and breakfast within walking distance to the theaters on Queen and Picton, and were pleased with the accommodation. The owner, a young gay man, had restored and decorated the house, which dated back to 1820. It was comfortable and elegant. Our room was snow white. White were the beds and covers, the chairs and tables, the tiles and fixtures in the bathroom, and the walls, on which a few paintings by contemporary local artists hung. The chair covers were so immaculate I hardly dared to sit on them, for fear of getting them dirty. But we spent very little time in our room. After a rich breakfast, served by the handsome young man, who was well connected with the actors in town, Liesl and I took off to look at the shops in early-nineteenth-century homes on the very picturesque main street, and to go for a ride in the countryside that held Ontario's much-praised vineyards and fruit orchards.

We had tickets for a performance of Edward Percy's *The Shop at Sly Corner* at the Royal George Theater, which we saw on the day we arrived, followed the next day by a matinee performance of a delightful George and Ira Gershwin musical in the same theater. In the evening we went to the Festival Theatre, where we attended a splendid performance of George Kaufman and Moss Hart's hilarious play *You Can't Take It with You*. Liesl rarely voiced her opinion and seemed to think it was cool not to laugh, but I did not let it bother me. I had fun at all the plays. The actors and performances easily rivaled London's and North America's renowned ensembles. –

After many phone calls, I had been able to get a reservation for two nights at the Prince of Wales Hotel, famous for the "intimate charm of its Victorian origins," its elegance, and its service. It was sought after by travelers from other countries. Trying to get to our richly decorated room was like meandering through a labyrinth. I asked Liesl to help with my suitcase, which she obviously did not appreciate, because it took her a while to stop pouting. She regained her composure in the elegant Queen's Royal Lounge, where I had made reservations for dinner, and sat next to the windowfront overlooking the well-kept gardens of Fort Simcoe State Park. Liesl even praised the dinner and approved of the wine I had ordered.

I am quite certain my teenage ex-stepdaughter also had fun when, the next day, we drove through the scenic Niagara Parkway, about fifteen miles along the Niagara River, to spend a day at Niagara Falls. Liesl had been there as a toddler, and, as you may remember, I had visited the Falls in the 50s. But one never gets tired of looking at this spectacular wonder of the world. We took the thrilling *Maid of the Mist* boat tour and saw the thundering cataracts from up close, but thanks to the plastic protection, we did not get too wet. – As we lingered in front of the huge Floral Clock, each year composed of different flowers, we overheard a couple raving about the Butterfly Conservatory and decided to pay it a visit before heading back to the hotel. – We both loved walking up and down the stony path that wound beneath the big glass dome, in which thousands of the most colorful butterflies swarmed around. They fluttered around our heads and up in the tropical vines and trees, rested momentarily on our shoulders, feasted on rotting fruits on rocks, and seemed to ignore a green iguana on a tree branch. – Some species were bigger than any butterflies I had ever seen, and I could have stood for hours and marveled at the striking patterns of their wings, were it not time to go.

Being so close to Canada's largest city, we decided to forego a play and drive instead to Ontario's capital, Toronto. We had no plans, and were immediately attracted to a jazz band playing on a stage, set up on the big plaza not far from the CN Tower, the world's tallest free-standing structure, with a rotating restaurant at the top. I thought of the TV tower in East Berlin, which was not as high. No, we did not take the elevator to the top. It was a sunny day, and I knew Liesl liked to go shopping with me. I had told her that the following year, as a graduation present, I would like to take her on a cruise to Alaska, for which she might need a couple of new dresses. She was also looking for a new wristwatch. Thus, we walked toward a shopping area on the harbor front, where we lunched before looking for watches and dresses.

I was very pleased that Liesl put forth an effort to say a few sentences in French every once in a while. She had spent ten days with her mother in Paris during spring vacation, and I was delighted that she was not too shy to speak with me. She told me about a prom dress she had found in Paris which she hoped her boyfriend would like. The chivalrous young man from Russia used to bring her flowers at school. Judging by the fax messages that awaited Liesl every night at the hotel and her consternation in the middle of the night about a misunderstanding (she quieted down only after I told her to call him), their friendship was intense. Liesl found a dress with a miniskirt in which she looked stunning. I asked her to keep it nice for our cruise, but told her I would understand if she first tried to impress Alex in it.

She did not wait until we were on the ship to wear the new outfit, but put it on the first night we went to the Shakespeare Festival Theatre in Stratford, Ontario, where we had driven to see another striking cast, this time in Shakespeare's *Julius Caesar*.

I had wanted to go to this Shakespeare festival for a long time, and was glad to have found last-minute lodging at the Victorian Inn on the Park. Since the main purpose of coming to Stratford was to see plays, we did not spend much time sightseeing. I laughed hard at the Avon Theatre, where we saw Shakespeare's *Much Ado about Nothing*, and the next day I allowed Liesl to talk me into going for a ride on a boat on the Avon River, which winds through the scenic park. We watched and fed the swans and a family of ducks and wished we had more bread with which to feed them. Our last play was a matinee performance of Anton Chekhov's *The Cherry Orchard* at the Tom Patterson Theatre, located along the river. We were supposed to change hotels that day, but when we saw the As You Like It Motel from the outside, even though all of their rooms were named after characters in Shakespeare's plays, we decided to cancel and start back home early, by way of Detroit. I bet Gustl, who had won a thespian pin at Howe for his acting skills, would have liked to come.

Liesl flew from Indianapolis to Florida on June 30 to be with her father and his family, but had to return to me to connect with the flight to the West Coast. I told her all about our neighborhood Fourth of July bash and that some had asked about her, but we avoided talking about her father. When Liesl told me his former boss from Miles, Doloris Cogan, the Ultra-Suede Queen, had sent him $200 for his birthday, I knew immediately that he had not only reconnected with her, but also manipulated her into sending him the money he had promised to pay me for his daughter's round trip. But he never reimbursed me. What else is new? Old habits die hard. As he was back to chain smoking, he probably used the money to buy cigarettes.

I did not understand why Tonio had sent along a photo, which Liesl handed me with greetings from Papa. Instead of looking at it right away, I put it face down on a chair in the entrance hall and almost forgot about it. When I picked the photo up, I was shocked – I could not believe what Antonio, the once so handsome and charming love of my life, looked like. His features had become hard and haggard, his skin dull and gray – and his black eyes had taken on a sinister stare. He wore a red cotton shirt, which contrasted with the long and wavy black hair hanging far below his shoulders, and sported a turquoise bead necklace but wore no glasses. I hid the photo, because the image I saw turned my stomach – and still does. Judging by what I saw, it was difficult to believe Liesl, who assured me her father was happy; but perhaps she was right. One thing was certain: by sending me the photo, Tonio reaffirmed that the narcissist in him was still alive. And he could undeniably pass for a genuine Native American.

When Liesl called to tell me she had returned home safe and sound, I thanked her for the lovely letter I found hidden under my pillow after she left. It was a beautiful, artistically crafted thank-you letter with a pink sweetheart rose over a painted blue flower in the upper-right-hand corner. She had taken the rose from the welcome bouquet I had put in her room. The contents of her letter touched me deeply, because she thanked me for all I had done for her over the years and on the trip we had just taken. She liked the plays, the ducks, the swans, the frogs, etc. and thanked me for being a friend and a second mother, for letting her visit her father, taking her around to see the world, and letting her call Alex. I had sent along a box of chocolate masks (tragedy and comedy) for her mother, as she had written her dissertation on Shakespeare, but if I had expected even a word of appreciation from her, I was wrong. The Nemesis had nothing to say, and neither did Alex's mother, for whom I had sent along a few jars of Ontario's well-known jams.

Trying Hard to Entertain Cousin Frank from Giesen

Frank had announced he would arrive on August 10, despite my having told him early on that August is about the worst time of the year to visit Southern Indiana. It is so hot and humid I dread going outside in the middle of the day. I was also disappointed that he had never acknowledged the literature I had sent him in response to his question about whether he could possibly attend an English course for foreigners while in Bloomington. I had spent hours on the phone trying to get him accepted into a course. When all my efforts met with silence, I gave up. – Well, he arrived around midnight, almost three hours late, in Indianapolis. I was tired, pulled myself together, and returned home after 1:00 a.m., and instead of going straight to bed, we sat outside on the terrace, talking. Frank was keyed up and highly optimistic about all the wonderful places he had told his friends I would take him to see during his three-week vacation with his second cousin in America.

I let him drive whenever possible, and we went to many of the places in the area that I have already described. But I had planned a special event for Friday, August 14, which I thought he might enjoy. I promised Dele's two lovely grandchildren, Jonathan (ten years old) and Daniella (thirteen), to host a more intimate summer Schubertiade for them to perform for their grandmother and her friends. They were mighty excited, created a fitting program on the computer, baked chocolate-chip cookies to complement the German cream cake and the ice cream, and invited about twenty guests. The Montesinos brought their children and toddler grandchildren. Daniella, a tall and rather skinny brunette with long hair, played *Minuet and Dance of the Blessed Spirits* by Gluck and Sonata no. 5 by Handel, and demonstrated that if she kept practicing, she would most certainly advance nicely. Master Jonathan, a darling youngster with blue eyes and a head full of white-blond curls, surprised everybody at the piano. He played several pieces, but earned the most enthusiastic applause for Beethoven's "For Elise." Grandmother Dele and her son Stefan were moved when brother and sister played Mozart's Variations on "Ah vous dirai-je, maman." When I introduced the young artists, I did not forget to remind them of their grandfather, Professor Jaeger, whose absence I regretted. Unfortunately, their mother too had been unable to come.

Frank was quite impressed by the entire event and grateful for being able to experience it. Deep down I was hoping a little culture might take him in a direction different from his barren trucker upbringing in the village of Giesen. I knew it would be difficult, because, from what I could observe, his apprenticeship at one of Germany's giant transport companies did not look very promising. – I was convinced he would love the spectacular show *Star of Indiana*, which Brass Theater was presenting at the MAC on our campus; the Arbutus Society had again sent two complimentary tickets for the show. This young brass, percussion, and visual-performance ensemble was again sensational, and kept us splendidly entertained from beginning to end. The year before, I had taken my friend Amber. As in 1997 the show was followed by a picnic, where we feasted on barbequed ribs, bratwurst, hamburgers, and much more under the huge tents set up on the shaded grounds behind the Lilly Library. The show was sponsored by Bill and Gail Cook, and it was nice to be able to thank them while they greeted the many guests, and their staff, as they walked past the tables. –

A deviation from the musical splash, but a splash nevertheless, was in store for Frank. I decided to give him a brief look into the gambling world. I let him drive for two hours in the blistering heat, because the air conditioning gave out in my car. We went on a senior citizens' day, when there was no admission charge. My neighbor friend, whose husband might well be a compulsive gambler, had taken me once before to the Grand Victoria Casino, a glitzy boat casino docked on the Ohio River close to the tiny town of Rising Sun. At that time, I tried the slot machine once. When I did not lose my one dollar, I quit. I was amazed that you can now charge everything to credit cards. Instead of gambling, I went around observing the greedy crowd waiting for the tokens to rain noisily into their buckets and talked to poker players at one of the tables. One man whose cards I watched liked me standing behind him, because he was winning, but I thought it was funny and sad at the same time. When I asked a woman behind a craps table about losers' behavior, she told me a gambler once got so mad he demolished the entire table. –

Neither Frank nor I was tempted to gamble. When I passed the poker table again, the same player was sitting in the very same chair. He recognized me immediately and asked me to bring him luck again. I told him I was sorry, but that if he stopped right away, especially if he was ahead, he would stay lucky as long as he stayed away. Gamblers do not appreciate such wisecracks. The boat pulled away from the dock to move up the river for about thirty minutes. The ship is required to move now and then while gambling goes on. Gambling on cruise ships is also not permitted when the ship docks.

We were ready to drive home before sunset. By some miracle, my air conditioning was functioning again. – We stopped at a jeans outlet, and continued our hunt for Levi's 501 jeans, an obsession which I certainly did not share. He had a few other strange habits, such as ironing blue jeans, putting sugar on popcorn, and not eating oranges in the summer because they were out of season. I thought it was weird that he drank gallons of orange juice, and he got upset when I asked him for the rationale.

I don't remember how many hundreds of miles we drove to find those jeans. We did not find them at the malls in Bloomington or even in Indianapolis, although he thought the malls were spectacular. On the way home from an outing to Conner Prairie, where we saw the Pilgrims' way of life, we detoured to the West Baden Springs Hotel, where he took the tour while I sat in a rocking chair, licking an ice-cream cone. I was disappointed that he had not asked the West Baden tour guide any questions when he did not understand her explanation, but that's not uncommon among young people. On another day we went to Columbus. While he was not much appreciative of the architecture, he did like the lunch at The Commons and the search for his jeans afterward, even though they did not have his size. He was about 6'3". –

Three weeks with a twenty-one-year-old youngster whose main interests are jeans and food can be trying. He did like my cooking and helped in the kitchen whenever I asked him. Much to my dismay, he turned out to be at a loss when it came to practical matters, which surprised me. I knew his father kept after him to help out whenever his crew was building a new house – and called him lazy. I lost my patience with him rather quickly when he asked for a pair of gloves to stain the cedar shingles on my birdhouse. I did it myself and was finished in less than twenty minutes without dirtying my fingers. I told him not to watch me. It was that evening, after I had called another outlet, thirty miles away, that we found the blasted blue jeans, of which he bought a bunch for himself and his friends, and was happy. I never asked how his little boyfriend liked the sweet-smelling cologne, which he had found at a mall and which could be used by either a male or a female.

As time went on, I doubted my young cousin had really come to improve his English. – He was impressed when I took him for dinner in the Tudor Room on campus, commenting that he felt as though he were in a movie, but he was not keen on visiting the fine-arts museum. We were invited to an afternoon garden party at the Montesinos, where a colorful group of guests, artists with their wives, colleagues, music students, and others were enjoying themselves and the delicious food. Dele's son Freddie and his wife Zinette were in town, which was good, because as it turned out, much to my dismay, Frank did smoke. I was not too pleased that he had not warned me before coming, and he promised to quit. But at the Montesinos he was happy to discover Zinette, who also smoked. They sat at a table removed from the crowd, and I was in no position to voice my disapproval.

– I felt increasingly stressed the longer my German guest was around. After eight years at school, he spoke English poorly. We had little to talk about, not even politics. I was embarrassed when one of the guests asked him what he thought about Saddam Hussein, since he was handling shipments to Iraq for his company. He shrugged his shoulders, not knowing who Hussein was. All he knew about chancellor candidate Schroeder was that he had been divorced several times. One of my friends asked me where Frank attended school, and when I told her he had just made the *Abitur* (diploma), I sensed she was as surprised as I was about his general ignorance. My respect for the once-high standards at German schools was greatly diminished. –

My biggest disappointment came on the day the renowned Leonard Hokanson was playing a sonata for piano on TV. We were both listening, but only a minute after he had started, Frank got up and left the room. – I felt deeply offended. – I must admit, I was impatient with my guest at times. It was partially related to the dreadfully sweet-smelling cologne he wore and which I could barely tolerate. It took a long time to air his room after I had dropped him off at the airport to fly home. I felt a bit guilty when I opened the door to his room and found a bottle of champagne wrapped in a garland made of my favorite candy with a sweet card of thanks. –

I had offered to help Frank with his English, and we had an agreement that thenceforth we would correspond in English exclusively, and that I would correct his mistakes. Though it's not something I enjoy, I was willing to help him, especially since his boss had instructed him to improve his language skills. I stuck to my side of the agreement, wrote him a long letter in English discussing Schroeder's election and Saddam Hussein, etc., and when he finally answered in English, I was amazed at the hundreds of basic mistakes. Yet, as promised, I spent much time correcting all of them and returned the pages via fax. He neither replied nor returned a rewritten copy. When he finally sent a letter in German, not even thanking me for my efforts, I did not respond. After lengthy deliberation, I decided to let Frank go. He had already hinted at wanting to visit me sometime at Christmas or on his honeymoon, but the thought of a repeat performance of his last visit, or the possibility of being once more manipulated into letting him come, had a definite paralyzing effect on me.

With Frank's departure I focused on the next Schubertiade, scheduled for September 11; and as soon as the exhilarating evening was behind me, I began to get ready for our Oktoberbest on October 3 and immediately thereafter for Bettina's much-awaited visit on October 15.

Bettina's Visit – Christmas with Friends in the Windy City – Visiting Doc's Offspring in the Big Apple

It was finally happening: after so many maybes since she had accepted a full-time position in Berlin, and after Constantin had decided not to come after all, she did arrive safe and sound. Tine and I did not fret about Constantin's absence. With fax and telephone conveniences, a separation of nearly three weeks could only make the heart grow fonder. Bettina was greatly in need of a relaxing vacation, and urged me not to plan too much. She just wanted to sit and talk, which we did often until late at night.

I brought her up to date about my hassles with the Veterans Administration. When the Veterans Administration in Washington had denied my claim, I scheduled a meeting with our congressman, John Hostettler, for May 29, asking him to introduce a new bill that reinstated the old law. When by the beginning of August I had not heard from him, I called his office in D.C. I thought I did not hear right when his assistant apologized for not having informed me that the old law had indeed been reinstated a few weeks earlier and that on October 1, I would receive my first DIC check and all privileges would be reinstated, including my eligibility to be buried in Arlington National Cemetery with Doc. Tine was as happy as I, and I was grateful to her for having encouraged me not to give up. It was the second time I prevailed against the Veterans Administration. Of course, they made another mistake and sent a check for much less than the correct amount, because they had listed Doc's rank as private instead of major, but they corrected the error as soon as I pointed it out. I feel sorry for women who are less determined and often unable to deal with matters of this nature, and am convinced the government does not go out of its way to help the poor souls. And the government never apologizes.

It was as though our Indian summer had donned its most colorful garments for Bettina's visit. The Cologners would have been green with envy if they had seen it. My own little forest radiated. The leaves were a mélange of purple, crimson, yellow, gold, ocher, chocolate, green, and shades in between. On the lookout for the deer, Bettina was elated when they lined up at the feeding station. She watched the chipmunks endlessly. They in turn seemed to enjoy entertaining their audience by sitting up on their hind legs to nibble as rapidly as they could on the sunflower seeds, the choice morsels they picked before the cardinals and blue jays could get to them. – I loved it when my young friend sat down at the Knabe and played sonatas she discovered in the piano seat, getting better each day. – We went for rides in the afternoon in our Brown County State Park or to admire the countryside. In the evening we dined alone and chatted in the library near the fire in the fireplace or in the winter garden, where another fire was burning, sipping a glass of wine or tasting an imported beer. One evening we saw Bizet's *Carmen*, on another we listened to our IU Jazz Ensemble at the MAC, and once I invited two of my neighbors and their wives to an ethnic restaurant downtown to meet Bettina. On a Friday we went to the College of Arts and Sciences annual awards banquet, at which a couple of outstanding faculty were recognized. I was anxious for Bettina to meet John and Amber Challifour, so I invited them as well, and they too enjoyed getting to know my charming friend. She spoke excellent English and was an exciting conversationalist. Unlike Frank, Bettina always contributed something of interest to a conversation.

I was grateful that several of my friends had invited us to lunch and was especially pleased about Harriet Calder's invitation. I knew Bettina would love their strikingly beautiful house, deep in the woods outside of Bloomington. It is a refuge surrounded by flowers where I myself would gladly live. While relishing a most delectable meal, served at the elegantly set table, I almost felt like I was sitting outside. We had a view toward the big windows that reached all the way up to the vaulted ceiling, thus letting in much light and emphasizing a big stone fireplace. You could see the ebony Steinway in the adjoining music room. The panorama of the fall trees outside was a symphony of colors. –

Bettina had wanted to spend a week basking on one of Florida's beaches, and after an extended effort, we were able to find a place where she could fulfill her wish. – While she was exploring the beach south of Tampa, I had to get ready for another concert evening, which meant getting the piano tuned and being available when either of the artists wanted to come over and get a feel for the instrument. – Sabine had enlisted the gifted Steven Spooner, a New Orleans native, who had performed throughout the United States, Europe, and Russia. He had started performing at age fourteen and had an astounding repertory under his belt, including a couple of CDs.

The twenty-two-year-old Hakan Ali Toker, from Turkey, also performed. He was pursuing a double major in piano and composition. He knew how to excite the audience with remarkable improvisations, a *novum* for us. He asked us for a melody from an aria or any composition, and from it evolved the most delicious and comical musical twists and turns. We were on the edge of our seats, laughed, mused, and jumped up at the end to shout our bravos. It was enjoyable to listen to and observe this young artist, who had tamed a full head of wild black curls with a colorful crocheted Nubian hat. Our audience hoped that both pianists would someday return to entertain us, and they did – two days before the writing of this paragraph, in fact – and again earned standing ovations. My guests wished the same when another extremely gifted Sebők student, the African-American Carl Gales, played Schubert's Sonata in A Major, op. 120, and J. S. Bach's Chromatic Fantasia and Fugue with much sensitivity and conviction on December 11, for the Christmas Schubertiade, at which Sabine enchanted us with Robert Schumann's *Carnaval*, op. 9.

I was glad it snowed on our Christmas Schubertiade night, because I was serving the forty-five guests my annual *Krambambuli*, for which Frank had brought sugar cones from Germany. Gunther Rodatz, a tall and handsome, recently divorced German exporter of choice woods, had generously brought four bottles of Moët & Chandon champagne, which I stored for another evening. Gunther, Rita's big-hearted employer for many years, always felt guilty when he had to miss a concert, especially when Sabine, whom he adored, was playing. – He himself rose to a sort of fame when after a successful triple bypass, our cardiologist persuaded him to pose for a cardboard poster advertisement, three times his size, which was plastered all over town.

The snow had tapered off by the time Amber and John picked me up in the early morning on December 21. They had invited me for a weekend trip to Chicago, to go shopping and visit the Mary Cassatt exhibition at the Art Institute of Chicago.

Their son Collin, a handsome chap attending Purdue University, had come along as well. It was raining on our drive up north, but as soon as John parked the car close to our hotel, right around the corner from the Magnificent Mile, it began to snow. We were glad to have bundled up, and could not wait to mingle with the Christmas shoppers on Chicago's spectacularly decorated streets. It was like old times, when Tonio and I used to look at the animated toy displays with the children, the snow first falling gently but then flying past our faces as soon as the winds off of Lake Michigan began to blow harder. It was great looking for a special item at Bloomingdale's, Water Tower Place, Nieman Marcus, and other department stores. Each place boasted a Christmas theme in its own fashion. Luncheon at Bistro 100 was out of this world, as was dinner at an Italian restaurant that night.

We had Sunday breakfast at the unique Corner Bakery, which offers a delectable assortment of breads, muffins, and coffee cakes. After we checked out, John drove to the Art Institute, where we spent several hours in Regenstein Hall admiring the American Impressionist paintings in the *Modern Woman* exhibition. Paintings of mothers and children and Mary Stevenson Cassatt's *At the Français, a Sketch*, which depicts a woman sitting in a gallery and watching the stage through opera glasses, fascinated me the most. Amber, who loves teaching art in her French classes, gave a highly informative and enthusiastic commentary as we toured the exhibit. I easily understood why her students thought so highly of her. –

John suggested we stop for dinner at a Chinese restaurant in Lafayette on the way back. It was late and dark when we returned home, and I could not thank my friends enough for a wonderful weekend in the Windy City. It was a Christmas gift I will never forget.

Though I had three invitations for Christmas dinner, I decided to stay near the fire and watch my deer outside. I had put a garland with Christmas lights on the A-frame bird feeder, and when on Christmas Eve I saw a deer standing next to it in the snow, turning his head and looking at me, the scene was reminiscent of the crib in Bethlehem. I was glad to be home when a call came from my cousin Klemens Jr. and another from Bettina's Constantin, which really surprised me.

*   *   *

The kind Internet chips had led Doc's oldest grandson to me, and I could hardly wait for the limo to take me to the airport, where I would board the plane that would take me to meet the handsome family, who had sent me a photo. As I spotted the Statue of Liberty and the Empire State Building from my seat on the plane, I felt a strange sensation come over me. I remembered the first time I landed in New York, at Idlewild Airport, on February 25, 1954. I was forty-four years older, but almost as nervous as I was then. As I left the gate at LaGuardia, I saw Doc's proud offspring, father and son, blue eyed and handsome, standing in front of me. Wayne looked as strong as Doc, while his light-brown hair and his smile seemed more like his mother's. He gave me a welcoming hug, and Peter, not quite as tall, but strong, blond, and blue eyed, with a smile more like Doc's and as sweet and charming as could be, gave me an even bigger hug. I felt relieved and elated at once and knew I would like them. – Unfortunately, my suitcase was missing.

As we approached their big and lovely white frame home sitting up high in a scenic cul de sac in one of Westchester County's most desirable residential locations, the afternoon sun broke through the snow-covered branches of the mature evergreens, blue spruces, and fruit trees in the park-like setting. – Wayne led the way up the path and the steps to the wide front door, which opened into a large, bright living room with vaulted ceilings. In front of a huge bay window towered a twelve-foot-high Christmas tree, more exquisitely decorated than any tree I had seen inside a home, and reaching all the way up to their high ceiling. It was much taller than the tree that tipped over at the Croft. The tree was a joy to look at from the soft black leather couches in the opposite corner. A big, rectangular glass-top table by an Italian designer, on which precious glass figurines and a collection of Murano glass objects were tastefully arranged, blended perfectly with the crystal and glass ornaments on the tree. Light-green wall-to-wall carpet contrasted soothingly with the white walls and ceilings. – The same simple elegance found in the living room characterized the rest of the house. As soon as Wayne's attractive wife, Diane, came to welcome me, I knew she was responsible for the smart interior of the home. She was petite, simply yet stylishly dressed. Her dark-brown hair was fashionably cut, and her smile radiated warmth, which explained the deep love Wayne feels for his wife. He adores her. I saw immediately that they had a sound marriage and were proud and devoted parents to their sons. When Eric came home, tall, dark, and handsome, taking more after his mother, I knew the four were a family of which Doc and his son Peter, Wayne's father, who died much too early, could have been proud.

My visit to their gracious home was filled with culinary and musical delights. New York City at Christmastime under a blanket of snow is an experience to behold in itself. I was thinking of Doc, especially when Wayne and his wife invited me to the *Radio City Christmas Spectacular*, featuring the Rockettes, and we stopped to stand in awe over the Christmas tree in Rockefeller Plaza, with its 26,000 lights. They had no idea Doc had insisted I see the Rockettes when he took me to the pier in 1956, on my way home to Bremerhafen. I must admit, though, that the *Nutcracker* performance by the New York City Ballet at Lincoln Center was the highlight of my stay. It was performed in tribute to Maria Tallchief, the New York City Ballet's original Sugarplum Fairy, a role danced in this production by Miranda Weese, supported by her cavalier Ethan Stiefel. It was an event filled with outstanding music, enchanting dancing, and winter-wonderland magic that rivaled the show I saw with the kiddies in Chicago.

My newfound relatives virtually showered me with Christmas extravaganzas. I was relieved my suitcase had arrived the evening of my arrival. After the Rockettes, they surprised me with a delicious dinner in the world-famous restaurant Tavern on the Green. located close to Central Park, where I had not previously been. It is surrounded by huge trees and includes several big glass pavilions. The big trees stretch out their knotty branches above the pavilions. Starting at the foot of the big trunks and ending in the last branches and twigs of the trees, tiny blue, white, and turquoise lights illuminate the park and transform it into pure magic as soon as it gets dark.

Diane emerged as an excellent cook when she served chicken à la king on pastries. They liked the German potato cakes I made for lunch one day, but there are so many gourmet restaurants close by that we took full advantage of them during the short time I was there. – A special event for me was when Wayne took me for a ride through the scenic neighborhood and stopped at Long Island Sound, where we watched Peter get into his new wet suit, step into the one-man sailboat, and disappear on the horizon in line with other sailboats participating in the regatta. It was too cold to wait until they returned. In the evening I suggested the boys invite some of their friends over and concocted a *Krambambuli* for them in the billiard room downstairs.

Whenever there was a moment, we talked. I even spoke on the phone with Christopher, Wayne's nephew, his brother Lee's son, and left him one of Doc's silver dollars I had brought for the boys. With so many years to cover, and because I had lived so many lives, by the time I had to leave in order to get ready for a New Year's Eve party at my house, I was almost hoarse. – I took with me my precious gift, a nutcracker who, in his lacquered blue-and-red uniform, looked just like the one who danced in *The Nutcracker* at Lincoln Center. He had awaited me wrapped in a pretty box that stood erect beneath the exquisite Christmas tree. When I first held him, I knew I had come full circle. He was part of the miracle, because his Uncle Drosselmeier was one of Hoffmann's master figures I had written about in the book that Doc's grandson, the sailor and computer genius, found while surfing the Web. If it had not been for Doc, I would never have researched and written that particular tome.

On the way home, I remembered Diane's last words and felt secure. The next time I would have to give out an address in a hospital about a relative nearby, I would not have to refer them to Paradise and God.

I had invited fewer friends to this year's New Year's Eve party, because there was little time to get ready. Everybody brought a dish, and we were as happy as always. We rang in the new year by toasting with champagne in front of the big-screen TV when the crystal ball was lowered at Times Square. I looked for Peter, Eric, and Chris, who were there, but you guess correctly: I did not see them on my screen. –

Tonio stopped calling. He had called toward the end of November and started to tell me about an announcement he had sent in the mail. I cut him off, told him I was not interested, and asked him to stop calling me. A small envelope with his handwriting, and without a return address, arrived several days later from Florida. I put it in my desk drawer, where it still is, together with the unopened letter Gustl had sent to me in Princeton in 1995. It was my last personal contact with Adonis, aka Tiger, Panther, etc.

Ten days later I sat again in the big limo, in which I always feel like a gangster, to start my annual retreat to Cancún. I chatted happily with another passenger, a professor who had visited his father. The flight from Indianapolis to Cancún takes only three hours, and the Cancún airport seems larger and more prosperous each year. The temperature was 86 degrees Fahrenheit. The studio suite looked familiarly inviting, and as soon as I opened the sliding glass doors, a strong ocean breeze flooded toward me. I looked down to the beach and watched the foaming waves with genuine enthusiasm. – I took it easy, soaking up the seashore atmosphere, while observing slender bronze-colored bodies strutting along the beach and grinning to myself when I noticed that the fat American tourists, who like to come here each year, tried hard to cover up their beer bellies, which wobbled so grotesquely when bare. From the distance, some looked as though they were pregnant with quadruplets. I went shopping at Sam's and Walmart, where the gourmet, tropical-fruit, and fresh-baked-goods selections, like elephant ears and croissants, are much more inviting than back home, and ever so cheap. During the day I ate fresh and juicy pineapples, avocados, papayas, mangoes, and other tropical fruits. At night I prepared a simple but tasty meal, usually pasta with peppered salmon filets or smoked trout, roasted potatoes with prosciutto and white asparagus, or fried plantains. I treated myself to a glass of piña colada or two, sat on the balcony watching the calm or stormy sea below, read and wrote letters, or tried to improve my Spanish.

Upon my return from the exotic getaway, I was greeted by a long, faxed letter from Arturo. It was filled with exciting news about his career, which I shared with the guests at the next Schubertiade. He had won first prize in the Angelica Morales National Competition, the most important piano competition in Mexico. It opened the way for more concerts in Mexico as well as in Europe and one with the San Antonio Symphony.

Local Gossip Lines among Friends and So-Called Friends

I always make my usual rounds after Cancún to keep the medical profession from starving to death. I hop from one doctor to the next, starting with a general checkup to learn whether or not my blood pressure and cholesterol are too high, how badly my arteries are calcifying or blocked, and whether arthritis is rearing its ugly head or some form of cancer has begun to nibble on a part of my body. This year, my blood pressure had normalized, my cholesterol was, as always, perfect, my bone density was normal, the stress test was good, and the prospect of needing a bypass was very slim. – I had a dispute with a bone specialist about a splinter that was lodged in my left ring finger. He insisted it was an arthritic cyst and not a splinter, and after lengthy deliberation I let him slice away. The little bubble was gone, but not the pain, which is still there because the supposedly best hand surgeon in town, according to his own admission, cut one of the many little nerves while slicing away at my poor finger. I put this doctor on my blacklist, to be avoided in the future at all costs. If I were a professional violinist, I would have sued him.

Don't think I let him forget his slip. Though I was discreet about it, when I ran into him again a couple of months later at a picnic sponsored by the Arbutus Society, I informed him, while holding my finger in front of his eyes, that it still hurt. I was disappointed that it left him cold. He turned away and focused on the attraction that brought us there in the first place, the historic Cedar Farm in Harrison County, the only antebellum plantation-style complex in Indiana, directly on the banks of the Ohio River and across from the forested bluff of Kentucky. The Pritchetts and Gail and Bill Cook, who cohosted the event, had renovated this beautiful plantation house with four big pillars. They spent most of their weekends at this estate, and were proud to give us a tour and answer questions about the place, built by Jacob and Elizabeth Kintner in 1837.

I had invited along three of my friends, Amber, Peggy, and Brunhilde. We split up and toured the mansion and the grounds on which the various buildings stood. There were tenant houses, barns, an underground milk house, a carriage house, and a smokehouse. Amber and I walked down one of the four alleys of mature cedar and maple trees toward the river, where we sat on a bench in the shade of a maple tree, watching a riverboat pass by. I told my friend, who knew the bone specialist, that I had been tempted to add him to my Schubertiades guest list since he was an ardent music lover, but was glad not to have done so. Had he attended the three Schubertiades we put on that year, I would have been reminded each time that due to his slip with the scalpel, I could play the violin no more.

It was a typically hot and humid Indiana summer day, and the picnic set up beneath big tents was most welcome. We had been taken in two buses through the picturesque countryside on rather narrow and steep roads, and were full of praise for our hosts, who secretly hoped their present-day generosity would fill the IU Foundation's coffers later. –

My friend Peggy, the widow of a successful architect, herself a jazz pianist and a newcomer in town, could be a future donor, I thought. She was kind and respectful, a genuine lady. Each time I saw her, she was dressed differently, and she was noticeably elegant in the finest selections shipped in from Neiman Marcus in Chicago. Her house is a true reflection of her personality. It is more tastefully decorated than others I have seen of the same style in the settlement where she resides. One of the pieces that stand out is her specially designed dining-room table. A Louis Sullivan screen from an elevator door in the Chicago Stock Exchange was placed on a large, thick, rectangular pane of cut glass. On the wall close to the table hangs a similar panel from the screen, which looks striking together with the tabletop. Peggy always points with pride to the different pieces of needlepoint her late husband had made. They never fail to remind me of the dining-room chairs Doc made after his early retirement from the Army. When I was first invited and saw her baby grand ready to be played, I liked her house at once. –

Peggy's greatest love is her little dog Pearl, who is more spoiled than many a child. Perhaps even Pearl is not as well off as the four-legged prince of my friends Bruce and Mary Ann, another Schubertiade couple, who are among my favorite guests. They are so devoted to their little dog that whenever he gets sick, they spare no expense or effort to save his life, if it is at risk. I look upon these dogs as a reminder to curb my appetite for a dog or pet. I will never forget when the Padre once pointed to an old lady walking through the park in Bonn with her little dog, dolled up so extravagantly with jewels and costumes that it was difficult to distinguish what kind of a body was above the four spindly legs. He mocked the old woman, saying she had "gone to the dogs." When my friend Renate's cat was put to sleep, she had already bought a new one, ready to take over when the firstcomer had to go.

I am always amazed at what science can do for humans, and was eager to help my Schubertiade friend Bruce Gingle, VP for the Cook Group, who on a Saturday came over with his stunningly attractive wife from the Philippines, Mary Ann. He asked for a quick translation of the name of a new device, the Enk Oxygen Flow Modulator, developed by Dr. Enk from Germany. I immediately recognized that this particular instrument was well suited for manufacturing by the Cook Group, who have made a name for themselves, not to mention fortunes, with their catheters designed for patients with heart problems. It is an emergency airway device for use in critical situations with patients experiencing complications in breathing. Subsequent to my suggestion, the device began to be mass produced by the Cook Group. I wondered if I should have asked for a commission, but was content for the time being with the bottle of wine the handsome couple brought over. Bruce hopes that someday his Dr. Enk may be in town for a Schubertiade. – The future will tell.

My friends thanked me for inviting them along to Cedar Farm. I would have liked to take along others, Anna, my younger neighbor, and Dicke. Dicke was short but strong, a bit rough around the edges, and wore pants most of the time. She was as tough as the General, who was five years older than she. While he played tennis and jogged, she hiked, exercised at the YWCA, and each year planted a large garden full of flowers; she also mowed her own lawn, liked to have people come to her cozy home for coffee and dinner, and drove to the East Coast several times a year to spend time with her children and three grandchildren. Like the General, she had many interesting stories to tell. Raised and educated in Germany, she came to America in 1947, after living in Turkey and Palestine, and met up with my friend Dele, who had come a year earlier. Dicke's husband passed away thirteen years after their arrival in Bloomington and three years after Doc died. But she was fortunate to have three lovely daughters, with whom she has healthy and enviable relationships to this day, at age eighty-seven.

I liked Ann and Dicke for their love of nature and curiosity about exploring. Anna and I did explore the area on several daytime trips. She was also responsible for my first encounter with the Ohio River. She loved to show off the historic sites and churches around her hometown, Huntingburg, where her aging parents live happily in a big trailer in a forest. They own a log cabin on the same land, in which they spend much time weaving carpets and blankets on two looms, which they sell at county fairs.

A highlight of our outings occurred the day Anna convinced me, after a long hike, to venture into the mysterious and somewhat eerie Wyandotte Caves, located not far from the Ohio River. This whetted our appetite to stop at Bluespring Caverns, outside of Bedford, where the White River had cut its way deeply into the soluble limestone and opened before man's eyes another myriad of wonders carved into the stone. Afterward I was curious to see more caves and soon thereafter persuaded Dicke to drive up to Marengo Cave. A walk through this federal natural landmark will not soon be forgotten. It was a sight to behold, stretched out before us, the fantastic scenery of Sherwood Forest, Mirror Lake, the Great Wall of China, and the breathtakingly spectacular Crystal Palace, with the most striking stalagmites and stalactites.

Brunhilde, another German I met, was from the Rhine region, like Pieps. Several of the other Germans forewarned me as soon as she joined the Schubertiade guest list. They were right. She had a major complex about her schooling in Germany and in the States, which boiled down to the fact that she never earned a degree, but raised one child instead. She tried to make up for the lack of education by memorizing each and every name of the professors and lecturers who came to campus or walked past her desk. She prided herself for being the secretary of the most intelligent man in the universe, whose name I need not mention since you most likely know who it is. Don't feel bad if you don't, because I too flunked the test. And most of the time, I had no idea who she was talking about when she dropped all those names as though they were presidents of the United States. Curiously she did not know prominent persons whose names I referred to at times. I did not hold it against her. It must be a trait of the Rhinelanders to boss people around once you give them an inch. Maybe they pick on me because I am from Northern Germany and came here by myself. When this domineering woman, perhaps twelve years younger than I, started telling me to polish my bathtub with car wax, and butted in when I was organizing the concerts, I retreated, hid behind my writing, and was mighty glad I had ignored the pleadings of the art museum's docent clique, to which she belonged, to join them. I did not feel the urge some of them appeared to have to compensate for a void in education and simultaneously gain some recognition in the academic theater.

Like Brunhilde, some people, women mostly, but men too, have a distinct drive to be seen at public gatherings. They always stroll down the aisle slowly and sit in the front rows in theaters and concert halls, even though the overall acoustics are better further back. Before they sit down they turn around, look for acquaintances further back, and if they spot someone, no matter how distantly known, they wave like mad until they know they have been recognized. They give the impression that it is more important to be visible than to derive the artistic benefits of a performance. They also join any club in town that will have them for a fee of $50 or less in the hope that the affiliation will be recognized in their obituary. It might sound a bit boastful, but one of the enjoyable features of writing is that you can finally express what you might have been too polite to say verbally. In all fairness to Brunhilde, who cannot help being the way she is any more than I, she did grow up without a father, because he divorced the mother, or vice versa. I have met several Germans who refuse to deal with the facts and conveniently blame the war for killing their husband or father, even if it is untrue. – Brunhilde is a great cook and keeps an impeccable house, though with the help of a cleaning lady, and maybe, once I decide to get someone to scrub my humble abode, she will stop butting in more than my own mother would have dared. One thing is certain: I will not polish my bathtub with car wax.

As I am having fun with the Rhinelanders, I must not overlook the Thistle, who shares with them the officious trait and eventually started needling me. My first year in town, I took pity on her when her assistant left her in the lurch on the biggest rose day of the year, Valentine's Day. I agreed to help and de-thorned hundreds of long-stemmed roses. Their leaves were very badly torn during the transport from Colombia; I would not have dared to charge such an exorbitant price. Being in the flower business, where she had a mixed reputation, especially among the Germans, as I mentioned before, the Thistle was all thorns, sticking them deeply into Dele at one of the Schubertiade evenings, blasting her, as our old friend told me before she joined the angels, for having greatly harmed her business by advertising among friends that her artistic creations were overpriced. The attack resulted in another major crack in a decades-long so-called friendship. When I found out accidentally that she gave a discount to senior citizens, I wondered why she never gave it unless you asked. I guess her store must have gone poorly. After I had gotten to know her better – more precisely, when she told me how much one of the flowers that she contributed to the table arrangement on Schubertiade nights cost her, quoting the retail instead of wholesale price – I was ticked off. I told her I would be glad to let her furnish the champagne instead of the flowers, but she shook her head. From then on I handled the flower arrangements myself. – I am still worried I may owe her something for past flower-favors.

I developed a regular complex. Whenever the Thistle entered my house, she gave it a once over, telling me what to do with this or that flowerpot or where to place a vase – whatever she could find to criticize. I had probably made a mistake when I first came to town and occasionally asked for her opinion. It's most likely the reason her husband told me to get rid of the blue curtains in the kitchen when he saw them for the first time. My curtains are still there. They go with the color scheme. He still has the same wife for whatever reason. But her store help was so fed up with her that one day she walked out on her without notice. Even my neighbor had had her fill of her before I came. She owned a cleaning agency at the time, and the Thistle, one of her customers, made her life so miserable with continuous complaints that she cancelled the contract.

There is probably something wrong with me too, because I would never have the guts to walk into their house and tell them to tear the roof out and replace it with glass to light up the sinister place. But then again, I am not from Cologne, and my hair is blond and not red like the fur of a fox, as is the Thistle's. By now, I have learned it is best to avoid people with such temperaments. I got my last hint when one day, as I stopped by her shop just to say hello, she was arranging a big shipment of poinsettias. The minute she spotted me, she demanded I go to the bakery across the street and make a fuss because they were selling a few bouquets of fresh flowers. She wanted me complain to the manager and tell him to stop competing with her flower shop at once. I told her I would do no such thing, that we have in this country a free economy, and that if she forbade the baker to sell a few flowers, he could forbid her to sell the few loaves of German bread she kept for sale on a shelf. She did not like my response, and I was glad when her husband walked in. I turned to him and suggested he fight his wife's battles. I was surprised when he turned on his heels and fled. Surprised, because I had observed that over the years he had adopted a bunch of her habits.

On the way home I kept thinking about the poinsettias she hoped to sell. As always when I see those pretty flowers, which on the island of Tahiti grow as tall as trees, I remember the time when Dele brought me a magnificent poinsettia in time for the concert, asking me not to tell the Thistle that she gave it to me, because she would be upset that she did not buy it at her shop, where it would have cost twice as much. Unfortunately, when the florist's husband came over to drop off the programs, he spotted the big pot of flowers in the library right away and asked who gave it to me. I did not want to lie and told him. As soon as the Thistle appeared on the scene, she started complaining about all those Germans who had boycotted her store for so many years, naming all of them alphabetically, I think. She took it a step further and attacked their children, who lived in other cities, for sending money to a friend here, asking him or her to buy a bouquet at Kroger for their mothers instead of ordering from her. From that time on, I developed a distinct dislike for poinsettias and was afraid that whenever someone brought me flowers from another source, she would get upset – and she did, blaming every other place in town for ruining her business.

She did not exactly treat her customers with kid gloves. I overheard her ridiculing a caller who wanted to send his girl a teddy bear with the flowers he planned to order. She turned him away, telling him in no uncertain terms that she did not stock such tacky items. No doubt he is one of many customers she alienated.

She was full of unsolicited advice when it came to the way I mowed my lawn and the flowers or bushes I planted outside, and she ceased to offer it only when I refrained from inviting them over for anything but concerts. I wonder how the Thistle would react if she ever observed my other neighbor, the one who vehemently dislikes lawn violets and dandelions and any other weeds that tend to raise their ugly heads on our lawns. I think she watches the grass grow from her kitchen window with binoculars. As soon as she spots any undesirable plant, no matter how tiny, she grabs her shiny bucket, tweezers, and digging tools and pulls out carefully, but firmly, each little weed that might taint her manicured lawn, which she mows like clockwork until it is exactly the height she prefers and not a millimeter higher. Any fallen twig or branch disappears minutes after it has landed on the green carpet. She breaks or clips each one, as evenly as if measured by a ruler, and not one blade of grass is an iota longer than the other. She bundles the twigs for collection by the garbage truck. I am forever tempted to sneak over to her place and bring home the bundles for kindling, but she has become so private over the years that I am afraid she would suffer a heart or hysteria attack if I dared to do something out of the ordinary. I know she would call the police and report a burglary, because she is scared to death of robbers. I can tell from listening to the greeting on her answering machine, which scares me away as soon as I hear it: "We are screening all calls." It sounds like an inquisition. By the way, the garbage collectors must love to pick up her immaculately stored garbage, which she keeps in plastic bags in the freezer during the summer.

I felt sorry for Violet when I first came to Bloomington. She was and still is afraid to drive more than five miles away from her home. I used to take her for a ride occasionally, and would call her on the phone and invite her to the Schubertiades, which she claimed to like. Little by little, because she waited several days to return the messages I left on that scary machine, I sensed that she preferred to be left alone. I never see her grandchildren play in the yard, but remember that she does not like the company of children or others, out of fear a pillow or chair might be displaced. We wave toward each other from a distance, but speak no more. I think it's all ridiculously sad, but I have learned that many women develop the weirdest habits as they age. I am sure they think the same of me. I am anxious to read their memoirs. Meanwhile, I wish Violet would stop chopping off the top of that pretty bush, which wants to branch out each spring. Before it gets a chance, she spends hours clipping away at it, stuffing the cuttings neatly into garbage bags, until it looks like something else, perhaps a stylized oversized broom top, a brush, not a bush. It's not unlike her hair, short, stubby, thick, exact – and exactly the same all over. Out of fear that a single strand may blow loose in the wind, she wears a triangular scarf that holds it securely in place. My neighbor Anna and I are betting she wears a wig, of which she probably has a whole closet full, and buys them *en gros*. I would not be surprised if she brushed her entire body for more than an hour, like my best friend Renate does after her shower, each and every day of the year.

Meanwhile, it's back to more exciting things and off to horizons other than lingering over eccentric neighbors, weed-free lawns, and butchered bushes. – It's off to Alaska, at last, for an eleven-day cruise and land tour to behold more treasures in God's vast museum.

Liesl and I Cruise the Love Boat – MS *Sea Princess* – to Alaska

Getting Liesl excited about what I considered to be a spectacular graduation gift was like pulling teeth. I had tried to put her in the mood by sending her, well in advance, any and all information that came my way in the form of pictures, a video, and catalogues with elaborate photos and trip descriptions. I hoped to a remind her of our honeymoon trip at the Seiser Alm in Tyrol, followed by the ocean voyage on the *QE2*, and sent her an Italian-made wooden jewelry/music box, which played our favorite song, "Edelweiss." Alaska had never been on my list of travel priorities, but I thought that Liesl, who likes the mountains, might enjoy this particular trip, and that the *Princess* advertised enough activities to keep the young crowd entertained. She was reluctant to commit herself, probably waiting for something better to come along, until I finally gave her a deadline.

I had the feeling she thought she was doing me a favor in coming along. I never again wish to experience a repeat performance of that ordeal. Of course, Ms. Ice Water, who never once attempted to communicate with me, or even to express some sort of appreciation, did not help. It was obvious to me that she wanted to hurt me, and, sensitive as I always have been and will be, she succeeded. – With her, it always seemed to boil down to envy. –

By the time I sat in the plane and looked down on the snowcapped Rocky Mountains peaking and sparkling in the blinding sunlight like giant diamonds, I was bursting with joyful anticipation to see Liesl again, who I hoped did not miss her plane. However, she had found her way to the stately 77,441-ton *Sea Princess*, docked in Vancouver's awesome harbor, before I arrived. – Liesl waved at me from the gangway, and came toward me, smiling. We hugged, and she led the way to our gorgeous ocean-view cabin with private balcony, where she had already parked her carry-on luggage. It was wonderful having Liesl, who had already gotten acquainted with the ship, lead the way. The *Sea Princess* was only one year old, built by the Italian company Fincantieri. This ship, known as the Love Boat from the popular TV series, ranks among the world's classiest ships by virtue of all it has to offer by way of ambiance, service, amenities, and food. A Chinese-American passenger, who was on his fortieth cruise with his wife, ranked it nine on a scale of one to ten. On our way to the reception desk, Liesl and I felt like we were in a palace as we walked down the lavishly carpeted floating staircase beneath the stained-glass dome in the circular marble foyer of the four-story Grand Plaza Atrium.

To make sure we were scheduled for late seating, we strolled past the elevated aisle on which stood a concert piano, music stands, and chairs for the ship's quartet. We took one of the sparkling, brass-trimmed glass elevators upstairs, where we peeked into the grandiose Neapolitan Dining Room, which, though large, provided intimate and charming dining areas, accentuated by decorative light sconces, rich wood tones, and etched glass. As in the Grand Plaza, potted palm trees enhanced the ambiance. We knew it would be dress-up time at 8:30 p.m. and that we would sit with three more couples at the oval table. Liesl was keen to investigate Lago's Pizzeria, and we agreed that the flagstone floors and the decorative wrought-iron grillwork gave it the Italian look; the variety of gourmet pizzas on the menu whetted our appetite enough to ensure that we would be back.

As we ventured toward the top deck, we stopped by the large Princess Theater, decorated in plush burgundy, art-deco style, and were looking forward to the nightly entertainment for which the Princess line is famous. It would give me something to do in case Liesl found a companion to take her to the disco. – The pool on the top deck, one of three, was big enough to accommodate a bunch of swimmers, and there were ample chairs on all the decks to satisfy the sun worshippers. If anybody preferred to just stay up there, they could simply walk toward the international Lido Café in the Horizon Court, with indoor and outdoor seating and a twenty-four-hour menu, and choose from a multitude of culinary delights. As on most cruise ships, almost everything was available to keep you from getting bored, or feeling lonesome. – My personal priority was to see as much of God's museum as time and opportunity would permit.

Our ship set out to sea, and the golden sun was setting behind the mountain ranges still rising out of the glistening waters of the Pacific Ocean. I remembered when last I had seen the panorama with Doc, in 1956, and felt a bit melancholic. – When I awakened early in the morning, I got my first view of the snow-topped mountain ranges, their valleys hugged by a white veil of fog and the woods tinted orange by the rising sun. I pulled the curtain carefully so as not to awaken Liesl. I opened the glass door, stepped out on the balcony, and was deeply moved by the closeness of the mountains. They were no more than several hundred yards away from the silently moving *Sea Princess*. –

Liesl and I agreed that we would give each other enough space to do whatever we liked best. We knew we had to eat and take shore excursions together. We traveled well together, like friends. I was proud of Liesl, who had developed into a well-mannered lady and was unafraid to get engaged in conversations with the adults at our table, who all liked her. Already on the second day, I got acquainted with a couple from Minneapolis, an airline pilot and his very attractive wife from the Philippines, and two young adults, an attractive daughter, who was a bright freshman in college, and a handsome son, just out of college and on his way to a very successful career with American Express. Liesl and the young man took an instant liking to each other, and thenceforth were inseparable. I was not at all worried, but to the contrary, relieved that she had found someone who I knew would treat her with respect.

Our adventure cruise, blessed by almost perfect weather and friendly passengers, could not have been more perfect, starting with the most exciting scenery as the ship cruised through the Inside Passage toward our first port of call, Ketchikan, situated on an island and known as Alaska's First City, rich in Indian heritage. It was raining when we arrived. – Due to my experience with Tonio's Indian conversion, I have avoided contact with totem poles and Indian artifacts because they give me stomach pain. You may consider that narrow-minded, with which I tend to agree, but it will take a while for me to put the Indians back into the right perspective.

The rain subsided when we were coasting in a floatplane over the Misty Fjords National Monument, which seemed eerier due to the recent rain. The pilot landed on the water in between the many small, wooded islands that emerged like flat or inflated green cushions from the waters along the fjords. I did not see the bear which two copassengers swore they spotted in the distance. Who knows – perhaps Liesl's bright-red jacket scared the grizzly away. I asked the pilot to take a photo of us two standing on the platform of the tiny plane. Liesl shrugged her shoulders when I asked her if she would like to be flown to school in one of these planes, as the children up here are, but she did not mind standing next to a huge polar bear outside a souvenir store so I could take a picture of the two.

Neither Liesl nor I had ever been in a floatplane, and we marveled at the striking landscapes that we saw through the windows from the sky. I felt like an eagle encircling the Juneau Icefield and combing the centuries-old glaciers with their deep ice crevasses in search of prey. The glacier fields with the ice peaks sparkled like blue aquamarines and diamond tiaras in the bright sun and brought back memories of the turquoise glacier at Mont Blanc, in Chamonix, Switzerland, which I saw on my way home from my year abroad in France. I wished Doc, with his deep love of nature, could have shared these moments with me. I was glad to have included another floatplane excursion on our itinerary instead of panning for gold beneath the ruins of a gold mine, which I had done on my trip with Doc and Maria in 1956. I knew we would not be as lucky as Richard Harris and Joe Juneau, who after climbing many mountains, forging streams, and overcoming countless difficulties, found nuggets "as large as beans" in 1880. Three of the largest gold mines in the world resulted from their discovery. It was always a special treat to have a bird's-eye view of the small port towns and the *Sea Princess* in dock. There were always small fishing boats coming and going, because several passengers, like our Minnesotan friends, went fishing for salmon to ship home. Salmon and the business of government now fill the coffers of Juneau, Alaska's capital, with money other than gold.

While Liesl was busy with her new friend Tysen, taking full advantage of the many activities scheduled throughout the day for all ages, I spent time on deck or on the balcony, always on the lookout for a whale, which, unlike other passengers, I never saw. Yet, one afternoon, a large school of graceful dolphins danced past my balcony, only fifty yards away. –

After having cleared the Gastineau Channel and cruised through Stephens Passage, Favorite Channel, and Lynn Canal after midnight, the ship was secured alongside a railroad dock in the scenic town of Skagway early the next morning. The sun was shining, and the town at the foot of the snowcapped mountains looked just like villages you find in Bavaria, Austria, or Switzerland. I fell in love with it instantly, and Liesl and I ventured out on our own, because we had no tour to catch until afternoon. It was enjoyable to walk down Broadway with its false-front buildings, peeking inside or looking for souvenirs, and to get a sense of what it must have been like in the gold-rush era, when about twenty thousand people lived here and the hotels, saloons, dance halls, and gambling houses prospered. Thousands lived in tents until 1900, when the gold began to dwindle. – You will recall that in 1978, I had been to the Klondike Days festival in Edmonton, Canada; I was therefore overjoyed to be here, where the fever had run high. A look into the Trail of '98 Museum, with all its memorabilia, gave my historical imagination an extra boost.

Liesl, who excelled in cross-country running, persuaded me to walk up several hundred steps to a section of the town on a more elevated plateau. I was proud of myself to have climbed the flight of steps without much trouble. Up there, we discovered small but neat cedar-paneled houses and peeked into rustic gardens, bursting with richly colored flowers, from which we had a view of the bay, snow-topped mountain peaks, and exquisite green forests. – We hiked up a narrow trail along a rumbling mountain stream, where we were alone until the ship's string quartet, who had had the same idea, surfaced. We talked a while, and Liesl and I headed back to the ship for another scrumptious lunch, before we hopped aboard the train that retraced the White Pass and Yukon Route along the original Klondike Trail on a very narrow-gauge railway, all the way up to the White Pass summit, which leads to the Klondike gold fields.

The train ride reminded me a bit of the one I took when going to Machu Picchu. The terrain along the track was rough, and at times treacherous, but it was very scenic when accentuated by such waterfalls as the Bridal Veil Falls, which cascade about six thousand feet from the glaciers on Mount Cleveland and Mount Clifford. Although the scenery pales in comparison to that of Machu Picchu, I found the commentary by the guide fascinating. We learned much about the obsessions of the gold diggers, who endured extreme weather conditions, intrigue, torture, and shoot-outs with fellow fortune hunters. The diggers did not hesitate to expose the pack animals that climbed up the rocky path to unheard-of cruelties, often sending them to their deaths as they tumbled down the cliffs. This was the case in the mad stampede of 1898 at Dead Horse Gulch, where three thousand pack animals fell victim to neglect and overloading. On the way back, the train stopped at the Gold Rush Cemetery, where early Skagway residents rest side by side with "Soapy" Smith, the gold-rush gangster, Jefferson Randolph, and the hero Frank Reid, who died defending the town's honor in a final shoot-out with Soapy.

Our *Sea Princess* sailed for Glacier Bay via Lynn Canal and Icy Strait while Liesl and I sat down for dinner after a reception hosted by the captain in the Grand Plaza, where a sparkling pyramid constructed of hundreds of champagne glasses filled with the golden bubbly greeted the passengers. Everybody was dressed as elegantly as possible and had their photo taken with the captain in his snow-white uniform before sipping champagne, mingling, and relishing mouthwatering hors d'oeuvres. Liesl wore one of the fancy dresses she had designed and sewn. She wanted to be a fashion designer and looked much like a model. The string quartet played Viennese waltz melodies in the background. – The captain's dinner climaxed when some thirty waiters paraded through the darkened dining room balancing blue-flaming baked Alaska on their raised arms and hands.

Liesl, who always got in late at night or in the morning, was still asleep when I went on deck to find an ideal spot from which to view the highlight of the cruise, Glacier Bay, with its magnificent concentration of glaciers. Margerie Glacier, which flows from the 15,320-foot Mount Fairweather into Glacier Bay, combined with the St. Elias Mountains, may well be the world's most spectacularly glaciated mountain range. More than one hundred alpine and valley glaciers flow from these mighty mountains, enhanced by the dramatic backdrop of the park and its striking scenery. This spectacular scene includes twelve or more active tidewater glaciers, some retreating, some advancing, and others "calving" icebergs, which thundered into icy waters, on which small and huge chunks of ice were floating around in the picturesque fjords. We were lucky to see a brown grizzly bear trotting across a glacier field.

We cruised alongside the Grand Pacific, Johns Hopkins, and Lamplugh Glaciers before leaving the magnificent bay and setting out on a northwesterly course in the Gulf of Alaska, at high speed, toward Prince William Sound and College Fjord. We gasped each time a gigantic glacier came into view, of which College Fjord alone boasts sixteen, where either ice or a sparkling waterfall moves toward the Gulf. – We searched for possible traces of the 1989 Exxon oil spill and were relieved to see none, but we could not miss a stretch of the unsightly Alaska pipeline as we looked out the window in Seward, where we had docked during the night alongside the cruise terminal. The line was a sore spot. It disfigured the harbor, which was otherwise pretty, with its colorful wood-frame houses and the soaring cliffs that looked out on Resurrection Bay in the background.

The first gloomy morning, which was very rainy, dampened any enthusiasm to walk around the small fishing town that, since 1903, was the southern terminus of the Alaska Railroad. It seems remarkable that the residents, whose primary income is derived from commercial fishing and tourism, survived the horrifying Good Friday earthquake of 1964, when a tidal wave over one hundred feet tall washed away most of the town's waterfront.

Liesl and I went shopping for smoked salmon, and while waiting to embark for our land tour into the heart of Alaska, which was delayed due to a major accident on the road to Anchorage, we went to one of the two theaters and saw, together with Tysen, the moving film *Shakespeare in Love*, which left me fighting back tears. – Good-byes are always hard, but Liesl and I promised our newfound friends we would stay in touch, and Tysen had already assured Liesl that he would come to the airport when she stopped over in Minneapolis on the way to college in San Antonio, Texas. The Marquettes continued toward the Kenai Fjords National Park to look for wildlife and get a glimpse of the colony of thousands of puffins, while we climbed on the bus to Anchorage, from which we stayed on the lookout for wild animals in the vast and mountainous countryside. The view was occasionally highlighted by a bunch of fire-red paintbrush flowers, which I insisted on photographing. The driver was kind enough to stop. We were running late, but our guide made sure we saw more wild animals than the few white Dall sheep climbing around in the mountains along the roadside. He stopped at a sanctuary where huge caribou, elk, and buffalo grazed or rested in a loosely fenced-in field.

Our view from the room in the Sheraton was soothing. The sun was setting over the bay, and when Liesl returned from her jog in the area, we enjoyed our sushi while talking to the Asian cook and his wife behind the bar. We were not quite sure we would want to live in Anchorage, where the winters are bitter cold and the summers short. We were more interested in the Midnight Sun Express rail trip to Denali National Park and Mount McKinley, which we were to start the next morning.

Everybody smiled as they were seated in the exquisite, open-air Ultra Dome train, which reminded me of the train ride I took with Mrs. Lowe on the Santa Fe Railway years before, traveling west across the country to Las Vegas. As expected, we saw more awe-inspiring scenery, enjoyed chatting with the couple across from us, and rushed out to the viewing platform of the train whenever the guide announced a forthcoming natural phenomenon, of which Mount McKinley was the last and ultimate. Everybody hurried to adjust their binoculars or cameras when the highest mountain in North America came into sight. Later, the train pulled into the station, from which the motor coach drove us to the very rustic but impressive Mount McKinley Princess Wilderness Lodge for a two-night stay.

The passengers and guides kept saying how lucky we were to actually see the top of Mount McKinley, which is so often hidden in the clouds. The guide had no problem convincing me to change the timing of our helicopter trip to the big mountain from the next day to the current afternoon. In no time at all, Liesl and I stood next to the brand-new helicopter and received our instructions. The trip sounded a bit scary, considering that only a couple of weeks earlier, a helicopter connected with the *Princess* had crashed in this very same region, killing all of its passengers. Our hearts were beating while we listened to the pilot's emergency-landing instructions. Another couple got into the flying machine with a glass bottom for an optimal view of what lay beneath. The woman weighed at least three hundred pounds, and the pilot directed her where to sit, and to stay put. I assume she had to pay at least double for the seat because she exceeded the limit of two hundred pounds. I was glad Liesl and I sat in the front, because she would have blocked the view badly.

As soon as the copter lifted off the ground, I felt better and concentrated on the fast-approaching wonders of Denali National Park. I glanced over at Liesl, who was noticeably quiet, but smiled faintly. Neither of us had ever flown in a helicopter, and I could hardly believe that this journey into the sky, above unexplored vistas, was real. We flew higher and higher over green-carpeted mountain ranges and brown, rusty-red, and purple mountain peaks and valleys. The pilot pointed to a big brown bear and a cub crossing a valley in this vast expanse. The higher we rose, the whiter the rocks turned beneath us and the brighter the sun shone in a blue sky. Here and there, pieces of soft white clouds wafted past the mountain peaks or lingered like veils in the valleys of grinding glaciers. As the copter hovered near the white-hooded peaks, the pilot said that to get all the way up to 20,230 feet, we would have to climb three hundred more feet, which he would not dare. We were all silent, looking down on God's pure and immaculate masterpiece, which sprawled out below, before, and above us in all its glory, bathed in blinding sunlight and blue-white skies. The closeness to God was immanent in the immense expanse of this king of the mountains, and it touched my soul. – My encounter with Mount McKinley together with Liesl was truly one of the most overpowering and sublime experiences of all my worldwide travels to date.

The next day, venturing by bus through rolling tundra and taiga in Denali National Park to search for wildlife, was anticlimactic but more or less relaxing. The guide had funny tales to spin, and impressed me with his extensive knowledge of the many different trees, bushes, plants, and flowers we encountered when walking to the ranger's log cabin. The ranger too had a few stories to tell about the development of this great park. Whenever someone spotted a caribou, elk, moose, or wild bird, we all had to be quiet to avoid scaring the animal away. We stopped for hot chocolate and cookies, and looked through a big scope for bears and birds, which I could never find, unlike the other tourists. I talked to a couple who had come to Denali by way of Banff National Park, Canada. They were delirious about Lake Louise, where I had been in 1980, and immediately awakened my desire to revisit that scenic landmark in the not-too-distant future.

I felt rejuvenated when we had landed safely. Now, nothing could scare me away from going white-water rafting with Liesl on the icy torrents of the Nenana River. The guides helped us seven adventurers put on the wet suits before the wild ride down the river began. All the others were younger than I. Liesl sat in the front of the raft with two other college-age girls. I had no idea what I was in for, but was rapidly initiated when the freezing water splashed all over us. We screamed and laughed and chatted, and we prayed to the Lord to keep us afloat when the raft hit big rocks that bounced us in the opposite direction. We had an experienced oarsman, who, after an hour's ups and downs, more wild than a rollercoaster trip, steered us safely to shore, where a van met us and drove us back to the lodge just in time to catch the bus that took us to the Midnight Sun Express.

The train went along the Nenana River for a while, so we could follow from the window the rugged path we had just rafted, and we thanked our guardian angel for saving us from tipping over. A few days earlier, four elderly women had met their tragic end by drowning and freezing to death in the icy water of the river when their raft turned upside down, leaving them underneath.

Liesl chatted away happily on the train, and we both loved the wild-salmon dinner served in the dining car. I had thought the salmon on the ship could not be surpassed, but on the Express it was superb. – When it came time to bid farewell to our travel companions, I was a bit disappointed when Liesl balked at helping me with my suitcase, at which our table partners raised their eyebrows. – By the time we checked in at the hotel in Fairbanks, it was too late to go sightseeing, because we had to catch our flight early in the morning. Liesl, always a bit detached and more and more like her mother, bade me farewell to fly to Oregon. I took off an hour later for hot and humid Indiana, where I arrived in the early afternoon on July 21, still keyed up about the Mount McKinley climax. I got wound up again when I met a tall, dark, and very handsome young man at the body shop who had repaired a dent in my car. I found it incredible that this man, who was a judge at the Winter Olympics two years before, had actually climbed that big mountain.

I got into an animated discussion with Mr. Handsome, relating a few stories of my life, including Doc's climbing of Mont Blanc, in which he became quite interested. When I mentioned I was seriously thinking of writing my memoirs as soon as I mastered the laptop I had acquired in April, he gave me his card and made me promise to notify him as soon as the opus was available.

Doc's Grandson and Wife Come to Visit – Plans for Lake Louise – More Music, Disappointing Friendships, and New Wunderkinder

Looking back, I realize I have always had the tendency to plan another adventure soon after one lies behind me. I had told Liesl a year earlier that I would like to show her the world and reiterated this wish on the cruise. I also explained that it would be prudent to keep going while I was still able. I had never watched her ski and expressed my desire to show her Lake Louise and stay once more at the impressive Chateau Lake Louise. She could try out the slopes in Canada right after her first freshman semester. I guaranteed she would be home for Christmas. We even considered that Tysen, whom she really liked, might come along. She was willing to use her frequent-flyer points, which were about to expire, for the flight. I too had enough rewards for the trip.

I had invited my newfound relatives, Doc's grandson and his wife, for a visit, and though their stay would be all too brief, I wanted to turn it into a special occasion. Sabine was in, and when she happily agreed to play the piano, I arranged for an impromptu summer Schubertiade, to which I invited about twenty of my favorite Schubertiade friends, asking everybody to bring a dish, because I knew I would be busy showing my relatives around. It was wonderful to greet them in my home, to be able to show them some of the antiques and memorabilia from the Croft, and to catch up on the boys. I was hoping with them that Eric would spend his year abroad in France, because I was intent on giving the boys a cruise to the Greek Isles as a graduation gift at the end of Eric's year in Paris.

Sailing and boating is Wayne's primary passion – he participates in and has accumulated numerous trophies at major regattas, including some to Bermuda. I therefore took them out to Lake Monroe, Indiana's biggest man-made lake, to show him and Diane that, if they decided to retire in the area, they would have a place to indulge their passion. They smiled politely as we gazed at the boats lined up on the shore close to the Fourwinds Resort, but I knew full well that Lake Monroe could not compare to Long Island Sound. Even the boys, who were sailing instructors during the summer, would most likely have raised their noses.

It was a bold attempt on my part to compete with what the Big Apple had to offer by way of music, but I was certain our special summer Schubertiade, with Sabine at my Knabe, could give New York at least a run for its money. I had wanted Wayne and Diane to meet my friends and vice versa, and since we had so little time, what better way to do it than in the form of a feast with good music, hors d'oeuvres, and champagne? I would have liked to show them more of what we had to offer, but the next morning they were already headed east, and thanks to the maps on Wayne's computer, they returned home in record time.

Shortly before the beginning of the fall semester, I was invited for dinner by Jane and Dick, two lovely Schubertiade friends, to meet a couple from the former East Germany and their two daughters. I had not yet been to their home, located in Bloomington's upscale neighborhood, and appreciated especially the beautiful and healthy plants and flowers they had placed both within and outside their large and tastefully decorated home. Jane, who definitely had a green thumb, of which I was envious, was from England, and I liked to listen to her accent. She and her

American husband, who lived in Australia for over twenty years, were genuine patrons of the arts. Jane, a docent at the IU Art Museum, continuously audited art courses and took under her wing gifted foreign students, such as Soon Ron Youn, a young Korean woman and a figure and fiber artist, whose extraordinary talents I admired at an exhibit at our museum. This time, the generous people had committed themselves to helping one of the daughters of the visiting German couple, both physicians, in exchange for their hospitality when they met on a trip to Germany.

Loreley was sitting diagonally across the big dining-room table from me, sipping wine. We drifted into discussions about East Germany, which led to my experiences in the GDR and, as so often, my immigration and marriage to Doc, at which point I heard Loreley's dark, masculine, and rather hoarse voice shouting in German for everybody's benefit, except the host's, remarks across the table to the effect that I had been married to an old codger. At this point I retaliated by raving about Doc's professional and human qualities, reminded her of the Duke of Thurn and Taxis, who married a girl more than thirty years his junior, and pointed out that she neglected to mention I also married the brilliant and handsome Tonio, who was much younger than I. I announced that eventually they could all read about it in the book I was about to write. Loreley turned red in the face, gulped down more wine, and in an even more disdainful tone of voice, began questioning the sanity of anybody (by whom she meant me) who would want to "undress" him- or herself, as she put it, before the public eye. I told her it takes guts to write honestly, and was tempted to add that she did not have what it takes, but dropped it. The guests soon forgot the incident, but I probably never will. Yet I continued to be polite whenever we were together. Since that time, I have considered Loreley just another so-called friend, of which I have several, including Rita, who on various occasions has cracked an age- and money-related remark about my benefiting from Doc's early demise, which really makes my blood boil, and which you will appreciate when you consider her marriage to a husband with a partial brain.

Oh, what petty rivalries among old wenches! Why, with the exception of my friend Renate and a few others who never once treated me with disrespect over the course of twenty years, does it more often than not happen with the Germans? – Of course, I could refrain from talking about it, but it is a part of life. So often, the little things cause longer-lasting pain than catastrophes.

But as soon as the Oktoberfest rolled around, all seemed forgotten, and Loreley, the Thistle, and Dele, who for a couple of years steered clear of her prickly opponent, always prepared a potato salad that all my American and foreign guests liked. Our Turkish pianist spiced the festival with his ingenious improvisations and turned it into another memorable event, filled with song and laughter. Hakan found what he was looking for, too: a replacement for his Scandinavian girlfriend. He and Tanja, the German girl from the GDR, fell almost too passionately in love, and for the duration of her stay in the States, they were, at times much to the dismay of her foster parents, who had helped her settle in an apartment with a rented piano, inseparable. I wished my friend Bettina and her parents, the Segebrechts, could have joined me for one of the Oktoberfests or musical soirees. I felt so sorry for Tine, who discovered a few months after she had returned from her vacation with me that her charming boyfriend of nine years had struck up a relationship with another law student, a girl from the former GDR. Ironically, it started when he was studying with the girl for the law exam announced during Bettina's absence – an exam he never took, because in midcourse his focus changed from courtroom law to nature's law. Had I known what the scoundrel had been up to, I would never have sent him the onyx dolphin from Cancún, for which he never thanked me.

Loreley, who is insatiable when it comes to both self-adoration and admiration bestowed upon her by others, had included me on her guest list for as grandiose a birthday party as you can imagine, even though she knew how I felt about such events of self-glorification. – Had the party been scheduled a week earlier, I would have had a good excuse, because my good neighbors, the Overlys, had invited me for a performance at the Brown County Playhouse, where we laughed heartily over Neil Simon's *Lost in Yonkers*. – More than thirty guests were gathered in the reception room leading to a big, somewhat sinister-looking banquet room in the Memorial Union at IU. Loreley was the mother queen, dressed in a jet-black, knee-length, long-sleeved, and waistless coatdress. You might have surmised she was commemorating the passing of someone dear. But we knew she wanted to celebrate her birthday and be toasted with champagne, which we all did with the expected reverence. She looked really nice, perfectly coiffed and mani- and pedicured, just as she does on days when she is scheduled for an operation at the local hospital. Even more attractive was the magnificent silver bowl (from her personal collection, I am sure) overflowing with several dozen dark-red long-stemmed roses and placed in the center of the long banquet table. Our tiara-less majesty, surrounded by her three biological sons, sat at the head of the table. Far away, at the opposite end, sat her oldest daughter, whose father had been and still is the subject of much speculation and gossip, as well as one of her daughter-in-laws, Rita, and I. I felt a bit sorry for the daughter, who was noticeably not among the favored offspring. The food was good, and I had fun with the daughter in an effort to dig deeper into the age question, which even to this date, when all the attention is naturally directed toward celebrating the fortune or misfortune of being alive rather than dead, she will reveal nothing about. I have never been to a birthday party where the celebrant hushed up the date that all were invited to celebrate. I have heard you can now find out anybody's age on the Internet, which at times I am tempted to do, but then I could not poke fun at my "friend."

Many of Loreley's guests came to the November 5 Schubertiade. The event also included a new guest, Ruth Hanner, whom I met in the Walmart parking lot. I noticed that an elderly lady was having trouble transferring a heavy bag of bird feed from the cart to her trunk and offered to help. We talked, and it turned out that she had a son living in Nuremberg, Germany. He was an opera singer, a baritone, and her grandson was with the conservatory in Graz, Austria. She gladly accepted my invitation and brought another pianist along as her guest. – It's one way to ensure a full house. The artists loved to have a big audience, which, due to the heavy competition with numerous performances at the School of Music, was not easily achieved. Yet, on November 5, more than forty people filed in.

I had already bought a dozen extra folding chairs, but had to borrow more from my other kind neighbors, the Greens, who came whenever their grown children and grandchildren did not keep them busy. I squeezed chairs into every free spot imaginable and was actually relieved when a few people had to cancel at the last minute because someone's mother had died.

Sabine and Fernando had planned another climactic evening from start to finish. Stephen Spooner played brilliantly again, and Fernando had gotten hold of two Brazilian sopranos, a mother and her daughter, who was twenty-two, and a Japanese violinist who also studied with Shkolnikova. Fernando, extremely well versed in the opera repertoire, accompanied Madame de Oliviera and her young, fiery, and beautiful daughter, Edlyn de Oliviera. She had recently competed in Placido Domingo's World Opera Competition in Puerto Rico, and, as a semifinalist, was invited by Domingo to return. Her voice was so overpowering and passionate that she brought the house down when she sang. Tears were flowing freely. One should perhaps not be surprised, because her father is an opera singer in Brazil. I am convinced she will dazzle the music world in the future. She had her sights set on New York, where she moved right after she earned her diploma.

The exhilarating soiree contrasted with my visit the next evening to the home of my colleague and comember on the International Studies Committee, Professor Albrecht Holschuh, whose specialty is German lyric poetry of the twentieth century, with a focus on the poet Ingeborg Bachmann, whom he personally met when he was at Princeton. Albrecht, whose second wife I remembered from the time I had been enrolled in German honors courses when pursuing the PhD, greeted us with his new, very attractive young wife, Debbie, at the front door of his spacious and rustic wooden house deep in the forest. Here calm and peacefulness reigned supreme. I had heard others rave about the place, and with my penchant for rustic places and scenery, I too was enchanted. I fell in love with the extra-large stone fireplace, which held logs so long they would not have fit into my fireplace. I was impressed when Albrecht told me he fells the trees for firewood himself. – I told them that a few days earlier I had been invited to Nelli Shkolnikova's home, where a gas fireplace was burning, to attend a recital by one of her students, the young Chernyavsky, from Russia. I felt ever so much more comfortable in the rustic home than at the villa of the celebrated Russian violinist. Her large modern home was filled with invaluable treasures, so artfully displayed that I thought I was in a museum.

The Piedmonts had picked me up, for which I was grateful, because the place was hidden so far away from other houses I never would have found it. We spent a pleasant evening at the hideaway, without my getting needled by the Thistle, and I got caught up on much of the German Department gossip. Of course, I already knew that Lou Helbig, former dean of International Studies, had divorced his wife in a rather devious way, after having a mistress hidden away in Germany for years. I bet the betrayed wife wished she had ignored him when his life hung in the balance after they removed I don't remember how many feet of cancerous intestines. Professor Weisstein, who had sat on my dissertation committee, had also divorced his wife and replaced her with another one in Austria. Steven Wales, the medievalist, had had the fortune or misfortune, depending on how you look at it, of bringing into this world a surprise baby from a student whom his wife had graciously invited to stay at their house while taking her husband's courses. So much for generosity. Some critiqued the age difference of thirty years or so. As you know, it's not at all important to me, and after all I am in "learned" company. The only difference is that I am a female professor.

The retreat to the Holschuh lodge had been badly needed. I also got a few new tips as to what I could learn through the Internet and how to cope with computer problems, and I was encouraged not to hesitate to consult the very knowledgeable IU computer assistants, who had already proven to be invaluable resources while I was delving to bring forth the miracles from my Pandora's box. I was about to start writing my memoirs. But, like so many times before, another invitation came my way, this one for the next day, Sunday, November 7, which I just could not refuse, since it came from my friends the Newmans. Lou had been elected president of the Friends of Music and invited me to the fourth-annual Auer Hall honors performances, where a number of scholarship recipients performed.

The highlight of that afternoon was the performance given by Leor Maltinski, a Russian-born twenty-two-year-old student of Madame Shkolnikova, who pursued his studies in Italy's greatest cities until Zubin Mehta sent him to study with Abram Shtern in LA. He had just won first place at the Carl Nielsen International Violin Competition in New York, which gave him a good start on his climb to the top. – He simply took my breath away at the first stroke. He and his outstanding young pianist, the French-born Julien Quentin, gave sizzling performances of Henryk Wieniawski's Polonaise in D Major, op. 4, and Niels Gade's Capriccio. I was instantly reminded of the time in Auer Hall when I heard Mark Kosower play the cello for the first time. Leor had something of Yehudi Menuhin's quality when he played.

I was so animated I simply had to ask the two if they would consider playing for us at a Schubertiade. I went to the reception and waited, together with many, in vain for their appearance. I decided to leave the building, but ran into some construction work. I had difficulty locating an exit door and found myself in a narrow room with huge glass panels that looked toward the parking lot. Suddenly I spotted Leor and Julien walking toward me from the parking lot. I started knocking loudly at the big window. They noticed me at once, and somehow I found a narrow door, which opened when I pushed. The two young men, both with dark-brown hair and very handsome, stood right in front of me, smiling from ear to ear. I congratulated them excitedly and gave both a big hug, and they hugged me in return. Their eyes were sparkling. I introduced myself and discovered to my surprise that they had already heard about the Schubertiades. It turned out that the Brazilians had befriended them and had raved about the Friday-evening event. I asked if they would consider playing at my place even though we would not pay them anything, and instantly they said, "Yes, Madame, we would love to play." – I was overjoyed. What a coup, and what an event to look forward to! I wondered how it was that, at times, I could be so lucky. – I invited the two new wunderkinder to come to the next Schubertiade, this one on Thursday, December 2, instead of the usual Friday. The event, I was convinced, promised to be another milestone in my own musical life, which, as I approach the end of my memoirs, it is high time for me to retrace briefly, just to refresh your memory.

Interlude

As I look back, it becomes evident that music was my first love. (For a couple of years I even deluded myself that I was in love with a professional musician – you will recall Amadeus.) A year or so before my father passed away at the age of seventy, I wrote him a letter thanking him for instilling a great love and sensitivity for music within me. When I was five years old I had started taking violin lessons on a half-size violin with the well-known teacher Frieda Ritter, who often let me stay after my lesson to listen to her play or watch her teach other students. She also sent me to hospitals to play for wounded soldiers. Each year my parents invited a number of music students for house concerts at our apartment on Kleine Düwelstraße. My older brother had started out with piano lessons, but switched to cello because my father was constantly yelling at him. My younger brother played the recorder. My mother had a beautiful voice, and I loved it when she sang, accompanied by my father, who played the piano very well. I was always ready to play sonatas with him. Mutti said she married my father because he played the piano. Papa had a love affair with his pianos, much like the one I had with my violins. During my first lesson, Frau Ritter impressed on me the importance of caring for it like a baby. I tucked my instrument into the pretty silk bag which Mutti had made for it, but Papa's pianos were the most dusted and polished pieces of furniture in the house. One could never find a speck of dust or a fingerprint on them. The one on Kleine Düwelstraße, which burned when our house was bombed, was black ebony, and the other one, the first piece of furniture he bought after the war, was dark mahogany, Queen Anne style. Once, when little, I climbed on the piano stool and reached for the cigar stump in the ashtray on top of the upright and took a puff. I suffered severe stomach cramps, ran downstairs, went to the bakery across the street, and asked for a cookie. I had no money and asked the lady to put it on a tab. Mutti was not pleased about it, but did not tell Papa. I did not get a licking that time.

Piano and violin playing ran in my father's family. His older brother, Artur, whom I never met because he lived in East Germany, was supposedly, as I pointed out earlier, very gifted. According to some reviews I found, he was an exceptional musician showing great promise. He also played the violin in the Leipziger Gewandhaus Orchestra, I was told. When the war was lost and the Soviet Union moved into Leipzig, his career went in reverse, and he found himself forced to earn a living playing in coffeehouses and the like. Later, after I had already immigrated to America, he and his wife defected. They sought refuge with my parents, arriving only with a couple of suitcases and a box of sheet music. Several months later they went to Zurich, Switzerland, and lived with his wife's relatives. I very much regret never having had an occasion to communicate with Uncle Artur about his musical experience. He had no children.

I used to think that my father felt he stood in the shadow of his bigger brother and that he secretly hoped one of us children would become a great musician. As early as I can remember, Papa took me to dress rehearsals at the opera house in Hannover. I was no older than five or six when we both stood on the highest balcony listening to Wagner's *Parsifal*. On other Sundays, after church, when we were dressed in our best outfits, Papa went promenading with us on the Maschsee, while Mutti was at home in the kitchen preparing the Sunday meal. We listened to the local bands playing marches and waltzes in a pavilion. Papa always accompanied the musicians by hitting a book or the seat of a bench with his knuckles. – Until we were evacuated, we always attended Humperdinck's *Hänsel und Gretel* at Christmastime.

When I had to join the BDM, the equivalent of Hitler Youth for girls, Mutti was instrumental in getting a dispensation from the doctor for me to play violin in, and learn how to conduct, a youth orchestra in lieu of marching on the big plaza in front of our church, Sankt Heinrich, on Sundays when Mass was celebrated inside. Even when we moved around due to mandatory evacuations or bombings, my parents saw to it that I continued with violin lessons. I had lessons in V. when we lived with Aunt Sissy and the tyrannical Uncle Adolf. At Sankt Ursula I took up instruction with the organist, who also taught violin. In addition I played in two school orchestras and sang in the choir. Most of all, I learned to respect and admire my best and most influential music teacher at the convent school, Marianne Schirduan. I will never forget the time we earned much applause for our performance of Mozart's *Bastien und Bastienne* in the auditorium.

I have previously described Marianne's fabulous soprano voice and her outstanding skills as a conductor, and I am convinced that my exposure to her teaching later gained me an entrance into the big Niedersachsen Chor (choir of Lower Saxony), where I met another professional singer, the soprano Maria Gärtner, who gave me free voice lessons in exchange for my accompanying her on the violin. Mrs. Gärtner introduced my family to a young pianist whose name I have forgotten. Occasionally, my parents would invite him for evening supper. He was a refugee from Kiev, Russia, now Ukraine, where he left behind his mother, an opera singer, and his father, a reputable attorney. He was slender and tall. His hair was dark brown and curly, and his eyes were black and melancholic. There was a certain sadness in him. It was my first time to hear a professional pianist play in our apartment. The experience was simply awesome when he played Alexander Scriabin's Nocturne no. 9 for one hand. The floor in the apartment trembled. I accompanied him to the electric streetcar later that evening. While waiting, he discovered that Mutti had put a sandwich in his coat pocket. He was so grateful. He always kissed my hand and stood up and bowed whenever we toasted with a glass of wine. When I was away on a vacation, he sent me a short composition I no longer have. I was nineteen years old at that time; the pianist was probably fifteen years older. Papa used to walk ten yards behind us when we went to the streetcar stop.

Shortly before my emigration, our choir performed in Mahler's Symphony no. 8 in E-flat Major in the opera house in Hannover and sang Beethoven's *Missa Solemnis* before an audience of approximately three thousand people in Stadthalle (City Hall), a huge hall with a dome near the Maschsee. The performances of both masterpieces were unforgettable. –

After I had immigrated to America, I traveled to Washington, D.C., and was invited to a concert by Mr. and Mrs. Guillermo Espinosa of the Pan-American Union, who were friends of Dr. Thierfelder, the conductor of the Niedersachsen Chor. He was there to conduct guest performances. But on that day, Palm Sunday, 1955, I was afforded the unique opportunity to co-critique with John Haskins, music critic of the *Washington Evening Star* (as well as the best man of J. F. Porter), the performance of the Washington National Cathedral Choir. They sang Bach's *St. John Passion* with the National Symphony Orchestra, conducted by Paul Callaway.

My arrival in America did not stop me from playing my violin. I played every day at Wetherbee Lake Farm, despite the fact that my sponsors treated me most shabbily. Whenever I played I felt at peace. I was fortunate to find an elderly lady, the mother-in-law of my sponsor, who loved to accompany me on their Steinway, much to the chagrin of the Neverbees. Playing with Mrs. D. had been much more pleasant than singing in the church choir in that tiny church in Cassopolis, Michigan. I don't recall that they ever sang an entire hymn in tune. I tried my best to help improve the quality, yet in vain. My hypersensitivity to dissonant sounds and noises stemming from humans in particular caused me to withdraw. I quit the choir and concentrated on my precious violin, which my parents had gotten for me by some mysterious means from East Germany, at considerable financial sacrifice. The cellist from the International String Quartet thought the bow was worth more than the violin.

My musical appetite was appeased once I found employment at Miles Laboratories in Elkhart, Michigan, with the help of the Beardsleys. Moving to the YWCA in Elkhart made it possible for me not only to continue with violin lessons, but to play second violin in the Elkhart Symphony. It was not exactly a perfect orchestra, but its status was low enough for me to be accepted. The conductor was also my teacher. It was wonderful to be among musicians in the New World and make friends who shared my interest. After our marriage, Doc drove me once a week to Mishawaka so I could continue lessons with my friend Mary Jo, who later joined the Denver Symphony Orchestra for a couple of years. Since Doc had bought the baby grand right after the wedding, I was happy to have an instrument on which I could be accompanied. Above all, I felt, like my parents, that a piano is the soul of the home. As soon as I had my own place in South Bend, Indiana, I bought the Knabe baby grand, which I took along wherever I moved, first to Princeton, New Jersey, and eventually to Bloomington, Indiana.

1999 Christmas Schubertiade

Wherever my Knabe moved, we found ways to draw musicians into our fold. We derived the ultimate pleasure from its presence when, in December 1999, the last Christmas month of the twentieth century and the millennium, we hosted another incredible event, which I call the Christmas Schubertiade.

Preparation for the event began at Thanksgiving. It was unseasonably warm when I started by hanging the more than one thousand tiny white Christmas lights over trees and bushes around the house. I draped Christmas garlands in the entryway leading from the front hall into the music room, where my Knabe reigns supreme. I hung a wreath decorated with the same lights next to the entrance to the garage, tied bright-red bows on the wreath and the five crystal globes illuminating the path leading to the main entrance, and placed one on my A-frame birdhouse. Shiny golden and crystal angels holding musical instruments intermingled with little wooden violins that dangled on the garlands. In the center hung a golden star, embraced by two angels, draped in white and dark-red robes, respectively. One was blowing into a trumpet and the other into a French horn. When the lights were turned on, the musical ornaments glittered festively.

With the exception of the Christmas tree, which I did not put up at that time in order to save room for the cellist and his instrument, the house was in its Christmas dress throughout. Red and white flickering candles were everywhere. It started in the entryway and continued into the music room, the dining room, the kitchen, the library, and the winter garden. Candles were on mantelpieces, in the kitchen and library, in the dining room on the big TV set, on every table, next to the piano, even on windowsills. On the mantel over the see-through red-brick fireplace paraded my various nutcrackers, which had been given to me over the years by people very close to me. All of them knew I had written my first book, my dissertation, about E. T. A. Hoffmann's fantastic fairy tales with a focus on the master figures, which include

Drosselmeier, the clockmaker from *The Nutcracker and the Mouse King*. Mutti, who gave me a sturdy nutcracker figure wearing a light brown and beige uniform, was aware of my fascination with Hoffmann and the "music and magic" in his works. Mutti's nutcracker could actually crack nuts without breaking his tongue or teeth. My good friends the Segebrechts gave the second nutcracker, which wore a shiny black uniform, to me. The third, a tall and slender chap, dressed in a shiny red, black, and white uniform, was the surprise gift after my trip to Seiffen in the former German Democratic Republic, a thank-you for bringing many sought-after dollars to them by way of my American students. I put him next to my most recently acquired nutcracker, the pretty clone of the one I saw dancing when Wayne and Diane took me to the memorable performance of *The Nutcracker* by the New York City Ballet at Lincoln Center.

The nutcrackers were my most treasured Christmas tokens until recently, when two precious angels joined them. One is handcrafted and made of golden tinsel. My friends from Bamberg had chosen it for me at the legendary Weihnachtsmarkt (Christmas Market) in Nuremberg, Germany. The other angel, sent from Doc's offspring in New York for Christmas, is of frosted crystal, by Mikasa from Austria, and arrived just before I left for Lake Louise. He has his place of honor on the piano. A long candle fits in a holder between his wings and shines down on the figurine like a star. It reminds me of Liesl walking into the room dressed as an angel, carrying a burning candle, and softly singing "We Wish You a Merry Christmas." How well these angels fit into my 1999 Christmas Schubertiade theme.

Our Christmas Schubertiade was so special not only because it was the twenty-seventh concert since Hie-Yon started the series in 1996, but because Mark Kosower, after five performances at my house, was one of our very favorite performers. He was flying in from New York, where he had a full scholarship at Juilliard. Jee-Won Oh, an international prizewinner and at that time a student of György Sebők as well as a studio pianist and assistant to János Starker, was Mark's accompanist. Still at Juilliard and rapidly making a major mark as a soloist with big orchestras, Mark is now happily married to Jee-Won.

The minute Mark and Jee-Won entered the house, he paused at the entrance to the music room, taking in its Christmas splendor. His eyes were sparkling when he said, "This really makes me want to play!"

At each Schubertiade, our young artists surprise us with even greater excellence than we thought possible. Just when we think they are close to the pinnacle, they soar higher. Mark and Jee-Won performed Robert Schumann's Adagio and Allegro, op. 70, Benjamin Britten's Sonata, op. 65, and Ernst von Dohnányi's Sonata in B-flat Minor, op. 8. It was a moving, sparkling, and explosive performance. The audience jumped to their feet. Their bravos and bravissimos were as passionate as their applause. Once again, these human miracles had transported us high into the realm of Regina Musica. – In keeping with our tradition, I handed each artist a long-stemmed red rose, accompanied by tight hugs and tearful eyes.

When the applause ceased, the guests got up to congratulate the artists, and to assist in clearing away the chairs in the dining room so we could place the food on the dining-room table, which is Queen Anne style, just like Papa's new piano. I put evergreen branches into the horns of the epergne, the centerpiece, and in keeping with the angel motif throughout the house, I had suspended from the branches small crystal angels holding golden instruments. They glittered in the light of the burning candles. The memories of the Croft are kept alive wherever I go, since I withheld a selection of Doc's favorite antiques when the rest were auctioned off at the time I felt compelled to sell the farm. Whenever I use them for social functions, especially the Schubertiades, these dishes remind me of our first and only anniversary party.

The big, golden tinsel angel from my friends in Bamberg crowned an evergreen branch arranged in a big crystal vase, which stood on the long cherrywood serving table behind the tan leather couch and in front of the dark-brown walnut shelf wall. The shelf wall holds the third of my library that I did not donate to Princeton's Firestone Library before moving to Bloomington. Opposite the SABA/Bang & Olufsen entertainment center is the glass door that opens onto the spacious winter garden, where the cobalt-blue-tiled wood-burning stove stands. Together with the Knabe and the SABA, it is a mover's nightmare.

As usual, artists and guests chose to socialize in the library/entertainment room or relax in the deep-cushioned wicker furniture in the winter garden. It harmonizes with the red-brown hue of the rough cedar walls and ceiling. Like the rooms in the Croft, the wide windowfronts create the illusion that the room extends outward to the wooded embankment, where the animals from the fields gather to feed whenever they feel the need. My music-loving guests got excited when they spotted the deer feeding at the crib and wagging their white, bushy tails at them in the yellow sheen of the floodlight.

For the Christmas Schubertiade, the big ficus trees in the winter garden, reaching up to the cathedral ceiling and skylights, were decorated with tiny white Christmas lights. Burning candles alternated with houseplants on the long, cobalt-blue-tiled windowsills. Instead of champagne, at Christmastime, my old favorite, *Feuerzangenbowle* or *Krambambuli*, is served, along with all the hocus pocus witnessed by the students at my Christmas parties on Southeast Drive. The more or less senior Schubertiade crowd enjoys it as much as the students. Mark and Jee-Won sipped the hot wine-rum concoction slowly. They were as happy as the rest of the guests, including Sabine, who had found a most able successor to replace her when it was time for her to leave for the Mozarteum, in Austria, to further her studies, and subsequently to embark on an extensive career as a concert pianist. She recommended the twenty-four-year-old Julien Quentin, whom I had invited to play at a future event. The charming French pianist had repeatedly excelled on the international concert stage, but promised to find room in his busy concert schedule to grace our circle with his talents. I guarantee the music world will hear more about Julien Quentin once he finishes his artist diploma in 2002. As I write, I can report that he did not disappoint us. In fact, we are planning our Schubertiaden Finale for April 5, 2002. If you don't believe me, ask my Knabe.

Winter Wonderland with Liesl at Lake Louise – Turn-of-the-Millennium Denouement at Home

The Christmas Schubertiade was the prelude to what would take place in December 1999. It would have been perfect in every way had it not been for the missing snow. Yet, in anticipation of a mild December, the minute I had returned from that fabulous cruise, I began planning the next adventure for us, to Lake Louise, Canada. As you know, the awesome snow-topped mountain peaks, the majestic and massive blue-green glaciers in Glacier Bay, and ultimately our helicopter trip to the highest mountain in North America were responsible for arousing my nostalgia for that scenic spot.

I have had a lifelong obsession with snow. Each winter season, even today, when I am almost seventy years old, childhood memories still linger and resurface at Christmas. Already as a child, when living on Kleine Düwelstraße, I thirsted for snow. One winter we had mountains of snow, and my male playmates were building a snow burgh on the playground opposite our house. To gain entrance into their kingdom I had to pass a test. It meant standing on top of the stairs leading down to the playground and, for several minutes, quietly allowing four somewhat older boys to shovel tons of snow in my face and all over my body. I passed gloriously, and they made me queen of their castle.

Although I was much older, I loved to play in the snow with Gustl and Liesl and watch them sledding at Southeast Drive, where we lived right in snowbelt country, close to the Great Lakes. I wish I had been able to keep a sketch Antonio made of me from the back, standing and looking out of the picture window in the nude. He entitled it *Christa wartet auf Schnee* (Christa Is Waiting for Snow).

I had seen Lake Louise with Ingeborg Guenther in the summer, and I was eager to see the mountains under a blanket of snow. I had decided to present this other place in the world to Liesl as a Christmas gift. She is a skier, and I was anxious to see her on the slopes just once. The closest I ever came to skiing was when we were evacuated and lived near V., in the low mountains of the Solling in Aunt Sissy and Uncle Adolf's luxurious mansion. Major Haas, the boarder from Vienna who supervised the Ukrainian female prisoners, put us on a couple of rough boards. They had been dipped into hot water to bend them at the end so they would resemble skis. He virtually dragged us through the snow. It was sheer torture, because he had perfect skis and was always fifty yards ahead of us.

1995–2000

Liesl had flown to Calgary from Trinity University in San Antonio, Texas, where she had finished her first semester. As we approached Banff National Park in our rented car, it began to snow gently, adding to the two feet of snow of the previous day. Winter wonderland was opening its gates for us to enter. There was very little traffic, and we coasted in at a moderate speed, admiring the snow-covered scenery. We drove up to the grandiose Chateau Lake Louise and were greeted by an attendant in uniform, who unpacked and parked the car. The temperature was a nippy 10 degrees Fahrenheit. We had a spacious room, furnished with Bavarian-style beds and wardrobes. It had a big window looking out toward the diamond-shaped lake, which was covered with snow, flanked by white mountain tops, and showing off a wide glacier mass, invisibly inching its way toward the frozen lake. The view was compelling and intoxicating each time you looked out the window.

Early the next morning, Liesl, bundled up in her bright-yellow-and-green ski outfit, skis in hand, was ready to head toward the slopes in a bus that picked her up. I watched the bus drive toward the rising sun, and went to the spacious English-style library of the Chateau. I sat at a desk in front of a huge window and, with my binoculars, traced the sun's movement up the mountaintops, painting them first bright orange and then yellow, lighter and brighter rather quickly, until the whole panorama bedazzled me. When clouds were hanging at the foot of the mountains, they created an eerie atmosphere. When the skies were clear, the rocky formations seemed closer. The lake was frozen, but a portion was cleared off for skaters, and two hockey goals had been set up. It reminded me of my skating days at the Maschsee. – In the center of the cleared portion was a big ice sculpture. It was a replica of a big gate to the Chateau, engraved with "1890–2000" above the arch. Other big and artfully carved sculptures were mounted between towering evergreens growing on the spacious grounds of the Chateau. Liesl and I felt drawn in particular to a large reindeer, hitched to a sleigh in which visitors could sit and have a snapshot taken. Liesl tried in vain to crawl on top of the slick deer. I reminded her of the fruitless attempts to crawl up a maple tree in our backyard when she was only five or six. Gustl had a favorite hiding place in the same tree, which he climbed when he was pouting or playing hide-and-seek.

When Liesl went skiing, I met her at the Lodge of the Ten Peaks for lunch. It was a beautiful structure with posts and beams and a huge, open-faced stone fireplace that reached the ceiling. Skiers huddled close to the fire to warm their cold hands and feet. In back of the lodge rose the slopes and the lifts that transported the skiers to the top, for more or less daring and at times dangerous trips back down. An extensive front of windows looking out to the slopes and landscape let in much sunlight, and I quickly got over a mild touch of stomach flu that had threatened to ruin it all for me. I loved seeing Liesl, tall and slender, mix in with the eager skiers dressed in their colorful outfits. They jumped on the lifts with their feet and skis dangling in the air, ready to start downhill as soon as they hit the ground on the top. I was thrilled to see my girl in action in this skiers' paradise. She had met a young man, and vowed she had never been challenged as much. Fortunately he helped her when she fell, which seems to be no big deal to skiers. When Liesl tried to teach me how to cross-country ski before we went home, I did not exactly enjoy my falls and was about to give up. She enjoyed challenging me in skiing – just as she had coaxed me into white-water rafting in Denali National Park, Alaska, a few months earlier.

The dogsledding venture at Lake Louise may have been my first and last, just like the helicopter and floatplane rides in Alaska. We had ample snow, and since we did not go dogsledding in Alaska, it was an absolute must, no matter how cold it got. I knew Liesl loved sledding. – I had been on some dangerous bobsledding trips with my teenage buddies on the curving downhill roads on the Bollert, a forest-covered mountain in the Solling. It was always a midnight venture. The guys tied together three sleds. We pulled the snake up the moonlit road for about an hour, took our seats, and sped down like lightning. The ultimate danger spot was a crossing road, followed by an even steeper decline. My cousin, the captain, always yelled, "Make your will!" just before he saw it. We zoomed across and down. Always lucky! –

To reach the dogsleds, Liesl and I had to walk downhill from the Chateau for about ten minutes. We had bundled up with layers of warm clothes, mittens, woolen caps, scarves, fur-lined boots, and goggles. We heard the huskies barking shrill and loud as we approached. The owner had hauled about one hundred of his 180 dogs to the station. The dogs had thick black, brown, or reddish-brown fur, with fluffy white hairs mixed in around their faces. They were tied to long cables anchored in the ground and pulled fiercely, anxious to whisk away the minute they were freed. Our guide chose eight dogs and introduced them by name and position as he hitched them in front of our two-seater sled and after he had tucked us in tightly with down covers. The sun was shining brightly. Ten degrees Fahrenheit was not warm, but a year before they had endured negative 40 degrees Celsius. At first the dogs were hampered from running swiftly, because some of the huskies pulling one of the sleds ahead of ours kept stalling and pooping until their guide rearranged their positions. Eventually all animals sped along the track through the soft white snow toward a spectacular and harmonious mountain range bathing in the golden afternoon sun. We passed through peaceful forests of snow-covered evergreens until we stopped at the Great Divide. We sank knee-deep into the snow as we struggled toward an open shelter for a thirty-minute rest, where hot chocolate and snacks were served at a warm fire. While we warmed our red fingers and noses, the dogs lay in the snow and enjoyed being pampered by their guides. On the way back we took a detour through an exquisite winter landscape, which reminded me of the scenes in *The Nutcracker* in New York. Now, when I see dogsledding in films, I immediately remember the venture in Canada. I would not want to have missed it for anything.

On December 22, the day before our return to Calgary, Liesl went skiing during the day, and in the evening we climbed on a horse-drawn sleigh for a ride along Lake Louise. We were tucked into warm blankets in the front seat of the sleigh, which held six. It was a beautiful ride through yet more magical winter scenery. A full moon almost double the usual size shone down on the snow, which seemed studded with tiny diamonds, just like the silvery snow on my Advent calendar on Kleine Düwelstraße. Little bells were jingling as the two horses pulled us along the path. The snow was crunching underneath the hooves, reminding me of the horses pulling wagons on the cobblestone streets of Hannover. In front of us lay the intoxicating mountain range, glistening in the moonlight. When the horses turned around on the frozen lake, the majestic Chateau resembled a fairy castle, with all its windows lit up and surrounded by giant spruces and evergreens covered with Christmas lights. In the peaceful solitude of this dreamlike spot in God's museum, it was a sight to behold.

After the sleigh ride, Liesl and I changed into our dressy outfits for dinner. In keeping with the traditional Christmas Eve dinner with the kiddies, we had made reservations at the Swiss Fondue Stuben in the Chateau. The rooms were paneled with cherrywood and the floors covered with plush carpets, and Tiffany lamps were shining down on solid cherry tables. A fire burned in the hearth and soft music played in the background as we enjoyed a hearty cheese fondue with a glass of wine in the rich Old World atmosphere. Coupled with our romantic sleigh ride, the evening was a perfect Christmas finale at the end of the millennium.

When I returned from Lake Louise to Bloomington on Christmas Eve, a white blanket of snow welcomed me. I could not have hoped for a more fitting gift.

The Christmas snow had melted by the time our traditional neighborhood New Year's Eve party rolled around. Out of respect for the last Christmas of the century and to appease my ever-nagging, oh-so-German friends, I had attempted to put up a genuine tree next to my Knabe right after the December 2 Schubertiade. It tipped over so many times the needles started dropping into the piano and onto the floor en masse. That was the final straw. I dragged it back to my car trunk, drove it to the place where I bought it, and much to the amazement of my friends, got my money back. In its place I put my pretty fake tree from Phoenix, Arizona, crowned with the golden tinsel angel from Nuremberg, Germany. It was in good company with a bunch of golden and silver balloons floating under the ceiling of the music room, and obviously did not mind the curly streamers hanging down from every ceiling lamp in the house. Under the garland in the entrance to the music room hung a string of silver letters reading *Happy New Year*. My friends filed in around 9:00 p.m., placing all their culinary specialties on the dining-room table. We served them hot *Glögg*, a more potent drink than *Krambambuli*, the preparation of which had to begin two weeks ahead of time. It took several bottles of port, three more of red wine, a couple quarts of brandy, an assortment of exotic spices, almonds, raisins, and such. It did the trick. Everybody was happy in a jiffy.

The evening really took off with my two new Korean *musikkinder*. One, Hee-Kyung Juhn, was a brilliant and attractive pianist. She was a doctoral student of Professor Leonard Hokanson at IU and now holds a position as collaborative pianist at the University of California–Santa Barbara. The other Korean was the stunningly beautiful soprano Hoo-Ryoung Hwang, student of the former Metropolitan stars Martina Arroyo and Costanza Coocaru. Hoo-Ryoung earned much applause at our own Musical Arts Center when she sang Mimi in *La Bohème* and Susanna in *The Marriage of Figaro*, and at this moment she is enrolled in the Vilar/Domingo Young Artist Program at the Washington Opera, where Placido Domingo placed her. She began to play and sing familiar operetta arias by Lehár and Strauss, known to all, but special to me, because Mutti used to sing them with Papa accompanying her on the piano. Hee-Kyung gave us a sampling of her solo expertise by playing Debussy's "Ca qu'a vu le vent d'Ouest" just before midnight. Hoo-Ryoung surprised us with a most moving performance of "Mi chiamano Mimi," which stirred our hearts profoundly.

At the turning of the millennium, we gathered around the big-screen TV, just as Tonio and I once did with the kiddies, distributed golden, blue, and green hats and noisemakers, and poured champagne for all. We watched the massive crystal ball at Times Square come down, joined the countdown, made a lot of noise at midnight, toasted, embraced, and called out, "Happy New Year!" It was almost disappointing that the electricity did not go out. There was no need for extra candles, flashlights, gasoline, cash, or water bottles. The computer did not crash. As a beginning to the year 2000, it could not have been surpassed. Above all, good friends and music surrounded me.

EPILOGUE IN TRANSIT

Fireball Lily – Victoria Falls – Zimbabwe, Africa

Is it providence that almost two years after I began writing my memoirs, on December 24, 1999, I should find myself on this vast continent in the eastern hemisphere – whose name has a spelling and sound very similar to *America*, where the impulse to write my memoirs was born – to compose in my mind, on November 24, 2001, the conclusion to those memoirs? I am convinced that divine intervention must have had a hand in it. After all, the 24th has over the years taken on a distinct significance in my life.

I am certain that destiny has led me to this remote yet thought-provoking place in the universe to pause and reflect at the end of this long and at times strenuous, but also exhilarating, journey, and to rejoice in having had the courage, the stamina, and above all the unwavering support and encouragement of my loyal friend the General to bring it to its end. – Writing is a lonely mission.

I cannot think of a more fitting place to rejoice than here at Victoria Falls, another natural wonder of the world, which for an entire lifetime I secretly longed to see, but could only dream about. Niagara Falls, in North America, was the first natural phenomenon I hurried to look at shortly after my immigration to the New World. Africa's Victoria Falls – God willing – will not be the last.

It was my passion for adventure and the search for a better future that brought me from war-torn Germany to America. The same passion has led me to seek out the wondrous creations of nature, man, and the gods that are exhibited in the great museums, and toward the end of my life, this passion has brought me to Zimbabwe and face to face with the fireball lily. It is a flower more stunning than any I have ever seen. Its bright, orange-red color shines from afar through the lush green grasses of the rainforest, which I last saw when cruising the South Pacific to visit Tahiti and other islands that belong to the Society Islands. This radiant flower cluster, about three inches in diameter and a foot high, held in relief by its blade-shaped leaves, is a miniature depiction of the rising or setting sun, the source of life and love.

It seems almost miraculous to stumble upon the fireball lily while standing close to the edge of the gorge of the thundering falls. The falls' eternal mists touch my face, fill the air, nourish the flora, and give the red beauty its alluring and highly intoxicating appearance. I am spellbound – because the flower speaks to me. This natural wonder typifies much of what has excited me in my life and still does. It touches my romantic inclinations, my fascination with the exotic, and my love of life. The ball shape of its flowering head reminds me of the globe, mirroring my zest for finding adventure all over the world. The lily's numerous pedicels point outward like rays, spikes, the tips of flames, or needles in a pincushion. They speak to the fiery and exhilarating, the passionate and sanguine, the treacherous and threatening episodes in my life as well as to those moments when pain, anger, fear, or sadness overshadowed all. The spikes, pins, or flames also strike a chord with my fighting nature, the temptation to tease, confront, incite, or mock those who inflict pain on my perhaps all-too-sensitive soul. They reveal my at times devilish nature, starting with my childhood on Kleine Düwelstraße (Street of the Little Devil). They come to my rescue when I struggle to survive.

It is common knowledge that one of the most striking mushrooms, the bright-red toadstool, is among the most poisonous umbrella-shaped fungi. Thus too does the vibrant fireball lily, whose pedicels radiate like the stays of an umbrella, supply a poison, which is coincidentally used on the tips of spears. Yet its bulb serves to treat poorly healing wounds, and it does no harm to a graceful butterfly that rests on its rays. The lily's sturdy, lush green stem, from which the leaves grow to protect the exquisite blossom, stirs within me the realization that man and woman must learn early on to stand proudly and optimistically alone among mankind and depend on no one but themselves. There is no guarantee that those you call friends or even family will stand by you when you most need support. – In the process of writing down the story of my life, I have come to realize that more often than not I was disappointed, that too many friends have undergone a metamorphosis into so-called friends. Thus, it might be safer to teach yourself to expect nothing from anyone, and then you will not be disappointed, but maybe pleasantly surprised from time to time. I have learned that avoiding pain requires shunning those who almost habitually inflict it. It requires a concerted effort to remain thus unencumbered and liberated. But the inner strength derived from such independence will give you that special license to feel free as a bird. Most of all, this freedom will rid you of the fear of death.

Free as a bird, or an angel, do I feel once more, even though I had thought it to be my last adventure in a helicopter when Liesl and I came face to face with the majestic Mount McKinley, in Alaska. This time, I let myself be persuaded to take the Flight of the Angels in order to marvel at the broad Zambezi River. It flows calmly along in its flat bed of black basalt toward the mile-wide brink, or lip, where its waters, depending on the rainfall (between 75,000 to four million gallons a minute), plunge abruptly, like a sheet or curtain, over 340 feet into an abyss. This wide crevasse not only causes a break in the long river, but also separates the countries of Zimbabwe and Zambia. Out of the vertical chasm emerges an eternal cloud of frothy, foamy spray. This sunlit mist is a white, waiflike veil that lends the gap an otherworldly hue.

The panorama below spreads out like a map of my life – as though it were the aggregate of my diverse experiences. The Zambezi brings to mind the big waterways in my native country, the Rhine and the Danube, and the great streams in America, such as the Mississippi and the Ohio, and it makes me wonder how it will measure up to the grand Nile, which I will cruise a few weeks from now. – Here at the falls, where Africa's fourth-largest river is so wide and flows so quietly, almost playfully, around the tree-clad islands that dot its blue waters, I am tempted to compare the settings to the happy and peaceful episodes in my life. As the river, the pulse of life, approaches the brink, it looks from up here like arteries leading to the heart and sustaining its function: to live. It seems like the calm before the storm. – And the Zambezi, within a split second, unexpectedly cascades and is transformed into turbulent waters that, at the bottom of the narrow and rocky ravine, flush, twist, and wind rapidly through a tortuous zigzag, until they meander and then flow again more gently for hundreds of miles until their river mingles with the waters of the Indian Ocean. Thus has been the stream of my life – more torrential than calm. Yet I look back on my years with no regrets. Here in Africa, where I am constantly confronted with the most devastating poverty, I cannot but realize how fortunate I am to have experienced, at least for a while, what it is like to suffer hunger. Only after having gone through hardship can I empathize with the poor and feel a deep gratitude for what life has shared with me so generously. I have learned it is impossible for most people to break out of their underprivileged surroundings without meaningful support. Not everybody is endowed with the physical or mental strength to fight for a better life. My life has taught me repeatedly to turn each negative into a positive, to profit from adversity and always get up when I am knocked down, like a tumbler doll, or like the rivers in this universe, which flow and flow regardless of the size of the stumbling blocks. Life goes on. It does not stop to challenge us with new problems. Life never robs us of hope for peace. I will always remember Doc's quote from Swinburne's "The Garden of Proserpine":

> ... *even the weariest river*
> *Winds somewhere safe to sea.*

As the Flight of the Angels descends, I spot in the water below a group of fat hippopotami, a couple of crocodiles on the shore, and only a few yards away, three elephants immersing their trunks in the river. I am eager to forge ahead on this journey, which will take me to other places of my dreams – to the Cape of Good Hope, to Botswana, where I will experience safaris with all the wildlife (elephants, giraffes, zebras, lions, etc.), to the vast Maasai Mara National Reserve, in Kenya, and finally to Egypt, where the Giza pyramids, the Great Sphinx of Giza, and the magnificent temples and tombs of pharaohs and kings will at least partially satisfy my appetite for Egyptian art treasures. This appetite was renewed only a few months earlier, when Doc's offspring, Peter and Eric, joined me to cruise the Aegean and marvel at the treasures of Greece.

As I leave the falls and listen to the birds' mysterious sounds in the tropical forest, I am startled by a most vibrant rainbow and see it as a final sign. It is a bridge connecting my two worlds. The rainbow touches the river on the west side of the falls in

Zambia, and on the east side, it ends in the crown of a tropical broad-leaved tree in Zimbabwe. Baboons are frolicking in its branches, and a lone long-billed crombec perched on a barren limb chirps happily. While the monkeys and the piping bird amuse me, as though wanting to remind me that music is everywhere, the warbler suddenly spreads its wings and soars across the blue sky, directly toward the fiery ball of the setting sun.